Diaspora Entrepreneurial Networks

Business, Culture and Change
Edited by Andrew Godley

Diaspora Entrepreneurial Networks

Four Centuries of History

**Edited by
Ina Baghdiantz McCabe, Gelina Harlaftis and
Ioanna Pepelasis Minoglou**

Oxford•New York

First published in 2005 by
Berg
Editorial offices:
1st Floor, Angel Court, 81 St Clements Street, Oxford OX4 1AW, UK
175 Fifth Avenue, New York, NY 10010, USA

Berg is the imprint of Oxford International Publishers Ltd.

Library of Congress Cataloging-in-Publication Data
Diaspora entrepreneurial networks : four centuries of history / edited by Ina
Baghdiantz McCabe, Gelina Harlaftis, and Ioanna Pepelasis Minoglou.
    p. cm.
    Includes index.
    ISBN 1-85973-880-X (pbk.) -- ISBN 1-85973-875-3 (cloth)
    1. Merchants, Foreign--History. 2. Business networks--History. I. McCabe, Ina
Baghdiantz. II. Harlaftis, Gelina, 1958- III. Pepelasåe Minoglou, Iåoanna.

    HF479.D53 2005
    338'.04'086910903--dc22

                          2004026841

British Library Cataloguing-in-Publication Data
A catalogue record for this book is available from the British Library.

ISBN 1 85973 875 3 (Cloth)
1 85973 880 X (Paper)

Typeset by JS Typesetting Ltd, Porthcawl, Mid Glamorgan
Printed in the United Kingdom by Biddles Ltd, King's Lynn

www.bergpublishers.com

To Frank Broeze

"...the real stuff of life is people"

Contents

Contents

Contents

Acknowledgements

Many but not all of the articles in this book were written after the outcome of two conference meetings, the first held in Corfu, Greece, in 2001 and the second held in Buenos Aires, Argentina, in 2002. The Corfu conference was an excellent forum for discussing ideas and exchanging concepts and forging a common language. Despite the individual signatures of the articles, all are an outcome of that common language. These papers are not conference proceedings, but due to the great interest in diaspora networks and in networks in general, this book project was launched in Buenos Aires. Special thanks must go to Jonathan Israel, who had chaired the session on the Armenians and the Jews in Corfu, both for his enthusiastic participation to the conference in Corfu and in the book, as is reflected here in the preface to Part I he later wrote.

We would like to thank William Gervase Clarence-Smith for his support in initiating these conferences for the XIIIth meeting of the International Economic Historians Association. This book is dedicated to Frank Broeze who was the instigator of this project. Frank Broeze passed away five months before the meeting in Corfu at the age of 55; his last piece is included in memoriam at the end of this book. Frank's premature death gave us some perspective about the fragility of life, a sentiment that was to continue to mark our meetings.

Both conferences were disrupted by world events, yet became more vibrant and meaningful experiences in the process. Our first meeting was scheduled just days after September 11 and many scholars from the East Coast missed Corfu, as their airports were closed. Despite the anxiety created world-wide, all the papers were sent via the internet on time and read by colleagues. Many thanks to Tony Reid both for getting there from California via Bangkok and for reading for his American colleagues. The next meeting in Buenos Aires presented another hurdle as half of the six hundred economic historians registered for the large conference did not come fearing political turmoil in Argentina. The turmoil was somewhat hastily predicted by CNN as 'civil war' during the IMF meeting. As a consequence our meeting became a small closed workshop, which turned out to be very fruitful for the book.

The following articles are an outcome of many exchanges. Many of these exchanges took the form of global e-mails, as the contributors and the editors of this book live across the world, in China, India and Greece, Europe, Canada and the US. For three years we were a network of scholars working on a common project; the editors thank all the contributors for their timely corrections and even tempers, especially during discussions over minutiae. There were extraordinarily few problems given the large number of people involved, so this was a successful and very efficient global network. Such an international project would have been impossible without instant and constant communication. One such crucial electronic link was to Andrew Godley in Oxford whose enthusiastic support was instrumental in endorsing this book for this new series at Berg. Our commissioning editor at Berg, Kathleen May, has done everything an editor could do to make the process a pleasant one and has greatly contributed to our happiness as editors. Special thanks go to Ian Critchley, Senior Production Editor, and George Pitcher for their editorial guidance. At Tufts, our gratitude goes to Margaret Casey in the History department for smoothing out many technical hurdles during the last stages of the manuscript.

Editing this book was an extraordinarily pleasant experience and forged many new friendships. This pleasure was greatly augmented by the outcome, as the anonymous but unusually generous referees of this book also unknowingly supported our wish for its length and scope. We truly thank them as we secretly would have wished for even greater length. We do acknowledge that some important regions and networks are not covered in the following articles, and we hope this will be remedied by other specialists one day. Eurasian trade is at the center of this book, and networks in the Americas and Africa deserve similar conferences and books.

The process of collaboration over the book was a tremendous intellectual experience for all but especially for the three editors. Many of our family members have helped and participated throughout. Credit for the cover photo belongs to Bill McCabe. He shot the image of the pomegranate in the snow on a cold Boston morning. Special thanks to the Harlaftis family, especially to Dimitri Chryssis and his friend Yannis, for lodging us and feeding us so luxuriously in Corfu during our initial collaboration on the book in August of 2003. To all our loved ones, especially our children, who patiently suffered our absence and absent-mindedness during the many working hours a book always requires, we owe more than words can express.

Contributors

Rajeswary Ampalavanar Brown is an economic historian at the School of Management Royal Holloway College, University of London. Her publications include *Capital and Entrepreneurship in South East Asia* (Macmillan 1994), *Chinese Big Business And the Wealth Of Asian Nations* (Palgrave 2002). She is currently working on a book on *The Failure Of Arab Capital in South East Asia*.

Ina Baghdiantz-McCabe has degrees from the Sorbonne and Columbia, and holds an endowed chair in Armenian History at Tufts University. Previously she has taught at Columbia University, the University of Chicago, Bennington College and at the EHESS in Paris. Her publications include *The Shah's Silk for Europe's Silver: The Eurasian Silk Trade of the Julfan Armenians in Safavid Iran and India (1590–1750)* (University of Pennsylvania 1999) and, as co-author, *Slaves of the Shah: New Elites of Seventeenth Century Safavid Isfahan* (I.B. Tauris 2003), and she has edited *Du bon usage du thé et des épices en Asie: Réponses à Monsieur Cabart de Villarmont* by Jean Chardin (L'Inventaire, Actes Sud, Paris 2002).

Chiara Betta holds a degree from the School of Oriental and African Studies, University of London. Since 1999 she has been teaching Asian studies at the Athens campus of the University of Indianapolis; she is also research fellow at the Institute of International Economic Relations. Her main publications on Baghdadi Jews have been published in many journals.

Maria Christina Chatziioannou holds degrees from the University of Athens and the Scuola di Perfezionamento di Storia Medioevale e Moderna, Università di Sapienza, Rome. She has published on Greek merchant houses and entrepreneurs, as well as on Greek regional history. Her latest publication is *Family Strategy and Commercial Competition: The Geroussi Merchant House in the Nineteenth Century* (Athens 2003) (in Greek). She is Director of Studies in the Institute for Neohellenic Research/National Hellenic Research Foundation.

Wai-keung Chung holds degrees from the New Asia Institute of Advanced Chinese Studies (Hong Kong) and the University of Washington (Seattle). A sociologist by training, his research focuses on the historical processes of institutional transformation in non-Western societies. He has published a few articles on the evolution of Chinese and Japanese business organizations and business practices. He is assistant professor at the Singapore Management University.

William Gervase Clarence-Smith holds degrees from Cambridge University, Institut d'Etudes Politiques (Paris), and the School of Oriental and African Studies (London), where he is currently Professor of Economic History of Asia and Africa. He has published on the Portuguese, Basque, Catalan, Gujarati, Hadhrami Arab, and 'Greater Syrian' entrepreneurial diasporas, and his books include *The Third Portuguese Empire, 1825–1975: a Study in Economic Imperialism* (Manchester UP 1985), *Hadhrami Traders, Scholars and Statesmen in the Indian Ocean, 1750s–1960s* (Brill 1997, co-edited with Ulrike Freitag), and *Cocoa and chocolate, 1765–1914* (Routledge 2000), *The Global Coffee Economy in Africa Asia and Latin America, 1500–1989* (Cambridge UP 2003, co-edited with Steven Topik).

Sushil Chaudhury recently held the University Chair of Islamic History and Culture at Calcutta University. He is a Fellow of the Royal Historical Society, England, and is presently Emeritus Fellow, University Grants Commission, New Delhi. He has a number of publications including *Merchants, Companies and Trade, Europe and Asia in the Early Modern Era* (Cambridge 1998, co-edited with M. Morineau); *The Prelude to Empire – Plassey Revolution of 1757* (New Delhi 2000); *From Prosperity to Decline: Eighteenth Century Bengal* (New Delhi 1995) and numerous research articles.

Maria Fusaro holds degrees from the University of Venice and Cambridge University. After three years in Oxford as Junior Research Fellow at St Hugh's College, she is currently Assistant Professor at the University of Chicago. She is the author of a book on the currants trade *Uva Passa: Una guerra commerciale tra Venezia e l'Inghilterra,* (Venice 1996) and of several articles on early modern trade and is preparing a monograph on Early Modern Trade.

Stathis Gourgouris teaches Comparative Literature at Columbia University. He is the author of *Dream Nation: Enlightenment, Colonization, and the Institution of Modern Greece* (Stanford UP 1996) and *Does Literature Think? Literature as Theory for an Antimythical Era* (Stanford UP 2003). He has also written numerous essays on contemporary politics and political theory, psychoanalysis, film studies, and music.

Gelina Harlaftis holds degrees from the University of Athens, Cambridge University and Oxford University, she has taught at the University of Piraeus from 1991 to 2002 and she is now Associate Professor and Head at the Department of History of the Ionian University in Corfu, Greece. She has been a visiting professor in universities in Canada and the UK and is President of the International Maritime Economic History Association. She is author of a number of articles and books, among them *Greek Shipowners and Greece 1945–1975* (Athlone Press 1993), and *History of Greek-owned Shipping* (Routledge 1996) which was honoured with the Runciman Award 1997.

Jonathan Israel holds degrees from Cambridge University and Oxford University. He has taught at Newcastle, Hull and at University College London before taking up his present post. He is an Early Modern Europeanist based since 2001 at the Institute for Advanced Study, Princeton. He has worked on the Dutch Golden Age and on seventeenth-century Jewish diaspora communities, and also on the Enlightenment. Among other books, he has published *European Jewry in the Age of Mercantilism* (Oxford 1985), *Dutch Primacy in World Trade* (Oxford 1989), *The Dutch Republic* (1995), *Radical Enlightenment* (2001) and *Diasporas within a Diaspora* (London 2002).

Ioanna Pepelasis Minoglou holds degrees from Harvard University and the London School of Economics and is an Assistant Professor of Economic History at the Athens University of Economics. She has published articles in international refereed journals on industrialization, entrepreneurship, international business and finance. She is the author of a book in Greek on consumption patterns in the nineteenth century.

Caroline Plüss received her doctorate in sociology from Oxford University. She worked as a Post-Doctoral Fellow at the University of Hong Kong and currently is an Adjunct Assistant Professor at the Chinese University of Hong Kong. She has published articles in international refereed journals on the Indian, Jewish and Muslim trade diasporas in Hong Kong and is preparing a book manuscript on the history of the Jewish community in Hong Kong.

Anthony Reid is a Southeast Asianist with history degrees from New Zealand and Cambridge. He has taught and researched at the University of Malaya, the Australian National University, and the University of California, Los Angeles. Since 2002 he has been founding Director of the Asia Research Institute at the National University of Singapore. His books include: *The Contest for North Sumatra: Atjeh, the Netherlands and Britain, 1858–1898* (1969); *The Indonesian National Revolution, 1945–1950* (Longman 1974); *The Blood of the People: Revolution and the End of Traditional Rule in Northern Sumatra* (Oxford UP 1979); *Southeast Asia in the Age of Commerce, 1450–1680*, 2 vols (Yale UP 1988–1993); *Charting the Shape of Early Modern Southeast Asia* (Silkworm 1999) and, as editor, *Sojourners and Settlers: Histories of Southeast Asia and the Chinese* (Allen & Unwin 1996); *The Last Stand of Asian Autonomies: Responses* *to Modernity in the Diverse States of Southeast Asia and Korea* (St Martin's 1997) and (with D. Chirot) *Essential Outsiders: Chinese and Jews in the Modern Transformation of Southeast Asia and Central Europe* (University of Washington Press 1997).

Huibert Schijf holds degrees from the University of Amsterdam. In 1975 he became a staff member at the Department of Sociology/Anthropology at the University of Amsterdam. He has published several articles and a book: *Netwerken van een financieel-economische elite, personele verbindingen in het Nederlandse bedrijfsleven aan het eind van de negentiende eeuw* (Networks of a business elite, personal interlocks in Dutch business life at the end of the nineteenth century) in 1993. He is the (co-) author of articles on various elites in the business world, and has also published on trading minorities such as the Mennonites, the Jews and the overseas Chinese.

Gabriel Sheffer holds degrees from Oxford University. He is a Professor of Political Science at the Political Science Department of the Hebrew University of Jerusalem. He has been a visiting Professor at Cornell University, University of Wisconsin-Madison, University of California-Berkeley, University of Pittsburgh, New South Wales University-Sydney and the University of Maryland. He has authored and edited numerous articles and books on foreign policy, leadership, conflict and diaspora politics, including *Diaspora Politics: At Home Abroad* (Cambridge University Press 2003); as co-editor, *Middle Eastern Minorities and Diasporas* (Essex Academic Press 2002); as editor, *Modern Diasporas in International Politics (*St Martin's 1986).

Carmel Vassallo holds degrees from the University of Westminster in London and did postgraduate work in Hispanic Studies and History at the Universities of Navarre and Barcelona. His publications include *Corsairing to Commerce: Maltese Merchants in XVIII Century Spain* (Malta University Press 1997) and *The Malta Chamber of Commerce 1848–1979* (Malta Chamber of Commerce 1998). He lectures at the Mediterranean Institute of the University of Malta and is coordinator of the Mediterranean Maritime History Network.

William D. Wray holds degrees from Harvard University where he taught from 1976 to 1978 before moving to the University of British Columbia where he is presently an Associate Professor. His main publications include *Mitsubishi and the NYK, 1870–1914: Business Strategy in the Japanese Shipping Industry* (Harvard University Press, 1984); as editor, *Managing Industrial Enterprise: Cases from Japan's Prewar Experience* (Harvard University Press 1989), and several articles on Japanese shipping.

Tribute to Professor Frank Broeze

This book is dedicated to Professor Frank Broeze. Frank Broeze was at the inception of this project and its main instigator; he passed away five months before the first meeting of the group on diaspora entrepreneurial networks in Corfu in September 2001.

Frank Broeze was a Dutchman, born in Amsterdam in 1945; he studied at the University of Leiden, a student of Professor Jaap Bruijn. And as a real Dutchman he followed the classic sea-routes of his country men. For many centuries Dutch ships led their way from Amsterdam, around the Cape of Good Hope, under the thirtieth parallel of south latitude to avoid the monsoons and then up to Batavia. Many Dutch ships that lost the trade winds to Indonesia were wrecked on New Holland's coast, where Perth is today. Frank Broeze's passenger ship arrived fine to Perth with his wife Uli, in 1970. So writes his friend and colleague Anthony Barker in Australia: 'In 1970 when the history department of the University of Western Australia selected Frank Broeze from the University of Leiden to introduce a course on maritime history, it had no idea how much its choice would enrich a much wider range of its teaching activities, strengthen its links to the community and enhance its international reputation for outstanding scholarship'.

I met Frank Broeze 21 years ago, in 1983, the year when I started my D.Phil. in Oxford, in a conference at Greenwich Maritime Museum. And it was there that I was introduced to the group of maritime historians and of what eventually became the International Maritime Economic History Association. During the last 20 years, Maritime History has emerged as an independent discipline and Frank Broeze has been regarded as the indisputable leading thinker of the group; he has been described by the other leading figure, Professor Lewis R. Fischer, "without question the pre-eminent maritime historian of his generation". Classic now, is his definition of maritime history in a seminal article in the *Great Circle*, the journal of the Australian Association for Maritime History, in 1989: maritime history in a broad sense rather than simply a study of ships, sailors and navies. A President of the International Commission of Maritime History, a Vice President of the International Maritime Economic History Association, Frank has always participated and supported all sessions on maritime history in the International Economic History Congresses, since Bern in 1986, in Leuven in 1990, in Milan in 1994, in Madrid/Seville in 1998. The last conference that he organized took place in his *absentia*, in Perth in December 2001, and was entirely in the spirit of Frank Broeze: "Maritime History beyond 2000: Visions of Sea and Shore", with representative historians from around the world.

Extremely well-read, with the deep knowledge of German, French and Dutch historical tradition of old Europe and the breadth of the Anglo-Saxon historical literature and the New World, Frank Broeze had a wide and rounded view of world history. A real historian to the core, he was a firm believer in a one-and-only history, not a history in pieces. He was equally comfortable with economic and social history, business history, urban and imperial history. He taught, as he characteristically said, on "whatever he could lay hands on", from European and American to Middle Eastern history. This breadth was invaluable, and his contributions in articles and in the discussion of the conferences were a source of inspiration to his colleagues.

A gifted writer, he left us with numerous publications in English, Dutch and French that have appeared in press in Australia, Great Britain, the Netherlands, the USA, Canada, India, France, Germany and Austria, while his works have been translated into Spanish, Arabic and Greek. He has published ten books, and 90 chapters or articles, while for ten years he was the editor of Australia's leading maritime journal. His articles have appeared in the *Economic History Review*, *Australian Economic History Review*, the *International Review of Social History*, the *International Journal of Maritime History*, the *Australian Historical Studies*, the *Journal of Transport History*, the *Indian Economic and Social History Review*, *Modern Asian Studies*, etc. A forceful and dynamic personality he was active in research and other committees within his university on a national and international basis. His world-wide reputation was recognized in Australia that honoured him by making him fellow of the Australian Academy of Humanities.

But honours was not what Frank Broeze sought. What was wonderful about Frank was that he was a man of passion and love for history and life. Frank was a frank man, honest, direct, never an antagonist but always a "synagonist". A popular teacher to his students, he was a popular and supportive man to his colleagues.

From the summer of 2000 his health was getting steadily worse. For the first time since I knew him, I received a message that lacked the optimism usual to Frank but was so brave. On 24 March he wrote:

It is abundantly clear that my tumours are incurable and that all that we can do is manage the process and try and delay the inevitable. I continue working at home on my Pacific History project (although I'll never finish it). I also try and maintain giving my honours seminar and next week I hope to be able to give a seminar to my colleagues about the Pacific Ocean project. In short: it goes very much up and down, but the highs are not that high any more and the down become more numerous. Even so, I'll hang on as long as I can.

Professor Frank Broeze

Frank Broeze was able to give his last seminar as he wanted. Thus report his colleagues from Australia:

> A select 25 of us – mainly staff and graduate students in the history department – had the moving experience of attending his last seminar exactly one week before his death. For weeks – as he went in and out of hospital – Frank's determination to give this seminar was a reminder of how much history and his work as a historian meant to him.
>
> In one sense it was a terribly sad occasion because by then he was a shriveled figure in a wheelchair, talking about a book on the Pacific Ocean he was not going to write. But though his appearance was a shock to those who hadn't seen him recently, his performance was inspirational: he spoke for an hour, with his usual command of sweeping issue, with his usual humorous anecdotes and – thank goodness – in his distinctive booming voice. It was an intensely moving, uniquely appropriate way for him to say goodbye.

Frank Broeze passed away early in the morning of Wednesday 4 April 2001 at the age of 55, very much in peace. His son Carsten and his wife Uli were at his side to the last moment.

Gelina Harlaftis

Introduction

National historiographies have masked the significance of trade diasporas and their entrepreneurial networks. During the last 400 years a succession of regional and long-distance trading networks, at first in Asia and Europe, from the Mediterranean to the northern European seas, the Indian Ocean, the southeast Asian seas but later also stretching across the Atlantic and Pacific Oceans, lay at the heart of the gradual integration of the world into one global system. The study of such networks, which often took the form of ethnic trade diasporas, is becoming a vibrant field for economic, business, political and social historians, sociologists and economists.

The purpose of this interdisciplinary book is to take stock of the current state of the art and to lay the foundations for new directions in the study of diaspora entrepreneurial networks by soliciting a broad range of case studies from varying regions and periods, some of which in a comparative perspective. We discuss organized groups of merchant families and their extended regional networks having the same ethnic origin, whether it be Arabs, Armenians, Chinese, Greeks, Jews, Japanese, Maltese, Parsis, Scots or Western Indians. Within some groups we study regional sub-groups with organized networks, such as the Julfan Armenians, Baghdadi Jews, and Hadhrami Arabs. As is amply clear from the list above, the book concentrates not only on the networks of diasporic people but also on trade diasporas. The three classical diasporas, the Jews, the Greeks and the Armenians, occupy a large part of this discussion. The term 'trade diaspora' was coined by Abner Cohen in Paris in 1971. It elicited great discomfort because of the usage of the term diaspora, habitually a term reserved for the Jewish diaspora with an implication of forced exile. Throughout the book we interchangeably use 'trade diaspora', 'entrepreneurial networks' and 'diaspora networks'. Many of the chapters deal with the definition and re-definition of these terms as last examined by the well-known historian Philip Curtin.

Historical diasporas – the three classical ones; those of the Armenians, the Greeks and the Jews – epitomize the resilience of traditional forms of association in certain groups who for centuries transcended the boundaries of nation-states. Over thirty new groups have now joined them under the umbrella term 'diaspora'. The problems associated with the massive migration of the modern period are beyond the subject matter of this book, where the focus is not even on classical diaspora but on trade diaspora and entrepreneurial elites and their networks. What these organized groups of diaspora merchants were able to do was to carry out cross-cultural trade mostly confined to the Eurasian continent in the early modern period. During the first period examined, the Christian-Islamic divide was the central axis of their activity. During the early modern period Eurasian trade was a common feature of the Armenians, the Jews and the Greeks, the three classical diasporas, because they developed trade diasporas within Muslim environments. Among the groups examined only the Sephardic Jews had any Atlantic trade. For the Arabs, the Baghdadi Jews, the Chinese, the Gujaratis, the Parsis and the Scottish in the Indian Ocean it was the Muslim-Hindu-Chinese divide that was a main axis of activity. These 'trans-territorial', 'trans-ocean', 'trans-cultural', 'transnational', 'international', or 'multinational' networks had business beyond national and imperial boundaries, and preserved an unfettered flow of information and communication that sustained a permanent competitive advantage for the service sector. This also holds true for the modern period.

Contrary to many a current belief, the integration of world economy, the so-called globalization of modern economic life, does not owe its present character solely to the actions (and omissions) of the colonialism and imperialism of prominent Western or Eastern powers. Trade diasporas have played a major role in the process of globalization. If they have been noticed, their role has often been misundertood. These trade diasporas that lived in the Ottoman, Safavid, Indian and Chinese empires and dealt with trade within the Western maritime empires, such as the Portuguese, the Spanish, the Dutch and the British, have sometimes erroneously been described as brokers of the West, as a service bourgeoisie, or as *compradors*. Or, on the contrary, it is often assumed that diaspora networks are a service bourgeoisie in their host societies and therefore the competitors or the antagonists of Western entrepreneurial or trading networks. Their significant political role as elites participating in empire- and state-building in the Muslim world has often been minimized in preceding scholarship. It is an outcome of binary thinking to oppose East and West, imaginary boundaries easily crossed by trade diasporas, or to juxtapose ethnic trade diasporas and national trading networks. Many contributors show the clear participation of several ethnic trade diasporas in national trading networks, including companies, such as the Sephardic Jews in the Dutch East Company (Verenigde Oostindische Compagnie [VOC]), and the Armenians in the French Royal East India Company (FREIC). To build their own commercial empires ethnic trade diaspora excelled at being on good terms with everybody. They were not merely cross-cultural brokers, they were building considerable political and economic spheres of influence for their own interests.

The second period examined in this book, the nineteenth and twentieth centuries, brings the question of the formation of nation-states and the importance of Western capitalism to the forefront. The nineteenth century is the era of industrialization, incredible technological achievements and quicker communications. Here we have to raise the question asked by Philip Curtin whether in the nineteenth century, traditional trade diasporas tended to disappear as a result of the Westernization of commerce. Many scholars in this book portray a continuity and adaptation within this transformed environment. The only reason why trade diasporas seem to have disappeared is that they long remained invisible to scholarship. It is amply evident from several contributions that, despite the enormous economic and political changes brought about by the nineteenth and twentieth centuries, not only do these ethnic trade diasporas not disappear but many of them follow the same trading methods as in the early modern period, as in the case of the Baghdadi Jews and others.

Diaspora entrepreneurship and international networks have to some extent preceded western European economic expansion. It appears that during the colonial and imperial expansion of Europe in the nineteenth century and first half of the twentieth century, trade diasporas continued to play an important role in the services sector, namely: trade, shipping and finance. The ethnic groups that interplayed between East and West became part of state building in European nations. For example, the Greek trade diaspora dispersed from Odessa to Trieste, Amsterdam and London was to be a fundamental element in the formation of the Greek state in 1830. Moreover, the multinational activities of trade diaspora in the Eurasian trade of the nineteenth century retained characteristics of the early modern period, integrating the old with the new, adapting to the modern economic reality.

In the international economy of the beginning of the twentieth century, particular characteristics prevailed that determined the path of the century. Firstly, the impact of the industrialization of the West became increasingly more distinctive and determined the path of world trade: inflow of raw materials from the non-European world and outflow of manufactured goods to the rest of the world. The result was the quest for non-European markets with intense international competition of British, German, French and American capital. Secondly, the formation of large national companies in Europe and the United States, with Japan joining the 'club' in the second half of the century, their concentration in huge industrial complexes leading to unprecedented quantities of mass production resulted in the formation of gigantic multinational businesses.

Throughout the four centuries trade diaspora were prominent in services, particularly trade, shipping and finance; however, in many cases they were intimately engaged in the control of the mode of production of the goods they traded, such as silk, cotton, grain and jute.

Both religion and culture have served as explanations for the success of trade diasporas. Several prominent thinkers hoping to understand the business behaviour of specific groups have used religion repeatedly. Recently scholars have used Confucius to help analyse Chinese entrepreneurship; a century ago, Werner Sombart used the Torah to explain Jewish economic success; the attitudes toward wealth expressed in the Torah were supposedly more positive than those found in the New Testament. Most notoriously Max Weber searched the key to the success of European capitalism in the Protestant Ethic. The Christianity of the Armenians has often been given as the key to their success in the Muslim world. Is it Zoroastrianism the cause of Parsis' success? Which religion could not be chosen to provide answers for the success of particular groups within the capitalist system? If for scholarship these explanations fall short, undeniably within the groups themselves they play an immense role enhancing group cohesion and maintaining distinct identities that separate diasporas from their host societies. Cohesion is at the heart of extensive commercial networks.

A common culture is what keeps a network together and gives it a particular ethnic identity. Here the term 'culture' does not mean a general and abstract interpretation of the 'external' process of the evolution of the 'culture' of a nation, but an alternative interpretation of an 'internal' process within a group, an evolution through time of their religion, art, family and personal life, which in turn construct the institutions, practices, values and way of thinking of a society. Most importantly for our purposes here, a common commercial culture is created which is transmitted from generation to generation. It is not the increase in the number of interconnected commercial establishments that made the network work, but rather the elaboration of a common commercial strategy which relied first on the organizational structure of the firms and second on the methods of trading.

Western economic literature has taken for granted that over historical time there is a gradual evolution of business organization from the individual entrepreneur (private proprietorship) at one extreme, to partnerships and eventually to joint stock companies and the managerial enterprise. This evolution is seen as inexorable linear progress toward more sophisticated business methods. It is assumed that the latter forms are more rational forms of organization and a sign of greater success. Recent research brings a new perspective demonstrating that the transformation from the family firm to the joint stock company is not self-evident or the only path to success. The two extremes, markets and hierarchies, are thought of as constituting the two poles of a continuum of organizational structures, into which other business structures can be placed, which can be described as hybrids, perfectly rational and efficient – a sign of creative adaptation to particular conditions. Some such hybrids are certain 'extended' trade diaspora networks, with units encompassing families from a regional unit defined as their homeland. The homeland can be a town, as in Julfa, an island like Chios, or an extended region as for the Baghdadi Jews who considered the Persian world to be Baghdad.

Trade diapora often combined the advantages of family firms as well of managerial capitalism by going into joint ventures with Western trading groups and hierarchies, be they the East India Companies or other later large multinational corporations. They also go into collaborative ventures with other trade diasporas. In the era of managerial capitalism there is a new wave of studies on what has been coined family capitalism which stress the positive attributes and resilience of family firms and closed networks of trust ranging from extended families to ethnic communities. In particular with reference to the difficult business conditions and volatility in pre-twentieth-century long-distance trade, family-based networks built on trust among partners are thought to have supplied the most effective governance structure as a solution to principal/agent problems and curbing agency and transaction costs.

From another perspective, part of the theoretical study of business organizations today is based on the role of knowledge and information. What is highly important at the dawn of the twenty-first century and the so-called rise of the network society is the flow of information and the dissemination of knowledge, the new 'God' of world economies. Business information has long been one of the main 'weapons' of trade diasporas. There was a great advantage to being cross-cultural brokers; since they controlled the flow of information between at least two societies, they could always withhold information or even misinform their competitors. Moreover, the fact that they kept accounts and wrote letters in scripts other than the Latin alphabet and that could only be read by a small group was an enormous advantage for keeping secrets and communicating within the network. Even in the age of telegrams some groups continued to use their own languages transliterated into the Latin alphabet. As Geoffrey Jones writes in his *Merchants to Multinationals* (Oxford University Press, 2001), 'in services, ownership advantages rest particularly in "soft" skills, embodied in people rather than in machinery or other physical products. Knowledge, information and human relationships often proved the ownership advantages of service sector firms'. Throughout the four centuries trade diaspora were prominent in services, particularly trade, shipping and finance. To conclude, this book is about international business, entreprises beyond boundaries. Its aim is to identify common patterns in the enterprises of trade diaspora, to trace similar characteristics of business practices of trading groups of common ethnic origin and to provide a framework for a comparative study.

Part I
Diasporas in Early Modern European Trade

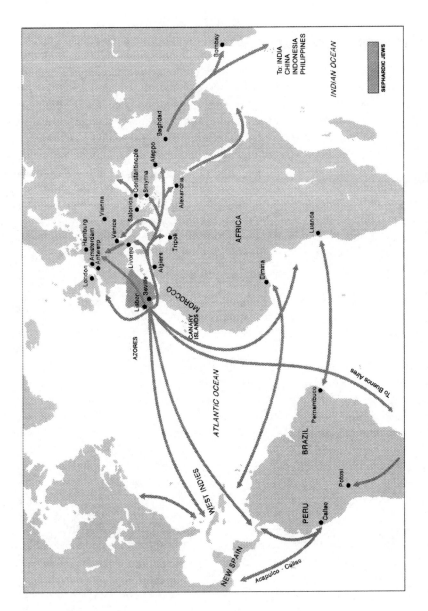

Map 1 Maritime trade diaspora of Sephardic Jews, 16th–18th centuries

Diasporas Jewish and non-Jewish and the World Maritime Empires

Jonathan Israel

Diasporas in the classic sense of scattered peoples dispersed – often in some degree forcibly – from their original homeland but not entirely cut off from it, and which then remain sharply distinct from their host societies, and united among themselves, by strong ties of religion, language and ethnicity, have undoubtedly played a major and remarkable role in many areas of social, cultural and intellectual as well as economic and imperial history. But the cultural roles of such groups – as, for example, the Jews in translation, medicine and philosophical debate in medieval Islam, or Greek scholars in Renaissance Italy, or the Huguenots in publishing, journalism and theological debates in early Enlightenment Europe – were so thoroughly steeped in the religious circumstances of that specific diaspora, as well as in the religious and cultural context of the host societies, that opportunities for broad comparative analysis in this sphere appear to be rather limited. By contrast, the roles of different diasporas in long-distance trade and empire building, even though these have in fact only rather rarely been systematically compared, offer excellent opportunities for a broad comparative approach as well as a particularly valuable vantage point from which to study major aspects of world history within a genuinely global framework.

In the fields of long-distance trade, finance and shipping, furthermore, there can be little doubt that diasporas have often, throughout the medieval and modern eras, been of fundamental importance sometimes affecting the basic structures of empires in ways which, as Maria Fusaro shows in Chapter 5 of this volume, in respect of Greek merchants and seamen in the Venetian *stato do mar* in the sixteenth and seventeenth centuries, have profoundly influenced the general development, indeed fate, of whole maritime trading systems. Yet traditional 'national' historiographies have, for rather obvious reasons, mostly been somewhat slow, or even distinctly reluctant, to acknowledge such non-national influences. Where the economic impact of diasporas has been strongly emphasized within national traditions and historiographies, this has often been – as in the case of the Expulsion of the Jews from Spain (1492) or that of Huguenots after the Revocation of the Edict of Nantes (1685) – where ideological opponents made use of the phenomenon for their own propaganda purposes. Thus, the Dutch and English were prone to point to these expulsions when offering explanations for the subsequent 'decline', absolute or relative, of formerly massively powerful adversaries such as Philip II's Spain or Louis XIV's France, explanations in large part derived from a wider polemical critique of the policies and religious attitudes of such eclipsed rivals.

Most of the existing historiography, in any case, with its inherent bias toward emphasizing national achievement, has long tended to play down the positive contributions of ethnic and religious minorities of all sorts. At the same time, while all the classic diasporas arguably shared a number of crucially important common features, some were obviously more flexible or able to function more effectively in a wider range of contexts than others. The range of contexts in which they could operate indeed varied significantly. The Greeks as Ottoman subjects and the Armenians who, though Christian, had over the centuries developed great confidence and skill in travelling through, and conducting business in, Muslim lands, were no less adept than the Sephardim in bridging the gap between the Christian and Islamic worlds (Aghassian and Kevonian 1999: 82–3; Kardasis 2001: 81, 93). The Huguenots, on the other hand, were well equipped to play a major part in maritime trade, banking and many specialized industries throughout the Calvinist and Anglican societies of western Europe and from the 1680s, when thousands of Huguenots settled in British North America and the Dutch Caribbean colonies, were for a time also the most important trade diaspora in the New World (Johnson 1998: 28–1; Goslinga 1985: 275, 353: Johnson 1998: 28). They were, however, for obvious confessional and cultural reasons, wholly unable to participate in the Catholic empires or operate effectively in Lutheran, Orthodox and Muslim countries. Similarly, Ashkenazic Jewry in early modern times never developed a flourishing trade diaspora ranging across the Balkans, the Ottoman Empire and the Middle East.

Seemingly, the single most flexible and widest-ranging, historically, of the classic diasporas, was in fact that of western Sephardic Jewry, a community network which for analytical purposes must be carefully distinguished both from Ashkenazic (i.e. the great bulk of central and eastern European Jewry), on the one hand, and most of the Asian and North African Jewish communities, on the other (Israel 2002: 1–39). Unlike the rest of the Jewish world, the western Sephardic diaspora fulfilled a uniquely vast range and versatile set of functions throughout the maritime, commercial and colonial expansion of Europe and the Levant from 1492 down to the late eighteenth century. This was particularly conspicuous with respect to Iberian trade, the mid- and southern Atlantic and the Caribbean, and in western Europe's relations with Islamic North Africa and the Near East. Over large expanses of the globe, Sephardic Jews, and the crypto-Jews of Iberian background associated with them, contributed in fundamental ways to the growing dominance over international trade, shipping and finance of the leading commercial imperial systems of the Western and Islamic worlds, hence also of the seven great maritime and imperial empires of the age – the Ottoman, Venetian, Portuguese, Spanish, Dutch, English and French. At the same time this group suffered frequent persecution, expulsion, harassment and other kinds of pressure not only from the Inquisition in the Spanish and Portuguese Atlantic empires and parts of Italy, but also, resulting from shifts and vacillations in state policy, in the empires of Venice, France and, to an extent – as in Tangiers under English rule (1661–84) or Gibraltar, in 1713 – even England. Throughout the early modern period this particular segment of the Jewish people can indeed be said to have been simultaneously, and to a unique degree, agents and victims of empire.

It seems, furthermore, that characteristic economic practices and commercial culture of the western Sephardic diaspora operating in the Ottoman Empire and the western maritime empires during the early modern age, had very little to do with any supposedly age-old characteristics of Jews *qua* Jews. The Sephardim of the West played an exceptionally wide-ranging and highly innovative role owing not to any supposedly ingrained economic skills, traditions or attributes but rather to something quite different: namely, broad structural changes in relations between empires. These shifts in international circumstances, then in turn impacted in an unprecedented way on traditional Jewish forms of community and social organization. In this respect, the post-1492 diaspora functions of the western Sephardim in the economic sphere arguably have more in common with those of the Armenian diaspora than they do with those of Ashkenazic and most of Middle-Eastern Jewry. It is remarkable, moreover, that the great reorganization and expansion of the Armenian trading diaspora – which had previously pivoted on the Ottoman empire – in the early seventeenth century also resulted from high-level political restructuring and imperial strategy in the Near and Middle East, indeed was caused by factors not unrelated to those which transformed the position of the Sephardim a century earlier.

During the later Middle Ages, we know, the Armenians were key intermediaries in the primarily overland trade between Mongolia, Central Asia and Italy. During the fifteenth and sixteenth centuries, the Armenians built on this experience and succeeded in establishing a flourishing commercial network ranging right across the Ottoman Empire, the Black Sea region and the Ukraine centring around the Armenian community of Lwow, and also gained footholds in the great Italian commercial emporia, including Livorno where, like the Sephardic Jews, they were from the outset among the groups of merchants expressly offered privileges (Engels 1997: 28, 30). Then, Shah Abbas I of Iran (ruled 1580–1629) deported and resettled large numbers of Armenians who had previously been under Ottoman control, particularly during and after his 1603–1605 campaign against the Turks, as part of a wider strategy of rivalry with the Ottoman Porte. As a result, numerous

Armenians were relocated to the interior of Iran, in the area south of the Caspian Sea and, from 1605, as Ina Baghdiantz McCabe describes, a core of elite families were resettled in New Julfa, a suburb of Isfahan where they became in some fashion court merchants or, more precisely, the 'Shah's merchants' integrated into the royal administrative system. New Julfa subsequently served as a hub of the now drastically reconfigured Armenian trade network which flourished so spectacularly in the seventeenth and eighteenth centuries (Baghdiantz McCabe 1999: ch. 5).

A striking consequence of this vigorous Iranian bid for imperial control over long-distance trade between Asia and the West was a marked further erosion of the ancient overland traffic linking Central Asia and the Near East. Like the Sephardim in Turkey and the Balkans, the prime function of the Armenian trade diaspora radiating outward from Iran and India was invariably to export local products westward and import European manufactures (Mauro 1990: 270–2). Part of Shah Abbas' – in this respect by no means wholly successful – strategy was to divert Persian silk exports away from Ottoman territory, by arranging for the silks to be shipped to western Europe (in practice mainly London and Amsterdam) via the Persian Gulf or else via the Caspian Sea and Moscow to Archangel from where, from the beginning of the seventeenth century onward, large quantities of high-value Persian silks and Caspian caviar were shipped each summer in Dutch vessels to the Amsterdam entrepôt (Israel 1989: 99, 153–4; 88–9). Negotiating sales of silk with English and Dutch buyers at Hormuz and Bandar 'Abbas, at the mouth of the Persian Gulf, became one of the classic Armenian commercial functions.

From the point of view of the Armenian diaspora, this focusing of their network on Iran – without, however, losing their footholds in Turkey and Italy – made possible an astonishing integration and expansion of their trade network in particular by linking India, the Far East, the Ukraine and Russia to New Julfa. In southern India, Madras under British control became a major focus of Armenian activity particularly with regard to distributing coral and purchases of rough diamonds (Israel 1989: 75). Although it is sometimes said that where the Sephardic Jews concentrated more on maritime trade while their Armenian counterparts concentrated more on overland trade, in fact the Armenians in Italy – and as Sushil Chaudhury demonstrates in Chapter 3 of this volume, in their flourishing Bengal trade – were just as apt as the Jews to employ the maritime routes and certainly much more adept in employing small Asian craft. In 1636, Armenian merchants established a foothold at Batavia (Jakarta), the chief Dutch maritime base in southeast Asia. They also exploited the fact that the Spanish authorities in the Philippines freely admitted Chinese and other Asian merchants while scrupulously excluding European rivals to establish a flourishing trade also in Manila. Nevertheless, in cases where these two diasporas, the Armenian and Sephardic, were direct competitors – as, for example, in the export of North African red coral via Livorno, London and Amsterdam to India, in exchange for rough diamonds, an indispensable element in the English (and Dutch) diamond trade with Golconda – there was a clear tendency toward division of labour, or at least to use of wholly different routes. The Sephardim being obviously far more dependent for the transportation of their wares, to and from India, on the large ships of the English and Dutch East India Companies, were restricted to the use of western vessels sailing round the Cape of Good Hope (Yogev 1978: 103–7).

Crucial to Armenian success in spanning the immense areas lying between western Europe and inner Asia, in early modern times, as Aghassian and Kevonian (1999: 74–94) and other specialists in Armenian commercial history have stressed, was their building of the commercial empire, like those of the other classic diasporas, on a system of trust supplemented by informal methods of enforcing family, religious and business discipline. For long-distance trade, spanning many states, this kind of commercial culture proved not just remarkably effective but indispensable. The tight family and religious community organization typical of the classic diasporas provided an informal judicial structure resilient enough not just to minimize transaction costs which others, in the absence of such ties, were unavoidably saddled with, but also to enable them to venture on commercial operations, relying on contracts, promises and undertakings, without the support of any state-based judicial apparatus or any institutional support other than that furnished by their own community network. Armenian community organization thus served as a dependable surrogate for the functions of the state in vast marginal zones, geographical, legal and military, which in any case often lay beyond the control of particular states.

Nevertheless, as Ina Baghdiantz McCabe stresses, there was a striking organizational difference between the Armenian Diaspora and that of the Sephardic Jews, Ashkenazic Jews and Greeks in that the Armenian Christian elite of New Julfa became an integral part of the regular financial and administrative machinery of the Safavid state. They therefore enjoyed, at any rate until the mid-seventeenth century, not just a privileged status but a defined set of quasi-administrative functions within the Iranian empire. Moreover, certain features of New Julfa's trade, such as the procedure for bullion imports, were carefully defined and directed by the Shah. However, the deterioration of the Armenian position as a specially favoured minority within the Iranian empire, in the 1650s, seems to have lent new momentum to Armenian emigration from Iran and therefore to the renewed spreading of the capital resources, demographic strength and religious vitality of the Armenian diaspora scattered across Asia and Europe.

In any case, the effective range of a diaspora's operations varied to a remarkable extent from period to period, and from diaspora to diaspora. No matter how important structural characteristics were, historical context, as always, was decisive. Certainly, all the early modern trade diasporas shared key features which account for how it was that these groups succeeded where others could not, in establishing enduring commercial networks over vast sections of the globe. All nurtured a culture of trust in commercial partners of the same community, and the systematic reduction (and in some instances complete elimination) of transaction costs incurred by others, generated by a geographically widely scattered but religiously and culturally close-knit international community possessing a distinctive language and communal institutions particular to itself. Greeks outside Greece, Armenians and Huguenots, no less than Yiddish-speaking Jews, could boast forms of legal autonomy existing independently of any particular state as well as finely tuned methods enforcing social discipline and maintaining strict standards of ethics and business practice within their own community wherever members travelled and traded.

Undeniably also, precisely the same set of structural changes and accompanying opportunities which forged the uniquely extended western Sephardic maritime trading diaspora within the wider Jewish diaspora was, initially at least, in its early formative stages, in the Ottoman context, offered equally to the Armenians and Greeks. For, as Philip Curtin (1984: 182, 197–8) has observed, restrictions placed in the sixteenth century by the Ottoman sultans on foreign traders, and especially West Europeans such as the Venetians, Genoese, French and later the English and Dutch, forced all the Westerners to rely in their dealings in Ottoman lands on what he called 'cross-cultural brokers', that is, intermediaries with the language, business, diplomatic and legal skills necessary to handle transactions for them, in other words, given the available business-orientated minorities in the Ottoman imperium, principally on the Greeks, Armenians and Sephardic (as distinct from Ashkenazic, Romaniote and Arabic-speaking) Jews.

Indeed, in some ways it might seem that the Romaniote and Arabic-speaking Jews, Greeks, and particularly the Armenians had an important edge over the Sephardim, for the Ottoman policy of easing the Venetians, Genoese and Florentines out of the markets which the Sultan controlled certainly began much earlier than 1492. In the Black Sea, for example, despite the fact that the Genoese and Venetians continued to provide the large ships which handled much of the region's long-distance maritime trade, the decay of the Genoese emporium centring on Caffa, at the mouth of the Sea of Azov, began around 1450, even before the Turks conquered the area in 1475, and seems to have been largely complete by the 1480s, the departing Genoese being replaced largely by Greeks and Armenians as well as Tartars and Turks (Ashtor 1983: 448–9, 480–1; Inalcik 1994: 209, 278, 286, 288, 315). The Greeks and Armenians also had many other apparent advantages over the Sephardic refugees, and not least their greater numbers and wider dispersal. Much of the mohair yarn which constituted the most valuable export product of Anatolia came from, or from near, the region of Armenia (Anderson 1989: 161).

Armenians also derived much commercial leverage from their experience and expertise in organizing trans-Anatolian caravans and supplying caravaniers.

It was not then either Ottoman policy, or the circumstances of local markets, which after 1492 rapidly placed the Sephardim in an unrivalled position, but rather the particular impact of this general elevation of cross-cultural brokers in the Ottoman empire on commercial relations between Italy and the Near East and the shifting of the Armenian centre of gravity eastward, to Iran. In particular, the Armenians and Greeks could not provide anything like so dense a network of connections as the Sephardim in Italy and the western Mediterranean. It was this, then, which during the mid-sixteenth century placed one particular Jewish society in a specially pivotal position which none of the other diasporas – including the rest of the Jewish people – could aspire to, at any rate not before the mid-eighteenth century. The shifting balance between Sephardic Jews and Greeks in the commercial politics of the Ottoman court was reflected in a tendency, pronounced by the mid-sixteenth century, for Jews to displace Greeks from many areas of tax-farming and managing state salt and other commodity monopolies (Inalcik 1994: 211–13).

Certainly, without the age-old continuity provided by the resilient ties of religion and family, it would have been totally impossible to form the particularly complex kind of diaspora with its unique religious tensions and ambiguities and highly specialized trading networks, which evolved among this section of the Jewish people following the Expulsion from Spain. But equally, without the specific sequence of developments, including the peculiar form of religious persecution to which Iberian Jewry was subjected after the setting up of the Spanish Inquisition, and the practice of mass forced baptism, the western Sephardim would never have acquired their peculiar versatility and adaptability leading to an unmatched capacity to span religious and cultural divides as well as continents and oceans, the characteristics which became their chief hallmark during the sixteenth century. For it was their religious duality and frequent ambivalence which above all differentiated the western Sephardim (many of whom had reverted to formal Judaism after several generations of living as Christians) from other Jewish societies and also from the Armenian and Greek Christians; albeit some Armenians also converted, often under duress, to Islam, particularly in Iran. Without the changed and more flexible European and intercontinental context created by the staged exodus from the Iberian peninsula and the rise of the Ottoman imperium, a context starkly different from that prevailing before the Expulsion from Spain, western Sephardic Jewry would have been no more successful, presumably, in traversing the continents, oceans and cultural spheres than any other Jewish or Christian diasporas.

The rise of the early modern maritime empires together with the resettlement of large numbers of Iberian Jews in the Ottoman Empire and the establishment of the Inquisition in Spain, Portugal and Spanish America, then, simply joined to produce a different set of effects among one part of the Jewish people – the western Sephardic and (associated) Portuguese *converso* diaspora – than it did among most of the Jews whether Yiddish, Greek, Arabic, or Persian-speaking or among Christian, Muslim or other trade diasporas of Europe and the Near East. During the Middle Ages, circumstances had encouraged large sections of the Jewish people to concentrate on trade and finance, and enabled them to spread their trading networks over considerable areas such as England, the Low Countries and Germany, and eastern Europe where they were newcomers. But the Middle Ages also divided the Mediterranean world between Christendom and Islam, and the Jews into corresponding Ashkenazic and Arabic-speaking categories which evinced, as Michael Toch stresses, despite what was long supposed, comparatively little capacity to interact and bridge the gap. It was only after the Christian reconquest of most of southern Spain in the thirteenth century, when a large, formerly Arabic-speaking Jewish population began to develop the specific skills needed to operate on both sides of the religious frontier between Christendom and Islam, that one section of the Jewish people began to acquire the expertise needed by any major 'cross-cultural' trade diaspora in early modern times. After 1500, stimulated by Ottoman policy, this section of Jewry developed its ability to bridge religions and cultures still further until it was equipped to handle a geographically and culturally (though not functionally) much wider field of operations than other kinds of Jews, or the other classic diasporas. In particular, they were equipped comprehensively to penetrate the new spheres of trans-Atlantic and colonial trade.

It is indeed a striking historical fact that neither the main body of the Jewish people nor the other early modern trade diasporas, however extensive, remarkable and important all of these in their different ways were, ever managed to span the gulf between all four of the main early modern religious spheres of Europe and the Near East – that is, Protestantism, Catholicism, Orthodoxy and Islam – all six of the western maritime empires, and America North and South as well as India and the Far East. Ashkenazic Jewry traversed all religions but by no means all the maritime empires, or continents, so that Yiddish-speaking Jewry played little or no part in the development of the maritime systems of the Ottoman Empire, Spain, Portugal, Venice, France, England or the Dutch, or in India or China. The Armenians similarly spanned all religions but not the Atlantic. The Huguenots traversed the Atlantic but not all religions or empires. Meanwhile, the Greeks outside Greece remained largely confined until the late eighteenth century to the Levant, the Balkans, Italy, Russia and the Black Sea. Only one particular sub-section of the Jewish people, the western Sephardic diaspora in combination with their forcibly converted (i.e. *converso)* relatives and associates in the Hispanic world contrived for some two centuries to span in structurally crucial ways all the great religious blocs with exclusive claims (i.e. Catholicism, Protestantism, Orthodoxy and Islam), all the western maritime empires and all the continents.

Although the impressive Sephardic contribution to European maritime expansion and colonization effectively began with the discovery of the Americas and with Portugal's initial exploratory efforts in coastal Africa and India in the late fifteenth century, it only assumed its mature form, extending also to the northern European maritime empires, from the end of the sixteenth century, and did not attain its fullest maturity until the second half of the seventeenth. At most, the Sephardic-crypto-Jewish world trade network remained at, or somewhere near, its fullest development for a century and a half. In fact, after about 1780, western Sephardic Jewry's contribution to the functioning of the West's by now overwhelming preponderance over world trade-routes, resources and markets began, fairly rapidly, to disintegrate.

The western Sephardic diaspora originated in medieval Spain and Portugal. It acquired its peculiar characteristics as a trading diaspora in Ottoman lands between 1492 and the mid-sixteenth century. By 1650, Sephardic Jewish communities scattered across western Europe and recently if still precariously established in the New World, together with the residual crypto-Jewish networks in the Iberian Peninsula and Ibero-America, as well as 'Westernized' Spanish-speaking elements scattered among Levantine and North African Jewry, had forged close and vigorous links with the Turkish dominions, the Persian Gulf, trans-Saharan Africa, the Atlantic Islands under Portugal and Spain, the Caribbean, Brazil, Spanish America and North America as well as, more tentatively, with the Portuguese, Spanish, Dutch, and British enclaves in India, China, the Philippines and Indonesia. In doing so they had created a startlingly new phenomenon in Jewish history. For theirs was a new type of Jewish commercial system which, while displaying some affinities with medieval Jewish patterns of trade and finance, dramatically differed in that it mainly used maritime rather than overland routes and was based principally not on local markets, or on dealings in agricultural produce, but rather on transporting non-European commodities vast distances. Also in marked contrast to circumstances during the Middle Ages, the Christian-Islamic divide now became a central axis of activity rather than, as in the past, a line of internal Jewish segregation, while reaching systematically across the Protestant-Catholic divide also became a typical feature, especially after 1590.

The colonial products shipped to the emporia of the West by this culturally specific and economically highly specialized diaspora consisted primarily of sugar, spices, bullion, diamonds, pearls, hides, tobacco, cacao, silks and American dye-woods (especially Brazil wood and Campeche wood) but included numerous other luxury and exotic commodities ranging from Saharan ostrich feathers to indigo, cochineal, ginger and coffee. In addition, western Sephardic Jewry from the late sixteenth century onwards, played a major part in the export of European textiles to the Near East and the Americas, the re-export of Asian spices to the New World and the shipping, as we have seen, of North African red coral to India. The Sephardim and the *conversos* with whom they formed trading partnerships, also played a not inconsiderable part, albeit eventually much less substantial than the big (Protestant and Catholic) slaving companies established by Dutch, English and French, in the transportation of African slaves to the Americas, and their sale to plantation, mine and *hacienda* owners.

The new global context which evolved from the end of the fifteenth century onward, and which enabled the western Sephardim to play their unique role in early modern times, owed much to the disruption of the characteristic late-medieval trade patterns across the Near East resulting from the early stages of Portuguese and Spanish colonial expansion, the Ottoman conquest of the Byzantine empire and the establishment of Turkish control in the Balkans and around the coasts of the Black Sea and Aegean. The combination of the rapid Iberian conquest and colonization of the Caribbean, Mexico, Peru, Brazil and West Africa with the extension of Turkish power in the eastern Mediterranean and the Middle East simultaneously connected the markets of the New and Old Worlds while drastically reshaping commercial contacts between Christendom and the Islamic World. It was a wholly changed context requiring new types of long-distance trade networks. The Spanish and Portuguese American markets, chiefly exporting such products as sugar and bullion to Europe, not only caused European commerce to re-orientate toward the West but placed a large premium on expertise and especially reliable channels of communication and trade able effectively to negotiate the vast new spaces – not just continents and oceans but also dramatically changed religious frontiers.

To cross the much greater distances now involved – political and cultural as well as geographical – required a range of specialized techniques which the old-established European Christian merchant elites, and also the majority of European and Near Eastern Jewry, largely lacked. By 1400, the Jews of Germany, Italy and Provence had been squeezed by the hostility of the 'host' societies among which they lived into an extremely narrow range of economic functions, chiefly moneylending and petty trading. It is true that the largest European Jewish community, that of Spain, remained despite the onset of systematic Christian oppression also there from the 1390s, more favourably situated than the rest of European Jewry. But prior to 1492 Spain was neither a great maritime nation nor yet a major military power. Furthermore, most of Spain's international trade lay in the hands of the Genoese, Flemish and other Christian nations. The commerce of Spanish Jewry though diverse was largely confined to the internal market in local products such as textiles, leather goods and grain. Relatively little of their commerce was orientated outward.

However, by the time of the expulsion of the Jews from Spain in 1492, much of Spanish Jewry had converted, under duress, at least nominally to Christianity, thereby not only retaining their immovable property and valuables of which those who remained stubbornly faithful to their old religion were largely deprived, but also thereby regaining the right to remain in their native land. Furthermore, they were also freed from the oppressive restrictions and pressures to which they had been subjected while living in the Iberian Peninsula as Jews. Hence, as nominal Christians, they enjoyed much more personal freedom than before. Meanwhile, the bulk of those Jews who left Spain in 1492 migrated either to the Ottoman empire where they settled in such maritime commercial centres as Salonika and Constantinople or else to Portugal where the entire community was forcibly baptized in 1497. Despite the emigration restrictions intermittently placed on them, the forcibly baptized Jews in Portugal, many of whom remained loyal to Judaism in secret despite their official status as 'New Christians', thenceforth also had more freedom of movement and profession at least within Portugal than before.

In the changed sixteenth-century context, Portugal and the Ottoman seaports were, at the same time, the two most decisively situated spaces from which to respond to the new commercial opportunities and participate in the reshaping of the world's trade routes. Hence, nearly all the Jews and crypto-Jews in the three key maritime and commercial crossroads of the early sixteenth-century world who were in a position to participate in long-distance trade could do so in a new context of freedom, having been liberated from all the usual restraints besetting medieval European Jewry either by the Turks or else by more or less forced conversion in the Iberian Peninsula. Furthermore, despite the distances and contrasting conditions they had to negotiate, the Jews and crypto-Jews in all three of these key zones were of Iberian background, speech and culture, and were frequently linked by close social and family ties

By 1550, Portuguese crypto-Jews had gained an important share in the burgeoning overseas commerce of Portugal with Brazil, India, West Africa, and the Low Countries, while Spanish-speaking Jews, migrating from Salonika, rapidly acquired a prominent and in certain respects hegemonic position – at the expense of the Venetians, Florentines and other Italians – in the internal trade of Greece and the Balkans. Where until around 1500, Venetians, Genoese and also Florentines still dominated the Balkan market and Black Sea markets, supplying high-quality woollen textiles and other Western products in exchange for the raw silks, wool and hides produced in these regions, between 1500 and 1540, Italian merchants rapidly lost their former ascendancy if not yet in the maritime trade of the eastern Mediterranean then certainly over the internal marketing of Western products within Ottoman lands and the buying up of Greek, Balkan Crimean, and Anatolian silks and wools.

During these decades, the Italians were progressively squeezed out of such regional trade emporia as Salonika, Belgrade, Sofia, Sarajevo, Edirne, Ankara, Bursa and Patras as well as the Black Sea and Dalmatian ports. As a matter of policy, the Ottoman court forced the shipping of the Italian trading republics out of the Black Sea region and compelled Westerners to pay higher tolls and customs than its own subjects were subject to in all the inland Balkan and Anatolian commercial centres (Cooperman 1987: 198; Emmanuel 1936: 254–61; Paci 1971: 33–5; Veinstein 1987: 785–7). This happened despite the fact that the Italian commercial republics continued to supply most of the European manufactures imported into the Turkish empire, as well as to ship the spices and pepper transported overland via India from south-east Asia to Aleppo and Alexandria, together with the Persian raw silks, Anatolian mohair yarn, and Egyptian cotton and sugar exported to the West.

In this way the Turkish ruling elite, determined to curtail the extensive trading privileges and freedoms possessed in the Near East for centuries by the Venetians, Genoese and other Westerners, forged a trading context in which ethnic Turks, Arabs, Kurds, Balkan Christians, Armenians, Greeks and Romaniote (Greek-speaking) Jews no less than the Sephardim theoretically found themselves in a greatly improved position. But the Sephardic Jews alone were able to take full advantage of the new circumstances. Like the Romaniote Jews, Ashkenazim and Turks they had the advantage of not being Christians; but in addition, as a result of their recent expulsion from Iberian and southern Italy, the Sephardim, unlike the Romaniotes and (Italian, Hungarian-Roumanian and Balkan) Ashkenazim, possessed knowledge of Western languages and writing, and continued to have connections with the maritime centres of the West. This clearly placed them in a near unique position in the Jewish as well as in the Christian and Muslim worlds: only the Armenians offered a comparable degree of versatility. While in some cases the Turks may have deliberately favoured the Jews in preference to other groups, as when Rhodes fell to the Turks in 1523 and Cyprus in 1571, and the Ottoman authorities seemingly issued orders for the settlement of Jews on those islands as a way of curtailing Italian and western Christian commercial influence (Israel 1998: 198; Levy 1992: 11, 28; Lewis 1984: 123), in general Sephardic pre-eminence in Balkan trade was simply an unplanned by-product of a broader context and set of circumstances.

The new arrivals from Spain, Portugal and southern Italy, then, were best placed to exploit the new circumstances. While the bulk of the Sephardic population in the Ottoman empire settled in the Greek lands and the littoral of Asia Minor, a few lesser Judeo-Spanish communities which took root to the north of the Greek lands attained considerable significance during the early sixteenth century. This rise of a new Sephardic trading network revolved not so much around the Ottoman capital in Constantinople – which was by no means the largest Sephardic centre in the empire – but rather around Salonika and the latter's numerous offshoot communities in Greece and the Aegean, as well as to an extent in the Balkans proper. Salonika Jewry's rising prosperity and importance in turn attracted further Sephardic immigration both from the new Spanish-speaking congregations in Italy and directly from Portugal. The largely Sephardic and Italian Jewish population of Valona, on the Dalmatian coast, for example, increased by over five times during the first two decades of the sixteenth century, reaching around 2,000 by 1520 (Veinstein 1987: 785–6), a considerable proportion of these consisting of ostensibly Christianized Jews escaping from the mass forced baptism in Portugal in 1497.

Ascendancy over the Balkan inland trade routes and emporia against the background of the growing Turkish power at sea, as well as on land, placed the immigrant Spanish-speaking Jews of the Ottoman imperium in an entirely new position with respect to international – and especially international maritime – trade. Having been progressively marginalized throughout the later medieval centuries in western, central and southern Europe, they now for the first time for generations again became a vital link between East and West and, in particular, an indispensable channel for trade relations between Italy and the Near East. By the 1540s, despite their reluctance to admit to having suffered a major setback, not to mention aversion to the prospect of having to adapt to it, the Venetians as well as the Ferrarese, Florentines and the papal states had been forced to acknowledge that if they wanted to preserve a major role in the Levant trade they had no choice but to learn to deal with and through the Sephardim of the Balkans, Greece and Aegean.

Before long, republics and principalities on the Italian mainland enacted measures to attract the settlement of Iberian Jewish expatriates. In 1538, the duke of Ferrara, perceiving that this might be a useful method of diverting some of the lucrative Levant traffic away from Venice, issued a charter permitting 'Levantine' and other Spanish- and Portuguese-speaking Jews special rights of residence within his territory. In a particularly striking move, resolved on only after much arduous deliberation, the Venetian senate, prompted by the senatorial council for trade, the *Cinque Savii alla mercanzia*, finally abandoned its long-standing policy of shutting out Jewish long-distance traders and permitted 'Levantine' Jews to settle, thereby adding another sizeable 'classic diaspora' grouping to their community of Greeks, consisting both of refugees from mainland areas as well as islands – latterly including Cyprus – under Turkish rule and also natives of the Greek islands under Venetian control.

The 'Levantine' Jews were allowed to settle in Venice and assume an important role in the Venetian emporium, because, as the *Cinque Savii* expressed it, 'the commerce of Upper and Lower Romania [i.e. of the whole Balkans] is being diverted from this city, being now principally in the hands of the Levantine Jews' (Archivio di Stato, Venezia: 1st series, vol. 137, fos 135v-136 and vol. 143, fos 20v-21; Israel 1998: 37). Venice could not change this unpalatable fact and had no choice but to adapt to it. Following the Venetians, in 1547, Pope Paul III accorded comparable permission for 'Levantine' Jews to settle in Ancona, again expressly for the purpose of promoting trade with Ottoman lands, while in 1551 the Grand Duke of Tuscany issued charters inviting Ottoman and other Jews practiced in the Levant trade to settle on his territory (Cooperman 1987: 73). As early as 1552, there were more than 100 Portuguese Jewish families residing in the papal port of Ancona, as well as 'Italian' and Spanish-speaking 'Levantine' Jews (Toaff 1974: 263–4).

It is true that the early growth of the new Italian Sephardic communities was subsequently disrupted by the change in papal policy, followed in part by the other states, from the mid-1550s. Pope Paul IV, one of the chief architects of the Counter-Reformation, reasserting the theological priorities of the Holy See, shifted to an unrelentingly anti-Jewish and anti-*converso* stance (Israel 1998: 14–18; Zorattini 1980: 11–14). But subject to this new pressure, the Ottoman Empire more than ever became the prime refuge and support of the exiles from Iberia. The economic and cultural development of the Spanish Jewish exiles in Ottoman lands, therefore, expanded further. Theirs was a social and commercial system combining new elements, especially as regards maritime and long-distance trade and the bridging function of Ottoman Jewry between East and West while also accommodating more traditional economic activities, such as the extensive artisan and textile skills of medieval Spanish Jewry. Especially in Salonika but also in Safed, in Galilee, a Jewish community which drew raw wool and silk supplies from as far away as the Peloponnese, cloth-making, leather, silk-weaving and dyeing industries took root in the wake of the mass migration from Spain, reaching a peak of vigour and prosperity during the third quarter of the century. After that, the Jewish textile industries in the Ottoman Empire, like the Ottoman Sephardic trading system itself, undermined in particular by textile imports from Italy, Flanders, Holland and England – lands where techniques were increasingly more sophisticated and transport costs lower – commenced its slow but inexorable decline.

The success of the Spanish exiles in the Ottoman imperium, then, was rapid but one followed by a premature decadence which was increasingly obvious by the early seventeenth century. Meanwhile, in Portugal the success of the forcibly converted New Christians was slower but ultimately had still greater ramifications. During the early phases of Lisbon's long-distance commerce, with Portugal emerging as the dominant European trading power in India, Indonesia, the Persian Gulf and West Africa and extending its grip over the coasts of Brazil, its overseas trade, largely confined to spices, pepper, jewels and Guinea gold, though valuable, was of low bulk and highly centralized in character. Participants in the traffic consisted of just a handful of front-rank merchants with very large capital resources, often Italian, Flemish or German.

Initially, then, few 'New Christian' businessmen shared to any significant extent in Portugal's spectacular maritime expansion, though this handful prospered and found opportunities for others, especially since they needed reliable agents and factors to help them exploit the business opportunities their new Asian, African and Brazilian trade opened up for them in the wider European market. Preferring to employ their own relatives, and in the case of those who remained loyal to the old faith, fellow crypto-Jews, as their correspondents abroad, the originally small group of Lisbon crypto-Jewish New Christian businessmen engaged in colonial commerce did not just amass wealth and far-flung contacts but created an entire new network of crypto-Jewish business agents to handle (in particular) their spice and jewel consignments to Italy, France, Germany and the Low Countries. For they needed trusted, experienced agents adept at dealing internationally, particularly in Venice, Florence, Rome, Bordeaux and Antwerp, the latter then the main entrepôt for Portuguese colonial goods in northern Europe. From a tiny group of fewer than twenty persons in 1511, the Portuguese *converso* community of Anwerp swelled by 1570 to a sizeable body of around 300 adults divided ideologically, the evidence indicates, into two sharply differentiated and inwardly warring factions, part faithful to their new Christian faith, others rumoured to be crypto-Jewish.

From the 1560s, the rising production of the newly established sugar plantations transplanted from Madeira and São Thomé vastly enhanced both the value of Brazil to Portugal and the importance of the Portuguese seaborne empire to such commercial centres as Antwerp, Livorno, Venice, Bordeaux and soon Hamburg. While a few Portuguese New Christians had already traded with Brazil in the early sixteenth century, in particular importing Brazil wood, a dye-stuff highly prized by Europe's textile industries, it was assuredly the rise of Brazilian sugar, after 1560, which rendered Brazil crucially important to both the Portuguese New Christians and the western Sephardic diaspora as a whole. For the Brazil sugar traffic generated a considerably larger network than had existed previously of partly or largely crypto-Jewish Portuguese New Christian merchants engaged in, and orientated toward, trans-Atlantic trade.

A little later, toward the end of the sixteenth century, tiny groups of crypto-Jews fanning out from Antwerp, or arriving fresh from Portugal, following the onset of the Low Countries Wars in 1572, established new crypto-Jewish communities in London, Rouen, Hamburg and (from 1595) Amsterdam. The Dutch Revolt particularly after the paralysing siege of Antwerp (1584–85) acted as an important agent of diffusion, spreading the incipient Portuguese Jewish business diaspora to various new locations in northern Europe. Among the factors which drove this process of extension and enlargement was the growing volume and diversity of the spice traffic handled by the western European trading powers, first the Portuguese but then, from the 1590s, also the Dutch followed soon after by the English. Pepper from Indonesia and the Malabar coast, nutmeg, cloves and mace were shipped in much larger quantities than before, while cinnamon from Ceylon was transported from Portugal to northern European ports from around 1570.

After their arrival in the Indonesian Spice Islands in the late 1590s, the Dutch rapidly gained control of the lion's share of the traffic, curtailing the Portuguese share of the trade drastically and largely cutting off the traditional flow of spices and pepper across the Middle East and via Aleppo and Alexandria to Italy, a traffic which despite the activities of the Portuguese had continued on a substantial scale throughout the sixteenth century and even experienced something of a revival during the late sixteenth century. By contrast, within a few years of 1600, this ancient traffic almost entirely ceased, a veritable catastrophe for the Italian trading powers as well as for the Portuguese. The rapid decline of Italy's and the Iberian Peninsula's long-distance commerce after 1600 in turn led directly to the undisputed hegemony of the north-west European Atlantic seaboard in the marketing of spices (and other south Asian products) throughout Europe and the Mediterranean with the western Sephardic diaspora from their bases in Amsterdam, Hamburg and Antwerp playing a key intermediary role in the commerce (Lane 1966: 33–4).

Meanwhile, yet another important cause of the expansion of the linked Portuguese crypto-Jewish and western Sephardic diasporas after 1580 was the political union of the Spanish and Portuguese crowns in that year and consequent dramatic increase in Portuguese 'New Christian' immigration into Spain and via Spain (and sometimes also via Brazil or Portuguese West Africa) into Spanish America. In the early seventeenth century, the Spanish crown consciously encouraged this kind of migration, seeking more financiers and tax-farmers to assist with collecting revenues and financing its military undertakings (Belinchón *n.d.*: 33–8; Contreras 1995: 196–200, 205–10). It was, moreover, in the 1580s that crypto-Judaism first deeply penetrated the viceroyalties of New Spain and Peru and first became a factor in the great Andean silver metropolis of Potosí as well as in the contraband traffic which began in the 1580s, linking Peru, via Tucumán and the River Plate, with Buenos Aires and the Portuguese outposts in southern Brazil (Canabrava 1944: 61–4, 87; Israel 2002: 18–19, 125–50).

The Portuguese New Christians in Spanish America specialized like their counterparts elsewhere, chiefly in long-distance trade, in particular in retailing European textiles, often circumventing the closely regulated framework of the official trans-Atlantic convoy system designed by the Spanish crown to restrict trade to officially approved routes, harbours, times and methods of shipping, so as to minimize the difficulty of exerting bureaucratic and fiscal control over vast distances with limited resources. Thus, the route to and from Potosí, via Tucumán and Buenos Aires, was in theory closed to trade, and was supposed to be used only by officials, soldiers and clergy. Likewise, numerous other Spanish imperial maritime and overland routes, such as the sea-lanes between Peru and Central America, Peru and New Spain, Venezuela and New Spain, and the river route from Buenos Aires to Peru via Paraguay, were heavily restricted. In 1604, New Spain's maritime trade with Peru was reduced to two vessels per year, with a ban on carrying oriental fabrics on the outward run or bullion on their return; and in 1634 this traffic was prohibited altogether (Israel 1975: 100–2, 196–7). New Spain's trans-Pacific China trade, via Acapulco, on the Manila galleons to the Philippines was, from 1593 onward, limited to only two vessels per year supposedly to prevent Chinese silk imports from Manila undercutting Spain's textile exports to Spanish America; later it was still more heavily restricted (Israel 1975: 75, 101). Meanwhile, the Spanish crown strictly prohibited commerce of any sort with Portuguese, English, Dutch or other foreign ships cruising along the coasts of the Spanish Caribbean or Spanish American mainland. All this provided ample scope for contrabandists not a few of whom, from the 1580s onward, were in fact Portuguese New Christians.

Bolstered by their expertise in unauthorized trade, it would seem that the Portuguese New Christians, some of whom were crypto-Jews, forged the earliest contacts between Spanish America and European countries other than Spain. The Dutch, in particular, initially began to trade with the Spanish colonies through Portuguese New Christian merchants based in Puerto Rico, Cuba, Hispaniola (Española) and such Venezuelan centres as Maracaibo, Río de la Hacha, and Caracas, a town where out of forty-six resident foreigners, making up a sizeable proportion of the adult male white population in year 1606, no fewer than forty-one were Portuguese, many or most of these being 'New Christians' (Israel 1989: 62; Sluiter 1948: 173; Vilar 1979: 155–6). However tenuously, the contraband route between Potosí and Buenos Aires, a port where many Portuguese *conversos* settled in the years around 1600 linked up with the Portuguese in southern Brazil and ultimately with Lisbon. Not only did large quantities of untaxed silver and other Spanish American products reach Brazil and eventually Portugal by this route but so, in reverse, did unregistered imports of textiles from Europe and slaves shipped by the Portuguese from West Africa via Brazil to Potosí and Peru.

The principal successor of Antwerp as the northern entrepôt for Ibero-American colonial products as well as the silks, mohairs, and other luxury goods of the Levant and North Africa was, of course, Amsterdam. This was true in general terms and also with respect to the further evolution of the trans-Atlantic and trans-Mediterranean Jewish-'New Christian' trading diaspora. As the Dutch Revolt continued to succeed, there began, especially from the 1590s, an unprecedented expansion in Dutch shipping and commerce and, at the same time, Amsterdam emerged as what soon became the chief centre for such specialized industries and services as sugar-refining, diamond-cutting, tobacco-spinning and blending, maritime insurance, commodity brokerage, all geared to the processing and distribution of colonial products. In introducing these new activities to the Dutch entrepôt without which it would have been hard for Amsterdam permanently to supplant Antwerp as the primary northern European depot for colonial products, Sephardic Jews, mostly former New Christians who had reverted from Christianity to Judaism in Holland or France, played a conspicuous part. By 1620, there were around 1,000 Portuguese-speaking Jews dwelling in Amsterdam.[1]

During the first quarter-century of the existence of the Amsterdam Portuguese Jewish community, down to 1620, this group handled the larger part of Dutch commerce with Portugal, Brazil, Madeira and the Azores, established a leading role in the Dutch trade with Morocco (De Bakker 1991: 17–18), and also gained a significant foothold in the Dutch trade with the Caribbean, Spain and Italy. The second period of war between the Dutch Republic and Spain (1621–48), however, severely hampered the commerce of the Portuguese Jewish community in Holland and their network of New Christian correspondents in Lisbon, Oporto, Seville, Malaga, Hamburg and Antwerp for more than a quarter of a century. Being more dependent on Iberian markets and the Iberian empires than were other sections of the Dutch merchant community, the Sephardic Jews together with the ostensibly Christian *conversos* who had settled in Antwerp were more seriously affected by the disruption than were other sectors of the Dutch trading system (De Bakker 1991: 116–32; Ebben 1996: 131–2; Fuks-Mansfeld 1989: 68–9; Israel 2002: 208–15). Nevertheless, not all the effects were damaging or negative. For by disrupting Dutch trade with the Iberian Peninsula, the war also stimulated commerce with Morocco, a country which served the Dutch Sephardim in some measure as a substitute. A still more valuable compensation was the rise of a Dutch colonial empire in the New World with the setting up of the Dutch West India Company, in 1621, and the conquest of north-eastern Brazil by Dutch forces during the early 1630s. The eager involvement of Dutch Sephardic Jews in the colonization of Dutch Brazil in the 1630s and early 1640s reflected the continuing depression in the trans-Atlantic transit traffic via Portugal.

The era of prosperity for the Portuguese Jewish community in Dutch Brazil, however, proved of short duration. It ended abruptly, in 1645, with that year's great revolt of the Portuguese planters and their slaves against Dutch rule. The Dutch colonial regime and military garrison, caught completely unprepared, could do little more than retreat behind the walls of the main towns and forts. Within months, the sugar plantations were devastated and the economy in ruins (Cabral de Mello 1975: 43–4, 273–5; Israel 1989: 168–70; Van den Boogaart et al. 1992: 127; Wätjen 1921: 322–3). Sugar and Brazil-wood exports slumped and never recovered during the remaining nine years of the Dutch presence in the area. Many of the Jews who had settled in Recife and neighbouring localities left Brazil during the late 1640s and early 1650s, dispersing in various directions though the majority returned, at least initially, to Amsterdam or Middelburg. During the bitter war which followed, the Dutch held on to Recife while, at sea, they heavily disrupted Portuguese Atlantic shipping; but they failed in every attempt to defeat the rebels in the field and thereby clear them from the sugar-producing zone. With the final collapse and surrender of Dutch Brazil during the First Anglo-Dutch War, in 1654, the remaining 600 Jews in the country were obliged to depart, some leaving for other parts of the Americas, chiefly the Caribbean and the Guyanas, most for the Netherlands.

Thus, the most remarkable Jewish social, economic and religious experiment in the New World ended in 1654. Nevertheless, something of what had been built up by the Jewish colonists in Brazil survived elsewhere, contributing in various ways to the development of other New World Jewish communities, notably in New Amsterdam (New York), Curaçao, Barbados, Jamaica, and Surinam. From the 1650s, onwards, the Sephardic community of Curaçao, emerged as a key entrepôt, not least for the shipping of Venezuelan cacao and tobacco, in the long-range commerce between Holland and Spanish America (Israel 1989: 240–2; Israel 2001: 335–49; Israel 2002: 400–1, 513–16, 528–34, 540–1, 554–6, 562–4; Klooster 2001: 353–68; Sánchez 2000: 107–10, 131–42). The exodus of Sephardim from Brazil likewise stimulated the founding of Sephardic communities in the French Caribbean which were allowed to take root, albeit precariously, during the period of relatively liberal social and economic policies pursued under Mazarin and the opening years of the personal rule of Louis XIV. During the 1660s and 1670s, Martinique rapidly outstripped Guadeloupe both in sugar production and general importance and had a flourishing Sephardic Jewish community (Arbell 2001: 287–313). The leading figure in the Sephardic community socially, economically and culturally, was Benjamin d'Acosta de Andrade who had been brought up as a *converso* in Portugal but had subsequently lived as a professing Jew in Dutch Brazil from where he arrived in Martinique in 1654.

In the early 1680s, however, Louis' attitude changed and French policy toward the Sephardim in the Caribbean was reversed. The growth of the Jewish presence in French America ended abruptly with an edict issued by Louis XIV in 1685 (the same year in which he revoked the Edict of Nantes). This measure, enacted in response to repeated efforts by the Jesuits and their allies to secure the expulsion of the Jews, referred back to the edict of his father Louis XIII, of 23 April 1615, denying Jews all right to live in France, proclaimed them 'declared enemies of Christianity' who therefore were a pernicious and undesirable presence in the French colonies. They were ordered to depart within three months of publication of the decree, on pain of imprisonment and confiscation of their goods. Most of the Jews of the French Caribbean, nearly one hundred from Martinique alone, did leave, most migrating to the now flourishing Sephardic community of Curaçao, taking with them the Torah scroll which had been presented to the Martinique community by the Portuguese synagogue in Amsterdam in 1676 (Van den Boogaart et al. 1992: 294). Nevertheless, Sephardic commerce was by no means totally eradicated from Martinique, Guadeloupe, Cayenne or Saint-Domingue then or later.

The exodus from Brazil accelerated the process of Jewish settlement in other parts of the New World. But it also stimulated the impulse to found new Sephardic communities within a mercantilist framework in Europe. There was, remarkably, a close connection between the spread of new Jewish communities in the Caribbean, Guyanas and North America during the 1650s and 1660s and the simultaneous efforts to resettle Sephardic communities in England, Zeeland, and the northern Italian states (see pp. 000–000). Discreetly, and behind the scenes, the Amsterdam Sephardic leadership, anxious to reduce the excess of poor and needy on their hands, and help rehabilitate those who had lost their homes and businesses, guided and presided over this remarkable trans-Atlantic colonization programme ranging from Italy to the Caribbean. England was then the fiercest rival of the Dutch for domination of world trade and shipping; and given the bitter and hard-fought background of the First Anglo-Dutch War (1652–54), a struggle fought mainly by the rival fleets in the North Sea and English Channel but with important clashes also in the Mediterranean, it was impossible for the Elders of the Portuguese Jewish congregation in Amsterdam directly to support projects for Jewish resettlement in London and the English empire. But even there, the evidence shows, behind the scenes the Amsterdam Sephardic elders were in fact directing the proceedings.

During the second half of the seventeenth and first half of the eighteenth centuries, the period which marks the high-point of Jewish involvement with Europe's global maritime empires, two great western European emporia – Amsterdam and Livorno – but not London were increasingly the leading Sephardic communal, cultural and religious centres, all the other Sephardic communities tending in various degrees to revolve around them and signally failing to grow to a comparable extent. The British overseas-trading system, in contrast to those of Venice, Portugal and the Dutch, never accorded the Sephardim an integral role in its inner mechanism. The London Sephardic community did play some part in England's burgeoning overseas trade and did expand to reach around 1,050 by 1720 and possibly as many as 1,700 by 1740. But structurally it remained marginal to the overall framework of the British Empire and British commerce. Even at its height, in the mid- and late eighteenth century, the London Sephardic community remained, from a cultural, demographic and religious point of view, of strictly secondary importance compared with those of Amsterdam, Venice, Livorno, Salonika or Constantinople (Diamond 1968: 40–1).

Only in a few isolated sectors of commerce, such as trade with Portugal, Barbados and Jamaica, the operations of the Gibraltar depot, and the buying of rough diamonds at Madras, did this community gain more than a marginal significance. And perhaps only in the diamond trade was it crucial. In the 1680s, the English East India Company was obliged to acknowledge that the London Sephardic community and its factors in southern India were indispensable to England's success in capturing and dominating the world market in Indian diamonds (Endelman 2002: 30; Yogev 1978: 92–6). Also, London for a time rivalled Amsterdam and Livorno in its capacity to draw crypto-Jewish immigration from Spain and Portugal, though by the 1740s when London Sephardic Jewry was at its peak, the major last wave of Portuguese New Christian emigration spent itself. After the 1740s, fresh crypto-Jewish emigration from Portugal and Brazil never rose above miniscule levels. The essentially marginal character of Sephardic participation in the British imperial system, compared to those of the Ottomans, Venetians, Portuguese, Spanish and Dutch, was mirrored in the eighteenth century both in the comparative paucity and insignificance of the provincial Sephardic communities outside London and in London Sephardic Jewry's loss of capacity to grow to any appreciable extent after the middle of the century.

Despite the progressive decline of the Dutch overseas-trading system after 1713, and especially from the 1740s, in Amsterdam there continued to be many more important Jewish merchants, financiers and brokers, a much larger Jewish diamond-cutting and polishing industry, and a far more substantial Jewish tobacco industry than in London. By 1700 there were no fewer than twenty-three tobacco-spinning and blending establishments in Amsterdam, around a dozen of which were Jewish-owned (Luzac 1780–83; Herks 1967: 175, 195). By 1720, the total number of tobacco-processing workshops there had risen to about thirty and the Jewish total to around fifteen, establishments which employed both Sephardic and Ashkenazic workers albeit usually with the former acting as supervisors and the latter in the more menial functions (Herks 1967: 164–6; Westermann 1943: 73). The Portuguese Jewish communities of Amsterdam and Livorno, where poor Jews often worked in the coral-polishing industry, both numbered well over 3,000 in the late seventeenth century. Indeed, according to the most expert recent estimates, Amsterdam Sephardic Jewry at its peak, around 1685, attained considerably higher levels than previously estimated, amounting to around 4,500, a level from which it declined only slightly during the course of the eighteenth century.[2]

After the end of the War of the Spanish Succession (1713), and especially during the second half of the eighteenth century, the western Sephardic trade diaspora rapidly lost its general impetus and importance in global trade. The Venetian and Dutch as well as the Ottoman maritime empires rapidly declined while the stream of crypto-Jewish emigration from Portugal and Spain dried up. Portuguese New Christians as an identifiable group ceased to play a significant or distinctive role in Spanish and Ibero-American commerce. The Sephardic community of Hamburg largely disappeared while that of London continued to stagnate. By around 1750, the western Sephardic merchant diaspora could no longer rely on a network of relatives among Portuguese New Christian merchants scattered in commercial centres dotted all over the Iberian Peninsula and Ibero-America and this, in turn, increasingly marginalized the Sephardic trans-Atlantic and international trade network as a whole. As the system lost its impetus and creative drive, and its capacity to adapt, it was increasingly deprived of its usefulness to the remaining great maritime empires, which, then, in turn, accentuated the commercial decline and added to the growing impoverishment and other social problems associated with the economic deterioration.

More and more, Sephardic congregations in Europe had to grapple not only with a serious increase in poverty and unemployment but a tendency for sons of wealthy families to become inactive gentlemen *rentiers*, and finally, also for wealthier Sephardim to move away from the main community centres such as Amsterdam, Venice and Livorno with their rising social burdens and responsibilities (Bernfeld 2002: 67, 71, 85–91, 96–102). The ultimate result of these combined processes of commercial decay, financial deterioration and abandonment of communal responsibilities was a trend toward communal dispersal especially to the New World and toward cultural assimilation, not infrequently culminating in the reconversion (of Jews who had reverted to normative Judaism after living for generations as New Christians) to Christianity, both Protestant and Catholic, a late eighteenth and early nineteenth-century phenomenon especially marked in England, Holland and Germany but discernable also in the Caribbean, Surinam and North America.

Notes

1. On the demographic development of the Sephardic community in the Netherlands, see H.P.H. Nusteling (2002: 43–62).
2. According to Nusteling's calculations (2002: 58–60), the Amsterdam Sephardic community reached its demographic peak around 1680 or 1685 at which date it numbered around 4,500.

Bibliography

Arbell, M. (2001), 'Jewish Settlements in the French Colonies in the Caribbean (Martinique, Guadeloupe, Haiti, Cayenne)', in P. Bernardini and N. Fiering (eds) *The Jews and the Expansion of Europe to the West, 1450–1800*, New York:

Baghdiantz McCabe, I. (1999), *The Shah's Silk for Europe's Silver: The Eurasian Silk Trade of the Julfan Armenians in Safavid Iran and India (1590–1750)*, University of Pennsylvania (Series in Armenian Texts and Studies), Atlanta: Scholar's Press.

Belinchón, B. López (n.d.), *Honra, libertad y hacienda: Hombres de negocios y judíos sefardíes,* Alcalá de Henares: 33–8, 141–78.

Bernfeld, T.L. (2002), 'Financing Poor-Relief in the Spanish-Portuguese Community in Amsterdam', in Jonathan Israel and R. Salverda (eds) *Dutch Jewry: Its History and Secular Culture*, Leiden: 67–102.

Cabral de Mello, E. (1975) *Olinda restaurada Guerra e açucar no Nordeste, 1630–1654*, São Paulo.

Canabrava, A.P. (1944), *O Comércio português no Rio da Prata, 1580–1640*, São Paulo.

Contreras, J. Contreras (1995), 'Cristianos de España y Judíos de Amsterdam. Emigración, familia y negocios', in J. Lechner and H. den Boer (eds) *España y Holanda*, Amsterdam.

De Bakker, J. (1991), *Slaves, Arms and Holy War: Moroccan Policy vis-à-vis the Dutch Republic during the Establishment of the 'Alawi Dynasty (1660–1727)*, Amsterdam.

Diamond, A.S. (1968), 'Problems of the London Sephardi Community, 1720–1733', *Transactions of the Jewish Historical Society of England*, 21: 40–1

Ebben, M. (1996), *Zilver, brood en kogels voor de koning: Kredietverlening door Portugese bankiers aan de Spaanse kroon, 1621–1665*, Leiden.

Endelman, T.M. (2002), *The Jews of Britain, 1656 to 2000*, Berkeley and Los Angeles.

Fuks-Mansfeld, R.G. (1989) *Sefardim in Amsterdam tot 1795*, Hilversum.

Herks, J.J. (1967), *De Geschiedenis van de Amersfoortse tabak*, The Hague.

Israel, J. (1975), *Race, Class and Politics in Colonial Mexico, 1610–1670*, Oxford.

—— (1990), *Dutch Primacy in World Trade, 1585–1740*, Oxford.

—— (2001), 'The Jews of Dutch America', in P. Bernardini and N. Fiering (eds) *The Jews and the Expansion of Europe to the West, 1450–1800*, New York: 335–49.

—— (2002), *Diasporas within a Diaspora: Jews, Crypto-Jews, and the World of Maritime Empires (1540–1740)*, Leiden.

Kardasis, V. (2001), *Diaspora Merchants in the Black Sea: The Greeks in Southern Russia, 1775–1861*, Lanham MD:

Klooster, W. (2001), 'The Jews of Surinam and Curaçao' in P. Bernardini and N. Fiering (eds) *The Jews and the Expansion of Europe to the West, 1450–1800*, New York: 353–68.

Luzac, E. (1780–3), *Hollands rijkdom* (4 vols), Leiden.

Nusteling, H.P.H. (2002) 'The Jews in the Republic of the United Provinces: Origin, Numbers and Dispersion', in Jonathan Israel and R. Salverda (eds) *Dutch Jewry: Its History and Secular Culture*, Leiden: 43–62.

Sluiter, E. (1948), 'Dutch-Spanish Rivalry in the Caribbean Area, 1594–1609', *Hispanic American Historical Review*, 28: 173.

Jonathan Israel

Van den Boogaart, E., Emmer, P.C. et al. (eds) (1992), *Expansión holandesa en el Atlántico*, Madrid.

Vilar, E. Vila (1979), 'Extranjeros en Cartagena (1593–1630)', *Jahrbuch für Staat, Wirtschaft und Gesellschaft Lateinamerikas,* 16: 155–6.

Wätjen, H. (1921), *Holländische Kolonialreich in Brasilien*, The Hague.

Westermann, J.C. (1943) 'Memorie van 1751 over de tabaksindustrie en den tabakshandel', *Economisch-Historisch Jaarboek*, 22: 73

Yogev, G. (1978), *Diamonds and Coral*, Leicester.

Global Trading Ambitions in Diaspora: The Armenians and their Eurasian Silk Trade, 1530–1750

Ina Baghdiantz McCabe

This chapter argues for the exceptional role of the New Julfan Armenians in Iran. During the Safavid Ottoman wars, the Persians practised a scorched-earth policy and deported the population of the Caucasus for strategic and economic benefit. The merchants of Julfa were among those deported by force. The collaboration of the silk merchants of Julfa once they were settled in Iran was among the biggest prizes won by the Persians during those wars. Julfa in historic Armenia was located on the river Arax on an old trade route. It had acquired fame as a village in the early Middle Ages, grew into a town in the tenth through thirteenth centuries, and by the sixteenth was an outstanding trade centre. This densely populated, prosperous town was often subjected to invasions by foreign forces and was devastated, plundered. After 1604 Julfa was set on fire and lay in ruins after its entire population was compelled to migrate to Iran. Although the Armenians of Julfa had been silk traders prior to their move to New Julfa, Isfahan, it was only after their arrival in Iran in 1604 and under Safavid political protection that their international network was perfected. The Julfan Armenians, renowned silk traders since the sixteenth century, settled in Safavid Iran's new capital of Isfahan. Their Eurasian trading network was important, and it spanned from Narva to the Philippines. Most of the raw silk spun in Europe in Early Modern times was produced on the Caspian shore and in regions that were integrated into northwestern Iran. European consumption of silk was around 200,000 to 250,000 kilograms of mostly raw silk per year. Eighty-six per cent of this silk came from Iran (Faroqhi 1997: 503). The Eurasian silk trade of the Armenians brought silver bullion imports to Iran. This silver was essential to Iran's early state building. Special measures were taken to accommodate the silk merchants of Julfa. Less than a decade after Isfahan was chosen as the capital of Safavid Iran, a wealthy new suburb was constructed south of the river for the deported merchants. In 1619 the Shah granted this land exclusively to the prominent Armenian merchants after they offered the highest bid for the shah's recently monopolized silk and won his silk auction against the English East India Company which had bid too low. No one else was allowed to reside in wealthy New Julfa, where they were allowed to practice their religion.[1]

New Julfa became the hub of Iran's silk trade and the centre of a vast commercial organization covering half the world: from Amsterdam in the west to the Philippines in the east, and from Arkhangelsk and Narva in the north to the coast of Coromandel in India, the Moluccas, and Siam in the south. Although the Armenians are often spoken of generically, it was a specific group that was involved in the trade of silk and silver, an organized group of merchant families who ran this worldwide commercial network of Iranian silk exchanged for silver and European manufactured goods. Within Iran, other groups of recently deported Armenians were involved in the silk trade before it came on the market, from the cultivation of mulberry trees to the many steps involved in producing silk from silkworm cocoons. The deportations from the Caucasus were the cornerstone of a planned Safavid political economy centred on silk. Within this political economy, the Armenians were crucial at every level from production to distribution to export (Baghdiantz McCabe 1999). The Armenians are often compared to the Jews, most famously perhaps by Fernand Braudel. Therefore some Jewish networks are also briefly discussed here, albeit not in the same depth, just in order to clarify certain points. Finally European factors in the East India or Levant Companies are also briefly and comparatively drawn into the concluding part of the discussion in an attempt to reshape, if not redefine, the concept of trade diaspora.

It has been assumed, save in Subrahmanyam (1992) on the Iranians in exile and in (Baghdiantz McCabe 1999) on the Julfan Armenians, which both point to two exceptions, that trade diasporas did not participate in the political life of their host country or directly in state building in Asia. Even when highly successful as financiers and brokers, trade diaspora remained, according to current definitions, outside the political elite. They served as a power base of outsiders, beneficial to one monarch or dynasty against other internal forces of political competition. The most comparative, comprehensive and broad study of this phenomenon to date is that by Daniel Chirot and Anthony Reid (1997). They concluded that minorities have played a crucial role in the development of trade, money management and capital accumulation everywhere except in Eastern Asia. They were needed by kings and magnates who found them less threatening than their own subordinate populations (Reid 1997: 333–75). Direct participation in the political life of the host country, or inclusion in a political elite, however, is not the same as the financing of a state or a potentate. Becoming a king's merchant or court merchant falls under this form of financing. Some merchants have been given peerage and titles of nobility in their host society. Even with access to court they have not been included in the political elite. Often the Armenians of Julfa have been erroneously seen as the 'Shah's merchants'. It will be argued here that the case for the Julfan Armenians was exceptional among the rest of the Armenian diaspora. Perhaps their case best illustrates the necessity of avoiding the study of diaspora as a unit. This group was made part of the Safavid Royal Household and was integrated within the palace government.

In order to study the Julfan Armenians, who served the Safavid state in Iran, it is also helpful to contrast and compare their trade diaspora with trading groups perceived as 'national' East India Companies, such as those trading in Iran and India in the seventeenth century, as well as to contrast them with court merchants elsewhere. European Company factors, we assume, were serving the home society's interests abroad, as indeed they did in later centuries. These Companies were rather unsuccessful competitors in the Iranian silk trade in the seventeenth century, where the Armenians were their main competition. Did these companies serve national interest in Early Modern times? Can they be perceived as national companies from their inception as they have been, or are they also trade diasporas? What if any differences might there be between European factors serving courts and trade diaspora at the service of monarchs?

Trade historians have come up with the notion of 'trade settlement' or 'trade diaspora', although now the word 'network' is much preferred. The term 'trade diaspora' was first coined in 1971 by Abner Cohen to refer to 'a nation of socially interdependent, but spatially dispersed communities'. Even as he defined it, he was criticized for his usage of the word 'diaspora' instead of the more neutral term 'network'. He argues that the usage of the term stands.

> A diaspora of this kind is distinct as a type of social grouping in its culture and structure. Its members are culturally distinct from both their society of origin and from the society among which they live. Its organization combines stability of structure but allows a high degree of mobility of personnel ... It has an informal political organization of its own ... It tends to be autonomous in its judicial organization ... Its members form a moral community. (Cohen 1971: 266–81)

The term 'trade diaspora' appears applicable to many groups. It could equally apply to the East India Company factors, such as the English in India and the Dutch in Southeast Asia. Yet, interestingly, the term 'trade diaspora' has been used only exceptionally for European factors. Therefore the question arises as to why the usage has been reserved by most scholars, with a few exceptions, for other trading groups and not for European factors. The Europeans, unless they settled and went through a form of 'nativization', could not, one supposes, be seen as a group distinct from their society of origin. In the past ten years, much has been written about the usage, the meaning and the implications of the concept of diaspora.[2] The criticism against Abner Cohen was that the term was a historically specific one.[3] The term 'diaspora', first found in the Greek translation of the Bible, was once exclusively reserved for the Jews. It implied a forcible scattering as it is described in Deuteronomy (28:25). As Robin Cohen argues, the Old Testament also carried the message that 'scattering to other land' constituted punishment for breaking with tradition (Vertovec and Cohen 1999: 267). Soon it was applied to two more groups, the three classical Diaspora being the Jewish, the Armenian and the Greek. Today the term is used for nearly thirty different groups (Vertovec and Cohen 1999). The Armenians are considered a classical diaspora.[4] The notion of diaspora, first used and coined in the classical world, acquired great importance in the late twentieth century (Vertovec and Cohen 1999: 267). The intensity of international migration, the phenomenon of globalization, and the imminent demise of the nation-state have been crucial to the creation of the current debate about diaspora.

Scholarship on diaspora trading-networks would have been entirely marginal and perceived as irrelevant in mainstream academic debates twenty years ago. The present and especially the future can now point to the problem of considering the nation as 'natural' to historical discourse. The nation-state, once the ubiquitous model for historical thought, has masked many elements, perhaps not least being the participation of outsiders or foreigners in state formation during Early Modern times. Today there is much preoccupation with globality; yet, many global networks existed well before the twentieth century. They have simply not been the focus of scholarship until recently.

One study that hoped to transcend the 'national' category was Philip Curtin's. In a world-wide study of cross-cultural trade, he argues for a clear dichotomy between host societies and outside trading groups: 'The traders were specialists in a single kind of economic enterprise, whereas the host society was a whole society, with many occupations, class stratification and political divisions between the rulers and the ruled' (Curtin 1984: 5). Curtin, who first started the debate, makes clear with other passages that he sees trade diaspora as exempt from political participation in their host societies (Curtin 1984). He uses the terms trade network and trade diaspora interchangeably and argues that these groups were only cross-cultural brokers helping to encourage trade between the host society and their own. He is also a pioneer in the second problem discussed here. In his discussion of trade networks in 1984 he includes the European militarized diaspora within the same category as the Armenians, the Banians, and the Fukein Chinese. To make his universal model Curtin chose the highly visible Julfan Armenians. Based on the secondary scholarship available to him, Philip Curtin has argued that the Armenian trading diaspora was a self-contained and self-regulating body, a commercial organization divorced from political participation in state formation (Curtin 1984: 179–207).

The fact that the Armenians are perceived as a classical diaspora has played a significant role in enforcing views about the political non-participation of trade diasporas in general. Even the best critic of this binary model conceived by Curtin,

Sanjay Subrahmanyam, still follows this pattern for the Armenians. He has had to rely on the usual secondary sources written about the Armenians, with the Julfan Armenian seen as a service bourgeoisie. In his innovative study on the contribution of the Iranian merchant elite to the early state formation in Golconda, the Deccan and Thailand, Sanjay Subrahmanyam uses the Armenian case as a classical diaspora to conclude that he cannot make a model of what he finds for Iranian merchants abroad:

> that this does not mean either that the 'Iranian model' can be used as paradigmatic, or that it is one that does away entirely with the concept of diaspora community. Clearly the functioning of the Armenian community – significantly also the one chosen by Curtin to illustrate his theory – does correspond far more closely to the self-regulated body, largely divorced from the world of politics. (Subrahmanyam 1992: 359)

Nevertheless, despite his hesitation to include the Armenians, a diaspora community, in the model he finds for the Iranians, Subrahmanyam notices that an Asian trade diaspora, specifically the Iranians, politically and not simply financially participated in state building in their host societies. Very little work has been done on Iranian merchants, leaving the false impression that they were not important. There existed no equivalent class to the European urban bourgeoisie in Iran until the twentieth century, yet Iran had many merchants, many of whom were prominent in the silk trade in the sixteenth century (Ashraf 1970: 308–33). Most importantly perhaps, the merchants and the aristocrats were not two different groups, but one. The richest merchants were also the richest landowners; there was no social stigma associated with trade (Aubin 1976–77: 79–132). They traded in gems, silk, wool or cotton with their surplus capital. There was no class equivalent to the European bourgeoisie in Iran save, of course, in the eyes of many scholars, the exceptional case of the Armenians forced to settle there in the seventeenth century. They did seem to become a real bourgeoisie, living in a 'burg', and appeared as outsiders distinct from the power network of the local land-owning nobility.

Most of the wealthy Iranian merchants were often feudal lords, whose power was a threat to the Safavids as demonstrated by a ten-year war of succession before Abbas I could come to power; after 1590, to consolidate his rule the Shah relied on a new power base. This was made of a large group of deportees from the Caucasus, not only the Christian merchants of Julfa, but converted royal slaves who would reach the highest ranks in the Safavid power structure. No official political links within the Safavid power structure were evident before the reading of three neglected Safavid royal edicts. These edicts, translated and published for the first time in *The Shah's Silk for Europe's Silver* (Baghdiantz McCabe 1999), demonstrate the direct participation of the Julfan elite in the Safavid political administration and their elevated political rank – one on par with their economic power. The New Julfan leader, Khwaja Nazar, was the Shah's banker and ran the Armenian organization of the silk trade. The leading families of New Julfa were in fact one of the pillars on which the organization of the Safavid Royal Household (*khassa-yi sharifa*) rested. Their financial contribution was essential in more ways than one to shaping the history of Iran in the first half of the seventeenth century. The Royal Household relied heavily on the deportees of the Caucasus, some of them even being converted Julfan Armenians, the mechanism of this political role is explored elsewhere.[5] One of the major arguments is their contribution to Iran's centralization and state building in the first half of the seventeenth century. They contributed both as administrators and as financiers.

It is interesting to note that at this time many prominent Iranian merchants were leaving Iran to emigrate to India. Subrahmanyam argues that many of the Iranian merchants left for India in the seventeenth century as they considered it a land of opportunity. He hypothesizes that the success of the Armenian merchants might have been responsible for the massive migration of Iranians to India (Subrahmanyam 1992: 340–63). This hypothesis is essentially correct, but the reason for migration is a political one: it is the Shah's centralization of power and monopoly of silk, and not the Armenians, which are responsible for this massive migration. A major Armenian family from New Julfa also leaves for India after losing its bid for power. The Safavid monarch's monopolization of the silk trade in 1619 and his integration of the Armenian merchants within the court was probably also a major reason why opportunities declined for local merchants in Iran. The revenues of silk were centrally collected under the responsibility of the head of the Julfan community and much of it went to the salaries of the army (McCabe 1999: Chapter 5). Before the war of 1580–90 the army was provided by the *amirs*, or feudal lords, and the Safavids were dependent on them. After 1590 a paid army of Caucasian converts commanded by generals of Georgian and Armenian origin won the Safavid wars against the Ottomans. They were paid in cash. The Caucasian administrator of the royal household was also paid his salary through a centralized mint system; much of the cash was brought in by the Armenian silk trade. There is direct financing of the administration and the army by the New Julfans and a communality of interest with the Caucasian administration. This system prevailed and after 1629 dominated the court and made the Royal Household powerful for nearly half a century.[6]

In 1943, Minorsky perceived them as a middle class, a service bourgeoisie. Many have followed suit. My own emendation to this analysis has prevailed – that is, that only part of this group can be viewed as a middle class. You cannot view all of the New Julfans as a middle-class bourgeoisie. They were not strictly middle-class, not simply because of the immense fortunes they amassed but especially because of their inclusion in the royal *khassa*, (Royal Household). This made them de facto part of the royal administrative system. The heads of the

New Julfan community functioned as bankers, but this isn't enough to make them exceptions to rules applicable to other trading diaspora. Banking is a common feature of classical trading diaspora. It is rather their formal status, accorded to them by the Shah, that gave them a political and administrative role within the government. Their inclusion in the Royal Household, and their association with the converted Caucasian deportees called *ghulams*, or royal slaves, opens a window that helps explore the structure of the previously neglected Safavid Household and its centrality to Iran's political economy. This new finding places Safavid Iran within the same household system of government that may be found in the Ottoman Empire, where there were household and military slaves in the highest administrative posts. Perhaps the best-known case of a powerful household is that of the Mamluks. Iran, however, has never been seen as having had a household.[7] Many Armenians, both as Christians and as converted *ghulams*, rose high in the political world of Safavid Iran, one even attaining the post of Grand Vizier; the ghulams and merchants were part of this Royal Household (Baghdiantz McCabe 1999: Chapter 5). Their integration into the Safavid Household, despite their Christianity, made them the financial wing of the Royal Household. Studying them also contributes to a better understanding of the yet unstudied Safavid Royal Household system. From the mid-sixteenth century on, increasingly this was becoming a household of administrators who were converted Caucasian royal slaves (Babayan 1993). It was never suspected that there could be a link between the Christian merchants, perceived as foreign by scholars, and the converted Caucasian administrators. These royal merchants controlled the Iranian silk trade for half a century, although prior to their arrival in Iran, they already were the most renowned silk traders in the Ottoman markets (Masters 1988).

Beyond their political role within the household there is an exceptional structure to their own merchant organization (Baghdiantz McCabe 1999: Chapters 3 and 7). More importantly, albeit only for a few generations, they had an autonomous city state within the Safavid realm. To the best of our knowledge today, there were no Armenian merchant city states formed in the Ottoman Empire and the merchants of Constantinople of Aleppo did not form a governing body to exercise autonomous municipal power. Except for New Julfa in Iran, whose autonomous organization I have compared to that of the far more famous Italian city states, I know of no others in Iran or the Ottoman Empire where many Armenians traded (Baghdiantz 1993). In my analysis, the city state of New Julfa became possible because of a unique political role played by the Armenian elite in seventeenth-century Iran, both Christian and converted, which I have studied in great detail elsewhere (Baghdiantz McCabe 1999). The Royal Household, of which the Julfan Armenians were a part, was a new political power base for the Shah.

The New Julfans were quite different from the Lvov Armenian merchants of Poland who had political autonomy but were not integrated into the structures of local power and never ran a city state. Their merchant organization was part of the organization of the *khassa* through their provost. The Armenian Provost of New Julfa is called a Shah in Safavid royal edicts, a title bestowed on him by the Safavids in an edict that perhaps reflected his Armenian title. The New Julfan Provost also had a princely title in Armenian, which might point to a recognition of the kingly title by the Safavids; a passage in Claude Markovits makes one think of another possibility (Markovits 2000: 159). Markovits writes of the *commenda* being called a *Shah-gumasthas* contract in the British period for the Sindhi network of Shikarpur. The *Shah* is the sedentary capitalist financing the mobile *gumasthas*. That this capitalist and associated travelling factor system was also the New Julfan system leaves no doubt, but Markovits cannot establish earlier usage of the term even for the Sindhi group, and extending it to Iran is equally, if not more, problematic. It remains nevertheless a serious hypothesis, one not to be dismissed, as the New Julfa network had the sedentary capitalist financiers living in a burg sending out factors with an established commission to the four corners of the world.[8] The Persian world was one familiar to the Sindhi network, and the vocabulary itself is Persianate, as discussed by Markovits, but the *Shah-gumastha* terminology he discusses is nineteenth-century, two centuries later. Furthermore the title of Shah for the Provost is found in a royal edict and not a commercial contract as in the case of the Sindhi merchants. This second possibility seems improbable, and one must remain quite certain that there was an Armenian prince in exile.

New Julfa was an extremely wealthy suburb which many European merchants describe; Jean Chardin wrote 'There are three thousand four or five hundred houses in Julfa, the most beautiful are along the water, and there are some that are very richly gilded in gold and blue and that could be called palaces'. He goes on to describe that Abbas I and his successor both dined and stayed there, as they much favoured the Armenians, and that certain merchants had a worth of over two million livres (Chardin 1735: II, 107). Other descriptions are more precise, describing the Shah dining in the house of the Provost, head of the suburb. One should note that in a highly hierarchical society, kings did not displace themselves for mere court merchants. The inclusion of the New Julfans within the palace itself is the only possible explanation for this behaviour, especially since Christians were considered *najas*, unclean, and one did not ordinarily dine with them. It is even more striking as one reads that within the palace the Shah ate at a table alone and did not share it with his courtiers (Chardin 1735: III, 373). If the provost was of princely blood, it makes these shared dinners more understandable.

The New Julfan Armenians in Iran, as members of the Royal Household, were in competition with the English East India Company and the Verenigde Oost Indische Compagnie (VOC) for the Iranian silk exports. The latter gained a minimal share in the trade, as they were outsiders. The unusual success of the Julfans in Iran has been explained by platitudes and prejudices such as their Christianity, by their hard work, and even by their avarice, or that elusive and quite ubiquitous factor of 'trust' among ethnic trading groups. The Julfan Armenians were insiders in the Safavid palace system, however, and their participation in Safavid Iran's political economy is perhaps the clearest and a more plausible factor in their immense success. One cannot simply call them merchant or bankers of the Shah as in a classical trade diaspora: they were part of a vast administrative system to which they formally belonged: the Royal Household, within which, together with the royal slaves, they functioned as the political heart of the palace. Under Abbas I (r.1587–1629) this new administration was a power entirely at the service of the Shah, but it even overshadowed royal power as is the case of Abbas I's successor Shah Safi (r.1629–1642). Under this shah this Caucasian elite was at its most powerful and ruled Isfahan. The fallacious notion that there are no Safavid sources on economy persists in some works (Mathee 1999).[9] As only the Safavid edicts demonstrate their participation in polity, the Armenians continue to be seen as outsiders conforming to what is expected of a trade diaspora.[10] Foreign company factors were not privy to a country's political mechanisms, and their accounts give no notion of this integration. There is, however, another major element at work in disguising the Armenian political role in Iran: that is, as demonstrated before, the general views held about trade diaspora. With documents in hand, now translated and published (Baghdiantz McCabe 1999: Annex), there will still be scepticism, especially among those who have a strong belief in the Weberian dichotomy between 'pariah trading communities' and rational capitalism (see Weber 1930). The concept of 'pariah communities', with which scholars of the German school associate the Jews, and by extension the Armenians, have continued to overshadow the real importance of these vast and highly organized and certainly rational networks. Also, rational capitalism and mercantilism are often reserved for Europe, and Iran does not fit into the model. Only the European merchants are seen as capable of achieving market transparency through their methods, yet as Jonathan Israel demonstrates in Chapter 1 of this volume, the Sephardic Jews became from the sixteenth century onward the intermediaries for many European traders on the Ottoman markets. My own work shows that the Armenians received and informed the Dutch, the French and the English in Iran and India; there is no question as to which networks controlled the flow of commercial information flowing between Asia and Europe in the early Modern period. This in itself is a mighty weapon for competing on the market, as one could chose not to share information that was to one's advantage. The role of intermediary, often seen as a subservient one in some studies, is in fact a position of power, as it means dependency on that intermediary for accurate information.

In addition there are good arguments that can be made for rational capitalism and even for mercantilist policies for Iran, despite what has been written to the contrary

(Matthee 1999), not to mention for planning and foresight. The deportations had a dual purpose: they were an element in the military strategy against Ottoman incursions into the contested areas between the two powers, and they functioned politically in the formation of a new internal power base for the Safavid shahs. Within this second purpose lay the consolidation of the silk trade in Armenian hands, although the Julfans had been powerful silk traders for two generations before they reached Iran. This move was as much political as economic, since it was a means of financing the Safavid Shahs' centralization plans. The formation of new elites, such as the one formed by the Caucasian converts called *ghulam* (slave, or royal slave), was the other aspect of this internal planning. Since the deported populations lacked any previous political power or political ties in Iran, they were given administrative and commercial powers by the Shahs in order to counterbalance the strife between the two main groups, the turkic Qizilbâsh and the Iranians. Their loyalty to the Shah had defined the extent of his power, as became evident during Shah Tahmasb's succession problems, which caused the civil war of 1580–90.

The *ghulams*, or royal slaves, integrated within the Safavid army were compared by Chardin to 'Enfants de Tribut' in Turkey. The 'Enfants de Tribut' were young Christian boys who were taken as tribute from their families at an early age and integrated into the Ottoman troops, the Janissaries. The Janissaries and these Iranian troops have much in common. If the role of the minorities in the Ottoman Empire is now better understood, the importance of Caucasian populations in Iran, both Christian and converted, remains relatively unknown even to scholars of the Middle East. In reality, not only did they have a role comparable to that of the Janissaries in the seventeenth-century Safavid army, they also managed nearly the entire administration of the Royal Household by the mid-1640s. In essence, the *ghulams* ran the palace itself, again mirroring the Ottoman and Mughal systems. They played several key roles: some reached high offices in the administration or the army, and others were the tutors of the Safavid princes. This group has only just been studied and a more detailed definition of this group remains to be made.[11] The silk trade was in the hands of the Christian Julfan Armenians settled in new Julfa for exports, and in the hands of certain converted *ghulam*, who served as governors of the silk growing regions, or as the Shah's main silk factor, or as head merchant. This group of converts also controlled the Iran mints, where all the silver had to be deposited. Most importantly, the mint paid out the salaries of the army and some of the administrators, showing the direct link between the bullion imported through the silk trade and the new centralized administration instituted by the Shah who named these officials. None of these deportees had kin or connections in Iran, and many lost a sense of their origins in the Caucasus; therefore they could never form allegiances or participate in conspiracies. Chardin writes that this was conscious and systematic policy under Abbas I (1580–1629).

This was true in theory during Abbas I's rule; later this group acquired some very serious power of its own and became a political force. Silver imports from the silk trade paid the salaries of this new slave administration and army (Baghdiantz McCabe 1999). Clearly the New Julfans with their silk trade and silver imports served state building in Safavid Iran. Did they, despite this integration into the Safavid palace, manifest 'national' interests of their own? Can one speak of ethno-national or national interests despite the absence of a homeland? Could it be that the merchants' sole aim, beyond simple survival, was the expedient pursuit of lucre, that they had no underlying political goals of their own?

Some years ago K.N. Chaudhuri postulated that the 'trade diasporas,' or settlements of a nation in diaspora, necessarily have a different outlook from merchants belonging to a nation, the assumption being that only the latter serve national interests. This immediately begs the question: how do the Armenians in India and Iran fit into this schema? How did they differ from the European factors in India? Did the East India Companies serve national interest in the seventeenth century? Merchants and traders in this period conducted business through close-knit groups, irrespective of their location. In the groups considered, Jewish and Armenian merchants alone had no proper homeland to which they eventually hoped to return. Were the behaviour and outlook of these particular members of a nation in diaspora likely to be very different from those travelling merchants with solid connections at home? According to K.N. Chaudhuri (1985: 225), the Armenians living in Kashgar, Delhi and Hugli in the seventeenth century could point to their own suburb in Isfahan, the little town of Julfa on the far side of Zayandah-Rud. Was it a national home? New Julfa, in Iran, was a second home, far from their original town of Julfa in historic Armenia, which was burnt to the ground. The creation of an entirely new calendar used in their worldwide silk trading network and dating from their settlement in Iran seems to indicate that they saw this new settlement as a new beginning. The titles held by their Provost indicate that they saw themselves as a kingdom within a kingdom, regardless of whether they were one, as no real independence was possible within the Safavid realm (Baghdiantz McCabe 1999: 366–7). They certainly had autonomy and the right to bear arms, and they seem to have possessed sophisticated European-made armament even as late as 1722, during the Afghan invasions, a time when New Julfa was no longer favoured by the Shahs.

When the Julfan Armenians settled elsewhere, did they serve the interests of their host societies such as Gujarat, Bengal, the Netherlands or Russia as they did the interests of Safavid Iran? It seems clear that up to 1646, they served the Safavid and the organization under their Provost over anything else, save of course their own share of the profits, which were immense. This changed, as they lost their status and privilege in Iran around 1646. In other societies they contributed as financiers and merchants but nowhere were they integrated into the local political system as in Iran. They much later contributed to the state-building efforts of Peter the Great, albeit on a smaller scale and as outsiders close to court circles. They received peerage, land and nobility in Russia, but they were never a financial wing of the court. In contrast to their status in Russia, in Iran they were at the heart of Iran's political economy and political system under Safavid rule; it was the first time that a large number of Armenians were forced to settle throughout Iran.

What then of national interest for the stateless Armenians? What were their goals beyond profit? The Julfans for Iran amassed surplus capital necessary to state formation. In 1646 the political faction, which they were associated with in the harem, as Julfa was the appanage of the Queen mother, fell from favour and lost power. The major event was the assassination of Saru Taqi, a Grand Vizier who had in the past been the governor of Mazandaran, where most of the silk was produced. There are no documents spelling the end of the inclusion of the New Julfans in the Royal Household, just the rise of a new political faction, which would now dominate Isfahan. After losing their role in the administration of the Royal Household, the Armenians of New Julfa formed their own company, and its capital and organization can be compared advantageously to those of the European companies. It has not been believed that Asian merchants, no matter how great their accumulated wealth, were capable of establishing a worldwide organization. The argument of wealth does not suffice when confronting orientalist scholarship, which argues for a lack of 'rational organization' among the Asian merchants: 'The peddler might have well possessed the habit of thinking rationally. But he had no possibility of making a rational calculation of his costs in a modern sense so long as the protection costs and the risk remained unpredictable and the market non-transparent' (Steensgaard 1973: 58).[12] The orientalist view contrasts them with the Europeans, who corresponded with a company's home base every few weeks, coupled with the argument that transport insurance and customs costs on the European side were predictable, presumably through an amalgamation of data. Given the difficulty that the Companies had in establishing themselves in India and in Persia, it is arguable whether they had accurate knowledge of the market, as the author supposes. It is wrongly assumed that the Asian merchants only knew of the prices as they reached the markets, and that they had no planning or organization with which to analyse the market (Steensgaard 1973: 30). There is clear proof to the contrary. Much work has been done on India, but there is still very little about Turkish and Iranian merchants who are part of this cliché of the peddler. The Indian merchant princes were known to trade historians and were never seen in the same light.

There certainly was a 'comprehensive and coordinated' organization for the Armenians; its headquarters were in New Julfa, a suburb of the capital of Safavid Iran. It had jurisdiction over other Julfans settled across the world from Paris to Tibet, and Amsterdam to Shanghai. As we have seen, the Armenians had a very important role in the economic and political history of Safavid Iran. Their integration was a conscious policy by a dynasty that strove for absolutist power over many feudal strongholds. Nevertheless, as the economic agents of Safavid royal power for ten years, then for the Royal Household in the first half of the seventeenth century, the Armenians, merchants and silk growers or simply taxable Christians, cannot be dissociated from the political economy and history of Safavid power in Iran. That they served Iran's interest is now established by documents; that they served their own national interest as they served Iran's is equally certain. The trading organization of the New Julfans was so elaborate that, allied with the administrative role of the Church, it served as an infrastructure for the diffusion and preservation of a common cultural identity. As such, using the term 'trade diaspora' implies a certain cultural cohesion because of the word 'diaspora'; the wording of 'merchant network' is devoid of such cultural connotations. Through the financing of scriptoria and presses and the diffusion of books in Armenian to their remotest churches and diaspora they assured the survival of their language, their accounting system and their artistic, religious and commercial culture. This form of support and diffusion of a common culture was a role played by early states (Anderson 1983: Chapters 2 and 3). As such, the trading network served Armenian interests as well, be they financial, administrative, political or cultural. I have studied their financial support of the first Armenian printing presses elsewhere, but it remains one of the most important stages in forming a cultural canon that would later serve a national discourse (Baghdiantz McCabe 1998: 58–73). Armenian books were financed by merchant money and carried and diffused through their merchant network.

This merchant network was also instrumental in rebuilding the main churches of historic Armenia, and in financing the Church. It can be argued that their wealth and Safavid protection saved the Apostolic Church of Edjmiadzin from conversion to Catholicism. Therefore there is no question that while they served the state-building aims of monarchs such as Peter the Great or the Safavids they also looked after their own ethno-national interests, interests that were well beyond immediate financial gain. The political autonomy they obtained in diaspora both in Lvov, Poland and New Julfa in Iran was due to their commercial skill. Their contribution as bankers to the King of Poland, or even to the Venetian Doge, gave them the autonomous jurisdiction common to trading diaspora as defined by Abner Cohen. Armenian merchants were given titles of nobility in several European courts. The political aspects of this autonomy are very important. Their high status was not uncommon elsewhere. Nowhere, however, were they directly integrated in the administration of an early state as they were in Iran. Nowhere did they achieve the same wealth or success. In Venice and Poland their local settlements in the network converted to Catholicism. Many Julfans ceased to be devoted to Safavid interests progressively by the late seventeenth century, while many of them still remained fiercely loyal, making it impossible to generalize. Again there was a diaspora within a diaspora, the Catholic Julfan Armenians were the ones looking to Europe, looking for liberation schemes from the 'Muslim yoke', while Apostolic Armenians remained close to the Safavid court: there may have even been two provosts at one time. Their vast network, probably not as united as before, took them to contact other courts which, however, never integrated them, never called their Provost 'King'. In Russia, Poland, India and elsewhere, even ennobled Armenians, to the best of our knowledge, remained outsiders, save for a few individuals who attained high ranks. Moreover, other major differences point to the danger of studying the Armenian diaspora as a unit simply put together because of a division along ethnic lines. The Armenians had very regional perceptions of themselves according to their town of origin, they referred to themselves as Julfans or Tabrizi Armenians, not as Armenians. In forming networks these regional identities were crucial and have been neglected. The element of class, viewed as essential during that century, also divided them ever more sharply.

Does the question of a common identity arise in this period? The question of serving national interests, ethno-national ones, is not a simple one for the early modern period – even when referring to the European Companies as serving the interests of nation-states. Commerce seen as a linear progress to colonization is a misleading view; during this period, France and England often objected to the cost of any overseas settlement of expansion and often had policy detrimental to the progress of their companies in Asia. Furthermore, traditional views contrast the Europeans, seen as peoples with homelands, to the Jews and Armenians in diaspora. Yet Bruce Masters, quite exceptionally, classifies the English Levant Company with trade diaspora:

> The Armenians, the Sephardi Jews, and Syrian Christians, Catholics and otherwise, all represent trading diaspora in the sense of the term suggested by Curtin. To them might be added the English Levant Company factors, who supply an illustrative example of the metamorphosis of a trading diaspora, supported by the bonds of religion or ethnicity, to one built on starkly profit motives, the forerunner of the multinational corporation as it were. (Masters 1988: 104)

He does not see it as serving national interest, or national interest as a bond in the Levant Company; rather, profit is the binding element. He does not commit the usual error of seeing the companies as national ones serving the state. As for defining trade diaspora, we have already disagreed over Curtin's model for the Armenians of Julfa, who are, in the main, the ones discussed by Masters in Aleppo although he identifies other groups of Armenians trading there.

It is extremely important to look at the trade diaspora that most ressembled that of the Julfan Armenians – that of the Sephardic Jews. The trade of the Sephardic Jews expelled in 1492 is explored on the markets of the Ottoman Empire and in their trans-Atlantic trade by Jonathan Israel in Chapter 1 of this volume. Some new light is also being shed on specific communities formed by these Sephardic Jews, such as the very important one of Amsterdam. Both of the studies made by Jonathan Israel and Daniel Swetschinski to some extent contradict Curtin's model and Masters's views on the Jews, but they certainly destroy Weberian ones (see Weber 1930). A large group of the Jews exiled from Spain first settled in Portugal as New Christians after 1492. In the seventeenth century, as the inquisition threatened even New Christians, they left for Holland. In Amsterdam, where, thanks to Protestantism, there was religious freedom from the inquisition, they slowly but surely returned to practicing Judaism. A masterful study of the Portuguese Jews of Amsterdam in this crucial century of state formation in the States General sheds light on their many endeavours. While this new study dismisses over-amplification of their commercial role, such as Fernand Braudel quoting a generalization that 'it was only in imitation of the Jews who had taken refuge among them, and who had set up counting houses everywhere, that the Dutch began to set up their own and send their ships all over the Mediterranean' (Swetschinski 2000: 108), it uncovers the many layers of their participation in Dutch society, many of which are political and go well beyond the purely commercial.

Some contributions are very important, such as the overwhelming contribution of the Portuguese Jews in the colonial settling of Brazil for the Dutch West India Company (ibid.: 114–17) and the introduction of sugar growing and the entire sugar production of Surinam, where they were the main settlers for the Dutch. There also was the quasi-monopolization of the import, manufacturing and distribution of chocolate, a new product which, like sugar, did not fall under established guild rules (ibid.: 126–9). Perhaps even more strikingly, there is the direct financing of William of Orange's conquest of England, as well as of his Irish wars. In this war for the throne of England, they played an active and direct political role as purveyors of food and equipment to the army. The Jewish firm Machado & Pereyra, which held investments from many prominent Portuguese Jews, was entirely responsible for horses and provisions to the Dutch army. The provisioning of William's Irish campaign against James, the Catholic contender to the throne of England, according to one source required at least twenty-eight bakers, 700–800 horses, and 300–400 wagons (ibid.: 139).

Just as in Iran, where the Armenians and the Safavids had common interests against the Spanish, Portuguese and French Catholics, the Portuguese Jews found common interests with the Protestant Dutch against the Catholic powers of Europe. Both groups had their own ethno-national interests in common with the new states forming in Iran and the States General, both of which gave them religious freedom and a chance for participation. As the Jews helped the Dutch in their state building, they rebuilt an identity that they had to hide for two centuries as New Christians. Much has been made of this community as the first community of Modern Jews, who nicknamed Amsterdam 'Mokum' (from the Hebrew word for place) and made the Amsterdam-Jerusalem analogy (ibid.: 2).[13] Finding a second home, religious freedom, and prosperity are parallels with circumstances of the Armenians of New Julfa.

Among the Amsterdam Jews was also a prominent banking family, as important as the family of Nazar, head of the Julfans, was in Iran. Although, unlike the Julfan Armenians, more than 10 per cent of Amsterdam's bankers were Jewish, the Suasso family stands alone because of their unparalleled wealth. Later, their house became the residence of the Queen of the Netherlands. Franciso Lopes Suasso lent the astronomical sum of 1.5 million Gulden to William of Orange in 1689 as he ascended the throne of England. Recently published figures of Portuguese Jewish trade show participation quite disproportionate with their number (ibid.: 113).[14] Even within the West India Company where their physical representation was no larger than 5 per cent among the main investors, their investment was very large, sufficiently large for them to have political clout. At their request the Dutch West India Company reprimanded Peter Stuyvesant, the governor of the New Netherlands, for his anti-Jewish measures (ibid.: 117).

There remains a serious difference, however, between these two cases of participation to state building that highlights the role of both these trade diaspora. There seems to have been no formal political integration for the Jews of Amsterdam, despite the fact that they did play a political role. Both groups, however, share a common characteristic: the way they are approached by scholarship. It is a problem that needs to be tackled when studying merchant networks. European merchants are studied differently from all others. Perhaps it is created by Weber's legacy, so well described by Anthony Reid (1997: 35–7). To reiterate: Weber drew a sharp distinction between the 'rational capitalism' that developed from puritan values and the 'pariah capitalism' of the Jews. Jewish and Armenian trade diaspora are viewed quite differently when they are studied. In studying the Sephardic networks for example, as for the Armenians, kinship and religion and ethnic solidarity are taken into account by scholars to explain the network's solidarity at the expense of looking for a rationally organized company. Family is emphasized as the largest possible body of organization, despite the fact that the provost seems to have acted as treasurer for the shah for the collection of silver on the Ottoman markets. The municipality was the administrative unit under the rule of the provost, not the family, although within the municipality the unit was the family. This was a hybrid system, where the provost acted as a central bank for both the network and, for two generations, the shahs on the Ottoman markets (see Barbaie et al. 2004).

What of the European Companies in this period? Would gain be the only purpose, before or even after they became joint stock companies? Do the factors serve their nation? Do they contribute to state building? The evident link between long-distance trade and the creation of surplus capital and state formation need not be stressed here. France, England and the Dutch Republic were at different stages of state formation. The Dutch had just won their independence at the end of the sixteenth century. In their case, the commercial success of the Dutch East India Companies and other trading groups and the formation of the Dutch Republic were parallel processes. Economic and political power in the Dutch Republic was in the same hands, and the City Council of Amsterdam was also entirely a group of merchants. The Dutch Republic, with its Calvinism and overt capitalism, seems the perfect example in support of Max Weber's thesis of the link between Protestantism and capitalism. Yet, as Sephardic Jewish participation clearly demonstrates, even in the most homogenous of European companies, there was no ethnic or religious uniformity to argue for such a thesis. I have discussed these problems in detail elsewhere, and after analysing several aspects have concluded that none of the European companies can be simply looked at as serving the State and cannot in this period be considered national. Nor do they serve 'national' interest even if sometimes they demand armies from the states they pretend to serve (Baghdiantz McCabe 1999: Chapter 7).[15] Bruce Masters in including the English Levant Company in the category of diaspora traders, defines it as an ancestor of the multinational corporations, having only profit as an aim for solidarity (Masters 1988: 75–9). He may well have been the first not to be misled by the national names of these companies.

In the end, the perception that these commercial companies were 'national' companies, which served the interest of nation states, is fallacious. All these fallacies arise from a nineteenth-century writing of history through the lens of national histories. In the Early Modern period this nineteenth-century model does not hold. Furthermore, the interests of participating individuals over and against those of the company complicate the equation. Many of the men at the service of the European companies were out for their own fortune, some of them even working for rival companies to the detriment of their national companies. One well-known example is the Dutchman François Caron, who was a Protestant and born in Brussels. He converted to Catholicism and was one of the first directors of the French East India Company, after years of work in the Dutch East India Company.[16] Hired by the French specifically for his knowledge and experience, he was naturalized French and given a patent by Louis XIV in 1665 (Caron and Schouten 1935: xv). Next to him the other director was an Armenian, Marcara, a New Julfan who was also naturalized French, which implied conversion to Catholicism for both directors. Colbert had recruited them from the two most successful groups in Asia in order to compete with the English and the Dutch (McCabe 1999: Chapter 10). Marcara's fascinating fate can be traced in the French archives, through the story he told the French courts during his suit against the French Company. Indeed François Caron, who had turned from collaborator into foe, had imprisoned him in the hold of a ship that took them both to Brazil and back. The emaciated Armenian

French director miraculously survived to sue his tormentor and the French Royal East India Company. Yet, while in India we find him with his entire Armenian network, Julfans exiled in the court of Golconda, successfully at the service of obtaining the French Company their first permission to trade on the Coromandel Coast of India (Baghdiantz McCabe 1999: ch. 10). This is a clear illustration of the collaboration and integration of diaspora networks into a European Company structure, for which the participation of the Jews of Amsterdam in the Dutch East India Company offers even more evidence.

In no way can one invoke the idea of national interest in this early period, be it for the European Companies often seen as national companies. Nor do diaspora merchants only work for their own interests, or that of their host societies, as we see them work within European companies. In addition to the fact that many diaspora networks did not always have their interests at odds with those of the European Companies, European Companies did not always have common interests with their national states. Therefore binary views about the interests pursued by trade diaspora on the one hand and Companies on the other do not hold up on closer scrutiny. The biography that closes this volume, an elegant essay by Frank Broeze about a Scottish merchant in diaspora, extends this argument into the nineteenth century. Between the interests of the Scotsman Gillean Maclaine and the Dutch colonial administration in charge of commerce in Batavia he finds a 'dialectical co-existence'.

The host society's policies toward a trade diaspora remain of primordial importance to their success. The imperial policies of the Ottomans increasing the taxation dues on Venetian and Genoan exports, as Jonathan Israel demonstrates in Chapter 1, were crucial to the rise of the Spanish and Portuguese Jews on the Ottoman markets. These measures also benefited the Armenians of Julfa before they came to Iran, still under Ottoman rule. As Braudel had noticed half a century ago, the Armenians in competition with the Jews replaced the Italians on the Ottoman markets, which were at the heart of a newly global Early Modern Eurasian trade. The imperial policies of the Safavids were instrumental to the success of the Julfan Armenians after the 1619 royal monopoly imposed on silk production and sales in Iran; they were given consignments of the annual yields of silk around the Caspian shore; they were integrated within the administration itself and exempted from many taxes imposed on other merchants (Baghdiantz McCabe: 1999). The Armenians of Julfa, just as the Sephardim explored here by Jonathan Israel, were given permission to settle in European cities only because they were intermediaries between East and West and important to French, Dutch or Italian trade. These trade diasporas should not be viewed through a parochial lens, but within the imperial histories of their host societies, as no amount of trust or honesty has ever made a whole network as rich and as visible as the Sephardim or the Julfans on the international markets. As nearly all the articles in this volume explore regional cohesion – as in the Julfan Armenians, the Chiot, the Baghdadi Jews – coupled with trust and collaboration and family ties are common to many networks, both European and Asian, yet without the specific historical conjunctures, their trading methods and cohesion cannot be the sole explanation for the immense success of these trade diasporas through time. After all, they faced competition from many other groups sharing these characteristics and hoping for commercial success: political opportunity, whether negotiated or offered to a network, remains the key to their economic success. To keep these political opportunities in the many worlds they could adapt in, these cosmopolitan networks excelled at forging congenial relations with courts and municipalities in both Asia and Europe.

Notes

1. In 1647 this changed and other Armenians were made to leave Isfahan and live there. They were artisans and came from a different region and a different class. This was a gesture to end the favoured status of New Julfans and create an Armenian ghetto.
2. Some of the best articles on the subject have been gathered in a hefty tome edited by Steven Vertovec and Robin Cohen (1999). The volume has the advantage of gathering articles written in English on both sides of the Atlantic. It contains many articles from the main scholarly journal devoted to the subject: *Diaspora: A Journal of Transnational Studies*, Khachig Tölöyan, editor. The journal explores many theoretical approaches to the subject and is multidisciplinary. Its contents clearly demonstrate that the term 'diaspora' is now applied to nearly thirty groups.
3. Abner Cohen adds a footnote making it clear that he was criticized during the conference of 1969, published in 1971.
4. The debate as to when the Armenians start being entirely in diaspora without a homeland has no place here, but the artificial date traditionally used by Armenian historiography has been the fall of the Crusading Kingdom of Cilicia in 1375. This small and fleeting kingdom, away from the lands of historic Armenia, was certainly not home to most of the Armenians. Another favourite date is 1071, the time of the Seljuk invasion of historic Armenia, but the same holds true for this date as many Armenians already lived out of historic Armenia even by this date: for example, many had left for Rome, Constantinople and Egypt well before that.

5. Baghdiantz McCabe 1999: Chapters 4 and 5, Annexes. Several Safavid edicts in the Appendix of the book are translated to demonstrate this.
6. See Baghdiantz McCabe 1999 for a demonstration of this mutual dependence. Also explored in Babaie et al. 2004.
7. Babaie et al. 2004 explores the Safavid household and its importance during the first half of the seventeenth century.
8. On merchants living in burgs see Bayly 1983: 11.
9. R. Matthee, despite his pertinent arguments against Eurocentric views and orientalist methods, uses a good amount of VOC documents but does not consider the Safavid documents related to Armenian trade, and for the Armenians relies on the conclusions of Herzig 1991.
10. These documents were published for the first time in the Annex of McCabe 1999. They were in the archives of All Saviours' at New Julfa, and were translated with the collaboration of Kathryn Babayan.
11. Babaie et al. 2004 should probably answer some aspects.
12. Quoted below is what was an accepted definition of Armenian trade:

> A peddling trade: buying and selling in small quantities on continuous travels from market to market. But if Hovhannes's journal and the indirect evidence does not deceive us, a peddling trade that makes use of very sophisticated organizational forms such as commenda, bottomry, partnership and combined credit transfers by means of bills of exchange [*sic*] Nevertheless the ordinary entrepreneur operates on the peddler level, and there is nothing in the sources to indicate the existence of comprehensive coordinated organizations – of an Armenian, Turkish or Persian version of Fugger, Cranfield or Tripp.'

13. See the song with the verse 'Amsterdam she [is] Jerusalem!' in Swetschinski (2000).
14. For 1634 Vlessing finds that they controlled 4–8 per cent of the entire trade that year and 10–20 per cent of the Amsterdam trade excluding the companies.
15. See also Baghdiantz McCabe 2001. A striking instance is the assistance that the English East India Company provided the Persians in capturing Hormuz away from the Portuguese in 1622. At the very time they were fighting the Portuguese, the English Crown was hoping for a rapprochement with Lisbon and the Spanish Crown.
16. François Caron (1597–1672) (see Caron and Schouten 1935) was the author of a travel account in Dutch of which there is an English translation; unfortunately it contains little about the author, which is typical of the style of the travel accounts of the time. It was compiled for the use of the Dutch East India Company for use in the Far East.

References

Anderson, B. (1983), *Imagined Communities: Reflections on the Origin and Spread of Nationalism*, London: Verso.

Ashraf, A. (1970), 'Historical Obstacles to the Formation of a Bourgeoisie in Iran', in M.A. Cook (ed.), *Studies in the Economic History of the Middle East: from the Rise of Islam to the Present Day,* London: Oxford University Press.

Aubin, J. (1976–1977), 'La propriété foncière en Azerbaydjan', *Le Monde Iranien et L'Islam: Sociétés et Cultures*, 4: 79–132.

Babaie, S., Babayan, K., Baghdiantz-McCabe, I. and Farhad, M. (2004), *Slaves of the Shah: New Elites of Seventeenth Century Safavid Isfahan,* London: I.B. Tauris.

Babayan, K. (1993), 'The Waning of the Qizilbash: The Spiritual and the Temporal in Seventeenth-Century Iran', unpublished dissertation, Princeton University.

Baghdiantz, I. (1993), 'The Merchants of New Julfa: Some Aspects of their International Trade in the Late Seventeenth Century', unpublished PhD Dissertation, Columbia University.

Baghdiantz McCabe, I. (1998) 'Merchant Capital and Knowledge: the Financing of Early Armenian Printing Presses by the Eurasian Silk Trade', *Treasures in Heaven: Armenian Art, Religion, and Society,* New York: Pierpont Morgan Library.

—— (1999) *The Shah's Silk for Europe's Silver: The Eurasian Silk Trade of the Julfan Armenians in Safavid Iran and India (1590–1750),* University of Pennsylvania (Series in Armenian Texts and Studies), Atlanta: Scholar's Press.

—— (2001), 'Trading Diaspora, State Building and the Idea of the National Interest', *Interactions: Regional Studies, Global Processes and Historical Analysis*, AHA and Ford Foundation Conference, March.

Bayly, C.A. (1983), *Rulers Townsmen and Bazaars: North Indian Society in the Age of British Expansion, 1770–1870,* Cambridge: Cambridge University Press.

Caron, F. and Schouten, J. (1935), *A True Description of the Mighty Kingdoms of Japan and Siam by François Caron and Joos Schouten,* London.

Chardin, J. (1735), *Voyages du Chevalier Chardin, en Perse, et autres lieux de l'Orient. Enrichis de Figures en Taille-douce, qui représentent les Antiquités et les choses remarquables du Païs. Nouvelle édition, augmentée du Couronnement de Soliman III. & d'un grand nombre de Passages tirés du Manuscrit de l'Auteur qui ne se trouvent point dans les Editions précédentes.* 4 vols. Amsterdam: Aux dépens de la Compagnie, Volume II.

Chaudhuri, K.N. (1985), *Trade and Civilization in the Indian Ocean and Economic History from the Rise of Islam to 1750,* Cambridge: Cambridge University Press.

Cohen, A. (1971), 'Cultural Strategies in the Organization of Trading Diasporas', in C. Mésailloux (ed.), *L'Evolution du commerce en Afrique de L'Ouest,* London: Oxford University Press.

Curtin, P. (1984), *Cross-cultural Trade in World History,* Cambridge: Cambridge University Press.

Faroqhi, S. (1997), *An Economic and Social History of the Ottoman Empire, Vol. II, 1600–1914,* Cambridge: Cambridge University Press.

Herzig, E. (1991), 'The Armenian Merchants of New Julfa, Isfahan: A Study in Pre-modern Asian Trade', DPhil dissertation, Oxford University.

Markovits, C. (2000), *The Global World of Indian Merchants,* Cambridge: Cambridge University Press.

Masters, B. (1988), 'Merchant Diasporas and Trading "Nation"', *The Origins of Western Economic Dominance in the Middle East,* New York: New York University Press.

Matthee, R. (1999), *The Politics of Trade in Safavid Iran: Silk for Silver, 1600–1730* (Cambridge Studies in Islamic Civilization), Cambridge: Cambridge University Press.

Reid, A. (1997), "Entrepreneurial Minorities, Nationalism and the State," in D. Chirot and A. Reid (eds), *Essential Outsiders: Chinese and Jews in the Modern Transformation of Southeast Asia and Central Europe,* Seattle: University of Washington Press.

Steensgaard, N. (1973), *Carracks, Caravans and Companies: The Structural Crisis in the European-Asian Trade of the Early Seventeenth Century* (Copenhagen), reprinted as *The Asian Trade Revolution of the Seventeenth Century: The East India Companies and the Decline of the Caravan Trade,* Chicago.

Subrahmanyam, S. (1992), 'Iranians abroad: Intra-Asian Elite Migration and Early Modern State Formation', *Journal of Asian Studies,* 51(2): 340–63.

Swetschinski, D.M. (2000), *The Reluctant Cosmopolitans: The Portuguese Jews of Seventeenth Century Amsterdam,* London: Littman Library of Jewish Civilization.

Vertovec, S. and Cohen, R. (eds) (1999), *Migration, Diasporas, and Transnationalism,* The International Library of Studies on Migration, 9. Cheltenham, UK: Edward Elgar.

Weber, M. (1930), *The Protestant Ethic and the Spirit of Capitalism,* London: Unwin.

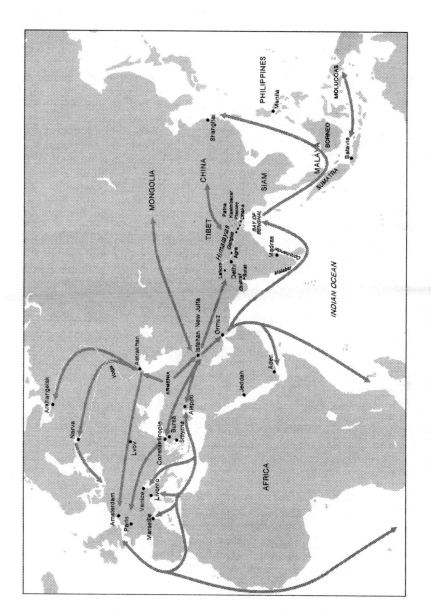

Map 2 Armenian trade diaspora in the Eurasian trade, 16th–18th centuries

–3–

Trading Networks in a Traditional Diaspora: Armenians in India, *c.* 1600–1800
Sushil Chaudhury

The observation of the Court of Directors of the English East India Company in 1699 (DB: vol. 94, f. 197, 17 April 1699) about the Armenians that 'most certainly they are the most ancient merchants of the world' was perhaps no exaggeration, as is now being revealed in the works of several scholars on the Armenian diaspora and their trading networks. Indeed, from the earliest times to the end of the pre-modern era, Armenian merchant communities engaged themselves in international and intercontinental trade in the Eurasian continuum. They ventured out of the homeland to different parts of Asia and Europe, and settled themselves not only in important cities, ports and trade marts but also in remote production centres far away from their own country. And thus they created the infrastructure for an efficient and successful long-distance trade and a commercial network with strong links to their main centre at New Julfa. This 'trading diaspora' of the Armenians was a unique feature of the trading world of the seventeenth and eighteenth centuries, as the preceding chapter by Ina Baghdiantz McCabe discusses. The aim of this chapter is to make an analysis of the trading networks of the Armenians in India, particularly Bengal, and their link with the Armenian diaspora in the region.

In this context it is pertinent to point out that there were several other trading diasporas like those of the Jews, Indians, Greeks, Arabs and Chinese in the early modern era, and all of them shared certain key features which explain why they succeeded in such remarkable ways in establishing enduring commercial networks over vast areas of the Eurasian continuum. A high degree of confidence, great trust among the members of the same community and the reduction in transaction costs through a scattered but well-knit international community which possessed a distinctive culture, religious tradition and communal institutions particular to itself, was largely shared alike by all these diaspora peoples – whether Armenians, Greeks, Jews or Indians. At the same time there were certain dissimilarities in the trading networks of the various diasporas. For example, while the Jewish people concentrated more on maritime activities, the Armenians were involved mostly, but not exclusively as this chapter attests, in overland trade.

The emergence of Armenian trading network and diaspora in the seventeenth century as discussed by Baghdiantz McCabe, was aided by the historical developments of the preceding century when the old Armenia fell victim to Perso-Ottoman rivalry. In the early seventeenth century, the Persian Emperor, Shah Abbas I, forcibly moved the professional Armenian merchants and artisans and settled them in the new township of New Julfa in the suburb of Isfahan. The Emperor's main objective was to utilize the services and expertise of the Armenian entrepreneurs in transforming his newly founded capital city of Isfahan into a major trade centre. The latter did not disappoint him. As they had the necessary capital and commercial networks in Asia and Europe, the Armenians were able to develop 'Persia's foreign trade in raw silk, create new markets and products and expand the scope of trade routes'. And they ceaselessly contributed to Persia's economic prosperity under the succeeding Shahs until the invasion of Persia by the Afghans in 1722 which dealt a severe blow to the Armenians of New Julfa and after which many of the prominent Armenian merchants migrated to other countries.

Be that as it may, it is perhaps needless to emphasize that India was one of the most important centres of international trade in the seventeenth and eighteenth centuries. As Indian textiles and raw silk were among the best and cheapest in the world market, merchants and entrepreneurs from various parts of Asia and Europe thronged there for procuring these and other commodities. Thus a conglomeration of traders and entrepreneurs from different parts of the world was to be found in the trade marts of India during this period. As such, seventeenth- and eighteenth-century India provides a unique case for studying the organization, ethics, culture and dynamics of the various entrepreneurial communities as reflected through their activities in India. A thorough study of the networks of enterprises and entrepreneurs of various groups and nationalities – how they organized their networks which extended over vast geographical areas stretching from Bengal to Delhi-Agra and even to Surat or from Surat to the Red sea and Persian gulf ports – will throw ample light on the different aspects of business organization, networks, credit mechanisms, and business techniques and 'culture' in the pre-modern era.

Though we shall be speaking in general of India as a whole, the case studies will be taken mainly from Bengal, which was the most prosperous province of the erstwhile Mughal Empire in the seventeenth and eighteenth centuries. By the early eighteenth century, the great Mughal Empire had already disintegrated, bringing in its train political chaos and economic decline in most parts of North India. But Bengal was a singular exception where trade, commerce and economy as a whole flourished under its almost independent *nawabs* (title of the rulers). It is to be noted here that it was Bengal textiles and silk, together with a few other commodities, which were most sought after in the world at that time. The conclusions arrived at from the case studies of Bengal, however, will be applicable, more or less, to India as a whole. In Bengal, again, we shall confine our analysis mainly to the Armenian diaspora and their networks as reflected in the enterprises of Khwaja Wajid, the Armenian merchant prince of mid-eighteenth-century Bengal.

I

It is more or less well known now that the Armenians played a significant role in the commercial and economic life of India, especially of Bengal. Though it is not possible to determine when the Armenians established their trading networks in India, it can be reasonably assumed that they began their trading activities in India long before the arrival of the Europeans, and that is why we call this a 'traditional diaspora'. They were active in Bengal trade from at least the late sixteenth and early seventeenth centuries if not earlier. As an important trading group, their presence was a common feature in all the prominent centres of trade and manufacture, cities and ports. What was most striking about them, however, was that if there were any possibility of profit in trade, they would go even to remote places and deal in any commodity, unlike many other trading groups in Bengal. Through their commercial acumen, their thorough knowledge of markets and products, a chain of connection with the important producing and consuming centres maintained through their own agents who were most often than not their own family members or kinsmen, their low overhead cost and capacity to thrive on a low profit margin, the Armenians could compete successfully with not only the Indian and other Asian merchants but also with the European companies trading in Bengal.

It was obviously the commercial expertise of the Armenians in Bengal that prompted the Directors of the English East India Company to enter into an agreement in 1688 with Khwaja Phanoos Kalantar in London by which the Armenians were to provide Bengali goods for the Company's investments in Bengal with their own capital and at their own risk at 30 per cent profit on their cost and charges (DB: vol. 94, f. 197, 17 April 1699; Chaudhury 1975: 131). It is significant to note that while writing to Bengal about this agreement, the Court of Directors of the English Company in London observed (DB: vol. 93, f. 38, 18 October 1690): 'Those people [the Armenians] are a thrifty, close, prudent sort of men that travel all India over and know almost every village in the Mughal's dominions and every sort of goods with such a perfect skill and judgment as exceeds the ancientest of our linen drapers'. A few years later, the Company made another agreement with the same Kalantar which stipulated that the Armenians would provide specially Patna[1] goods for the Company with their own money and deliver them to the Company either at Hughli[2] or Calcutta for which they were to be allowed 15 per cent upon the prime cost and necessary charges (*Home Miscellaneous Series*: vol. 36, ff. 81–2). Here again the Directors of the Company noted that the Armenians 'are diligent, frugal and very experienced merchants' and asked their employees in Bengal to try to procure some fine Bengal piece-goods through the Armenians as they would 'know how to buy better than you can' (DB: vol. 93, f. 148, 15 February 1690). Again it was in recognition of the economic and political importance of the Armenians that Khwaja Surhaud Israel was made a member of the famous Surman embassy which was despatched from Bengal to Delhi by the English East India Company in 1715 and which obtained the controversial *farman* (Imperial edict) from the Mughal Emperor Farrukhsiyar in 1717.[3]

Thus it is not surprising that there were many important Armenian merchants and traders in the flourishing Armenian settlement of Saidabad (a suburb of the capital Murshidabad), Hughli, Calcutta, Kasimbazar, Dhaka and Patna with their own localities and churches.[4] Among the Armenians in Bengal, however, it was Khwaja Wajid who played the most significant role in the commercial economy and political life of Bengal in the 1740s and 1750s. What is significant to note here is that the Armenians in Bengal were not dissociated from their mainstream community in New Julfa. There are several instances[5] which show that the Armenians in Bengal were in touch with New Julfa and that there was regular traffic between Bengal and New Julfa, which only reinforces the notion that cultural and ethnic ties were extremely important in the entrepreneurial networks built by the Armenians. The vast networks of enterprises created by the Armenians in Bengal in the seventeenth and eighteenth centuries will be more than evident from a close look at Bengal's silk and textile markets during this period. They were conspicuous even in the remote parts of Bengal, wherever there was the possibility of good profit in mercantile activities.

II

Khwaja Wajid was one of the three merchant princes (the others being Jagat Seths[6] and Umichand[7]) who collectively dominated the commercial life and hence, to a great extent, the economy of Bengal in the last three decades of the first half of the eighteenth century. An idea of the nature of the Armenian diaspora and Wajid's extensive networks can be formed from the fact that he not only was involved in inland trade in saltpetre, salt and opium but was also quite active in maritime trade extending over a vast space from Bengal to Surat, and the Persian Gulf and Red Sea ports. He operated his extensive business empire from Hughli, the then commercial capital of Bengal. Like several other Armenians of Bengal at the time, it is possible that he too had links with New Julfa. According to *Zamia-i-Tadhkira-i-Yusufi*, though Wajid was born in Azimabad (Patna), his forefathers were from Kashmir, and he settled in Hughli (Khan 1978: 17). The early career and activities of Wajid are not very clear to us as of yet. It is probable that he was the son of 'Coja Mahmet Fazel', an influential Armenian merchant in the 1730s and early 1740s (Hume 1730). However, it is known from the Calcutta Mayor's Court Proceedings that around the early 1740s, Wajid obtained a foothold at the *darbar* (royal court) of the Hughli *faujdar* (an administrative official in the Mughal bureaucracy) as the representative (*vakil*) of the Armenian community of merchants. It was deposed in the case of Teneseause *vs* Khwaja Manuel that there was a move by many of the Armenian merchants at Hughli in 1741 to replace Khwaja Petruse with 'Coja Avid' as [Khwaja Wajid] as their *vakil* (*Mayor's Court Records, Calcutta*: Range 155, vol. 24, f. 30vo, 7 May 1741). From then onward, there was no looking back for Wajid, who rose in power and position throughout the 1740s to be reckoned not only a merchant prince, but by the late 1740s also one of the most important figures in the commercial and political life of Bengal.

It is to be noted here that in the first half of the eighteenth century, politics and commerce was closely intertwined in Bengal. The main prop of the prosperity of the three important merchant princes was their close connection with the *darbar*. Thus Wajid too seems to have consolidated his position through political connections and extended his influence to the court at Murshidabad. Through subtle diplomacy and judicious financial support to Nawab Alivardi Khan, he built up a powerful position at the *darbar*. It seems that by the mid-1740s, he had developed from being a 'creature' of the Hughli *faujdar*'s *darbar* to being one of the central figures at the Murshidabad court. In the late 1740s, he began to reap the fruits of his *darbar* connections and managed to gain virtual control of the economy of Bihar. It is significant that he was not only the leader of the Armenian merchants but also of the community of merchants in Hughli. This is borne out by the fact that when the English fleet captured two ships of the Hughli merchants including the Armenians, the merchants comprising 'Syeds, Mogulls, Armenians, &ca.' had an audience with the Nawab through Wajid and it was he who spearheaded the protest against the English (*Factory Records, Kasimbazar*: vol. 7, Consultations, 24 December 1748, 9 January 1749 and 12 January 1749; BPC: Range 1, vol. 22, f. 49vo, 19 December 1748 and f. 64vo, 31 December 1748).

Khwaja Wajid operated his business empire from his main base at Hughli. He was actively engaged in the inland trade of Bengal both on his own account and as a supplier to European companies. He had extensive business transactions with the French and the Dutch, and through Umichand with the English. Robert Orme, the official historian of the English East India Company and who lived in Bengal in the early 1750s, observed (1803: II.I.138) that 'Coja Wazeed [Khwaja Wajid] managed the greatest part of the French trade in Bengal with great profit to himself'. Extremely devious as he was, he had a passion for extending his commercial hegemony at any cost and was ready to swing his allegiance at the slightest prospect of commercial advantage. Utilizing his close connection with the *darbar*, he tried to operate his business with a monopolistic design.

The main props of Khwaja Wajid's extensive operations in Bengal's internal trade were the monopoly of the saltpetre and salt trade. Through his influence with the Bengal administration, he actually gained a virtual monopoly of the trade of Bihar (a division of the Bengal *suba*) from at least the late 1740s. He secured the monopoly of saltpetre, one of the most important commodities in the export lists of the European companies, in 1753 (*Bengal Letters Received*: vol. 22, para. 18, f. 410; BPC: Range 1, vol. 26, f. 110, 2 April 1753). Of course, he was already involved in the saltpetre trade long before this, through his close association with Umichand and his brother Deepchand who was the *faujdar* of Chapra, the main saltpetre-producing centre of Bihar. The Dutch Director Jan Kerseboom noted that in 1747 the Dutch company had procured 21,000 sacks of saltpetre – 42,000 mds, each sack weighing 2 mds[8] – sent from Bihar by Deepchand to his authorized dealer (*gemagtigden*) Khwaja Wajid in Hughli. In his 'Memorie' (VOC: 2849, f. 103vo, 14 February), he also refers to the fact that Wajid later obtained the 'privilege' of a monopoly trade in saltpetre from the Murshidabad court. He further comments that as a result 'this trade [in saltpetre] has fallen entirely in his hands and completely under his control'. Wajid's monopoly of the saltpetre trade was a great irritant to the European companies who were the main buyers of the commodity. Hence the next Dutch Director in Bengal, A. Bisdom, dwells at length on the mechanism of Wajid's operations in saltpetre trade in Bihar. He mentions that Wajid obtained a *parwana* (letter patent) from the Bengal Nawab Alivardi Khan by which he got the 'special privilege' to deal in saltpetre for which he paid only a paltry sum of Rs 25,000[9] to the Nawab (VOC: 2849, ff. 498–501vo, 10 January 1755). He operated the saltpetre trade through his agents Mir Afzal and Khwaja Ashraf (his brother) who were based in Bihar.

The European companies no doubt tried every means to get out of Wajid's stranglehold on the saltpetre trade but only in vain. So immediately after the British conquest of Bengal at Plassey in 1757, the English factor Mr Parkes at Patna wrote to the Council at Calcutta to 'apply to the New Government to set aside Coja Wazeed's exclusive parwannah for saltpetre' (BPC: Range 1, vol. 29, f. 133, 18 July 1757). But the Company's resident representative at Murshidabad wrote back to Calcutta that 'they cannot with propriety apply to the Darbar for abolishing Wazeed's monopoly or regulate the Patna trade' (BPC: Range 1, vol. 29, f. 170vo, 2 September 1757). Wajid managed to obtain a *parwana* from the new Nawab, Mir Jafar Khan, 'for the entire possession of the saltpetre trade at Patna', of which the English were informed by the Dutch Director at Hughli in October 1757 (BPC: Range 1, vol. 29, f. 245, 31 October 1757). Wajid, however, did not live in a fool's paradise. He knew that it would be almost impossible for him to continue the monopoly trade in saltpetre under the vastly altered circumstances after the British became the virtual rulers following their conquest of Bengal. So he was quick to assure the English representative at Murshidabad that he would use his power to the utmost to assist the English in procuring saltpetre at the cheapest rate, provided they 'assisted him in return to make the Dutch purchase from him'

(BPC: Range 1, vol. 29, f. 285, 24 November 1757). That was the last straw to which he desperately hoped to cling and save at least part of his commercial empire. But that was not to be. In 1758 he lost his saltpetre monopoly which was now grabbed by the English company.[10]

The most important prop of Wajid's trading empire, however, was the more lucrative monopoly of the salt trade which was farmed by him in 1752 for a mere Rs 25,000 to Rs 30,000 a year. Writing as late as 1763 Batson, an English factor, noted (Orme Mss: OV, 134, f. 13): 'Coja Wazeed of Hughli had the salt farm of Bengal for many years for an inconsiderable sum.' The anonymous author of an English manuscript 'Historical Sketches of Taxes on English Commerce' wrote the following under the year 1752 (Mss Eur. D: 283, f. 22): 'Salt on account of Coja Wazeed is exempted from ... duties and pays only

> Import per 100 md. One rupee which is Rs 0.8 per cent
> Export per 100 md. One rupee which is Rs 0.8 per cent
> Total: per 200 md. Two rupees which is Rs 1.00 per cent'.

When an estimate made in 1773 of the annual proceeds of salt production and sale in Bengal put the value at Rs 1 million, one can easily guess how much Wajid earned from the virtual monopoly of salt trade in the 1750s (Orme Mss: OV 134, ff. 21–2).[31]

The extent of Wajid's deep involvement in the inland commerce of Bengal is evident from the fact that he also tried to monopolize the opium trade of Bihar through his close link with the Murshidabad *darbar.* Though the detailed mechanism of his operations in the opium trade is not very clear, it is known from the Dutch records that Wajid managed the opium trade through his brother Khwaja Ashraf at Patna. The Dutch Director Huijghens reported that the Company could buy only 1479 mds of opium in 1749/50 because Khwaja Ashraf had already bought or contracted for all the opium in December 1749. Drabbe, the Dutch factor at Patna, however, managed to influence the administration (actually the *diwan* or officer in charge of revenue) by giving a bribe of Rs 1,000 which prevented Ashraf from sending the opium out of Patna and thus the Dutch were able to procure the said amount (VOC: 2763, f. 458, 20 March 1750; VOC, 2732, ff. 9–10, Hughli to Batavia, 27 January 1750). It seems that as the Dutch, who were the principal buyers of opium in Bihar for export to Batavia, and the English did not have much liquid cash to contract for or buy opium in the proper season, Wajid through his brother cornered (of course, with the assistance of the Bihar administration) most of the produce with ready money and later sold the commodity to the Dutch, English and Indian merchants (the last two having only marginal interest during the period) at a high premium.

III

It is no wonder that this Armenian merchant prince who settled in Hughli, with its rich tradition of handling Bengal's maritime trade, also ventured into intra-Asian and coastal trade. In the shipping lists of the Dutch records there are many instances of Armenian merchants sending their trading vessels to different parts of India and West Asia with rich Bengal commodities and bringing back bullion and other cargoes from those parts in the first half of the eighteenth century.[11] The rapid growth of Calcutta notwithstanding, Hughli was the traditional Asian port, which was frequented by most of the Asian ships besides those of the Dutch, French and other Europeans except the English.[12] It seems that after consolidating his position in the inland commerce of Bengal, Wajid embarked on overseas trade. In all probability, he was engaged in the beginning in sea-borne trade in partnership with other Hughli merchants. This is evident from the fact that the ship *Chandernagore* captured by the British navy in 1744 or 1745 on its return voyage from Basra and Mocha, on the pretext of its flying French 'colours', was owned by Wajid and other Hughli merchants. The merchants, led by Wajid, made a strong complaint to the Nawab Alivardi Khan who directed the British to compensate the merchants (BPC: Range 1, vol. 17, f. 702, 3 October 1745, f. 706vo, 14 October 1745, f. 717, 24 October 1745; vol. 18, f. 165vo, 9 April 1746, f. 318vo, 6 August 1746).

Soon after, however, he began his own venture in overseas trade and we find in the lists of the Dutch records that his first ship *Salamat Ressan* left Hughli in 1746 for Surat with a considerable cargo of rice, sugar, textiles and silk (VOC: 2661, f. 163). In July 1747, his ship *Salamat Manzil* returned from a successful trading voyage to Surat with cotton, rosewater, coral, almond, porcelain, etc. and it left Hughli in January 1748 with a large cargo bound for Surat again (VOC: 2689, ff. 136, 140). Unfortunately, there is a gap in the shipping lists of the Dutch records from 1748 till the end of the monsoon in 1754 and hence we cannot enumerate the total strength of Wajid's trading fleet. But there is little doubt that by the early 1750s Wajid had acquired a fleet of trading vessels, which dominated the Asian maritime trade of Hughli. Between 25 November 1754 and 28 January 1755, his ships were engaged in five voyages: two inbound from Basra and Jeddah; three outbound to Masulipatnam and Jeddah (VOC: 2862, ff. 837, 1079, 1080). The gap in the shipping lists notwithstanding, we come across six ships owned by Wajid, namely, *Salamat Ressan, Salamat Manzil, Mobarak, Gensamer, Medina Baksh* and *Mubarak Manzil* (see shipping lists in VOC: 2661, 269, 2862). These ships operated from Hughli to Jeddah, Mocha, Basra, Surat and Masulipatnam. Significantly Wajid had a trading house at Surat which was referred to by the Dutch Director Jan Kerseboom and also by the Fort William (Calcutta) Council of the English Company (Hill 1905: II.87; VOC: 2763).

It is interesting to note that Wajid, like the two other merchant princes of his time, also played a significant role in the crucial period of the 1750s in Bengal politics. As has been pointed out earlier, all these merchant princes owed their prominence and rise to great heights of wealth and power mainly to their closeness to the Nawabs of Bengal (Chaudhury 1995: 109–23). The Persian chronicler, Yusuf Ali, wrote that Wajid who was a 'favourite personal friend' of Nawab Alivardi flourished as a great merchant of Hughli and that his 'business prospered so well that he built up a vast amount of wealth and affluence'. He also stated (Khan 1978: 17) that Wajid was commonly known as 'Fakhru'l-Tujjar' (Pride of the Merchants). That Wajid had already become a key figure in Bengal politics by the late 1740s is evident from the fact that the Dutch Director Huijghens wrote in his 'Memorie' in early 1750 that the Dutch should maintain good relations with Wajid because he was held in high esteem (*groot aanzien*) at the Murshidabad court (VOC: 2763, f. 467, 20 March 1750). In the early 1750s, Robert Orme described him as the 'principal merchant of the Province' (1803: II.I.58). Wajid's close connection with the ruling elite is clearly reflected in numerous references in the Dutch and English records. In the course of Fort William (Calcutta) Council's debate in 1753 whether the contract for saltpetre should be made with Wajid or Umichand, Wajid's link with the government comes out clearly. Most of the Council members referred to him either 'as an officer of the government' or 'intimately connected with it' (BPC: Range 1, vol. 26, ff. 131vo–132vo, 3 May 1753). That the merchant prince Wajid was also a political heavyweight in mid-eighteenth century Bengal is abundantly clear from Jan Kerseboom's 'Memorie' of 1755 (VOC: 2849, f. 128vo, 14 February 1755): 'While mentioning those persons whose friendship would be very useful to your honour I cannot neglect Coja Mahmet Wazit, recently honoured with the title of Faqqur Tousjaar meaning the supporter of the treasure because he is truly the maintainer of the riches of the rulers. He gives them a lot willingly rather than under compulsion.' In that very year Louis Taillefert (VOC: 2849, f. 264, 27 October 1755), who succeeded Kerseboom as Director in Bengal, significantly remarked while commenting on the residents of the Company's village, Chinsurah, that the Company should not have admitted 'respectable persons of so high standing as the Moorish merchant Coja Wazeed who trade overseas or who have such internal trade that in some respects they can be considered as competitors of the Company and who deem themselves to be on an equal footing with the Directors (of the Dutch Company) if not their superiors'.[13]

IV

By the early 1750s Wajid had emerged as an extremely powerful political figure and seems to have tied his fortunes with the heir-apparent Sirajuddaula.

Along with the Hughli *faujdar,* he seems to have essentially forced the English Council at Hughli to pay obeisance to Sirajuddaula upon his investiture as heir to Nawab Alivardi Khan (BPC: Range 1, vol. 25, f. 229vo, 31 August 1752). But the relation between the English and Wajid soured by the early 1750s mainly because of Wajid's monopoly of saltpetre and his virtual domination of the Bihar economy, both of which were hampering the cheap investments of the Company. The relation was further strained because of a dispute between the English and Deepchand, Umichand's brother and ex-*faujdar* of Chapra (the most important production centre of saltpetre in Bihar) in which Wajid was involved as security for Deepchand. The case was referred to England but Wajid made repeated demands on the English Company for payment of his security deposit of Rs 78,000 (BPC: Range 1, vol. 17, f. 429vo, 24 December 1744; vol. 22, f. 126vo, 13 February 1749). As he now had considerable political influence, Wajid threatened the Company in 1752 to have its business stopped if he was not satisfied, and in 1755 he bluntly told the English that if he was not paid, he would not use his good offices to stop the Hughli merchants from raising a serious complaint against them at the *darbar* (BPC: Range 1, vol. 28, f. 122, 12 May 1755).

It is against the backdrop of these circumstances that the crucial role played by Wajid in Bengal politics in the pre-Plassey period assumes great significance. The assertion of Karam Ali (1952: 56, 63), the author of the near-contemporaneous Persian chronicle *Muzaffarnamah,* that Wajid incited both Alivardi and Sirajuddaula against the English is nothing but an echo of the English attitude (including that of Robert Clive, who later conquered Bengal) and can hardly be relied upon.[14] Wajid knew well his own interests and that he would hardly gain much by turning out the English. His saltpetre and salt monopolies, exclusive trade in opium and maritime ventures would have benefited little from their removal. True, he was more inclined to the French and the Dutch than to the English, but his relations with the former two vis-à-vis those with the latter were not mutually exclusive. As Jean Law, the chief of the French factory at Kasimbazar, pointed out, Wajid 'wanted to be on good terms with everybody' (cited in Hill 1905: III.190). Governed by a strong passion to extend his commercial empire at any cost, he nonetheless threw his lot in with Sirajuddaula probably because he knew that the main support of his commercial prosperity was the *darbar* backing. Thus he soon became an important member of the inner circle of Siraj's advisers.

That Wajid was a key figure at the Murshidabad *darbar* is evident from the fact that Sirajuddaula appointed him as his emissary to negotiate with the English soon after his accession in April 1756, and before his march against them in Kasimbazar and the subsequent attack on Calcutta. Wajid's diplomatic mission came to nothing, but for that he was certainly not responsible. The chief of the English in Bengal, Governor Drake, treated him with ignominy and turned him out of Calcutta (Chaudhury 1986/7: 111–34; Hill 1905: I.58). Thus it is amply clear that

Wajid bore no special enmity toward the English and that he was eager to bring about a rapprochement between the English and the Nawab. The expeditionary force, which came from Madras in the wake of the fall of Calcutta, realized well the influence of Wajid in Bengal economy and politics. Thus, Colonel Clive and Major Killpatrick, who were in charge of the expedition to Bengal, wrote to Wajid, among a few others, to mediate between the Company and the Nawab (Gupta 1962: 89–90). Meanwhile the English, after recapturing Calcutta from the Nawab, sacked the premier port of Hughli allegedly on the grounds of avenging the Nawab's earlier attack on Calcutta. This severely jeopardized the commercial fortune of Wajid, as Hughli was the principal base of all his business operations. But it appears from available evidence that even after that he was eager for a negotiated settlement between the English and the Nawab. He wrote to Clive:

> Though I have always been a well-wisher and an old friend of the English Company, yet no person has been so great a sufferer in the last disturbance [meaning the British sack of Hughli] as I am. Notwithstanding this I still look upon your interest as my own. I will use my utmost endeavour with the Nawab for the success of your affairs. (*Home Miscellaneous Series*: vol. 193, f. 14, Wajid to Clive, 10 January 1757)

A few days later he wrote to Clive again to 'consider and weigh ... the consequences of continuance of the present disturbances' and whether it would not be in the interest of the Company 'to put an end to these troubles by an amicable composition'. He assured Clive that he would 'not be wanting in my endeavours in conjunction with Juggutseat to adjust matters' to the advantage of the Company (*Home Miscellaneous Series*: vol. 193, f. 15, Wajid to Clive, 17 January 1757). On his side, Clive replied to Wajid that he could safely rely on the 'integrity and friendship' of Wajid, and expected that Wajid and the Seths would act as mediators between the Nawab and the English (*Home Miscellaneous Series*: vol. 193, ff. 125–6, Clive to Wajid, 21 January 1757; Hill 1905: II.125–6), though he always suspected Wajid to be a French agent (Orme Mss: India X, f. 112vo, Clive to Watts, 4 August 1758).

In all probability, Wajid became worried about the prospects of his commercial empire after the British onslaught on Hughli, and had suggested to Sirajuddaula an alliance with the French against the British. The report of William Watts (Orme Mss: India V, Select Committee Consultations, f. 1210; Orme Mss: OV, 170, f. 215), the English chief at Kasimbazar, following the fall of French Chandernagore at the hands of the British in March 1757, that the Nawab was 'very angry with Coja Wazeed for telling that the French were superior in everything and that we should be able to do nothing against them' suggests that Wajid's hope of survival was pinned on the French. Even so, he was the last one to join the bandwagon of the Indian conspirators who joined hands with the British to bring about the downfall

Sushil Chaudhury

of the Nawab leading to the British conquest of Bengal. In fact Wajid was a serious obstacle to the success of the coup until May 1757. It was in recognition of his power and influence in Bengal polity and economy that Hazari Mal, Umichand's *vakil* at Murshidabad, reported in November 1756 that Wajid was obstructing the British interests in opposition to the Jagat Seths (*Bengal Secret and Military Consultations*: Select Committee Consultations, Range 1, vol. 1, 23 November 1756). Though he was outside the 'revolutionary movement', there should be little doubt that several of the influential persons at the *darbar* were involved in the conspiracy. Umichand, one of the main conspirators, as Robert Orme points out (Orme Mss: OV, 28, f. 52, Robert Orme to John Payne, 3 November 1756), was ' the friend and in most trade his partner' and sure to have divulged it to Wajid.

Besides, in view of his close link with the *darbar* officials and his network of agents throughout the country, it is unlikely that Wajid was in the dark about the conspiracy. But extremely shrewd and calculating as he was, Wajid took the final leap when he saw no hope of the Nawab's survival. He joined the conspiracy as late as May 1757 (the so-called Battle of Plassey taking place on 23 June 1757) since he badly needed a revolution to restore the political backing for his commercial empire, and since by then, with the expulsion of Jean Law from Murshidabad, the chances of French intervention on behalf of the Nawab had already vanished. At the same time, with the failure of his policy – the suggestion to the Nawab of an alliance with the French – the Nawab's confidence in the Armenian merchant prince ended and he was discarded like a broken toy. By early May, his position at the *darbar* had deteriorated so much and he felt so insecure at the court that he apparently took refuge in the English factory at Kasimbazar (Hill 1905: II.379). Unfortunately for him, as for other merchant princes, Wajid's gamble in joining the Plassey conspiracy failed. Plassey brought about the downfall, sooner or later, of all three of the merchant princes. With Plassey went the foundation of their commercial empires – court backing for monopolies of various sorts and contracts for investments with the European companies.

The fall of Wajid was no less spectacular than his rise. As we have seen, he had taken energetic steps to avoid a commercial crash and joined the Plassey conspiracy at the last moment. But the British dealt a great blow to his fortune in January 1757 when they sacked Hughli, burning his salt warehouses and destroying his commercial headquarters. Soon after Plassey, he suffered a further blow from the piratical activities of the British naval squadron off the Bengal coast when one of his trading vessels, loaded with rich cargo, was captured in September 1757 on the pretext – as in the case of the *Chandernagore* mentioned earlier – of its flying French 'colours' (BPC: Range 1, vol. 29, f. 173, 5 September 1757). In the completely altered political situation after Plassey, he was unable to turn to the *darbar* for redress, something he had successfully done from about the mid-1740s until 1757. Of greater consequence for his doom was the destruction of his control over much of Bengal's internal commerce. The main foundations of his commercial empire were either swept away or undermined after Plassey. The domination of the English Company at the Murshidabad *darbar* led to the loss of his saltpetre monopoly in 1758 (HR: 246, f. 274, 17 November 1763). More disastrous for his commercial supremacy was the open flouting by Company servants of his control over the salt trade, which was soon to become the Company monopoly. At the same time, his position as a supplier to the European companies faded away with the destruction of the French and decline of the Dutch Company in Bengal. His ruin was completed by 1758 when he bitterly complained that the English had destroyed his commerce and had driven him to the brink of ruin.

In general terms, the fall of Wajid was a logical conclusion to the English victory at Plassey and hence it is difficult to subscribe to Jean Law's observation (cited in Hill 1905: III.190 n.1) that Wajid 'finally fell a victim to his diplomacies, perhaps also to his imprudences'. If any single factor accelerated his doom, it was the wrath of Clive who wanted to ruin the Armenian merchant prince whom he considered to be a 'villain' for his support to the French. Clive had a strong suspicion that Wajid was connected with the plan for French intervention in Bengal in 1757 and wrote to William Watts (Orme Mss: India, X, f. 112vo, Clive to Watts, 4 August 1758): 'There is among the papers one to Coja Wazeed, mentioning these matters. I wish you could effect the ruin of that villain who is a Frenchman in his heart.' The opportunity for the British to complete Wajid's destruction came in 1759. By then it must have dawned on Wajid that with the British at the helm of affairs in Bengal, he had absolutely no chance of rescuing his crumbling commercial empire. In desperation he gambled again, perhaps realizing that he had nothing to lose but everything to gain if he could succeed in his venture. So he now plotted with the Dutch for them to invade Bengal and act as a counterpoise to the British. Like Plassey, his second gamble failed and that, too, miserably. With the failure of the Dutch expedition, his doom was beyond retrieval. Clive described, as if joyfully, the destruction of the great Hughli merchant:

> As I know that rascal Coja Wazeed was the principal cause of our late troubles at Calcutta, and was even now doing his utmost to set the Dutch and us at variance, I thought proper to lay hold of him that he might not attempt to break the firm friendship which subsists between his Excellency [Mir Jafar, the new Nawab], you (Miran, Mir Jafar's son) and myself. (Clive Mss: vol. 269, no. 982, Clive to Miran, 27 November 1759)

On his capture, Wajid was jailed, where he conveniently poisoned himself (Mss Eur. G: 37, Box 22). With Wajid's death, his rival in the 1740s and one of the early Plassey conspirators, Khwaja Petruse, took his place as the leader of the Armenian community in Bengal.

Sushil Chaudhury

V

The presence of the Armenian diaspora and the extent of their trading network in Bengal will be apparent from the evidence of their involvement not only in the various trade marts but also in the numerous production centres (especially of textiles and silk) of Bengal throughout the seventeenth and eighteenth centuries, and is well borne out by documentation in European records of the period. Their prominent role in the silk and textile trade of Bengal is beyond any doubt. Though we are not in a position as yet to make any estimate, in quantitative terms, of the Armenian involvement in Bengal's export trade in silk and textiles, there is no dearth of qualitative evidence indicating a significant role played by them in this particular area. The extraordinary diffusion of silk and textile industry, especially the textile industry, in Bengal was perhaps best paralleled by the Armenian diaspora and their extensive network which made them one of the most important groups of merchants in Bengal, often competing successfully with even the most powerful local merchant groups. As the textile industry in Bengal was basically a rural domestic-handicraft industry (Chaudhury 1995: 135–44), the natural corollary was its extreme diffusion which suited the Armenians with their extensive networks throughout Bengal. That was why they could become formidable rivals of the local/Indian merchants, not to speak of the European trading companies, in procuring textiles for export markets. In an estimate of the textile export from Dhaka in 1747, the Armenian share, among the Asian merchants, is said to have been as large as 23 per cent (*Home Miscellaneous Series*: vol. 456F). In the silk market too, they along with other Asian merchants (mainly Gujaratis and North Indian merchants from Lahore, Multan, Delhi, Agra, etc.) were the dominant buyers, often responsible for pushing up prices with their heavy purchases with little concern for even high prices, and to the detriment of the European companies (Chaudhury 1995: 228–36).

The above scenario prevailed until the mid-eighteenth century after which the British, with their victory in the Battle of Plassey in 1757 and their consequent mastery over Bengal politics and economy, tried to eliminate their Asian competitors, including the Armenians, from Bengal trade. William Bolts, one of the important officials of the English Company in Bengal in the 1760s, wrote that (1772: 196–7), as the Company tried to establish a monopoly over the export of piece-goods to Basra, Jeddah and Mocha especially, and attempted to force the Armenians to send their goods as freight in English ships, 'by all which circumstances there have been in Bengal many instances of families of Armenians, principal traders in this branch [of trade] to Persia and Arabia who have been totally ruined'.

But the Armenian diaspora and their trading networks were so extensive that it was quite difficult to write them off. Despite some setbacks, the Armenians thrived in Bengal trade and their influence was quite significant even in the 1770s.

The Supreme Court of Calcutta observed in 1775 that the Armenians were 'a very rich body of people, whose extensive dealings and universal correspondence make them particularly useful in this country'. The Chief Justice of the Supreme Court, Sir Elijah Impey, noted in the same year (*Home Miscellaneous Series*: vol. 212, pp. 289–91) that 'the greatest part of the foreign trade of this kingdom [Bengal] is managed' by the Armenians and English free merchants and that 'except a little silver imported by the Dutch and French, the only resource for keeping up the currency of this country lies in the honesty, integrity and perseverance of the English and Armenian independent merchants residing in Calcutta'. In fact the importance of the Armenians and the benefits of their trade in Bengal was such that earlier, in the late 1740s, there was a proposal to expel the Armenians from Calcutta following a dispute regarding the compensation the Company had to pay to the Armenians of Hughli for the alleged seizure of two Armenian ships by English ships, and the Company's attempt to realize the money from the Calcutta Armenians. The proposal, however, was ultimately dropped in consideration of the fact that the French at Chandernagore would then give shelter to the Armenians and deprive the Company of the huge benefit the Company derived from the Armenian trade in the form of 5 per cent tax paid by them in Calcutta for their imports and exports (BPC: Range 1, vol. 23, f. 12vo, 2 January 1750 and f. 22vo, 9 January 1750).

Though the Armenians had close links with the English and often assisted them in their trade and procured commodities for them on commission, nevertheless there was no love lost between them. The English were often very critical in their observations about the Armenians which of course was a reflection of the former's frustration arising out of their failure to make the latter subservient to them. Thus in 1768 a Company official observed that 'it is well known how designing and intriguing a set of people the Armenians are' (*Verelst Papers*: no. 67, Harper to Verelst, Faizabad, 14 March 1768) while the Bengal Council of the Company wrote to the Directors in London in 1771 of 'the intriguing spirit of the Armenians' (*Verelst Papers*: no. 68, Fort William Council to the Court of Directors, 17 April 1771). However there is no denying the fact that the Armenians in general, as the Bengal case will bear out clearly, were driven by a strong passion for extending their commercial hegemony at any cost and were ready to swing their allegiance at the slightest prospect of commercial advantage.

The case of Khwaja Wajid, as analysed earlier, is a point in illustration. In the mid-eighteenth century, trade and politics were closely intertwined, and all the successful merchants tried to cultivate close relationship with the ruling authorities so that they could extract special privileges for themselves. Thus, all three merchant princes of mid-eighteenth century Bengal, including Khwaja Wajid, had developed close links with the ruling power and the main backing of their business prosperity was the support of the ruling court (Chaudhury

1995: 92–131). Realizing this well, Wajid threw his lot in with the heir apparent, Sirajuddaula, as soon as it was announced that the latter would succeed the old *nawab*. Soon he became one of the closet confidants of the new *nawab* but later on when he saw that the young *nawab* had little chance to survive in the face of the onslaught from the English Company which roped in some of the powerful courtiers of the *darbar* in their 'project' of a revolution in Bengal, he deserted the *nawab* and joined the bandwagon of the British who nevertheless ruined him after the revolution. Some of the Armenians of Calcutta joined the British side in the so-called Plassey Revolution, as they thought it would enhance their business prospects. Later on when the British had absolute sway in Bengal politics and economy, some of the Armenians shifted their place of operations from Bengal to the independent kingdom of Oudh (in North India) where they tried to cultivate the friendship of the *nawab* there vis-à-vis the British (*Verelst Papers*: no. 67, Maddison to Verelst, 23 October and 26 November 1767).

VI

As noted earlier, the Armenians in Bengal were not dissociated from their main community in New Julfa. They had regular traffic with New Julfa and, more interestingly, sometimes the Armenians in India borrowed money from rich merchants in New Julfa by executing bonds (*Verelst Papers*: no. 67, Khwaja Petruse's petition to the Court of Directors in London, 5 February 1760). Again, they transacted business with bills of exchange in such faraway places as Surat or Agra and Delhi (BPC: Range 1, vol. 1, f. 410vo, 6 September 1762). In fact Khwaja Wajid had a trading house in Surat. The vast networks of enterprises created by the Armenians in Bengal in the seventeenth and eighteenth centuries are evident from the analysis of Bengal's silk and textile markets made earlier. And we have seen that they were conspicuous even in the remote parts of Bengal wherever there was the possibility of good profit in mercantile activities. It is pertinent to point out that they did not enjoy any special concessions in Bengal as an ethnic and minority foreign religious group of merchants, and yet they were able to compete successfully with the local and other foreign group of merchants operating in the region.

That the Armenians often acted as a group rather than as individual entre-preneurs is a result of the pride they took in their identity. That they had one language, one culture and one religion was the most crucial factor, and one which helped them develop and extend their networks. Unlike other groups of Indian or foreign merchants, the Armenians had built their own colonies and settlements with their own churches in different parts of India, something that underlines the strong ethnic and cultural overtones of the Armenian entrepreneurs and their enterprises. Thus we find that the Armenians had their own settlement in Saidabad where they built their own churches. Similarly, they had their own communities with churches in Kasimbazar, Hughli, Patna and other important centres of trade in Bengal. An area in Calcutta still bears the name of the Armenians (*Armanitola* – the habitat of the Armenians), as does an Armenian church and even a place on the banks of the Ganges where the goods of the Armenians were off-loaded or on-loaded (*Armani ghat*).

While speaking about the entrepreneurial networks of the Armenians and their enterprises, the question that naturally arises is whether the Armenians were mere peddlers, as typified by the famous (made so by Niels Steensgaard as an example of Asian peddlers) Armenian Hovhannes Joughayetsi who had travelled widely in India and Tibet for business transactions as factors of his masters in New Julfa (Khatchikian 1966: 153–86). Though J.C. van Leur (1955) was the first historian to challenge the Eurocentric view that the Indian Ocean trade in the sixteenth and the seventeenth centuries was dominated completely by the Europeans, his thesis of Asian trade being entirely pedalling trade, later reinforced by Steensgaard (1974), can hardly be accepted now.[15] Among the Armenian merchants, as among the Indians, there were small peddlers alongside the wealthy and powerful merchants, with varied and extensive business operations, who can easily be compared with the Medicis, Fuggers or Tripps of Europe. Hovhannes was not really a pedlar working on his own, as one may gather from a rather summary account of his activities by Steensgaard, but a cog in a very large commercial wheel operated by the wealthy merchant families of New Julfa. In fact, the way the networks of Armenian entrepreneurs functioned and the way they organized the circulation of capital and commercial intelligence will only reinforce the proposition that the Armenian entrepreneurs were not 'insecure men', made so 'by limitations of information and vagaries of commerce' as Das Gupta (1979) would have us believe in the case of Mulla Abdul Goffur, the greatest merchant-trader of the Mughal Empire in the third quarter of the seventeenth century.

The crucial question that remains to be answered, however, is that of what the reasons were for the fabulous success of the Armenian merchants vis-à-vis even the advanced organizational form of the European joint stock companies – a question which has been raised earlier by Fernand Braudel (1984) and Philip D. Curtin (1984). It has been suggested recently that the success of the Armenians was primarily due to 'organizational form or arrangements' which seems to be quite tenable (Baladouni and Makepeace 1998: xxxiv–xxxv). Indeed, the widely spread but highly interrelated Armenian enterprises operated under the 'ethos of trust' which served as human capital, accrued to the community as a result of their 'collective socio-political experiences over many generations' (ibid.: 34). The structuring of their business enterprises, based as it was on family kinship and trusted fellow-countrymen, gave the Armenian merchants two significant advantages – organizational cost savings and organizational innovations. In all probability, the Armenians succeeded because they were able to create networks of trust, shared information and mutual support based upon the fact that they were a distinct ethnic and religious minority. This very characteristic differentiated them from other merchant groups in Bengal. There is no doubt that some of the other diaspora peoples such as the Jews had all these characteristics as well, but perhaps the Armenians were ahead of the others in these respects and hence their success was more spectacular than that of the others. The political aspects of their role remain key to their success as Baghdiantz McCabe has made clear in Chapter 2.

However, the Armenian commercial system, based as it was on close family ties, was not something extraordinary. The well-known Italian merchant families are European examples of the same family system. This was a common trading pattern in the early modern period. The Indians, especially the Marwaris and Gujaratis, and also the Parsis in India, had the same system of operations. And all of them were quite successful in their enterprises. In fact, one of the main factors that contributed to the fabulous success of the Armenians was their will to better their situation in exile, which fostered their drive to acquire knowledge of the languages and customs of others. Their flexibility was an asset. They were capable of assuming multiple identities as and when required for the sake of their commercial prosperity (Baghdiantz McCabe 1999: 358–9).

At the same time the Armenians had a higher level of awareness of the international scene and the expertise to link up local and regional markets to intra-Asian markets. In this context the observation of Georges Roque is worth quoting:

> These people are shrewder than the Indian sarrafs, because they do not work alone, when it comes to evaluating their merchandise and money. More enterprising amongst them deal with all that is there [to trade in], and do not ignore the price of any merchandise, either from Europe or Asia, or any other place because they correspond with all others and receive rapid information on current prices wherever they are. Thus they do not get cheated in their purchases, and are very economical, and work unbelievably hard to trade so as not to overpay on the merchandise. They spend very little towards living. They are by nature accustomed to living frugally. (cited in Husain 1994: 394)

In fact the Armenian merchants, as has been rightly pointed out by K.N. Chaudhuri (1978), were highly skilled arbitrage dealers who were forced, through historical circumstances, to develop very flexible and geographically mobile forms of commerce. An ability to measure the risks of overland trade and a readiness to vary the size of commercial transactions were the special skills that the Armenians brought to the trading world of the Middle East, India and even Europe, and this was one of the secrets of their tremendous success. Indeed, the ability of the Armenians to thrive on low profit margin, their readiness to deal in any commodity and move into even remote producing centres when there was the prospect of a profit, and their ability to adopt to the language and culture of their trading country without losing their own identity were some of the important factors behind their phenomenal success in interregional and international trade in the seventeenth and eighteenth centuries.

Notes

1. Patna in Bihar was the most important trade centre in that province and was famous for the production of saltpetre, opium and textiles in the seventeenth and the eighteenth centuries.
2. Hughli was the premier port of Bengal in the seventeenth and early eighteenth centuries.
3. For the Surman embassy and the *farman* of 1717, see Chaudhury 1975: 41–3.
4. While Saidabad was an exclusive Armenian colony, founded around 1665, Kasimbazar, another suburb of Murshidabad, was the most important centre of silk production. Dhaka was the most important centre of the finest and most expensive textiles, especially the legendary muslins.
5. That the Armenians of Bengal had links with New Julfa is evident from the fact that after the death of 'Coja Avatook Cunnon and Coja Surhaud Cunnon', their brother, 'Coja Turcawn Cunnon Armenian' came to Bengal from New Julfa to claim their 'effects' from Khwaja Nazar Jacob of Calcutta (see BPC Range 1, vol. 5, f. 451, 16 March 1723). In all probability Khwaja Surhaud was connected with one of the greatest merchant families of New Julfa, the Sharimans (or Surhaud?), c.f. Herzig 1987: typed mss.
6. For Jagat Seths, the greatest banker of his day in India and possibly Asia, see Chaudhury 1995: 109–16.
7. For Umichand, ibid.: 116–20.
8. Indian unit of weight: one maund is equivalent to 75 English lbs.
9. At that time one pound sterling was equivalent to Rs 8.
10. The Dutch Director Louis Taillefert also mentioned that the English Company obtained the saltpetre monopoly from Mir Jafar in 1758, c.f. the 'Memorie' of Louis Taillefert (1763: HR 246, f. 174, 17 November).
11. For details, see the shipping lists in the VOC records in Algemeen Rijksarchief.
12. Peter Marshall's assertion that by the 1720s Hughli was completely overshadowed by Calcutta port (1976: 54–8; 1987: 65) is not beyond doubt. The lean period of the 1720s and the 1730s was only a temporary phase for

the Hughli port which recovered from the late 1730s and the early 1740s with considerable increase in French and Asian shipping, c.f. Chaudhury 1995: 24–5, 314–19.

13. It is obvious from this reference that Wajid lived in Chinsurah for some time. But this must have been for a short period because in early 1750, in a letter from Bengal (VOC: 2732, f. 9vo, Hughli to Hereen XVII, 11 February 1750), Wajid was referred to as 'the merchant who was removed' (from Chinsurah). It is of interest that in the Dutch records, Wajid was frequently referred to as 'Moor Merchant' (*Moors Koopman*). There can be hardly any doubt that Wajid was an Armenian, and there is no evidence that he was ever converted to Islam. It might have been possible that because of his close connection with the Muslim rulers, the Dutch referred to him as 'Moor Merchant' or 'Coja Mhamet Wazid'. There is evidence that Armenian merchants changed their names often for the sake of convenience in trade. Thus in the early seventeenth century, Khwaja Philipos of New Julfa was known as Philippe de Zagly in Courlande while in Persia his name was Imam Kuli Beg (Gulbenkian 1970: 361–9). So it might be possible that Wajid also added Muhammed to his name, perhaps like his father, Khwaja 'Mhamet' Fazel, to enhance his business prospects.

14. The author states that Wajid told Nawab Alivardi Khan that if the latter drove the English out of Calcutta, he would have gained Rs 3 crores (Rs 30 million). He again asserts that Wajid who 'bore enmity' to the English incited Sirajuddaulla to attack the English (Ali 1952: 163). As Siraj dismissed Karam Ali from the office of the *faujdar* of Ghoraghat and imprisoned him later in Purnea (Bihar), he had every reason to be biased against young Nawab Sirajuddaulla and also against Wajid who belonged to the inner circle of the Siraj (Ali 1952: 70). That Karam Ali echoes the sentiment of the English is evident from the fact that even Orme and Clive thought that Wajid was behind Siraj's attack on Calcutta (Orme Mss: OV, 28, p. 52, Orme to John Payne, 3 November 1756). For Clive's attitude see Clive Mss, vol. 269, no. 982, Clive to Miran, 27 November 1759.

15. For an opposing view, see Chaudhuri (1978) and a recent assertion in Chaudhury and Morineau (1999) and also in Baghdiantz McCabe (1999).

References

Abbreviations used in text and references

BPC   Bengal Public Consultations
DB   Despatch Book
HR   Hoge Regering, Algemeen Rijksarchief

IOL&R   India Office Library and Records
VOC   Verenigde Oost Indische Compagnie

Ali, K. (1952), *Muzaffarnamah,* in J.N. Sarkar (ed.), *Bengal Nawabs,* Calcutta: Asiatic Society.

Baghdiantz McCabe, I. (1999) *The Shah's Silk for Europe's Silver: The Eurasian Silk Trade of the Julfan Armenians in Safavid Iran and India (1590–1750),* University of Pennsylvania (Series in Armenian Texts and Studies), Atlanta: Scholar's Press.

Baladouni, V. and Makepeace, M. (eds) (1998), *Armenian Merchants of the Seventeenth and Early Eighteenth Centuries: English East India Company Sources,* Philadelphia: American Philosophical Society.

Bengal Letters Received, relevant volumes, India Office Records, British Library.

Bengal Public Consultations, Range 1, relevant volumes, India Office Records, British Library, London.

Bengal Secret and Military Consultations, Select Committee Consultations, Range 1, India Office Records, British Library.

Bisdom, A. (1755) The 'Memorie' of Bisdom; (VOC) 2850.

Bolts, W. (1772), *Considerations on Indian Affairs,* London.

Braudel, F. (1984), *Civilization and Capitalism,* New York.

Chaudhuri, K.N. (1978), *The Trading World of Asia and the English East India Company,* Cambridge: Cambridge University Press.

Chaudhury, S. (1975), *Trade and Commercial Organization in Bengal, 1650–1720,* Calcutta: Firma K.L.M.

—— (1995), *From Prosperity to Decline: Mid-Eighteenth Century Bengal,* New Delhi: Manohar.

—— (1986/7), 'Sirajuddaullah, the English East India Company and the Plassey Conspiracy: A Reappraisal', *Indian Historical Review,* 13(1–2).

—— and Morineau, M. (eds) (1999), *Merchants, Companies and Trade: Europe and Asia in the Early Modern Era,* Cambridge: Cambridge University Press.

Clive Mss. Vol. 269, no. 982, India Office Records, British Library.

Curtin, P.D. (1984), *Cross-Cultural Trade in World History,* Cambridge: Cambridge University Press.

Das Gupta, A. (1979), *Indian Merchants and the Decline of Surat,* Wiesbaden: Franz Steiner Verlag.

Despatch Book, relevant volumes, India Office Records, British Museum.

Factory Records, Kasimbazar, relevant volumes, India Office Records, British Museum.

Gulbenkian, R. (1970), 'Philippe de Zagly, marchand arménien de Julfa, et l'établissement du commerce persan en Courlande en 1626', *Revue des arméniennes,* n.s. 7.

Gupta, B.K. (1962), *Sirajuddaullah and the East India Company, 1756–57,* Leiden: E.J. Brill.

Herzig, E. (1987), 'The Armenian Commercial Documents in the Archivo di Stato of Venice', typed mss.

Hill, S.C. (1905), *Bengal in 1756–57,* 3 vols, London.

Home Miscellaneous Series, relevant volumes, India Office Records, British Library.

Huighens, A. (1750), 'The Memory of Huighens...', VOC 2763.

Hume, A. (1730), 'The "Memorie" of Hume', General Indische Compagnie, 5768, Antwerp: Stadsarchief Antwerpen.

Husain, R.K. (1994), 'The Armenians in India', *Proceedings of the Indian History Congress,* 55th session, Calcutta.

Khan, Y.A. (1978), *Zamia-i-Tadhkira-I-Yusufi,* A. Subhan (ed.), Calcutta: Asiatic Society.

Khatchikian, L. (1966), 'The Ledger Book of the Merchant Hovhannes Joughayetsi', *Journal of the Asiatic Society of Bengal,* 4th series, 8.

Kerseboom, J. (1755), 'The "Memorie" of Kerseboom...', VOC 2849.

Marshall, P.J. (1976), *East Indian Fortunes,* Oxford: Oxford University Press.

—— (1987), *Bengal: the British Bridgehead,* Cambridge: Cambridge University Press.

Mayor's Court Records, Calcutta, India Office Records, British Library.

Mss. European D. 283, India Office Records, British Library.

Mss. European G 37, Box 22, India Office Records, British Library.

Orme Mss., relevant volumes, India Office Records, British Library.

Orme, R. (1803), *History of the Military Transactions of the British Nation in Indostan,* vol. II, sec. I.

Steensgaard, N. (1974), *The Asian Trade Revolution of the Seventeenth Century,* Chicago: University of Chicago Press.

Taillefert, L. (1755), VOC 2849.

—— (1763), 'The "Memorie" of Hoge Regering', 246, Algemeen Rijksarchief.

Van Leur, J.C. (1955), *Indonesian Trade and Society,* The Hague.

Verelst Papers, Mss. European F 218, India Office Records, British Library.

The Seventeenth-century Japanese Diaspora: Questions of Boundary and Policy

William D. Wray

Introduction

In the period between the 1580s and the 1630s Japan sent several hundred vessels into Southeast Asia to participate in trade there. The size of this undertaking was unprecedented in the country's history. The maritime context in which it occurred can be defined by three developments: a suspension of direct trade between China and Japan in the 1550s, the arrival of European traders in Asian waters, and a resurgence of Chinese trade into Southeast Asia. Earlier trade between Japan and China had been in two forms: private trade, meaning mostly pirate activity carried out by what were called 'Japanese pirates' (*wakō*) who were actually often Chinese attempting to circumvent China's maritime restrictions, and officially recognized trade based on governmental agreements between the two countries. This last form collapsed as a result of violent competition for the permits that the trade required. In the aftermath of this collapse the Portuguese arrived in East Asia and acted as intermediaries carrying goods between China and Japan, which meant primarily an exchange of Chinese silk for Japanese silver. They were later joined by the Spanish (in the Philippines), the English and the Dutch. In 1567 China removed a ban on private trade to the south which had the effect of making Southeast Asia a meeting place for both Asian and European maritime enterprises. The Japanese initiated their overseas expansion partly to take advantage of this entrepôt function of Southeast Asian ports where they could exchange their exports for Chinese goods exported there. That enabled them to circumvent the Chinese ban on direct China-Japan trade.

This era of expansion that produced a widespread Japanese diaspora came to an end in the 1630s when the Tokugawa *bakufu*, the central government of Japan since 1603, issued a series of edicts, traditionally characterized by the term 'seclusion' but more recently described as 'maritime prohibitions', which among other measures included a ban on overseas travel and a refusal, after a certain interval, to allow Japanese abroad to return to Japan.[1] These edicts thus set up limitations on overseas Japanese communities that in effect created a 'boundary' in thematic terms to their experience. How we characterize the Japanese diaspora depends in part on its relationship to the seclusion policy. Conversely, our interpretation of that policy should be affected by the conditions of the diaspora.

In recent decades the study of seclusion has focused on issues of policy (the sequence of *bakufu* decisions on foreign relations), perception (how Japanese intellectuals viewed Japan's position in the world), and trade (the expansion of foreign trade after the 1630s). The general consensus is that the *bakufu*'s measures in restricting overseas travel conformed to those of many other East Asian countries, especially China. Furthermore, as the decades wore on, Japanese intellectuals did not perceive their country as being 'closed', but rather viewed the policy of maritime prohibitions as helping to secure a peaceful environment among East Asian countries. Finally, as trade continued to grow after the 1630s, the regulatory measures of that decade appeared simply as part of a sequential process rather than firm indications of new policy directions (Arano 1994; Toby 1984). These interpretations, of course, differ substantially from earlier conclusions that Japan's banishment of Iberian traders signified a condition of seclusion. Nevertheless, recent scholarship has not fundamentally incorporated into its interpretive perspective the experience of Japanese who traded abroad either on vermilion-seal voyages [government-licensed voyages] or as emigrants.

Our consideration of the Japanese diaspora essentially involves three phases: *expansion* from Japan into Southeast Asia lasting from the late sixteenth century through to the mid-1630s, *integration* into the local communities from the 1630s to roughly the 1660s, and *absorption* into these societies from the 1670s onward, as incidence of intra-Japanese marriage declined. The characterization of each of these phases raises issues of boundary, that is, whether the Japanese abroad conform to standard definitions of diaspora.[2]

In the phase of expansion before the 1630s the Japanese communities in Southeast Asia seem to have been more vertically linked to Japan than horizontally associated with one another. That linkage, being part of Japan's expansion, might invalidate their status as a diaspora insofar as diaspora are not regarded as part of a state's expansion. On the other hand, they did have important functional connections with the commerce and administration of the states where they resided, activities that are typical of diaspora.

In the second phase, that of integration, which followed the implementation of the seclusion policy in the 1630s, the overseas Japanese expanded on their roles in their communities. No longer part of the Japanese state's expansion – they were cut off from Japan and Japan itself was no longer expanding – they conformed to standard diaspora experience. There were, however, important variations from that standard. First, one definition, employed by Philip Curtin, terms a diaspora 'a nation of socially interdependent, but spatially dispersed communities' (cited in Reid 1998: 36). Second, a characteristic diaspora usually retained ties with its homeland (see Harlaftis in Chapter 7 of this volume). It could thus replenish itself by emigration either from the state from which it originally emerged or from other parts of its existing dispersed community. The post-1630s Japanese diaspora in Southeast Asia probably met neither of these two criteria. The primarily vertical linkage to Japan before the 1630s likely made it harder for them to draw on inter-community ties after seclusion. Furthermore, unlike the experience of overseas Chinese, there were no 'periodic new waves of emigration' (Reid 1998: 39) from Japan. Under the seclusion policy there was basically no ethnic home territory from which it could draw.

Although relations between the overseas Japanese and the homeland had largely been cut after the 1630s, some tenuous connections remained in the form of financial and commercial ties through intermediaries and sporadic correspondence with ageing relatives in Japan (Blussé 1986). In the third phase of absorption even these links seem to have disappeared. Within Southeast Asia itself, although some data suggest the communities retained substantial resilience for several decades following the 1630s, in general, with their relatively small numbers, they appear not to have followed a strategy of autonomous growth but instead to have allowed themselves gradually to be absorbed into the local society. Whereas individual Japanese entrepreneurs became integrated into Southeast Asian societies after the 1630s, by the 1660s their offspring were for the most part of mixed blood. Given that outcome, it is reasonable to conclude that even though the overseas Japanese met sufficient criteria to be termed a diaspora, their experience as such ultimately proved abortive.

In the context of the seclusion policy, at least with respect to those who left Japan in the 1630s, the diaspora can be viewed as the product of an expulsion. The phenomenon of specific social groups (as opposed to simply ethnic communities) being expelled from countries has recently been the subject of an increasing comparative analysis. Benjamin Kedar has used the term 'corporate expulsion' to characterize 'the banishment of an entire category of subjects *beyond the physical boundaries of a political entity*'. What 'differentiates corporate expulsion from other types of displacement' is, says Kedar, 'the applicability of expulsion orders to a category of persons, rather than to specific individuals'. Banishment of this kind, the rationale for which was the presumed danger they represented to their home society, 'was deemed to be permanent' (Kedar 1996: 167–74). Kedar suggests that a Japanese proclamation of 1614 aimed at the expulsion of Christians may have been influenced by similar actions in European countries against Catholic priests.

If 'expulsion' can be thought of as a partial model for the Japanese case, a possible comparison might be the expulsion of Jews and Moors from Spain subsequent to the Christian reconquest. Changes in commercial policy accompanying the transition from Islamic to Christian rule suggest both social and economic parallels with

Japan's case. Earlier Muslim rulers in Spain had sought to promote international trade as a source of profit, but their Christian successors, partly because of papal restrictions against trading with Muslims, were more inclined toward regulation (Constable 1994: 256–7; Kedar 1996: 167–74). Like some Islamic governments, the *bakufu* also sought to profit from trade during and after the 1630s, but its policies encompassed dimensions of expulsion and increased regulation.

Nevertheless, the Jews and Moors were not only religiously but also ethnically distinct from the surrounding population in Spain. While a religious expulsion of Christian leaders was part of Japan's seclusion policy, in contrast to the Spanish case, there was really not, in any general sense, a separate *ethnic* expulsion resulting in a diaspora. On a more specific level, however, there was also a gender dimension in that the Japanese wives of Western traders, and their children, were expelled. The distinction between ethnicity and gender here is, of course, blurred in the offspring of the mixed marriages. The 'foreignness' of these children makes ethnicity at least a part of the characterization of the diaspora (Innes 1980: 146–7, 192).[3]

In a broad sense, however, in these comparisons religion represents a similarity and ethnicity a contrast, that is, in both cases the religion of the expellees was different from that of the home country. However, their ethnicity was different in the case of Spain but the same in the Japanese case. If we were to seek an inverse analogy, where the ethnicity was the same but where the 'religion', or its modern functional equivalent, ideology (with its accompanying military danger) was different, an example would be the 'White' Russians, the counter-revolutionary forces who sought to overthrow the new Soviet ('Red') government after the Russian Revolution of 1917. Following their defeat, anywhere from one to two million left Russia, departing either through fear or expulsion, thereby being characterized, respectively, as either émigrés or expellees (Johnston 1988: 1–5; Stone 1983: 379).[4]

The common element in the Russian and Japanese cases, then, is that the ethnicity of the expellees and the home country was the same. If we break down the components of the White Russian emigration, however, certain contrasts may be made with circumstances in Japan. First, on a macro level, the comparative scale of the White Russian emigration was far larger, constituting perhaps 2 per cent of the Russian population, while the Japanese diaspora probably never exceeded 0.04 per cent of Japan's population. The religious, ideological and military component was, however, similar in that many left Japan after defeat in the early seventeenth-century battles. A comparison at the entrepreneurial level would be thin at best. Although there were many émigré Russian entrepreneurs, just as there were many Japanese entrepreneurs in Southeast Asia, Japanese could remain in Japan in the seventeenth century as entrepreneurs without the same level of restrictions imposed in the Soviet Union. Religious suppression constituted a common element in the two cases, but the portion of émigrés leaving Russian for religious reasons was far lower than among those who left Japan in the seventeenth century.

While the religio-ideological factor offers useful comparisons, as in the Russian case, religion itself cannot be a sufficient characterization for the generation of the Japanese diaspora because not all who went abroad were Christians.[5] Ultimately such a characterization must be judged against the sequence of events and how they affect the interpretation of expulsion. As Anthony Reid has noted (1998: 66), the concept of expulsion is one of the defining roots of diaspora, particularly through the biblical passage referring to the Lord removing 'into all the kingdoms of the earth' those whom he had smitten. Nevertheless, the expulsion model, while certainly suggestive, has obvious limitations in its applicability to Japan. Most historical diaspora have arisen after either a growing awareness of a threat to well-being or a specific expulsion order. In the movement of Japanese abroad, those leaving for political and religious reasons conform to this pattern. However, there was a twenty-year gap between the anti-Christian edict of 1614 and the crucial measures of the 1630s. These decisive measures of state were issued *after* the departure of emigrants. Many Japanese abroad, who were prevented from returning because of the edicts of the 1630s, were at that time being *kept* out rather than being *forced* out. The decisions of the 1630s, then, perhaps constitute less an expulsion than a closing, meaning that many Japanese abroad, at least those who were not Christians, were technically not expellees. What is unusual about the Japanese diaspora, then, is the reversal of the common sequence when the policy precedes the departure. In Japan, to an extent, the departure preceded the policy.

The Diaspora

A great variety of Japanese went abroad in the late sixteenth and early seventeenth centuries. There were three major categories of emigrants. First, some whose voyages were part of the vermilion-seal ship business had commercial experience before their departure from Japan. However, probably most of those who ended up in Southeast Asia lacked that experience before their arrival. Their development as an entrepreneurial minority within Southeast Asia was a form of adaptation to a new lifestyle. A second category was the Christian refugee, that is, the Japanese Catholics fleeing persecution under the increasingly repressive policies of the Japanese authorities toward Christianity in the early seventeenth century. Many of these settled in Manila. The third consisted of mercenaries or political exiles from the unification wars that had culminated in the Battle of Sekigahara in 1600 in which Tokugawa Ieyasu was victorious. Many of these exiles were also veterans of the Korean wars of the 1590s and carried their military lifestyles into the new towns they were creating. This category also included many *rōnin*, that is, samurai who had lost their master. As a *daimyō*, losing in the unification wars did not inevitably mean losing status. Many who were on the losing side had their domains reduced in size. They retained their status but were placed in a category of *tozama* (meaning 'outside') *daimyō*. Others, however, were dispossessed. When that happened, their samurai automatically lost their status and thus became *rōnin*. These were the exiles who constituted the mercenary groups. The *bakufu*'s fear of the disruptions they might cause was one of the considerations behind the seclusion policy (Gaimushō 1934: 548–9). Apart from these three main categories, there were many others who settled abroad. These included labourers, crew members of foreign vessels, servants (many served the Spanish in Manila), bondsmen, and slaves (Massarella 1990: 134).

On a broad macro level, the principal role of the diaspora was to participate in the entrepôt trade of Southeast Asia, exchanging imports of Chinese silk for Japanese silver. However, this is not the easiest route to describing the Japanese entrepreneurial activities there. One reason for this is that the principal silk-exporting area in the region was Tonkin. Because of its rulers' concern about the Japanese mercenaries importing weapons, they discouraged the development of a full-scale Japanese town there. What we can learn about the diaspora lies more in the commodities in which they traded, the positions they held in the local administration of commerce, and their functions as intermediaries (before seclusion) between the vermilion-seal vessels and the local economy.

One of the institutional arrangements designed to handle the business of foreign merchants in Southeast Asian countries was the port master, or *syahbandar*. This was an office held by a foreign merchant usually to service his own community. The identity of many of the Japanese who served in this post in the numerous Japanese towns in Vietnam, Cambodia and Siam is known. In some ports, however, where the Japanese seem to have held a dominating hold over the local economy, the Japanese *syahbandar* may have played a more general role in local port administration (Reid 1993: 120; Iwao 1985: 366–7).

Certainly Japanese entrepreneurial residents played a crucial role in the smooth and productive operation of the Japan-local trade. In the case of Hoi An in central Vietnam, when a vermilion-seal vessel arrived, its merchant crew would report to the chief of the Japanese town and local authorities. They would then notify the king who would retain some of the cargo, especially copper and copper coins, and then issue a discharge for the remainder of the cargo. The Japanese town chief was also involved in the inspection of the ship. Japanese residents participated in the local government's selection of goods for purchase, and they transported and sold to the public the rest of the cargo. Purchasing of local products for the return voyage of the vermilion-seal vessels was also carried out by Japan town residents. In Manila, where there were many Japanese shops, Japanese residents sold the cargo of the Japanese ships and sometimes serviced Chinese ships. As a result of these activities, some Japanese residents became very influential (Iwao 1966: 25–8).

Although the Japanese did not develop a large town in Tonkin, it was a major destination for Japanese ships. One of the most active Japanese traders there was Wada Rizaemon, who had been one of the Christians exiled to Macao. After working in the raw silk trade in Quang Nam as a representative of a Portuguese vessel he moved to Tonkin where he became a member of the Emperor's staff. Wada also dealt in raw silk and silk fabrics and imported copper coins (Abe 1993: 68–9).[6]

Japanese had an important role in Siam in both military and commercial spheres. The key military figure was Yamada Nagamasa. He had an army of 700 Japanese under his leadership, which played a decisive role in a Siamese civil war and aided in suppressing rebellion. Through this support for the King, Yamada gained high official rank, and he also served as head of the Japanese town. The most important commercial function performed by Japanese in the Siamese capital, Ayutthia, was the handling of deerskin. Their position in this trade was strong enough that the competing Dutch had to rely on them as brokers. When the large Japanese military population there, which provided service to the Siamese king, was off duty, it too participated in the deerskin trade. One resident, Itoya Taemon, who apparently had ties with Nagasaki traders, established such a large position in the deerskin purchasing and brokerage business that he became head of the Japanese town (Gaimushō 1934: 537–78, 893; Ishii and Yoshiharu 1987: 46–51; Iwao 1966: 175–8).

Although the principal activity of the Japanese in the Southeast Asian towns covered here was probably handling the vermilion-seal ship business, they were obviously heavily involved with local commerce and government administration in these towns. These functions, as well as their military role, demonstrate that they had an important connection with the political systems in the countries where they resided. Activity of this kind is usually considered typical of classic diaspora. In particular, the Japanese role in Southeast Asia has many similarities to the functions performed by Armenians in seventeenth-century Iran where the profits from their silk trade provided support for the government there (see Baghdiantz McCabe, Chapter 2 in this volume). In general, then, even though the overseas Japanese were part of Japan's own expansion, they also possessed certain characteristics of a diaspora in the years prior to seclusion.[7]

The Seclusion Policy

Debate remains about whether the edicts governing trade, which, in addition to the banning of overseas travel and the ending of the vermilion-seal voyages, included the expulsion of the Portuguese in 1639 and the confining of overseas[8] trade to Nagasaki in 1641, should be thought of as having a collective meaning, as expressed in the term 'seclusion'. Ronald Toby (1984: 71–2) calls them 'more properly a series of memoranda and orders'. Even if that view were regarded as a form of reductionism, it is hard to find an alternative characterization. Yoko Nagazumi (1998: 170 n2) suggests that 'there is no consensus to replace the still widely-used term sakoku [seclusion] with another, less anachronistic term'. Given that uncertainty, I am employing the term 'seclusion' in this chapter more out of convenience than of commitment to an older view.[9]

Certainly today there is a general consensus about its motives, namely, that it was implemented to enhance the security and legitimacy of the Tokugawa regime, and that goal entailed excluding the *daimyō* from independent access to foreign trade and showing that the *bakufu* had established its control over that trade. 'Control', however, did not mean that there was a single uniform set of measures applied to the outside world. On the contrary, Japan had a distinctive policy for virtually every country or area with which it traded. There were far more Chinese than Dutch ships coming to Nagasaki, and while the Dutch were kept under strict control in Deshima, the artificial islet in Nagasaki harbour, the Chinese, until 1689, were free to reside in Nagasaki with few restrictions.

Furthermore, in the evolution of trade management over the first four decades of the seventeenth century, elements of 'process' were almost as important as those of 'policy'. One such element was bureaucratization. In the early decades of the century trade administration in Nagasaki was rather informal and personal. Zen monks, who had close ties to the *shōgun*, prepared the vermilion-seal permits and the Nagasaki magistrates who had authority over trade there were often *daimyō* who were also close associates of the *shōgun*.[10] By the 1630s Nagasaki magistrates were usually retainers (*hatamoto*) more subordinate to the upper levels of the *bakufu* bureaucracy. They imposed more regulation over the issuance of vermilion seals by requiring an addition certificate (*hōsho*) beginning in 1631. The degree to which this process had become bureaucratized is indicated by the fact that the formal edicts of the 1630s regarding overseas trade were sent to the Nagasaki magistrate without any separate, formal notification to the *daimyō*, that is, through normal administrative, rather than political, channels (Innes 1980: 125–56; Yamamoto 1995: 20–4, 26–67). This suggests that the measures taken relative to seclusion were part of a long process of political evolution and not the product of sudden decisions in the 1630s.

These matters of policy and process are viewed in recent historiography as examples of normal statecraft as contrasted with a paranoid anti-foreignism. This view, however, often overlooks the details of the actual physical implementation of the seclusion policy. Enforcement of this policy was carried out through a form of coast guard consisting of corvee labour conscripted from domains close to Nagasaki. In one case in 1647 when two Portuguese ships came to Japan, a contingent of over 50,000 was assembled at Nagasaki to confront them. This compares favourably to the 110,000 soldiers who actually fought at Sekigahara in 1600, the most decisive land battle in Japanese history (Kalland 1995: 44; *Kodansha Encyclopedia of Japan*: 7. 56; Ooms 1985: 44).

Reactions on this scale, indeed displaying a sense of paranoia, form an interesting contrast to the *bakufu*'s purposeful disconnection from the Japanese abroad. After the 1630s the Japanese diaspora was left on its own with no protection by governments in Japan. That environment has an important bearing on how we characterize the Japanese in Southeast Asia. As part of a working definition, Jonathan Israel has argued that diaspora are essentially stateless and are neither protected by a state nor part of a state's expansion.[11] On the basis of these points, the Japanese communities in Southeast Asia after the 1630s would qualify as a diaspora.

This concept of 'no-state protection', however, also has at least some connection to both the motivation for seclusion and the overseas experience before the 1630s. One of the reasons for the suspension of the vermilion-seal voyages was the *bakufu*'s fear that they might be attacked by the Spanish, who had been forced out of Japan.[12] Even before the 1630s, though, the *bakufu* offered no physical protection to the vermilion-seal ships. They were left unarmed on the grounds that retaliation against any attacker would come through suspension of trade privileges at Nagasaki. As long as Japan remained open to trade with Iberian nations, that policy was a sufficient deterrent. Was it, however, a policy of 'state protection'? If not, then based on Jonathan Israel's definition, the Japanese abroad might be characterized as a diaspora even before the 1630s. It would, however, probably be more accurate to view the *bakufu*'s policy as diplomatic rather than military protection – still enough, in other words, to argue that there was indeed a form of protection extended to the Japanese community insofar as the vermilion-seal vessels could be regarded as integral to the community's existence prior to the 1630s. In that sense the suspension of their voyages would be regarded as a necessary condition for the community's transition into 'diasporahood'.

The elimination of direct contact between the diaspora and Japan itself does not, however, appear to have lessened trade between Southeast Asia and Japan. Recent historiography has stressed Japan's relative openness to trade within the framework of its maritime prohibitions and, through a comparative approach, has sought to demonstrate their similarity to the policies of other Asian countries. For example, the Chinese were the only Asians allowed to trade through Nagasaki, but Siam carried on trade with Japan in the seventeenth century after the seclusion edicts not directly but through ships handled by Chinese merchants (*tōsen*). To a degree, however, that was a preferred option, for the Siamese government, like the Tokugawa, discouraged their own merchants from operating overseas (Viraphol

1977: 8, 58–69). Furthermore, from the perspective of some Koreans, Japan's policy appeared quite liberal. Korea, of course, could trade through its land border with China, but its maritime policies were more restrictive than Japan's. By the mid-eighteenth century some Korean reformers who favoured contact with the West looked favourably on Japan's trade administration through Nagasaki precisely because of its openness to the West through the Dutch (Kang 1997: 195–6). In asking whether Japan's policies converged with those of China, I would draw more of a distinction between Japan's maritime prohibitions and the various dimensions of the Chinese tribute system which included policies on maritime prohibitions on which the Japanese ones were modelled. While the intent of these policies in the two countries may have been similar, their results were not. The waxing and waning over the centuries of these Chinese policies did not prevent the substantial diaspora into Southeast Asia of Chinese who defied them. There was nothing in Japan's experience after the 1640s that resembled the flow of Chinese abroad. Compared to Japan, southern China was more like a sieve.

Another way of assessing Japan's seclusion policy is to place it within longer-term national and global patterns of protectionism and regulation. For example, even before seclusion there was a regulatory component to the issuance of vermilion-seal licences in that the ships had to have at least some Japanese among their crews (Innes 1980: 114). This requirement, of course, was one of the components of mercantilist policies adopted in Japanese shipping subsidies of the late 1890s (Wray 1984). These programmes, in turn, explicitly borrowed from the English Navigation Acts which had been abolished in the 1840s. From a global comparative perspective, it is interesting that the English Acts, which sought to promote British shipping, came into effect in the 1650s roughly fifteen years after Japan shut down its own overseas shipping.

From the domestic Japanese perspective, the edicts of the 1630s can be seen as one phase in a long wave of policy measures stretching from the initial prohibition against *daimyō* acquiring vermilion-seal permits in 1612 through the prohibition of silver exports in 1668 to regulations against Chinese shipping in the 1680s and the explicit adoption of import substitution measures in the 1720s. Collectively, these measures affirmed policies of protectionism, regulation and government assertions of control. The edicts can also be viewed as part of a long regulatory cycle. Over the past four centuries there have been several such cycles in Japanese economic history, with certain points in the cycles being characterized by phases more oriented to less restrictive economic measures, that is, freer trade.

If the edicts were thus a series of measures occupying a phase in a longer pattern of cycles, they should not be regarded as a variable, that is, initiatives leading the economy off into a new or unprecedented direction. This proposition, at face value, would appear to support the revisionist view that also sees these edics as consistent with long-term Japanese policies and not being opposed to trade itself in the 1630s. On the contrary, my argument could open the way for a new perspective on seclusion that might undercut the thrust of the revisionist contentions. If the edicts were not a variable in Japanese economic history, then their full significance cannot be evaluated by reference to their purely economic content. The revisionist argument is that the edicts did not 'close' Japan because trade continued unabated, and in fact increased in volume after the 1630s. This, however, is logically inconsistent with the above proposition, for seclusion cannot be assessed simply on the basis of trade.[13] Indeed, the key element in the several-centuries-long discussion of seclusion is not *trade* but rather *people*, that is, the controls on the movement of people in to and out of the country, or the regulations governing who should be the carriers of Japan's trade.

From this perspective, for the *bakufu* to have allowed further commercial expansion into Southeast Asia with the potential of developing links with the powerful Japanese figures within the diaspora active in the affairs of local states would have, by implicitly recognizing the legitimacy of their continued activity there, partially nullified the hegemonic meaning of the battles of Sekigahara (1600) and Osaka (1615) through which the Tokugawa gained and consolidated their power. Sanjay Subrahmanyam has commented on the tendency in the seventeenth century of Asian states allowing a form of elite immigration where foreigners from outside the region came to occupy important posts in their administration. He concludes that Japan was the most reluctant to permit this (Subrahmanyam 1993: 20–6). However, numerous Japanese in the diaspora were among the elite that served Southeast Asian countries. The key point here is that these were not at all representative of Japan's political leadership at the time. Indeed, many were former opponents, even enemies, of the *bakufu*. The *bakufu* may well have feared these diaspora figures. If so, the momentum toward seclusion may have been directly proportional to the growth in the influence of the diaspora within Southeast Asia.

The role of these *bakufu* opponents also reinforces the proposition that the overseas Japanese could be considered a genuine diaspora even before the 1630s. An overseas community that is protected by the state of its homeland is not usually considered a diaspora. However, these opponents had broken their association with Japan. They were, in a sense, stateless and were not part of the expansion of the Japanese state.

The Post-Seclusion Diaspora

The suspension of the vermilion-seal ships and the ban on overseas travel by the *bakufu* cut the Japanese diaspora's direct physical ties with Japan. Nevertheless, as distinct communities they were able to sustain their commercial enterprises in Southeast Asia for several decades. These years were marked by substantial changes in the context of trade in the area. One major shift involved a range of territorial and policy matters involving China and Japan. Another change, related to the withdrawal of the vermilion-seal ships, was in the identities of the carriers of the key commodities traded in the area.

The question of territory and policy can be divided into two periods: the 1630s to the 1660s and the 1660s to the 1680s. During the first of these periods the absence of Japanese ships and the disruptions in China's trade during the collapse of the Ming dynasty gave the Verenigde Oost Indische Compagnie (VOC) an extra advantage in the trade between Japan and Southeast Asia. That these years marked the peak of Dutch hegemony was in no small part due to the financial success of the VOC's position in Japan.[14] In 1649, for example, the VOC had net profits of 709,603 guilders in Japan, well above the level of their other posts in Asia. Profits from Taiwan and Persia, the only other factories that could be considered large, were, respectively, 66 per cent and 46 per cent of the Japanese figure. To protect their position in Japan, the Dutch remained vigilant in trying to dissuade other Asian countries, such as Siam, from establishing links to Japan (Iwao 1971: 391; Iwao 1976: 14–19). As many have observed, however, Dutch strength in these years was built on developments beyond their control, the seclusion policy in Japan and the wars in China. As an offshoot of these wars, the Ming-loyalist Cheng family took over Taiwan in 1662, expelling the Dutch from the position they had used to dominate the silk and silver exchange within Asia. Then, in the late 1680s China removed its own ban on overseas private trade. It was about this time, when the renewed Chinese maritime dominance in the South China Seas forced a further Dutch retreat, that references to the Japanese diaspora as distinct entrepreneurial communities seem to fade away.[15]

In the shift in the identity of commodity shippers after the implementation of the seclusion policy, one noticeable trend is the continued participation, even if indirect, of the diaspora in Japan's trade. Much of the trade of Japanese towns in Southeast Asia, previously handled by the vermilion-seal ships, was now taken over by the VOC ships. The silk trade best illustrates this. Because of disruptions in China and competition from the Cheng family, the Dutch had to find new sources of silk to ship to Japan. In the early 1640s they succeeded through connections with the Japanese community in Tonkin which controlled much of that area's export trade. The silk they obtained there and shipped to Japan enhanced their capacity to export silver from Japan until later in the decade when price increases of silk within Tonkin undercut the trade. However, in the 1640s the Tonkin raw-silk trade had accounted for one-third of the profits earned by the VOC's Nagasaki station (Abe 1993: 69: Blussé 1996: 62–71; Klein 1989: 80–1). With regard to Japanese exports, probably much of the export cargo carried by the vermilion-seal ships was dispatched directly to Japanese importers in the towns of Southeast

Asia. Following the maritime restrictions of the 1630s, these importers, such as copper dealers in Cochin China, switched to Japan-based Dutch suppliers. In the case of silver, the two largest export carriers through to the late 1630s were the vermilion-seal ships and the Portuguese. As Chinese and Dutch ships took over their cargo in the 1640s, similar supplier-importer relationships likely changed (Reid 1993: 100; von Glahn 1996: 136–7).

Another dimension of economic activity that straddled the pre- and post-seclusion eras and that in some respects created linkages between internal Japan and the external diaspora was foreign financing. This took several forms. One was investment by Japanese in the trade of the Portuguese and the Dutch. A second, lending by diaspora Japanese, seems to have been focused primarily on the communities where they resided. A third involved the diaspora in international ventures within Southeast Asia. And finally, some of this financing may have sustained links between the diaspora and Japan after the 1630s.

The analytical space I am trying to occupy on this issue is the connection between financing and both the diaspora experience itself and its relationship to seclusion. In that sense, lending by Japanese merchants based in Japan to Portuguese or Dutch enterprises seems irrelevant. However, during this period money was flowing in many different directions, often without any national focus and between groups with close linkages horizontally within Southeast Asia and vertically from there to Japan or Chinese merchants trading through Nagasaki. This overall context provides some necessary background to the diaspora experience in financing.

At least since the 1610s Japanese had been financing Portuguese trade. The substantial risks relating to natural disasters or piracy coupled with the potential for huge profit enabled the Japanese to charge high interest rates, often in the 25–30 per cent range, but sometimes even higher. Even the Macao municipal government had a large debt to Japan, while the overall Portuguese debt to Japanese exceeded that to any of its other Asian operations. Consistent with these close financial connections are suggestions that after 1635 there was a flood of new Japanese money into Portuguese trade coming largely from former vermilion-seal ship investors that financed a surge in Portuguese imports until the Portuguese were expelled in 1639. Even after that the Portuguese may have continued their trade temporarily by lending to Chinese merchants trading with Japan (Boyajian 1993: 234–6; Innes 1980: 131–3, 162–3). Also, the Japanese had sustained a long-term pattern of investing in the VOC trade, although by the 1630s the identity of the investors had shifted from port merchants and Western *daimyō* to *bakufu*-related figures. In specific cases in the late 1630s, when the Dutch were still stationed in Hirado, Japanese merchants lent money to the VOC to pay Chinese merchants in Taiwan for imported goods destined for Japan (Kato 1976: 34–84; Nagazumi 1990: 5, English summary 167–73; Nagazumi, 2001: 209–21).[16]

Investment activity within the diaspora seems to have been most prominent in Vietnam. This was an area where the diaspora had a strong influence over the local economy and where the competition between the Chinese and the Dutch created the need for Japanese services. One of the leading Japanese merchants in Tonkin, Wada Rizaemon, apparently invested in both VOC and Chinese ships. In Quang Nam a 1637 Dutch report showed Japanese merchants investing heavily in Chinese ships and making large profits exceeding 15,000 *taels*. In the late 1630s the Dutch seem to have had a difficult time increasing their dealings with the Japanese because of the close ties the latter had already established with Chinese merchants. In Central Vietnam resident Japanese had shipped goods to Nagasaki through Chinese junks. In Tonkin, according to Dutch suspicions, Chinese operations were being financed by Chinese residents of Nagasaki who had borrowed from Japanese merchants (Abe 1993: 68, 75–6; Iwao 1966: 76–7; Innes 1980: 186–91). This last example, which involves a continuing linkage between capital within Japan and commerce in Southeast Asia, is interesting in the light of other accounts that suggest Japanese in the diaspora continued to send wealth back to Japan (Abe 1993: 77). If transfers like this did occur, it is not clear whether the *bakufu* was aware of, or on what grounds it might have tolerated the practice. However, this would have been consistent with its intelligence-gathering activities and a liberalization of family correspondence in 1656. This would also, with respect to the seclusion debate, strengthen the proposition that in the economic sphere Japan was still relatively open.

These financial activities of the diaspora were, of course, based on the capital they had accumulated in the years before the suspension of the vermilion-seal ships. Although the suspension of their voyages removed a large portion of the diaspora's business, for some time they were able to maintain their capital by performing other business functions and utilizing their position in the local economy. For example, in Siam many Japanese worked for the Dutch, who had taken over the profitable leather trade with Japan. Heads of the Japan towns as well as other leading businessmen were in fact large-scale brokers of deerskin, sharkskin and sappanwood. They also supervised labourers who sorted out, took care of, and packaged these goods. Many Japanese were engaged in brokering and selling other goods such as lead, tin and rice (Ishii and Yoshiharu 1987: 69; Iwao 1985: 355–6; Iwao 1966: 202–6). Another way Japanese merchants survived in the post-seclusion environment was to act as agents between the Dutch and local authorities. For example, in central Vietnam in the late 1630s, the chief of the Hoi An Japanese town, Hiranoya Rokubee, served as port administrator, having been appointed to that position by the Nguyen ruler. At the same time he was acting as an agent for the Dutch (Iwao 1966: 79).

Since the diaspora Japanese still participated in the lucrative trade with Japan by investing in or consigning export goods to Dutch and Chinese vessels, it is not surprising that they were also engaged in regional shipping within Southeast Asia. For example, in 1654 Wada Rizaemon, the influential Tonkin businessman, took part in negotiations with the Governor of Luzon for the conclusion of a Tonkin-Manila navigation and trade treaty. In Siam the chief of the Japanese town in Ayuthia between 1642 and 1671, Kimura Hanzaemon, was also a large-scale tin merchant who engaged in Southeast Asian regional trade. Between 1633 and 1663 the number of voyages undertaken by diaspora ships from Ayutthia to other Southeast Asian ports is reported to have been about twenty. Diaspora vessels visited Luzon, Taiwan, Manila and Cambodia (Ishii and Yoshiharu 1987: 82; Iwao 1966: 289).

Demographics and Family

Despite the success of this entrepreneurial diaspora for several decades following seclusion, the Japan towns experienced a rather rapid decline in the last third of the century. Their eventual withering away probably had less to do with any lack of commercial opportunity than with the fundamental failure to reproduce themselves. Before that decline set in, however, their numbers had held up rather well through the 1650s. In Hoi An there had been eighty Japanese households in 1633. Late that year a fire gutted much of the town, but it was rebuilt and by 1651 there were still sixty households. The Japanese in Manila were at one point much more numerous, reaching a peak of about 3,000 residents in the early 1620s. However, following the suspension of the vermilion-seal ships their numbers fell more quickly than those of other towns. By 1637 there were only 800, compared to 2,000 Spanish residents, and 200,000 Chinese, but they also seem to have survived longer than Japanese in other towns. In a rather suggestive incident in 1767 about sixty to seventy were deported back to Japan. That would seem contrary to Japan's ban on return from abroad, but the rationale may have been their rejection of Christianity (Iwao 1966: 246–56, 289, 303–4). Ayuthia was the most military-oriented of the Japanese towns with the presence of Yamada Nagamasa and his roughly 800 followers, who made up perhaps four-fifths of the population. When Yamada was reportedly killed in 1630 the town was annihilated. But it was reconstructed shortly thereafter because of previous Japanese involvement in the deerskin trade. By 1637 it had grown to about 300–400 residents (Gaimushō 1934: 533, 561, 641–59; Ishii and Yoshiharu 1987: 65–8; Iwao 1966: 167–74).

Most of the key historical diaspora, whether of Jewish, Islamic or Parsee background, have been characterized by strong religious traditions that provided cohesion to their communities. Their particular form of Christianity played a similar role for Armenian and Greek diaspora. The Chinese did not possess a similarly distinctive religion, but their extended family system provided some of the same functional supports as religion. In contrast to the above examples, the fact that the Japanese lacked both a single orthodox religious tradition and an extended family system may have had some bearing on the failure of the overseas Japanese to perpetuate themselves as a long-term diaspora.

The principal reason for the eventual decline of the Japanese Southeast Asian towns was the relatively small number of Japanese women who went overseas. In a rough survey of the Japan towns, Iwao Seiichi estimated that there were twenty-three men to every seven women (1966: 335).[17] In this context, as long-term Japanese residents tended to marry local women, over the decades the towns lost their Japanese identity. The situation in Batavia was slightly different because that city had never been a port for the vermilion-seal ships. Japanese came to Batavia primarily as employees of the Dutch whom they had served in Japan. This is borne out by data on their origins. At least half of all Japanese in Batavia came from either Hirado or Nagasaki, the Dutch posts in Japan. However, this figure rises to 88 per cent if the category for emigrants whose origins were unclear is omitted. These emigrants originally came to Batavia as labourers or reinforcements for the Dutch military. They were mostly unmarried men, but since many women came as well, the sex ratio was only 2:1, making Japanese women proportionately more numerous than in the Japan towns. When the emigrants had completed their terms of employment with the Dutch they remained in Batavia and entered various occupations involving agriculture or commerce. As a community less dependent on the vermilion-seal vessels than the Japan towns, it did not suffer as much from the suspension of those voyages (Iwao 1966: 335–6; Iwao 1970: Iwao 1971: 348). Nevertheless, although it may have retained its identity longer, the same marriage dynamics eventually undermined it. At its peak the Japanese population in Batavia numbered around 300–400. The number of Japanese who married in Batavia between 1618 and 1659 was 106, but only 11 marriages occurred between Japanese. Most marriages took place on a multi-ethnic basis (Blussé 1986: 187).[18] This pattern places the overseas Japanese at the opposite extreme to the Parsees, who survived as a distinct entrepreneurial diaspora in Asia by following an intra-group marriage strategy.[19]

In all of the Japanese diaspora there was clearly a variety of marriage types; quite possibly that of Japanese men marrying Japanese women constituted a minority. There were, of course, many Japanese women who married Western men in Japan and who were forced to leave with their husband and children in the context of the seclusion policies. Other Japanese women married Southeast Asian men, but because of the sex ratio among Japanese, the most common pattern was that of Japanese men marrying Southeast Asian women. Of particular interest in all of these marriage types is the contribution to trading activity in Asia made by the wives or the daughters of these marriages. It is often assumed that the Portuguese retained certain advantages within Japan because so many of them had Japanese wives. Many sources portray women as interpreters, bookkeepers, traders, brokers and money-lenders (Blussé 1986: 172–6; Boxer 1951: 305–6).

One interesting case was the wife of Wada Rizaemon, the key Japanese trader in Tonkin. Known at the time as Ursula, she was a translator-interpreter who served also as an agent for the Tonkin emperor. When the Dutch entered the Tonkin silk trade in the late 1630s, they employed Ursula as an agent and interpreter, which in that case meant translating from Portuguese to Vietnamese. Wada himself, of course, had continued to trade with Japan subsequent to seclusion. One of the sources of his capital was Ursula's mother, who had an account from which Wada drew about 1,000 *taels* a year to transport commodities to Japan aboard Dutch ships. In this sense, Ursula's mother was an agent in the trade between the diaspora and Japan (Nagazumi 1992: 79–82).[20]

Another key Japanese woman was a pious Catholic who married Constance Phaulkon, a talented Greek who had handled negotiations over Siam's deerskin exports to Japan and who became a key adviser to King Narai. Phaulkon was killed in a succession dispute in 1688, but his Japanese wife survived him and eventually became the head of the royal kitchen staff (Gaimushō 1934: 583–92; Iwao 1966: 198; Reid 1993: 306–7).

These final examples of female entrepreneurship stand by themselves as a sufficient conclusion to this chapter. If Japanese women of such talent could not return to Japan, then whatever the revisionist historians have said, Japan was closed. Of course, there may be some who would argue that the Tokugawa *bakufu* saw pious Catholic women as functionally equivalent to what centuries later Western governments would view as communist subversives or religious terrorists. This view might even invite the conclusion that Japan, in its seclusion policy, got it right after all. I would differ. Look at it this way: Wada's mother-in-law was a good capitalist.

Notes

1. The following political categories are important for the background to this chapter: (1) *bakufu*: This was the term for the government of Japan before 1868. It was technically a military government, but in real terms Japan was, before the 1850s, probably less militarized than any major country in the world. The *bakufu* directly controlled about one-quarter of all the land in the country (based on assessed yield), including major cities, ports, and mines. (2) *shōgun*: the leader of the *bakufu*. (3) *daimyō*: the *daimyō* were technically vassals of the *shōgun*. Each *daimyō* was the lord of a domain.

In the seventeenth century there were about 300 domains in the country and collectively they controlled about three-quarters of the land in the country. The largest was about one-sixth the size of the *bakufu* territory, but most were quite tiny. Through the early seventeenth century the *daimyō* in western Japan had been active investors in trade. Had they been able to develop long-term profit from independent access to trade, they might have constituted a regional economic threat to the *bakufu*. That is one reason why the *bakufu* placed all trade under its own authority. After the Restoration in the nineteenth century the domains were reduced in number and converted into prefectures.

2. I am utilizing definitions primarily from Chapter 7 in this volume by Gelina Harlaftis and from the conference's wrap-up discussion.

3. See Harlaftis and Minoglou in this volume.

4. I have discussed this matter through some examples in the 'post-Seclusion' section of this chapter.

5. For example, around the year 1620 Christians constituted a majority of the residents of the Japanese town in Manila and about half of the Japanese in Cambodia. That still means there were many non-Christian Japanese (Iwao 1966: 118–19, 299).

6. For more on Wada, see the section below on post-seclusion diaspora.

7. I have not included a separate discussion here on Korea. I do not view Japanese in Korea as part of the diaspora because their status there was primarily that of representatives of Japan rather than as a resident diaspora. This is because from the early sixteenth century the Korean government had prohibited actual residence by Japanese. See Kang 1997.

8. I am here excluding trade through Korea and the Ryukyu Islands from the definition of 'overseas'.

9. 'Maritime prohibitions' as a more concrete and accurate description of the policy is a term that is beginning to stick as a replacement for 'seclusion', but it would be preferable to find a single word that would convey a broader meaning.

10. Unusually close, one might say, for the younger sister of one such magistrate was the *shōgun* Ieyasu's favourite concubine (Boxer 1951: 263).

11. Comments made in conference wrap-up session.

12. This point does not apply to the Portuguese, for they were not expelled from Japan until 1639, four years after the end of the vermilion-seal voyages.

13. In this view, one could include 'information gathering' as part of trade. Also, see Innes 1980: 208, which asserts the 'fundamental continuity throughout the seventeenth century' of Japan's economic policy.

14. For background, see de Vries and van der Woude 1997: 382–96, 429–36, esp. 396, which refers to the 'exceptional' profitability of the period 1630–50, and Israel 1989: 171–87, 244–58.

15. On the background to Chinese maritime expansion after the late 1680s, see Blussé 1996: 51–76.
16. Hirado was a port in northern Kyushu from which the Dutch could trade with relatively few restrictions. They were moved in 1641 to Deshima, an artificial islet in Nagasaki, where they were subject to tight control.
17. Interestingly, mainly because of the alternate attendance system (under which *daimyō* and their retainers had to spend alternate periods in Edo), the male: female ratio in Edo in 1800 was 6:4, making the city 'a predominately male society with an unquenchable thirst for pleasure and entertainment' (Hur 2000: 135).
18. See Iwao 1970: 2–3, 17, where Iwao notes that the highest frequency of marriage was in the decade following the prohibition against overseas voyages, probably reflecting the fact that emigrants no longer could hope to return to Japan.
19. See Chapter 11 in this volume by Caroline Plüss. It is interesting to contrast the marriage patterns of the early seventeenth-century Japanese overseas with those of the 1920s when Japanese male emigrants maintained the ethnicity of their community by importing 'picture' brides.
20. There is some question whether Ursula the translator and Ursula the financier were the same, or two separate people. Regardless, the roles performed illustrate the functions women performed.

References

Abe, C. (1993), 'Junana seiki no Vietnam-Nihon bōeki: shuinsen bōeki o chōshin ni', *Tōyō shigaku ronshō*, 1: 63–79.

Arano, Y. (1994), 'The Entrenchment of the Concept of "National Seclusion"', *Acta Asiatica*, 67: 83–103.

Blussé, L. (1986), *Strange Company: Chinese Settlers, Mestizo Women and the Dutch in VOC Batavia*, Dordrecht: Foris.

—— (1996), 'No Boats to China: The Dutch East India Company and the Changing Pattern of the China Sea Trade, 1635–1690', *Modern Asian Studies*, 30: 51–76.

Boxer, C. (1951), *Christian Century in Japan*, Berkeley: University of California Press.

Boyajian, J. (1993), *Portuguese Trade in Asia under the Hapsburgs, 1580–1640*, Baltimore: Johns Hopkins University Press.

Constable, O. (1994), *Trade and Traders in Muslim Spain: The Commercial Realignment of the Iberian Peninsula, 900–1500*, Cambridge: Cambridge University Press.

de Vries, J. and van der Woude, A. (1997), *The First Modern Economy: Success, Failure, and Perseverance of the Dutch Economy, 1500–1815,* Cambridge: Cambridge University Press.

Gaimushō Chōsa-bu (1934), *Jōnana seiki ni okeru Nissha kankei,* Tokyo.

Hur, N. (2000), *Prayer and Play in Late Tokugawa Japan: Asakusa Sensōji and Edo Societv,* Cambridge MA: Harvard University Press.

Innes, R. (1980), 'The Door Ajar: Japan's Foreign Trade in the Seventeenth Century', PhD Dissertation, University of Michigan.

Ishii, Y. and Yoshiharu, T. (1987), *Nichi-Tai kōryō 600 nenshi,* Tokyo: Kōdansha.

Israel, J. (1990), *Dutch Primacy in World Trade, 1585–1740,* Oxford: Oxford University Press.

Iwao, S. (1966), *Nanyŏ Nihon-machi no kenkyū,* Tokyo: Iwanami shoten.

—— (1970), 'Japanese Emigrants in Batavia During the 17th Century', *Acta Asiatica,* 18: 1–25.

—— (1971), *Sakoku,* Tokyo: Chōō Kōronsha.

—— (1976), 'Foreign Trade in the 16th and l7th Centuries', *Acta Asiatica,* 30: 1–18.

—— (1985), *Shuinsen bōekishi no kenkyō,* new edn, Tokyo: Yoshikawa Kōbunkan.

Johnston, R. (1988), *'New Mecca, New Babylon': Paris and the Russian Exiles, 1920–1945,* Kingston: McGill-Queen's University Press.

Kalland, A. (1995), *Fishing Villages in Tokugawa Japan,* Richmond: Curzon Press.

Kang, E. (1997), *Diplomacy and Ideology in Japanese-Korean Relations: From the Fifteenth to the Eighteenth Century,* London: Macmillan.

Kato, E. (1976), 'The Japanese-Dutch Trade in the Formative Period of the Seclusion Policy:

Particularly on the Raw Silk Trade by the Dutch Factory at Hirado, 1620–1640', *Acta Asiatica,* 30: 34–84.

Kedar, B. (1996), 'Expulsion as an Issue of World History', *Journal of World History,* 7: 165–80.

Klein, P. (1989), 'The China Seas and the World Economy between the Sixteenth and Nineteenth Centuries: The Changing Structures of Trade', in Carl-Ludwig Holtfrerich (ed.), *Interactions in the World Economy,* New York: New York University Press.

Kodansha Encyclopedia of Japan (1983), Tokyo: Kōdansha.

Massarella, D. (1990), *A World Elsewhere: Europe's Encounter with Japan in the Sixteenth and Seventeenth Centuries,* New Haven CT: Yale University Press.

Nagazumi, Y. (1990), *Kinsei shoki no gaikō,* Tokyo: Sōbunsha.

—— (1992), 'Saikō: Tonkin no Nihonjin tsōshi Urusura', *Nihon Rekishi,* 532: 79–82.

—— (1998), 'From Company to Individual Company Servants: Dutch Trade in Eighteenth-century Japan', in Leonard Blussé and Femme Gaastra (eds), *On the Eighteenth Century as a Category of Asian History*, Aldershot: Ashgate.

—— (2001), *Shuinsen,* Tokyo: Yoshikawa Kōbunkan.

Ooms, H. (1985), *Tokugawa Ideology: Early Constructs, 1570–1680,* Princeton: Princeton University Press.

Reid, A. (1993), *Southeast Asia in the Age of Commerce, 1450–1680, vol.2: Expansion and Crisis,* New Haven CT: Yale University Press.

—— (1998), 'Entrepreneurial Minorities, Nationalism, and the State', in Daniel Chirot and Anthony Reid (eds), *Essential Outsiders: Chinese and Jews in the Modern Transformation of Southeast Asia and Central Europe,* Seattle: University of Washington Press.

Schurz, W. (1939), *Manila Galleon,* New York: Dutton.

Stone, N. (1983), *Europe Transformed, 1878–1919,* London: Fontana.

Subrahmanyam, S. (1993), *The Portuguese Empire in Asia, 1500–1700: A Political and Economic History,* New York: Longman.

Toby, R. (1984), *State and Diplomacy in Early Modern Japan: Asia in the Development of the Tokugawa Bakufu,* Princeton: Princeton University Press.

Viraphol, S. (1977), *Tribute and Profit: Sino-Siamese Trade, 1652–1853,* Cambridge MA: Harvard University Press.

Von Glahn, R. (1996), *Fountain of Fortune: Money and Monetary Policy in China, 1000–1700,* Berkeley, University of California Press.

Wray, W. (1984), *Mitsubishi and the N.Y.K., 1870–1914: Business Strategy in the Japanese Shipping Industry,* Cambridge MA: Harvard University Press.

Yamamoto, H. (1995), *Sakoku to kaikin no jidai,* Tokyo: Kōkura Shobō.

–5–

Coping with Transition: Greek Merchants and Shipowners between Venice and England in the Late Sixteenth Century

Maria Fusaro

This chapter is concerned with the activities of some of the Greek Diaspora merchants and shipowners who were active in the Republic of Venice during the last quarter of the sixteenth century. It will focus on the Greek merchants who traded directly with England in that period and on their connections with English and Italian merchants who were based in London and active in the eastern Mediterranean. My goal is to show how, in times when the Venetian state was no longer able to keep open the sea-route to the north of Europe, some private merchants, coming mostly from the Venetian dominions in Greece, fought to keep this trade in their hands against the increasing English involvement in Mediterranean trade. The analysis of the multifaceted economic activities of these Greek subjects of the Republic in this transitional time, especially their active involvement in ship owning and international carrying trade, allows us also to antedate by two centuries the debut of Greek entrepreneurs on the international stage. This is in itself a very interesting episode of the economic history of the eastern Mediterranean, which until now has been under-researched.

The last quarter of the sixteenth century was a period of intense activity in the eastern Mediterranean. After the end of the war with the Turks (1570–3), the Venetian state found it rather difficult to rebuild its commercial maritime strength, particularly because of the pre-existing crisis in its shipbuilding industry. Throughout the second half of the sixteenth century, concerns over the issue of defence, paired with problems of forest-management in the territories of the Republic, had pushed the Senate toward a policy that privileged the needs of military shipbuilding against the ones of private mercantile shipping (Knapton 1986: 233–41). Because of these and other circumstances, it has been estimated that the Venetian commercial fleet halved in size between 1560 and 1600 (Sella 1968: 92). In such a crisis, substantial opportunities for commercial gain opened up for private merchants ready to provide ships and capital to be employed on the trade routes of the eastern Mediterranean, and on the sea route to northern Europe.

While in earlier periods the Venetian government had always tried to define policies for its eastern dominions before the crisis struck, after 1571 all decisions were taken on a 'reactive' basis, as if a real project was lacking for the territories. If in the past the dominant attitude of the Venetian government in regard to its Eastern dominions had been an extreme attention to trade and commercial issues (Zakythinos 1977: 61–75), after the fall of Cyprus the issue of defence engulfed every other consideration. The Greek subjects of Venice, on the other hand, were always extremely proactive, constantly finding ways to cope with the incoming crisis, but their requests nearly always ended up being dismissed by the Senate, even when they had the support of other Venetian governmental bodies like the *Cinque Savi alla Mercanzia* – the Venetian Board of Trade – or the Venetian governors in its overseas territories.

For these Greek merchants active in the Venetian dominions, war therefore acted as a creator of new opportunities, and the northern demand for the goods that were produced in the Ionian Islands and in Crete put them in a very privileged position to take advantage of the new opportunities afforded by the crisis of their overlord. The principal items of the export trade to the north of Europe – wine and currants – came from the Venetian Greek dependencies, places where these merchants could fully employ the strength of their personal and family networks to overcome the disruptions and problems of the trade. This phase of international success for these Greek merchants was not long-lived. By the beginning of the seventeenth century their impetus had substantially weakened, trade was expanding faster than they could cope with, and this, paired with the pervasive establishment of English merchants and ships in the area, served to price these operators out of the market.

The main protagonists of this chapter are Diaspora Greeks, settled between the Ionian island of Zante and Venice itself. That there were merchant-shipowners among the Greeks established in the Venetian Republic is not a novelty in itself. What I hope to highlight in the following pages is how the range and scope of their commercial enterprise has before now been underestimated (Leon 1972: 15; Moschonas 1988: 189–96), and how crucial a role they played in connecting the north and south of Europe in the transitional period between the onset of the maritime crisis of Venice and the beginning of the English dominance of these trades at the outset of the seventeenth century.

In talking about diasporas there is always the risk of simply producing a list of individuals who have risen to prominence (Clogg 1999: 2), but as much as I will be mostly c-oncerned with just a few families of Greek merchants-entrepreneurs, I would like it to be clear that behind them there were many more, and that the history of the commercial activities of the Greek community in Venice is a field which still has incredible riches to offer.[1] Studying the economic activities of these individuals, we find them to be an excellent example of the transition from the pre-capitalist merchant, who simply negotiated local surpluses of agricultural goods, to the merchant-entrepreneur actively involved in the organization of both the whole process of production and its commercialization. As we will have occasion to see in the next pages, other factors make them a particularly worthy subject of investigation. On the one hand their involvement in the long-distance and large-scale provision of shipping services for third parties allows us to antedate such activities among Greek shipowners from the eighteenth to the late sixteenth century. On the other hand their patterns of diversification of reinvestment, both in the commercial and in the production sector, provide us with evidence that points toward a reassessment of their economic role throughout the Venetian state, not only in its eastern dominions – the *Stato da Mar* – but also in the Italian mainland.

Choosing among the wealth of scholarly definitions of 'entrepreneur' available (Casson, 1982; Klep 1994: 59–79; Schumpeter 1989: 253–71), the one that I favour in this chapter, because it fits very well the activities of the group of merchants investigated here, defines the 'entrepreneur [as] someone who specialises in taking judgemental decisions about the coordination of scarce resources' (Casson 1993: 31). This well describes the situation in which they operated. If we define judgemental decisions as decisions for which no obvious correct procedure exists, this also fits very well with the nature of the economic transition in which they operated. Moreover, this definition stresses the importance of coordination rather than allocation, therefore emphasizing the dynamic aspect of their business activities, something crucial to consider especially when analysing periods of such fast and profound economic and social change. This allows us to underline the variety of their commercial activities and the diversification of their investments, bringing to light the multifaceted mediating role that these Greek merchants played for all traders active in the Venetian economy.

The Greek Diaspora and the Republic of Venice

Because of its close links with the Byzantine Empire, the Republic of Venice since its origins had a sizeable Greek community established in the capital, mostly taking care of the commerce between southern Europe and the areas under the Empire. The size of this community grew slowly but steadily after the events of the Crusade of 1204, when Venice's direct presence and active role in the eastern Mediterranean increased dramatically. By the sixteenth century, as a consequence of the steady Ottoman advance in the territories of the eastern Mediterranean, the majority of Greeks who established themselves in Venice were either subjects of the Republic, or refugees who declared as their place of origin territories which were previously held by the Republic itself. Frequently mentioned as places of origin were Lepanto (lost in 1499), Modone and Corone (1500), Monemvasia and Napoli di Romania (1540) and Cyprus (1571). Only a minority seemed to have escaped from areas under direct Ottoman rule (Geanakoplos 1976: 60; Manousakas 1989: 323). Classification is not so easy though. With the Ottomans advancing for such a long time, and therefore causing a constant movement of people into the Venetian-held territories in Greece, it becomes extremely difficult – not to say impossible – to distinguish exactly where these people came from. What is possible to hypothesize is that to arrive as refugees in the Venetian territories in the Levant was just the first step toward a more drastic move to Venice/Italy/the West (Harris 1995: 25; Plumidis 1972: 219–26; Spiridonakis 1977: 124–27; Thiriet 1977: 218–19; Vacalopoulos 1976: 45–6 and 1980: 272–83). What we can say with certainty is that the Greek presence in Venice was a mix of 'real' refugees and subjects from Venice's dominions, and to distinguish between them is rather difficult.

The Ionian Islands were a favourite destination for people escaping from mainland Greece. In the islands of Zante and Cephalonia, which were almost completely deserted when they entered into Venetian control, the influx of new inhabitants created a peculiar social environment characterized by the absence of feudal structures; amongst the Ionian Islands only Corfu had some feudal jurisdiction, albeit of late creation (Pratt 1978: 3). When first Zante in 1485, and then Cephalonia in 1500, became part of Venice's dominions, the main concern of the Senate had been first to repopulate them and then to promote agriculture, especially grain production (Fusaro 1996: 79–106). To achieve this, Venice had put a great deal of effort into implementing fiscal incentives which would favour the immigration of people from territories under Ottoman control – a large number came, for example, from the outposts of Modone and Corone which had just been lost by the Venetians to the Ottomans. To these immigrants the Republic granted the ownership of parcels of land, advantageous long-term fiscal incentives and commercial privileges.[2] A sizeable percentage of these settlers were *stradioti*, a light cavalry corps mostly composed of Morean Greeks (Manousakas 1989: 323; Vlassi 1995: 274–5; Zakythinos 1976: 116), which had been organized by the Venetians in their Levant territories during the Middle Ages. Throughout this period, the Islands were also the destination of a small but steady stream of immigrants from the nearby territories under Ottoman control. All these factors contributed to create the peculiar property situation mentioned above, based on a large proportion of small landowners. This was at the base of a unique land structure on which the currants boom would later have dramatic consequences.

Zante and Cephalonia benefited from an extremely advantageous strategic position which made them central to the routes between the western and eastern Mediterranean. For this reason, commercial activity immediately thrived on the islands (Vacalopoulos, 1976: 270–90). Wine, oil and currants were their main products, but from the middle of the sixteenth until the end of the seventeenth centuries their economies ended up being completely dominated by currants (Fusaro 1996). Their geographical position at the crossroads of the Mediterranean trade routes, which made them a favourite stop-over for ships, paired with the Venetian presence which had important cultural, economic and social consequences, made the Ionian Islands extremely exposed to Western influence, and Ionians, particularly active within the Venetian system and beyond, for example the Greek community in the commercial entrepôt of Leghorn, also had a strong presence of people from Zante (Frattarelli Fischer 2001: 49–61; Zakythinos 1976: 107–9).

The Greek community in Venice was the largest and longest-lived in the West (Fedalto 1967; Imhaus 1997; Manousakas 1989 and 1991: 1–12), and the Greeks were the largest foreign community established in the city during the early modern period. At the end of the sixteenth century their numbers were estimated to be between 4,000 and 5,000 (in a population roughly estimated at around 150,000); the main problem of trying to assess these estimates is the very fluid nature of part of the community. The presence of captains and sailors, and of people frequently moving between Venice and the dominions, makes it very difficult to be precise about their total numbers (Beltrami 1954; Fedalto 1977: 147–9; Thiriet 1977: 219). Particularly because of the important economic role the Greeks played in trade with the eastern Mediterranean, the traditional area of Venetian economic activity, the Venetian government had always welcomed them. From 1271 special legislation favouring Greeks resident in Venice had been put in place by the Great Council and in 1513 the Council of Ten permitted a church of the Greek rite to be built in Venice (Fedalto 1967: 16, 29). The community itself acquired juridical status as a confraternity in 1498 and by 1573 the beautiful church of St George, focal centre of the Greek presence in town, was completed, thanks also to the 'Greek shipowners, captains and seamen who, on each voyage to Venice, made a more or less voluntary contribution to the treasury of the colony' (Geanakoplos 1976: 62; Manousakas 1989: 322–6; Panaghiotopoulou 1974: 284–352; Vacalopoulos 1976: 49–52). The presence of their Church and confraternity acted as a focal point for Greek settlement in the city. Consequently the majority of Greeks lived in ten parishes within the *Castello* wards, with the greatest number concentrated in the five parishes bordering or closest to the Arsenal the state-owned shipbuilding factory (Burke 2000: 10–16).

The Greek presence in Venice has been thoroughly studied in regard to the cultural impact that the intellectual emigration from Byzantine territories had on the development of Humanism and the Renaissance (Geanakoplos 1989 and 1972; Harris 1995; Vacalopoulos 1976: 180–1; Zakythinos 1976: 116–19); however, its economic and social history has been until now rather neglected. Still, it was their crucial economic role that had made them welcome in the Republic, and merchants undoubtedly constituted the backbone of the Greek presence in Venice, immediately followed by sailors and skilled artisans, several of whom worked in the Arsenal (Geanakoplos 1976: 61).[3] Greek merchants acted in Venice especially as mediators and organizers of Balkan and eastern Mediterranean trade. Apart from the cultural affinities with Venice, which certainly helped their settling, the main circumstance that persuaded the Greeks to remain was the opportunities offered by Venice in its position as a 'colonial power' in the eastern Mediterranean world. This, paired with the collapse of the Byzantine Empire and the consequent establishment on its territories of the Ottoman Empire, had provided the Greeks with splendid opportunities to perform the role of economic middlemen, connecting their places of origin with western Europe, while taking advantage of the Venetian trade structure and network. This allows us to apply also to the sixteenth century the comments written by Traian Stoianovich (1960: 305) forty years ago on the role played by the Greek merchants during the eighteenth century:

> the Greek merchants of the Mediterranean, ... were constantly in contact with the underdeveloped areas of the eastern Mediterranean and economically well-developed area of the West, [therefore] developed new business habits and a new business outlook as a result of the dual nature of their business relations.

For the Ionian subjects of the Republic it was easier and more profitable to run their business from Venice than from their islands (Geanakoplos 1972: 54; Harris 1995: 57), and this was particularly true for those who were involved in long-distance trade. Being part of the Venetian network also offered a certain level of protection, as the government was interested in keeping alive the trade with the area, and legislation was implemented to prevent the depopulation of its eastern Mediterranean dominions (Vacalopoulos 1976: 75). Above and beyond this, being a Venetian subject guaranteed that an individual would be part of a commercial system that, albeit in crisis, was still powerful and had a capillary presence in the Mediterranean, something that afforded good opportunities to people who were ready to take advantage of them. These Greek merchant-entrepreneurs, active under Venetian protection and sailing under the Venetian flag, had therefore every interest in keeping good relations with their overlord, and although there were instances in which their economic interests diverged, in the long term the relationship between the Republic of Venice and its Greek subjects remained a mutually profitable one. The Greeks always behaved as 'active' subjects of the Republic, and were constantly engaged in lobbying, aiming at influencing the public policies of their host society to suit their own economic interests, particularly in the eastern Mediterranean (Fusaro 1996). As 'subjects' – hardly any Greeks applied to become Venetian citizens in the sixteenth century[4] – they could already take full advantage of the privileges available to Venetian merchants in the eastern Mediterranean (consuls, tax rebates, customs discount), and their role in keeping open the trade with that area was well appreciated by the Venetians. These Greeks described themselves as 'Venetians', and as such they were described abroad in documentary sources, thereby acquiring invisibility to the historian. In reality they were 'Venetian subjects' not 'Venetians'; this ambiguity was maintained on the one hand because it was probably not seen as such, but also because it carried substantial economic advantages. The Greek commercial network was strong and geographically widespread, ethnically homogenous and with a very strong common religious affiliation. All these were factors that gave it a very strong internal cohesion which made it very effective in the handling of commercial activities over long-distance trades. Its major strengths were in its surviving connections in the former Byzantine territories, in its existing commercial networks with the Balkan Jews, maintained through its correspondents in Venice (Tenenti 1959: 14), and in its specific knowledge of the languages and customs of these areas. All this made it essential in this phase of western European capitalism in which some ethnic minorities – Jews, Greeks, Armenians – found themselves better equipped to provide economic services, thanks to their scattered geographical presence and to the strong bonds of mutual trust that develop in such communities, something which served very well to guarantee, among other things, effective contractual enforcement and a lowering of transaction costs (Subrahmanyam 1996).

The Ionian Islands and Crete

The economy of the Ionian Islands had, from very early on, been dependent on foreign markets as an outlet for production. This was not a novelty for the Venetian eastern dominions. Both Cyprus and Crete had produced massive quantities for the export market, above and beyond what was exported to Venice, and both had been under the influence of market forces that tended to privilege other crops at the expense of grain. In Crete, taking advantage of the decline of Syrian and Egyptian sugar production, sugar had been produced from the fourteenth century, but also cotton and wine were widely exported from the island as well (Ashtor 1981: 91–132; Jacoby 1994: 167–80; Tucci 1998: 183–206 and 1994: 199–211). The trade in 'malmsey' wine between Crete and England had even been at the centre of a short tariff war between the two countries during the late fifteenth century (Fusaro 1996: 13).[5] And it was only the great productivity of the lands of Cyprus that allowed it not only to produce for the export market – mainly cotton and oil – but also to be known as the granary of the Republic.

From an economic perspective Crete, especially, bears marked similarities to the Ionian Islands (Manousakas 1973: 473–514). Like Zante and Cephalonia, Crete had a large share of its agricultural output destined for export, and there too local merchants and shipowners tried to keep active the trade route to their major export markets in the north of Europe. Furthermore, as we will have occasion to see later on, in several cases their attempts went hand in hand with the activities of the Ionian merchants who are the main subject of this chapter. From the mid-sixteenth century, as the Turkish threat to Venetian possession grew, Venice implemented in Crete a series of economic measures designed to improve the economic situation of the local population, hoping to maintain their loyalty to Venice. Seafaring benefited relatively from these measures, with local shipowners enlarging the scope of their trades beyond the eastern Mediterranean and the routes to Venice.

Cretan wine was rather popular in England and Flanders; during the reign of Henry VIII wine exports to England had increased to such an extent that an English consul was appointed in Candia to take care of this specific trade (Maltezou 1991: 29–32). Because of its importance, by the middle of the fifteenth century legislation had been implemented in Crete prohibiting the transport of the wines of the island westward to England, Flanders, Hamburg and Danzig, chiefly as an attempt to keep the traffic on 'Venetian' vessels.[6] This had some positive effect on local shipowners, and in the next century these policies of strengthening the local shipyards and naval constructions helped the emergence of some Greek operators of international stature. Unfortunately the problems of the Venetian merchant marine were structural and could not be solved by these occasional legislative attempts mostly concerned with offering tax rebates for people willing to build galleons (Baroutsos 1999: 187–223; Costantini 1998: 207–31). If the policy of the mid-fifteenth century had met with some success, its later counterpart did not achieve the desired result, as by then the English were getting a tight grip on naval traffic in the area, and the Venetians were no longer able to counteract it effectively (Fusaro 1996: 13, 27–44; Tucci 1998: 201–4).

It can certainly be hypothesized that the presence of a buoyant export market can be considered as an incentive for producers to own ships and become directly involved in the commercialization of their goods, thereby reducing their reliance on third parties and buyers to transport them. Venice itself had traditionally taken care of the commercialization of the goods produced in its dominions, but by the second half of the sixteenth century, the crisis of the Venetian merchant marine certainly acted, in Crete and in the Ionian Islands, as a catalyst to encourage the locals to get involved in shipping.

Greek Shipping, English Shipping, Anglo-Greek Shipping

The eighteenth century has always been considered the century that saw the beginning of the fortunes of Greek-owned shipping, something that also had great significance in the development of the movement for the creation of the Greek state. Greek shipping never ceased to be active under the Ottoman rule but it saw its great prosperity in the 'Adriatic economy' and particularly in the sea-trade of the Ionian islands with the Italian peninsula at the beginning of the eighteenth century; a prosperity that quickly expanded to the Aegean islands (Harlaftis 2001, ch. 1). By the end of the eighteenth century,

> merchants of Greek origin or culture came to dominate imperial [Ottoman] trade, exporting raw materials and importing western manufactures and colonial wares. Greek became the *lingua franca* of Balkan commerce. Greek mercantile *paroikies*, or communities, were established throughout the Mediterranean, the Balkans, central Europe and southern Russia and as far afield as India. At the same time Greek sea captains, based principally on the three 'nautical' islands of Hydra, Spetsai and Psara, were busy laying the foundations of what, in the twentieth century, was to become the largest merchant fleet in the world. The continental blockade imposed by the British during the French revolutionary and Napoleonic wars afforded highly profitable opportunities to those prepared to risk running it (Clogg 1992: 24–5).

But new research has indicated that the birth of modern 'Greek shipping' has its roots in the developments in the Ionian Islands during the sixteenth century (Pagratis 2002). Therefore the roots of 'Greek shipping' have to be traced to two centuries before the date typically given, at least as far as the Greek territories under Venetian rule are concerned. This is extremely interesting because, although we have ample evidence for such activities on the part of the Greek entrepreneurial networks for the later period – mostly the eighteenth century – this late sixteenth-century Anglo-Venetian evidence allows us to antedate this phenomenon while at the same time, enriching the picture of Greeks' economic activities in the previous two centuries. The strength of the maritime traditions of the Ionian Islands does not come as a surprise; Cephalonia is recognized as one of the cradles of Greek ship-ownership, and the Ionians' activities in the Black Sea in the eighteenth and nineteenth centuries are considered fundamental in the development of Greek-owned shipping (Harlaftis 1993: 11 and 1996: 3). It is interesting to note, especially for the purposes of this chapter, that the Ionians' involvement in shipping seems to have been particularly strong in times of transition, probably because at these times the inner cohesiveness of these ethnic diasporas was exceptionally effective in overcoming the disruption in long-distance trades. In the late sixteenth-century economic transition, the Greeks acted as a bridge between the periods of Venetian- and English-dominated traffic; in the last quarter of the nineteenth century 'they covered the transitional period from sail to steam and from combined profession to specialization' (Harlaftis 1996: 70).

The roots of the Anglo-Greek alliance which was at the basis of the trade between England and Venice's territories are to be found in the web of contacts established with English merchants by the Greek traders who sent their ships to England in the last quarter of the sixteenth century. Only private ships kept the sea-route to England open in the central part of the sixteenth century after the state galleys abandoned their trips to the north in 1533 (Fusaro 1996: 9–19). In the last quarter of the sixteenth century very few Venetians were active in London. Two of them are particularly interesting for us: Placido Regazzoni and Giovanni da Riviera. As the Republic did not have an official representative in England at that time, Placido Regazzoni acted unofficially as Venetian consul. After his return to Venice in the early 1580s, the only remaining 'Venetian' in London was Giovanni da Riviera, a native of Zante. Da Riviera was in London as agent of the Seguro, an important Greek mercantile family of Zante, although sometimes he also represented another Zantiot firm, the Sumacchi.[7] Da Riviera informally inherited Regazzoni's position, and he was the key man who helped build a lasting commercial alliance between his fellow-countrymen and the founding members of the Levant Company. In 1591 his efforts to keep this trade alive were acknowledged by the Venetian government and he officially became consul.[8] These early commercial contacts between English and Greeks in London were maintained and reinforced when the English started to penetrate the Mediterranean themselves. Therefore, especially in the earlier phase of their direct presence in Venice, English merchants favoured commercial partners who were indeed Greeks and Venetian *cittadini*. Extremely few Venetian patricians were involved in these trades; the Corner family which was quite active because of their Cretan possessions[9] and only a handful of other Italian and Ragusean merchants complete the picture. To understand the mercantile web of the English, and their behaviour in the islands, it is therefore essential to understand their connection with the Greek network. Giacomo[10] and Placido Regazzoni, Giovanni Da Riviera and the Florentine merchant based in London Bartolomeo Corsini were the links between the English and the Ionians,[11] and they were connected to a tight web of merchants who operated within the triangle: Venice – Zante and Cephalonia – London.

The Protagonists

The powerful Greek family of the Seguro, both merchants and shipowners, were very prominent among these merchants. The Seguro family had been for a long time one of the most powerful families on the island of Zante. Already in 1542 the *Rettore* at that time wrote of them 'they are the first in this place, connected by blood with all other citizens, they control half of the Island'.[12] The family was divided between Venice and Zante, but some members had some connections with Crete, mostly through marriage. Here the focus will be on the commercial activities of two brothers of the family: Agesilao acting from Zante and Marco moving between Zante and Venice. They used Venetian-built ships, but also bought and commissioned some to be built abroad. They seem to have enjoyed particularly close contacts with Danzig, where they commissioned a number of large vessels to be built for them.[13] Buying ships abroad was a classic way in which Venetian and Greek merchants and shipowners responded to the crisis in shipbuilding in Venice. The ships were then naturalized and could be used taking full advantage of the benefits that were in place for Venetian ships. It was, of course, a policy open to abuse and which certainly did not help to overcome the shipbuilding crisis. From the last quarter of the sixteenth century the Senate had authorized the buying of foreign ships to try to respond to this need, but still in 1627 legislation was being put into place to try to properly regulate these issues.[14]

Marco Seguro and his brother had been involved in importing grain to Venice and we also know that they had trade contacts with Genoa.[15] Marco had very close links with England; Thomas Sanders was a guest of Marco Seguro on Zante in 1584, and some of his party remained on the island waiting for a passage back to England on one of Marco's ships.[16] These reached England well into the late 1580s carrying currants and oil, not only for the Seguro family but for other merchants of Zante as well.[17] From the papers of the only currants-smuggling trial that have survived, Marco Seguro's image as a merchant and shipowner of international stature comes out strengthened.[18] His ships appear to have been trading regularly with England, and on this route he employed Englishmen as captains.[19] Even the ship he bought specifically for the deal at the origin of the trial was crewed by Englishmen.[20] He certainly enjoyed an equal partnership with his English counterparts. In addition to his activities as a merchant-entrepreneur and shipowner, Marco Seguro was active in other economic endeavours. For example, he was particularly interested in a project for the development of new technical solutions for windmills in the islands of the Venetian Lagoon, in which he reinvested some of his trade profits.[21] After the death of Marco and Agesilao in the late 1580s, a nephew also called Agesilao took over. At some point in the early 1590s he suffered bankruptcy, but quickly recovered. Although he never reached the international stature of his uncles, the breadth of his interests and of his reputation in Zante is exemplified by the fact that in 1618 he was nominated consul for the 'merchants subjects to the Turk' (a charge he kept until 1650) and in 1623 he became consul for the English as well.[22] He lived a very long life and played a large role in the economy of Zante until the middle of the seventeenth century.[23]

Another Greek family that played an important role in these international trades were the Sumacchi, particularly Giorgio and his son Michele. The Sumacchi too were both merchants and shipowners, also dividing their interests between the Ionian Islands and Venice and trading also with Candia, whence they exported Muscat wines to England.[24] Giorgio was based in Zante, where he acted as an intermediary between Venetian, English and local merchants.[25] Michele was based in Venice and was the owner of several ships employed mostly on the northern routes. He also invested part of his earnings in landed property in Venice and in the *Terraferma*.[26] Michele Sumacchi appears active in Venice from the late 1570s, initially as the agent of Bartolomeo Zanoli, a Venetian merchant active in the northern European markets, particularly in Antwerp, but also with strong connections in London.[27] In the early 1580s Michele stretched himself financially to build his own fleet,[28] so much that in 1583 he had to sell one quarter of one of his new ships – the *Sumacchia* – to the Venetian patrician Taddeo Moresini to gain some liquidity. Only two years afterward he was able to buy it back after a very successful commercial trip to Constantinople.[29] A few years later the roles were reversed and it was a Venetian patrician, Piero Alvise Barbaro, who was in debt to Michele. Interestingly, he repaid his debt by renting him, at a nominal sum, all his properties on the island of Zante, where Michele's father, Giorgio, took care of their administration.[30]

When in 1582 Acerbo Velutelli lost his monopoly on currant imports to England, which the following year was granted to some English merchants who were later among the founders of the Levant Company, it was the Sumacchi whom he accused of having colluded with the English merchants to rob him of the monopoly.[31] And from the papers of the above-mentioned smuggling trial it is evident how crucial the Sumacchi were in the trade with England.[32] Michele was also active in Constantinople where he appears as a leading importer (on his own ships) of luxury Venetian goods, especially textiles. In a letter to his agent there, Sumacchi seems to be concerned more with the quality of the imported goods, rather than with exporting specific goods. When asked about which merchandise he wanted bought for the return trip to Venice, he declared that either textiles or leather would be fine, what mattered to him was the speed of the transaction and dealing with good-quality merchandise 'as good quality goods always sell very well'.[33] Apart from the typical comments regarding the need for a merchant-entrepreneur to keep capital active and never idle, what is interesting in his instructions is the old-fashioned stress on the quality of the merchandise as a guarantee of successful trading. This stress on quality, typical of Italian production, was to be proven wrong by the resounding successes of the cheaper products that the English were so successfully introducing in the Levant in the same period. Michele's adventure into large-scale enterprise ended in 1595 with a massive bankruptcy, after which time he disappears from the documentation. We later find his son engaged, on a far smaller scale, in trade and custom administration in Zante.

The Seguro and Sumacchi were frequently in active commercial partnership,[34] particularly in the English side of their businesses. They took care of shipments of goods not only from Venice and Zante, but also from Crete.[35] Both the English merchants dealing with Zante, and the Florentine based in England and interested in traffic with the Republic of Venice, openly acknowledged the prominent position that these two families had in the commerce of the areas of the Mediterranean under Venetian control.[36] It can certainly be said that these Greeks, taking advantage of their own diaspora commercial-network, acted as an intermediate network for English penetration into Mediterranean trade, and this had very important consequences for the economic development of the whole area (Fusaro 2003). If currants from Zante and Cephalonia and wines from Crete were the dominant cargoes to London,[37] the favourite goods for the return journeys of these Greek ships from England were lead, tin, iron and kerseys.[38] Most of the time the cargoes were destined for Venice, but on some occasions the return journey involved a stopover to unload in Leghorn or in the Kingdom of Naples.[39] But their interests were not confined to direct traffic to and from Venice and its dominions, they also shipped to Ragusa, where they had contacts with the local leading merchant Nicolò de Gozzi.[40]

Both the Seguro and the Sumacchi families were also serious players on the international stage. In Venice they performed a crucial role as a link connecting northern traders with the Jewish commercial web. The English took advantage of the Jewish Mediterranean trade network extremely rarely, and it can be argued that the Greek network played the mediating role traditionally associated with the Jews. The Seguro and the Sumacchi also traded in partnership with the Portuguese Jews based in Venice, and through them sometimes English merchants participated in those trades too. Trading in association with English merchants was certainly financially convenient in those days when Anglo-Spanish hostilities were at their height. On the other hand, it could also lead to problems with the Spanish authorities, as the following episodes amply demonstrate. In 1588 the ship *Sumacchia* had been stopped in Palermo because local authorities believed it to be carrying merchandise belonging to English subjects, while instead it was carrying goods belonging to the Portuguese Jews Gerardo Malines and Garzia Pimentel.[41] The following year it was the turn of the *Segura* to be stopped in Cadiz, also wrongly suspected of carrying English goods.[42] Another similar episode took place in 1592 when the *Sumacchia* was itself thought to be English and was captured by the Spanish, who suspected secret dealings between the Republic and England. In the end, this turned into a complicated diplomatic case as on this occasion part of the cargo actually belonged to English merchants.[43]

Apart from providing shipping for third parties, another 'service' area in which these Greek merchant-entrepreneurs were active was the insurance business. For merchants active within the Venetian mercantile system it was rather common to branch out in the insurance business. The Greeks specialized in insuring ships for trips to the eastern Mediterranean, which was also the trade route in which they were most active themselves (Gofas 1979: 54–88), but we also have documentary evidence for Greek merchants, in association with Venetian merchants, insuring ships bound for London (Stefani 1956: 270). Being involved in the insurance business on the one hand was a traditional and profitable diversification of investment, and on the other was an excellent way to keep in close touch with both the movements of the market and the state of the trade. Michele Sumacchi appears as an insurer active on several routes – from the Adriatic to the north of Europe – frequently in partnership with the same members of the English mercantile community in Venice, or with Florentine merchants still based in London, the same people with whom he was conducting business in England (Tenenti 1959: 61, 87–9).

Several other Greek merchants with profiles comparably as high as those examined here appear in the Venetian documentation. Andrea della Vigna, the Cubli and Samariari families – all from Zante – are classic cases of mercantile-entrepreneurial dynasties. Active in Venice for several generations, they were involved in international trade and owned large estates both in Zante and in the Venetian mainland. Their commercial interests ranged from wine to wheat, for which they entered into a major contract to supply the Venetian State in 1550; were involved in the salt industry of Zante; and owned a small fleet of commercial vessels.[44] Other Ionian families also traded internationally in those years, although on a smaller scale. Among them the Balsamo of Zante concentrated mainly on inter-Mediterranean trade, but they also sent their goods directly to Holland, albeit on Dutch ships.[45] The very important role played by the Balsamo family in the history of Zante was not matched by the scope of their international presence.

The Metaxà family of Cephalonia also played an important role as well. They kept commercial contacts with the Flemish community in Venice and they also bought Flemish ships for their trade. As the Greeks generally seem to have been absent from the international financial markets, it is interesting to note instead that the Metaxà family was also present at the international European financial fairs.[46] Furthermore, they displayed a wide range of commercial interests; a member of the family in 1627 asked for and obtained Sir Thomas Roe's help in setting up a Greek press for him in Constantinople.[47]

The Copio family was probably the most important Jewish family of Zante, and they too were part of this commercial network. In the Ionian Islands they acted as brokers between shipowners and merchants,[48] and in Venice they arranged some of the major deals that involved consignments of goods in exchange for currants. The Copio, taking advantage of the Jewish mercantile networks in the Ottoman territories, were in a prime position to commercialize large consignments of goods in the Morea, and to sustain this strategy they acquired large warehouses for the storage of goods in Zante.[49]

The Nomicò family of Zante kept a lower profile, never rising to the level of international traders or shipowners. They concentrated instead on increasing their landholdings in the islands, where they were heavily involved in the salt-works and provided loans to the fiscal Chambers.[50] And, like all the other Greek merchants of their day, they invested heavily in Venice itself.[51]

Conclusions

Giacomo Regazzoni when asked in 1584, alongside the other principal Venetian merchants, what was the situation of trade with England, replied that the recent increase in customs duty in England had killed trade, making it unprofitable for foreigners to import goods to England. In other words, the direct trade had entirely stopped in the preceding few years. All the other Venetian merchants consulted on the same issues agreed with him.[52] But from the 'Corsini papers' kept in the Guildhall archives a different picture emerges which supports the notarial documents found in Venice. Traffic had diminished substantially, but was not interrupted, and Venetian and Greek ships kept on reaching the English shores. What would have been interesting to see, and unfortunately is not possible due to the loss of the Port Books for this period, is how much of the goods were imported under English names, and how much under those of foreigners.

The mercantile network whose activities I have sketched was characterized by an impressive connectivity. All the merchants and shipowners involved in it – Venetians, Venetian Greek subjects, Florentines and English – all cooperated frequently and in a flexible manner. The brothers Placido and Giacomo Regazzoni had long been involved in trade between the islands and England, on Venetian and Greek ships,[53] and their trade continued throughout the 1580s and well into the 1590s. The Florentine Bartolomeo Corsini and the Venetian Giacomo Regazzoni were in business together during those years,[54] often in conjunction with Paolo Labia, also from Venice. Regazzoni himself frequently rented ships from the Seguro.[55] But their trade with Northern Europe always involved either wines from Candia,[56] or currants from the islands. In all these cases there were Greeks involved: as merchants, brokers, or shipowners. In the last quarter of the sixteenth century, the Zantiot Zuanne Da Riviera, acting in London as agent of the Seguro family, was the hinge of these trades.[57] English merchants were also involved. For example, William Garway and others were among the insurers of a ship coming from Zante.[58] Even the Flemish made an early appearance in a contract about a cargo of currants and rice.[59] All the above-mentioned merchants also took advantage of the grain shortage that hit the Italian peninsula in the 1590s.[60]

The portrait that emerges from even such limited sources is still very clear. The Venetian documentation confirms what we see in the Guildhall documents. There was a small group of Greek merchants fully involved in international trade both as merchants and as shipowners. They enjoyed fruitful business contacts with Venetian merchants and throughout the Mediterranean basin, but they were also very active in trade with England, where they were able to send their ships both earlier and for a longer period of time than previously thought. Their trading was characterized by an extreme flexibility in their choice of carriers and by an interesting mix of shipowners and crews.[61] English merchants themselves were using and insuring Greek ships, and dealing with them on an equal basis. Their alliance with the English newcomers, which had started as an attempt to keep trade in Greek/Venetian hands, ended up instead being instrumental for the successful commercial penetration by the English into the Mediterranean.

This complex series of connected contracts shows a strong willingness and attempt to keep trade in Venetian hands as much as possible in the face of ever-mounting difficulties. Ultimately this strategy was not successful. That the Seguro and Sumacchi were employing English crews on their ships, adds further to the proof of the serious decadence of Venetian seamanship. That they were providing English pilots for other merchants proves the strength of their connection. And the fact that not only were English ships active in inter-Mediterranean trade, but that English crews were hired to man non-English ships, sheds some new light on English activities in the Mediterranean.

The major Greek diaspora merchants based in Venice and in the Ionian Islands took advantage of the English presence to enlarge the scope of their trades, and to strengthen their own trading and shipping webs thanks to the general increase in trade in the area. Apart from the advantages these brought to larger merchants, from the documents that have been analysed it also appears that smaller merchants had much to gain from the presence of foreign merchants, as this allowed them to move their goods to Venice, and therefore to increase their chances for income, taking advantage of the presence of foreign ships which they could use as carriers. The necessity to keep open the direct trade route between northern Europe and the islands had been the reason for some Greek merchant-entrepreneurs and shipowners to make their debut on the international stage, where they had stepped in to counteract the disappearance of Venetian ships from these routes. Although this ended up being a short-term episode, lasting roughly for the second half of the sixteenth century, it is extremely interesting because it presents an early example of the entrepreneurial spirit that characterized Greek diaspora merchants living in Venice and the *Dominio da Mar*, and their awareness of the opportunities afforded by the crisis in the Venetian mercantile fleet and by the arrival of new commercial players in the area.

Notes

1. I would particularly like to highlight here the forthcoming work of Ersie Burke on the Greek community in Venice. I also wish to thank her deeply for the

time she dedicated to my questions, and for the generosity with which she discussed her own work in progress. This chapter owes a lot to these talks. I also wish here to acknowledge the useful critical comments made on this text by Maria-Christina Chatziioannou and Leslie Peirce, and the generous help provided by Mary Coulton.

2. On the repopulation of Zante and the issues surrounding it, see the second part of Archivio di Stato di Venezia (hereafter *ASV*), *Miscellanea Codici*, serie ii diversi, no. 42, 'Storia antica e moderna del Zante, scritta già in latino da Monsignore Baldassar Maria Remondini Bassanese, vescovo del Zante, e di Cefalonia. Ed ora tradotta in italiano, e accresciuta di molte considerabili aggiunte da Niccolò Serra nobile Zacintio, Ricopiata l'anno 1793'.

3. Ersie Burke estimates merchants and shopkeepers as constituting 30 per cent of the community, 'maritime jobs', in which she includes captains and crews as 24 per cent, and artisans as 14 per cent. I wish to thank her for providing me with this information. On the Arsenal see Davis 1991.

4. I owe this information to Ersie Burke, who discusses this issue in her forthcoming PhD dissertation. Venetian citizenship was of three kinds: *de iure*, limited to the so-called 'cittadini originari', *de intus* and *de intus et de extra*. The second one allowed them to claim all the benefits of being a Venetian in all commercial endeavours. For a short analytical description of the issue of citizenship see Bellavitis 1995: 359–83. On the issue of citizenship for foreigners see Fedalto 1977: 151 and Mueller 1981: 75–7.

5. On avoiding customs for foreigners exporting wines from Candia, more than a century afterwards, see Guildhall Library, Ms 21317, Vol. 10, No. 907, 6 April 1596.

6. Michele Sumacchi in the early 1590s still exported Rethimno wines to Danzig (*ASV: Notarile Atti*, b. 7866, Gerolamo Luran, cc. 27r/v, 11 February 1590; Tucci 1998: 187). This legislation had been reinforced in 1488 (*ASV: Senato Mar*, reg. 12, carte 156r–157v, 18 November 1488).

7. We know that Da Riviera was an agent of the Seguro from the defence memorial written by Ottaviano Volterra on occasion of his trial for smuggling in 1589: 'Zuanne Darevera ... per ritrovarse a Londra alle facende di essi Sicuri, per li quali teniva casa' (*ASV: Quarantia Criminale*, b. 103, fasc. 73, cc. 77v–80r).

8. *Archivio di Stato di Venezia* (*ASV: Cinque Savi alla Mercanzia, Risposte*, reg. 138, c.166v; b.34 n.s., fasc.v, cc.n.n, 27 February 1591). The regulations for the election of consul had been published in 1586 (*ASV: Cinque Savi alla Mercanzia*, b. 34 n.s., fasc. v, cc. n.n., 7 March 1586). On Da Riviera's efforts see Fusaro 1996: 25, 109–10.

9. *ASV: Notarile Atti*, reg.7850–7869.

10. Giacomo Regazzoni is a classic case of a Venetian merchant-entrepreneur, extremely representative of a new kind of non-noble Venetian merchant, who managed to acquire a large fortune with an intelligent diversification of investments. Equally interested in landed investments in the Venetian *Terraferma* and in commercial enterprises all around Europe. (While still very young he set up a company with Giacomo Foscarini for trading between Venice and England.) He was also active in the insurance business and in the Venetian financial market; on him see Pezzolo 1991: 986–7.

11. For an example of these connections see Guildhall Library, Ms 21317, Vol. 10, No. 995, 23 July 1599, where Giovanni da Riviera received instructions about some deals with the Corsini in London so that they could pay back some credit they had with the Sumacchi. Such documents are scattered throughout the 'Corsini papers' in the Guildhall Library in London.

12. *ASV: Capi del Consiglio dei Dieci, Lettere di Rettori e altre cariche,* b.296, Zante 1506–1749, fasc.i, cc.n.n., 25 August 1542. Some additional information on the Seguro family can also be gathered from Rangabés 1927: 242–70 and Zois 1963: 585–9, and 603–4 for the Sumacchi family. It has to be noted that both these texts, and especially the genealogies, are studded with mistakes and imprecisions, particularly for the early period up to the end of the eighteenth century. Therefore, any information gathered from them needs to be thoroughly vetted through other documentary evidence.

13. *ASV: Collegio, Risposte di dentro,* filza 7, cc.n.n., 27 May 1581 and 29 July 1581.

14. *ASV: Senato Mar,* reg.44, c.149 r/v, 23 August 1579 and filza 260, cc.n.n, 22 December 1627.

15. *ASV: Notarile Atti,* b.6533, Luca Gabrieli, cc.6v-7v, 4 January 1586 and cc.16v-17v, 10 January 1586.

16. They will then find an earlier passage on an English ship. See 'The voyage made to Tripolis in Barbarie, in the yeere 1584, with a ship called the Iesus, wherein the adventures and distress of some Englishmen are truly reported, and other necessarie circumstancies observed. Written by Thomas Sanders' (cited in Hakluyt 1965: 198–9).

17. *ASV: Notarile Atti,* b.6534, Luca e Giulio Gabrieli, cc.34r/v, 6 February 1587; Guildhall Library: Ms. 22,274, no.1394, 8 March 1591.

18. *ASV: Quarantia Criminale,* b. 193, fasc. 73. The smuggling trial was about a very complex deal between Greeks and English merchants that involved the delivery of currants – free of customs – in exchange for textiles. Several of these deals, forbidden by reiterated Venetian legislation, characterized the currants trade. Few were discovered, and even fewer were prosecuted successfully. The trial is recounted in detail in Fusaro 1996: 108–15.

19. We know of a shipment of tin on the ship '*Segura*, patron Danes Carpenter', from *ASV: Quarantia Criminale*, b. 103, fasc. 73, cc. 37r/v. Trut and Daelnes, agents of Baying and Holmden, hired the 'nave *Madonna di Schioppo*, parcenevole Marco Sicuro, patron Danit Carpenter inglese' for another delivery of currants (*ASV: Quarantia Criminale*, b. 103, fasc. 73, cc. 37v–39r; *ASV: Notarile Atti*, b. 6533, Luca Gabrieli, cc. 16v–17v, 10 January 1586).

20. 'Havendo il quel tempo salariato un patron Inglese con alquanti Marinari, tenendoli in questa Città comprò con detto Volterra essa nave parignota per 3300 ducati...' (*ASV: Quarantia Criminale*, b. 103, fasc. 73, c. 9v). Volterra was in partnership with Marco and Zuanne Seguro for deals with England (*ASV: Notarile Atti*, b. 7866,Gerolamo Luran, cc. 422v–424r, 12 April 1590).

21. The petition for implementing his new design for windmills on the Lido is in *ASV: Collegio, Risposte di dentro*, f. 6, cc. n.n., 1578; about the technological issue concerning wind and water mills in Venice see Pitteri (2000: 15–39).

22. As consul for the merchants subject to the Turk see *ASV: Collegio, Risposte di dentro*, f. 15, cc. n.n., 23 June 1618; *ivi*, f. 41, cc. n.n., 3 August 1650; and *ASV: Cinque Savi alla Mercanzia*, b. 44 n.s., fasc. vii, cc. n.n., 9 July 1618. As consul for the English see: *ASV: Cinque Savi alla Mercanzia*, b. 23 n.s., fasc. iii, cc. n.n., 12 August 1623.

23. He was mainly involved in trade between the Ionian Islands and Venice (*ASV: Avogaria di Comun, Civile*, b. 152, fasc. 48).

24. Their ship *Salvagna* was blocked in Muros (Galitia) fully loaded with muscat wines (*ASV: Notarile Atti*, b. 7867, Gerolamo Luran, cc. 657v–658v, 19 May 1590). One of the insurers of the ship was the same Antonio Tizzone, a Venetian, who at the beginning of the seventeenth century was still exporting wines to England on Venetian ships (*ASV: Cinque Savi alla Mercanzia, Risposte*, b. 140, cc. 149r/v; *ASV: Senato Mar*, f. 117, cc. n.n., 20 September 1592; Brulez and Devos 1965: no. 1294, p. 423, 23 May 1602).

25. See, for example, *ASV: Notarile Atti*, b. 6529, Luca e Giulio Gabrieli, cc. 110v–111r, 1 April 1583. They also rented Flemish ships jointly with the Seguro (Brulez and Devos 1986: no. 3803, p. 670, 12 November 1618; no. 3805, pp. 671–2, 17 November 1618; and no. 3808, pp. 672–3, 22 November 1618). Michele was also extremely active in the insurance business (Tenenti 1959).

26. Large properties in Portobuffolè, next to Treviso, appear in his name from the beginning of the 1580s (*ASV: Notarile Atti*, b. 7647, Gerolamo Luran, cc. 99v–100r, 2 July 1580). In 1594 he sold, for what looks like a 'favourable' price, these rather large properties to his sister Caterina (*ASV: Notarile Atti*, b. 7882, Gerolamo Luran, cc. 1193v–1194v, 5 August 1594). Michele also bought land and water mills in Friuli (*ASV: Notarile Atti*, reg. 7877, Gerolamo Luran, cc. 595v–597v, 5 February 1593). From this deed it appears that he

also owned several houses in the *Castello* area of Venice. For his activities in Rovigo see *ASV: Notarile Atti*, b. 7861, Gerolamo Luran, cc. 84r/v, 29 April 1588. For his other activities in the *Terraferma*, see *ASV: Notarile Atti*, b. 7865, Gerolamo Luran, cc. 476r–478r, 8 August 1589.

27. *ASV: Notarile Atti*, b.11886, Gerolamo Savina, cc.201v-202v, 27 January 1576.

28. For one such contract, in this case for a medium-sized ship (600 *botti*) see *ASV: Notarile Atti*, b. 7854, Gerolamo Luran, cc. 385v-386v, 386v–389v, 5 February 1584.

29. *ASV: Notarile Atti*, b.7854, Gerolamo Luran, cc.421v-422v, 15 March 1584 and 7 November 1585.

30. *ASV: Notarile Atti*, b.7864, Gerolamo Luran, cc.169r-170v, 15 March 1589.

31. On Velutelli's short-lived monopoly (1575–82), see Fusaro (1996: 19–22). Velutelli in a supplication to the Queen after the loss of his monopoly, would accuse the 'Italian' merchants Nicolò de Gozzi Pange and Innocenzo Lucatelli to have colluded with the Sumacchi in pushing for new custom duties for foreigners in the islands (Public Record Office: *State Papers* 99, 1, c. 16r, 1583–4). Nicolò de Gozzi was in reality from Ragusa, and he was a leading merchant in England at the time, probably one of the wealthiest foreigners, along with Sir Oratio Pallavicino (Abulafia 1994: 286–7).

32. Thomas Daelnes, in his testimony, mentioned a deal between the Sumacchi and Thomas Baxter for 200 *miara* of currants to be consigned in Venice (*ASV: Quarantia Criminale*, b. 103, fasc. 73, cc. 14v–17v). The original contract of that deal must be the one in *ASV: Notarile Atti*, b. 7852, Gerolamo Luran, cc. 535r–536v, 23 September 1583. All the details correspond to the description of it given by Daelnes in the testimony at the trial. Daelnes was acting for Holmden and Bayning.

33. This informations is taken from the papers with which the *Bailo* was ordering the confiscation of his goods in Constantinople, after Sumacchi had been declared bankrupt in 1595. These papers in the *Avogaria* are an extremely long list of inventories of merchandise, and some commercial correspondence of the same Sumacchi (*ASV: Avogaria di Comun, Civile*, b. 203 fasc. 16., cc. n.n. , 10 September 1595). On Michele Sumacchi's bankruptcy see also *ASV: Notarile Atti*, Gio Andrea Catti, b. 3366, cc. 411r/v, 23 October 1595.

34. For example see *ASV: Notarile Atti*, b. 7851, Gerolamo Luran, cc. 300r/v (12–11–1583); or *ivi*, b. 7864, Gerolamo Luran, cc. 200r–201v, 21 April 1589; ibid., cc. 241r/v, 27 June 1589.

35. On their shipments from Crete see Guildhall Library, Ms. 22274 *passim*.

36. For example see the letters of Orazio Rucellai and Alfonso Strozzi to the Corsini brothers in London on this subject, in Guildhall Library, Ms. 21317,

vol. 1, no. 114; vol. 3, no. 239, 16 June 1581; no. 283, 16 February 1581; and Ms. 21317, vol. 2, no. 188, 21 August 1579.

37. For example see the bills of lading at Zante for the ship *Reniera e Sumacchia* (Guildhall Library, Ms 24482/1 vol. 1 no. 26, 27 March 1589), where Zorzi Sumacchi was lading currants to be consigned to Giacomo Regazzoni in Margate.

38. Guildhall Library, Ms. 21317, vol. 7, no. 689 9 June 1589, about the *Reniera e Sumacchia* from Crete via Zante to London with wine, and with a cargo of tin on the way back. In Guildhall Library, Ms. 21317, vol. 3, no. 201 3 October 1579, Michele Sumacchi orders a shipment of kerseys and tin to be delivered in London to his brother Zorzi. These goods were then to be loaded on the English ship *Giona* and are destined for Zante. Another shipment of tin for the Sumacchi brothers is found in *ASV: Notarile Atti*, b. 6534, cc. 464v–467r and bb. 6535 and 6536, *passim* 1588–9.

39. For one of such journey see the bill of lading of the ship *Santa Maria di Scoppo* (patron David Carpenter) in Guildhall Library, Ms. 24482/1 vol. 1 no. 8, November 1584.

40. Guildhall Library: Ms. 21317, no.193, 14 August and 22 August 1579.

41. On the ship there were also goods belonging to Flemish traders based in London such as Thomas Coteels, and this led local authorities to believe that the ship was English and acting under a cover name: on this see Brulez and Devos (1965: no. 195, p. 69). This episode can be also followed in *CSPVe*, vol. viii (1581–1591), London, 1894, no. 624, p. 336; no. 647, pp. 347–8; no. 664, p. 357; no. 676, p. 362; no. 769, p. 409; no. 774, p. 412; no. 821, pp. 430–2; no. 854, p. 455.

On the relations between the Sumacchi and the Portuguese Jews based in Venice, see Ruspio (1999: 142–9). On the contacts between Michele Sumacchi and the Ribeira family of Portuguese Jews, see also *ASV: Notarile Atti*, b.7847, Gerolamo Luran, cc.74r/v, 20 May 1580 and ibid., b.7849, Gerolamo Luran, cc.115v-116v, 7 June 1582. Their contacts are also mentioned in Scammell (1972: 396). There he wrongly called Michele Sumacchi 'nominal owner of the *Santa Maria*' in his line of interpretation by which English merchants kept the trade open in markets otherwise closed to them, like the Spanish one.

42. The *Segura* was going from Crete to Lisbon, and probably afterward to London. After being freed it remained in the harbour of Cadiz to avoid the English corsairs who were raiding the area. On this episode see *CSPVe*, vol. viii (1581–1591), London, 1894, no. 901, p. 476; no. 906, p. 479; no. 966, p. 504.

43. On this see *CSPVe*, vol. viii (1581–1591), London, 1894, no. 85, p. 40; no. 101, p. 46; no. 125, pp. 55–6; no. 129, p. 57; no. 132, p. 58; no. 147, p. 65; no. 161, p. 71; no. 162, p. 72; no. 163, p. 72. On the ship there were also

goods belonging to Hamburg and Cologne merchants. On the episode see: *CSPVe*, vol. ix (1592–1603), London, 1897, *passim*.

44. On Della Vigna's business as ship owner, slave merchant and landowner see his will in *ASV: Notarile Testamenti*, Agostino Pellestrina, b. 768, no. 41, 13 January 1545. On the activities of the Cubli and Samariari families see Burke forthcoming.

45. See, for example: *ASV: Notarile Atti*, b. 11919, Andrea Spinelli, cc. 469v–470v, 2 November 1598; *ivi*, reg. 3386, Gio Andrea Catti, cc. 268v, 5 July 1608; also *CSPVe*, vol. xii (1610–1613), London, 1905, no. 111, p. 73; no. 115, p. 78; no. 132, p. 91; no. 153, p. 101; no. 171, p. 112; no. 186, p. 121. They had frequent contacts with Flemish merchants, for some of whom they acted as procurators: see Brulez and Devos 1965: no. 1421, p. 461, 18 July 1603; 1986: no. 2022, p. 82, 5 May 1607; 1986: no. 3852, p. 687, 11 February 1619 and no. 4073, pp. 760–1, 1 August 1620). And, interestingly, it is to Dutch merchants that some Venetians gave power of attorney to recuperate assets of the Balsamo in Amsterdam (Brulez and Devos 1986: no. 3990, p. 731, 17 August 1619). Another example of Greek goods on Dutch carriers is in Public Records Office: *State Papers* 105, 147, cc. 70r/v, 18 December 1615.

46. *ASV: Notarile Atti*, b. 3400, Gio Andrea Catti, cc. 140v–141r, 23 July 1621, and *passim*. They shipped currants to the Netherlands on Flemish ships (Brulez and Devos 1986: no. 2910 and 2920, pp. 389, 393, 1 and 18 February 1613; no. 3442, p. 558, 30 December 1616ns). They also bought Flemish ships for their trades (*ASV: Collegio, Risposte di dentro*, f. 17, c. 351, 18 October 1626).

47. 'He had affluent merchant relations in his native Cephalonia and in London', commented Roe upon him (Strachan 1989: 172–5).

48. See for example the bills of load in the papers of the trial between Nicolò Tomà and Demetrio Cutrica, where the Copio always mediated for the hiring of English ship (*ASV: Avogaria di Comun, Civile*, b. 152, fasc. 91; and b. 48, fasc. 13). They also rented Flemish ships to trade with the Netherlands (Brulez and Devos 1986: no. 2584, p. 281, 7 April 1610; no. 2734, pp. 332, 27 July 1611; no. 2763, p. 343, 9 January 1612; no. 2772, p. 345, 1 February 1612; no. 2840, p. 366, 22 June 1612; no. 2907 e 2908, p. 388, 1 February 1613; and no. 2924, p. 394, 4 March 1613). They were also active in the insurance business (Tenenti 1959).

49. *ASV: Notarile Atti*, b.6531, Luca e Giulio Gabrieli, cc.181r/v, 28 May 1584; *ASV: Collegio, Risposte di dentro*, filza 30, cc.n.n., 4 February 1639mv.

50. *ASV: Collegio, Risposte di dentro*, filza 30, cc.n.n., 17 October 1639.

51. Eustachio Nomicò quondam Zuanne, son of a Zante merchant, transferred to Venice where he opened a 'drogheria'. At his death he left a massive

inheritance, properties in Venice, landholdings in the *Terraferma*, a staggering amount of bullion, and 30,000 ducats invested in his shop. His will is in *ASV: Notarile Testamenti*, b. 770, Giacomo Profettini, no. 46, 15 December 1620, and added codicil in *ivi*, b. 1242, Giulio Ziliol, no. 239, 9 March 1622.

52. *ASV: Cinque Savi alla Mercanzia*, b. 836b, fasc. ii, 3 November 1584 and 27 October 1584. The latter is signed by all the 'parcenevoli di navi per Inghiltera': 'Hieronimo Corner quondam Andrea, Todorin Lombardo, Raphael Sumachi, Jacomo et Placido Regazzoni, Domenego da Gagliano, Paolo Tabiò, Alvise Balanzer, Vincenzo Costantini, Piero Grataruol, Domenego et Piero Innocenti; Zuanne Muscorno, Marin Tressa, Zeb. no [*sic*] Balbianij'. For a comparative overview of custom duties paid in England, and the debate on the traffic, see Fusaro 1996: 27–44.

53. On Regazzoni using Greek ships to collect currants from the islands and the Morea, see *ASV: Capi del Consiglio dei Dieci, Lettere di Rettori ed altre cariche*, b. 297, fasc. ii, no. 64, 16 December 1574.

54. Guildhall Library: Ms. 22274, no.439, 9 March 1582 and *passim*.

55. See for example Guildhall Library: Ms. 22274, no.104, 10 March 1590.

56. See, for example, Guildhall Library, Ms. 22274, no. 947, 12 April 1582: Paolo Labia in Venice to Bartolomeo Corsini in London, for 200 barrels of superior quality muscat wine from Candia on the ship of Costantin di Michiel Episcopopolo. The quality was deemed to be so good that Labia wanted them sold separately from the other wines loaded on the same ship, and made arrangements accordingly. Paolo Labia appears also in Guildhall Library, Ms. 22274, nos. 468, 687, 948, 963, 979, 1050 and 1061.

57. See for example Guildhall Library, Ms. 22274, no. 456, 10 March 1582: a contract involving also Paolo Labia. In this case payment was to be made with letter of exchange, an infrequent occurrence for Greek merchants.

58. There are a few insurance contracts among the 'Corsini papers', mostly dealing with Leghorn and Naples, only one with Zante for the ship *Santa Maria di Scoppo* (belonging to the Seguro family). The contract was for a total of £1,450, and the insurers were thirty in total, among whom William Garway and Thomas Cordell of the Levant Company (Guildhall Library, Ms. 22281, 20 February 1582).

59. Guildhall Library: Ms. 22274, no.1068, 29 February 1589.

60. Guildhall Library: Ms. 22274, no.1195, 31 August 1590.

61. For contracts that confirm this interpretation, see *ASV: Notarile Atti*, reg. 11920, Andrea Spinelli, cc. 42r/v, 16 January 1599; reg. 3371, Gio Andrea Catti, c. 121v, 29 March 1600; reg. 11923, Andrea Spinelli, cc. 73v–74r, 28 January 1602; reg. 11925, Andrea Spinelli, cc. 569r/v, 11 August 1604; reg. 7868, Gerolamo Luran, cc. 351v–352v, 17 May 1591.

Maria Fusaro

References

Abulafia, D. (1994), 'Cittadino e "denizen": mercanti mediterranei a Southampton e a Londra', in M. Del Treppo (ed.), *Sistema di rapporti ed élites economiche in Europa (secoli XII–XVII)*, Naples: Liguori.

Ashtor, F. (1981), 'Levantine Sugar Industry in the Late Middle Ages: A Case of Technological Decline', in A.L. Udovitch (ed.), *The Islamic Middle East, 700–1900: Studies in Economic and Social History*, Princeton: Darwin Press.

Baroutsos, F. (1999), 'Sovention per fabricar galeoni. Ο Βενετικός μερκαντιλισμός και οι αντανακλάσεις του στην Κρητική κοινωνία του ύστερου 16ου αιώνα' ('Sovention per fabricar galeoni: O Venetikos merkantilismos kai oi antanaklaseis tou sten Kretike koinonia tou usterou 16ou aiona') ('Financing Galleons: Venetian Mercantilism and its Consequences on Late Sixteenth-century Cretan Society'), *Thesaurismata*, 29: 187–223 [in Greek].

Beck, A.G., Manoussacas, M. and Pertusi, A. (1977), *Venezia centro di mediazione tra Oriente ed Occidente (secoli XV–XVI): Aspetti e problemi*, Vol. 1, Florence: Olschki.

Bellavitis, A. (1995), '"Per cittadini metterete...": La stratificazione della società veneziana cinquecentesca tra norma giuridica e riconoscimento sociale', *Quaderni Storici*, 89: 359–83.

Beltrami, D. (1954), *Storia della popolazione di Venezia dalla fine del secolo XVI alla caduta della Repubblica*, Padua: CEDAM.

Borsari, S. (1963), *Il dominio veneziano a Creta nel XIII secolo*, Naples: F. Fiorentino.

Brulez, W. and Devos, G. (1965, 1986), *Marchands Flamands à Venise*, 2 vols, Bruxelles-Rome: Institut historique belge de Rome.

Burke, E. (2000), '"Your humble and devoted servants": Greco-Venetian view of the Serenissima', in F.W. Kent (ed.), *Street Noises, Civic Spaces and Urban Identities in Italian Renaissance Cities*, Monash Publications in History, 34: 10–16.

—— (forthcoming), *The Greek Neighbourhoods of Sixteenth Century Venice: Daily Life of a Foreign Community*, PhD thesis, Monash University.

Calendar of state papers and manuscripts, relating to English affairs, existing in the Archives and collections of Venice: and in other libraries of northern Italy (1890), R. Brown, vol. vii (1558–1580), London: Public Record Office.

Casson, M. (1982), *The Entrepreneur: An Economic Theory*, Oxford: Robertson.

—— (1993), 'Entrepreneurship and business culture', in J. Brown and M.B. Rose (eds), *Entrepreneurship, Networks and Modern Business*, Manchester: Manchester University Press.

Clogg, R. (1992) (ed.), *A Concise History of Greece,* Cambridge: Cambridge University Press.

—— (1999), *The Greek Diaspora in the Twentieth Century*, London and New York: Macmillan.

Costantini, M. (1998), 'I galeoni di Candia nella congiuntura marittima veneziana cinque-seicentesca', in G. Ortalli (ed.), *Venezia e Creta: Atti del Convegno Internazionale di Studi (Iraklion-Chianà, 30 settembre–5 ottobre 1997),* Venezia: Istituto veneto di scienze, lettere ed arti: 207–31.

Davis, R.C. (1991), *Shipbuilders of the Venetian Arsenal: Workers and Workplace in the Pre-industrial City,* Baltimore and London: Johns Hopkins University Press.

Fedalto, G. (1967), *Ricerche storiche sulla posizione giuridica ed ecclesiastica dei Greci a Venezia nei secolo XV e XVI,* Florence: Olschki.

—— (1977), 'Le minoranze straniere a Venezia tra politica e legislazione', in *Venezia centro di mediazione tra Oriente ed Occidente (secoli XV–XVI): Aspetti e problemi,* vol. i, Florence: Olschki: 143–62.

Frattarelli Fischer, L. (2001), 'Alle radici di una identità composita: La "nazione" greca a Livorno', in G. Passarelli (ed.), *Le iconostasi di Livorno: Patrimonio iconografico post-bizantino,* Pisa: Pacini.

Fusaro, M. (1996), *Uva passa: Una guerra commerciale tra Venezia e l'Inghilterra, 1540–1640,* Venice: Il Cardo.

—— (2003), 'Un réseau de coopération commerciale en Méditerranée vénitienne: Les Anglais et les Grecs', *Annales ESC,* 3: 605–25.

Geanakoplos, D.J. (1972), *Greek Scholars in Venice: Studies in the Dissemination of Greek Learning from Byzantium to Western Europe,* Cambridge MA: Harvard University Press.

—— (1976), 'The Diaspora Greeks: the Genesis of Modern Greek National Consciousness', in Nikiforos P. Diamandouros et al. (eds), *Hellenism and the First Greek War of Liberation (1821–1830): Continuity and Change,* Thessaloniki: Institute for Balkan Studies: 59–77

—— (1989), *Constantinople and the West: Essays on the Late Byzantine (Palaeologan) and Italian Renaissances and the Byzantine and Roman Churches,* Madison: University of Wisconsin Press.

Gofas, D.C. (1979), 'Ασφαλιστήρια του 16ου αιώνος εκ του αρχείου του εν Βενετία, εληνικού ινστιτούτου' (Asphalisteria tou 16ou aionos ek tou archeiou tou en Venetia ellenikou instituotuo), ('Insurance Policies of the Sixteenth Century Preserved in the Archive of the Hellenic Institute in Venice'), *Thesaurismata,* 16: 54–88 [in Greek].

Hakluyt, R. (1965), *The Principal Navigations: Voyages and Discoveries of the English Nation,* D. Deers-Quinn and R.A. Skelton (eds), Cambridge: Hakluyt Society.

Harlaftis, G. (1993), *Greek Shipowners and Greece, 1945–1975: From Separate Development to Mutual Interdependence,* London: Athlone.

—— (1996), *A History of Greek-owned Shipping: The Making of an International Tramp Fleet, 1830 to the Present Day,* London and New York: Routledge.

—— (2001), *The History of Greek-owned Shipping during the Nineteenth and Twentieth Centuries* (Η Ιστορία της Ελληνόκτητης Ναυτιλίας, 19ος-20ος αι), Athens: Nefeli.

Harris, J. (1995), *Greek Emigres in the West, 1400–1520,* Camberley: Porphyrogenitus.

Imhaus, B. (1997), *Le minoranze orientali a Venezia, 1300–1510,* Rome: Jouvence.

Jacoby, D. (1994), 'La production du sucre en Crète vénitienne: L'échec d'une entreprise économique', in *Ροδωνιά: τιμή στον M.I.Μανούσακα, (Studies in Honour of M.I. Manousakas),* Rethymno: Panestimio Kretes [in Greek].

Klep, P. (1994), 'Entrepreneurship and the Transformation of the Economy, an Introduction', in P. Klep and E. Van Cauwenberghe (eds), *Entrepreneurship and the Transformation of the Economy (10th–20th Century): Essays in Honour of Herman Van der Wee,* Leuven: Leuven University Press.

Knapton, M. (1986), 'Lo stato veneziano fra la battaglia di Lepanto e la guerra di Candia', in *Venezia e la difesa del Levante: Da Lepanto a Candia, 1570–1670,* Venice: Arsenale.

—— (1992), 'Tra Dominante e Dominio', in G. Cozzi, M. Knapton and G. Scarabello, *La repubblica di Venezia nell'età moderna,* Vol. 2, Turin: UTET.

Leon, G. (1972), 'The Greek Merchant Marine, 1453–1850', in S. Papadopoulos (ed.), *The Greek Merchant Marine,* Athens: National Bank of Greece.

Maltezou, C. (1991), 'The Historical and Social Context', in D. Holton (ed.), *Literature and Society in Renaissance Crete,* Cambridge: Cambridge University Press.

Manousakas, M.I. (1973), 'L'isola di Creta sotto il dominio veneziano: problemi e ricerche', in A. Pertusi (ed.), *Venezia e il Levante fino al secolo XV,* Vol. I, Book 2, Florence: Olschki.

—— (1989), 'The History of the Greek Confraternity (1498-1953) and the Activity of the Greek Institute of Venice (1966–1982)', in *Modern Greek Studies Yearbook,* 5: 321-94.

—— (1991), 'Οι μεγάλες Ελληνικές παροικίες της Ιταλίας (Βενετίας, Νεάπολης, Λτβόρνου, Τεργέστης) από την άλωση της Κωνσταντινούπολης (1453) ως σήμερα', (Oi megales Ellenikes paroikies tes Italias (Venetias, Neapolis, Livornou, Tergestes) apo tin alose tes Konstantinoupoles (1453) Os simera), *(The Principal Greek Communities in Italy [Venice, Naples, Leghorn, Trieste] from the Fall of Constantinople [1453] to Today),* in J. M. Fossey (ed.), *Proceedings of the First International Congress on the Hellenic Diaspora:*

From Antiquity to Modern Times, Vol. II, *From 1453 to Modern Times,* Amsterdam: J.C. Gieben [in Greek].

Moschonas, N.G. (1988), *Navigation and Trade in the Ionian and Lower Adriatic Seas in the Eighteenth Century,* in A.E. Vacalopoulos, C.D. Svolopoulos and B.K. Király (eds), *Southeast European Maritime Commerce and Naval Policies from the Mid-eighteenth Century to 1914,* Boulder, CO: Social Science Monographs: 89–96.

Mueller Reinhold, C. (1981), *Stranieri e culture straniere a Venezia: Aspetti economici e sociali,* in M. Muraro (ed.), *Componenti storico-artistiche e culturali a Venezia nei secoli XIII e XIV,* Venice: Ateneo Veneto.

Pagratis Gerassimos, D. (2002), 'Greek Commercial Shipping (Fifteenth to Seventeenth Centuries): Literature Review and Research Perspectives', *Journal of Mediterranean Studies,* 12/2, December.

Panaghiotopoulou, K. (1974) Έλληνες ναυτικοί και πλοιοκτήτες από τα παλαιότερα οικονομικά βιβλία της Ελληνικής Αδελφότητας Βενετίας (1536–1576)' (Ellenes nautikoi kai ploioktetes apo ta palaiotera oikonomika vivlia tes Ellenikes adelfotetas Venetias (1536–1576)), ('Greek sailors and shipowners in the oldest account-books of the Greek Confraternity in Venice'), *Thesaurismata,* 11: 284–352 [in Greek].

Pezzolo, L. (1991), 'Sistema di valori e attività economica a Venezia, 1530–1630', in S. Cavaciocchi (ed.), *L'impresa, l'industria, commercio, banca, secoli XIII–XVIII,* Atti della XXII Settimana di Studi, Florence: Monnier.

Pitteri, M. (2000), 'I mulini della Repubblica di Venezia', *Studi Veneziani,* n.s. 40: 15–39.

Plumidis, G. (1972), 'Considerazioni sulla popolazione greca a Venezia nella seconda metà del '500', *Studi Veneziani,* 14: 219–26.

Pratt, M. (1978), *Britain's Greek Empire: Reflections on the History of the Ionian Islands from the Fall of Byzantium,* London: Rex Collings.

Ramsay, G.D. (1973), 'The Undoing of the Italian Mercantile Colony in Sixteenth Century London', in N.B. Harte and K.G. Pointing (eds), *Textile History and Economic History: Essays in Honour of Miss Julia De Lacy Mann,* Manchester: Manchester University Press.

Rangabés, E.R. (1927), *Livre d'or de la noblesse ionienne,* 3 vols, Athens.

Ruspio, F. (1999), *La comunità portoghese a Venezia (1567-1618),* Dissertation, University of Venice.

Scammell, G.V. (1972), 'Shipowning in the Economy and Politics of Early Modern England', *Historical Journal,* 15: 385–407.

Schumpeter, J.A. (1989), 'Economic Theory and Entrepreneurial History', in R.V. Clemence (ed.), *Essays on Entrepreneurs, Innovations, Business Cycles and the Evolution of Capitalism,* New Brunswick NJ and London: Transaction.

Sella, D. (1968), 'Crisis and Transformation in Venetian Trade', in B. Pullan (ed.), *Crisis and Change in the Venetian Economy in the Sixteenth and Seventeenth Centuries*, London: Methuen.

Spiridonakis, B.G. (1977), *Essays on the Historical Geography of the Greek World in the Balkans during the Turkokratia*, Thessaloniki: Institute for Balkan Studies.

Stefani, G. (ed.) (1956), *L'assicurazione a Venezia dalle origini alla fine della Serenissima*, Trieste: Assicurazioni Generali.

Stoianovich, T. (1960), 'The Conquering Balkan Orthodox Merchant', *Journal of Economic History*, 20: 234–313.

Strachan, M. (1989), *Sir Thomas Roe 1581–1644: A Life*, Salisbury: Russell.

Subrahmanyam, S. (ed.) (1996), *Merchant Networks in the Early Modern World*, Aldershot: Variorum.

Tenenti, A. (1959), *Naufrages, corsaires et assurances maritimes à Venise, 1592–1609*, Paris: S.E.V.P.E.N.

Thiriet, F. (1977), 'Sur les communautés grecque et albanaise à Venise', in A.G. Beck, M. Manoussacas and A. Pertusi, *Venezia centro di mediazione, tra Oriente ed Occidente (secoli XV–XVI): Aspetti e problemi*, Vol. 1, Florence: Olschki.

Tucci, U. (1994), 'Le commerce vénitien du vin de Crète', in Klaus Friedland (ed.), *Maritime Food Transport*, Cologne: Böhlau Verlag.

—— (1998), 'Il commercio del vino nell'economia cretese', in G. Ortalli (ed.), *Venezia e Creta: Atti del Convegno Internazionale di Studi (Iraklion-Chianà, 30 settembre – 5 ottobre 1997)* Venice: Istituto veneto di scienze, lettere ed arti.

Vacalopoulos, A.E. (1976), *The Greek Nation: The Cultural and Economic Background of Modern Greek Society*, New Brunswick NJ: Rutgers University Press.

—— (1980), 'The Flight of the Inhabitants of Greece to the Aegean Islands, Crete, and Morea during the Turkish Invasions (Fourteenth and Fifteenth Centuries)', in Angeliki E. Laiou-Thomadakis (ed.), *Charanis Studies: Essays in Honour of Peter Charanis*, New Brunswick NJ: Rutgers University Press.

Vlassi, D. (1995), 'La politica annonaria di Venezia a Cefalonia: il fondaco delle biade (sec. XVI–XVIII)', *Thesaurismata*, 25: 274–318.

Zakythinos, D.A. (1976), *The Making of Modern Greece, from Byzantium to Independence*, Oxford: Basil Blackwell.

—— (1977) 'L'attitude de Venise face au déclin et à la chute de Constantinople', in A.G. Beck, M. Manoussacas and A. Pertusi (eds), *Venezia centro di mediazione tra Oriente ed Occidente (secoli XV–XVI): Aspetti e problemi*, Vol. 1, Florence: Olschki.

Zois, L.K. (1963), *Λεξικόν ιστρρικόν και λαογραφικόν Ζακύνθου*, (Lexikon istorikon kai laografikon Zakunthou), *(Dictionary of the History and Folklore of Zakynthos)* 2 vols, Athens [in Greek].

–6–

Maltese Entrepreneurial Networks
Carmel Vassallo

The Jewish, Armenian and Greek diasporas are the archetypal or classical ones but there have been others. A hitherto little-known network was the Maltese one. Although endowed with certain special characteristics, it nevertheless shared with the Jews, Greeks and Armenians what could be considered one of the principal distinguishing features of the classical diasporas: liminality, the occupation of a position at, or on both sides of, a boundary or threshold. The Maltese, in fact, lived on the mental and spatial frontier between the two mighty empires which dominated the Eastern and Western halves of the Mediterranean Sea, the Ottoman and the Habsburg. Though linguistically Semitic and thus sharing the quality of 'Easternness' with historical diaspora peoples, the Maltese were, like the Greeks and Armenians, Christianized very early on. With the 're-conquest' of Sicily by Christendom, they settled down to become fervent Catholics. This condition would eventually prove to be the key that would permit them easy access into a Catholic southern Europe which was somewhat more suspicious of non-Catholic Greeks, Armenians and others.

Malta, a tiny, crowded island south of Sicily should, by right, not have attracted any more attention in history than many islands the same size were it not for its strategic location and superb harbour. Until the early sixteenth century it was just one more Sicilian domain, and a small one at that. Probably aided by its insularity, it had been left, more or less, to fend for itself. The local elite, of Sicilian or Aragonese origin, had repeatedly and successfully managed to 'buy off' the feudal lords to whom the island had been pawned by the King, always desperately strapped for cash. It was off the main trade routes but was, nevertheless, in possession of a modest merchant fleet which brought in supplies of grain to make up for the already considerable shortfall in its own production (Bresc 1991). It paid for these food imports partly from its exports of cotton and cumin and partly from the earnings of a long-established corsairing sector.

The arrival of the Hospitaller Order of St John in 1530 accompanied by 500 Rhodiots, opened up completely new horizons. Initially resentful of the imposition of yet one more feudal lord, who proceeded to establish himself by the harbour, away from Mdina, the island's seat of power in the centre of the island, the traditional elite eventually saw themselves shunted to the side and displaced by a new commercial and service elite whose welfare depended on attending to the wealthy scions of Europe's noble families and the activity they generated in and around the new city of Valletta. The income from the Order's far-flung European estates in fact permitted population growth, particularly around the harbour area, far beyond what would have corresponded to the arid island's 315 square kilometres. And, after one of the best-publicized sieges in early modern Europe (in 1565), the island became firmly established as the southernmost outpost of the Habsburg Empire (see Mallia-Milanes 1993).

In the seventeenth century it was the base for considerable corsairing activity. This and its policing role produced a lively economic climate which translated into fast population growth, albeit not devoid of setbacks resulting from plagues, famines, and the like. The second half of the seventeenth century saw, first, France's *rapprochement* with the Sublime Porte in the 1670s and eventually, in 1699 with the Treaty of Karlowitz, an end to the general hostilities between Christians and Muslims. To a military order whose *raison d'être* had been the confrontation with Islam and a civilian population which had grown completely out of proportion to what the island's own tiny rural hinterland could sustain, the future looked bleak. The consequence was a desperate attempt to adjust to new realities. Men and resources previously devoted to corsairing would seem to have been increasingly applied to exploring the possibilities of peaceful trade beyond the traditional victualling trade with Sicily and Southern Italy. The *Consolato di Mare*, set up in 1697, provided swift settlement of litigation involving merchants and seafarers. Its establishment must be taken as the result both of increasing trade and as a factor aiding its growth.

The late seventeenth century and the eighteenth century also saw the development of a widespread network of consuls which went well beyond the island's immediate surroundings to encompass Northern Italian, French, Spanish and Portuguese ports. The Hospitallers had their own long-established network of agents but with the exception of Barcelona, where the representative of the Order played a notable role in defence of Maltese merchants in the early decades of the eighteenth century, these were typically located on the estates which the Order possessed, far away from coastal cities. As the correspondence relating to consular appointments demonstrates, the consular network was established to attend to the needs of merchants and seafarers (see Vassallo 1996).

Maltese merchants were, in general, very welcome in Catholic Europe. Subjects of the Grand Master whose highly-regarded Order was made up of knights coming from all over Christian Europe, they were guaranteed preferential access to practically all of Southern Europe (Vassallo 1997: 98, 126 n. 86). This contrasted somewhat with the experience of Greeks, Armenians and others who were, on the one hand, non-Catholics and, on the other, subjects of the Ottomans.

In 1791 there were only two Greeks out of a total of 3,216 foreigners established in Spain's foremost commercial centre, Cádiz (see Collado Villalta 1981). About a decade earlier, in 1782, a community of around two hundred Greek families who had prospered in Minorca during the British occupation of the island was obliged to leave (Domínguez Ortiz 1955: 251–2). They were considered schismatics and thus not very amenable to 'assimilation'. As Ottoman subjects, the Greeks and the Armenians were also considered politically unreliable elements whose economic activities only benefited the Turk's exchequer. Edicts of expulsion were decreed for Greeks and Armenians in 1663 and 1753, although these very acts are a clear indication that some, at least, always managed to filter back in, despite official obstacles (Domínguez Ortiz 1955: 252).

The situation in nearby France seems to have been somewhat analogous to the one prevailing in Spain, despite France's favourable disposition to the Ottomans. Fernand Braudel (1982: 156) makes reference to the opposition of the Marseilles consuls to the presence of Armenians selling silk in the city in 1623, but Charles Carrière (1973) makes no mention of Greeks or Armenians in his monumental work on Marseilles. Out of a total of 489 foreign merchants established in Marseilles during the eighteenth century, only 29 are noted down as from the Levant and most of these, like the 14 from Barbary, would seem to have been Jews (Carrière 1973: 266–78).

In overall terms therefore, it would seem that the Maltese might have had a bit of an edge over other eastern minorities by virtue of the island being governed by the politically neutral – at least vis-à-vis intra-European political struggles – Catholic Order of St John.

The Maltese in Spain

Early modern Spain, point of entry for much silver and gold from the Americas, was an important focus for trade networks from all over Europe. Domínguez Ortiz (1955: 237) has claimed that the seventeenth was the century when the number of foreigners and their economic weight were at their highest point in Spain. But he had in mind all foreigners, including agricultural labourers, artisans and such, and not only those involved in mercantile activities.

The total number of foreigners may have decreased in the following century but there is no doubt that much of eighteenth-century Spain's trade, both foreign and domestic, was still dominated by foreigners, according to most researchers. There were a total of 27,502 heads of households in a detailed census of foreigners taken in 1791 (Lafuente 1887–1890, 15: 184–5). Made up mostly of Frenchman (48.47 per cent) they also included Italians (26.85 per cent), Portuguese (12.79 per cent), Germans (5.82 per cent) and Maltese (4.46 per cent), among many others.

But these aggregate figures include all professions. In a study of detailed returns for 12,180 householders out of the above-mentioned 27,502, Salas Ausens and Jarque Martínez (1990: 993) show commerce as being the occupation of only 2,104 or 17.27 per cent of them.

By way of contrast, the relatively small Maltese presence in Spain was almost exclusively devoted to trade. Excluding Cádiz, where a quarter of the 217 Maltese heads of households there had other occupations, the Maltese in other localities in Spain for which we have information were engaged overwhelmingly in trade (96 per cent in Malaga, 100 per cent in El Puerto de Santa María and 100 per cent in Játiva [Vassallo 1997: 256–7]). As a consequence, the Maltese represented a much higher proportion of those involved in commerce than the meagre 4.46 per cent of *all* foreigners would seem to indicate.

The Maltese, in fact, conform to Curtin's criterion, based on his worldwide study of cross-cultural trade, that members of a trade diaspora were 'specialists in a single kind of economic enterprise' (1984: 5). In contrast to the host society, which was a whole society, with many occupations, class stratification and so on, the Maltese, more than any of the other foreign communities in Spain, was a merchant colony with a very specific niche – the sale of cotton and cloth (Vassallo 1997). Extensive research has already been carried out concerning the Maltese mercantile presence in eighteenth-century Spain and a brief sketch will suffice here.

Probably as a consequence of initial contacts established while serving in the Order's navy or on board of corsair vessels, Maltese sailors/traders are known to have been established in Majorca and Barcelona in the mid-seventeenth century, trading in a wide range of goods and benefiting from special privileges granted to the Maltese out of consideration for the Order (Pons and Bibiloni 1991: 31). It is worthwhile noting, in passing, that this privileged access was not limited to Spain but extended to Portugal, France and other places too (Mallia-Milanes 1974: 31).

During the course of the latter half of the seventeenth century, occasional sightings became more and more frequent and in 1699 there were at least 13 brigantine expeditions to Spain and Portugal (National Archive of Malta, *Consolato di Mare, Manifesti*: Bundle 1, 1698–1701). The phenomenon of the brigantine expedition has been described in detail elsewhere (Vassallo 1997: 69–130) and for our present purpose it will be sufficient to set out the description of the brigantine and its trade in eighteenth-century Malta as entered in the *Nuovo Dizionario della Marina*, an eighteenth-century manuscript found in the National Library of Malta.

> *Brigantino, Brigantin.* It is a small and light vessel that serves both for corsairing and
> for trade and which is cut fairly deep in its bottom to permit it to go better under sails
> and with oars. One could say it is a small galleon with the same sailing characteristics,

the speron and the masting. These are the vessels which, albeit small, carry on Malta's big business, earning for the country considerable sums. They start their trade in Sicily where they take on large quantities of silk in Messina. They then sail up the coast of Italy to France, and always hugging the coast, trade in all the small places until they get to Spain which is where they ordinarily do the best business. In the past they used to be considered foolhardy if they ventured beyond the Straits of Gibraltar but nowadays they have arrived as far as Lisbon. They have managed to fill that vast city with fine Maltese cotton products which used to be a rarity in those lands but are now commonplace. These vessels normally have twenty oars and around twenty-two men. Some of them have two small cannon in the bow but their strength is in their musketry and swivel-guns of which they have as many as six and as a consequence they can defend themselves very well from Turkish galleons which in the main do not dare to attack them. (National Library of Malta: Lib. Ms.223)

It is a succinct description difficult to improve upon as a portrayal of the vessel which first as a corsair ship and subsequently as a merchantman constituted the centrepiece of Malta's maritime economy: a highly adaptable craft manned by a highly adaptable captain and crew who were at the same time merchants, mariners and musketeers.

The Iberian Peninsula, and more specifically Spain, emerged as the most important area of operations for Maltese brigantines and so they remained, even in the latter decades of the eighteenth century when the trade became both more important and more settled. We shall, once again, refer to the testimony of two contemporaries to sum up the phenomenon. The first is by an anonymous German gentleman who travelled through Spain in the years 1764 and 1765, around the time when the brigantines reached their era of maximum splendour. He wrote that:

The Maltese do a lot of trade in Cádiz and you will not find any important city all over Spain where you cannot find them. They have more privileges and rights than Spanish shopkeepers who only sell small amounts... They take their merchandise from Genoa, Marseilles and other ports of the Mediterranean. They take everything and arrive with entire loads of all kinds of goods of which only a few are from Malta; they secretly use neutral ships in the ocean; in the Mediterranean they also take their own ships. These people live very badly, eat little, sell for low prices and take large sums of cash back home from Spain. (cited in Von Den Driesch 1972: 241 (trans. Steffi Anzinger))

Shortly after that was written, the Maltese mercantile network in Spain was subjected to a spate of adverse legislation that caused Maltese merchants to become, seemingly, established in Spain. The reality was somewhat different, as borne out in a memorandum read by José Guevara Vasconcelos, in 1778, to Madrid's Real Sociedad Económica. He said:

Every two years the members of these companies return to their countries and are replaced by others, whom they eventually replace, taking turns. Those who belong to these companies bring the clothes they will need with them and take out all the coin they can and it is feared much of it is smuggled. They establish themselves in the principal villages where it is not difficult for them to get a low tax assessment by securing the favour of those in authority. They give their wares on hire purchase to the women without the knowledge of their husbands and recover the debt at exorbitant rates. They exclude from their companies those who marry in Spain. Their internal regulations are unknown but not even those excluded have ever appealed to local magistrates... (1787: 42–3 (trans. the author))

Even allowing for the fact that the commentator is opposed to Maltese and other foreign trading companies it is clear that he is describing a very pervasive phenomenon and I have described elsewhere how the Maltese retail and pedlar network opened up considerable areas of eighteenth-century Spain to the market (Vassallo 1997: 131–83).

Maltese merchants in Spain were characterized by: a high level of literacy compared to other foreigners; reliance on kith and kin at all stages of the conduct of their business; regular travel to and from their island to settle accounts and attend to other business matters, as well as spending time with their families; a tendency to set up in business and live in close proximity to each other in veritable enclaves in the communities where they were established; a high regard for honour and trust in the conduct of business with each other and the tendency to settle any differences which arose during the course of dealings with their fellow nationals abroad, in their own home country (see Vassallo 1997).

On a somewhat wider plane but serving to reinforce their sense of community, one must note that they often undertook not to marry while on foreign business trips and we, in fact, note a considerably lower tendency, compared to that of other foreigners, for the Maltese merchants established in Spain to be married to non-Maltese. When the community was large enough they established their own religious confraternities, with both spiritual and material welfare concerns, and separate burial arrangements, and secured the services of their own priests who could assist them in their own language. Finally we note that at all stages Maltese merchants were expected to give, and gave, considerable support to each other in return for a high degree of social control (Vassallo 1997).

It must be emphasized that many of the characteristics I have mentioned are not peculiar to the Maltese and have been noted for classical trading diasporas as well. Indeed, they have been shown to apply even beyond these to many other cases (Fontaine 1996).

Each diaspora, whether relating to entrepreneurial networks or otherwise, has its peculiarities but the Maltese network established in Spain during the eighteenth century clearly fulfils the basic criteria of dispersal, a collective identity which centred on an alien tongue and a very real need to return to the homeland deriving in the main from the credit-dependent nature of their business and families left behind.

The Wider Picture

Although the Maltese mercantile network in the eighteenth century centred on Spain and Portugal there is, nevertheless, ample confirmation that it extended to other parts as well. A 1776 Chamber of Commerce report described Malta's trade in the following manner:

> For clarity's sake we can divide commerce into two branches; the first is that of the Maltese in Sicily, the second in Spain. Malta supplies the Sicilians and the Calabrians with sugar, coffee, cocoa, cinnamon, herbs, drugs, iron nails, glass, paper, planks, lead shot, powder and other goods and the Maltese purchase from Sicily the soda ash, sulphur, alum, pulses, barley, wheat and carob beans which they resell in Spain, Italy and Marseilles. The second branch to Spain consists of those who buy silk from Catania, Messina and Naples and all sorts of cloth from Leghorn and Genoa for resale in Alicante, Malaga, Seville, Valencia, Ferrol, Cádiz and the Canary Islands. (National Library of Malta: Ms 1020, item 20)

Barcelona is mentioned further on in the report in connection with the trade in cotton yarn.

In France, the Maltese were entitled to the same civil and commercial rights enjoyed by the indigenous population and had a long-established presence in Marseilles, but its nature and extent is still to be determined (Godechot 1951: 71).

The same applies to the Italian Peninsula. We know that Maltese merchants bought and sold goods and obtained credit in ports such as Genoa, Leghorn and Naples, but information is still fragmentary. Maltese traders had long been active in southern Italy buying provisions for their densely populated island but, as we saw above, they were also important articulators of a trade which supplied the Sicilians and Southern Italians with a wide range of goods. There is no reference, in the above citation, to a trade in woollen cloth but we have encountered evidence for Maltese merchants taking considerable quantities of this product from Catalonia and selling it in Sicily and Southern Italy (Vassallo 1997: 210–16). An eighteenth-century report by Saverio Scrofani cited by Calogero Messina (1986: 290–1) gives details of goods originating in Spain, particularly woollen cloth, supplied to Sicily. The relevant table is entitled 'Mercanzie di Spagna che s'immettono in Sicilia principalmente per la via di Genova e pel mezzo dei Maltesi, Napolitani, Genovesi ec.' It is noteworthy that of the various 'nations' responsible for the trade the Maltese are mentioned first. We have still to find out the nature of the Maltese trading network responsible for this business.

But Malta's mercantile network was not limited to Catholic countries. Malta was an important quarantine and rallying point for French mercantile shipping to the Levant; but despite official belligerency, it also had a notable entrepôt role of its own. The movement of goods and people to and from the North African Regencies and the Levant was constant during the seventeenth century (Cutajar 1988). Cotton from ports in the Levant (Gaza, Haifa, Saida, Tripoli-in-Syria, Alexandretta, Cyprus) and Anatolia (Satalia, Smyrna, Constantinople) was a very important item and contacts in the seventeenth century probably laid the foundations for Malta's near-monopoly status as supplier of cotton to the emerging *Indiane* manufactories in France and Spain during the eighteenth century. Despite repeated official prohibition of imports of cotton from the East it is very probable that some, if not most, of the prized 'Maltese' cotton may have originated elsewhere (Vassallo 1997: 190–5). Malta's geographical proximity was clearly critical in determining the island's role as an intermediary between north and south and east and west but equally important must have been cultural factors which could both divide and bring people together.

Christian corsairing based in Malta and portraying itself as engaged in a just and holy war against Islam was a continual irritant to Muslim shipping and eventually drove the transport of Muslim goods and passengers into the arms of French shippers. Muslim corsairing, on the other hand, preyed on Maltese vessels. But this perpetual state of war was more in the nature of skirmishing and was not a total war. There was ample opportunity to carry on with the other, more mundane, aspects of life. Business is business and even corsairing is, when all is said and done, a kind of business. Maltese merchants could be found in Tunis purchasing prize ships and cargoes during the seventeenth century (Bono 1990: 141–2). But this was probably outweighed by other types of business. Using safe-conducts and neutral shipping Maltese merchants were continually tapping the Maghreb and the Levant for merchandise for consumption on the island or for re-export. In the middle of the eighteenth century, Maltese-flagged vessels arriving at the island from Muslim territories were far outweighed by vessels with goods consigned to the island but flying other flags, sometimes under the supervision of Maltese supercargoes and crewed and captained by Maltese (Vassallo 1998: 24–5). Boubaker (1987: 175) has, in fact, highlighted the 'privileged' position of the Maltese in Tunis compared to that of 'other Europeans' during the seventeenth century. This privileged position must have had a lot to do with an important cultural component – language.

Despite sharp religious antagonism the Maltese and Muslims in fact shared a common linguistic heritage. Originally a dialect of Tunisian Arabic, Maltese was first cut off from its roots and then subjected to Romance and other influences. It has, over time, developed into the unique and hybrid language that it is today. Its literature is young and it has only been regulated into its present form in the last hundred years or so (and only achieved official status in 1934). One of the earliest written renditions of it was actually in Hebrew but for many hundreds of years it was relegated to being the 'secret' linguistic code of the indigenous population, which nevertheless kept its records, conducted its religious rituals and communicated with the outside world in Latin, various forms of Italian and most recently English. It is this linguistic and spatial proximity to the Muslim world that was probably the most important factor behind Malta's mediatory role in the early modern and contemporary periods but all we have to go on at the moment are occasional glimpses. We are far removed from being able to describe the nature of the Maltese presence in Muslim lands.

Summing up, we can say that although it can be asserted with a considerable degree of certainty that Spain was the focal point of much of eighteenth-century Malta's trading network, there are clearly many missing pieces in the puzzle concerning their presence in Sicily, mainland Italian states, France, the Maghreb and the Levant. And while we can, in principle, anticipate being able to fill in some of the blanks for Europe, the scant archival material available in Muslim countries does not bode well for the possibility of doing the same for the latter.

The *débâcle* at the end of the Ancient Regime resulted in a near-complete reworking of the system we have described, although for a few years the momentum acquired during the eighteenth century spilled over into the nineteenth century.

The End of an Era

The establishment of British dominion over the Maltese archipelago, after a brief French interregnum, closed off Continental markets to Maltese-supplied cotton, but for a brief period Maltese merchants used trade contacts they had established in the previous century to distribute other goods, particularly agricultural produce (Martínez Shaw 1991: 227–41). It must, nevertheless, be stressed that the Maltese presence in the opening decades of the nineteenth century was but a shadow of what it had been in the closing decade of the previous century, although it showed greater resilience on Spain's southeastern seaboard than was the case in the southwest. The population of Cádiz's Maltese mercantile colony, for example, decreased from 217 in 1791 to 41 in 1801 and that in Málaga went down from 35 in 1771 to 11 in 1817 (Vassallo 1997: 291–2). Further east, on the other hand, Almería's declined from 32 in 1791 to 20 in 1808, Murcia's from 41 in 1791 to 32 in 1807 and Játiva's from 32 in 1791 to 22 in 1807 (Vassallo 1997: 291–2). In the city of Valencia, the core group of Maltese retail-cloth guild merchants around whom was constructed the large Maltese mercantile community there, only decreased from 39 in 1793 to 35 in 1805 (Vassallo 1997: 40).

Some of the Maltese merchants established on Spain's eastern littoral in fact proved very adroit at adapting themselves to the new circumstances. They were the few who stayed on in contrast to the majority who appear to have gone home. The Cachia, Seiquer, Scicluna, Cardona and Camilleri in the City of Murcia; the Butigieg in Cartagena; the Borja and Cachia in Lorca; the Cutajar in Alicante and the Attard, Mifsud, Piscopo, Busuttil, Formosa and Caruana in Valencia all played an important role in the economic development of their respective cities in the nineteenth century (Vassallo: forthcoming). Starting out as humble pedlars and shopkeepers in the eighteenth century, they branched out into a whole range of activities during the course of the nineteenth century. They are a clear vindication of Eva Morowska's claim (1990: 203–5) that first-generation migrants often accumulate economic and human capital which, once released by the relaxation of the attitudes of the host society, is used by following generations to move into the mainstream society in a spectacular display of accomplishment. The Caruana of Valencia are a prime example of this phenomenon.

From Rags to Riches: the Caruana of Valencia

The founder of the dynasty, Antonio Caruana Brignone, was born in 1753 in Senglea, the mercantile part of the Grand Harbour of Malta. His mother's side of the family had been in the Spanish trade for at least three generations and Antonio and his brother Pedro Pablo were apprenticed in 1768 in the *Gremio de Mercaderes de Vara*, or Cloth Retailers Guild, to their uncle on their mother's side, Joseph Brignone.

Pedro Pablo, the elder brother, continued in the Cloth Retailers Guild, appearing as a full-fledged member in 1793, and indeed achieved considerable success in this line until 1805, when he decided to retire to Malta. His brother Antonio, on the other hand, left cloth retailing very early on and went into manufacturing. His silk factory was awarded prizes and Royal Patronage for its technological innovations and the quality of its goods as well as for creating employment. In 1806 he still retained contact with his native land, Malta, to where he exported some of his products. He died in 1819. His sons Peregri, Antonio and Josep continued building on their father's success. From 1855 to 1867 they were among the principal beneficiaries of the sale of confiscated Church property, acquiring sixteen agricultural properties and five urban ones for a total of 1,341,650 *reales*, a huge amount for the time (Pons Pons 1987: 324–49).

The eldest of the three brothers, Peregri, who had been involved in his father's manufacturing concern, became a particularly active figure in the economy of nineteenth-century Valencia. Apart from property speculation he was also the driving force behind the project to establish Valencia's first issuing bank and was heavily involved in railway and potable-water development (Rodenas 1978: 240 and 1982: 16–22).

But the Caruanas and all those descended from the first generation that had taken the first step in a new land and stayed on eventually lost their Maltese connection. As Philip D. Curtin points out 'one immediately striking generalisation is that trade diasporas tend to work themselves out of business' (1984: 63). But as the descendants of the eighteenth-century Maltese trade network were being absorbed into the indigenous populations other possibilities were opening up elsewhere.

The Continental Blockade set up by the Berlin decree of 1806 was a disaster for British trade but it provided a window of opportunity for Malta, and for a number of years the island became an important centre of contraband. As many as one in five of those living on the island in 1807 were foreigners wheeling and dealing in a brisk trade in the sale and purchase of licences and goods, most of which probably never touched the island. Malta was also considered a good place for Greek ships to offload cargoes of corn from the Black Sea, which were then taken up by Maltese and other merchants and taken to the western end of the Mediterranean.[1]

The arrival of the British may have contributed to the closure of European markets for Maltese cotton and may have rendered Maltese merchants unwelcome by virtue of their newly-acquired British status, but it also ensured the protection of the British flag for Maltese shipping and British papers and British Consular protection for Maltese merchants. It must also be noted, however, that during the nineteenth century this same British status would act as a mantle that creates not inconsiderable problems when we are seeking to identify the Maltese and distinguish them from others enjoying British 'nationality'. This is, fortunately, somewhat offset by the increased availability of statistics and other sources for this epoch.

The Nineteenth Century

Braudel (1981: 158) has noted that emigration is the commonest way in which Mediterranean islands have entered the life of the outside world. This is certainly true for Malta but in its case one can also talk about how immigration was probably the commonest way for the outside world to enter the life of Malta. The movement of people to and from the island is recorded from very early on but is more clearly a constant feature of early modern Malta, as Carmel Cassar has demonstrated (2000: 94–120). Apart from members of the Order, Malta also saw a continual inflow of commoners. Sicilians and other Italians were the most prominent but others came from all over Europe as servants to the Knights, artisans, soldiers, corsairs, etc. Also worth mentioning were the Greeks, to whom I made reference earlier, and the French, who were particularly important in mercantile circles (Mercieca 2000: passim).

The reverse flow, namely emigration from the island, was just as important a phenomenon and became more so with the passage of time. Toward the end of the eighteenth century, the island may have had in excess of 15 per cent of its adult male population trading in Spain, Portugal, France and other parts of the Mediterranean, or serving in foreign navies, and this does not include those working as sailors on the short-range Malta–Sicily route (Vassallo 1997: 284 n. 5).

In the harbour towns the situation appears to have been even more dramatic. A *Ruolo degli Uomini della Città Senglea e Conspicua,* which seems to belong to the middle of the eighteenth century, gave the total number of able-bodied men for Senglea, the home town of most merchants and mariners, as 1,109, of whom 471 were away trading or serving in foreign navies, compared to 191 serving in the Order's armed forces (National Library of Malta: AOM 1067). In other words, 42 per cent of Senglea's adult males were away from the island. The corresponding figure for nearby and more populous Conspicua was 30 per cent. It is clear that in the eighteenth century, the highly urbanized island already had a migratory mechanism that provided Maltese labour and capital with openings lacking in the mother country.

The closure of the traditional markets for Maltese cotton yarn at the beginning of the nineteenth century had consequences that reached well beyond the mercantile sectors of the population. The cultivation of cotton, its spinning, the manufacture of some of the yarn into sail cloth, caps and other products and all the mercantile activities associated with its marketing had at one time occupied up to three-quarters of the population, according to one estimate (Price 1989 [1954]: 65). The loss of traditional markets in the nineteenth century resulted in a massive manpower surplus that was released in the migration of tens of thousands of people to nearby territories.

The presence of Maltese communities in the Muslim Mediterranean in the Contemporary period is a well-documented phenomenon, but the more settled existence of the latter part of the nineteen century and the earlier part of the twentieth needs to be distinguished from the much less documented earlier part of the nineteenth century, before the process of European colonization had started. Fallot, writing in 1896, declared that 'during the second and third quarters of this century [nineteenth] Malta had practically monopolised the commerce of a large part of Barbary' (1896: 10).

More recently Price (1989: 50–2) has pointed out the opportunities that emerged in Mehemet Ali's pashalik in the early decades of the nineteenth century when a Maltese tradesman could make a good living in Cairo, Alexandria or Constantinople and even set money aside, but he also noted the openings for small merchants from Malta in the smaller North African ports. Price then goes on to observe (1989: 61) that from these modest beginnings emerged men of not inconsiderable fortunes in the space of fifteen or twenty years, men who qualified for the term 'merchant', not just in North African towns but also in Constantinople, Rhodes and Alexandria. Price's work centres mainly on aggregates of migratory flows and he limits himself to describing how

> the small Sicilian or Maltese trader found it easy to fill his *speronara* (sailing ship of 50 to 150 tons) with European textiles, metal-ware, tobacco and wine and distribute these goods along the African coast in exchange for oil, dates, hides, cattle and cereals: the large European merchant would then take over in Valetta or one of the Sicilian entrepôt ports (1989: 50–2).

Relatively little is known about what, by all accounts, was a very large Maltese presence in, for example, the Regency of Tunis. Ganiage, in his study of the parish records of the main Catholic church of Tunis, St Croix, in the middle of the nineteenth century, has given a minimum figure of 9,150 Europeans in Tunis alone, and this may need to be doubled to account for those with no fixed address or for celibate men who typically did not appear in church records (1960: 19). Of the 9,150 Europeans, 60 per cent were Maltese.

In a recent article Andrea L. Smith suggests that, 'Knowledge of the Maltese has been hampered in part by the fact that they remained largely an exotic curiosity to most Europeans writing about Tunisia' (2000: 187). Most authors were apparently struck by the closeness of the Maltese in language, dress and habitat to the indigenous population. The Maltese were even said to be as 'intolerant' as Arabs regarding their faith. Smith goes on to provide valuable new material based on both British Consular correspondence and National Archives of Tunis material.

If we know relatively little about the general Maltese population, we know even less about their trade networks and especially about the highly mobile petty traders or *paccottiglieri* who may have functioned in a manner not unlike the Maltese retailer/pedlar network developed a century earlier in Spain. The Maltese, in fact, often reached areas where no other 'Europeans' ventured (Smith 2000: *passim*).

In 1854, the Bey of Tunis issued an Ordinance which, among other things, stipulated that the Maltese arriving in the Regency were to do so at one of the major ports where a British Consulate existed, namely Tunis, Sousse and Sfax (*Malta Government Gazette* No. 1804, Tuesday 18 April 1854: 67–8). At the behest of no fewer than one hundred commercial houses, the recently-established Malta Chamber of Commerce reacted immediately and, in a letter of 4 May 1854 to the Chief Secretary to Government, highlighted that Malta had for a long time been the channel via which British manufactured goods reached Barbary through the hands of Maltese petty traders who would no longer be able to attend to their business at different points of the North African littoral (Chamber of Commerce Copy Letter Book 1848–1854: 4 May 1854). Some idea of the scale of Malta's entrepôt trade was given by Miège in 1841 (1841, II: 46). He calculated that Malta's transit trade in the late 1820s and early 1830s was already worth around three times the value of Malta's domestic trade. Some sixteen years later Michele Dedomenico confirmed that, 'It is not the product or local consumption or industry to which we have already referred, which constitute the principal basis of the commerce of this island, but the transit [trade] which is truly of interest' (1857: 51).

Regrettably, no reliable figures on the value of the trade in the earlier part of the century have been encountered but we do have some shipping figures. Counts taken from Customs records of vessels arriving in the Grand Harbour of Malta at five-to-ten year intervals show arrivals from Barbary (Regencies of Tunis, Algiers and Tripoli) increasing from 70 in 1801 to 449 in 1848, a near-sevenfold increase, while total arrivals only increased by 70 per cent (Vassallo 2001: 172). Commercial exchanges with Barbary ports were clearly very brisk. A breakdown of arrivals from Barbary in 1848 shows Tunisian ports to have been by far the most important with 246 out of the total of 449, with Malta Register English vessels accounting for half the tonnage followed by Greeks with nearly 20 per cent (ibid.: 177–9).

An 1857 description of the nature of Maltese/Tunisian trade indicates that in the mid-1850s Malta imported grain, olive oil, hides, wool, ivory, cattle, plumes, animal bones, Turkish berets, spices, rags, wax, sponges, dried squid, dates, rope, straw mats, etc. (Dedomenico 1857: 53). It exported or re-exported groceries, worked and leaf tobacco, English and Maltese manufactured goods, raw and manufactured metal, planks and other wood, glassware, paper, wines and spirits and occasionally grain as well.

A more detailed description of the nature of the cargo carried by Maltese *scunne* and *speronare* arriving in Sfax in the middle of the century indicates that, like Maltese brigantines going to Spain and Portugal in the previous century, Maltese merchants arriving in Tunisia apparently carried considerable quantities of cloth, an item which accounted for nearly half the value of the Regency of Tunis's imports (Finotti 1856: 378–86). There was English cloth transhipped into Malta but also Maltese calico commonly known in Tunisia as *Malti* or *Kham.* There were two types; *Kham Soukri,* a finer cloth preferred by Europeans in Tunisia and *Kham Halouffi,* a longer-lasting and stronger material which fetched a better price than the former and was preferred by the Arab population. Stocks of *Malti* were also kept in Tunisia for further shipment to the interior. Other cotton products included muslin, sail cloth, packing cloth and so on. Late in the century, when Malta's trade with Tunisia would seem to have declined considerably, the six million francs worth of exports from the former to the latter still included three million francs worth of cotton cloth (Fallot 1896: 24).

Other goods exported or re-exported from Malta to Tunisia, according to Finotti (1856: 378–86), included rope; anchors and chains; nails, wrought iron and other iron products; furniture; spices and other tropical products such as sugar, coffee, rice and dried fruit; Maltese stone; wine and spirits; potatoes, beans and other agricultural products; alum, rubber, soap and other chemical products; fish and fish extracts; and so on.

Finotti also points out the existence of a not inconsiderable contraband trade in gunpowder and tobacco (ibid.: 378–86). Both were carried by caravan, via Giered, into the interior where the former was exchanged for wax, a prohibited export. Smith (2000: 196–7) has noted that Maltese involvement in contraband was considerable, especially in the smaller ports such as Mahdia, Sfax, Sousse and Djerba. Consular correspondence indicates the presence of Maltese boats and vessels lying for years in most Tunisian ports being used as 'floating Depots for contraband' with the Maltese using the British, Jerusalemite, Tunisian and Turkish flags according to circumstances. While the British dealt severely with those Maltese accused of dealing in arms, gunpowder and military uniforms, they were less concerned with the traffic in substances such as tobacco controlled by state monopolies.

From the above there seems to be no doubt that the Maltese were extremely important intermediaries in North Africa, in both licit and illicit goods. They clearly utilized their ability to communicate with the local population to forge fruitful partnerships but we know very little about the nature of this trade network which seems to have endured for most of the nineteenth century but which declined considerably with the partition of Northern Africa between France and Italy.

During the latter part of the late nineteenth century Malta's role as an entrepôt actually waned considerably. Dependent mostly on defence expenditure and the victualling and coaling of vessels on their way to and from Suez, the Maltese mercantile class became more introspective and remained more or less so until the advent of independence, a process which started in 1964 and ended, with the departure of the last foreign troops, in 1979.

In the post-colonial era Malta has sought to break out of foreign relations and trade ties conditioned by its colonial past and to move toward a wider network of diplomatic and commercial relations. The social democratic Malta Labour Party led by Dom Mintoff and elected to power in 1971 immediately set about trying to complete the process of independence by working toward the closure of the foreign military bases around which much of the tiny island's economy centred. In order to achieve this it embarked on a series of diplomatic initiatives which in less than six months brought no fewer than twenty-one foreign delegations to the island state. Of particular interest for our purposes is the close relationship established with the Socialist People's Libyan Arab Jamahariya. The political and economic cooperation that took place between Libya and Malta during the Mintoff regime is well known. Not so well documented, on the other hand, is the spin-off for entrepreneurs who, particularly during the long years of the UN-imposed embargo, seem to have benefited from preferential access to the Libyan market. Approaches to institutions that would, in principle, have some data on the subject have met with little success. The Maltese-Arab Chamber of Commerce's main function, according to the declaration of one of its officials, is the issue of Certificates of Origin, with particular regard to certifying that the goods are not of Israeli origin. It is difficult to forecast, at this stage, how fruitful our quest for information concerning the Maltese entrepreneurial network in Libya is going to be.

Conclusion

In this chapter I have sought to examine the evolution of a trade diaspora – the Maltese – which shares many of the characteristics of the 'classical' diasporas. Eastern by virtue of their language and living at the margin between the eastern and western Mediterranean, the Maltese were, nevertheless, singularly Western by virtue of their Catholicism. In an age when religion was probably the most important mark of identity, the Maltese were able to access southern Europe in the early modern period with considerably more ease than Jews, Armenians or Greeks.

But the Maltese were different from the 'classical' diasporas in that they also had the benefit of powerful sponsors in the form of the Hospitallers who governed their island and were respected and held in high esteem by the Catholic monarchs of Europe. In an age when much trade was considerably conditioned, if not determined, by peace and commercial treaties, the Maltese were practically given *carte blanche* to trade to their hearts' content in the Italian states, France, Spain and Portugal. In the nineteenth century they built upon long-established contacts in the Maghreb to carve out an intermediary role for themselves under the British flag. In both the early modern and contemporary periods we are still lacking information about the nature of the network in France, Italy and the Maghreb.

As regards the conduct of their affairs we have found that the Maltese were not distinguished by any particular way of doing business. Relative latecomers to the field of international trade, they were content to adopt well-proven strategies and methods centring on kith and kin.

Diaspora entrepreneurial networks, at least as represented by the 'classical' cases, were clearly an attempt by 'outsiders' to participate in the process whereby

Christian Europe overwhelmed the planet between the fifteenth and the nineteenth centuries. In taking stock of the current scholarship and laying the foundations for new directions, as we were encouraged to do by the late Professor Frank Broeze, I feel that we must seek to incorporate into the picture those who up till now have had little or no exposure. This must be done at both the macro and micro levels.

At the macro level we must seek to incorporate the diaspora entrepreneurial networks of other peoples or ethnicities that have not achieved the prominence and durability of Jews, Armenians and Greeks.

At the micro level we must be wary of allowing successful individuals and/or families to hog the limelight. It is perhaps inevitable that these should set the pace but we must not overlook that diaspora entrepreneurial networks are composed mostly of a legion of micro-operators. In the case of trade, these were pedlars, stall operators in markets and small shopkeepers. For every multi-millionaire who set up benefices or foundations to be remembered by, and left copious documentation which can be consulted, there were thousands, nay tens of thousands, who just got by or even went under, eventually ending up buried in some unmarked grave in a corner of some foreign field and for whom we encounter, if we are lucky, only some brief reference in a notarial or other document. To these stories not crowned by success we also have a responsibility.

Notes

1. Though the Rhodian community, established in the early sixteenth century, was eventually assimilated into the general population, Greeks continued to be regular visitors to Maltese shores. There is ample evidence of the increasing presence of Greek shipping in Malta throughout the early modern period but this phenomenon would become particularly important during the final decades of the eighteenth century (Debono 2000: 80–2, 174–84). The advent of the British period saw a resurgence of permanent Greek *and* Jewish communities on the island. In 1829 the Greeks of Malta received two hundred ducats from the Czar in order to build a place of worship. (National Archive of Malta: GOV.02 Despatches from Secretaries of State, Murray to Ponsonby, No. 76, 12 November 1829). Jews already had a 'committee' in 1815 and sought assistance with a site for a new synagogue in 1851 (Davis 1981–82: 158; National Archive of Malta: GOV.02 Despatches from Secretaries of State, Grey to Reid, No. 15, 5 December 1851). A police report recommended against the granting of any aid as it was felt that the members of the 130-strong community enjoyed 'very

easy circumstances' despite the assistance they rendered to 'a great number of poor Jews' who passed through Malta (National Archives of Malta: CSG.01 Vol. 2, No. 178 Police, 22 December 1851).

References

Bono, S. (1990), 'Guerra Corsara e Commercio nel Maghreb Barbaresco (Secoli XVI–XIX)', in G. López Nadal (ed.), *El Comerç Alternatiu: Corsarisme i Contraban (SS XV–XVIII),* Mallorca: Prensa Universitaria.

Boubaker, S. (1987), *La Régence de Tunis au XVIIe siècle: ses relations commerciales avec les ports de l'Europe méditerranéenne, Marseille et Livourne,* Zaghouan: CEROMA.

Braudel, F. (1981), *Civilisation and Capitalism 15th–18th Century,* Vol. I, *The Structures of Everyday Life,* London: Fontana.

—— (1982), *Civilisation and Capitalism 15th–18th Century,* Vol. II, *The Wheels of Commerce,* London: Fontana.

Bresc, H. (1991), 'Sicile, Malte et monde musulman', in V. Mallia-Milanes and S. Fiorini (eds), *Malta: A Case Study in International Cross-Currents,* Malta: Malta University Publications.

Carrière, C. (1973), *Négociants marseillais au XVIIIe siècle,* Marseilles: A. Robert.

Cassar, C. (2000), *Society, Culture and Identity in Early Modern Malta,* Malta: Mireva.

Collado Villalta, P. (1981), 'El impacto americano en la bahía: la inmigración extranjera en Cádiz 1709–1819', in *Primeras Jornadas de Andalucía y América,* Huelva: Instituto de Estudios Onubenses, D.L.

Curtin, P. (1984), *Cross-cultural Trade in World History,* Cambridge: Cambridge University Press.

Cutajar, D. (1988), 'The Malta Quarantine: Shipping and Trade 1654–1694,' in *Mid-Med Bank Limited: Report and Accounts 1987,* Malta.

Davis, D. (1981–82), 'The Jewish cemetery at Kalkara, Malta', *Transactions of the Jewish Historical Society of England,* 28: 145–70.

Debono, J. (2000), *Trade and Port Activity in Malta 1750–1800,* Malta: PEG Ltd.

Dedomenico, M. (1857), *Manuale del commerciante,* Malta: S.G. Vassalli.

Domínguez Ortiz, A. (1955), *La Sociedad española en el siglo XVIII,* Madrid: Consejo Superior de Investigaciones Científicas.

Fallot, E. (1896), *Malte et ses rapports économiques avec la Tunisie,* Tunis: Impr. Rapide.

Finotti, G. (1856), *La Reggenza di Tunisi,* Malta.

Fontaine, L. (1996), *History of Pedlars in Europe,* Cambridge: Polity.

Ganiage, J. (1960), *La population européenne de Tunis au milieu du XIXème siècle: Etude démographique,* Paris: Presses Universitaires de France.

Godechot, J. (1951), 'La France et Malte au XVIIIe siècle', *Revue Historique,* 25, April–June: 67–79.

Guevara Vasconcelos, J. (1787), 'Memoria sobre el recogimiento y ocupación de los pobres formada en informe por una comisión de 16 individuos y extendida por el señor D. Josef de Guevara Vasconcelos, Censor Perpetuo de la Real Sociedad, leida en Junta General de 20 de Marzo de 1778', in A. de Sancho, *Memorias de la Sociedad Económica,* Madrid: Impresor de la Real Sociedad, 3: 42–3.

Lafuente, M. (1887–1890), *Historia general de España desde los tiempos primitivos hasta la muerte de Fernando VII,* Vol. 15, Barcelona: Montaner y Simón.

Mallia-Milanes, V. (1974), 'Some aspects of Veneto-Maltese trade relations in the eighteenth century', *Studi Veneziani,* 16: 503–53.

—— (1993), *Hospitaller Malta 1530–1798,* Malta: Mireva.

Martínez Shaw, C. (1991), 'Del gran comercio al pequeño comercio: El comercio entre Cataluña y Malta, 1808–1823', in C. Martínez Shaw (ed.), *Actas Primer Coloquio Internacional Hispano Maltés de Historia,* Madrid: Ministerio de Asuntos Exteriores.

Mercieca, S. (2000), 'Commerce in Eighteenth-century Malta: The Story of the Prepaud Family', in C. Vassallo (ed.), *Consolati di Mare and Chambers of Commerce,* Malta: Malta University Press.

Messina, C. (1986), *Sicilia e Spagna nel settecento,* Palermo: Società Siciliana per la Storia Patria.

Miège, M. (1841), *Histoire de Malte,* vol. 2, Brussels: Gregoir, Wonters et Co.

Morowska, E. (1990), 'The Sociology and Historiography of Immigration', in V. Yans McLaughlin (ed.), *Immigration Reconsidered: History, Sociology and Politics,* New York and Oxford: Oxford University Press.

Pons, J. and Bibiloni, A. (1991), 'Las relaciones comerciales entre Malta y Mallorca durante la segunda mitad del siglo XVII', in C. Martínez Shaw (ed.), *Actas Primer Coloquio Internacional Hispano Maltés de Historia,* Madrid: Ministerio de Asuntos Exteriores.

Pons Pons, A. (1987), *La Desamortizació i els seus beneficiaries: un procés de canvi de propietat a les comarques centrals dels Pais Valencià (1855–1867),* unpublished Doctoral Thesis, University of Valencia.

Price, C. (1989 [1954]), *Malta and the Maltese: A Study in Nineteenth-century Migration,* Melbourne: Georgian House.

Rodenas, C. (1978), *Banca i Industrialització: El Cas Valencià,* Valencia: Tres i Quatre.

—— (1982), *La Banca Valenciana: Una aproximación histórica*, Valencia: Institució Alfons el Magnanim, D.L.

Salas Ausens, J.A. and Jarque Martínez, E. (1990), 'Extranjeros en España en la segunda mitad del siglo XVIII', in *Coloquio Internacional Carlos III y su Siglo,* Actas Tomo II, Madrid: Universidad Complutense.

Smith, A.L. (2000), 'The Maltese in Tunisia before the Protectorate, 1850s–1870s: Towards a Revised Image', *Journal of Mediterranean Studies,* 10: 183–202.

Vassallo, C. (1996), 'The Consular Network of XVIII Century Malta', in *Proceedings of History Week 1994,* Malta: The Malta History Society.

—— (1997), *Corsairing to Commerce: Maltese Merchants in XVIII Century Spain*, Malta: Malta University Publishers.

—— (1998), *The Malta Chamber of Commerce 1848–1979: An Outline History of Maltese Trade*, Malta: Malta Chamber of Commerce.

—— (2001), 'Trade between Malta and the Barbary Regencies in the Nineteenth Century with Special Reference to Tunisia', in A. Fehri (ed.), *L'Homme et la Mer: Actes du Colloque des 7–8–9 mai 1999 à Kerkennah,* Sfax: Faculté des Lettres et Sciences Humaines de Sfax.

—— (forthcoming), 'From Petty Traders to Big Businessmen: The Saga of the Caruana of Valencia', in *Proceedings of International Conference on Foreign Elites, Minorca, 11–14 September, 1998.*

Von Den Driesch, W. (1972) *Die aüslandischen Kaufleute wahrend des 18. Jahrhunderts in Spanien und ihre Beteiligung am Kolonialhandel,* Cologne and Vienna: Böhlau Verlag.

Part II
Diasporas in Modern Eurasian Trade

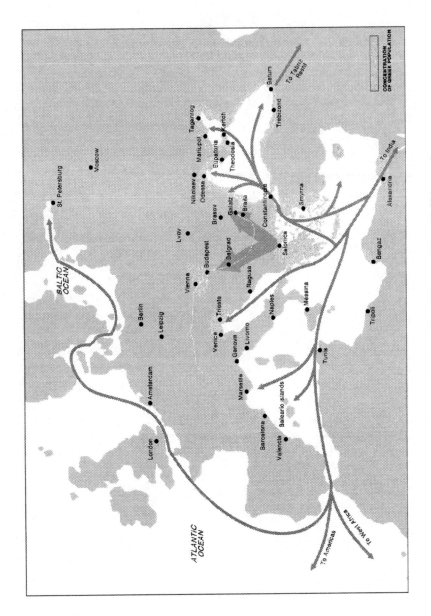

Map 3 Greek maritime entrepreneurial diaspora, 18th–early 20th centuries

Mapping the Greek Maritime Diaspora from the Early Eighteenth to the Late Twentieth Centuries

Gelina Harlaftis

The cartography of the Greek maritime diaspora reveals a wide entrepreneurial network of Greek involvement in international business: Eurasian sea trade in the eighteenth and nineteenth centuries and global sea trade in the twentieth century. To map the Greek maritime diaspora is to follow the routes of ships owned by Greeks. Following Greek ships along international sea routes is to trace Greek merchant and maritime communities in the world's main port cities. In the main port cities of Europe, Africa, Asia and America, a number of Greek entrepreneurial families can be identified: families who followed maritime rather than overland routes, and families who were involved in a triadic form of international business, i.e. trade, shipping and finance. It is obvious that the focus here will be the 'elite' of the Greek diaspora, not the Greek 'proletarian' diaspora – the waves of thousands of Greek immigrants who left the Ionian and Aegean seas from the late nineteenth century to the last third of the twentieth century to the Americas, Australia and western Europe (Clogg 1999: 1–17).

So, this chapter will concentrate on mobile groups of organized Greek entrepreneurial families involved in international sea trade over the last three centuries. It will trace continuity and change by way of the sea, identifying the various phases and analysing the main factors that formed the circumstances under which they functioned within a broader comparative dimension. The first part will handle the issue of the Greek diaspora and its role in the formation of the Greek State; the second part will map the maritime diaspora of Greek entrepreneurs according to different historical periods; and the last section will indicate possible points of comparison with the other historical entrepreneurial diasporas.

Greeks as a Diaspora People

Greeks have always lived in lands of the eastern Mediterranean, on the Greek peninsula and dispersed in what we today call the northern Balkans, Turkey and the Near East. Regular professional groups of travelling merchants (*emporoi*, a word we still use today), have been part of Greek culture and have influenced the whole of the Mediterranean coastline. The starting point here is in the modern period, or what Greek historians have commonly called neo-Hellenic history, the conventional chronology beginning with the fall of Constantinople to the Ottomans in the mid-fifteenth century. This of course coincides with the modern European era, the era of the development of capitalism and the expansion of the Europeans to the rest of the world. Conventionally two main periods are distinguished in order to analyse Greek history, two periods that share common characteristics: the first, long one, covers most of the period of Ottoman rule from the mid-fifteenth century to the early nineteenth century; and the second consisting of the period from 1833 to the present day, which includes the development and existence of the Greek State.

The idea of an independent national state emerged from the 'dark' in the age of Greek Enlightenment, conventionally dated from 1750 to 1830. It is in the merchant diaspora communities on the northern shores of the Black Sea and in the main cities of western Europe that the intellectual and cultural awakening known as the Neohellenic Enlightenment took place (Dimaras 1977; Kitromilidis 1996). Alongside their mercantile transactions with the West, Greek merchants were exposed to and assimilated ideas and mentalities of the European Enlightenment. Regular communication through sea trade with the eastern Mediterranean allowed them to maintain close links with relatives and compatriots, nurturing the growing sense of Greek consciousness. Greeks, whether in Odessa, Tanganrog, Vienna, Bucharest, Trieste, Livorno, Marseilles, Paris, London or Amsterdam cultivated their faith, language and heritage by establishing their own social life in close-knit neighbourhoods, with schools, churches and theatres. All Greek-diaspora merchant communities in Europe, beyond Ottoman lands, became hotbeds of Greek revolutionary ideas. Odessa in particular became the nucleus of a secret society formed by three Greek merchants in 1814, the *Philiki Etaireia* (Society of Friends), that became a vehicle for expanding the idea of armed insurrection and independence. The *Philiki Etaireia*, via conspiratorial methods, attracted recruits from a broad spectrum of diaspora and Ottoman Greeks: merchants, clergy, peasants and influential landowners from southern Russia, the Danubian Principalities, Constantinople, the Greek mainland, and the islands of the Aegean and Ionian seas (Proussis 1994; Vakalopoulos 1975). As a result of the formation of an independent Greek kingdom in 1833, the Greek diaspora issue took on another dimension and now revolved around the relationship between the Greeks 'inside and outside' as Elli Skopetea so simply and vividly put it (1988: 65–85). The new Greek State was an 'incomplete' state, however, extremely small, including half of the Greek peninsula, and only a small portion of the Greek population dispersed around the eastern Mediterranean and in the Balkans. Despite its continuous expansion and the final formation of the boundaries at the end of the Second World War, still, Hellenism *extra muros* – 'the brothers outside' (Skopetea, 1988: 67) – is supposed to encompass an additional 50 per cent over the present population of Greece.

As Constantine Tsoucalas very rightly notes 'except for scholarly discourses, the Greek word "diaspora" is seldom, if ever, referred to in Greece other than in the sense of the recent groups of emigrants in industrialized countries' (Tsoucalas 1997: 297). Greeks have used various words to describe the Greeks 'outside'. The word *homogeneia* has been very commonly used, a word that has no translation in the English language.[1] It means men of the same breed. This notion of the Greek *'genos'* (breed) might be the result of these 'spaceless' linguistic, cultural and religious communities within the Ottoman Empire which formed the Ottoman *millet* system, and this 'imagined community' of *genos* has evolved in the modern notion of nation (Anderson 1983; Gourgouris 1996). In the same way that there was the *genos* of the Greeks (Hellenes), there was the *genos* of the Jews (Hebrews) and the *genos* of the Armenians that co-existed and collaborated within the eastern Mediterranean. The use of the term 'merchant communities settled abroad' is also common among Greek historians when describing the Greek-diaspora merchant communities beyond the traditional territories in the eastern Mediterranean, for example in Southern Russian, Italian, French, English, Dutch or Austro-Hungarian lands, not to mention those in India dating as far back as the eighteenth century. Instead of the word 'community' the ancient word *'paroikia'* is used; *'paroikia'*, untranslatable too, means something like temporary settlement, or *'paroikoi'* meaning the 'sojourners', those in temporary settlement but having in mind to return to the homeland.

The issue of the diasporic nature of Greek people and the boundaries of their 'homeland' has attracted the attention of many a Greek scholar. Although it has been written repeatedly that Greeks form part of the so-called 'classic' diaspora people, it has also been argued that 'Greece is not a diaspora nation', except only for the new emigrant 'diaspora' which acquired significance in the twentieth century and expanded in all continents – in America, Australia, Africa (Tsoucalas 1997: 287–304). So, all the Greeks dispersed within the territory of the Ottoman Empire until the first third of the twentieth century are not considered as 'diaspora', because Greeks have always lived there. Ioannis Hasiotis has written the most comprehensive definition of Greek diaspora along this line of thought: by Greek 'diaspora' he means this part of the Greek people that for various reasons have left the traditional lands of the Greek Orthodox East and have settled, even temporarily, in lands and countries far away but continue to keep close cultural ties with their land of origin (Hasiotis 1989; Hasiotis 1993: 19–20).

But what has been highly interesting is the debate raised in the last thirty years over the issue of the impact of the Greeks 'outside' on the Greeks 'inside'. Traditional national Greek historiography until the 1970s had dealt only with the

Greeks 'inside' and there had been minimal research on the Greeks beyond Greek boundaries. Only since the 1970s has there been a growing interest in diaspora Greeks and their relation to the Greek State. In a seminal article written in 1983, Christos Hadziiossif presents an overview of this discussion of the diaspora Greeks and their relation to the development of the Greek State. He presents central arguments of the so-called new Greek historiography that followed a Marxist approach. Central to this approach is the notion that 'Greek history cannot be understood as the history of the Greek State but as the history of Greek people' (Svoronos 1987: 36). An emphasis was thus given to the importance of the diaspora merchant communities and hence the importance of trade and shipping as the main link between this populace, dispersed around the world, and the small Greek State. The issue was about the effect of diaspora Greeks on the socio-economic evolution of Greece during the nineteenth and twentieth centuries. The debate was closely connected to the appearance of the Dependency School, which emerged in the late 1950s to explain the development of capitalism in backward nations, particularly in Latin America (Hadziiossif 1983: 28, 34; Palma, 1978). Greek-diaspora merchants of the nineteenth century and Greek shipowners of the twentieth century have assumed the role of 'internal' forces that function as 'go-betweens' and sell their compatriots out to the 'external' forces, i.e. the developed capitalist countries. As such, diaspora-Greek entrepreneurs have been described as an 'adulterated bourgeoisie', 'Trojan horses of foreign consortia', 'agents of imperialism', and 'comprador bourgeoisie' (Harlaftis 1993b: 65–6).[2]

The same argumentation has been applied to Jews. The successful Jewish business paradigm did not fit Max Weber's interpretation of the mechanisms of capitalism and he defined the capitalism of the Jews as 'pariah' capitalism in an attempt to analyse the Jewish role in European capitalism (Reid 1997: 35). The simple fact is that these people did not conform to the edifice of national historiographies and their economic activities, beyond borders, have served their own economic survival. Political alliances were made to serve economic interests. As Hadziiossif (1980: 185) indicated in his analysis of Greek merchants in Alexandria,

> it is the common economic origin, the characteristic business strategy and the organization of these commercial houses more than the ethnic origin of the merchants that characterize them as Greek and that distinguish them from their competitors. The citizenship of the merchants is connected with the advantages that it can bring to the commercial house, that is, more or less opportunistic.

The subject of diaspora Greeks and their impact on the formation and development of the Greek State has drawn increasing interest in the last thirty years. Indicative of this trend that encompasses a wider notion of Hellenism, the diaspora Greeks included, is the new multi-volume opus under the title *The History of*

Modern Hellenism, 1770–2000. It is worth noting that thirty years ago the first and most prestigious multi-volume opus, published under the title *The History of the Greek Nation* (*Istoria tou Ellinikou Ethnous*, 1975), did not consider the effect of Greek diaspora on the Greek state. So, Greek-diaspora activities are now regarded as part of Greek historiography and are analysed through the theories of commercial and family networks, as Olga Katsiardi-Hering very lucidly points out in her most recent work (Katsiardi-Hering 2003b: 88). Movements of internationally oriented groups of merchant families are no longer interpreted only through the Marxist approach of 'the exploitation of foreign powers' or 'centre-periphery' dependency theories. During the eighteenth and nineteenth centuries, Greek mobility and the formation of Greek merchant communities beyond the Ottoman State, or Greek State boundaries, were the result of a mobility organized within family and commercial networks, with profit as the sole purpose for their movements, and much less due to an organized, massive immigration instigated by 'push and pull' factors. (Katsiardi 2003b: 87–112).

The Maritime Diaspora

We can distinguish three phases of the Greek maritime diaspora. The first one covers the period from the beginning of the eighteenth century to the formation of the Greek State in 1833. The second one covers the period from 1833 to the First World War. The third period includes the inter-war era and the second half of the twentieth century. Archival research in Greek maritime history has mapped the routes of tens of thousands of ships from the early eighteenth century to the late twentieth century, and has analysed the cargoes these ships carried, the international trade in which they were involved, the seamen who manned the ships, the local island communities from which they came, the shipowners and merchants who owned the ships, the communities in which they lived (dispersed in the main port cities of the Mediterranean and northern Europe, the ports where these ships were registered), the formation of their extensive commercial networks and their organization and strategies (Harlaftis 1990, 1993a, 1993b, 1996; Harlaftis and Vlassopulos 2002; Harlaftis et al. 2003; Theotokas and Harlaftis 2004).[2]

Although Greek merchants and seafarers have been active in the European seas since the early modern period (see Fusaro in Chapter 5 of this volume), it was in the eighteenth century that they experienced an impressive growth in sea and land trade; their activities formed an organic part of the Ottoman Empire and, more particularly, of the eastern Mediterranean, or what Westerners have called the Levant (Inalcik and Quataert 1992; Kremmydas 1985; Svoronos 1956). The expansion of organized groups of trade and shipping families to western Mediterranean and northern European ports, and the formation of entrepreneurial networks extended to all main ports of the Mediterranean and northern Europe, began from the areas of the Ottoman Empire at the beginning of the eighteenth century. It witnessed an impressive growth with the opening of Black Sea navigation and the Black Sea grain trade, and the consolidation of the Greeks as the main sea traders of the area came about as the result of the fierce competition of Europe's Great Powers for control of the decaying Ottoman Empire.

Initially it was in the Adriatic, and in direct connection with the decadence of the Venetian merchant fleet, that Greek merchants and shipowners from the Ionian Islands were carrying the cargoes to and from the port cities of the Italian peninsula (Katsiardi 1987). The first period of Greek maritime diaspora during the modern era really starts from the Treaty of Utrecht in 1713, in the West, followed by the Treaty of Passarowitz in 1718, in the East, both of which marked a new era in the Mediterranean. During this period the Venetians and Austrians hired Greek traders and shipowners as privateers under their flags to compete with rival shipping nations; existing archival evidence indicates the importance of the Greeks in sea trade during this period. Throughout the eighteenth century, Austrians and Russians were able to conquer Ottoman lands and secure the gateways to the Mediterranean, establishing two new big ports, Trieste in the Adriatic and Odessa in the Black Sea, whereas the English competing with the French, advancing by sea, vied for supremacy in the Mediterranean sea trade. This eastward expansion and the competition of the Great Powers came to be to a great advantage to the entrepreneurial families involved in the export sea trade of the Ottoman lands.

The British overseas colonial trading system seems to have accorded the Greeks an integral role in its inner mechanisms from the early eighteenth century, a role that expanded and was consolidated in the first third of the nineteenth century. The War of Spanish Succession, which marked the end of any further claim of the Spanish for power in Europe and ended with the Treaty of Utrecht, gave the British their first colonial acquisitions in the Mediterranean: Gibraltar and Minorca. In their attempt to promote the establishment of non-Catholic, non-Spanish seafaring communities on the island, the British supported the establishment of a Greek community on the island of Minorca (Hasiotis 1994; Svoronos 1956) They offered incentives: land for cultivation, saltpans, religious freedom and the right to build their own Orthodox church. What is more, they gave them the right to use the British flag, as well as their own, the 'Mahonian' flag – an equivalent of what was to be called a 'flag of convenience' in the second half of the twentieth century. Under these conditions a large number of Greek families had settled by the 1730s in Port Mahon on Minorca. These were all highly experienced seafaring people from places with long traditions in sea commerce and commerce-raiding of the seas and who maintained close links with their compatriots and relatives in the Levant. They built a sizeable fleet, with which they carried trade between the West and the East. This fleet, under the jurisdiction of the British, connected Port Mahon and Livorno, the main emporeion of the British in the Mediterranean, and thus controlled part of the sea traffic between the western and eastern Mediterranean (Harlaftis 2001: 68–9).

Moreover, the conquests of the Ottoman lands by the Habsburg and Russian Empires were followed by policies that ultimately favoured Greek traders. Both countries needed to expand their commercial and maritime activities and consolidate their influence in the Ottoman lands. At the beginning of the century, the Austrians conquered half of Serbia and part of Wallachia, resulting in the Treaty of Passarowitz in 1718 which secured a century-long peace in south-eastern Europe, during which time trade and navigation thrived. One of the main consequences of the Austrian victory was their access to the Mediterranean and the formation of the port of Trieste as a *porto franco* in which political, economic and religious freedom was guaranteed. Special concessions were provided to Greek immigrants, who were among the best-known merchants and shipowners in the Levant (Katsiardi-Hering 1986: 27–32). The formation of a thriving Greek community in Trieste ensured Austrian prosperity, as well as close economic relations with the prospering Greek trading communities in Smyrna, Constantinople and Alexandria. The expansion of maritime trade was also fed by the increase in importance of the land routes of the Balkan Peninsula (Chatziioannou, Chapter 17 of this volume; Stoianovich 1960).

Russians also used Greek traders and seafarers in the Russo-Turkish wars of the second half of the eighteenth century. What Peter the Great was not able to achieve in the beginning of the eighteenth century, i.e. establish the Russian borders on the Black Sea, was achieved by Catherine the Great after the Russian victory in the Russo-Turkish War of the 1770s. The treaty of Kutchuk-Kainardji (1774), its Explanatory Convention (1779), and the Treaty of Commerce (1783) not only established Russian dominance on the northern coast of the Black Sea but also secured a long-desired direct sea route to southern and western Europe. The Black Sea, which was viewed by the Ottomans as a *mare nostrum* and restricted navigation to Turkish subjects, was opened to Russian subjects and ships flying the Russian flag. Another fifty years were needed, however, to secure the right of free navigation for ships of all nations. The Russo-Turkish War of 1828–29 ended with another Russian victory, codified in the Treaty of Adrianople, which provided Russia absolute freedom of trade in the Ottoman dominions and guaranteed all peaceful nations complete freedom of navigation.

The first concern of the Russians was to establish a large port in the area, and thus Odessa was founded in 1792. However, this vast new area, the New Russia (Novorrossia), was almost totally unpopulated and the fertile soil uncultivated. Colonization schemes were put into effect to attract immigrants, using land, agricultural equipment and even building materials as inducements. In addition to encouraging native Russians to move to the new territories, new settlers were attracted from the Aegean archipelago and other parts of the Ottoman Empire.

Gelina Harlaftis

The encouragement of Greek settlements in southern Russia coincided with the establishment of a Russian protectorate over the Ionian Islands. As a result, a great number of Greeks migrated to southern Russia from the Aegean and Ionian Islands. The Greek revolt in the 1770s (which was supported by the Russians), the eventual Russo-Turkish war, the Greek war of independence (1821–29) and the second Russo-Turkish war (1878–79) stimulated continuous waves of Greek immigrants, not only to southern Russia but also to that part of Rumania under Russian protection, into the ports along the Danube. The economic prosperity of the Black Sea ports encouraged immigration that lasted until the end of the nineteenth century. In this way members of shipowning families from the Ionian and Aegean islands were established in all Blacks Sea ports.

However, despite the Austrian, Russian and British penetration, France's primacy in the eastern Mediterranean before the French Revolution was still indisputable; in 1784 the French carried 36 per cent of the Ottoman external trade, the Austrians 25 per cent, the Dutch 18 per cent, the Venetians 12 per cent and the British just 9 per cent (Inalcik and Quataert 1992: 699). Apart from external trade, the French carried most of the internal Ottoman sea trade in convoys. The Ottoman merchants preferred French ships because they considered them safer and more reliable, in addition to the fact that, unlike Maltese ships, they were not attacked by Christian corsairs. The Greeks, also involved in the intra-Ottoman sea trade of the eastern Mediterranean, expanded gradually to the western Mediterranean and the Black Sea. But the big leap forward took place after the 1790s and during the first couple of decades of the nineteenth century. The wars following the French Revolution, from the 1790s until the 1810s, ousted once and for all the fleets of Venice, Malta and France from the sea of the Levant. The neutrality of the Ottoman flag until the conquest of Egypt gave a great impetus to the development of the Greek island fleets, which were involved in carrying the trade of the Levant from north to south, from Odessa to Alexandria, from east to west and from Smyrna to Cadiz. Within less than thirty years, the Greek-owned fleet doubled its size: from 400 ships in 1786 to more than 800 ships in 1813 (Harlaftis 2001: 78–9). The story of the Greek fleet during the French wars from 1790 to 1815 was written by grain. Greek merchant-shipowners were carrying – in fact smuggling through the British naval lines – grain from the expanding markets of the Black Sea to the French, along the long coastline from Venice to Cadiz (Kremmydas 1985). The data we have are located in the archives of Trieste, Livorno, Firenze, Malta, Marseilles, Venice, Corfu and Hydra. During this period, Greek shipowners expanded their maritime network to all Mediterranean ports on the Asian, African and European shores.

During the war of Greek Independence (1821–29), a new wave of prosperous Greek merchant families from Smyrna, Chios and Constantinople who were involved in Ottoman export trade, moved westward and established themselves

–154–

in Trieste, Livorno, Marseilles, Amsterdam and London – the cities where they already had family connections and business arrangements. It is evident that during the eighteenth century a number of Greek trading and shipping families became the ethnic group in the Mediterranean who developed as 'independent' sea carriers of the Western European powers, and were able to serve a significant portion of the Mediterranean trade from the Levant to the west.

The second phase of the maritime diaspora covers the period from 1830 to the First World War. The dispersal of Greek merchants and shipowners among the main Mediterranean and Black Sea ports meant the creation of prosperous Greek communities in all the main port cities, not only in the Mediterranean but also in northern Europe. In this way, a tight commercial web, which had started in the Ottoman Empire, by the 1830s had assumed a wider Eurasian character. During this period, and until the First World War, sea trade was increasingly characterized by a small number of bulk commodities in all the world's oceans and seas. Grain, cotton and coal were the main bulk cargoes that filled the holds of the world fleet. At the same time, the transition from sail to steam, apart from increasing the availability of cargo space at sea, caused a revolutionary decline in freight rates. Bulk sea trade increased the importance of the Mediterranean Sea, placing it next to that of the Atlantic Ocean (Harlaftis and Kardasis 2000). The Black Sea was the most important granary of Europe during most of the nineteenth century, and Alexandria an important source of cotton. During the nineteenth century Greeks became the main carriers of Black Sea grain to the industrializing western Europe. The main strength of Greek shipowners, who during the sailing-ship era were still established in the Ionian and Aegean islands, were the networks of Greek diaspora merchant communities that stretched across the Mediterranean and northern Europe, networks that eventually opened the way to the worldwide expansion of the Greeks in all the oceans in the twentieth century.

The archival material has led to the distinction of two phases of the Greek commercial and maritime networks in the nineteenth century, in a rather 'cubistic' approach: the 'Chiot phase' and the 'Ionian phase' (Harlaftis 1993b; Harlaftis 1996: chapters 2 and 3). The merchant/shipowners from the island of Chios who prospered between the 1830s and the 1860s founded the Chiot network, only to be succeeded by the shipowner/merchants from the Ionian Islands, who formed the Ionian network from the 1870s to the beginning of the twentieth century. The Ionians successfully made the transition from the combined profession of merchanting and shipowning, to the specialized profession of shipowning that characterized Greek entrepreneurial diaspora activities in the twentieth century.

The Chiot network was formed by members of about sixty Greek families. Although almost half were not from the island of Chios, most were either related to the Chiots by marriage, or started their careers in Chiot offices and had their support. Nonetheless, the Chiot families were the largest and richest. The trade involved mainly bulk cargoes, such as grain, wool, cotton, linseed and tallow, from the East and manufactured goods, especially thread and textiles, from the West. The main nodes of the network were England and the Black Sea, with a chain of branch offices throughout the Mediterranean: in Marseilles, Livorno and Trieste; in the cotton markets of Alexandria and Cairo; in the maritime centre of the Aegean archipelago, Syra; and in the two financial markets of the eastern Mediterranean, Constantinople and Smyrna. Vital to the network's success was its ability to penetrate not only the main markets of the recipient western European countries, particularly England, but also the difficult and unexploited hinterland of the Black Sea.

The Rallis were the largest and most influential family within the Chiot network. The Ralli Brothers were the most senior, the wealthiest, and the most imperious of the Greek houses. Its founder and *pater familias* was Sir Pandia, who was also considered the titular head of the Greek community in London. For every occasion, the rest waited for the pronouncement of 'Zeus' so they could follow his example. There were sixty-six members (siblings and first and second cousins) of the Ralli family active during this period who married within the twenty-four families. The Rodocanachis, the most important family in the Black Sea ports, were the second most numerous, followed by Schilizzi, Scaramanga, Negroponte and Sevastopoulo. The other non-Chiot families in the network worked the same way. Imitation and internal competition were two of the first rules of network.

The typical structure of a Greek merchant house in some ways resembled that of a modern multinational firm. One office fulfilled the function of a mother company while the others acted as branches. The partners divided the direction of the various divisions while the role of the central house, which determined the 'nationality' of the firm, was given to the most capable. All directors appeared equal to third parties and all had signing authority. A variant occurred when the branches were legally independent but shared profits. But in either, the multinational character of these companies often created legal complications. Yet this multinationality and complexity have served as the bases in the twentieth century from which Greek shipping companies have avoided taxes in all countries. At a time when the post was the only means of communication, family control was a prime characteristic of the network. Kinship and common place of origin implied trust and facilitated entrance into the 'club'. Even more than with other Greeks, the power of the Chiot families derived from the discipline dictated by the hierarchy and cohesion of the family. Intermarriage was extensive as each family sought to mix with equals, and because the circles were so limited, competition for appropriate matches began early. Intermarriage made the family even more powerful.

It will be useful to have a more detailed account of the operations of a Chiot firm to see how the Greeks functioned. We shall examine here the network of the Ralli firm based in England. The House of the Ralli brothers was probably established during the first decade of the nineteenth century (Vourkatioti: 2004). In 1814 we have the first archival evidence where the branch of Zannis Rallis and Co. in Malta appears and is seen keeping other branch offices or close contacts with Smyrna, Constantinople, Trieste, Venice and Messina. In 1817 they established a branch office in Livorno and in 1818, John (Zannis) and Stratis Ralli went to London, while their brother Augustis was already established in Marseilles. In 1823 the firm of Ralli and Petrocochino was founded and in 1824 the other younger brother, Pandia, joined the others in London, and in 1826 Ralli Brothers was established. Pandia, the main 'brain' of the firm, remained in London, Stratis went to Manchester, John to Odessa in 1827 and Tomazis to Constantinople. The various branches of the firm as they were consolidated in the mid-nineteenth century were: Ralli Brothers in London; E. Ralli in Manchester; St. P. Schilizzi and Co. in Liverpool; Ralli, Schilizzi and Argenti in Marseilles; Tomazi Ralli and Co. in Constantinople and Trebizond until the early 1850s and thereafter replaced by St. P. Schilizzi and Co.; Ralli Brothers in Odessa; Ralli and Scaramanga in Taganrog; St. Scaramanga in Rostov-on-Don; Ralli and Agelasto in Tauris; Petros Pandia Ralli in Resht (Iran). The Rallis covered the main Mediterranean ports, while in those where they did not have branches they had connections via other relatives. They were thus always consignors and consignees.

Ralli Brothers widened their commercial horizons and successfully entered the cotton trade from Calcutta, Bombay and New York where they opened branch offices in 1851, 1861 and 1871, respectively. The death of John Ralli in the late 1850s and of Pandia in 1863 led to the total reorganization of the firm. The Levant trade was abandoned by closing down the branches in Trebizond, Constantinople, Resht and Tauris, while the Russian grain trade was handed over to the Scaramanga family. The new man in charge, Stephen Ralli, turned instead to the much more lucrative and open East Asian and American trades. Eventually, the firm let its activities in the American continent diminish, and in the twentieth century it expanded to Africa while it kept its activities in East Asia and particularly in India and Pakistan where it continued trading up to the early 1960s when the firm closed down. Thus we can see that the Greek firm of Ralli Brothers was an international trading house that operated for almost 150 years, with interests extending from New York to Russia, India and Japan, and a commercial bank in the City of London (Harlaftis 1996; Vourkatioti 2004).

By the 1870s the dwindling of the Chiot network in the trade of the Black Sea and the Levant and its replacement by Ionian shipowners and merchants was evident. The archival material presents us with new names, new shipowners and new merchants, the largest number of whom came from the Ionian Islands. The Ionian network lasted from the 1870s to the beginning of the 1900s and covered the transition from a combined profession to specialization. By the beginning of the twentieth century the final exodus from commercial activities and a specialization in shipowning was manifest. The most successful Greek shipowning families of the early twentieth century were directly linked with the Ionian network.

The Ionian network was concentrated in the Black Sea ports and Constantinople and it extended to Marseilles and London. It comprised about 140 families, half of which were Ionian. Although Greeks from other islands and areas were part of the network (as was the case with the Chiots), we call it Ionian since it was mainly Ionian families – and more specifically Cephalonians and Ithacans – that were the most powerful members. The majority of the families were based in the Danubian ports of Braila, Galatz and Sulina and were involved in shipowning and commercial companies as well as shipping agencies. Besides the Danube, the Ionian network was also strong in the cities of southern Russia (Nicolaieff and Odessa), in the ports of the Sea of Azov (Taganrog, Rostov-on-Don, Berdiansk, Yeisk and Kertch) and in the Caucasus ports (Novorossisk and Batum). Members of the Ionian network were established in the largest economic centre of the eastern Mediterranean – Constantinople. In western Europe, the branch offices of twenty-seven families were concentrated in Marseilles and thirty-six in London. As was the case with the Chiots, the Ionians devised a common business strategy and an organizational structure along the same principles of the Chiots.

The Vagliano Brothers was the family firm that succeeded the Ralli Brothers in the leadership of the Greek entrepreneurial network between the Levant and western Europe in the last third of the nineteenth century (Harlaftis 1996: 92–3). Possibly no other Greek family combined all three aspects of business – trade, shipping and finance – to such an extent. The eldest brother, Maris Vagliano, left his native Cephalonia in the early 1820s as a seaman on an Ionian sailing ship, and disembarked at Taganrog in the Sea of Azov, where he settled himself for life and was fully engaged in exporting grain. He was joined shortly after by his brothers Andreas and Panaghis. The Vagliano were the owners of more than twenty sailing vessels before the 1860s and are known to have exploited the Crimean War to enhance their business by illegally transporting grain exports from the Azov to Constantinople, thereby earning exorbitant profits. In the 1850s Panaghis Vagliano was sent to England and Andreas to Marseilles. Panaghis in London in the 1860s went a step further than his contemporaries, establishing the first Greek shipping office in London. This office, which served as a model for other Greek shipping offices in London in the twentieth century, was for forty years the main link between Greek shipping and the London maritime market. Throughout their entrepreneurial lives the Vagliano family owned and operated the largest Greek-owned fleet. From 1870 to 1905, the Vagliano family continually possessed between thirteen and twenty-one vessels, accounting for more than 10 per cent of the Greek-owned fleet each year.

What has not been known in the literature until recently is the fact that the Vagliano were also known in the City of London as merchant bankers. It seems that the Vagliano office carried out the usual business of international merchants and functioned as an accepting house/merchant bank for their compatriots in the Levant (Chatziioannou and Harlaftis 2002). In London, as the sources reveal, the Vagliano family kept accounts with the Bank of England for many years. Their transactions assumed great proportions for a sustained period of time, according to *The Banker's Magazine* reports. In 1886, for example, 4,000 payments were made by the Bank of England on Vagliano accounts, with a value of £3,500,000 in this one year. Through a court case, 'The Vagliano case', are presented extraordinary transaction details which reveal from inside the way Greek and non-Greek merchant bankers operated. It seems that after they lost their case in the House of Lords, and were excluded by the Bank of England, the Vagliano family concentrated their activities in shipping. The 1890s were the period of the transition from sail to steam, and the Vagliano family pioneered in private shipping finance: they granted loans at 7–8 per cent interest for the purchase of steamships if the borrower provided half the necessary amount in cash and put up the ship as collateral. Some of the largest twentieth-century Greek shipowning dynasties were financed by the Vagliano brothers, who have been repeatedly described as the 'patrons' of Greek steam shipping.

At the turn of the twentieth century most of the diaspora merchant houses were transformed into shipping companies that competed in the international shipping markets. By concentrating their activities to the axis Piraeus/London, they expanded into activities beyond European waters and entered into the Atlantic sea routes in the inter-war period and to global sea routes in the post-Second World War period. After the Second World War Greek-owned shipping offices were established in almost all the main ports of Europe, North and South America, Southeast Asia, South Africa and Australia. In the first two post-war decades, London and New York were home to the largest number of offices, followed by Piraeus. The adoption of flags of convenience (cheap flags of developing countries), the rapid increase of tankers and the close relations of Greek shipowners to the US in the immediate post-war era made the American city the second most important operating centre after London (Harlaftis 1993b: 41–5, 52–7). From the mid-1960s onward, Piraeus started slowly but steadily to resume its pre-war importance as the main operational centre of the Greek-owned fleet; from 18 per cent in 1958, the tonnage operated from Piraeus rose to 34 per cent in 1975 and more than 70 per cent by 2000. Thus, the phenomenon of Greek shipowners is in reality a twentieth-century trade diaspora 'par excellence', a prime example of the 'new age' of old diasporas which is characterized by great mobility and cosmopolitanism.

As in the previous centuries, the structure of Greek-owned shipping firms has been heavily based on family and common-island ties. The management, as well as all the branch offices, was in the hands of members of the same family or co-islanders. The main sources of shipowners from the 1910s to the 1960s were the Aegean islands and particularly Andros, Chios and Kassos, and the Ionian Islands of Cephalonia and Ithaca. The shipowning groups of 1910 represented the structures of the nineteenth century; a large number of Ionian grain merchants (Stathatos, Svorono, Vagliano, Dracoulis and Lykiardopoulos, from the islands of Cephalonia and Ithaca), established in the Black Sea in the last third of the nineteenth century, formed the most powerful shipowning groups of the early twentieth century. For the next fifty years, from the 1920s to the 1970s, the same shipowning groups belonging to traditional shipowning families from the Aegean and the Ionian Islands feature in the top ten: Kulukundis, Goulandris, Livanos, Lemos, Chandris, Nomikos, Embiricos and Lykiardopoulos. The only two notorious newcomers to the business, in the late 1930s, and known world-wide, were of course Aristotle Onassis and Stavros Niarchos. And even these two had to enter the traditional circles: they both married the daughters of Stavros Livanos, a powerful shipowner from the island of Chios. There were about one hundred families from the Aegean and Ionian Islands, a large proportion of whom came from sailing-ship owners in the nineteenth century, who were the main shipowning families of the Greek-owned fleet until the last third of the twentieth century, when they were replaced, and enhanced, by the entrance of new Greek shipowners, mostly ex-officers or employees of shipping companies (Theotokas and Harlaftis 2004a; Harlaftis and Theotokas 2004).

Despite the fact that these cosmopolitan entrepreneurs have always retained some part of their activities in Greece, in reality they have made international alliances according to their economic interests. Indicative of this is their exploitation of various political crises and a disregard of the state policies of European nations and the Unites States. Greek-diaspora merchants and shipowners, for example, have developed a certain 'tradition' of ignoring blockades, a practice continued to the present day, and one which significantly contributed to the increase of their business. Early in the nineteenth century, they broke the French blockade during the Napoleonic wars; this led to an important increase in the fleets of some of the Aegean islands like Hydra and Spetses. In the mid-nineteenth century, the Vagliano brothers made their fortune by exporting grain from Russia during the Crimean War, despite the blockade by the Great Powers. In the Russo-Turkish war of 1877–78, similar actions were repeated. The British consul in Odessa in 1877 reported that 'loading of five Greek vessels and their safe arrival at Constantinople was freely commented upon and severely criticized by the Russian press. It was even rumoured that the wheat was destined for the Turkish troops in Bulgaria'. During the First World War, when Greece was neutral until 1917, Greek shipowners sold 30 per cent of their pre-war tonnage to foreigners, many of whom were Germans, at very high prices. Greek shipowners transported weapons and other materials during the Spanish Civil War in the 1930s for both sides. During the Korean War the leading shipowner, Stavros Livanos, was accused by the Americans of carrying cargoes for both South and North Korea. When China was embargoed by the Americans during the 1950s, Greek ships continued to carry its trade; China became one of the main charterers of Greek dry-cargo ships throughout the 1960s. When Cuba was embargoed by the US at the beginning of the 1960s, Greeks invented the Cypriot flag under which to carry sugar between Cuba and the USSR. They did the same during the Vietnam War in the late 1960s. Vardinoyannis, a leading shipowner of the last thirty years, started his successful career by breaking the British blockade of Rhodesia in 1965. Hadjiioannou, the greatest shipowner of the past decade, profited enormously in the Iran-Iraq war at the beginning of the 1980s (Harlaftis 1996: 278–9). Greek maritime diaspora business transcended both borders and political alliances.

The Comparative Perspective

International business has always implied cultural minorities and the European 'miracle' would never have taken place without entrepreneurial minorities (Reid 1997: 33). It is now a common knowledge that the European maritime trade since the age of European expansion was linked with the establishment of foreign merchants of 'Levantine origin' such as the Jews, the Armenians and the Greeks, in big ports such as Antwerp, Amsterdam, London, Seville, Marseilles, Livorno, Venice or Trieste, where the terms 'merchant community' and 'community of foreign merchants' were synonymous (Mauro 1990: 285). Greeks, Jews and Armenians co-existed under Ottoman rule, and undertook the foreign trade of the Ottoman Empire from the sixteenth century, when the Ottoman Porte placed restrictions on European traders (Israel 2002: 3). The Armenians were extremely important in the Safavid Empire from the sixteenth to the eighteenth centuries as Ina Baghdiantz McCabe in Chapter 2 of this volume indicates, and in the trade of the Indian Peninsula in the eighteenth century as Sushil Chaudhury reveals in Chapter 3, whereas Baghdadi Jews were highly involved in the trade between Chinese, Indian and Arab ports in the nineteenth century as Chiara Betta indicates in Chapter 12.

It is evident that in all three diasporas, there were organized groups of merchants and shipowners involved in Eurasian trade with affluent communities from the Far East to all Western trading capitals, and their relation to the political establishment of their host countries was highly important to their economic strength. As Jonathan Israel clearly indicates, the Sephardic Jews that moved eastward from the Iberian peninsula in the sixteenth century and were established in the main port cities of the Adriatic (mostly in the islands of the Ionian sea and particularly Corfu and Zante), and in the main port cities of the Ottoman Empire (namely Constantinople, Salonica and Smyrna, but the Aegean islands as well), became closely connected to the Sultan (Israel 1989: 45–9; Israel 2002: 4–15; Israel, in Chapter 1 of this volume). On the other hand, Jews were established and consolidated as a cohesive cultural group in the main European cities, notably in Prague, Frankfurt, Hamburg, Amsterdam, Mantua, Venice and Livorno in the seventeenth century, the century of peak prosperity for European Jewry. Jews became the most important entrepreneurial minority in the European Courts with a wide involvement in statecraft, state finance and large-scale military supplies, a central feature of Jewish activity to the mid-eighteenth century (Israel 1989: 87–9, 109).

Since the seventeenth century, Greeks dispersed away from the Greek main-land, in the Balkans and Asia Minor, also found access to the Ottoman State mechanisms. A particular group, the so-called Phanariot Greeks who lived in the part of Constantinople where the Greek Patriarchate was established, because of their knowledge of European and Eastern languages were used as dragomans by the Porte dealing with all the transactions of the Ottomans with the Westerners. The Phanariots became necessary in the Ottoman administration, taking the posts of 'Dragoman of the Porte' since 1661, and 'Dragoman of the fleet' since 1701; moreover, between 1709 and the War of Greek Independence, Greeks became the rulers, or *hospodars*, of the Danubian Principalities.

Of equal interest is the case of the Armenians in the Safavid Empire who played a prominent role in the Eurasian silk trade from the sixteenth to the eighteenth centuries (Baghdiantz McCabe 1999). This trade, that until recently was believed to have been under European control in the seventeenth and eighteenth centuries, was almost entirely in the hands of an organized group of extremely rich Armenian merchants established in New Julfa, and expanded from the Far East to western Europe via land and sea routes. Armenians, through land routes via the Ottoman Empire, reached the Mediterranean and chartered ships for the goods to be taken to Venice, Livorno or Marseilles. Over the Russian land route, or via the Volga, the silk cargoes reached the Baltic and eventually Amsterdam. Through the maritime route from the Indian peninsula and the Persian Gulf, Armenian silk cargoes reached western European ports via the Cape of Good Hope. What is even more interesting was the importance of this group of merchants in the Safavid Court. Armenians became the main financiers of the Iranian Shahs, providers of silver for the exchange of silk. They were highly involved in the state mechanism of the Safavid Empire and were the main administrators of the Safavid Court in charge of the finances of the Court and the Royal Mint (Baghdiantz McCabe 1999: 141–3). Their vast entrepreneurial network and their economic strength and connections with the West gave them a prominent political role.

It is not surprising then, that the role of Greeks, Jews and Armenians continued to be highly important in the external trade of the Ottoman Empire in the eighteenth century. These cosmopolitan entrepreneurs, established in the main trading cities of southern Asia and the eastern Mediterranean, were in direct contact with the international financial and trading networks of the Jews, Armenians and Greeks in western Europe. All three had established large merchant communities in western Europe, keeping strong links with each other as cohesive cultural groups. They participated in an extensive financial network from Venice, Livorno and Genoa to Vienna and Amsterdam (Inalcik and Quataert 1992: 729). Western merchants, in order to form local networks of penetration in the markets of Anatolia, used Ottoman subjects, namely Greeks, Jews and Armenians, in the sales and purchases of cargoes of cotton, silk or grain. In 1768, for example, three-quarters of all cargoes loaded from Smyrna to Amsterdam belonged to the merchants of these three *millets*. In 1730, the Dutch had already given to the Greek, Jewish and Armenian merchants established in Smyrna (the main Ottoman export port) the same rights and advantages as their own subjects (Inalcik and Quataert, 1992: 702–3).

By the mid-nineteenth century, Greeks might not have been involved in high administrative posts of the Ottoman State, but under the now new and different circumstances, they formed part of the top bourgeoisie in the main Ottoman cities and were among the chief bankers of Constantinople, lending to the Ottoman State along with the Armenians and Jews (Exertzoglou 1986; Pamuk 1987). The activities of the Greeks went hand in hand with those of the Jews and Armenians within and outside the Ottoman Empire. According to the testimony of one of Constantinople's foremost Greek bankers, Andreas Syngros, the Jew Isaac Camondo and the Armenian Antonio Pirianz were among the top bankers of his time (Syngros 1998 [1908]: vol. 2, 15–16, 19–20, 64, 157, 178, 163–4, 196). Jews and Armenians were also involved, at least since the eighteenth century, in the administration of the finances of the Ottoman State. Particularly, they served the finances of the Ottoman State as customs officials in addition to their activities in the internal and external trading and financial networks dealing with trade and lending. The Armenians, traditionally placed in eastern Anatolia and Syria, were deeply involved in Ottoman public life by the nineteenth century (Krikorian 1977). Aside from their involvement in trade and customs, they traditionally were active in the mint, and industry of the Ottoman Empire.

There are hundreds of parallel cases from the nineteenth century. In the 1800s, for example, the Chiot Geroussis house from Smyrna was entering the consolidated East-West network by opening branch offices in Trieste and later in London; at the same time the Alhadeff family, a Jewish family from Rhodes, founded their house in the 1810s and became among the most important merchant and banking houses of the eastern Mediterranean with branch offices in Smyrna, Mersina, Athens and Milan: a leader among a network of another dozen Jewish families from the same area (Chatziioannou 2003; Efthimiou 1992).

At exactly the same time as the five Jewish brothers, the Rothschilds, were starting their activities from the ghetto in Frankfurt and soon expanding to Vienna, Paris and London, the five Greek brothers, the Rallis, established their own firm starting from their island Chios expanding from Smyrna and Constantinople to Malta, Livorno and London. It was at about the same time that the Armenian brothers, the Toumantiantz, started from Baku on the Caspian Sea expanding to Odessa, Moscow, Vienna and Paris, and the five Chinese brothers, the Chen from Qianxi village in South China, expanded to Hong Kong, Bangkok, Singapore and Saigon. All clung to their family character and were involved in trade and shipping, and turned to merchant banking.

The Jewish Rothschilds were referred to as 'an authentic multinational, with a business empire which expanded during the 1850s as far afield as the new goldfields of California and Australia' (Ferguson 1999: 89). And if the Rothschild brothers might seem to us an exception and a famous case, they were in fact the leading family in a large network formed by a number of Jewish family firms in banking between 1850 and the inter-war period in Europe. As in the case of the Greek commercial and maritime firms, the organization of the Jewish banking houses in the nineteenth and early twentieth centuries was based on extended families with international financial networks, using agents and correspondents between their diaspora communities in various European cities. Intermarriage was used as an important strategy in keeping the business together and the heirs were selected and educated carefully among this international family business elite, at the heart of which lay personal contacts and trust (Schijf, Chapter 9 of this volume). A striking example is that of the Dutch Jewry based in Amsterdam, whose traditional role had been that of importing and processing colonial goods, and re-exporting them to Europe, along with trade in precious metal and precious stones. And of course we have the example of the Jewish bankers in Amsterdam with their far-reaching contacts in Frankfurt, Vienna, Antwerp, Brussels, Paris and London.

The Greek Rallis, as mentioned earlier, were a multinational family trading company with interests extending from New York to Russia, India and Japan, with investments in all parts of their activities and a commercial bank in the City of London. In particular the London-based Ralli Bros attained great wealth. In 1860 it was among the largest companies in the City with an estimated wealth of over one million Pounds Sterling at a time when the wealth of Baring Bros was placed at two million Pounds Sterling and Rothschilds at eight million Pounds (Chapman 1992: 131).

The Armenian Toumantiantz family is another example of 'an authentic multinational, with a business empire' which expanded from central Asia to western Europe. The Toumantiantz brothers were extremely wealthy bankers who had established extended networks from Iran to France. In the last third of the nineteenth century their bank was based in Baku, and they kept branch offices in Moscow, Odessa, Tiflis in Azerbaijan, in the Iranian cities of Tabriz, Resht and Mashad, in France and in Austria. They owned oil wells in Baku, a rice refinery and steamships in the Caspian and traded in silk, wool, animal skins, almonds and raisins. They were reputed to be worth several million Tumans (Iranian currency) and apparently formed one of the largest international banking forces of the area.[3]

Further east, at about the same time as the Rallis, the Rothschilds and the Toumantiantz, another five closely bonded brothers founded the commercial dynasty of the Chen of Qianxi village in the Chaozhou area. They were involved in the rice trade and by the mid-nineteenth century had opened branch offices in Hong Kong, South China, Bangkok, Singapore and Saigon. In the same way as the Greek Rallis emphasizing the authority of 'Zeus', the patriarch, with only the males involved in the business, the Chens too retained patriarchal authority and patrilineal inheritance. They also combined trade with shipping; in the 1930s the shipping section of the firm ran a fleet of a number of cargo vessels. Choi Chi-Cheung wrote in 1998, 'Family, together with kinship, region and dialect ties, construct the inner circles of the fiduciary community which serve as prime criteria for recruiting employees, securing a firm's internal harmony and establishing business relations. Overall, the consensus of opinion is that wherever successful Chinese businesses have been found they have operated within extensive networks based on kinship' (see also Chung and Brown, Chapters 13 and 14 in this volume). It is striking how those who research the international businesses, particularly trade, shipping and finance of diaspora people, drawing their results from different archives and different cultures thousands miles apart, trace similar patterns of behaviour and similar strategies.

Key to the understanding of international diaspora business is the use of the concept of networks, in this case, relations of people who share a common culture and common economic interests. Culture is what keeps a network together and gives it its cohesion and longevity along with its particular ethnic identity. And by the term 'culture' we do not mean a general and abstract interpretation of the 'external' process of the evolution of the 'culture' of a nation, but an alternative interpretation of an 'internal' process of evolution through religion, art, family and personal life, which formulate the institutions, practices, values and ways of thinking of a society (Williams 1961). Interest in networks, as a theoretical concept, has grown dramatically since the 1970s, particularly in Sociology and Anthropology and expanding rapidly into related fields of Social Sciences. *Relations* are the essence of network analysis. A network is defined as a specific type of relation linking a defined set of people: thus we have transaction relations, communication relations, kinship relations (Harlaftis 2002). Power relations based on the growth of powerful 'invisible' world networks built the world 'Empire' of the United States, according to Hardt and Negri in their greatly discussed recent book (Hardt and Negri 2000).

We can trace certain common characteristics among the development of the business practices of historical diasporas whose practices facilitated the integration of the new economic world system of the modern capitalist era. They all developed in big-multiethnic empires and, apart from the Greeks, they are all Asian. They all speak languages that are not Latin-based, they are all ancient people who have retained their own culture, religion and language, they are all multi-lingual with an 'overinvestment' in education. They are all organized in enclave groups based on kinship and intermarriage wherever they established themselves. And we can distinguish in all of them a continuity of old structures and success in transnational business. The business strategies of the diaspora people have much in common: on the one hand is the organizational side – family, kinship, a particular culture that makes them feel their uniqueness, that brings cohesion to their efforts, and an identification of their particular practices by the 'others'; on the other hand there are their entrepreneurial practices, with the development of transnational networks at the head of which there is always one of their own, since at the core of this business lies 'trust'. They have all clung to their own identities and cultures for their business success. Their 'Greekness', 'Jewishness', 'Armenianness', 'Chineseness' meant an entry ticket to an international business network, because the diaspora entrepreneurs were always more loyal to international capital than to the nation in which they lived (Chirot 1997: 13). It is interesting to note that non-classic entrepreneurial diasporas behaved in similar ways (Wray and Vassallo, Chapters 4 and 6 in this volume), while the exceptional example of the Parsees in the Indian ocean really stands out in the similarities it shares with the 'classic' entrepreneurial diaspora (Plüss, Chapter 11 in this volume).

The modern international entrepreneurial practices of the Greeks, the Chinese, the Jews and the Armenians do not fit the model of Western capitalism or that of nation-building. Armenians, Jews, Greeks and Chinese have produced incredible business-success stories of family firms that have attracted attention, all of which put together form a highly interesting puzzle, the pieces of which will keep being filled in to give a much clearer picture, as seen from a comparative perspective.

Entrepreneurs of historic diaspora people, then, have formed since very old times vibrant entrepreneurial merchant communities around the world, vehicles for the flow of goods and the development of transactions between people, during the whole era of the European expansion. It seems that within Western capitalism and serving Western capitalism all entrepreneurs who belonged to diaspora people have retained all the characteristics of their own entrepreneurial tradition.

Notes

1. The word 'homogeneia' is also commonly used for the modern immigrant diaspora of the twentieth century; the Greek-Americans are referred to

as the American 'homogeneia', or the Greek-Australians, the Australian 'homogeneia'.

2. In order to map maritime networks a vast amount of statistical material was used: more than 50,000 entries of ships over a period of three-centuries containing detailed information were processed by computer. In order to analyse nineteenth-century eastern Mediterranean trade, British consular reports for 25 ports over a 70-year period were examined. To trace the destination of Greek-owned ships clearing eastern Mediterranean ports, details on tonnage, captains, crews, destinations, ports of origin, cargoes, merchants and agents involved were required. Through the French journal, *Sémaphore de Marseille*, valuable daily information was unearthed on arrivals from all eastern Mediterranean ports for every decade from 1840 to 1910. The same was done from another extremely valuable source, the *London Customs Bills of Entry*. Statistical research concerning the identification and full listing of Greek-owned vessels from various sources has been recently systematized and organized in three major databanks under a research project (1998–2003) sponsored by the Niarchos Foundation. The databanks with a full catalogue of Greek-owned ships, sailing ships, steamships and motor ships are called *Pontoporeia*, after the name of the nereid that was a protector of deep-sea-going (*pontos*) ships. *Pontoporeia 1700–1829* is still undergoing research and covers a still unknown and difficult period. Until now, 3,500 sailing ships have been identified as Greek-owned from local Greek historical archives, particularly those of Hydra and the Ionian Islands, in addition to the Archives of Venice, Malta, Florence and Marseilles. The second data-base, *Pontoporeia 1830–1939*, is completed and published in Harlaftis and Vlassopulos 2002. The data was drawn from twelve sources from Greece and abroad: Ship Registries, Classification Societies, Customs Archives, commercial and shipping newspapers, etc. and contains 21,000 Greek-owned sailing ships and steamships, every five years from 1830–1939. The third data bank *Pontoporeia 1947–2000*, E.L.I.A., 2003, still unpublished, contains detailed information on 25,000 Greek-owned motor vessels, every five years.

3. I am indebted to Ina Baghdiantz McCabe for this valuable information derived from the British Foreign Office, Persia: Bibliographical Notices of Members of the Royal Family, Notables, Merchants and Clergy, by Lieutenant H. Picot, 67–8, 1897.

References

Anderson, B. (1983), *Imagined Communities*, London: Verso.

Baghdiantz, McCabe I. (1999), *The Shah's Silk for Europe's Silver: The Eurasian Silk Trade of the Julfa Armenians in Safavid Iran and India (1530–1750)*,

University of Pennsylvania (Series in Armenian Text and Studies), Atlanta, Georgia: Scholars Press.

Chapman, S. (1992), *Merchant Enterprise in Britain: From Industrial Revolution to World War I*, Cambridge: Cambridge University Press.

Chatziioannou, M.C. (2003), *Family Strategy and Commercial Competition: The Geroussi Merchant House in the Nineteenth Century*, Athens: M.I.E.T. (in Greek).

—— and Harlaftis, G. (2002), 'From the Levant to the City of London: Mercantile Credit in the Greek International Commercial Networks of the 18th and 19th Centuries', paper at the Conference of the European Association for Banking History, 'Centres and Peripheries in Banking', Stockholm, 30 May–1 June 2002.

Chirot, D. (1997), 'Conflicting Identities an the Dangers of Communalism', in Daniel Chirot and Anthony Reid, *Essential Outsiders: Chinese and Jews in the Modern Transformation of Southeast Asia and Central Europe*, Seattle WA: University of Washington Press.

Choi Chi-Cheung (1998), 'Kinship and Business: Paternal and Maternal Kin in Chaozhou Chinese Family Firms', *Business History*, 40(1), January: 26–49.

Clogg, R. (ed.) (1999), *The Greek Diaspora in the Twentieth Century*, Oxford: Macmillan/St. Antony's College.

Dimaras, C.Th. (1977), *Neohellenic Enlightenment*, Athens: Ermis (in Greek).

Efthymiou, M. (1992), *Jews and Christians in the Ottoman-ruled Island of the Southeast Aegean: The Difficult Aspects of a Fruitful Co-existence*, Athens: Trochalia Publications (in Greek).

Exertzoglou, H. (1986), 'Greek Banking in Constantinople, 1850–1881', PhD thesis, King's College, University of London.

Ferguson, N. (1999), *The House of Rothschild. The World's Banker, 1849–1999*, London: Viking.

Frangakis-Syrett, E. (1992), *The Commerce of Smyrna in the Eighteenth Century (1700–1820)*, Athens: Centre for Asia Minor Studies.

Gourgouris, S. (1996), *Dream Nation: Enlightenment, Colonization and the Institution of Modern Greece*, Stanford: Stanford University Press.

Hadziiossif, C. (1980), 'La colonie greque en Egypte (1833–1856)', doctorat de troisième cycle, Université de Paris-Sorbonne (Paris IV), École Pratique des Hautes Études, IVe section.

—— (1983), 'Commercial Settlements and Independent Greece: Interpretations and Problems', *O Politis*, September (in Greek).

Hardt, M. and Negri, D. (2000), *Empire*, Cambridge MA: Harvard University Press.

Harlaftis, G. (1990), 'The Role of the Greeks in the Black Sea', in Lewis R. Fischer and Helge W. Nordvik (eds), *Shipping and Trade, 1750–1950, Essays in International Maritime Economic History*, Pontefract: Lofthouse.

—— (1993a), 'Trade and Shipping in the Nineteenth Century: the Entrepreneurial Network of the Diaspora Greeks, The Chiot Phase (1830–1860)', *Mnimon*, 15 (in Greek).

—— (1993b), *Greek Shipowners and Greece, 1945–1975: From Separate Development to Mutual Interdependence*, London: Athlone.

—— (1996), *A History of Greek-Owned Shipping: The Making of an International Tramp Fleet, 1830 to the Present Day*, London: Routledge.

—— (2001), *History of Greek-owned Shipping, Nineteenth to Twentieth Centuries*, Athens: Nefeli.

—— and Kardasis, V. (2000), 'International Shipping in the Eastern Mediterranean and the Black Sea: Istanbul as a Maritime center, 1870–1910', in Sevket Pamuk and Jeff Williamson (eds), *The Mediterranean Response to Globalization before 1950*, London: Routledge.

—— (2002), 'Greek maritime business in the nineteenth and twentieth centuries. A paradigm for comparative studies on family capitalism and diaspora networks' in Ferry de Goey and Joy Willem Veluwenkamp (eds), *Entrepreneurs and Institutions in Europe and Asia, 1500–2000*, Amsterdam: Aksant.

—— and Theotokas, J. (2004), 'European Family Firms in International Business: British and Greek Tramp-shipping Firms', *Business History*, April.

—— and Vlassopulos, J. (2002), *Greek Historical Register, Pontoporeia 1830–1939*, Athens: E.L.I.A.

—— Haritatos, M. and Beneki, E. (2003), *Ploto: Greek Shipowners from the Late 18th Century to the Eve of WWII*, Athens: E.L.I.A.

Hasiotis, I.K. (1989), 'Continuity and Change in the Modern Greek Diaspora', *Journal of Modern History*, 6: 9–24.

—— (1993), *A Survey of the History of Modern Greek Diaspora*, Thessaloniki: Vanias.

—— (1994), 'The Alexians of Minorca: Contribution of History of Sojourners in the 18th Century', *Rodonia*, vol. 2, Rethymno: 650–60.

Herlihy, P. (1986), *Odessa: A History, 1794–1914*, Cambridge, MA: Harvard University Press.

Israel, J.I. (1989), *European Jewry in the Age of Mercantilism, 1550–1750*, Oxford: Clarendon.

—— (2002), *Diasporas within a Diaspora: Jews, Crypto-Jews and the World Maritime Empires (1540–1740)*, Leiden: Brill.

Inalcik, H. and Quataert, D. (eds) (1992), *An Economic History of the Ottoman Empire, 1300–1914*, Cambridge: Cambridge University Press.

Katsiardi-Hering, O. (1986), *The Greek Community in Trieste, 1751–1830*, 2 vols, Athens: University of Athens, Department of Philosophy (in Greek).

—— (1987), 'The Austrian Policy and Greek shipping, 1750–1800', *Parousia*, V.

—— (2003a) 'The Greek Diaspora: Geography and Typology' in Spyros I. Asdrachas (ed.), *Greek Economic History 15th–18th Centuries*, vol. 1, Athens: P.I.O.P.

—— (2003b), 'The Greek Diaspora: Trade as a General National Specialisation', in Vasilis Panayatopoulos (ed.), *The History of Modern Hellenism*, vol. 1, 87–114.

Kitromilidis, P.M. (1996), *Neohellenic Enlightenment*, Athens: M.I.E.T. (in Greek).

Kremmydas, V. (1985), *Greek Shipping 1776–1835*, Vol. I, Athens: I.A.E.T.E. (in Greek).

Krikorian, M.K. (1977), *Armenians in the Service of the Ottoman Empire, 1860–1908*, London: Routledge.

Mauro, F. (1990), 'Merchant Communities, 1350–1750', in J.D. Tracy (ed.), *The Rise of Merchant Empires: Long-distance Trade in the Early Modern World, (1350–1750)*, Cambridge: Cambridge University Press.

Palma, G. (1978), 'Dependency: a Formal Theory of Underdevelopment or a Methodology for the Analysis of Concrete Situations of Underdevelopment', *World Development*, July/August.

Pamuk, S. (1987), *Ottoman Empire and European Capitalism, 1820–1913: Trade, Investment and Production*, Cambridge: Cambridge University Press.

Proussis, T.C. (1994), *Russian Society and the Greek Revolution*, De Kalb: Northern Illinois University Press.

Psiroukis, N. (1976), *Greek Settlers in Modern Times*, Athens: Epikairotita (in Greek).

Reid, A. (1997), 'Entrepreneurial Minorities, Nationalism and the State', in Daniel Chirot and Anthony Reid, *Essential Outsiders: Chinese and Jews in the Modern Transformation of Southeast Asia and Central Europe*, Seattle: University of Washington Press.

Skopetea, E. (1988), *The 'Original' Kingdom and the Great Idea: Aspects of the National Problem of Greece, 1830–1880)*, Athens: Polytypo (in Greek).

Stoianovich, T. (1960), 'The Conquering Balkan Orthodox Merchant', *Journal of Economic History*, 20: 234–313.

Svoronos, N. (1956), 'The Greek settlement in Minorca: Contribution to the History of Greek Merchant Shipping of the 18th Century', *Mélanges Merlier*, Vol. A.

—— (1987), *The Unsaid on Modern Greek History and Historiography*, Athens: Themelio.

Syngros, A. (1998 [1908]), *Apomnimonevmata*, Angelou Alkhs and Maria Christina Hadziioannou (eds), 2 vols, Athens Estia Publication (in Greek).

Theotokas, J. and Harlaftis, G. (2004), *Eupompe, Greek Shipping Companies 1945–2000: Organization and Strategy*, Athens: E.L.I.A. (in Greek).

Tsoucalas, C. (1997), 'Transterritorial Imageries and Symbolic Antinomies: The Greek State, Bureaucracy, and the Diaspora', in Chr. P. Ioannides (ed.), *Greeks in English-speaking Countries. Culture, Identity, Politics*, New York/Athens: A.D. Caratzas.

Vakalopoulos, A. (1975), 'The Hellenism of Diaspora', in *The History of the Greek Nation*, Vol. 10 (in Greek).

Vourkatioti, K. (1999), 'Anglo-Indian Sea-Trade and Greek Commercial Enterprises in the Second Half of the Nineteenth Century', *International Journal of Maritime History*, 11(1), June.

—— (2004), 'The House of Ralli bros, *c*. 1814–1961. The archetype of Greek diaspora entrepreneurship', ph.D. thesis, Panteion University, Athens.

Williams, R. (1961), *The Long Revolution*, London: Chatto & Windus.

–8–

Toward a Typology of Greek-diaspora Entrepreneurship

Ioanna Pepelasis Minoglou

Introduction

The origins of the Greek mercantile diaspora[1] date back to antiquity but for the modern era can be traced to the beginnings of the rise of the world economy in the sixteenth century, if not earlier (Clogg 1981: 93–4; Fusaro in Chapter 5 of this volume; Hassiotis 1993: 35; Stoianovich 1960: 234). This diaspora, which by the eighteenth century controlled the commerce of the Balkans and the Levant, experienced its 'golden age' from circa 1780/1820 to the early 1900s/1912. During this era the Greeks became internationally prominent in the long-distance maritime trade of staple goods and financial intermediation between the Black Sea-Eastern Mediterranean and the West. Let it be noted that by the mid-nineteenth century the Greek mercantile diaspora was (with the exception of the merchant community of Vienna and of a few other less important inland cities) almost exclusively a maritime diaspora.[2] Thus, during the 'golden age' the flourishing Greek mercantile communities *paroikies* were linked by the seas. They spread from Alexandria, Constantinople, Odessa, Smyrna and Taganrog in the East, to Livorno, London, Marseilles, and Paris in Western Europe.[3] These *paroikies* were large in size and their elite members attained dazzling wealth. The Ralli Bros, Rodocanachis, Scaramangas, Petrococcinos and Vaglianos became known as lesser Rothschilds. The business operations of these and other Greek-diaspora 'merchant barons' developed autonomously from the Greek economy, were of a multinational scale and, perhaps not surprisingly, attracted the attention of one of the early great economists. Jean Baptiste Say, in his *Cours Complet D'Economie Politique Pratique* (1828), devoted a special section to the merchants of only two nations: the Greeks and the Americans.

Although the general study of the Greek diaspora has yet to become a well-established academic discipline (Clogg 1999), the unabated fascination of the educated public with diaspora merchants eventually spread out into the academic world. As a result, a relatively extensive bibliography has emerged concerning their wealth and business affairs. This chapter draws together the diverse evidence from the literature and attempts to construct a typology for the entrepreneurial method and organization of the Greek mercantile diaspora during the 'golden age'.

The Sources and the Literature

First-hand information on the business operations and methods of the diaspora can be drawn from the occasional private papers of individual merchants and their Houses, the archives of some of the diaspora merchant communities and a variety of published sources. Prominent among the latter are 'autobiographical' accounts (Schilizzi 1871; Syngros 1998 [1908]; Vikelas 1997 [1908]; Xenos 1869); didactic treatises on the 'the art/technique of being a merchant' composed by renowned Greek literary figures (Papageorgiou 1990: 7–23; Sklavenitis 1991: 11–53) and contemporaneous official pamphlets describing aspects of the socio-economic organization of the merchant diaspora communities (Kapsambelis 1912; Kiozes-Pezas 1912).

Regarding the literature, the mercantile diaspora initially attracted the interest of contemporary educated observers (Dendias 1919; Paraskevopoulos 1898), diaspora descendants and prominent novelists (for example Argenti 1922; Roidis 1878). Academic research in this area began in the 1950s. At first, the focus was on the eighteenth century and the immediate pre-independence years (Svoronos 1956). The 'golden age' began to draw more attention during the 1960s and 1970s, and in the last twenty years there has been a boom in the field. Apart from the continuous stream of work produced by independent 'scholars', more than twenty academic studies have been written on the subject since 1990. Moreover, a few of the nineteenth-century autobiographies and treatises have been republished. It should be noted here that the scholarly contribution is not only of Greek origin. Already from the 1950s the mercantile diaspora has been one of the very few areas of Greek economic history to have attracted the attention of foreign scholars, the most notable of such examples being Susan Fairlie (1959), Traian Stoianovich (1960 and 1992), Stanley Chapman (1977, 1984, 1992 and 1995) and Patricia Herlihy (1979/80, 1986 and 1989).

The rich and growing body of knowledge has evolved around the activities of a Greek-diaspora mercantile community in a single city (or region/country): Alexandria, (Hadziiossif 1983; Kitroeff 1989); Smyrna (Frangakis-Syrett 1992); Odessa (Herlihy 1989; Kardasis 1998; Pepelasis Minoglou 1998); Danube (Fokas 1975); Venice (Pepelasis 1969; Xanthopoulou-Kyriakou 1978); Trieste (Katsiardi-Hering 1986); Vienna (Seirinidou 2002); Livorno (Vlami 2000); Marseilles (Mandilara 1998); Minorca (Svoronos 1956; Hassiotis 1993); London (Catsiyannis 1993). Although it may seem to be assumed that there were strong interlinkages among the diaspora merchant communities, few attempts have been made to embed in a systematic matter the specific 'segmented' information into the wider 'geographical' whole of the international Greek diaspora (Exertzoglou 1988, Hadziiossif 1983, Hasiotis 1993). To the extent that scholars attempt to place their diaspora case studies within a wider reference, the context chosen is usually either the host country or socio-economic ties with the motherland – meaning the Greek state after independence in 1830. Through shipping, which has been the main line of communication of diaspora communities, Harlaftis (1993, 1996) was able to construct the first unified canvas of the international activities of merchant diaspora communities, and to identify common business strategies that defined the different phases of entrepreuneurial networks formed by Greek merchant houses in the nineteenth century.

Studies of entrepreneurial groups or merchant houses are limited. Exceptional still remains the work of Exertzoglou on Greek bankers in Constantinople (1988, 1989) and other studies that have dealt with bankers (Dertilis 1995; Pepelasis Minoglou 2002). The first study of a Greek merchant Diaspora House was by Chatziioannou (1989, 2003) and most recently by Papaconstantinou (2002). A limitation of all the above literature is that entrepreneurship per se was never a central issue. However, beginning with Hadziiossif (1980) and Katsiardi-Hering (1986) a growing number of scholars have addressed the basic issues of business strategies, i.e. organization, structure and business methods of Diaspora commercial houses. These last studies, as well as all previous research on the mercantile diaspora, cover the success stories and the elite merchant-entrepreneurs. Hopefully, in the future the uncovering of 'new' archival material may permit and even incite researchers to examine and compare these findings with the business method and organization of the smaller Greek-diaspora merchants.

Business Organization and Strategy during the 'Golden Age'

In spite of the literature's aforementioned limitations, the juxtaposition of the rich yet scattered findings for the various geographical and occupational subgroups of the mercantile diaspora makes possible a general overview of business practices during the 'golden age'. Such an exercise reveals that the Greek mercantile diaspora at the time was basically characterized by a high degree of homogeneity (see Harlaftis in Chapter 7 of this volume). The diaspora merchant – regardless of where he was based – adopted a uniform style of business organization and strategy. Of course there were some differences among merchants. However, these were minor and a by-product of the variations among the local environments in which they operated, such as the legal system, political system and business practices of the ports and countries where they operated (see Chatziioannou, Chapter 17 in this volume). In order to form a diaspora entrepreneurial typology, two conceptual tools will be used, the 'Traders' Coalition' and the 'Chiot Method', analysed below.

a. The Traders' Coalition

Greek-diaspora merchants during the 'golden age' formed a peer group of international scale.[4] They were integrated into a 'larger whole' which can be described as a 'Greek traders' coalition'. I have adopted this terminology from the work of Avner Greif (1989) on medieval Maghribi traders. In a formal manner the term 'traders' coalition' was first applied to the case of the Greek diaspora five years ago (Pepelasis Minoglou 1998). However, to my knowledge, allusions have been made to it since at least 1815 (Chapman 1977, 1984, 1995; Papadopoulos 1815–17).

The Greek traders' coalition was organized on the principles of trust, reputation and reciprocity. The best way to perceive this traders' coalition (which can also be interpreted as another approach to 'commercial networks' analysed in the international historical literature from many perspectives) is to visualize it as a large circle enclosing smaller sub-circles. Each sub-circle was a mini-coalition in itself, representing merchants/traders from a specific area of Greece, as for example Cephalonia or Mytilene. Merchants from Chios formed the most prestigious sub-circle within the Coalition. The Chiots operated on the principle of constant inter-collaboration with other nearby and far-away Chiots. 'Cohesion' was encouraged through the institution of intermarriage (endogamy), special emphasis being given to business considerations (Harlaftis 1993, 1996). Contemporaneous observers noted that for the largest part of the 'golden age', on the one hand, the Chiots formed the majority in the diaspora mercantile communities and, on the other hand, the members of the communities were grouped either as Chiots or non-Chiots (Vikelas 1997 [1908]: 192–3). Indeed, non-Chiot diaspora merchants recognized in the 'Chiot capitalist miracle' the prototype of the successful merchant, and although they were envied, relations with them were much sought after (Chatziioannou 2003).

The traders' coalition operated according to a set of unwritten requirements and rules. That a merchant trader be of Greek descent, and indeed within each sub-circle that he preferably originated from the same region, was a necessary but not sufficient precondition for entrance into the Coalition. That he belong to a family of merchant traders was a *desideratum*, but again it was not sufficient. The only absolutely indispensable requirement was that a merchant have a reputation for being honest. Moreover, there was a long list of unwritten rules of correct commercial conduct which member merchants had to 'abide to'. They had to be loyal and display deep solidarity. They were expected to have the ability to keep commercial secrets, work diligently, be thrifty, have capital liquidity, be creditworthy and complete on time their obligations toward other parties. It was also assumed that a merchant would go through a period of tutelage (Harlaftis 1993: 91, 110–11; Papageorgiou 1990: 105–7, 133; Vourkatioti 1999: 125–6).

What services did the Coalition provide to its members? It operated as an informal banking and insurance organization. When a merchant faced a crisis, the other members of the Coalition (and especially Chiots who were renowned for their capital liquidity) would provide financial assistance (Chatziioannou 2003; Kardasis 1998: 136–7). The principle of reciprocity and mutual assistance among members concerned not only pure financial matters. To clarify, when members of the Coalition were in trouble with the legal and notarial authorities of the host countries, the members of the Coalition would act as guarantors or witnesses (Vlami 2000: 194). More importantly, the Coalition provided two cost-reducing functions: it guaranteed the exchange of exclusive market information, and acted as a pool from which prospective 'trustworthy' business collaborators could be drawn. Among the members of the Coalition, fraud-dishonesty did exist at times, but it did not remain secret and was exposed. (Katsiardi-Hering 2003: 184; Kremmydas 1996: 126, 154). Apart from the existence of an informal 'who is who' evaluation system, honesty was constantly being checked through the reliance of each merchant trader on *ad finitum* renewable collaborations (Mandilara 1998: 131). This commercial mechanism was not a Greek discovery or exclusivity. The first scholar to codify this process in terms of the modern terminology of business history was Avner Greif, with reference to eleventh-century Maghribi traders. In his work he explained how by establishing *ex ante* a linkage between past conduct and a future utility stream, a trader agent could acquire a reputation as honest. Namely, he could credibly commit himself *ex ante* not to breach the contract *ex post*: 'The agent acquired a reputation of being honest, the merchant could trust him' (Greif 1989: 859). In a similar fashion, the nineteenth-century Greek traders' coalition limited post-contractual opportunism and ensured the proper ethical conduct of collaborators among partners and agents, most of whom were based in distant locations.

As a result of the existence of the Coalition, which operated as a closed circuit of 'trust and reputation', Greek Merchant Houses internalized transaction costs. In contrast to Western merchants and Trading Companies engaged in the long-distance reciprocal trade between East and West, they did not rely on outsider-agents (Fairlie 1959; Kremmydas 1996: 52, 67,141). Instead, they established their own agents along the trade route: the local producing hinterland, depot centres such as Livorno, and large western ports (i.e. consumption centres) such as Marseilles and London (Greif 1989: 857; Harlaftis 1993: 103). The Greek merchant or House, by penetrating the market at both ends, was able to reduce the cost of trade and attain efficiency gains. Through the existence of agents in the production areas, the merchant or House was able to follow local market conditions closely and take advantage of the peasantry's need for cash by pre-purchasing crops and providing usurious loans (Frangakis-Syrett 1995: 58; 179; Stoianovich 1992: 324, 334). In the ports, the business associates performed a number of tasks: 'loaded and unloaded the ship; paid the customs, bribes, and transport fees, gathered and delivered information; decided when and how and to whom to sell the goods' much like the eleventh-century Maghribi traders (Greif 1989: 863–4). The importance of exchange of commercial secrets between the heads of the Houses and far-away agents was well appreciated. Apparently, at least in one case, that of the Marseilles Houses, the Greek Houses in their correspondence with their agents had 'invented' two types of letters: the common (*koini*) written in French which was addressed to the company, and the particular-private (*meriki*) written in Greek which was of a confidential nature and addressed to one person and contained 'some commercial secrets' (Mandilara 1998: 178).

Without the existence of the traders' coalition it is doubtful that the Greek merchant would have developed the high degree of flexibility that characterized his entrepreneurial method during the 'golden age'. In a constant state of renewal, the Greek merchant at the time was 'peripatetic' and 'polytropos', to use a Homeric expression. Peripatetic because rarely did he spend his whole life working/living in one place. Mobile and with a supranational outlook, his business operations followed the geographical shifts in the trade routes: 'polytropos', a man of many resources and ways, the Greek-diaspora merchant was. He had a wide range of activities and simultaneously combined the long-distance maritime trade in bulk cargoes with formal and informal banking, shipping and, less often, manufacturing and land cultivation. Partial diversification as a means to securing permanently high profits became a required ingredient for success for two reasons. First, because Greek merchants operated under the following constraint: they depended on self-finance, and not outside funds. Second, because of the high instability and volatility in the environment of the long-distance trade in bulk goods at the time. The characteristic 'polytropos' also concerned the organizational framework. Namely, the merchant would operate as a freelance privateer while simultaneously he would belong to one or more merchant houses. But this last observation brings us to the next section.

b. The Chiot Method: Organization and Business Methods of the Merchant House

The multinational empires of the more successful Greek diaspora entrepreneurs took the shape of agglomerations of a variety of organizations. At the centre of each of these empire-agglomerations stood a Merchant House, which would persist over time throughout the growth of the empire. This core House did not have the rigid structure of a firm. Instead, it was an 'amorphous' network-based entity involving a large number of actors and renewable ad hoc collaborations. We propose to describe here the business strategy (organization and business methods) of the Greek Diaspora House as the 'Chiot Method'.[5] Merchants originating from the island of Chios constituted the core elite of the Greek mercantile diaspora, and they were the first to formulate this method which was then copied by other subgroups of the Greek traders' coalition such as the Ionians. What were the key features of the Chiot Method?

The House would take the legal shape of either a private proprietorship or more usually – after the mid-nineteenth century – a family-based general or limited partnership (Katsiardi-Hering 1986; Mandilara 1998: 173–6; Vlami 2000: 184–5) There would be cases where the original legal framework might become more advanced and transform to a higher form of organization. A single proprietorship might evolve into a general partnership, or a general partnership might have transformed into a limited partnership. However, with the exception of some merchants who moved into a near exclusive diversification into banking, almost never would their original House evolve into a *société anonyme* over time (Pepelasis Minoglou 2002: 127–31).

In the limited partnerships, the head of the House and the major actors would have unlimited liability. The limited-liability partners, the so-called secret partners, were not involved in the day-to-day running of the firm. They could be relatives or the heads of 'autonomous' Houses, who were (semi)competitors and for reasons of tactical alliances would be made partners. For example, merchant A who was the head of House X set up as a limited partnership would have in his House merchant B as a limited-liability partner. Simultaneously this merchant A would appear as a limited-liability partner in the House Y of merchant B, which would also be set up as a limited partnership. In this way competitors kept an eye on one another. The formation of limited-liability firms/houses enabled the more affluent merchants to finance new ventures. Moreover, up-and-coming entrepreneurs could find supplementary sources of capital (Chatziioannou 2003).

Within the context of the 'Chiot Method', the internal organization of the merchant houses displayed two variations (Hadziiossif 1980: 185). Either (a) one branch of the House acted as the head office – the other international branches being equal toward third parties. Such for example was the case of the House Tositsas Bros, Mavrocordato Varsami et Cie and 'Ralli Bros'. In these cases it appears that head-offices were most often organized as general partnerships and that branches were set up as limited partnerships (Kardasis 1998: 213–15; Mandilara 1998: 174, 189–91; Vlami 2000: 182). Or (b), as was the case in the Rodocanachi House and Geralopoulos and Bros, the various international branches were equal associates – legally autonomous – their basic tie being the sharing of profits and losses. (Kardasis 1998: 207–12; Vlami 2000:182). The evolutionary path of the Houses shows that in both in cases (a) and (b) there was a tendency toward a more amorphous type of organization. The House would evolve into a hybrid entity. Far removed from the rigid structure of a proper firm, it took the guise of a loose network-based organization. On the one hand, its international branches were in substance not branches, but separate entities (Kardasis 1998: 225 and Pepelasis Minoglou, 1998). On the other hand, as the House expanded it would spread its tentacles not only by increasing its number of branches, but also through building a web of opportunistic collaborations with other Houses or merchants most of whom belonged to either other members of the same family or the Greek traders' coalition. Not so rarely collaborations would be established with members of other Diaspora groups, mostly Jews and Armenians. Collaborations with Westerners were sparse and basically involved syndicated joint ventures.

External collaborations involved a mixture of informal partnerships, often based on oral agreements, short term joint ventures with a specific objective such as the chartering of ships, or even sea loans; commenda type deals; the formation of limited partnerships or even *Société anonyme* companies. Notably, these external collaborations would be undertaken either by the House as an entity or by individuals belonging to the House. For it was the custom for merchants (and sometimes for agents) to maintain a privateer entrepreneurial status in parallel to their participation in a House (Chatziioannou 2003; Kremmydas 1996: 81, 84, 222; Mandilara 1998: 133, 151–2; Vlami 2000: 183–5).

External collaborations acted as a popular venue for diversification into banking, shipping, industry and other areas. Notable examples of extensive diversification strategies are, among others, the Ralli Bros, the Rodocanachi and Scaramanga merchant houses and the Merchant Banking House of 'Zafiropoulo and Zarifi' (Herlihy 1979/80: 406; Pepelasis Minoglou and Louri 1997; Vlami 2000: 183–5). Let it be noted that this diversification often involved a geographical shift in the focus of activities of the House. In some cases, diversification was passive, a response to changing market conditions. But, more often it was aggressive in that it occurred before there was a fall in profits in the core sector of the House, i.e. the long-distance trade in grain (Kardasis 1998: 225–6).

Before moving on to the conclusion, we should note that the traders' coalition and the 'Chiot Method' – the two foremost features of the 'golden age' entrepreneurial typology – were the products of a long process of evolution (Hadziiossif 1983). It may be argued that during the first three-quarters of the eighteenth century the business methods and organization of the mercantile diaspora suggest that the 'Chiot Method' and the traders' coalition were beginning to form but were still in their incipient stages of formation. Notably, before the 1780s business ties were formed basically within the family and although there was affiliation among merchants from the same region it was still loose and it is not possible to detect *strictu sensu* a traders' coalition.[6] Moreover, the scale of the business operations of merchant entrepreneurs was smaller. The international trade and financial transactions of these merchants were bilateral and not multilateral, as they basically involved exchanges between the lands of the Ottoman Empire and a specific city or region in Europe. There was less diversification. Merchants and their Houses had few branches and permanent agents established abroad. Business was conducted almost exclusively on the basis of informal contracts and partnerships and commenda-type deals. New methods of European business organization, such as the formation of partnerships and *sociétés anonymes*, were still absent. Another difference of the 'golden age' with the first three-quarters of the eighteenth century was the incorporation of the double-entry system in accounting and the acquaintance with the French commercial code which was translated into Greek and published in Vienna in 1817 (Dertilis 1995; Papaconstantinou 2002; Papageorgiou 1990: 72–86; Seirinidou 2002; Sklavenitis 1991: 33–8).

Conclusion: The Greek Diaspora Entrepreneurial Typology in a Wider Context

The synthesis of the various findings of the literature on the business activities of Diaspora entrepreneurs during the 'golden age' demonstrates that the international Greek mercantile diaspora was an integral, unified corpus. At this stage the following preliminary working hypothesis may be formulated. Success during the 'golden age' was not a matter of historical accident or conjuncture. The 'golden age' coincided with the evolution toward a uniform entrepreneurial typology within the Greek mercantile diaspora. This suggests that the two phenomena were interrelated, and that perhaps the typology 'brought about success'. Although we are just in the very beginning of understanding and mapping this interrelationship, it appears that the twin key features of the entrepreneurial typology were related to success in the following manner: The traders' coalition enabled the Greek mercantile-diaspora merchant house to acquire a powerful competitive edge vis-à-vis Western trading companies. This institution 'solved agency problems', while also allowing for the internalization of transaction costs and the use of scarce resources such as management skills, entrepreneurial know-how, and finance. Significantly, the Coalition facilitated the exchange of information in what was at the time an environment of uncertainty and high asymmetric information. Regarding the 'Chiot Method', through its network-based *ad finitum* renewable collaborations it allowed for the constant reworking of capital, the tracking down of new profits, diversification, fast growth, and flexibility – all features that became the hallmarks of success of the Greek mercantile diaspora during the 'golden age'.

It is clear that although endogenous features (the traders' coalition and the 'Chiot method') possibly played a prime role in bringing about the 'golden age', it is nevertheless obvious that two exogenous factors worked to the advantage of Greek-diaspora entrepreneurship. These were the formation in the half-century prior to the First World War in the eastern Mediterranean of 'a rather unified economic space under a remarkably liberal economic regime and the Western Enlightenment, the ideas of which spread among the Greek-diaspora mercantile communities c.1774–1821 (Dimaras 1964; Hadziiossif 1999: 175; Pepelasis Minoglou 2002: 125–7, 144–6). The creation of commercial schools, the publication of a commercial encyclopedia and numerous commercial textbooks/guides by the more prosperous diaspora mercantile communities from the end of the eighteenth century onward serve as the most obvious testimonies of the influence of the Enlightenment on Greek-diaspora merchants (Papageorgiou 1990; Sklavenitis 1991). Placed in a wider historical and theoretical context, what is the significance of the findings presented in this chapter regarding the Greek-diaspora 'golden age' entrepreneurial typology?

Relatively recent research on the evolution of nineteenth-century international business indicates that a great deal of international business activity at the time was organized through collaborative or network arrangements (Boyce 1995; Jones 1996: 20). This is in contrast to the traditional view which associated the rapid expansion in the volume and flexibility of international trade and capital movements in the nineteenth century with the rise of the impersonal market, which in turn was seen as a function of the emergence of the 'anonymous' businessman as an important economic agent (Condliffe 1951: 290, 408). I would argue that the evidence on Greek-diaspora entrepreneurs supports the newer interpretation and serves as an example whereby a non-market economic institution – a traders' coalition – contributed to the nineteenth-century development of long-distance maritime trade and the internationalization of the market in staple goods.

From the perspective of the literature on the history of the firm, the analysis here confirms that the transition from the individual entrepreneur (and family-based partnerships) to the corporate firm cannot be treated as a 'stylized historical' fact. The Greek-diaspora Merchant House is historical proof of the fact that big business need not be equated with the managerial/corporate firm. This study has shown how network-based 'amorphous' business organizations can operate as hybrids, combining traditional elements (such as family partnership and informal, short-term deals) with modern features. The form of hybrids in business operations is not an exclusive feature of the Greek diaspora as can be seen from other studies in this volume such as that of Raj Brown (Chapter 14). However, even outside the world of the diasporas, hybrids have been observed (Colli 2003: 59). The nineteenth-century international-business organizations which displayed the strongest similarities with the Greek-diaspora merchant houses are the Western trading companies. These 'multinational' organizations may have been less amorphous than the Greek-diaspora merchant houses, but, similar to them, they largely took the shape of family partnerships, had a short time horizon and were network-based and embedded in investment groups (Chapman 1984: 230–51; Jones 2000: 80, 97, 99).

At a theoretical level, entrepreneurship has been approached from various perspectives. Among the interpretations that stand out are those that have explained entreprenurship in terms of innovation (Schumpeter 1934); the ability to detect and exploit opportunities for profit (Kirzner 1973); and the superior access to information (Casson 1997). The 'golden age' Greek-diaspora entrepreneur was a mixture of the Kirznerian and the Cassonian interpretations in that he was more an intermediator than an innovator. This, in a sense, made him a typical specimen of nineteenth-century minority-group entrepreneurs who played an important part as intermediaries in the expansion of economic relations between the East and West as, for example, the Chinese in Southeast Asia, the Indians in Burma and East Africa, and the Lebanese in West Africa.

Moreover, the emphasis placed on knowledge and information in the analysis of this chapter is of relevance also to the literature on the economics of diasporas (Brenner and Kiefer 1981) and ethnic entrepreneurship (Light and Gold 2000; Schrover 2001), all of whom focus on human and socio-cultural capital in their interpretations of comparative advantage. Hopefully, this chapter will incite more researchers to consider the Greek case, thus allowing for the opening of a debate among the diverse scholarly traditions. Moreover, in the future the uncovering of new primary material and archival sources might allow this exercise in the 'construction' of a typology for Greek-diaspora entrepreneurship to take new directions. For example, the analysis in this chapter suggests that if further research on contracts and transaction costs were possible we would have an even clearer understanding of how Greek-diaspora entrepreneurship operated and acquired its competitive edge.

Looking at the Greek paradigm from a comparative perspective, one can easily note that the peculiarities of the Greek entrepreneurial typology can easily apply to the Armenians (Baghdiantz McCabe and Chaudhury, Chapters 2 and 3 in this volume), the Jews (Schjif and Betta in Chapters 9 and 12), in the Scottish (Broeze in Chapter 19), the Parsees (Plüss in Chapter 11) and Chinese (Chung and Brown in Chapters 13 and 14) diaspora merchant houses. Perhaps these methods perceived as so uniquely Greek within Greek networks were not unique after all, but were a common feature to the diaspora networks studied in this volume.

Notes

1. Mercantile here meaning an entrepreneurial diaspora which, although basing its activities on long-distance commerce, was in parallel involved in related/complementary activities such as banking, shipping, insurance primarily and secondarily, landowning/cultivation and industry

2. For the diverse perspectives regarding the periodization of the rise and fall of the Greek mercantile diaspora see Exertzoglou 1988; Hadziiossif 1983: 28–34; Karanasou 1999: 39–43; Louri and Pepelasis Minoglou 1998: 71.

3. For the immense wealth amassed by Greek-diaspora merchants by the opening of the 'golden age' see Frangakis-Syrett (1987: 73, 82; 1995: 23; 1987). For the international spread of Greek Merchant Houses by the mid-nineteenth century see P. Argenti, *Istoria tou Chiakou Oikou Argenti* (1922: 190).

4. Notably, the elite diaspora merchants did not spring from or intermarry with the 'indigenous' Greek-diaspora lower classes, such as the petty bourgeoisie and peasants in the areas where they settled; see Pepelasis Minoglou 1998 and Hadziiossif 1983.

5. I have adapted the term 'Chiot Method' from the term 'Chiot Phase' which Gelina Harlaftis (1996) employs in order to describe at heart the network and methods of Greek-diaspora merchants during the 1830s and up to the 1860s

6. However, new research on the eighteenth-century Greek-diaspora merchant reveals that there was an exception. In the Hapsburg Monarchy Greek merchants had already developed at least one feature of the 'Chiot Method' in that it was usual for them to belong to a House while also working on the side for their own benefit. Moreover, this specific group, through adjustment to the local institutions, had become part of the local merchant guilds. Thus, in a way this land-trade Greek-diaspora merchant group, which went into decline circa the 1850s, was the closest to the ensuing nineteenth-century Greek-diaspora traders' coalition (Diamandis 2004).

References

Argenti, P.P. (1922), *History of the Chiot Argenti House,* Athens (in Greek).

Boyce, G.H. (1995), *Information, Mediation and Institutional Development: The Rise of Large-scale Enterprise in British Shipping, 1870–1919*, Manchester: Manchester University Press.

Brenner, R. and Kiefer, N.M. (1981), 'The Economics of the Diaspora: Discrimination and Occupational Structure', *Economic Development and Cultural Change*, 29(3): 517–34.

Casson, M. (1997), *Information and Organization: A New Perspective on the Theory of the Firm*, Oxford: Clarendon.

Catsiyannis, T. (1993), *The Greek Community of London*, London.

Chapman, S. (1977), 'The International Houses: The Continental Contribution to British Commerce, 1800–1860', *Journal of European Economic History*, 6(1): 5–48.

—— (1984), *The Rise of Merchant Banking*, London: George Allen & Unwin.

—— (1992), *Merchant Enterprise in Britain: From the Industrial Revolution to World War I*, Cambridge: Cambridge University Press.

—— (1995), 'Ethnicity and Money Making in 19th Century Britain', *Renaissance and Modern Studies*, 38: 20–37.

Chatziioannou, M.C. (1989), 'The Merchant House Gerussi (1823–1870): From the Ottoman Empire to the Greek State', University of Athens, PhD thesis (in Greek).

—— (1997), ' The Development of a Traditional Firm in the First Half of the Nineteenth Century', in Ch. Agriantoni and M.Ch. Chatziioannou (eds), *Metaxourgeion: The Athens Silkmill*, Athens: Institute of Neo-Hellenic Research, National Hellenic Research Foundation.

—— (2003), *Family Strategy and Commercial Competition: The Geroussi Merchant House in the Ninettenth Century*, Athens (in Greek).

Clogg, R. (1981), 'The Greek Mercantile Bourgeoisie: Progressive or reactionary?', in R. Clogg (ed.), *Balkan Society in the Age of Greek Independence*, London: Palgrave.

—— (ed.) (1999), *The Greek Diaspora in the Twentieth Century*, Oxford: Macmillan/St Antony's College.

Colli, A. (2003), *The History of Family Business, 1850–2000*, Cambridge: Cambridge University Press.

Condliffe, J.B. (1951), *The Commerce of Nations,* London: George Allen & Unwin.

Dendias, M. (1919), *Greek Settlements around the World*, Athens (in Greek).

Dertilis, G. (1981), 'La Conjoncture économique au Levant et le comportement des capitaux de la diaspora hellénique', *Cahiers de la Méditerranée*.

—— (1988), 'Réseaux de crédit et stratégies du capital', in G.B. Dertilis (ed.), *Banquiers, usuriers et paysans réseaux de crédit et stratégies du capital en Grece (1780–1930)*, Paris: Fondation des Treilles.

—— (1995) 'Entrepreneurs Grecs: trois générations, 1770–1900' in F. Angolini and D. Roche (eds), *Cultures et formations négotiantes dans l'Europe moderne*, Paris: E.H.E.S.S.

Diamandis, A. (Forthcoming 2005), *Types of Greek Merchants in the Eighteenth Century*, Athens (in Greek).

Dimaras, K.Th. (1964), *The Greek Enlightenment*, Athens (in Greek).

Exertzoglou, H. (1986), 'Greek Banking in Constantinople, 1850–1881', PhD Thesis: King's College, University of London.

—— (1988), 'Greek Historiography and Diaspora Capital: Problems of Method and Interpretation', *Syghrona Themata*, 35–7: 152–60 (in Greek).

—— (1989), *Adaptability and Policy of the Expatriate Capital in Constantinople, the House of 'Zarifis Zafiropoulos' 1871–1881*, Athens (in Greek).

Fairlie, S. (1959), 'The Anglo-Russian Grain Trade 1815–1861', PhD Thesis: University of London.

Fokas, S.G. (1975), *The Greeks in the River-traffic of the Lower Danube*, Thessaloniki: Institute of Balkan Studies.

Frangakis-Syrett, E. (1987), 'Greek Mercantile Activities in the Eastern Mediterranean, 1780–1820', *Balkan Studies,* 28(1): 73–86.

—— (1992), *The Commerce of Smyrna in the Eighteenth Century (1700–1820)*, Athens: Centre for Asia Minor Studies.

—— (1995), *Chiot Merchants in International Exchange (1750–1850)*, Athens: Agricultural Bank of Greece (in Greek).

Greif, A. (1989), 'Reputation and Coalitions in Medieval Trade: Evidence on the Maghribi Traders', *Journal of Economic History*, 49(4): 857–82.

Hadziiossif, C. (1980), 'La colonie greque en Egypte (1833–1856)', doctorat de troisième cycle: Université de Paris-Sorbonne (Paris IV), École Pratique des Hautes Études, IVe section.

—— (1983), 'Commercial Settlements and Independent Greece: Interpretations and Problems', *O Politis*, September (in Greek).

—— (1999), 'Issues of Management and Sovereignty in Transnational Banking in the Eastern Mediterranean before the First World War', in K.P. Kostis, *Modern Banking in the Balkans and Western European Capital in the Nineteenth and Twentieth Centuries*, Aldershot: Ashgate.

Harlaftis, G. (1993), 'Trade and Shipping in the Nineteenth Century – The Entrepreneurial Network of the Diaspora Greeks, The Chiot Phase (1830–1860)', *Mnimon*, 15 (in Greek).

—— (1996), *A History of Greek-Owned Shipping: The Making of an International Tramp Fleet, 1830 to the Present Day*, London: Routledge.

Hasiotis, I.K. (1989), 'Continuity and Change in the Modern Greek Diaspora', *Journal of Modern Hellenism*, 6: 9–24.

—— (1993), *A Survey of the History of Modern Greek Diaspora,* Athens (in Greek).

Herlihy, P. (1979/80), 'Greek Merchants in Odessa in the Nineteenth Century', *Harvard Ukranian Studies*, 3/4: 399–420.

—— (1986), *Odessa: A History, 1794–1914,* Cambridge, MA: Harvard University Press.

—— (1989) 'The Greek Community in Odessa, 1861–1917', *Journal of Modern Greek Studies*, 7.

Jones, G. (1996), *The Evolution of International Business: An Introduction*, London: Routledge.

—— (2000), *Merchants to Multinationals: British Trading Companies in the Nineteenth and Twentieth Centuries*, Oxford: Oxford University Press.

Kapsambelis, A. (1912), 'Report on Agriculture, Commerce, Industry and Shipping in Russia in General and Odessa in Particular', *Bulletin of the Ministry B of Foreign Affairs*, Issue 10, Athens.

Karanasou, F. (1999), 'The Greeks in Egypt: From Mohammed Ali to Nasser, 1805–1961', in R. Clogg (ed.), *The Greek Diaspora in the Twentieth Century*, Oxford: Macmillan/St Antony's College.

Kardasis, V. (1998), *The Greek Diaspora in Southern Russia 1775–1861*, Athens (in Greek).

Katsiardi-Hering, O. (1986), *The Greek Community in Trieste, 1751–1830*, 2 vols, Athens: University of Athens, Department of Philosophy (in Greek).

—— (Forthcoming 2004), *Migration and the Transfer of Techniques to Central Europe (Mid-eighteenth to Early Nineteenth Centuries). Post scriptum: The Syntrofia of Ampelakia*, Athens (in Greek).

Kiozes-Pezas, S. (1912) , 'Report on the Commerce Industry and Shipping in the area of Taiganion for 1910 and 1911', *Bulletin of the Ministry B of Foreign Affairs*, Issue 9, Athens (in Greek)

Kirzner, I.M. (1973), *Competition and Entrepreneurship*, Chicago: University of Chicago Press.

Kitroeff, A. (1989), *The Greeks in Egypt, 1919–1937: Ethnicity and Class*, London: Ithaca Press.

Kremmydas, V. (1996), *Merchants and Merchant Networks during the War of Independence (1820–1835): Merchants and Shipowners from the Cyclades*, Athens (in Greek).

Light, I. and Gold, S. (2000), *Ethnic Economies*, San Diego: Academic Press.

Mandilara, A. (1998), *The Greek Business Community in Marseilles, 1816–1900: Individual and Network Strategies'*, unpublished PhD Thesis: European University Institute, Florence.

—— (2000), 'The Penetration of Greek Entrepreneurial Networks in the Markets of the Western Mediterranean: The case of Marseilles (1860–1890)', *Ta Istorika*, 33: 266–8 (in Greek).

Papaconstantinou, K. (2002), 'Greek Commercial Enterprises in Central Europe in the Second Half of the Eighteenth Century: The Pondikas Family', Unpublished PhD dissertation, Department of Philosophy, Athens University (in Greek).

Papadopoulos, N. (1815–1817), *Ermis-Commercial Encyclopedia*, Venice (in Greek).

Papageorgiou, G. (1990), *The Modernization of the Modern Greek Trader according to the European Prototypes Late Eighteenth to Early Nineteenth Centuries: A Textbook of Commerce of Athanasios Psalidas*, Athens (in Greek).

Paraskevopoulos, G.P. (1898), *Greater Greece*, Athens.

Pepelasis, A.A. (1969), *Venice and East Mediterranean Trade in the Eighteenth Century*, Berkeley: Bureau of Business and Economic Research at Berkeley.

Pepelasis Minoglou, I. (1998), 'The Greek Merchant House of the Russian Black Sea: A 19th century example of a Traders' Coalition', *International Journal of Maritime History,* 10(1): 1–44.

—— (2002) 'Ethnic Minority Groups in International Banking: Greek Diaspora Bankers of Constantinople and Ottoman State Finances *c.*1840–1881', *Financial History Review*, 9(2): 125–46.

—— and Louri, H. (1997), 'Diaspora Entrepreneurial Networks in the Black Sea and Greece, 1870–1917', *Journal of European Economic History*, 26(1): 69–104.

Roidis, E. (1878), *The Complete Works, 1860–1904*, Athens (in Greek).

Schilizzi, P.H. (ed.) (1871), *A Freetext Biography*, Athens (in Greek).

Schrover, Marlou (2001), 'Entrepreneurs and Ethnic Entrepreneurs: What is the Difference? German Entrepreneurs in the Netherlands in the Nineteenth Century', unpublished paper: N.W. Posthumus Institute, Netherlands Graduate School for Economic and Social History.

Schumpeter, J.A. (1934), *The Theory of Economic Development*, Cambridge MA: Harvard University Press.

Seirinidou, V. (2002), *Greeks in Vienna, 1750–1850*, unpublished PhD Thesis: University of Athens.

Sklavenitis, T. (1991), *The Commercial Textbooks during the Venetian and Ottoman Periods and the Commercial Encyclopedia of Nikolaos Papadopoulos*, Athens (in Greek).

—— (1998), 'The "Traders Coalitions" of Smyrna and Constantinople (1806–1820)', in *The Outside Hellenism: Constantinople and Smyrna 1800–1922*, Athens: Society for the Study of Modern Greek Civilization and General Education (in Greek).

Stoianovich, T. (1960), 'Conquering Balkan Orthodox Merchant', *Journal of Economic History*, 20: 234–314.

—— (1992), 'Between East and West: The Balkans and Mediterranean Worlds', in S. Vryonis (ed.), *The Greeks and the Sea,* New Rochelle: Aristide D. Caratzas.

Svoronos, N. (1956), *La Commerce de Salonique au XVIIIe siècle*, Paris: PUF.

—— (1983), 'The Consequences of the Economic Activity of the Greeks of the Balkan Peninsula in the Eighteenth Century', *Analekta Ellinikis Istorias kai Istoriographias* (in Greek).

Syngros, A. (1998 [1908]), *Apomnimonevmata,* A. Angelou and M.C. Chatziioannou (eds), 2 vols, Athens.

Vikelas, D. (1997 [1908]), *Compiled Works. Vol. 1: My Life*, Athens (in Greek) (2nd edn ed. A. Angelou).

Vlami, D. (2000), *Greek Merchants in Livorno, 1750–1868*, Athens (in Greek).

Vourkatioti, K. (1999), 'Anglo-Indian Sea-Trade and Greek Commercial Enterprises in the Second Half of the Nineteenth Century', *International Journal of Maritime History*, 11(1).

Xanthopoulou-Kyriakou, A. (1978), *The Greek Community of Venice (1797–1866)*, Thessaloniki

Xenos, S. (1869), *Depredations on Overend, Gurney and Co. and the Greek Oriental Steam Navigation Company*, London.

–9–

Jewish Bankers 1850–1914:
Internationalization along Ethnic Lines
Huibert Schijf

Jewish Bankers

The phenomenon of Jewish diasporas involved in trading routes is an old one. The cosmopolitan Jewish merchants from the eleventh to the thirteenth centuries in Cairo showed a variety of long-range contacts with merchants all around the Mediterranean and as far as India. Dealing with money and banking was also among their activities, but Goitein warns not to overrate these activities and not to see them as the Rothschilds of the Islamic world (1967: 229–30). Financial business was usually part of a much wider range of commercial activities by the merchants in Cairo. According to Goitein the banker's vocation was highly honoured in the Jewish community. He concludes from the records in the *Geniza archive* that 'the need for capital and perhaps also the complicated nature of the banking was conducive to co-operation. References to partnerships in banking are frequent' (Goitein 1967: 248). It is a characteristic of banking we will see time and again.

Another example is the Sephardic Jewry who played such an important role as traders and bankers in the maritime empires of the sixteenth and seventeenth centuries and who created 'Diasporas within a Diaspora', as Israel (2002) titled his book on the subject. After migrants left Portugal they settled down in such diverse places as Morocco, the Ottoman Empire, northern Europe and even Brazil. Their economic activities 'had little to do with any imagined age-old characteristics of Jews *qua* Jews, or possessing certain ingrained economic skills or attributes' (Israel 2002: 10). It evidently resulted from very specific and complex international circumstances.

There are other reasons to believe that no specific Jewish characteristics (whatever these may be) were of importance, because many non-Jewish minority groups in the past acted as specialized actors in trade and finance as well. Among them were – or still are – overseas Chinese in Southeast Asia, Greeks in the Black Sea (Pepelasis Minoglou and Louri 1997), Parsis in Bombay, Indian trade communities keeping trading routes between India and Russia in the past (Dale 1994) or the Sindhis (Markovits 2000), another group of international Indian merchants. In each case, the position of these trading minorities is due to specific circumstances. The networks of Jewish bankers operating internationally are an example of how these worked in nineteenth-century Europe and America.

It is beyond the scope of this chapter to describe the historiography of Jewish bankers, but the variety in background of studies on the subject is enormous, ranging from anti-Semitic tirades or hagiographic publications – some German publications in the 1930s clearly wanted to prove the crucial role played by the Jewish business elite in the German economy – to careful academic studies. Very useful are local studies on banking, such as Jonker (1994; 1996) for the Dutch situation, Chapman (1984) and Cassis (1994) for London, and Reitmayer (1999) for German studies on banking and banking houses. Also invaluable are the studies by Mosse (1987; 1989) who studies the Jewish business elite within Germany in a more general context. To the best of my knowledge there does not exist a modern overview of international Jewish bankers in nineteenth-century Europe or the United States, but there are many studies on separate Jewish banks and banking families. Some families, such as the Warburgs from Hamburg (Chernow 1993; Rosenbaum and Sherman 1976), the Oppenheims from Cologne (Stürmer et al. 1989) or Bleichröder from Berlin (Stern 1977), are well documented. So are, of course, the Rothschilds with the famous five brothers from Frankfurt in the first decades of the nineteenth century.

With their huge success the Rothschilds belong to a league of their own and are one of the very few families, together with the Warburgs and the Mendelssohns (Treue 1972), to have kept their wealth and position in international finance over several generations (Ferguson 1998; Landes 1975). The Rothschild brothers, with their offices in various European cities, acted as a multi-national banking house using agents, correspondents and, from the 1830s onward, satellite banking houses in other cities. For instance, in the Netherlands, *Becker & Fuld* became a satellite banking house in Amsterdam, *Moses Ezechiëls & Zoonen* acted as correspondent in Rotterdam for the Rothschilds and received from them substantial orders (Stevens 1970: 71). Around 1830 the Rothschilds did business with M.M. Warburg & Co. in Hamburg (Pohl 1986: 66), in the same period the incipient Bleichröder bank acted as an agent for Rothschild (Stern 1977: 6) in Berlin.

In the 1820s the Rothschilds already owned a wide-ranging business network all over western Europe, which provided them with a constant stream of information (Ferguson 1998: 296–304). The brothers usually had a keen eye for new chances but not all five brothers had the same financial competence. In practice, Nathan Rothschild in London became the leader of the international banking house. Ferguson's magnificent and voluminous study on the Rothschilds as the world's bankers saves me from having to tell their story again, but the disadvantage of so much attention to one particular family is that the more 'ordinary' bankers of the day are perhaps ignored even though they followed the same strategies and were also very successful in creating their own, and sometimes intertwining, networks in this period. Frankfurt sent a remarkable number of Jewish bankers and entrepreneurs abroad. Based on A. Dietz, *Stammbuch der Frankfurter Juden*, Chapman (1992: 139) provides the following information: 'Of 356 men who left the town in the early nineteenth century, 113 went to France (nearly all to Paris), eighty-nine to Britain (London sixty-six, Manchester fourteen), fifty-two to the USA (of which New York thirty-one), forty-seven to the Low Countries, forty-one to Vienna, and fourteen to various Italian cities.' Kirchholtes (1989: 50) points to the fact that banking houses abroad offered possibilities for worldwide financial business and at the same time a safe base from political unrest at home. Sometimes poor success at home was a push factor in the decision for a son to migrate.

During the nineteenth century a large majority of the Jewish bankers operating internationally were of German origin. They usually kept their contacts with agents and correspondents or financial partners in Germany, as we will see. The following examples should give an impression of how their spatial arrangements started. Several banking families from Frankfurt sent their sons to European capitals such as Amsterdam, Brussels, London, Paris and Vienna (Grunwald 1967: 177) to start branches of the family bank. The English Sir Ernest Cassel, 'the last Court Jew', as he was called by Grunwald, a friend and business partner of the American banker Schiff, was born in Cologne into a family of Rhineland bankers and already had experience in banking when as a young man he arrived in Liverpool (Grunwald 1969; Thane 1986). A.J. Rothstein was the manager of an international merchant bank in St Petersburg at the very end of the nineteenth century. He was born in Berlin, but learnt his banking in England. Conversations with his Russian clients were conducted in French (Barth 1999: 95).

Important bankers in the capitals of the Habsburg Empire arrived from various German regions as well: Moritz Königswarter from Fürth, Salomon Rothschild (one of the five brothers) from Frankfurt; Zsigmund Kornfeld, who as an employee of the Viennese *Creditanstalt* (Rothschild) ran a branch bank in Budapest, but came from Bavaria and learnt the bank trade with Thorsch in Prague (Karady and Kemény 1978: 33; Michel 1976: 227). Another example is Karl Morawitz who also left a small town in Bavaria to join the *Banque de Paris et des Pays Bas* (Bischoffsheim & Bamberger) in Paris. In 1885 he went to Vienna and joined the board of the Anglo-Austrian Bank in which both Ernest Cassel and Maurice de Hirsch had interests (Ronall 1977: 211). Finally, a group of American banking houses, among which *Kuhn, Loeb & Co.* was the most prominent one with its partner Jacob H. Schiff (born in Frankfurt), were also managed by bankers of German-Jewish descent (Carosso 1967; Supple 1957). Many bankers remained connected through marriage or other personal relations with banking houses in

Germany. 'Banking ... was for aspiring young Jews from modest background a most promising avenue of upward social mobility', as Mosse concludes (1987: 382). That is certainly true for some of the examples, but the majority of the international bankers were descendants of established families who had been active in all kinds of financial transactions.

International banking by Jewish banking families is a thing of the past, but their banking power remained the subject of anti-Semitic stereotyping for a long time afterwards (Tanner 1998) and which had its origin in 'the fear that demonstrable Jewish pre-eminence proved hidden Jewish *domination*', as Fritz Stern has aptly put it (1977: 503). The reason for Jewish success in banking has been sought in the intrinsic values of the Jewish religion comparable to the correlation Max Weber saw between Protestantism and the rise of capitalism. The most prominent defender of this thesis was Werner Sombart in his *Die Juden und das Wirtschaftsleben* (1911), but one of his earliest and most extensive critics (Guttman 1913) already argued convincingly that Sombart's thesis does not hold up against empirical evidence. Many other critics have argued in the same direction (see also Barth 1999: 105, n. 32). There is therefore no reason to pursue Sombart's arguments for the nineteenth century any further in this chapter.

Here I want to look at Jewish bankers as an example of a transnational community and to see which patterns of migration can be found, how national and international contacts were kept and how a sense of community – if any – developed. Of course, it remains worthwhile to look at the religious and ethnic background of the bankers because their way of operating might be explained by their position as members of a minority which for a long period of time was excluded from many sectors of economic life. The emancipation of the Jews due to new legalization enacted around 1800 in many European countries opened more and other economic and academic opportunities. Still, many families continued their long-standing economic activities and some became even more specialized in financing. Moreover, Jewish bankers can be seen as members of a trading diaspora in the past. The emphasis, therefore, is on the position of the bankers as members of extended families who, with far-reaching international contacts, were able to create and sustain extensive financial networks. This approach allows us to raise questions such as whether they were in any way distinct from other bankers and businessmen in that period. By looking specifically at the business strategies of the Jewish bankers we can probably get a better insight into the strategies used by other diaspora minorities elsewhere in the past and present as well.

In this chapter hardly any attention will be paid to the bankers' economic transactions as such. Suffice it to say that in the first decades of the nineteenth century many Jewish bankers were descendants from families with no particular financial specialization. Several future banking dynasties began as traders in precious commodities like silver, gold or diamonds. Many operated in a niche economy of money exchange. There also existed the tradition of the so-called court Jews who acted as the financial operators of kings and princes, particularly in Germany. During the nineteenth century the character of their financial activities changed considerably. Quite a few bankers became involved in financing railway lines all over Europe (Grunwald 1966, 1967; for Germany, Mosse 1987: 108–18), in the placement of numerous loans to states, and they played an innovative role in financing new industries by founding (not always successfully) new banks based on the principle of the French *Crédit Mobilier* (Cameron 1953). They usually did not operate as money-lenders themselves but as organizers of loans, or they participated through syndicates in the placement of new bonds and stocks. In this respect the bankers can often better be seen as dealers in stocks and bonds than as the performers of the financial operations we usually associate with a modern bank. Personal contacts always played an important role in their networks, as we will see with Wertheim in Amsterdam or Arnhold in Dresden.

In a few cases certain transactions are described in more detail because they provide information regarding the connections between particular banking houses. The chapter focuses on the spatial arrangements of the Jewish bankers and the way connections between them were cemented. In the next section the focus lies on Amsterdam as a case study of Jewish bankers. The Dutch capital had already had experience with an earlier group of Jewish merchants and bankers, the Sephardic Jews, who had arrived mainly from Antwerp at the end of the sixteenth century. Dutch examples of international contacts among Jewish bankers in the nineteenth century can be supplemented with many others from all over Europe, as I will sometimes – but certainly not exhaustively – do in the following sections which contain more general topics such as strategy and the position of the bankers as a religious and ethnic minority. The chapter ends with a discussion of how far the Jewish bankers can be seen in the light of concepts like 'middlemen minority' or 'diaspora'.

Jewish Merchants and Bankers in Amsterdam

In the seventeenth century Amsterdam became the centre for commerce and finance in Europe. Among other reasons this was because of the arrival of a group of Sephardic Jews who already had a long experience with immigration. After they left Spain for Portugal, they again left Portugal for Antwerp. After the closure of Antwerp's harbour in 1585 they finally arrived in Amsterdam where they settled down for many generations and became part of the local economic elite. Other merchants left for Frankfurt while maintaining their old commercial routes. Thanks to them, Frankfurt became a financial centre in its own right, comparable to Amsterdam in the same period (Forstmann 1996: 182).

Their migration movements were partly forced and partly induced by the wish to find better economic opportunities. The Portuguese Jewish merchants in the seventeenth century did not necessarily specialize in commodities but in routes where trustworthy associates at both ends of the route were of crucial importance. 'The trust that underlies these international commercial associations resided most powerfully in kinship relations' (Swetschinski 1981: 59–67). Originally, there was a route to Portugal, later another one to Brazil and, after the Dutch lost Brazil, a new one to Curaçao and New Amsterdam. Based on his research in the notarial archives in Amsterdam, Swetschinski points out that firms usually consisted of several partners situated in various geographical locations and that these partners were usually related. Smaller networks were intertwined with larger ones to form a hierarchy of networks. A rare case of a banker performing as a court Jew in Holland was the Jewish Portuguese banker Francisco Lopes Suasso, who, together with Pinto and Medina, raised loans for Stadholder William III to enable him in 1688 to sail to England and claim the English throne (Stern 1985: 63; Swetschinski and Schönduve 1988: 53–7). In Amsterdam economic decline settled in around 1713 and the Sephardic community lost much of its vitality in trade and banking (Israel 1985: 241).

Almost none of these early Sephardic merchant houses survived into the second half of the nineteenth century, but their pattern of operating can be seen again at the first half of the nineteenth century with the arrival of German-Jewish banking houses in Amsterdam. But they were not the first bankers from Germany. Around 1760 Lazarus Kann arrived in the Hague from Frankfurt where his ancestors had been part of the Jewish banking world. The banking house *Lissa & Kann* became a successfully operating local bank with many contacts in the Netherlands and Germany (Stevens 1970).

The doings and dealings of the Jewish bankers have always attracted many negative comments. On 4 January 1856 a leading article in the *New York Tribune*, titled 'The Russian Loan', criticized the Jewish bankers in Amsterdam. The author was Karl Marx, who in an anti-Semitic scolding saw an 'immense stock-jobbing machinery between the various European gathering points of the loan-mongering confederation now all connected by telegraph communication, which, of course, vastly facilitates all such operations. Moreover, almost all the Jew loan-mongers in Europe are connected by family ties (Marx 1897: 605).' Marx characteristically overstated his case, but with respect to family ties he had a point, as we will see, and he was well informed, as van den Berg (1992: 135–41) has shown.

In the first half of the nineteenth century German-Jewish bankers such as Königswarter and Bisschoffsheim came to Amsterdam, and Karl Marx named these and some other banking families: Hollander, Lehren and Raphael (the last two were Dutch Jewish families). *Raphael & Co.* had branches in London and Paris as well. As there was no successor for the Amsterdam branch, *Raphael &*

Co. was discontinued in 1881 and the family moved to Paris. The new arrivals from Germany brought a cosmopolitan culture and international financial contacts to Amsterdam (Jonker 1994; Jonker 1996: 249–53; van den Berg 1992: 135–41). Thanks to these internationally operating Jewish bankers, Amsterdam was able to keep its position as financial market, a market that had been in decline for a long time. The new bankers remained, however, more internationally than locally oriented, especially toward Germany. The ancestor of the Königswarters, for example, had started a banking house in Fürth and later his five sons opened offices in Amsterdam, Frankfurt, Vienna and Paris. The Bisschoffheims had their settlements in Frankfurt, Amsterdam, Antwerp, Brussels and Paris and from 1846 also in London. Their business connections were thus widespread and manifold (Emden 1938: 325). Through marriage the Antwerp Bisschoffsheims became also related to Benedict H. Goldschmidt, a banker from Frankfurt. Their financial position can easily be compared with that of the Rothschilds at that time. Königswarter left already for Paris in 1858, leaving a replacement behind. Others followed in the 1850s and 1860s and left for either Brussels or Paris, while keeping an office in Amsterdam. The reasons for leaving Amsterdam were probably quite simple: Brussels and Paris offered a more attractive life style and better chances for financial success than Amsterdam which had became a relative financial backwater at that time.

Of course, failure was another motive to leave. After acquiring his knowledge of banking in London, the future politician and co-founder of the *Deutsche Bank* Ludwig Bamberger tried his luck in Rotterdam in the 1850s, but failed completely after only a couple of years (Koehler 1999: 62). Leaving the Netherlands he went to the banking house of his relatives, the Bisschoffsheims in Brussels. His move would be the start of a successful career. But it was not the end of his contacts with banking in the Netherlands. While in Paris he became involved in the foundation of a *Crédit Mobilier* bank in Amsterdam. After the bank was dissolved, the Paris branch was merged with the Bisschoffheims' bank in Paris and became the *Banque de Paris et des Pays Bas*. Many of these early bankers' families completely disappeared from the financial world after one or two generations because they were unable to find appropriate successors, a great problem in this era where the personality of the banker and his personal contacts made all the difference.

At the end of the 1880s a few Jewish bankers still played prominent roles but due to competition their positions had certainly become more limited. In his research on Dutch business elites at the end of the nineteenth century Schijf (1993) defines an economic elite by using the number of directorates an individual holds as an indicator. Multiple directors, i.e. persons with positions in more than one company, the so-called *interlockers,* from Amsterdam held prominent positions compared to those in other parts of the Netherlands. In 1886, one hundred *interlockers* (of the nearly two hundred *interlockers* in total) lived in Amsterdam, representing almost all sectors of business life in the capital. But among these hundred members of the business elite there were only four Jews: three bankers (Fuld, van Nierop and Wertheim) and the manager of a diamond factory, a large industrial sector in Amsterdam, which was dominated (as in Antwerp) by Jews. On the other hand there was a huge overrepresentation of another religious minority, the Mennonites. Among the hundred members in Amsterdam there were sixteen Mennonites. They had directorships in traditional Dutch economic sectors: trade, transport and finance. Mennonite merchant families had a long history in Amsterdam dating back to the seventeenth century and during their heyday around 1900 some were not only specialized as merchants but in banking as well (Schijf 1993: 97–9). However, their activities differed from those of the Jewish bankers and they were predominantly focused on the Dutch colonies. Still, examples of financial cooperation between the two religious groups can be found.

There were many contacts between Amsterdam and German-Jewish bankers. To give some examples: in 1888 Max Moritz Warburg decided to spend six months with the private banking house *Wertheim & Gomperts* in Amsterdam, as he remembers in his memoirs (Warburg 1952: 10). Warburg, a future partner of the banking house *M.M. Warburg & Co.*, was still in his apprenticeship years. After his time in Amsterdam he would spend two more periods abroad. His father used his connections with the French Rothschilds to place Max with the *Banque Impériale Ottomane* in Paris, and in London he spent his time with N.M. Rothschild & Co. (Chernow 1993: 38). In the second half of the nineteenth century *M.M. Warburg & Co.* developed into a prominent banking house in Hamburg with many international contacts (Chernow 1993; Pohl 1986: 66–8; Rosenbaum and Sherman 1978). As with the Rothschilds there were five brothers, but the eldest would not take part in the family business. Through the marriages of two brothers with daughters of partners of *Kuhn, Loeb & Co.* in New York they acquired an unmatched access to Wall Street capital.

Unfortunately Warburg does not inform us why he preferred *Wertheim & Gomperts*, but his choice must have been a well-informed one and it is likely that the two banking houses had direct business contacts, or through mediators participated in common business projects. Wertheim's biographer (Rijxman 1961) does not refer to the apprenticeship of Max Warburg in Amsterdam either. Warburg also mentions his first business success in Amsterdam where he became a correspondent for the Dutch Central Bank (*Nederlandsche Bank*). It is most likely that he had to thank Wertheim for this success, because his host kept very good banking contacts with the *Nederlandsche Bank* and Wertheim was even invited to take a seat on the bank's Board of Directors in 1892. It was a unique success for a Jewish banker in this era. *Wertheim & Gomperts* operated internationally on a wide range: in 1884 the banking house invited *Kuhn, Loeb & Co.* in New York to join them in a syndicate for underwriting bonds and shares. The New York bank was only willing to conduct negotiations in the US provided that Ernest Cassel would do the same in London. The plans ultimately changed and the syndicate became interested in the Louis-Nashville Railway by the end of 1887 (Grunwald 1969: 127–8). In this venture alone three international banks were involved.

In 1890 Carl Fürstenberg, the famous Jewish banker of the joint-stock bank *Berliner Handels-Gesellschaft*, telegraphed to *Lippmann, Rosenthal & Co.*, another Jewish banking house in Amsterdam which also kept good business contacts with *Wertheim & Gomperts*. Fürstenberg wanted to organize new loans to the Russian state and needed the cooperation of the Amsterdam banking house, which was one of Europe's specialists in Russian loans and the leader of a consortium of earlier loans to the Russian state. In this respect *Lippmann, Rosenthal, & Co.* was the successor of Hope's banking house, which was the specialist in Russian loans in the early nineteenth century. Fürstenberg (1934: 252) remembers that the Dutch were rather demanding and new negotiations were required before he could proceed with his own deals. As so often happens in difficult business negotiations, Fürstenberg started the meeting with personal questions, among others on the well-being of Milli Fuld, who would marry another banker from Berlin and become one of the leading ladies of Jewish high society but was never fully accepted into Berlin high society (Augustine 1994: 206). Fürstenberg had met her before on earlier business visits to Amsterdam. She was the daughter of a Jewish Amsterdam banker of yet another banking house, *Becker & Fuld*, which had been founded by the Rothschilds in 1853. Both Becker and Fuld were employees in the Rothschild banking house in Frankfurt. (Becker was the only Protestant among them.) Having mutual acquaintances and friends smoothed things and a business deal was successfully concluded.

Wertheim & Gomperts and *Lippmann, Rosenthal & Co.* also participated together in a wide variety of national and international activities. On an international level, for instance, one can find both banks involved in the placement of Russian Railway Company bonds (Anan'ich and Bovykin 1991: Table 12a-1) or in the international consortium for raising money for the development of the ill-fated Baghdad Railway in 1904 (Barth 1995: 222, n. 94). Earlier on, the banker Lippmann also participated in the foundation of some Dutch railway companies as many other Jewish bankers did all over Europe in the first half of the nineteenth century (Grunwald 1967).

The last example has a somewhat different character. In 1871 a joint-stock bank the *Amsterdamsche Bank* was founded. German banks (Jewish and non-Jewish) and the three above-mentioned Jewish banking houses in Amsterdam were the main initiators (Brouwer 1946: 32–5). There was also an Austrian bank involved: the *K.K. Priv. Oesterreichische Creditanstalt für Handel und Gewerbe* from Vienna. 'With its branches in Prague, Budapest, ... and later Trieste and Lemberg, the *Creditanstalt* swiftly established itself as the dominant financial institute of the

Habsburg Empire... Nothing did more to re-establish the Rothschild's economic influence in Central Europe' (Ferguson 1998: 598). The Rothschilds owned at least 40 per cent of this important bank. So through both *Becker & Fuld* and the *Creditanstalt* the Rothschilds participated in the founding of the *Amsterdamsche Bank*. The Eltzbachers from Cologne were also involved. These Jewish bankers were the descendants of court Jews (Krüger 1925: 84–7) and already had a branch in Amsterdam. Another Jewish banker was Rudolf Schultzbach from Frankfurt who at the same time also participated in the foundation of a bank in Florence (Hertner 1977: 6). Although founded with the help of 80 per cent German capital, a Dutchman would become the first director. But the German influence remained in place for a long time to come as can be seen from the number of Germans on the Board of Directors, among them Adolph B.H. Goldschmidt, member of the banking house B.H. Goldschmidt in Frankfurt, and a Dutch member from the Eltzbacher family. As noted before, the Goldschmidts were related through marriage to the Bisschoffsheims in Antwerp.

The young Dutch lawyer F.S. van Nierop became the first director of the bank and he would become a prominent banker in Dutch economic life in the early twentieth century (Rijxman 1967). Van Nierop was a descendant of an Amsterdam Jewish regent family. After the early death of his first wife (she was the daughter of a Berlin banker) he married a daughter of Leon Gomperts, the co-founder of *Wertheim & Gomperts*. The example of van Nierop has nothing to do with the fame of a banking family but shows the business success of a well-educated professional of Jewish origin. In Germany these new professionals occupied many seats in modern joint-stock banks as well (Barth 1999: 103; Mosse 1987: 219–36). For our story the importance of the third example lies in the large number of German and Dutch banking houses, both Jewish and non-Jewish, that participated in the foundation of the bank. From these and many other examples one sometimes gets the impression that the founding of new banks was among the key activities of bankers for a period in the nineteenth century (Schijf 1993: 69–72). For example, in 1856 Mevissen and Oppenheim, important private bankers in the Rhineland, together with Mendelssohn, Bleichröder and Warschauer from Berlin, founded the *Berliner Handels-Gesellschaft* (Treue 1972: 39) of which the above-mentioned Carl Fürstenberg would become the most prominent director. Usually the new banks were specialized in financing a particular economic sector or were oriented toward a specific region.

London and Paris in a nutshell

The examples from Amsterdam show us almost all the patterns, strategies and spatial networks one can find among Jewish bankers in Europe in the nineteenth century. In Amsterdam, Jewish bankers certainly predominated in the early nineteenth century: eight out of fourteen banking house were Jewish (Stevens 1970: 62). In the early decades of the nineteenth century Amsterdam lost to London its central position as financial market. The rise of the City is largely associated with the migration of foreigners. 'In the early and middle nineteenth centuries this heterodox company were further diversified by the arrival of a large contingent of Germans, 'Greeks' (Ottoman Christians), Americans and various Continentals', as Chapman writes (1986: 181). Before 1914 there were fifteen merchant banks with a capital of over one million pounds (Chapman 1986: 182; see also his slightly different table in Chapman 1984: 44; for the whole of Great Britain, Chapman 1992: 133–49). Six had Jewish backgrounds and two of these a German Jewish background: Baron Hirsch and N.M. Rothschild & Son. Apart from their international networks each bank became part of local and regional networks in Great Britain.

At the beginning of the nineteenth century there were only a few German Jewish banking houses in Paris: Eichthal who arrived from Munich, Heine and Fould. The last was a French family who came from Lorraine (Barbier 1989: 161–2). All maintained close networks with Germany. These connections were not exclusively toward business partners but involved close ties with family as well (Espagne 1996: 135–8). The arrival in 1812 of James Rothschild and of Königswarter in 1830 intensified these international networks even further. A few examples give us an idea of the patterns we have already seen. In 1803, when Prussia was still under Napoleon's rule, a son from the Mendelssohn's banking house in Berlin held a position as cashier with the Foulds in Paris (Barbier 1989: 167; for Mendelssohn's part of the story, Treue 1972: 29). In 1813 Bénédict Fould, son of Berr Léon, married a daughter of the Oppenheim family, bankers from Cologne, and founded his own bank in Paris: the *Fould-Oppenheim Bank*. The bride was only fifteen years old and the marriage was closed by proxy (Stürmer et al. 1989: 41). Another son, Achille, married a daughter of Goldschmidt from London, a banker Fould already conducted business with. Through these two marriages the banking house Fould expanded its already substantial financial network in France and became fully integrated into the international Jewish banking world.

Strategies

From the examples presented so far we can conclude that many connections between the bankers often went much further than strictly business matters. Two characteristics of the bankers' behaviour will be discussed in more detail: creating networks and marrying an appropriate partner. Banking houses were usually rather small, except maybe the offices of the Rothschilds and some others. Apart from competence and sheer hard work (and, of course, a little bit of luck), knowing the right things at the right time and above all having a network of fellow bankers and businessmen were the key elements to success in banking in the nineteenth century. The personal contacts maintained by the bankers were thus of eminent importance and an apprenticeship abroad was often a first step to create them. But maintaining a network successfully requires a substantial amount of *social capital*. And in its turn social capital implies mutual trust in the members and the ability to sanction misbehaviour by partners. The importance of relations also depends on the content of information passed, the quality of the goods and services delivered and, perhaps above all, on the mutual expectations of the actors involved (Aldrich and Zimmer 1986: 11). Speaking of merchants in English ports and abroad Chapman formulates these problems elegantly, 'So long as communication between trading centres continued to be slow and uncertain, the only way in which merchants could repose confidence in their correspondents' discretionary decision making was to employ members of their families, or, failing that, the "extended family" of co-religionists' (Chapman 1992: 93; for Greek merchants, Pepelasis Minoglou and Louri 1997). To put it in economic terms: cooperation between members of one's own family usually lowers the transaction costs because trust is usually assured.

We have already seen this strategy among Sephardic traders in Amsterdam in the seventeenth century. Early nineteenth-century bankers faced exactly the same difficulties or even more so. Starting a new banking house abroad usually began with an extensive kinship network. Furthermore, trust was best created between people with the same religious and ethnic background and people who had a language in common. Almost all German-Jewish bankers spoke German or French and both languages functioned as a *lingua franca* in this period (but the first generation of Rothschilds still wrote their letters in an archaic Hebrew). Another benefit of participating in a network of trustees is the opportunity for gathering useful information. The fortune of the Rothschilds can perhaps be partly explained by their early excellent network of foreign correspondents that gave them an advantage over later newcomers. Others bankers presumably copied these information networks. Bleichröder, as Bismarck's banker, at least was sometimes able to provide him with better and more recent information than his own services (Stern 1977). As railway lines developed extensively, travel became easier and from the biographical studies of bankers we can see how much business travelling was going on in the 1850s, helping to cement international contacts.

However, the great advantage of the information network of the Rothschilds over other bankers might have been only temporary: the introduction of a good working telegraph made international contacts faster and cheaper. 'It appears', James Rothschild complained in 1851, 'that yesterday a great many German scoundrels sold [French] railway shares in London with the telegraph. Since the telegraph became available, people work much more. Every day at 12 they send a despatch, even for trivial deals, and realise [their profit] before the bourse close the same day' (cited in Ferguson 1998: 573–4). A last network strategy we have already seen with the *Amsterdamsche Bank*. The purpose of founding new banks or creating syndicates for loans again and again was simply sharing the risk. But sharing risks requires again a network of trustees. In this respect the Rothschilds were extremely successful by creating their own satellite banks with employees who learnt their business in one of the Rothschild branches.

Intermarriage within the group of international bankers was another strategy to create trust and these marriages made it possible not only to keep capital within the family but also to keep their financial partners in line, although there always was the chance of having a black sheep in the family. Cassis (1994: 214–17) makes a helpful tripartite classification of the marriages of the Jewish bankers in London in the period 1890–1914. At the level of the firm there are the marriages of the daughter of a partner; secondly, there were marriages between English-Jewish families not necessarily engaged in banking or finance; and at the third level there were international marriages with the possibility of staying within the same family. The Rothschilds knew, for instance, a relatively high percentage of intermarriage between cousins. 'Out of the nineteen cousins in the third generation – the children of the "five brothers" – fourteen married a Rothschild' (ibid.: 215, n. 28). The second level was the most important one in the London case because that made possible the integration of the bankers and merchants with Jewish dynasties not necessarily active in banking in England. Although the Jewish bankers certainly formed a close-knit group, Cassis (ibid.: 210) points to another group in the City as even more close-knit through marriages: bankers with a Quaker background. So had the successful Mennonites who became involved in banking at the end of the nineteenth century in Amsterdam. Intermarriage within the same group of businessmen was a widespread phenomenon in nineteenth-century Europe and probably to a certain extent still is.

Of course, success also depended on the personal qualities of a particular banker. In the 1880s and 1890s A.C. Wertheim became the leading personality of the banking house *Wertheim & Gomperts*. Wertheim's uncle Abraham Wertheim together with Leon Gomperts, a German cousin of the latter, founded the banking house. Originally the house operated mainly as stockbrokers with good financial connections to the internationally operating banking house of J. Königswarter & Co, where Wertheim had spent his own apprenticeship in the 1840s with Heyri Königswarter. As a banker he made many important contributions to the Dutch economy and to the Amsterdam economy in particular. Through his directorships he was very well connected in Dutch business life (Schijf 1993: 112), among others, in shipping companies and railway lines. This kind of creative personality can be seen in many other cities, as the example of another Jewish banker, Max

Arnhold, in Dresden shows us (Lässig 2000). Together with his brother he was the leading banker of the private banking house *Bankhaus Gebr. Arnhold*, founded in 1864. Both of the Arnhold brothers developed innovative policies for financing new industrial companies. As did Wertheim in Amsterdam, they became active participants in the Board of Directors of many industrial companies and thereby created a substantive network of interlocking directorates. Their use of this social capital created a prominent position for the bank which originally started as a local financial institution.

Finally, solving the problem of continuity was far from easy, as is the case with all family businesses, and there are no strategies to guarantee success. Competent sons or cousins were sometimes in short supply and many private banks went broke. Others lost their international prestige with the arrival of a successor of the founder of the banking house. Successful banking dynasties like the Mendelssohns, the Rothschilds and the Warburgs were in this respect very lucky families. The Bleichröder family was not (Landes 1975). In Amsterdam A.C. Wertheim's prestige as a creative banker was not reproduced by his son and successor and *Wertheim & Gomperts* declined into a decent but hardly influential banking house. A second factor was the profound change within the financial world itself starting at the end of the nineteenth century, particularly in Germany. Many of the financial activities were taken over by the new and much larger joint-stock banks founded all over Europe. Only a few of the most prestigious private banking houses remained; others became modest local banks and quite a number merged with the new large joint-stock banks, one of the explanations for why a relatively large number of Jewish bankers were members of the Boards of Directors of these banks in the 1910s and 1920s in Germany and elsewhere. The consequence of this new form of banking was that networks generated through apprenticeships and marriages declined. They were replaced by other networks and a new kind of social capital which, for instance, were created through interlocking directorships (Schijf 1993; for Germany, Mosse 1987: 260–322).

Migration

To understand the patterns of migration, two concepts from literature on migrations might be of use. Tilly (1990: 84) argues convincingly that individuals or households migrate but that the focus should be directed on the networks that migrate with them. Although he uses his concept *transplanted networks* somewhat differently than I do, it can be applied to the migration movements of the bankers as well. Although some went alone they almost always had the backing of local, regional and international networks, for fathers' connections were usually of great help to them in finding a place. The young men acquired their international experience, learned foreign languages and sometimes cemented their future business relations by marrying a daughter of their host, and cultivated future business connections abroad as well. Price (1969: 210–12) coined the term *chain migration* to describe a process of migration where the first migrants settle down somewhere creating favourable circumstances for others to follow. We see the same with younger bankers who followed in the footsteps of older brothers, uncles or cousins. They almost never started as isolated immigrants. An example from Amsterdam illustrates this point nicely: Rosenthal married the daughter of a Jewish civil servant from Hamburg. Her brother Amandus May immigrated to Amsterdam as well and he became an employee in *Lippmann, Rosenthal & Co.* Later on he became a partner in the bank and in due time his two sons also became partners.

Ludwig Bamberger may have failed with his own small bank in Rotterdam, but he had a kinship network to fall back on and was able to leave for Brussels to join a branch of the family bank. The early years of Ernest Cassel (Grunwald 1969) are even more telling. He started as an apprentice with *Eltzbacher & Co.* in Cologne. In 1869, when he was only seventeen, he arrived in Liverpool where he started to work with a grain merchant; in 1870 he left for Paris to work at the *Anglo-Egyptian Bank*. At the outbreak of the Franco-Prussian war he returned to London where he acquired a position at *Bischoffsheim & Goldschmidt*. For such a young man he seemed to have been very well connected indeed. His transplanted network must have been based on that of his family and its business contacts. Transplanted networks also imply that networks that are already in existence in the homeland are transferred to the host country, helping but also restraining the new immigrants. Working together with other Jewish bankers in Europe is a striking characteristic of their business. Networks were further strengthened by international marriages, which in fact were to a large extent marriages with families back in Germany. In this way local and regional networks were transformed into international ones.

In order to place the Jewish bankers among the many migrants it might be helpful to categorize them in two ways. On the one hand we can divide migration groups into 'voluntarily' and 'forced or expelled' minorities (compare Rubinstein 2000: 22). The position of Jewish diasporas contains both elements. Almost all these diasporas experienced long periods of expulsion and restrictions. The second distinction is between migration groups offering labour and groups providing service in the most general sense of the word (Gross 1992: 12). The Jewish bankers belonged obviously to a group, which left their homeland, Germany, voluntarily to look for new opportunities elsewhere, although we should not ignore other push factors at home. They offered specialized services that were very much in demand, as they were able to offer knowledge and international contacts and routes to be used. Ultimately their migration comes down to career migration. Many migrants often start in a kind of niche economy. So did the German-Jewish bankers with their specialization in exchange business in Amsterdam. The margin of profit in these dealings might have been small, nevertheless it required international contacts and up-to-date information and the Jewish bankers were able to offer both. The spatial arrangements of Jewish bankers within Europe have therefore little in common with the usual flows of immigrants in the past or present.

Jewish Bankers as Trading Minority

Did Jewish bankers work together because they were in the majority among their banker colleagues and therefore it was easier to find a Jewish banker elsewhere than a non-Jewish one in the nineteenth century? To understand how the position of Jewish bankers was, two questions have to be answered. The first one is directed at the representation of Jewish bankers among all bankers in this particular space and time. A second question is whether banking and other financial activities really were a dominant activity within the Jewish diaspora as a whole. To answer these questions one needs census tables where distributions of occupations are divided by religion in order to see how many Jews were present in specific occupations. It turns out that such tables are very rare indeed for the nineteenth century. Reliable statistics for Germany are only available for the years 1895 and 1907. What follows is a brief presentation of published German data.

According to Prinz (1984: 134) the number of Jewish bankers was in decline at the end of the nineteenth century in Germany. In 1882 there were 2,733 bankers in the state of Prussia of whom 43 per cent were of Jewish descent; in 1895 the number of bankers had grown to 2,982, whereas the proportion of Jewish bankers had declined to almost 38 per cent (the absolute number slightly declined as well; from 1,182 to 1,122). Prinz sees the data for Prussia as representative for the whole of Germany, but it is far more informative to look at the financial centre, the capital Berlin, separately. According to the same type of census data Prinz used 790 bankers or bank managers who were active in Berlin in the year 1895. The proportion of Jewish bankers was 434, or 55 per cent. It might well be that in 1895 this proportion was lower than the one in 1882, but 55 per cent was still completely out of proportion when we look at the employed Jewish population as a whole which was nearly 5 per cent at that time in Berlin (*Stat. Jahrbuch* 1895: 236–8). Based on a sample of the German *Hochfinanz* for the period 1877–1912 Reitmayer (1999: 166–7) shows that Jewish bankers dominated (with 80 per cent) the world of the private family banks, but their proportion was only about a third in the joint-stock banks.

But these data answer only one question, namely whether there was an over-representation of Jewish bankers at the end of the nineteenth century. For a city such as Berlin the answer is definitely yes. But that certainly does not mean there was an overrepresentation within the Jewish minority as such. As can be expected, other economic sectors with a Jewish overrepresentation were various kinds of trade and commerce, and in Berlin the clothing industry. The same is true for Hamburg. According to the same kind of census statistics for the year 1907, 63 per cent of the employed Jewish population worked in various sectors of commerce and trade, and almost 9 per cent were employed in the financial sector (Krohn 1974: 70–2). In none of these sectors were Jews dominant. In whatever way we look at the international banking families it should be clear that they formed just the top of the pyramid of Jewish financial activities. Simple loan houses or change offices were also included in the census data and those financial operators were completely out of range in comparison with the Jewish banker families.

Other countries knew a substantially larger proportion of Jewish bankers as well. For bankers in top positions in Vienna, Michel (1976: 312) names the almost unlikely high percentage of 80 per cent of Jewish participants at the beginning of the twentieth century, although the number is more or less confirmed by McCagg (1992: 74). Following Rubinstein's argument (2000: 6) that the highest Jewish percentages of the wealthy elite can be found in the most feudal societies without a well-developed middle class, we should not be surprised at this high percentage of Jewish bankers in central Europe (and Russia). Moreover, it is exactly in cities such as London – where a group of prominent Quaker bankers existed – or Amsterdam – with its strong group of Mennonites – or Hamburg – where traditional Protestants merchants became steadily more involved in banking – that the proportion of Jewish bankers remained relatively small. There was stiff competition from these groups. In this respect Hamburg looked more like Amsterdam or London than Berlin. As in Amsterdam, a number of Protestant merchant families who had lived in the city for centuries really dominated economic life in Hamburg. Over the eighteenth and early nineteenth centuries some merchant houses slowly converted into banking houses (Pohl 1986: 30–1).

Jewish bankers might have a different past from that of other groups of bankers but it is unlikely that this particular group used different strategies than those of other bankers. Trust is always a key element in the relationship between a banker and his client. The Jewish bankers almost never had an exclusive Jewish clientele. And there are numerous examples where they cooperated with non-Jewish bankers in the financing of a railway or the foundation of a bank. In would also be wrong to think that belonging to the same religious or ethnic group implies that there was at the individual level no competition or animosity among the bankers. Commercial communities, of course, are never fully homogeneous in this respect. A.C. Wertheim had a very disappointing meeting with James Rothschild in Paris. The banker from Amsterdam wanted the participation of the French Rothschild in a Dutch colonial bank (*Javasche Bank*) that was then in an economic crisis. But James Rothschild thought nothing of the proposal, the amount of money was simply too small to make an interesting venture and he arrogantly refused (Rijxman 1961: 126). The same Paris Rothschilds with their almost monopolistic position very strongly opposed the Pereire brothers with their new type of bank, the *Crédit Mobilier,* in 1852 (Graetz 1989: 213), although they had cooperated with them before in financing railways. The French Jewish financier Jules Isaac Mirès saw the Rothschilds as representatives of the German and the Pereires of the Portuguese Jews and he hated both (Redlich 1967: 64). In the 1850s he preferred Pereire's *Crédit Mobilier.* In the eyes of Mirès, James Rothschild was defending his power whereas the Pereires defended the general 'interest' (Redlich 1967: 65). The career of Mirès shows us that there were spectacular failures in the financial world of that era. As a young upstart he had a meteoric rise to his career, but in the end he failed completely and went bankrupt (Redlich 1967).

But the bankers also differed in their attitudes toward general topics such as dealing with anti-Semitic states. In the 1880s *Wertheim & Gomperts* in Amsterdam refused to introduce Russian bonds because of the pogroms which were taking place in the Russian Empire, whereas his Amsterdam colleagues *Lippmann, Rosenthal & Co.* were very active in this market (Rijxman 1961: 133). Perhaps the most striking example were the different attitudes among several international bankers toward the Russo-Japanese war of 1904–1905 (Aronsfeld 1973; Best 1972; Sherman 1983). *Lippmann, Rosenthal & Co.* in Amsterdam continued with their speciality, namely organizing loans to the Russian state. In 1905 a Tsarist's decree authorized another loan, which was underwritten by German and Dutch banks: among them were the Jewish banking houses of Bleichröder and Mendelssohn in Berlin and again *Lippmann, Rosenthal & Co.* (Anan'ich and Bovykin 1991: 263). These loans were no great success, however. Their activities are in striking contrast with the behaviour of *Kuhn, Loeb & Co.* in the United States. Schiff personally asked the Rothschilds and other Jewish bankers in Europe to block loans to the Russia state. He himself organized subscriptions of Japanese bonds and kept warm contacts with the Japanese special finance commissioner. Both subscriptions organized by Schiff were a great success in the United States. This probably was the last time Jewish bankers had such an important but conflicting impact on international affairs (Best 1972). Just before the First World War, Schiff wanted to support the German side, but 'at this time, although Schiff and other American-Jewish bankers of German origin favoured Germany as an enemy of Russia, they had little influence on the loans they floated' (Best 1972: 324; also Aronsfeld 1973).

In Germany, private Jewish banking houses remained in existence till the end of the 1930s, even after the beginning of Nazi rule in Germany (Fischer 1994; Walter 1992), but then international Jewish banking had already been in decline since the end of the nineteenth century, and, of course, not all German-Jewish private bankers had an international career. Moritz Pauk who in 1908 owned one of the largest Berlin fortunes lived his whole life modestly in Berlin. As a banker he did not do anything out of the ordinary and mainly specialized in exchange dealings (Schwartz 1958). The rise of the national state had its drawbacks for the international activities of the Jewish bankers. Crossing borders became stricter. But the process of state formation also improved the standards and requirements of schooling and it became easier for Jews to follow an academic course of studies and from the 1880s on we see a steadily increasing number of Jews across Europe as professionals such as doctors and lawyers. For bankers' sons the necessity to follow in their father's footsteps became less urgent. With the outbreak of the First World War many of the international Jewish networks disappeared for good. This decline can further be explained by two additional factors.

Jewish Diasporas

'There is little doubt that the Jewish people represents the classical Diaspora phenomenon of all time,' as Elazar has remarked (1986: 212). This might be true, but the position of Jewish diasporas in nineteenth-century Europe was far from straightforward, and this position also raises questions with respect to this particular use of the modern concept of a diaspora. Safran (1998: 255) distils from the example of the Jewish diaspora the following general attributes: collective forced dispersion, a collective memory with respect to the dispersion, the will to survive as a minority and the 'persistence of an "externally oriented" collective identity after the lapse of several generations of residence in a "host" country'.

First of all, European Jews had no homeland to keep in contact with. Certainly, as part of their religion and cultural past they referred to the *imagined community* from which they all were exiled, but there were almost no real contacts with Palestine. Only after the foundation of the Zionist movement in the second part of the nineteenth century did returning to Palestine became an option to reckon with. But for better or worse the European host countries became the home country for European Jewry. Moreover, Jewish communities adapted to these countries, which led to a variety of diasporas depending on where Jewish communities had settled, a development which parallels the creation of various diasporas by Sephardic Jewry in the sixteenth and seventeenth centuries (Israel 2002).

Markovits criticizes the modern concept of 'diaspora' by pointing to his finding that many of the Indian traders, the Singhis from a region which is now called Pakistan, did not remain permanently abroad but returned regularly to their homeland: they were not '...permanent but temporary migrants. Most of them did actually return, even if only to leave again' (2000: 4). For the Jewish bankers this migration pattern is generally not the case. On the contrary, many bankers displayed a great loyalty to the rulers of their respective host countries, sometimes receiving noble titles in France and peerages in England as a reward. Some were also very good in adapting to new political circumstances and rulers, as James Rothschild demonstrates. He started out as a banker for Louis XVIII and Charles X and converted himself into the banker of Napoleon III (Graetz 1989: 199). But if physical separation from the homeland on the one hand, and remaining in contact with a homeland on the other hand, are crucial characteristics of a diaspora, circumstances of Jewish bankers pose an interesting problem. Although the bankers kept their contacts with people who remained in the homeland, it seems that these contacts with Germany were meant for relatives and above all business partners and not necessarily for the German towns and regions they came from. It is very unlikely that those relations implied any political connotation, although in England Jewish bankers were suspected of German sympathies (Young 1990: 7) just before the outbreak of the First World War.

Belonging to a Jewish diaspora is partly forced by the social environment because others see the particular ethnic-minority group as separate from society as a whole. Almost all Jewish diasporas experienced long periods of exclusion from certain locations and professions in the past. In many countries their experience changed more or less for the best at the end of the eighteenth century. Finally, we can see movements from one diaspora community to another. Sephardic Jews are again an interesting example. They were originally expelled from Spain, moved to Portugal, later to Antwerp and, after the fall of Antwerp, to Amsterdam and other towns, but they also moved to other regions. Their economic success was partly due to keeping contacts with their homeland Portugal and to a lesser extent Spain. Without the 'resilient ties of religion and family which invariably underpinned Jewish involvement ... it would almost certainly have been impossible to form ... the highly specialized trading networks' (Israel 2002: 1).

The image of the success of trading minorities is often inspired by newcomers who started off as small shopkeepers or pedlars, some of whom would become the successful founders of large companies. In the eighteenth century, Jewish pedlars from neighbouring German regions dealing in textile began to settle as textile industrialists in Twente. Their families would become very successful Dutch textile industrialists in the nineteenth and early twentieth centuries (de Vries 1989). Only among the German bankers in the United States can such persons be found in substantial number. Supple (1957) makes a distinction between a very small number of bankers who as such emigrated to America and others belonging to large groups of immigrants from Germany arriving in the United States in the 1850s. Some of these were successful, became bankers and merged through marriages and business contacts with the earlier banking group. Together they formed one financial group in New York.

In medieval times, and to some extant in the seventeenth and eighteenth centuries Jews had played an important role as so-called court Jews, especially in Germany (Karsten 1958; Stern 1950). They operated as lenders of money to kings and princes, a dependent but beneficial relationship. Germany with its many kingdoms and principalities must have known hundreds of these functionaries over the centuries. The court Jews from the period between the fourteenth and eighteenth centuries might have functioned as an example for future generations of bankers in the nineteenth century. The Rothschilds and some other families were direct descendants of court Jews, although others were not.

Jewish international bankers used the same strategies that were common in the economic life of that era. In this respect they do not differ from non-Jewish bankers. Moreover, it would be worthwhile to investigate such dependent but beneficial relations in other diasporas, because they are not restricted to the Jewish experience in Europe. For instance, Wu Xiao An (1999: 89) describes the relation that a local Chinese businessman in Penang (Malay) had with a regional sultan around 1890. The sultan also relied on him to get access to finance from Penang and the market there. This way of operating in Malay looks very similar to the way court Jews acted in Europe.

However, the societies the bankers lived in sometimes seemed eager to remind them of the fact that they were Jewish and they remained the objects of much negative attention, an aspect which can also be seen with many other trading minorities. Normally highly valued as business partners, their social acceptance was almost never complete. 'In the centre but nevertheless at the margin' is the way Jonker (1994) characterizes the position of Jewish bankers in Amsterdam between 1815 and 1940. This characterization can be applied to many of the bankers in Germany and elsewhere in Europe (Augustine 1994; Barth 1999). Identity and integration remained the twin problems which many bankers were never able to solve entirely (Mosse 1989: 331). Although they had a Jewish background their attitudes toward Jewish religion and Jewish positions within European societies varied widely. As the Rothschilds, many of them acted as local philanthropists for their co-religionists and participated in the foundation of synagogues and libraries or other local Jewish institutions such as orphanages or religious schools. Others did not participate in religious activities at all but nevertheless lived exclusively within Jewish circles.

To conclude: Jewish bankers at the end of the nineteenth century created international networks in a way which was very similar to the methods which earlier Jewish diasporas had used, the Sephardic Jewry being the best example: through close-knit family networks, international marriages and the choice of business partners abroad with whom they at least had a religious and cultural background in common. It was not necessarily intrinsic Jewish values that mattered, but social circumstances that interacted with the economic experiences and examples which were part of the social circumstances of Jewish communities. In these strategies, however, they hardly differed from other trading minorities in other social circumstances. Trading minorities, as economic agents, react to the circumstances in which they live, while trying to make the best of it. Jewish bankers did exactly the same and some became, in the process, very successful indeed.

References

Aldrich, H. and Zimmer, C. (1986), 'Entrepreneurship through Social Networks', in D.L. Sexton and R.W. Smilor, *The Art and Science of Entrepreneurship*, Cambridge MA: Ballinger.

Anan'ich, B.V. and Bovykin, V.I. (1991), 'Foreign Banks and Foreign Investment in Russia', in R. Cameron and V.I. Bovykin, *International Banking 1870–1914*, Oxford: Oxford University Press.

Aronsfeld, C.C. (1973), 'Jewish Bankers and the Tsar', *Jewish Social Studies*, 35: 87–104.

Augustine, D.L. (1994), *Patricians and Parvenus*: Wealth and High Society in Wilhelmine Germany, Oxford: Berg.

Barbier, F. (1989), 'Les Origines de la Maison Fould: Berr Léon et Bénédict Fould (vers 1740–1864)', *Revue Historique*, Tome CCLXXXI: 159–92.

Barth, B. (1995), *Die deutsche Hochfinanz und die Imperialismen: Banken und die Aussenpolitik vor 1914*, Stuttgart: Steiner.

—— (1999), 'Weder Bürgertum noch Adel- Zwischen Nationalstaat und kosmopolitischen Geschäft: Zur Gesellschaftgeschichte der deutsch-jüdischen Hochfinanz vor dem Ersten Weltkrieg', *Geschichte und Gesellschaft*, 25: 94–122.

Best, G.D. (1972), 'Financing a Foreign War: Jacob H. Schiff and Japan 1904–05', *American Jewish Historical Quarterly*, 61: 313–24.

Brouwer, S. (1946), *De Amsterdamsche Bank 1871–1946*, Amsterdam.

Cameron, R.E. (1953), 'The Crédit Mobilier and the Economic Development of Europe', *The Journal of Political Economy*, 61: 461–88.

Carosso, V.P. (1967), 'A Financial Elite: New York's German-Jewish Investment Bankers', *American Jewish Historical Quarterly*, 66: 67–89.

Cassis, Y. (1994), *City Bankers 1890–1914*, Cambridge: Cambridge University Press.

Chapman, S. (1984), *The Rise of Merchant Banking*, London: George Allen & Unwin.

—— (1986), 'Aristocracy and Meritocracy in Merchant Banking', *British Journal of Sociology*, 37: 180–93.

—— (1992), *Merchant Enterprise in Britain: From the Industrial Revolution to World War I*, Cambridge: Cambridge University Press.

Chernow, R. (1993), *The Warburgs*, New York: Random House.

Dale, S.F. (1994), *Indian Merchants and Eurasian Trade 1600–1750,* Cambridge: Cambridge University Press.

De Vries, B.W. (1989), *From Peddlers to Textile Barons: The Economic Development of a Jewish Minority Group in the Netherlands,* Amsterdam: North Holland.

Elazar, D.J. (1986), 'The Jewish People as the Classic Diaspora: a Political Analysis', in G. Sheffer, (ed.), *Modern Diasporas in International Politics*, London: Croom Helm.

Emden, P.H. (1938), *Money Powers of Europe in the Nineteenth and Twentieth Century.* London: Low, Marston.

Espagne, M. (1996), *Les Juifs allemands de Paris à l'époque de Heine,* Paris: PUF.

Ferguson, N. (1998), *The World's Banker: The History of the House of Rothschild*, London: Weidenfeld & Nicolson.

Fischer, A. (1994), 'Jüdische Privatbanken im "Dritten 'Reich'', *Scripta Mercaturae*, 28: 1–53.

Forstmann, W. (1996), 'Frankfurt am Main, a City of Finance: Banking Systems in Frankfurt in the 18th and 19th Centuries', in H. Diederiks and D. Reeder (eds), *Cities of Finance*, Amsterdam: North Holland.

Fürstenberg, C. (1931), *Die Lebensgeschichte eines deutschen Bankiers 1870–1914*, Berlin: Ullstein.

Goitein, S.D. (1967), *A Mediterranean Society: The Jewish Communities of the Arab World in the Documents of the Cairo Geniza,* Vol I. Economic Foundations, Berkeley: University of California Press.

Graetz, M. (1989), *Les Juifs en France au XIXe siècle*, Paris: Seuil.

Gross, N.T. (1992), 'Entrepreneurship of Religious and Ethnic Minorities', in W. Mosse and H. Pohl (eds), *Jüdische Unternehmer in Deutschland im 19. und 20. Jahrhundert*, Stuttgart: Franz Steiner.

Grunwald, K. (1966), *Türkenhirsch: A Study of Baron Maurice de Hirsch Entrepreneur and Philanthropist,* Jerusalem: IPST.

—— (1967), 'Europe's Railways and Jewish Enterprise', *Leo Baeck Institute Year Book*, 12: 163–209.

—— (1969), '"Windsor-Cassel" – The Last Court Jew', *Leo Baeck Institute Year Book*, 14: 119–61.

Guttmann, J. (1913), 'Die Juden und das Wirtschaftsleben', *Archiv für Sozialwissenschaft und Sozialpolitik*, 36: 149–212.

Hertner, P. (1977), 'Deutsches Kapital im Italienischen Bankensektor und die Deutsch-Italienischen Finanzbeziehungen in der zweiten Hälfte des 19. Jahrhunderts', *Bankhistorisches Archiv. Zeitschrift zur Bankengeschichte*, 3: 1–29.

Israel, J.I. (1985), *European Jewry in the Age of Mercantilism, 1550–1750*, Oxford: Clarendon.

—— (2002), *Diasporas within Diasporas: Jews, Crypto-Jews, and the World Maritime Empires (1540–1740)*, Leiden: Brill.

Jonker, J. (1994), 'In het Middelpunt en toch aan de Rand: Joodse Bankiers en Effectenhandelaren 1815–1940', in *Venter, Fabriqueur, Fabrikant: Joodse Ondernemers en Ondernemingen in Nederland 1796–1940*, Amsterdam: NEHA.

—— (1996), *Merchants, Bankers, Middlemen: The Amsterdam Money Market during the First Half of the 19th Century*, Amsterdam: NEHA.

Karady, V. and Kemény, I. (1978), 'Les Juifs dans la structure des classes en Hongrie: essai sur les antécédents historiques des crises d'antisémitisme du XXe siècle', *Actes de la Recherche en Science, Sociales*, 22: 25–61.

Karsten, F.L. (1958), 'The Court Jew: A Prelude to Emancipation', *Leo Baeck Institute Year Book*, 3: 140–56.

Kirchholtes, H.D. (1989), *Jüdische Privatbanken in Frankfurt am Main*, Frankfurt am Main: Kramer.

Koehler, B. (1999), *Ludwig Bamberger: Revolutionär und Bankier*, Stuttgart: Deutsche Verlach-Anstalt.

Krohn, H. (1974), *Die Juden in Hamburg*, Hamburg: Hans Christians.

Krüger, A. (1925), *Das Kölner Bankiergewerbe: Vom Ende des 18. Jahrhunderts bis 1875*, Essen: Baedeken.

Landes, D. (1975), 'Bleichröders and Rothschilds: The Problem of Continuity in the Family Firm', in C.E. Rosenberg (ed.), *The Family in History*, Philadelphia: University of Pennsylvania Press.

Lässig, S. (2000), 'Jüdische Privatbanken in Dresden', *Dresdner Hefte*, 18: 85–97.

Markovits, C. (2000), *The Global World of Indian Merchants 1750–1947: Traders of Sind from Bukhara to Panama*, Cambridge: Cambridge University Press.

Marx, K. (1897), *The Eastern Question*, London.

McCagg, W.O. (1992), 'Jewish Wealth in Vienna 1670–1918', in M.K. Silber (ed.), *Jews in the Hungarian Economy 1760–1945*, Jerusalem: Magnus.

Michel, B. (1976), *Banques et banquiers en Austriche du debut du 20ᵉ siècle*, Paris.

Mosse, W.E. (1987), *Jews in the German Economy: The German-Jewish Economic Elite*, Oxford: Clarendon.

—— (1989), *The German-Jewish Economic Élite 1820–1935: A Socio-cultural Profile*, Oxford: Clarendon.

Pepelasis Minoglou, I. and Louri, H. (1997), 'Diaspora Entrepreneurial Networks in the Black Sea and Greece 1870–1917', *Journal of European Economic History*, 26(1): 69–104.

Pohl, M. (1986), *Hamburger Bankengeschichte*, Mainz: Hase & Koehler: Hase & Koehler.

Price, C. (1969), 'The Study of Assimilation', in J.A. Jackson (ed) *Migration*, Cambridge: Cambridge University Press.

Prinz, A. (1984), *Juden im deutschen Wirtschaftsleben: Soziale und wirtschaftliche Struktur im Wandel 1850–1914*, Tübingen: Mohr.

Redlich, F. (1967), 'Two Nineteenth Century Financiers and Autobiographers: A Comparative Study in Creative Destructiveness and Business Failure', *Economy and History*, 10: 37–128.

Reitmayer, M. (1999), *Bankiers im Kaiserreich: Sozialprofil und Habitus der deutschen Hochfinanz*, Göttingen: Vandenhoeck & Ruprecht.

Rijxman, A.S. (1961), *A.C. Wertheim 1832–1897: Een Bijdrage tot zijn Levensgeschiedenis*, Amsterdam.

—— (1967), 'Mr. Frederik Salomon van Nierop 1844–1924', in *Bedrijf en Samenleving*, Alphen aan den Rijn: N. Samson.

Ronall, J.O. (1977), 'German and Austrian Jews in the Financial Modernisation of the Middle East', *Leo Baeck Institute Year Book*, 22: 209–18.

Rosenbaum, E. and Sherman, A.J. (1978), *Das Bankhaus M.M. Warburg & Co. 1798–1938*, Hamburg: Hans Christians.

Rubinstein, W.D. (2000), 'Jews in the Economic Elites of Western Nations and Antisemitism', *Jewish Journal of Sociology*, 42: 5–35.

Safran, W. (1998), 'Comparing Diasporas: A Review Essay', *Diaspora*, 8: 255–92.

Schijf, H. (1993), *Netwerken van een Financieel-economische Elite: Personele Verbindingen in het Nederlandse Bedrijfsleven aan het Einde van Negentiende Eeuw*, Amsterdam: Het Spinhuis.

Schwarz, W. (1958), 'A Jewish Banker in the Nineteenth Century', *Leo Baeck Institute Year Book*, 3: 300–10.

Sherman, A.J. (1983), 'German-Jewish Bankers in World politics: The Financing of the Russo-Japanese War', *Leo Baeck Institute Year Book*, 28: 59–93.

Statistische Jahrbuch für die Stadt Berlin (1895), Berlin.

Stern, F. (1977), *Gold and Iron: Bismarck, Bleichröder, and the Building of the German Empire*, New York: Alfred A. Knopf.

Stern, S. (1950), *The Court Jew: A Contribution to the History of Absolutism*, New Brunswick.

Stevens, Th. (1970), 'De Familie Kann en haar Financiele Activiteiten gedurende vier Eeuwen', *Studia Rosenthaliana*, 4: 43–95.

Stürmer, M., Teichmann, G. and Treue, W. (1989), *Wägen und Wagen: Sal. Oppenheim jr. & Cie. Geschichte einer Bank und einer Familie*, München: Piper.

Supple, B.E. (1957), 'A Business Elite: German-Jewish Financiers in Nineteenth-century New York', *Business History Review*, 31: 143–78.

Swetschinski, D.M. (1981), 'Kinship and Commerce: the Foundation of Portuguese Jewish Life in Seventeenth-century Holland', *Studia Rosenthaliana*, 15: 2–74.

—— and Schönduve, L. (1988), *The Lopes Suasso Family, Bankers to William III*, Amsterdam: Waanders.

Tanner, J. (1998), '"Bankenmacht": politischer Popanz, antisemitischer Stereotyp oder analytischer Kategorie?', *Zeitschrift für Unternehmensgeschichte*, 43: 19–34.

Thane, P. (1986), 'Financiers and the British State: the Case of Sir Ernest Cassel', *Business History*, 28: 80–99.

Tilly, Ch. (1990), 'Transplanted Networks', in V. Yans-McLaughlin (ed.), *Immigration Reconsidered*, Oxford: Oxford University Press.

Treue, W. (1972), 'Das Bankhaus Mendelssohn als Beispiel einer Privatbank im 19. und 20. Jahrhundert', *Mendelssohnstudien*, 1: 29–81.

Van den Berg, N.P. (1992), 'Een Geschenk aan de Stad Amsterdam: Achtergronden van de Bibliotheca Rosenthaliana', *Jaarboek Amstelodanum*, 84: 131–58.

Walter, R. (1992), 'Jüdische Bankiers in Deutschland bis 1932', in W. Mosse and H. Pohl (eds), *Jüdische Unternehmer in Deutschland im 19. und 20. Jahrhundert*, Stuttgart: Franz Steiner.

Warburg, M.M. (1952), *Aus meinen Aufzeichnungen*, Glückstadt.

Wu Xiao An (1999), 'Chinese Family Business Networks in the Making of a Malay State: Kedah and Region 1882–1941', PhD dissertation, Amsterdam.

Young, G.F.W. (1990), 'Anglo-German Banking Syndicates and the Issue of South American Government Loans in the Era of High Imperialism, 1885–1914', *Bankhistorisches Archiv. Zeitschrift zur Bankengeschichte*, 16 : 3–38.

–10–

Middle Eastern Entrepreneurs in Southeast Asia, *c.*1750–*c.*1940

William Gervase Clarence-Smith

Asian entrepreneurs were skilled traders and financiers, as well as precocious manufacturers, probably more developmental in their impact on the 'periphery' than many Western rent-seeking capitalists. This has been increasingly emphasized in the Southeast Asian context for communities from southern China, Japan and southern India, and the older appellation 'trade diaspora' is now seen as too limiting (Brown 1994). However, little attention has been paid to dynamic immigrants from further west, fragmented into small 'communities of trust'. They originated from a wide arc of land that stretched from Bombay to Istanbul. This chapter concentrates on those originating from southern Arabia and Greater Syria, with some reference to other Middle Easterners, but setting aside the complex issue of communities from the northwestern areas of British India.

Southern Arabians were most numerous in Southeast Asia, perhaps 100,000 at their height in the 1920s and 1930s. Overwhelmingly Sunni Muslims of the same Shafi'i rite that predominated in Maritime Southeast Asia, they almost all hailed from Hadhramaut in modern Yemen. From around the middle of the eighteenth century, Hadhrami Arabs went in increasing numbers to the Malay World. Their main bastions were Surabaya, on Java, and Singapore, at the southern tip of the Malay Peninsula. A few were also scattered around the southern fringes of Mainland Southeast Asia and the Philippines (Freitag and Clarence-Smith 1997). A number of Arabs in the Dutch East Indies were reputed to be 'multimillionaires' at the end of the 1930s (Vandenbosch 1944: 371).

A smaller group of Arabic-speakers came from Greater Syria, including not only Syria as it is today, but also Lebanon, Alexandretta, Palestine, Israel and Jordan. Almost all went to the Philippines, which they probably reached in the 1870s. There they were usually lumped together as Syrians or Turks. Their numbers reached a peak of around 10,000 in the late 1970s, as a result of the Lebanese civil war, but there were only around 2,000 in earlier years. They were mainly Maronite, Greek Orthodox, Druze or Jewish by religion (Clarence-Smith forthcoming).

Some of the wealthiest entrepreneurs were Oriental Jews from Iraq, Arabic-speakers often referred to as Baghdadi Jews. They emigrated to India during the eighteenth century, and pushed on to Southeast Asia in the first decades of the nineteenth century. Like the Hadhrami Arabs, their major bases were in Singapore and Surabaya, and a few landed up in northern Borneo and the Moluccas. They numbered around a thousand in Java and another thousand in the Malay Peninsula in the inter-war years of the twentieth century (Goldstein, forthcoming; Nathan 1986). Rangoon, in close commercial contact with Calcutta, was home to another 500 or so in 1921 (Cohen 1956: 211).

Armenian Christians, mainly Orthodox but including some Uniates, typically spoke their own language and Persian, indicating their probable New Julfan origins in Iran (see Baghdiantz McCabe in Chapter 2 of this volume). Like the Baghdadi Jews, they entered Southeast Asia via India, and were found chiefly in Burma, the Malay peninsula and Java (Seth 1988; Papazian 1979; Sarkissian 1987). Usually accepted as 'European' or 'White', most of them left Southeast Asia from the end of the nineteenth century (Aghassian and Kévorian 2000: 39). By the 1930s, there were only about a hundred Armenians in Singapore, their main Southeast Asian stronghold (Sarkissian 1987: 8, 29).

Other Middle Easterners were of less significance. There were Shi'i Muslims from the Persian Gulf in Burma and Thailand, albeit less prominent than in former centuries (Yegar 1972). The odd Greek appeared here and there, notably in Thailand, but the Greek presence in Bengal does not appear to have spilled over into Burma (Norris 1992; Wright and Breakspear 1908: 280–1). A sprinkling of Latino-speaking Turkish Jews found their way to the Philippines (late Cesar Majul, *pers. comm.*).

The presence of Middle Eastern entrepreneurs dated back to the earliest days of the fabled spice trade. Muslim links briefly faltered with the advent of the crusading Iberians, but Armenians exploited their Christian faith to extend their networks (Clarence-Smith forthcoming). The Muslim connection, which never disappeared, expanded again in the eighteenth century, as the Dutch East India Company tottered on the edge of bankruptcy (Clarence-Smith 1997). Colonial regimes, and independent Thailand, welcomed diasporas during the long nineteenth-century economic boom engendered by the adoption of free trade, although barriers began to go up after 1914.

The region thus proved a magnet for Middle Eastern entrepreneurs, who were probably wealthier than their better-known Chinese competitors. To be sure, it was estimated that the Chinese had 340 million guilders invested in 'large concerns' in Indonesia in 1921, compared to only 36 million for the Japanese and 24 million for 'Arabs, Armenians, etc.' (Cator 1936: 64). However, the average 'other Foreign Oriental' paying income tax in the Dutch possessions, a label that encompassed Middle Easterners and South Asians, earned around 3,000 guilders in 1936.

This compared to a little over 2,000 guilders for Chinese, a little under 2,000 for 'natives', and just over 4,000 for 'Europeans'. The latter category introduces particular statistical uncertainty, as it covered all Japanese, and any individual who had acquired European status, including the wealthiest among Chinese and Middle Eastern entrepreneurs (Tinbergen and Derksen 1941: 517). Another straw in the wind is that Hadhrami Arabs and Oriental Jews had greater real estate holdings than the Chinese, according to the 1931 census for the Malay peninsula (Vlieland 1931).

Hawkers, Peddlers and Shopkeepers

Commerce was the sector in which all Middle Eastern communities could be found, and this was often how immigrants began their careers. Negligible Southeast Asian trade with their homelands put Middle Easterners at a certain disadvantage, compared to Indian and Chinese competitors. However, a strong prior implantation in South and East Asia acted as a palliative for Armenians and Baghdadi Jews, while Hadhrami traders occupied niches in southwestern India. For earlier implantations of the Armenians in India, some instances are discussed at length by Sushil Chaudhury in Chapter 3 of this volume. The Syrian bastion lay across the Pacific in the Americas, and they developed a useful presence in Australia.

Syrians were initially particularly dependent on peddling. The French Consul in Manila described their experience thus in 1892:

> Most of the time, to launch their careers, they have only their readiness to work and a pack of goods of little value. These modest traders scatter around all the provinces of the archipelago, seeking their fortune. They try to persuade the natives of the worth of their numerous goods, including cheap jewellery, rosaries, scarves, handkerchiefs, fans, combs, chains, watches and so forth. They are not put off by the protracted bargaining of the natives, and the endless discussions necessary to sell the least of objects. Under a burning sun, made even less bearable by the weariness of walking in the great heat of this country, they wander about thus, struggling against competition from the Chinese. When these peddlers are methodical and patient, qualities that most of them possess, they make a considerable profit in relation to the value of their wares. After a few years, most of them settle in some part of the Philippines, open a store, and progressively extend their businesses. (*Moniteur Officiel du Commerce,* 11 January 1894: Annex, my translation)

Syrian peddlers attempted to attenuate the hardships of this life. They preferred to deal in lighter and more valuable objects, especially jewellery and watches, leaving heavier textiles to the Chinese. Occasionally they rode horses, or hired a 'coolie' to carry their wares. They went about in pairs, and stayed with parish priests whenever they could (late C. Majul, *pers. comm.*). They were the subject of some hostility, compared unflatteringly to the Jews of Europe in the Cagayán Valley in the 1890s (Rodríguez and Álvarez 1998: IV, 1581).

The initial impact of the American take-over of the Philippines was positive. The new authorities made it difficult for Chinese competitors to enter the archipelago, and abolished remaining legal disabilities for aliens, in terms of travel, residence and trade (Jensen 1956: 46). They also completed the 'pacification' of the archipelago. By the 1900s, 'Syrian traders located on the crocodile-infested river bank' of the Agusan River, in northeastern Mindanao, were buying jerked venison from an American renegade (Gleeck 1974: 187). However, Spanish and American elites considered peddling unfit for Whites, and this led to a growing reluctance to follow this profession (late Cesar Majul, *pers. comm.*).

The Philippine political environment also became increasingly hostile to 'alien pedlars and hawkers'. The Itinerant Traders Law of 1913 restricted their activities, and made them apply for licences from district governors. The newly elected Democrat administration in Washington declared that it sought to protect non-Christian tribes from unscrupulous foreigners, but probably mainly wanted to curry favour with Filipino nationalists (Gowing 1977: 229–30). With legislative autonomy after 1916, Filipino politicians increased the pressure on alien traders, although there were still some Syrian 'wandering traders' in the early 1930s (Agpalo 1962: ch. 1; Miller 1932: 543).

Hadhrami Arabs with established shipping connections were able to eschew ambulatory trade, but the same was not true of their poorer brethren, who often acted as hawkers and peddlers (Berg 1886: 113–20). As late as the 1920s, recent arrivals from Hadhramaut hawked and peddled goods obtained on credit, especially in rural areas of Java, hoping to rise further on the commercial ladder (Alatas 1923: 49). However, many petty traders became insolvent in the 1930s crisis, dragging their creditors down with them in some cases (Ingrams 1937: 147).

Syrians settled down to shopkeeping in the Philippines, as this activity was not denied to aliens till 1954. In 1908, 'well established Syrian merchants in Manila supply their countrymen who are scattered in the Islands doing the retail trade', mainly in Bikol and the Visayas (Abdou 1910: 434). Syrians came to be particularly associated with bazaars, whereas Chinese and Filipinos were typically seen as running smaller shops:

Bazaars in the Philippines usually exert considerable selling effort and do very satisfactory business. They are owned largely by Indians, Japanese and Syrians, and function as retailers, jobbers and importers. The management generally operates one or more branches and is in a position to dispose of considerable quantities of goods. [They] sell goods when some of the less developed retail establishments find difficulty in doing so. (Rohrer 1930: 23)

There were risks involved. The Salem family store burned to the ground, and the Gabriel family closed theirs in the 1930s depression (late Cesar Majul, *pers. comm.*).

Shopkeeping was also important for Hadhramis, including those of Sayyid status. During the Cultivation System in Java from 1830 to 1870, Hadhrami shops around state warehouses sold consumer items to peasants after they had been paid by the authorities for their crops (Elson 1994: 255–8). There were many Arab 'petty merchants and shop-keepers' in Singapore in the late 1850s (Wallace 1986: 32). Sayyid Masim b. Salih al-Jifri was among those who rose in the world by opening a small shop on Arab Street (Buckley 1965: 563–5).

For Armenian Eurasian trade in an earlier period Ina Baghdiantz McCabe (1999) has demonstrated how at the height of their glory, the elite in New Julfa Iran, from which network this group probably originated, was dependant on an organized system of lesser merchants, themselves dependant on peddlers, who were in fact at times the most visible ones on the road. Armenians and Oriental Jews were less often associated with petty trade, but a concentration on the fabulously wealthy leading figures in these communities is misleading. The poorer Baghdadi Jews of Singapore, who lived close to the synagogue, were often hawkers and peddlers. Abraham Penhas was one Singapore Jewish peddler who gradually improved his economic situation. Indeed, the Jews were unusual among Middle Easterners in having a fringe of professional beggars, of whom wealthy Baghdadis disapproved (Nathan 1986: 26–7; 76–7, 84–5).

Import-export Merchants

Both Oriental Jews and Armenians were initially heavily involved in Singapore's lucrative opium business, complementary to their operations in China, and also dealt in spices. Some Oriental Jews moved into general import-export functions as the opium trade was gradually suppressed from the 1880s (Nathan 1986: 3, 8–9, 28; Sarkissian 1987: 13). Wealthy Armenian merchants of Penang and Singapore, notably Agah Catchatoor Galustaun, contributed to Calcutta's Armenian Philanthropic Academy in the first half of the nineteenth century (Seth 1988: 131–4). George Manook, born of poor parents in Persia, was the greatest Armenian merchant in Java at this time, lending money to the cash-strapped Dutch government and leaving a fortune of five million guilders when he died in Batavia in 1827 (Seth 1988: 132). Armenians sold opium in the islands to the east of Java in mid-century, and they continued to be prominent merchants in Java up to the First World War (Goor 1982: 239; Sarkissian 1987: 10–14). South Persian merchants of Isfahan and Shiraz were also heavily involved in trading opium to Java, where they bought sugar, although it is not clear whether they settled on the island at this time (Abbott 1983: xviii, 86, 101).

Armenians in Burma suffered over time from their close association with independent Burmese monarchs. Major Armenian traders were employed as officials, especially in charge of maritime customs and relations with foreigners from across the sea. The British blamed their intrigues for the Negrais Massacre of 1759, and in the 1820s portrayed them as 'the Jews of the East, a description of men subtle, faithless and indefatigable' (Sarkissian 1987: 19–22). They survived the first Burmese defeat of 1826, when the British only annexed the fringe provinces of Arakan and Tenasserim (Papazian 1979: 39; Seth 1988: 131–4, 159). However, the British conquest of Lower Burma, the commercial heart of the country, in 1852, led to renewed accusations that Armenian merchants were anti-British, and even pro-Russian. There were further tensions when the British completed their conquest of Burma in 1885–86 (Sarkissian 1987: 24–6). Nevertheless, a new Armenian church was built in Rangoon in 1862 (Aghassian and Kévorian 2000: 159).

The import and wholesale sectors were a speciality for wealthier Syrians in the Philippines, both Lebanese and Jews placing a strong emphasis on jewellery and textiles (Gleeck 1975: 181; Gleeck *n. d.*: 4; Griese 1954: 49; Yoshihara 1985: 117). A commercial directory from 1908 indicated that Syrian wholesaling and importing operations were exclusively concentrated in Manila, and made no mention of exports (Abdou 1910: 434). By 1927, half a dozen Middle Eastern families were prominent in Manila's import-export trade, albeit still with an emphasis on imports (*RMCD 1927–28*). These families appear to have been mainly Christians from Lebanon, Damascus and Bethlehem (Clarence-Smith forthcoming).

Hadhrami wholesaling and importing was focused on the north Javanese ports, Sumatra and Singapore. In the 1880s and 1890s, reputable Hadhrami firms with good distribution networks obtained supplies on two to six months' credit from European importers (Berg 1886: 113–20, 134, 142–7; Fernando and Bulbeck 1992: 69, 71). However, the authorities backed a handful of large Dutch concerns in the import trade, and attempts by a group of Western-educated Hadhramis to break into direct importing from Europe were hard hit by the recession of the early 1920s (Alatas 1923: 49). In the 1920s, Hadhramis competed fiercely in Palembang, Sumatra, with Chinese, Europeans, Armenians, Indians and Malays (Vleming 1926: 241–2). Diamonds and coral were a Hadhrami niche market, together with perfumes (Berg 1886: 144; Deventer 1904: 102; Fernando and Bulbeck 1992: 69).

Japanese commercial penetration, particularly marked from 1914, helped to buttress the Hadhrami position. Japanese firms sought links with established Asian distributors, especially in textiles, and politically motivated Chinese boycotts of Japanese concerns made Arabs and Indians privileged intermediaries (Post 1993: 149–50; Huff 1994: 266–9; Cator 1936: 76; Vuldy 1987: 137–8). A Japanese newspaper, published in Batavia in 1928, called for the elimination of Chinese intermediaries and their replacement by European, indigenous and Arab merchant houses. In the same year, the Arab owner of the Rasjid Kanaekan Trading Company of Sibolga in Sumatra, went to Japan to enquire about importing Japanese products directly (Post 1996: 87, 93).

Japanese commercial penetration intensified after the devaluation of the Yen late in 1931, despite Dutch and British countermeasures. Moreover, Japanese reliance on non-Chinese intermediaries increased after the Manchurian crisis in that year, which further increased tensions between Japanese and Chinese entrepreneurs (Post 1993: 149–50, 159). There was even an Arabic and Islamic printing press in Osaka in 1937, run by one Mansur bin Sulayman Mar'i al-Kathiri al-Hadrami (Ulrike Freitag, *pers. comm.*).

Arab and indigenous merchants benefited particularly from Chinese boycotts in Java and South Sumatra, whereas the boycott movement was little followed by Chinese merchants in eastern Indonesia (Post 1993: 149–50; Vuldy 1987: 137). In the Malay peninsula and East Sumatra, the more numerous Indians were the main beneficiaries (Huff 1994: 268–9). Dutch moves to protect their own enterprises from 1933 shored up a cartel of five Dutch importers in the main ports, but did little to help European firms at lower levels of trade (Vuldy 1987: 138).

A handful of Arab trading associations set up branches throughout the archipelago, as well as in India. One of them, Jibul Fitr, was said to have 'rivalled the larger Chinese corporations in size and volume of operations' (Kroef 1953: 316). This firm does not appear in any other account, but it may have belonged to 'Awad b. Marta', from Haynin, who built up the most successful Hadrami wholesaling business in Indonesia, based in Surabaya (Meulen 1947: 155, 163, 215–6; Meulen and Wissman 1932: 101, 105). His clan became the leading Arab family in independent Indonesia (Serjeant 1957: 27). The N.V. Handelmaatschappij Antara-Asia was the joint-stock trading vehicle of the Bin Marta' family after 1945, possibly a new name for the company (Post 1996: 105). More generally, the larger Hadhrami trading firms in Java began to set themselves up as joint-stock companies in the 1930s, although in practical terms the control remained with the founding families (Clarence-Smith 2000).

The famous *batik* dyed fabrics of Java were a pillar of Hadhrami commerce from the early nineteenth century, but Chinese competition in finer grades intensified from around 1900, as did the Chinese grip on vital supplies of cambric and aniline dyes (Van Niel 1960: 86, 89; Vuldy 1987: 74, 106, 146, 156–9). To meet this perceived threat, leading Hadhrami families were at the forefront of the Sarekat Dagang Islam, a 'trade protection' movement which developed from 1909. Sarekat Islam emerged from these local trade associations in late 1912 as a Muslim political organization for the whole of Indonesia. This attempt to protect the Hadhrami position in the *batik* sector by political means went tragically wrong. Relations with the Chinese degenerated into rioting in 1912, and Marxist elements increased their influence in Sarekat Islam. Hadhrami entrepreneurs withdrew from the organization altogether after the Garut Incident of 1919, when radicals tried to foment an armed uprising (Algadri 1994: 106; Van Niel 1960: 86–94, 120–1, 145–6, 149).

The Hadhrami-Japanese alliance proved a better bet for *batik* traders. Arabs obtained plain Japanese cloth to sell to *batik* workshops, and sold the finished textiles directly to consumers around the Malay world and beyond (*HCHONI 1940*: 1378, 1447, 1455; Ingrams 1937: 147, 150; Ingrams 1942: 172; Meulen and Wissman 1932: 44–5). Business was good for some, even in the 1930s recession, for Sayyid H. b. Husayn Bin Shihab, a major Pekalongan trader in *batik* and checked cloth, endowed a *waqf* [charitable trust] for the Madrasah Arabiyah Islam school in the Arab quarter of the town in 1935 (Vuldy 1987: 216–7). *Batik* still figured high for Hadhrami traders in Java and Singapore on the eve of the war (Ingrams 1937: 147, 150; Ingrams 1942: 172).

In terms of exports, Middle Easterners were less visible, albeit with some exceptions. Neither Armenians nor Oriental Jews were prominent in this sector, although the Jewish Elias family were an exception. Indeed, Moshe Elias came to be known as the 'copra king' of North Sulawesi (Nathan 1986: 27). The Syrian presence in the Cagayán Valley was closely tied to purchasing tobacco for export, but speculation at the end of the First World War ruined many families (late Cesar Majul, *pers. comm.*). The concentration of Syrians in provincial towns in 1918 suggests that *abacá* (Manila hemp) and copra (dried coconut flesh) were the main raw materials that passed through their hands (Miller 1920: 416–17). However, the greatest export specialization of Manila's Middle Eastern community was embroidery, considered below under manufacturing.

Hadhrami exporters were also rare. The al-Saqqaf firm of Singapore was unusual in its emphasis on this sector, notably dealing in timber and spices, with a possible connection to its shipping interests (*SMD 1940*: 396; Wright and Cartwright 1908: 705–7). Coffee was something of a speciality, albeit one long-frustrated by Dutch government marketing in terms of the Cultivation System (Elson 1994: 37, 260; Clarence-Smith 1994: 245–50; Dobbin 1983: 103; Fernando and Bulbeck 1992: 69; Vleming 1926: 242). Hadhrami exporters also benefited to a limited degree from the gradual dismantling of similar government monopolies on pepper and spices in the Moluccas and Sumatra (Dobbin 1983: 167; Reid 1972: 39; Wright and Cartwright 1908: 707). In the key rubber sector, Hadhramis trailed far behind their Chinese and European competitors (Kroef 1953: 311; Vleming 1926: 241–3, 258).

Hadhramis played a larger role in the internal trade of the Dutch East Indies. They gained a stranglehold over the export of horses from southeastern Indonesia to Java, chiefly destined for transport and military purposes. Arab firms in East Java initially sent agents to the Lesser Sundas to purchase horses, but the major company of the inter-war years, Mohamat Aldjuffrie & Co., had its headquarters on the island of Sumba, with representatives in East Java (Clarence-Smith 2002a). The al-Jifri brothers who ran this firm were of the same Hadhrami Sayyid clan as the Arab representative on the Volksraad (advisory council) before the war (Ingrams 1940: 122). Hadhramis were also quite active in the internal rice trade, especially that from Bali in the early nineteenth century (Berg 1886: 146; Broersma 1934: 133–4; Elson 1994: 259). Sales of slaves and guns led to occasional confrontations with the authorities (Kniphorst 1885: 291; Reid 1972: 38).

More modern commercial niches emerged in Manila in the inter-war years. Thus, the Ysmaels, probably the foremost Lebanese family in the Philippines, represented the American pharmaceuticals company of Winthrop-Stearns before the Second World War (Gleeck 1975: 145). The related Hashim family appears to have had a stake in the importation of automobiles in 1927 (*RMCD 1927–28*: 512).

Real Estate, Finance and the Media

Diversification out of trade was uneven, with Middle Easterners overrepresented in urban real estate in relation to their numbers. In contrast, their presence in other services was patchy. Hadhramis were prominent moneylenders, but not bankers, whereas other Middle Eastern communities appear to have been altogether absent from financial services.

One easily underestimated factor in urban real estate was timing. The Chinese were surprisingly slow off the mark in Singapore, the beacon of free enterprise founded by Raffles in 1819. Of the 43 merchant houses recorded there in 1846, 6 were Oriental Jewish, 5 Arab, 2 Armenian and only 5 Chinese (Nathan 1986: 1). This partly explains the extraordinary Middle Eastern prominence in Singapore's real-estate sector in later years, though it cannot explain why European entrepreneurs failed to make much headway. Armenians were important early on, but seem to have pulled out. Sarkis (Sarkies) Brothers, active in business in Singapore since 1828, built the Raffles Hotel there, perhaps the most famous of all the great hotels of Southeast Asia (Papazian 1979: 39; Sarkissian 1987: 6).

Oriental Jews were making fortunes in Singapore's real-estate market by the end of the nineteenth century, as they moved out of the declining opium trade. Salleh Manasseh Salleh, who left Baghdad in 1862 and went to Singapore via India, was one of the pioneers. However, the great plutocrat Manasseh Meyer, undisputed leader of the community for many years, was the largest owner. From real estate, it was a natural progression to hotels and stables. Manasseh Meyer owned both the Adelphi and Sea View hotels in Singapore, and Nissim N. Adis was famous for building what became the Grand Hôtel de l'Europe (Nathan 1986:

Table 10.1 Estimated value of Arab investment in real estate, *c*.1885

Town	Millions of guilders	per cent of total
Singapore	4	25.0
Surabaya	3	18.8
Batavia	2.5	15.6
Pontianak	2	12.5
Semarang	1	6.3
Penang & rest of Malaya	1	6.3
Palembang	0.5	3.1
Rest of Indonesia	2	12.5
TOTAL	16	

Source: Berg 1886: 136

6–9, 21–5, 28–30). Meyer Mansions was also a famous block of flats, 'built by the Meyer family, one of several Jewish millionaire families in the business life of the city' (Peet 1985: 84).

Hadhrami prominence in real estate was equally renowned (Alatas 1923: 49; Peeters 1994: 32). The estimates in Table 10.1 are probably more useful in indicating geographical spread than actual quantities of capital invested. Among the cosmopolitan pioneers of Singapore, Hadhramis excelled in buying prime land and property at advantageous prices (Buckley 1965: 563–5). In 1887, leading Hadhramis joined with Chinese property owners to protest a proposal to levy rates on vacant houses (Song 1923: 232). The al-Saqqaf family owned the prestigious Raffles Hotel by the 1900s, while the al-Kaf were second only to the Dock Board as rate payers. Sayyid 'Umar b. Shaykh al-Kaf owned the Grand Hôtel de l'Europe in the 1930s, and the family firm in Singapore in 1940 styled itself 'Alkaff and Co., House and Landowners and Estate Agents [Real]' (Meulen and Wissman 1932: 137; *SMD 1940*: 395; Wright and Cartwright 1908: 707, 710). Arabs and Jews were the 'largest owners of house property' in the town in 1931 (Vlieland 1931: 87). Despite the 1930s recession, urban property made Arabs the wealthiest community per head in Singapore, with thirteen principal families owning assets valued at £2.5 million. Whole streets were owned by Hadhramis, there and in Penang (Ingrams 1937: 150). Indeed, there was resentment against Arabs for allegedly pushing up land prices and crowding Malays out of Singapore (Roff 1967: 192).

The Hadhrami stake in urban property in Java was also impressive. As early as 1860, the al-Saqqaf family of Singapore owned twenty houses in Surabaya, three in Batavia, and undeveloped land in the latter city (Al-Saqqaf 1993: 192–3). In 1914, Shaykh Salih b. 'Ubayd b. 'Abdat owned the luxurious Hôtel des Galeries, the second largest in Batavia (Mobini-Kesheh 1997: 237; Mobini-Kesheh 1999). The al-Kaf had a subsidiary in Batavia at the end of the 1930s, the N.V. Bouw

Maatschappij Alkaff (*SMD 1940*: 395). In the same decade, the well-known capitalist, Ba Suwaydan, originally from Shibam in Hadhramaut, possessed 'hundreds of houses in Singapore and Batavia' (Meulen and Wissman 1932: 80–2, 116).

The 1930s recession hit this sector hard. As late as 1939, Sayyid Abu Bakr bin Shaykh al-Kaf of Tarim, the religious centre of Hadhramaut, was suffering from low returns on his extensive property portfolio in Singapore and Batavia. Similarly, Shaykh Salim bin Ja´far bin Talib, of al-´Uqda, was reported to be 'in trouble with regard to his houses in Surabaya, the rents of which had diminished because of the world economic crisis' (Meulen 1947: 159, 219–20). A mixed story came from al-Hurayda, the family town of the al-´Attas family. The local school operated in 1934 with the rents of a building in Batavia, but was closed in late 1937 as 'the house in Java whose rent was its mainstay is empty because of the slump' (Stark 1945: 60). Two years later, however, the school was open again, still on the basis of revenues from the house in Batavia (Meulen 1947: 145). Indeed, for Hadhramis with abundant capital, steep falls in the prices of all other factors of production presented tremendous opportunities in the real-estate sector (Clarence-Smith 2000).

Urban real estate held a similar appeal for Syrians in the Philippines. The Ysmael (Isma'il) family came from Lebanon to trade, but later generations were largely involved in property (Yoshihara 1985, 117). Possibly the most successful of all Lebanese immigrants, they gradually became Catholic and Spanish-speaking, intermarrying with the Hashim and Hemady families. Magdalena (Wadi'ah) Ysmael Hemady bought a large parcel of land, in what was known as New Manila, later subdivided and sold in smaller lots at great profit (Quirino 1987: 53). A street in what became Quezon City was named after her, and there was a 'Magdalena subdivision' in affluent New Manila in the late 1930s (Benito Legarda and Dan Doeppers, *pers. comm*s.). The Ysmaels, at some point after 1912, put up 'their own edifice' (Gleeck 1975: 44). The Awads of Davao did the same in 1927, though the building was destroyed in the Second World War (Doeppers 1969: field notes).

Tourism and entertainment were related to real estate. The Hashim brothers owned the Manila Grand Opera House, which specialized in vaudeville and musical presentations, and they established a bicycle-race track (Gleeck 1975: 96, 181; Gleeck *n.d.*: 4). The Gabriel family ran a hotel in Bontoc, northern Luzon, and the Bichara family owned cinemas in Bikol. Elie Akrass ran a night-club for Americans after 1945, where he was murdered in mysterious circumstances (late Cesar Majul, *pers. comm.*).

Moneylending was central to Hadhrami economic activity, especially for the community in Tegal, North Java. Rich Hadhramis lent to the wealthy of all races at yearly interest rates of 25 to 30 per cent. The rescheduling of bad debts was preferred to foreclosure. Smaller operators, obliged to lend on dubious assets, pushed interest rates up to 200 per cent, extracting labour services in case of default. Koranic prohibitions on usury were side-stepped by fictitious sales and the 'renting' of money (Berg 1886: 136–8; Fernando and Bulbeck 1992: 49–51; Ingrams 1937: 147; Kroef 1953: 312–6). Critics nevertheless denounced this as 'usury', including reformist Hadhramis in the 1930s (Algadri 1994: 6–7). However, rescheduling lowered real interest rates, and great losses were incurred in the 1930s recession (Kroef 1953: 312–16). Arabs themselves often obtained credit from Indian or European firms (Berg 1886: 139–41, 146, 168–70).

Moneylending never developed into full-fledged banking, possibly because it would have been more difficult to avoid the ban on taking interest, and other financial activities did not figure much in Hadhrami activities. Singapore Arabs exchanged notes of the Java Bank, together with Indians, a significant business because of the port's pilgrim traffic (Fernando and Bulbeck 1992: 141). Tax farming, so important for the Chinese, attracted few Arabs (Clarence-Smith 1997).

Another growth area for Hadhramis was newspapers in the British possessions. They were first associated with *al-Imam*, appearing in Singapore in 1906–09, but it was in the 1930s that 'hard-headed Arab press barons' emerged in Singapore and Penang, employing mainly Malay journalists and selling copies in the Dutch possessions. The foundation of the Warta Malaya group of newspapers in 1930 by the al-Saqqaf family of Singapore was a milestone. Sayyid ʿAlawi b. ʿUmar al-Bar was another Singapore press baron of the time, while Sayyid Shaykh b. Ahmad al-Hadi owned the Jelutong Press in Penang, which published two influential papers. Indeed, there was Malay resentment by the end of the decade at the degree of Hadhrami financial control over the press, despite the pro-Malay political stance of papers (Roff 1972: 8–10, 51; Roff 1967: 64–5, 168–9).

Transport

Hadhrami shippers prospered from the late eighteenth century, especially under the cover of European flags, and this activity overshadowed trade in the middle decades of the nineteenth century (Clarence-Smith 2002b). The port records of Java show that although Arabs accounted for only 2 per cent of sea captains in 1774–77, they operated larger vessels and covered longer distances than all competitors except the Dutch East India Company. Since at least the mid-1750s, Arabs specialized in sailing between Java and Palembang and Malacca, on either side of the Straits of Malacca. The average size of ship owned by Arabs was only just over 50 tons, but some of their vessels were much larger. Arab captains resident in Java were mostly to be found in the central and eastern ports of the North coast, notably Semarang, Pekalongan, Gresik and Surabaya. Crew members were mainly Javanese, and were probably free. Arab ships were a mixture of types, at a time when older

Southeast Asian models were giving ground to ones of European design built in local yards (Knaap 1996: 33–7, 65–73, 83, 155–6, 212–13).

The British occupation of the Dutch colonies from 1795, effective in 1811 for Java, stimulated an inflow of Hadhrami shippers, and they proved better able than the British to cope with the return of the Dutch in 1816. From 1818, all coastwise shipping was legally restricted to Dutch-flagged vessels owned by residents of the Dutch colonies, to which ships registered in the Netherlands were added in 1850. International shipping was initially confined to the port of Batavia, though Riau, Semarang and Surabaya were opened in 1825. These regulations were tightened in 1834, to prevent foreigners with only a few years' residence from flying the Dutch tricolour and engaging in coastal shipping (Broeze 1979: 251–2).

This legislation helped to propel Hadhramis, legally Dutch subjects, to the forefront of coastal shipping. Not only British but also Dutch concerns declined, while ships owned by locally resident Chinese were confined to short hops, and were on average much smaller than those belonging to Arabs. Over medium and long distances within the Dutch East Indies, Hadhrami ships gained supremacy. From 22 per cent of the registered tonnage of European-rigged ships in 1820, Arabs went to just over 50 per cent in 1850, compared to 29 per cent for the Chinese, 9 per cent for the Dutch, 9 per cent for the British, and 3 per cent for 'natives'. Arabs had no European-rigged ships in Batavia in 1820, but they possessed nearly 2,000 tons of such shipping in the port by 1850. However, it was the twin harbours of Gresik and Surabaya in eastern Java which witnessed the fastest progression, with some 11,500 tons owned by Arabs in 1850 (Broeze 1979: 257–60, 266–7).

Hadhramis were able to expand shipping links not only between Dutch ports but also with British settlements in Malaya from the 1830s. Flying the Dutch flag, these 'fine vessels', built of teak and ranging from 150 to 500 tons, engaged in much contraband to avoid Dutch tariffs (Buckley 1965: 324). Furthermore, independent Muslim rulers allegedly accorded Hadhrami Sayyid shippers a remission of duties, on account of their 'superior sanctity' as descendants of the Prophet (Earl 1971: 68).

There was a gradual concentration of ships into fewer hands, with the complete disappearance of the formerly dominant Arab skipper-owner in Batavia and Surabaya by 1850. However, seven Arab captains out of twenty-five still owned their ships in Gresik in 1850, and the practice remained somewhat more common among Arabs than among Europeans. The average size of vessels rose, with the number of Arab ships of over 200 tons in Gresik going from nine in 1830 to sixteen in 1850. Shipping became a more specialized business, rather than a mere appendage of commerce (Broeze 1979: 264–6).

Sayyid families involved in the great Javanese shipping boom included the al-Saqqaf and the Ba Raqbah, but the most notable among them were two members of the al-Hibshi family, Hasan and ʿAlawi, who received the coveted Javanese title of Pangeran in the 1840s. By 1850, they possessed half the Arab tonnage of Surabaya, as well as owning ships registered in Gresik and Batavia. All seven al-Hibshi ships in Surabaya were barks, totalling over 2,000 tons (Broeze 1979: 265–6). Sayyid Hasan was also the greatest Arab trader in Java in the 1820s and 1830s (Earl 1971: 67–8). He was entrusted by the Dutch with delicate diplomatic missions as far away as Siam (Thailand), where he probably had trading interests (Broersma 1934: 133–4).

Not all major Hadhrami ship-owners in Java were of Sayyid status, for the Ba Hashwan also possessed several European rigged ships in Gresik and Batavia by 1850 (Broeze 1979: 266). In the 1860s, Muhammad b. ʿUthman Ba Hashwan did a flourishing trade in horses, transported from Sumba to Java in one of his ships (Parimartha 1995: 214). This family was drawn from the Maskin social stratum, the most lowly in Hadhramaut's free population. That said, the Ba Hashwan belonged to a 'bourgeois' group within the Maskin, who claimed to have immigrated from Iraq together with the founder ancestor of the Hadhrami Sayyid families (Berg 1886: 49–50).

Outside Java, Palembang in southern Sumatra was the main rival to Surabaya as a centre of Hadhrami shipping (Berg 1886: 147–8). Only three Arab shipowners were registered in Palembang in the 1830s, but from 1840 there was a rapid growth in Arab barks, brigs and schooners, generally between 200 and 600 tons. Foremost among the Hadhrami shipowners of the port was Sayyid ʿAli b. Abu Bakr b. al-Shaykh Abu Bakr b. Salim. He and his family owned about half the total Palembang Arab fleet by 1850. The Dutch appointed him Captain of the Palembang Arabs from 1833 till his death in 1878, and granted him the title of Pangeran. The other half a dozen major Arab shipowners in Palembang in 1850 were also of Sayyid origin, initially linked to Java, but with much of their business directed to Singapore after 1819 (Peeters 1994: 27–30). In 1823, Arab ships also controlled much of the traffic with Penang, in vessels locally built with elements of European schooner design, or in brigs (Dobbin 1983: 94). The al-Qadri sultans of Pontianak, West Borneo, owned a brig and other merchant vessels in the 1810s (Moor 1968: App., 101–6). In eastern Indonesia, Ternate, Ambon and Banda were centres of Hadhrami sailing ships, with close links to Surabaya (Clarence-Smith 1998: 39).

The British flag was a rival attraction. Among the Arabs who flocked to Singapore after 1819 were shipping families of Sayyid origin, notably the al-Kaf (Alkaff) and the al-Junayd (Aljunied). Most prominent was Sayyid ʿAbd al-Rahman al-Saqqaf (Alsagoff), who had earlier traded between Malacca and Java, and was from an influential Hijazi family with a branch in Hadhramaut (Berg 1886: 122; Morley 1949: 155; Buckley 1965: 85, 563–5). Sayyid Ahmad made a shrewd marriage into the royal family of Gowa in South Sulawesi, which drove much trade with Singapore, denounced as 'contraband' by the powerless Dutch (Alsagoff 1963: 9–11; Buckley 1965: 564; Wright and Cartwright 1908: 707). Sayyid Ahmad then initiated a regular pilgrim service to Jiddah in the 1850s. Singapore was the hub of the rapidly growing pilgrim flow from Southeast Asia, because the Dutch stubbornly attempted to limit numbers for political and social reasons (Lee 1991: 165).

Steamers provided competition to Hadhrami sailing ships from around 1850. The number of European-rigged sailing ships owned by 'Dutch Arabs' continued to rise between 1850 and 1864, reaching a total of ninety-six in 1860–64, but the Arab percentage fell slightly, as Chinese shippers expanded their operations. The aggregate number of such ships in Arab hands then fell for the first time in 1865–69 (Mansvelt 1938: 98; Campo 1992: 367, 683). Nevertheless, Arabs still owned seventy-five such ships around 1885, amounting to some 16,000 tons in all. They were concentrated in Palembang and Surabaya, and specialized in less-frequented routes, especially in eastern Indonesia (Berg 1886: 119, 147–50). The schooner became the preferred Arab ship, easier to manoeuvre than a square-rigged brig or bark, and requiring a smaller crew per ton. Up to 1914, Arab schooners operated between the small islands of the Moluccas and the Lesser Sundas, serving ports and islands at which steamers did not call (Broersma 1934: 144–5, 325–6; Broersma 1935–36: 425).

A functional niche which Arab sailing ships retained for a long time was the transport of live animals, pride of place being taken by horses brought from the Lesser Sundas to Java (Berg 1886: 150; Clarence-Smith 2002a). However, sailing vessels could only leave the Lesser Sundas when the monsoon was blowing in the right direction, for fear of horses losing condition (Kuperus 1936: 28). Arab shipowners held their own until special facilities for the transport of live animals were introduced on steamers around 1900. By the inter-war years of the twentieth century, European-rigged ships had become obsolete in this trade (Clarence-Smith 2002a).

Arab *perahu*, rigged and built in the local manner, survived for longer, for example to bring horses to larger ports visited by steamers. In the 1930s, they transported bulky but low-value chalk and lime from Sulawesi and the Lesser Sundas, for use in the Javanese construction industry, possibly a cost-cutting response to economic recession. Arab *perahu* were also of some importance in fishing in East Java and pearling in the eastern archipelago (Clarence-Smith 1998: 38–9; Kroef 1953: 316).

While harming established interests, steamers in theory provided new opportunities, and the Dutch possessions witnessed the beginnings of Hadhrami steam navigation. In the early 1860s, a group of Arabs from Ambon were the real owners of the *Menado*, which operated between Java and eastern Indonesia. The steamer was registered in the name of an Ambonese with European legal status, and had a European captain. Despite somewhat scanty return freight, consisting mainly of spices and coffee, the *Menado* undercut subsidized mail boats in the 1870s (Clarence-Smith 1998: 39–40). In 1878, two Arabs and a European founded the N.V. Voorwaarts Company for a weekly Batavia-Semarang service along the coast of Java. A year later, the company purchased a small 300–ton steamer in Singapore, able to carry seventy passengers, and extended its services to Surabaya. However, the venture collapsed a year later, allegedly for lack of sufficient capital (Berg 1886: 148–9; Campo 1992: 46). Two Arab firms still owned a single steamer apiece in the Dutch possessions in 1886, one in Ambon and the other in Palembang (Berg 1886: 149).

The foundation of the Koninklijke Paketvaart Maatschappij (KPM), in 1888, sounded the death knell of Hadhrami steam navigation in Indonesia. The Dutch were determined to eliminate 'Foreign Oriental' competition in coastal shipping. Financed by the major Dutch shipping companies and benefiting from generous official subsidies and assistance, the KPM became a quasi-monopolistic force, closely linked to the Dutch programme of military 'pacification'. Arab steamer services within Indonesia were thus almost entirely choked off by the end of the 1890s, although the KPM could not control routes to Singapore, or other foreign ports, as effectively as those lying entirely within Indonesia (Campo 1992). In the 1910s, an Arab steamer service still ran from southeastern Sumatra to Singapore, and Arabs owned a few small tramp steamers in North Sulawesi (Jansen 1990: 19; Purwanto 1992: 54, 89–90). Indeed, one Arab owner of motorboats in North Sulawesi, Sayyid ʿAbd al-Rahman b. Shaykh al-Hasni, remained defiant till the eve of the Second World War, exploiting links with Japanese shipping companies purchasing copra (Dick 1989: 257–8, 266).

Singapore, more liberal in its administration, thus became the bastion of Hadhrami steam navigation. As early as 1871, Sayyid Ahmad al-Saqqaf's Singapore Steamship Company ferried pilgrims to Jiddah, with a European captain (Sherry 1966: 47). Three years later, the company had four steamers and conveyed 3,476 pilgrims to Jiddah. After Sayyid Ahmad's death in 1875, his son, Sayyid Muhammad, continued the business (Lee 1991: 165–7).

In 1880, a major scandal befell the Singapore Steamship Company's *Jeddah*. This was an eight-year-old steamer of over 1,000 tons, built in Dumbarton, Scotland. The European captain together with European crew members and Sayyid ʿUmar al-Saqqaf, abandoned the stricken vessel in the Gulf of Aden, following a bad storm. They reached Aden in a lifeboat, and reported to the authorities that the ship had gone down with nearly a thousand pilgrims on board. To general astonishment, the ship was then towed into Aden by another steamer. The *Jeddah* was found to have had only six lifeboats on board, but accusations that the incident was staged to gain £30,000 in insurance money proved groundless (Sherry 1966: 43–64).

Despite this scandal, there were still two Arab steamer companies active in Singapore in the mid-1880s, the al-Saqqaf firm and Sayyid Masim b. Salih al-Jifri (Jeoffrie). Arab capital from Surabaya and some Chinese funds were invested in one of these companies. They owned two steamers apiece, employed European captains and engineers, and were locked in fierce competition with two Dutch lines for the pilgrim traffic to Jiddah. They also ran services to the east, as far as China. However, Sayyid al-Jifri's business collapsed some time before his death in 1894 (Berg 1886: 149–50; Buckley 1965: 564–5).

The long-term problem for Hadhrami steam navigation was that British liberalism failed to prevent the emergence of powerful cartels, the shipping 'conferences' or 'rings' which enmeshed the Indian Ocean in their coils from the 1870s. One solution was to join these cartels. Sayyid ʿUmar al-Saqqaf was a founding member of a pilgrimage syndicate in 1896, in alliance with the British company Holts, several Dutch shippers, and the Sharif of Mecca. The syndicate enjoyed a monopoly over the transport of pilgrims from the Straits Settlements to Jiddah (Lee 1991: 165–6). How long this arrangement lasted is not certain, but the al-Saqqaf company was still transporting pilgrims to Jiddah in 1908 (Wright and Cartwright 1908: 707).

The cartelization of steam navigation in Asian waters increased greatly from the turn of the century, leading Singapore Arabs to join an unsuccessful public protest in 1910 (Huff 1994: 135). Moreover, rapid technological change led to larger and more costly ships, raising barriers to entry. Nevertheless, some Arab involvement persisted into the inter-war years. Salim b. Muhammad b. Talib, of tribal or Qabili origins, was among the wealthiest Arab entrepreneurs in Singapore. He owned several steamers until his death in 1937, when his family sold them (Ulrike Freitag, *pers. comm.*).

The Armenian Apcar Line threw in the towel shortly before the First World War. The Apcar family was one of the great Armenian business dynasties in Asia. Originally settled in Persia, they came to be centred in Calcutta from the early nineteenth century (Seth 1988: 126). They ran a 'small fleet of tolerably fast vessels' to Rangoon and Singapore, and on to southern China and Japan. Their steamers specialized in the transport of Chinese 'coolies' to and from Singapore. In 1912, the family offered to sell the business to the British India Steam Navigation Company (BISN), part of the Scottish McKinnon group, and enjoying the support of the British authorities. The offer was accepted with alacrity, with the intention of gaining a greater share of the traffic with Japan, and the Apcar name was maintained by the BISN up to the Second World War (Blake 1956: 171–2). The antecedents of the Apcar Line, and the family's reasons for approaching the BISN, are not explained.

Land transport attracted a few Syrians in the Philippines, as the internal combustion engine replaced the horse. Businesses based on buses, lorries and petrol stations were centred on Manila, or on major provincial towns in Luzon (late Cesar Majul, *pers. comm.*).

Manufacturing

The 'third wave' of diversification out of trade focused on manufacturing. Middle Easterners were less prominent than Chinese in processing raw materials for export, and tended to specialize in consumer goods for the internal market, notably textiles.

Hadhramis were drawn early into the famous *batik*-dyeing business of Java, but their progress from trade to production was slow and cautious. In the 1840s, Pekalongan Arabs simply advanced imported cotton cloth and wax to Javanese women for home production, and sold the finished product. From around the 1860s, they financed workshops for individually drawn *batik tulis*, and for the cheaper *batik cap*, produced with metal stamps. At some point in the later nineteenth century they set up their own workshops, often run by their wives (Vuldy 1985: 106–9; Vuldy 1987: 107, 110–13, 138–42).

As the number of Hadhrami workshops grew, the centre of gravity of the business shifted inland to the old capital city of Surakarta. Of the 130 Arab *batik* workshops in Java in 1930, 88 were in Surakarta and 25 in Pekalongan. The Hadhramis of Pekalongan compensated in the 1930s by creating workshops weaving *palekat*, a checked cloth formerly imported from India. Arabs accounted for only 3 per cent of the 4,384 *batik* workshops in Java in 1930, compared to 16.5 per cent for the Chinese and a mere 0.3 per cent for Europeans. However, Arab workshops were usually larger than those of the Javanese, and Hadhramis indirectly controlled many of the 3,515 Javanese enterprises through supplies of inputs and credit (Cator 1936: 117–18; Vuldy 1985: 108–9; Vuldy 1987: 124–5, 129–32, 138–42).

A few Hadhramis owned larger and more modern units by the 1930s, moving from *batik* to cotton textiles themselves. One of the effects of the 1930s recession was to push the Dutch authorities into supporting industrialization, notably on Java (Clarence-Smith 2000). In 1939, enterprises owned by 'Foreign Orientals' other than Chinese were responsible for 16 per cent of the 56.8 million metres of cloth produced by large-scale weaving units (Segers 1987: 155). In 1942, Europeans owned 40 per cent of installed power looms, compared to 31 per cent for Chinese, 22 per cent for Arabs, and 7 per cent for indigenous entrepreneurs. Moreover, three of the seven largest textile concerns on Java belonged to Arabs (Matsuo 1970: 47–8).

The most significant Hadhrami textile empire was that created by the Bin Marta' family. The Firma Alsaid bin Awad Martak set up a weaving plant in Surabaya in 1934, on the advice of a Javanese engineer working as government industrial adviser. A year later, the brothers Faraj and Ahmad set up a second and larger weaving mill at Kesono in eastern Java, which was managed by a Dutchman. At the end of the 1930s, the Firma Alsaid bin Awad Martak had become the largest non-European textile concern on Java. The Kesono plant alone had 1,000 looms, of which 600 were Suzuki power looms imported from Japan (Post 1996: 104–5; Matsuo 1970: 48). The Surabaya plant employed nearly 2,000 workers (Ingrams 1940: 113). Under the Japanese occupation, the family dominated the Textile Control Board created in 1942 to monopolize the purchase, storage and sale of yarn in East Java (Post 1996: 104–5).

There were other Hadhrami textile pioneers. The Bin Sungkar (Soengkar) family combined weaving with *batik* production in their Surakarta factory by the end of the 1930s, and helped to finance a school in Pekalongan (Ingrams 1940: 123; Vuldy 1987: 217). The N.V. Textielfabriek en Handel Maatschappij Baswedan, set up in Surabaya in 1938 with a partly paid-up capital of 300,000 guilders, was headed by Ibrahim Ba Suwaydan (Brahim Baswedan) (*HCHONI 1940*: 1011). An unnamed Arab founded the first weaving factory in Pekalongan, and the E.K.J. Muallim factory in Tjermee had 560 power looms, 2,200 hand looms and 2,700 workers by 1942 (Matsuo 1970: 30, 48). The al-Kaf family attempted to emulate these developments in Singapore, but the business foundered when war broke out (Ulrike Freitag, *pers. comm.*).

An earlier involvement in ship-building declined in tandem with the Hadhrami sailing fleet. During the short British occupation of Java from 1811 to 1816, Hadhrami shipping entrepreneurs of Gresik exploited the renowned teak forests of east-central Java to build vessels, but the returning Dutch slapped restrictions on teak (Broeze 1979: 256–7). One Arab nevertheless built a ship of over 1,000 tons upstream from Surabaya, the largest ship ever built in Java at the time. He lacked the funds to fit her out, and was thus obliged to sell her at a loss, but she probably remained in Hadhrami hands as the *Fait Allam*, registered in Semarang at 1,120 tons in 1850 (Broeze 1979: 264; Earl 1971: 71–2). The Bin Shihab sultan of Siak also built his own vessels in the 1820s (Dobbin 1983: 94).

Other Arab workshops and factories turned out diverse goods for the local market, chiefly in Java and Sumatra. In the 1880s, Hadhramis were engaged in printing and brick making (Berg 1886: 153). Of the ten factories making cement tiles in Batavia in 1940, one belonged to the al-ʿAydarus (Alaydroes) family and another to the Ba Hashwan (Bahasoean) family, linking up with their real-estate businesses (*HCHONI 1940* :1280). In later decades, Arabs produced foodstuffs, clove-flavoured cigarettes, garments, sandals, umbrellas, perfume, furniture, candles, matches, torch batteries, religious texts and construction materials. Arab enterprises typically employed ten to twenty women and children, labouring under rudimentary conditions (Cator 1936: 117–20; Jonge 1993: 78; Kroef 1953:

316–17; Purwanto 1992: 86–7). Some units were larger, however, such as Zayn Ba Jabir's factory in Surabaya in the late 1930s, which produced tin trunks and fibre suitcases (Ingrams 1940: 113).

Processing raw materials was less common, although the al-Saqqaf family again proved exceptional. The Handel- Industrie- en Cultuur-Maatschappij S. Alwi Assegaf, in Palembang, was founded as a joint-stock company in 1928. Managed by Sayyid ʿAlawi bin Shaykh al-Saqqaf in 1940, its main assets consisted of the Prinses Juliana sawmill and rice mill (*HCHONI 1940*: 769–70). In the 1900s, the al-Saqqaf Express Saw Mill in Malaya was 'one of the largest sawmills in the East' (Wright and Cartwright 1908: 707). Of the five rubber mills processing smallholder rubber in southeastern Borneo in 1925, one belonged to the Arab Shaykh Mutlaq (Mutlek), and there were Arab sawmills in southern Sumatra (Purwanto 1992: 54, 86–7; Vleming 1926: 266).

The Syrian contribution to Philippines manufacturing developed with exports of embroidery after 1909, when the Philippines gained unimpeded access to the American market. Firms in the USA, mainly run by Lebanese and Jews in New York, sought to make the islands a supplementary source of embroidery from Japan, China and Europe. Some importers thus set up branches or subsidiaries in the Philippines (Gleeck 1975: 69–73; Kayal 1975: 88; Safa 1960: 32–3, 216). However, importers seem to have relied more on trusted agents. Oriental Jews were active exporters of embroidery, as well as of buttons, and there was a close correlation between their immigration and the rise of embroidery exports from the islands (Griese 1954: 49). Syrians of all faiths were represented in the late 1920s, and one firm also dealt in hats, produced in much the same way (*RMCD 1926–27*).

From just over 0.2 million pesos in 1912, the first year in which they were separately recorded, the value of embroidery exports rose to some 12 million pesos in 1929 (Miller 1920: 370, 402, 461; Miller 1932: 473–4; Philippines 1933: 219). Helped by the impact of the First World War, and by a stiff import duty on European products entering America, embroidery made up about 5 per cent of the Philippines' exports by value in the 1920s and 1930s (Doeppers 1984: 13, 22–3). Nineteen 'concerns' employed some 60,000 women in 1918, and there were about 1,700 salaried women in Manila factories, as well as 350 peripatetic agents (Doeppers 1984: 22–3). By 1930, about 50,000 women worked in eighteen 'factories' in Manila, and another fifty-three establishments produced 'hand-made embroidery', though the number employed was not stated (Mendinueto 1930: 9–10).

Embroidery was no more than semi-industrial in nature. Firms in America bought cotton or linen cloth, which they bleached and sent out to the Philippines, where the only textile mill collapsed in 1923. In Manila, the cloth was cut and stamped in factories, according to specifications of American purchasers.

Travelling agents or contractors provided advances of cloth, other inputs and cash to local women, who worked part-time. They embroidered principally lingerie, handkerchiefs, tablecloths and children's clothing. The business began in suburban Manila, but soon spread out over southwestern Luzon. Agents, many of them women in the early years, bought finished products by the piece, at a previously agreed price and time. They took them to Manila factories, where they were graded and prepared for export, with further 'sewing, trimming, ribboning, ironing and packing'. Some women were brought together in large buildings, but this was for greater supervision and division of labour, rather than to apply mechanical power (Doeppers 1984: 17, 22–3; Gleeck 1975: 69–73; Miller 1932: 472–9).

Primary Production

Hadhrami entrepreneurs were chary of tying up capital in risky primary production, about which they knew little, making them more akin to Indians than to Chinese. Even the exceptions tended to prove the rule. A handful of wealthy Hadhramis owned *partikuliere landerijen* around Batavia, enjoying quasi-feudal rights over local inhabitants, but the authorities began to buy these lands back in the inter-war years (Abeyasekere 1989: 106; Heuken 1996). Hadhramis occasionally grew coconuts, as well as tea in upland Java (Clarence-Smith 1997; Clarence-Smith 1998). British land policies in Malaya were more favourable than those of the Dutch, but only the al-Saqqaf family took much interest, focusing on rubber, while trying out a variety of crops (Wright and Cartwright 1908: 707; *SMD passim*). A Western craze for mother-of-pearl offered rich pickings off New Guinea from the 1890s, making a fortune for Shaykh Sa'id b. 'Abdallah Ba Adilla, Lieutenant of the Banda Arabs, but the boom collapsed with the advent of war in Europe (Clarence-Smith 1998: 38–9).

Much the same was true of Oriental Jews and Syrians. Among Baghdadis, the Elias family was unusual in investing in Malayan tin and rubber (Nathan 1986: 78). In the Philippines, Juan Awad married a wealthy local woman in eastern Mindanao, and grew Manila hemp and coconuts from around 1885. However, falling hemp prices led his heirs to sell the estate to pay off debts (Abdou 1910: 434; Doeppers 1969: field notes). Timber, pearling and mining tempted no more than the odd Syrian here and there (Clarence-Smith, forthcoming).

Conclusion

Much remains to be discovered about Middle Eastern entrepreneurs in Southeast Asia, not least why they flourished in particular economic niches. However, it is abundantly clear that the neglect of this group in standard economic histories of the region is unwarranted, for they were a force to be reckoned with. Moreover, Middle Eastern communities in Southeast Asia were part of wider diasporas, and further research needs to place them in this broader context.

The latter point is particularly important in attempting to assess why Middle Easterners did not hang on to their early nineteenth-century lead in Southeast Asia. Arabs, Jews and Armenians were generally quicker than their South Chinese and Tamil rivals to grasp the new opportunities flowing from nineteenth-century free trade, and yet they tended to lose ground toward the end of the century. The material above shows that there is no substance in the popular explanations that Middle Easterners were less well endowed with capital or entrepreneurial flair. If anything, their experience indicates that the praise heaped upon Chinese businessmen in recent decades has been exaggerated.

The material in this chapter suggests a better explanation, namely that many Middle Easterners were able to seize opportunities elsewhere, as the free-trading horizons opened up by Britain in the early nineteenth century began to narrow in the 1880s, and were seriously undermined by the First World War and its aftermath. While South Chinese and Tamils faced major and growing hurdles in emigrating to Western countries, many Middle Easterners managed to achieve the coveted status of Whites. This was especially important for Christians and Jews, who moved on to greener pastures in the Americas, Europe and Australia. Hadhrami Arabs, as Muslims, were less able to follow these avenues for upward social and economic mobility, although the story of Hadhrami migration to the West remains to be written. Hadhramis thus consolidated their position as the chief Middle Eastern business community of Southeast Asia in the inter-war years.

Independence after the Second World War made even this haven unsafe, as Sukarno was possessed of a deep hatred of Hadhrami Arabs, and proceeded to nationalize their assets and clamp down on trading and financial connections with the outside world. Some families rode out the storm, cruising back into prominence under General Suharto after 1965 or taking refuge in Malaysia. Others turned to the petrodollar manna of Sa'udi Arabia, exploiting the Yemeni nationality which retreating British colonialists had imposed upon them. In Sa'udi Arabia, one Maskin family by the name of Bin Ladin made a colossal fortune, and spawned an internationally infamous black sheep, but that is another story.

References

Abbott, K.E. (1983), *Cities and Trade; Consul Abbott on the Economy and Society of Iran, 1847–66*, ed. by Abbas Amanat, London: Ithaca Press.
Abdou, N. (1910), *Dr. Abdou's Travels in America*, Washington DC: author's edition [date of publication given as 1907].

Abeyasekere, S. (1989), *Jakarta: a History*, 2nd edn, Singapore: Oxford University Press.

Aghassian, M., and Kévorian, K. (2000), 'Armenian Trade in the Indian Ocean in the Seventeenth and Eighteenth Centuries', in Denys Lombard and Jean Aubin (eds.), *Asian Merchants and Businessmen in the Indian Ocean and the China Sea*, New Delhi: Oxford University Press.

Agpalo, R.E. (1962), *The Political Process and the Nationalisation of the Retail Trade in the Philippines*, Quezon City: University of the Philippines.

Alatas, I.b. A. (1923), 'De Arabieren', in L.F. van Gent (ed.), *Gedenkboek voor Nederlandsch-Indië*, Batavia: G. Kolff.

Algadri, H. (1994), *Dutch Policy against Islam and Indonesians of Arab Descent in Indonesia*, Jakarta: Pustaka LP3ES.

Alsagoff, S.M. (*c.*1963), *The Alsagoff Family in Malaysia, AH 1240 (AD 1824) to AH 1382 (AD 1962), with Biographical and Contemporary Sketches of Some Members of the Alsagoff Family*, Singapore: privately printed.

al-Saggaf, J. (1993), 'A Legal Document from Saywun in Relation to Vessels, Houses and Carriages owned by a Saggaf Sayyid in Nineteenth-century Java', *New Arabian Studies*, 1: 189–202.

Berg, L.W.C. van den (1886), *Le Hadramout et les colonies arabes dans l'archipel indien*, Batavia: Imprimerie du Gouvernement.

Blake, G. (1956), *B.I. Centenary, 1856–1956*, London: Collins.

Broersma, R. (1934), 'Koopvaardij in de Molukken', *Koloniaal Tijdschrift*, 23: 129–47 and 320–50.

—— (1935–36), 'Land en volk in Molukken-Zuid', *Koloniaal Tijdschrift*, 24: 416–34, and 25: pp. 42–71.

Broeze, F. (1979), 'The Merchant Fleet of Java, 1820–1850: a Preliminary Survey', *Archipel*, 18: 251–69.

Brown, R.A. (1994), *Capital and Entrepreneurship in South-East Asia*, London: Macmillan.

Buckley, C.B. (1965), *An Anecdotal History of Singapore in Old Times*, 2nd edn, Kuala Lumpur: University of Malaya Press.

Campo, J.N.F.M. à (1992), *Koninklijke Paketvaart Maatschappij, stoomvaart en staatsvorming in de Indonesische archipel, 1888–1914*, Hilversum: Verloren.

Cator, W.J. (1936), *The Economic Position of the Chinese in the Netherlands Indies*, Oxford: Basil Blackwell.

Clarence-Smith, W.G. (1994), 'The Impact of Forced Coffee Cultivation on Java, 1805–1917', *Indonesia Circle*, 64: 214–64.

—— (1997), 'Hadhrami Entrepreneurs in the Malay World, *c.*1750 to *c.*1940', in U. Freitag and W. G. Clarence-Smith (eds), *Hadhrami Traders, Scholars and Statesmen in the Indian Ocean, 1750s–1960s*, Leiden: Brill.

—— (1998), 'The Economic Role of the Arab Community in Maluku, 1816 to 1940', *Indonesia and the Malay World*, 26(74): 32–49.

—— (2000), 'Arab Entrepreneurs in the Malay World in the 1930s Recession', in Peter Boomgaard and I. Brown (eds), *Weathering the Storm: the Economies of Southeast Asia in the 1930s Depression*, Leiden and Singapore: KITLV Press and ISEAS.

—— (2002a), 'Horse Trading: the Economic Role of Arabs in the Lesser Sunda Islands, *c*.1800–1940', in Huub de Jonge and Nico Kaptein (eds), *Transcending Borders; Arabs, Politics, Trade and Islam in Southeast Asia, 1870–1990*, Leiden, KITLV Press.

—— (2002b), 'The Rise and Fall of Hadhrami Arab Shipping in the Indian Ocean, *c*.1750–*c*.1940', in David Parkin and Ruth Barnes (eds), *Ships and the Development of Maritime Technology in the Indian Ocean*, London: Routledge Curzon.

—— (forthcoming), 'Middle Eastern Migrants in the Philippines: Entrepreneurs and Cultural Brokers', in *Asia Journal of Social Science*.

Cohen, I. (1956), *A Jewish Pilgrimage, the Autobiography of Israel Cohen*, London: Valentine Mitchell.

Deventer, C.T. (1904), *Overzicht van de ekonomischen toestand der Inlandsche bevolking van Java en Madoera*, The Hague: M. Nijhoff.

Dick, H. (1989), 'Japan's Economic Expansion in the Netherlands Indies between the First and Second World Wars', *Journal of Southeast Asian Studies*, 20(2): 244–72.

Dobbin, C. (1983), *Islamic Revivalism in a Changing Peasant Economy: Central Sumatra 1784–1847*, London: Curzon.

Doeppers, D.F. (1984), *Manila 1900–1941, Social Change in a Late Colonial Metropolis*, Quezon City: Ateneo de Manila University Press.

Earl, G.W. (1971), *The Eastern Seas*, Singapore: Oxford University Press, reprint of 1837 ed.

Elson, R.E. (1994),*Village Java under the Cultivation System, 1830–1870*, Sydney: Allen & Unwin.

Fernando, M.R. and Bulbeck, D. (eds) (1992), *Chinese Economic Activity in Netherlands India: Selected Translations from the Dutch*, Singapore: ISEAS.

Freitag, U. and Clarence-Smith, W.G. (eds) (1997), *Hadhrami Traders, Scholars and Statesmen in the Indian Ocean, 1750s to 1960s*. Leiden: Brill.

Gleeck Jr., L.E. (1974), *Americans on the Philippine Frontier*, Manila: Carmelo and Bauermann.

—— (1975), *American Business and Philippine Economic Development*, Manila: Carmelo and Bauermann.

—— (n.d.), *The history of the Jewish Community of Manila*. No place: no publisher.

Goldstein, J. (forthcoming), 'Singapore, Manila and Harbin as Reference Points in Asian Jewish Identity; Questions Raised by the Sorkin "Port Jews" thesis', *Jewish Culture and History* [paper presented at conference on 'Port Jews and Jewish Communities in Cosmopolitan Maritime Trading Centres', University of Cape Town, January 2003].

Goor, J. van (1982), 'The Death of a Middleman: Scheming in the Margins of the Dutch East Indies', in G. Schutte and Heather Sutherland (eds), *Papers of the Dutch-Indonesian Historical Conference, 23–27 June 1980*, Leiden and Jakarta: Bureau of Indonesian Studies.

Gowing, P.G. (1977), *Mandate in Moroland: the American Government of Muslim Filipinos, 1899–1920*, Manila: University of the Philippines.

Griese, J.W. (1954), 'The Jewish community in Manila', MA thesis, University of the Philippines.

HCHONI = Handboek voor Cultuur- en Handelsondernemingen in Nederlandsch-Indië, Amsterdam: De Bussy.

Heuken, A. (1996), 'Arab Landowners in Batavia/Jakarta', *Indonesia Circle*, 68, 65–74.

Huff, W.G. (1994), *The Economic Growth of Singapore: Trade and Development in the Twentieth Century*, Cambridge: Cambridge University Press.

Ingrams, W.H. (1937), *A Report on the Social, Economic and Political Conditions of the Hadhramaut*, London: HMSO.

—— (1940), 'Report on a Tour to Malaya, Java and Hyderabad', al-Mukalla, unpublished typescript.

—— (1942), *Arabia and the Isles*, London: John Murray.

Jansen, W.H.M. (1990), 'De economische ontwikkeling van de Residentie Menado, 1900–1940', Doctoraal Scriptie, Rijksuniversiteit te Leiden.

Jensen, Khin Khin Myint (1956), 'The Chinese in the Philippines during the American Regime', PhD thesis, University of Wisconsin.

Jonge, H. de (1993), 'Discord and Solidarity among the Arabs in the Netherlands East Indies, 1900–1940', *Indonesia*, 55, 73–90.

Kayal, P.M. and Kayal, J.M. (1975), *The Syrian-Lebanese in America, a Study in Religion and Assimilation*, Boston: Twayne.

Knaap, G.J. (1996), *Shallow Waters, Rising Tide: Shipping and Trade in Java around 1775*, Leiden: KITLV Press.

Kniphorst, J.H.P.E. (1885), 'Een terugblik op Timor en onderhoorigheden', *Tijdschrift voor Nederlandsch Indië*, 14(1): 355–80, 401–83, and (2): 1–41, 81–146, 198–204, 241–311, 321–62.

Kroef, J. van der (1953), 'The Arabs in Indonesia', *Middle East Journal*, 7(3): 300–23.

Kuperus, G. (1936), *Het cultuurlandschap van West-Soembawa*, Groningen and Batavia: J.B. Wolters.

Lee, E. (1991), *The British as Rulers: Governing Multiracial Singapore, 1867–1914*, Singapore: Singapore University Press.

McCabe, Baghdiantz, I.(1999) *The Shah's Silk for Europe's Silver: The Eurasian Silk Trade of the Julfan Armenians in Safavid Iran and India (1590–1750)*, University of Pennsylvania (Series in Armenian Texts and Studies), Atlanta: Scholar's Press.

Mansvelt, W.M.F. (1938), 'De prauwvaart in de 19e eeuw', *Koloniale Studien*, 22(1): 89–102.

Matsuo, H. (1970), *The Development of Javanese Cotton Industry*, Tokyo: The Institute of Developing Economies.

Mendinueto, S.R. (1930), 'Industrial Development in the Philippines', *The Philippine Finance Review*, 3(6): 8–10 and 26.

Meulen, D. van der (1947), *Aden to Ḥaḍhramaut: a journey in South Arabia*, London: John Murray.

—— and Wissman, H. von (1932), *Ḥaḍhramaut: Some of its Mysteries Unveiled*, Leiden: E.J. Brill.

Miller, H.H. (1920), *Economic Conditions in the Philippines*, Boston: Ginn & Co.

—— (1932), *Principles of economics applied to the Philippines*. Boston: Ginn & Co.

Mobini-Kesheh, N. (1997), 'Islamic Modernism in Colonial Java: the al-Irshad Movement', in U. Freitag, and W.G. Clarence-Smith (eds), *Hadhrami Traders, Scholars and Statesmen in the Indian Ocean, 1750s–1960s*, Leiden: Brill.

—— (1999), *The Hadrami Awakening, Community and Identity in the Netherlands East Indies, 1900–1942*, Ithaca NY: Cornell University Press.

Moor, J.H. (ed.) (1968 [1837]), *Notices of the Indian Archipelago and Adjacent Countries*, London: Frank Cass, reprint.

Morley, J.A.E. (1949), 'The Arabs and the Eastern trade', Journal *of the Malayan Branch of the Royal Asiatic Society*, 22(1): 143–76.

Nathan, E. (1986), *The History of the Jews in Singapore, 1830–1945*, Singapore: Herbilu.

Norris [Nicachi], P.B. (1992), *Ulysses in the Raj*, London: British Association for Cemeteries in South Asia.

Papazian, K.S. (1979), *Merchants from Ararat: a Brief Survey of Armenian Trade through the Ages*, New York: Ararat Press.

Parimartha, I.G. (1995), 'Perdagangan dan politik di Nusa Tenggara, 1815–1915', Doctoral dissertation, Vrije Universiteit, Amsterdam.

Peet, G.L. (1985), *Rickshaw Reporter*, Singapore: Eastern Universities Press.

Peeters, J. (1994), 'Kaum Tuo – Kaum Mudo: sociaal-religieuze verandering in Palembang, 1821–1942', PhD Thesis, University of Leiden.

Philippines (1933), *Statistical Handbook of the Philippine Islands 1932*, Manila: Bureau of Printing.

Post, P. (1993), 'Japan and the Integration of the Netherlands East Indies into the World Economy, 1868–1942', *Review of Indonesian and Malaysian Affairs*, 27(1–2): 134–65.

—— (1996), 'The formation of the pribumi business elite in Indonesia, 1930s to 1940s', *Bijdragen tot de Taal-, Land- en Volkenkunde*, 152(4): 87–110.

Purwanto, B. (1992), 'From *dusun* to Market: Native Rubber Cultivation in Southern Sumatra, 1890–1940', PhD Thesis, University of London.

Quirino, C. (1987), *Philippine Tycoon: the Biography of an Industrialist, Vicente Madrigal*, Manila: Madrigal Memorial Foundation.

Reid, A. (1972), 'Habib Abdurrahman az-Zahir, 1833–1896', *Indonesia*, 13: 37–60.

RMCD = Rosenstock's Manila City Directory, Manila: Philippine Education Co. Inc.

Rodríguez Rodríguez, I. de, and Álvarez Fernández, J. (1998), *La revolución Hispano-Filipina en la prensa: Diario de Manila y Heraldo de Madrid*, Madrid: Agencia Española de Cooperación Internacional.

Roff, W.R. (1967), *The Origins of Malay Nationalism*, New Haven CT: Yale University Press.

—— (1972), *Bibliography of Malay and Arabic Periodicals Published in the Straits Settlements and Peninsular Malay States, 1876–1941*, London: Oxford University Press.

Rohrer, H.V. (1930), 'Merchandising Methods in the Philippines', *Philippine Finance Review*, 3(11): 14–15, 23.

Safa, E. (1960), *L'émigration libanaise*, Beirut [supplementary volume to *Annales de l'École Française de Droit de Beyrouth*].

Sarkissian, M. (1987), 'Armenians in South-East Asia', *Crossroads: an Interdisciplinary Journal of Southeast Asian Studies*, 3(2–3): 1–33.

Segers, W.A.I.M. (1987), *Manufacturing Industry, 1870–1942*, Amsterdam: Royal Tropical Institute (Vol. 8 of *Changing Economy in Indonesia*).

Serjeant, R.B. (1957), *The Saiyyids of Hadramaut*, London: SOAS.

Seth, M.J. (1988), *History of the Armenians in India*, 3rd edn., Delhi: Gian.

Sherry, N. (1966), *Conrad's Eastern world*, Cambridge: Cambridge University Press.

SMD = Singapore and Malayan Directory, Singapore: Printers Ltd. (yearly).

Song Ong Siang (1923), *One Hundred Years' History of the Chinese in Singapore*, London: John Murray.

Stark, F. (1945), *A Winter in Arabia*, 3rd edn., London: John Murray.

Tinbergen, J., and Derksen, J.B.D. (1941), 'Nederlansch-Indië in cijfers', in W.H. van Helsdingen and H. Hoogenberk (eds), *Daar werd wat groots verricht: Nederlandsch-Indië in de twintigste eeuw*, Amsterdam: Elsevier.

Van Niel, R. (1960), *The Emergence of the Modern Indonesian Elite*. The Hague and Bandung: W. van Hoeve.

Vandenbosch, A. (1944), *The Dutch East Indies: its Government, Problems and Policies*, 3rd edn., Berkeley: University of California Press.

Vleming, J.L. (1926), *Het Chineessche zakenleven in Nederlandsch-Indië*, Weltevreden: Volkslectuur.

Vlieland, C.A. (1931), *British Malaya: a Report on the 1931 Census and on Certain Problems of Vital Statistics*, London: Crown Agents for the Colonies.

Vuldy, C. (1985), 'La communauté arabe de Pekalongan', *Archipel*, 30: 95–119.

—— (1987), *Pekalongan: batik et islam dans une ville du nord de Java*, Paris: EHESS.

Wallace, A.R. (1986), *The Malay Archipelago, the Land of the Orang-utan and the Bird of Paradise*, 2nd edn., Singapore: Oxford University Press.

Wright, A. and Breakspear, O.T. (1908), *Twentieth Century Impressions of Siam*, London: Lloyds Greater Britain Publishing Co. Ltd.

Wright, A. and Cartwright, H.A. (1908), *Twentieth Century Impressions of British Malaya*, unabridged edn., London: Lloyds Greater Britain Publishing Co. Ltd.

Yegar, M. (1972), *The Muslims of Burma*, Wiesbaden: Harrasowitz.

Yoshihara, K. (1985), *Philippine Industrialisation: Foreign and Domestic Capital*, Singapore: Oxford University Press.

Globalizing Ethnicity with Multi-local Identifications: The Parsee, Indian Muslim and Sephardic Trade Diasporas in Hong Kong

Caroline Plüss

Diaspora, Globalization and Ethnicity

This chapter investigates how cultural processes sustain transregional diasporic networks as necessary conditions for globalized trade.[1] The ethnicity, or sense of cultural belonging, of a diaspora is characterized as cosmopolitan, flexible, deterritorialized and transnational, and as incorporating multiple identifications and loyalties.[2] A number of authors, including some writing in this volume, regard these characteristics (especially the transnational, or transregional, networks of members of diasporas with a homeland, or with members of the same ethnic group in further places of residence) as crucial factors to explain the success of their economic activities. Kotkin (1993) observes that because diasporas incorporate global networks of mutual trust, this provides members of diasporas with a competitive advantage over people lacking such links. In Cohen's opinion (1997: 176), members of diasporas are particularly well suited to succeeding in a globalizing economy because they already have family, kin, clan and ethnic networks in different areas, and this allows an 'unencumbered flow of economic transactions and family migrants' into these regions. Members of diasporas occupy insider positions in transregional networks and have privileged access to the resources and skills enshrined in them. An entrepreneur possessing connections with co-ethnics living in a different region may be able use these links not only to transfer and mobilize workers but also to draw on the skills and knowledge of co-ethnics who settled elsewhere.

In order to benefit from the resources enshrined in such trading networks, the diasporic entrepreneur needs to maintain relationships with the other network members that are based on trust and mutual obligations. Maintaining shared ways of doing things, based on common understandings, is a necessary condition to maintaining insider positions. Bourdieu's concept of *habitus* (1977: 72), which he defines as shared ways of interiorizing exteriority and exteriorizing interiority, expresses well the sense in which diaspora members maintain a common culture.

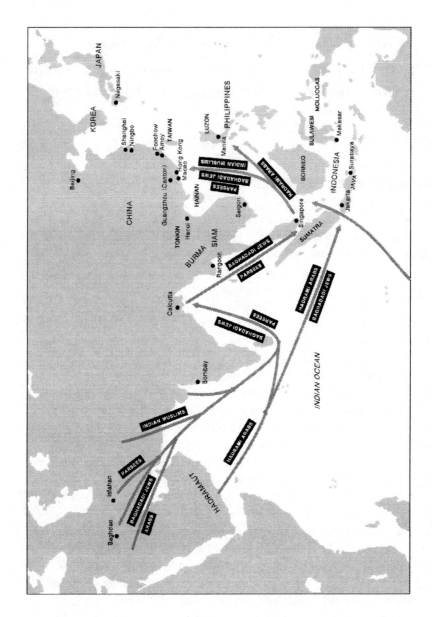

Map 4 Trade diasporas in the Indian ocean: Baghdadi Jews, Parsees, Hardrami Arabs and Indian Muslims in the 19th and 20th centuries

This is what makes a diaspora a diaspora, and differentiates it from a group of people connected throughout several regions by shared interests alone. Silliman gives an illuminating account of the role that shared ethnicity played for diasporic traders. She points out that for Sephardim in smaller trading ventures in India, it was crucial to maintain the characteristics they shared with co-religionists in South, Southeast and East Asia in order to pursue their businesses. They lived in each other's homes for extended periods of time, during which they not only finalized business transactions but also shared meals, rituals, news and gossip to renew kinship and patronage networks (Silliman 1998: 61). Maintaining shared values based on a common *habitus* was such a strong characteristic of these traders that they hardly identified at all with the majority cultures in the places where they lived.

For the more prominent diasporic traders, the pursuit of transregional trade was linked to processes of Anglicization. They needed to assimilate some of the characteristics of the British elite in order to gain more acceptance, and thereby access resources largely controlled by that elite group (ibid.). Prominent groups of entrepreneurs needed to address the fact that the cultural identity of the British colonial power was strongly '[self-] centred, highly exclusive and exclusivist' and that it placed the 'colonized Other' into a marginal space (Hall 1991: 20). A description of what constituted respectable society in Hong Kong in 1869 reveals the attitude of the British elite toward traders from other ethnic groups residing in the territory (Welsh 1977: 380): 'Within this society, but knowing their place, were a handful of Jews, Armenians, Portuguese and Parsees who knew which fork was which and who were admissibly rich.' British colonial expansion and trade throughout the Empire, however, was also dependent upon co-optation of local 'elites'. As ethnic minorities in their places of residence, members of trading diasporas were often an ideal choice. Their minority position had already placed them into some degree of conflict with the majority, and they often experienced discrimination in their social, economic and political pursuits. As outsiders in the societies where they lived, enterprising diasporic traders saw considerable advantages in entering networks with the colonial power, and they were willing to adopt some of the cultural characteristics of the British elite to increase their acceptability and to display their commitment to cooperation. Processes of Anglicization, however, entailed complex shifts in identification because they led diasporic traders to experience some contradictions and tensions in relation to the necessity, and their wish, to maintain shared characteristics with co-ethnics in the diaspora. For some of the entrepreneurs, especially the more prominent ones, entering and maintaining networks with both groups was at times essential to realize their goals. The question arising, then, was how to construct identities in ways that would support and maintain network building with both groups, that is, without jeopardizing their insider positions in either of them.

This chapter seeks to analyse how diasporic traders shifted identifications in order to support transregional trade in a colonial setting. Examples from Parsee, Indian Muslim and Sephardic traders, over a time period of over 150 years, will show how they constructed multi-local identifications, that is, identities that integrated cultural characteristics located in different networks. It will investigate how the entrepreneurs reconciled their often deep-felt attachment to, and need for, their co-ethnic diasporic groups, with their aim to explore the opportunities afforded by the expansion of the British Empire. This discussion will show that the confluence of different cultural systems did not necessarily lead to the absorption of a minority culture by the majority culture, but that a multi-faceted process emerged which changed, at least to some extent, both cultures (Papastergiadis 2000: 107–11). It will also show that by constructing multi-local identities the traders were able to sustain diasporic networks and enter new ones, and that these multiple identifications by themselves generated and sustained some acceptance (although undeniably also some rejection) by the colonial power. This was because such multi-local identities helped entrepreneurs not only to display some of the characteristics of the British elite, thus demonstrating points of similarity, but also to stress characteristics that other members of the colonial elite did not necessarily possess, and which therefore provided diaspora entrepreneurs with desirable qualities in the eyes of the British majority.

Data Collection and Historical Background

The sources for this chapter come from ongoing research on ethnic minorities in Hong Kong that started in 1997. The chapter focuses predominantly on the more prominent individuals of the Parsee, Indian Muslim and Sephardic merchant communities, because their lives are better documented than those of their less prominent co-ethnics. As far as possible, however, the processes by which less renowned community members (not all of whom were traders) constructed their identities are included to provide a more complete understanding of the inter-relations between the ethnicity of a diaspora and the cultural identifications of members engaged in transregional trade. Primary sources stem from archival research, notably in the Hong Kong Collection of the University Libraries of The University of Hong Kong; the private collection of the Reverend Carl Smith in Hong Kong; the private archives of Mr Jal Soli Shroff, President of the Incorporated Trustees of the Zoroastrian Charity Funds of Hongkong, Canton and Macao; the archives of the Jewish Community Centre of Hong Kong, and the archives of the Islamic Union of Hong Kong.

To survey the interrelations between transregional trade and ethnicity, one would ideally uncover the oral histories of several generations of family members to detect how social, economic and political changes affected these relations. This cannot easily be achieved in relation to the ethnic minorities in Hong Kong because only a few families residing in the territory today are the offspring of nineteenth-century traders in the region. These include, for example, the Ruttonjees, descendants of the Parsee trader Hormusjee Ruttonjee, who came to Hong Kong in 1886; the Kadoories, tracing their settlement in the territory back to Eleazer Silas Kadoorie's immigration of 1880; or the Ebrahim family, the progeny of the Bohra Muslim Ebrahim Noordin, who started trading in Hong Kong as early as 1841 (Pavri n.d.: 1; Kadoorie 1985: I, 84; Kadoorie Family, *pers. comm.*). Interviews with members of fourteen different Parsee, Indian Muslim and Sephardic trading families, most of whom have resided in the territory for several generations, are sources for the settlement histories of these ethnic communities in Hong Kong, their trading activities, their relations with British and Chinese majority, and their association with members of their co-ethnic groups in Hong Kong and other places of residence. A resident of Hong Kong who worked for Lord Mountbatten, the last Viceroy of India, volunteered information on the relations of the minorities with the colonial power in the Subcontinent. Secondary sources on Hong Kong and Indian history yield insight into the trading activities of the Parsee, Indian Muslim and Sephardic diasporas, their associations with co-ethnics, and their relations with Chinese and British majorities.

Chinese and foreign traders started opening offices in Hong Kong after the British occupied the island in 1841 as a result of the First Opium War between Britain and China, lasting from 1839 to 1842. The British won the war and the right to continue selling opium to China. As a result, China needed to agree to treaties with Britain, which made Hong Kong a British colony in 1842, and which gave foreigners extra-territorial rights in the Chinese trading ports of Canton, Amoy, Foochow, Ningpo and Shanghai, which became known as the Treaty Ports (Welsh 1977: 120–5). Traders settled in Hong Kong because of its free-trade policy and political stability. Four Parsee merchants, Dhunjibhoy Ruttonjee Bisney, Hirjibhoy Rustomjee, Pestonji Cawasji and Framjee Jamsetjee, were among the first purchasers of land in Hong Kong when it became a British possession (Bard 1993: 86). Before that, Parsee, Muslim and Sephardic entrepreneurs from India already operated offices in the nearby southern Chinese city of Canton, selling cotton and opium from India in return for tea, spices and other goods from China. Parsee merchants from India had actually engaged in trade with southern China since the eighteenth century, with the first Parsee trader to enter this region being Hirji Jivanji Readymoney in 1756. The Parsees came to form a large part of the temporary settlements of foreign merchants in Canton in the nineteenth century. For example, in 1831, there were forty-one Parsee and thirty-two English traders in Canton. A number of the foreign traders in Canton subsequently settled in the colony. Some of them moved to avoid the instability of the second Opium War, lasting from 1856 to 1858 (Dobbin 1996: 84). David Sassoon, Sons & Co., a branch of the Bombay-based company that Sephardim David Sassoon opened in Canton in 1844, re-located to Hong Kong in 1857 (Plüss 2003: 60). Ebrahim Noordin, a Bohra Muslim and one of the earliest traders from India to open offices in Hong Kong, also first traded in Canton before he opened Abdoolally Ebrahim & Co. in the colony in 1841 (Bard 1993: 90).[3]

Parsees: From Being Middlemen to Asserting Transregional Identifications

Parsee traders from Persia were long engaged in commerce between the Middle East and India and settled on India's west coast in the seventh century, if not earlier (Dobbin 1996: 84). Being an ethnic minority in Hindu surroundings, they had restrictions placed on them. A number of these conditions served to conceal Parsees' distinct religion and traditions so that they would appear more similar to the Hindu majority. Women were required to change their dress to saris, and wedding ceremonies had to include a section in Sanskrit and could only be performed in the evening. Parsees were not allowed to convert people to Zoroastrianism, and were required to give up their language for Gujarati. They were also prevented from carrying arms (Dobbin 1996: 79).[4] Partial exclusion from Indian society was a reason why Parsees, in the seventeenth century, were keen to cooperate with Portuguese, French, Dutch and British traders who came to India, first in the city of Surat and later in Bombay. Their previous residence in various villages and towns in the wider Gujarat region gave them the necessary contacts to become commodity brokers for the Europeans (Dobbin 1996: 78). Such Parsees rose to elite positions in their own group and improved their standing in Indian society. Typically for middlemen, their economic role was to be the intermediaries between high and low social, economic and political ranks, concentrating in occupations such as agent, labour contractor, collector, money-lender and broker.[5] To enter networks with Western traders and the British colonial elite, Parsees changed parts of their identities. They learned English manners, acquired a Western education and became cultivated in Western arts, especially music.[6] Cultural critic Homi Bhabha, whose ancestors were Parsees from Bombay, recounts that in the nineteenth century, this community formed a 'Westernized bourgeois class' whose cultural codes restricted them less than Hindus and Muslims from adopting components of Western culture. These processes did not lead to a loss of Parsee culture and group cohesion, as Parsees combined Westernization with their own traditions. For example, they spoke Gujarati in their families, but used English in their public lives (Dobbin 1996: 102). The importance they attached to maintaining 'purity' remained a 'very significant principle' of their lives (Thompson 1994: III, 84). For example, a central tenet of Parsee identity was that children born to non-Zoroastrian fathers were not easily accepted into their religious life.[7] Combining elements from several cultures provided Parsee entrepreneurs with a newly formed *habitus* – they had a 'cosmopolitan feel about them', and they were the carriers of a 'multi-vocal culture' (Thompson 1994: III, 183).

A willingness to engage in long-distance trade provided a further competitive advantage to Parsees when compared to Indian traders, who preferred to stay in their region of origin. Parsees are said to have been among the first traders from the subcontinent to recognize the potential of sea trade with China (Bard 1993: 86). Having accumulated substantial fortunes, in the early eighteenth century a number of Parsees, such as the Readymoneys and Jijibhais (Jejeebhoys), invested in dockyards and built their own ships, which they deployed for trade between India and Asia. They also made their boats available to the British, especially for commerce with China. This cooperation was highly profitable for both sides. Parsees provided access to raw material; manpower; expertise in trading in raw cotton and opium in the East; and finances and means of transport; while the British helped with political support for trading ventures (Vaid 1972: 51). Bombay-based Framjee Cowasjee, through his collaboration with Thomas Wedding, an agent for the British trading family Jardine, helped the Jardines to enter trade with cotton and opium in India (A. Reid 1982a: 16). Jamsetjee Jejeebhoy, who started to explore the commercial potential of China in 1799, became a close associate and life-long friend of the British trader William Jardine. This association played a large role in helping to establish the agency house Jardine, Matheson & Co., first in Canton and then in Hong Kong (M. Reid 1982: 17). Actually, Jardine and Matheson were agents for Jejeebhoy in Canton, and they jointly owned ships with the Parsee. Jejeebhoy was also one of the principal shareholders of an insurance company that Jardine and Matheson founded with Parsees and Portuguese traders in Hong Kong (A. Reid 1982b: 53; A. Reid 1982c: 69, 79; Keswick 1982: 181).

An indication of Jejeebhoy's importance to trade in Hong Kong was that he took the initiative to have the first 'foreign' ship constructed in the territory, and became the owner of the Lamont Dock on Hong Kong island (A. Reid 1982d: 196). However, he did not live in the colony. By 1860, a substantial number of trading companies in Hong Kong (seventeen out of a total of seventy-three merchant firms) were owned by Parsees (Bard 1993: 86). These firms recruited Parsee employees from India.[8] An enterprise jointly owned by Parsee and British traders was Rustomji, Turner & Co., which owned twenty-seven cargo ships sailing between London, Calcutta and China (Vaid 1972: 55). Recognizing the importance of Parsees for trade in the Empire, Britain bestowed a number of honours on them. For example, Jejeebhoy received a knighthood in 1842. He was the first Indian and the first Parsee to receive this honour (M. Reid 1982: 17). Traders in Hong Kong also recognized Parsees' expertise in moneylending and banking. An example of how their characteristics had some impact on transforming the culture of the British elite in Hong Kong is the observation that, at some unknown date, offices and counters where bills needed to be paid were re-named 'shroff offices', after the Parsee family name Shroff.[9] A descendant of the Shroffs (*pers. comm.*) in Hong Kong explains that this name probably came from the fact that his forefathers were village bankers in India. The Anglicized features of Parsees in Hong Kong not only supported traders' networks with the British, but also Parsees' employment in British firms and in the colonial government. In 1867, a man named E. Sapoorjee became the fifth clerk in the Government Treasury, probably the first Parsee in the civil service of the colony (Smith 1995: 396). Nevertheless, the social acceptance of Parsees by the British elite remained incomplete. British administrators saw Parsees as orientalized 'others'. For example, the *Anglo-Chinese Calendar* of 1832 classified Parsee merchants residing in Canton as 'Asiatic British Subjects' (Smith 1995: 390). Precise information on the number of Parsees in Hong Kong in the early colonial days is lacking, but it is estimated that it was never more than 200 individuals (Incorporated Trustees of the Zoroastrian Charity Funds of Hongkong 2002: 8).

With the gradual cessation of the opium sea trade between India and China in the early twentieth century, networks of Parsee merchants in the colony with their co-ethnic communities in India became less crucial to their economic activities. Parsee traders staying in the territory continued to import cotton yarn from India, but this was less lucrative than opium, and a number of firms, including Cowasjee Pallanjee & Co., closed their offices in the mid-1920s (Bard 1993: 87). The remaining firms continued to use the networks they established with China, importing silk, and a few started to produce embroidered goods in factories they owned in Canton, employing Chinese middlemen.[10] Investment in Hong Kong-based ventures, such as for example dealing in properties and stocks, was common for Parsee companies in the twentieth century, and Parsees could no longer be easily characterized as middlemen for the British, like their predecessors in India. Rooting economic activities in Hong Kong and China, rather than in commercial exchange with India, corresponded with the general development of trade in the colony at the turn of the twentieth century (Bard 1993: 49, 86). An example of the transition to Hong Kong-based economic activities, which was accompanied by changing cultural identifications, is the Ruttonjee family. Hormusjee Ruttonjee came to the territory in 1884 from India, and took up employment as an assistant with the firm P.F. Davar & Co. Eight months later, he became the manager of the Canton branch of B.P. Karanjia & Co. (Anonymous, n.d.: *Late Mr. J.H. Ruttonjee*). He returned to Hong Kong and established H. Ruttonjee & Sons, with the help of his son Jehangirjee (Jehangir). This wine and spirit business was closely connected to Parsees' relations with the British elite. Parsees were awarded liquor licences as part of the privileges they enjoyed for cooperating with the British.[11] The Ruttonjees then founded the Hong Kong Brewery and invested in property and hotels, which made them less dependent on British endorsement of transregional trade. Despite decreasing economic links with India, Jehangirjee Ruttonjee's connections with the Parsee community in Hong Kong remained strong. During the Second World War, he housed nearly the entire Parsee community in Dina House, his residence in Duddell Street, and supported the smuggling of food parcels into Stanley camp, where Indians were interned during the Japanese occupation (Pavri n.d.: 1). His son Dhunjisha (Dhun) Ruttonjee, who was born in Hong Kong in 1903, became more of a peripheral member of the Parsee community. He was one of the few who broke with orthodoxy by marrying a Chinese woman. This was also the case for Homaje Kotwaj in the nineteenth century and his son, Samuel Kotewall, in the twentieth century (Hall 1992: 188–9).[12] Dhun Ruttonjee's involvement in Hong Kong politics was a further unusual feature among Parsees in Hong Kong. He was an Urban Councillor from 1950 to 1957, and a Legislative Councillor from 1953 to 1968 (Pavri n.d.: 2). Although he was marginalized from the Parsee community and more integrated into Hong Kong society in these respects, he nevertheless served two terms as president of the Hong Kong Zoroastrian association, emphasizing the importance he attached to maintaining close links with this community.[13]

Despite decreasing economic significance, the diasporic links of Hong Kong Parsees with their co-ethnics in India remained important because they relied on the Parsee communities in India to find spouses. In the second half of the nineteenth century, Parsees coming from India to Hong Kong usually married cousins from India (Smith 1995: 397). The Parsee community was and remains small. In the early 1950s, there were around 80 to 90 Parsees in Hong Kong (Ingrame 1952: 248). Today, there are around 190 individuals. Hong Kong-born Parsees are keen to maintain their connections with the Parsee community in Bombay, the largest one in the world (numbering around 76,000 individuals in the year 2000) to assure their survival as a distinctive group (Taraporevata 2000: 9; Incorporated Trustees of the Zoroastrian Charity Funds of Hongkong 2002: 13).[14] For the same reason, Parsees migrating from Hong Kong to other places, such as Europe, North America and Australia, continue to be listed in Hong Kong Zoroastrian directories. When I asked five Parsees about the ethnicity of their five closest friends in Hong Kong, as well as their five most important professional contacts, the respondents always included other Parsees among their five closest friends, but they did not often list Parsees among their five most important professional contacts, indicating the group's strength of social and emotional ties, as well as the cosmopolitan nature of their working life. Diasporic links with India have little influence upon Parsees' professional lives today, but they serve increasingly as markers of group identification, assuring the continuity of the community. In this sense, transregional identification with Parsees in India came to serve as an important factor for cultural identification, and for maintaining a cohesive group identity.

Indian Muslims: Constructing Localized Identifications

The settlement of Indian Muslim traders in Hong Kong has its roots in the activities of the East India Company which brought them from India to Canton, and the 1833 withdrawal of the company's monopoly for licensing British traders in China, whereupon a number of these Muslims opened independent businesses, trading especially in cotton and opium (Bard 1993: 21, 90). Such a firm was Cassumbhoy Nathabhoy & Co., operating in Canton in the 1830s and moving to Hong Kong in the 1950s (Bard 1993: 91). These Muslim traders were from different regions in India, but prominent among them were Bohras from Gujarat. While residing in Gujarat, Bohras did not engage in such strong processes of Anglicization as did the Parsees (Dobbin 1996: 82). Their centralized religious leadership, under the authority of a *dai*, a spiritual leader, was one factor that made Bohras less inclined to change their traditions. Abdoolally Ebrahim & Co., possibly the earliest Indian firm operating in Hong Kong, was a Bohra firm. Established in 1841 by Ebrahim Nordin from Bombay, it dealt in sugar, raw silk, cotton yarn, beans and spices between China and India.[15] Presumably, the firm also traded in opium. Among the Indian Muslims, including Bohra merchants, who moved from Canton to Hong Kong in the 1850s were Currimbhoy Ebrahim, the Kaymally and Tyeb families, Solomon Ebrahim, Ahmad Hadjee Essacbhai, Cassumbhoy Nalhanbhoy, Jadjee Abdoola Nathan and Anerally Abdoolally (Vaid 1972: 56). Most of the Bohra companies that moved from Canton to Hong Kong, such as Cassumbhoy Nathabhoy & Co., closed in the 1860s (Bard 1993: 91). They had their opium confiscated by the Viceroy of Canton in 1839 during the disputes over the legality of the opium trade, and they then moved to Hong Kong to wait for compensation, while trading in the territory. Once they were reimbursed, they moved back to India, or ventured to further places (Vaid 1972: 57). The few Bohra companies staying in the colony remained under the control of this ethnic group, and I found no records of joint holdings with non-Bohras. Until at least the early years of the twentieth century, these firms employed exclusively family members and co-religionists from India.[16] Kaymally & Co., established in Hong Kong in 1885, and specializing in trading in cotton and silk, became an informal gathering-place for Bohra traders (White 1994: 71).

In 1920 there were 240 Bohra residents in Hong Kong, but by 1938 their number had decreased to 60 (Weiss 1991: 424). Many of them had decided to partake in the expansion of trade in Shanghai and Bombay, but they maintained close links with the Bohra merchants in Hong Kong. After the communist victory in China in 1949, for example, a number of Bohra families from Shanghai returned to, or settled in, Hong Kong. Among them were the Barmas and Tyebkhans. The Tyebkhans specialized in retail trade, especially in furnishing material, such as upholstery. Together with the Ebrahims and Kaymallys, these families became the leading members of the Bohra community in the twentieth century. In its latter part, they no longer exclusively employed family members and co-religionists, and traded frequently with non-Bohras in import and export. Their descendants also assimilated to characteristics of the Chinese population. One community member (*pers. comm.*) describes them as having become 'more Chinese than Indian'. Although older generations of Bohras would prefer their offspring to marry Bohras, there were intermarriages with Chinese residents who converted, and members of the present-day generation of the sixty or so Bohra families in Hong Kong do not frequently marry co-religionists from India.[17] There are marked differences today between newer migrants from India, many of whom came to the territory during its economic expansion in the 1970s and who tend to observe their traditions more strictly, and longer-standing trading families who, although remaining committed to certain aspects of their religion, such as rituals and food, have assimilated more closely to the Chinese and Westernized features of Hong Kong.

Bohras were not the only Shi'ite Muslim traders in the colony, but the size of the other groups is unknown. The number of Sunnis who came from various regions in India is not recorded in the Hong Kong government's annual reports, which do not differentiate between ethnic sub-groups. Some of the Sunni traders provided supplies for the British garrison in Hong Kong. Since they were less prominent members of Hong Kong society than the Parsees and Bohras, little information is available on them. They formed associations in order to look after their welfare, and information on the characteristics of their representatives and organizational history provides some insight into who they were and how their identities evolved. In the 1850s, the Hong Kong government provided a plot of land so that Sunni Muslims could build a mosque. In order to ensure the appropriate use of the land, four trustees had to be appointed. They were Shaik Mosdeen, Mohamed Arab, Shaik Carther and Hassan Malay. All of them kept boarding houses for Muslim sailors and deckhands who worked on the ships plying the waters between India and China. Shaik Mosdeen was a merchant, originally from Madras, who opened an import and export office in Hong Kong in 1842, after having traded in the nearby Portuguese enclave of Macao (Smith n.d. a: 11–20). Evidence for the diverse regions of origins of Sunnis in the early colonial days is found in a description by Weiss, who explains that they 'originally came as sailors with the East Indian Company from Campbellpur (now Attock), Hazara (now Abbottabad), Lahore and Gujarat and as traders and contractors in the wake of the growing British Empire' (Weiss 1991: 421–2). Different dialects and religious sub-differences among Sunnis further explain why they did not constitute a tightly knit community with strong social cohesion supported by shared business and family ties with India. Although such common diasporic networks were weak, these Muslims, as well as the other ethnic minorities from India, settled in the same area of the colony, south of and uphill from the central Victoria district. This region remained the seat of most Indian trading companies until well into the twentieth century. This proximity of habitation rarely resulted in the founding of joint companies between different ethnic groups from India, but it was certainly a reason favouring cooperation. For example, the Kohja Muslim trader Ramtoola Devjee, who is estimated to have settled in the territory in 1873 as a merchant and share broker, named two Parsees, Hormusjee Nowrojee Mody and Hormusjee Cooverjee Setna, among the five trustees for his estate (Smith n.d. b: 71–2).

The absence of shared links with regions of origin among Indian Sunni Muslims is one reason why a number of them felt that bringing relatives as wives to the colony was undesirable, as the women would lack the extended family networks they were used to. Intermarriages between Sunni Muslim traders and Chinese women in Hong Kong were common. English skills, despite significant cultural differences, gave Indians access to employment in British firms and the colonial government, providing privileges that Chinese residents in Hong Kong did not necessarily enjoy, and facilitating the prospects of marriage between the two groups. For example, Ahmad Rumjahan, who was likely to have come to the colony as a sailor from Calicut, took a Chinese spouse who converted to Islam, and so did his Hong Kong-born son. Three of the latter's sons also took Chinese wives, whereas the fourth married a Hong Kong-born Muslim woman. These male descendants worked as traders or military contractors, or for the government. Most of their sons, in turn, married Chinese women (Weiss 1991: 421–2). Muslim settlers in the colony expected their Chinese wives to adopt the Islamic way of life. One man named Sheik Abdool Sepher, an employee of the Hong Kong and Kowloon Wharf and Godown Co. in the early twentieth century, specified in his will that his wife Ayesha, whose maiden name was Tang Yau-kam, could only be a beneficiary if she were to remain a Muslim (Smith n.d. b: 42). Nevertheless, the descendants of these cross-cultural marriages maintained few links with India (Weiss 1991: 417–18). Hong Kong-born Muslims, often born to Chinese mothers, came to be known as 'local boys', familiar with both British and Chinese cultures. For example, Ranasamy Soonderam, born in Hong Kong in 1862, became a Chinese teacher in the Wanchai Government School in 1888, and stayed there for 21 years. He then worked in the Chief Contractor's Office of the naval yard, and one year later joined the Royal Army Service Corps, where he was employed for three years. Subsequently, he became a reception clerk for the Hong Kong and Shanghai Hotel Co., where he worked for 25 years (Smith n.d. b: 60).

Sunni traders were not as prominent as the Parsees, and their less influential position in Hong Kong's trade explains why it was not essential for either the

British elite or the Muslims to establish close networks. Rather, Muslims at the turn of the twentieth century focused on establishing stronger relations with China, and used the support of their own community to do so. In 1905, they founded the second Hong Kong Muslim association, the Islamic Union, whose aim was to unite Sunni traders who were engaged in commerce with China (Incorporated Trustees of the Islamic Community Fund of Hong Kong 1985: 8). The reorganization of the trustees in 1911 is evidence of this commercial priority. The trustees represented the Islamic community as follows: out of a total of six trustees, four represented the Sunni Muslims and two represented the Shi'ites (who were predominantly Bohras).[18] Of the four Sunni trustees, two represented Muslims associated with the Islamic Union, and two represented Sunni Muslims who were not linked to that organization (see also Plüss 2000: 21; Toraval 1991: 225). Despite this emphasis on trade with China, the Indian Muslims in Hong Kong did not establish significantly closer relations with the growing number of Chinese Muslims who migrated from Mainland China to Hong Kong, a number of whom were traders (Tang and Tian 1995: 51). Contacts between the two groups existed because in the early twentieth century, Chinese Muslims started to use the mosque and to pay subscriptions to the trustees, but in 1949, Indian Muslims voted against the proposition to include a representative of the Chinese Muslims on the Board of Trustees (Toraval 1991: 227–31).

This distinction between business pursuits and ethnic identification, the first one indicating inclusion in Chinese culture and the second one indicating exclusion from it, raises the complex question of whether, and to what extent, the transnational identifications of Indian Muslims with the subcontinent were a merely symbolic ethnicity (i.e. a nostalgic allegiance to one's culture of origin that is not incorporated into everyday conduct and not requiring its modification) (Gans 1996: 146–7). Such identifications would certainly not have been symbolic for newer Muslim migrants from Pakistan and India, who relied heavily on their diasporic networks to migrate, find employers, and find social support in Hong Kong. Local boys, on the other hand, who had a more powerful voice within the Islamic community, hybridized their understanding of Islam with Chinese culture and saw themselves as part of Hong Kong society, rather than as members of the societies their forefathers came from.[19] They largely adhered to an Islamic lifestyle, consciously distinguishing themselves from non-Muslims in Hong Kong, not only in thought but also in practice, especially with regards to food, piety and sometimes dress. They spoke Cantonese, and were familiar with, or adopted, Chinese ways of behaving. The fact that these local boys considered Chinese Muslims as outsiders from the Islamic community indicates that their largely imagined links with the sub-continent served as a strong identity element for them. The change of classification of many Muslims of Indian origin into Pakistani Muslims after the 1947 partition of India is further evidence of this. Hong

Kong Muslims felt that those who had become Pakistani Muslims should be given a stronger representation in the trustees than Chinese Muslims, who continued to be excluded.[20] As with the Parsees, community cohesion among Hong Kong Muslims was maintained by invoking primordial conceptions of ethnicity.

Sephardic Jews: Anglicizing Identities and Re-invoking Tradition

Most members of the Sephardic trading community in the second half of the nineteenth and the early twentieth centuries were closely connected to the activities of two firms in Hong Kong: David Sassoon, Sons & Co. and E.D. Sassoon & Co. Most Sephardim came to the colony from India, mainly from Bombay and Calcutta. They had relocated from Mesopotamia to India because the Ottoman rulers in the Middle East threatened their livelihoods. The most well-known Sephardic traders participating in this migration were descendants of Sheik Sassoon, a renowned leader of Sephardim in Baghdad and a banker to its Muslim rulers. When Daoud Pasha was appointed as the *Vali* of Baghdad in 1821, the Sheik's son, David Sassoon, came under a death sentence (Roth 1941: 31–6). Fleeing the verdict, David Sassoon settled in Bombay in 1833, where he founded David Sassoon, Sons & Co. (Roth 1941: 35–6).[21] He became the leader of the Sephardic community in Bombay, which was culturally Arab, multilingual and partly Anglicized (ibid.: 44). Making use of his diasporic networks with co-religionists in the Middle East, David Sassoon led the trade between India and the Gulf, and then started to explore the mercantile opportunities of China (ibid.: 45, 48). It was the export of opium and cotton to China that made the company one of the largest businesses in India, and it opened branches stretching from the Far East to London (ibid.: 49). Considerable financial assets, eight sons and strong links with Sephardim in the Middle East, made David Sassoon, Sons & Co. independent of close collaboration with other traders. The strength and Jewish characteristics of the firm were clearly recognized by the West, and the Sassoons became known as the 'Rothschilds of the East' (Jackson 1968: 1).

In 1844, David Sassoon sent his second-oldest son, Elias David, to Canton to open a branch of the family business (Roth 1941: 48). The office relocated to Hong Kong in 1857 and several of David Sassoon's sons took turns in running it. In 1867, Elias David Sassoon, who founded a firm rivalling his father's, established a branch of his company, E.D. Sassoon & Co., in Hong Kong (Criswell 1991: 137). Both Sassoon companies staffed their offices with Sephardim recruited from the Middle East and India. In 1898, E.D. Sassoon & Co. employed 40 Jews, a large proportion of the predominantly Sephardic Jewish community in the colony at that time. In 1897, the Jewish community in Hong Kong consisted of 52 men, 25 women, 26 girls and 14 boys (*The China Mail*, 2 December 1897).

Other Sephardic firms in nineteenth-century Hong Kong were E.R. Belilios (one of the leading opium merchants in the colony); S.J. David & Co. (which, like the Sassoons, owned cotton mills in India); Sir Elly Kadoorie & Sons; N.N.J. Ezra; Gubbay & Co.; Moses & Co.; Joshua, Gubbay & Co. and Judah & Co. (Bard 1993: 92–5). Like the Parsees and some of the Indian Muslim firms, most of these companies initially traded in cotton and opium, and in the nineteenth century a number of them diversified into stockbroking, property and the hotel business. What was more unique among the Sephardic firms was that nearly all of the families owning these firms, as well as their employees, had very close social and economic ties dating back to their residence in Baghdad and in the Middle East.[22] Elias David Sassoon's wife, for example, was Leah Gubbay. The Gubbays were also prominent residents in Baghdad and intermarriages between the two families had existed for generations (Roth 1941: 27, 97). The migration of Eleazer Silas Kadoorie (Sir Elly) to Hong Kong was partly tied to the Sassoons. Born in Baghdad in 1867, Eleazer was recruited by E.D. Sassoon & Co. in Bombay and the firm transferred him to its office in the Chinese city of Ningbo, probably in 1880. Soon after, he returned to Hong Kong and set up his own business as a stockbroker (Kadoorie 1985: I, 84).

The Sassoons strongly connected their Jewish tradition with the ways in which they directed their firms. Arabic was commonly spoken in the nineteenth century and the books of the company were written in Arabic with Hebrew characters. Like David Sassoon's firm, E.D. Sassoon & Co. printed its cheques with the Sassoon name in both Hebrew and English (Roth 1941: 98). England (1998: 60) alludes to the fact that speaking Arabic also helped Sephardim to maintain a degree of business secrecy. In Hong Kong, the firms provided synagogue services for their employees, who could settle in the colony without having to make major changes to the ways of life they were used to.[23] The substantial contributions of the Sassoons to trade in the colony and the Empire were recognized in Hong Kong. A number of its institutions, such as the Hongkong and Shanghai Banking Corporation and the Legislative Council, appointed members of this family in the second half of the nineteenth century (Plüss 2003: 74–5). Processes of Anglicization supported their positions in the networks of the elite. Abraham Sassoon, the provisional committee member of the Hongkong and Shanghai Bank, changed his name to Arthur Abraham Sassoon. In front of his orthodox father, however, he maintained his Hebrew name (ibid.: 74). Eleazer Silas Kadoorie changed his name to E.S. Kelly when he became a stockbroker in Hong Kong. First operating under the name of E.S. Kelly, the firm then merged with Solomon Sassoon Benjamin and operated under the name Benjamin & Kelly. In 1896, Briton George Potts, who was not Jewish, joined the firm, which was renamed Benjamin, Kelly & Potts. The firm was dissolved in 1906, whereupon 'Kelly' reverted to his Hebrew name, establishing E.S. Kadoorie & Co. (England 1998: 63–4). This latter process of reversing Anglicization is remarkable, expressing the ambiguities involved in combining elements from different cultures when constructing identities to enter into networks with majority while maintaining connections with one's society of origin. Although Sephardim altered the composition of the networks of the political and economic elite in Hong Kong, they were assigned a status of being outsiders on the inside. Frederick David Sassoon, for example, despite being a Legislative Councillor from 1884 to 1887, was not accepted as a member of the Hong Kong Club, the centre of informal political power in the colony (Endacott 1964: 103–4).

Emanuel Raphael Belilios settled in Hong Kong in 1862 and prospered quickly, engaging in a number of creative strategies to make his Sephardic origins more acceptable to the British elite. He did not share the Arabic origins of the Sassoons and the Kadoories. His father was from Venice, and he himself was born in Calcutta in 1837 (Bard 1993: 92). To strengthen his social and political position in Hong Kong, Belilios tried to establish links with the British Prime Minister Benjamin Disraeli, who managed to attain this office without having to deny his former Jewish roots.[24] Belilios proposed the construction of a marble and bronze statue of Disraeli in Hong Kong, but the Prime Minister declined the offer (*The Jewish Chronicle* (1879) 29 August: 13). Belilios then found another way to become known as paying respect to Disraeli, by constructing a row of houses close to the Legislative Council that carried the name of the Lordship Disraeli received, the Beaconsfield Arcade.[25] Belilios served on the Legislative Council from 1881 to 1900 (Endacott 1964: 94). He established his reputation as a philanthropist, sponsoring several schools and donating a number of scholarships. In 1893 this brought him recognition from Queen Victoria, who awarded him a CMG (Companion of the Order of St Michael and St George). He was the first Hong Kong resident to receive this recognition (Plüss 2003: 75). Despite the considerable influence that Belilios had in Hong Kong (including being the Chairman of the Hongkong and Shanghai Banking Corporation in 1877), and despite his alleged financial contributions to, and previously prominent position in, Jewish community life, the fact that he was an outsider in Sephardic networks originating in the Middle East prevented him from taking over the leadership position of Sephardim from the Sassoons at the turn of the twentieth century (Eitel 1983: 491; Plüss 2003: 68–71). The undivided loyalty of nearly all Sephardim in Hong Kong to the Sassoons, and not to Belilios, indicates the strength of their long-standing and closely interwoven diasporic networks, which not only brought them employment and opportunities in the colony but also accounted for the high degree of social cohesion of their community in Hong Kong, where maintaining insider positions in their historical social networks counted more than establishing relations with a prominent outsider. Nevertheless, with the departure of many Sephardim, including the Sassoons, from Hong Kong in the twentieth century, the few prominent traders remaining in the colony, such as the Kadoories, engaged in increasing processes of Anglicization and their diasporic links became less relevant to their economic pursuits.

Comparative Findings

Processes of Westernization strongly supported Parsees' ascension into more prominent social and economic positions in India. Diasporic linkages with co-religionists outside India did not account for this initial economic success. Parsees had lived in India for more than ten centuries. They maintained networks with co-religionists who were active in areas in which the British did not operate. This provided a number of Parsees with characteristics the British did not possess but were in need of, and this was one of the reasons that promoted them into middlemen roles for the British. These roles allowed them to prosper. Sephardim in India, on the other hand, achieved leading economic roles almost exclusively through the networks they maintained with their co-religionists in the Middle East and Asia, which made them economically more independent from the British colonial elite. Sephardim did also engage in processes of Anglicization, but this was mainly in order to mobilize political support for their ventures, and unlike some of the Parsee merchants, they did not engage in joint ventures with British companies once they started trading with China. Given their substantial contributions to the colonial economy in India and in Hong Kong, both Parsees and Sephardim received numerous honours and awards from Britain. This indicates that some of their characteristics were valued by the colonial elite who, therefore, made the boundaries of who could enter its circles more permeable. Muslim groups in India did not engage in equally strong processes of Westernization to enter into networks with British traders. It is debatable whether their status in Indian society was that of a diaspora or simply a minority. Nevertheless, their outsider status in relation to the Hindu majority, together with their regional knowledge, made them desirable employees for the British. Unlike the Parsee and Sephardic traders, who set up their ventures in the Far East with a relatively large degree of independence from the British elite, a number of Muslim traders in this region often started out by working first for British companies, and then established their own businesses. Bohra Muslims were an exception; they operated more independently from the British in Canton and Hong Kong. It was probably the support of their tightly knit organizational structure in India that facilitated a higher degree of self-reliance in diasporic trade.

Parsees, different groups of Indian Muslims and Sephardim all used their transregional diasporic networks to staff their companies in Hong Kong. They drew on the skills and resources enshrined in their connections with co-ethnics in India and China to engage in trade in the East. In the case of Sephardim, these networks were dominated by a smaller number of families, linked by kinship and economic ties that had previously been established during their residence in the Middle East. The Sassoons were the most influential of these families. Until the early twentieth century, most Sephardim ran their businesses in Hong Kong in accordance with Sephardic traditions. This facilitated the transfer of resources within the Sephardic diaspora. Parsee merchants in Hong Kong were not as tightly knit a group as the Sephardim. They stemmed from a wider circle of co-religionists in India. Nevertheless, Hong Kong Parsees remained attached to their distinct religion and lifestyle, binding them with co-ethnics residing in other places and facilitating the transfer of resources. Although information on the characteristics of Bohra Muslim traders in Hong Kong is more sparse, we can assume that their connections with Bohras in India fulfilled similar roles, especially since we know that they also staffed their offices with co-religionists from India. Prominent Sephardim, especially the Sassoons, stressed that the ethnic characteristics of their firms were largely responsible for the success of their trading ventures. Parsee traders in Hong Kong also did not seek to hide their distinct cultural roots. The involvement of prominent Parsees and Sephardim in leading Hong Kong institutions indicates that their cultural specificities were at least partly appreciated, or seen as useful, by the British elite, and that they also had some impact upon changing the characteristics of the ethnic composition of the elite circles in Hong Kong.

With the exception of Bohra Muslims, who retained strong diasporic links with their home community in Bombay, community cohesion among Indian Sunni Muslim traders in Hong Kong was not high because they came from different regions in India. The lack of shared family and long-standing business ties in Hong Kong, and the absence of common links with a community of co-religionists outside Hong Kong, explain why the economic activities of Sunni Muslims were not necessarily linked to diasporic trade. Sunnis generally lacked such a base from which they could have asserted distinctive characteristics in order to negotiate their positions in networks with the British in Hong Kong. Being less prominent than Parsees and Sephardim also made their knowledge and expertise less important in the eyes of the colonial elite. In order to more closely connect their trading interests and assets, Sunni Muslims in Hong Kong formed an association to support and promote their activities in China in the early twentieth century. The absence of shared kin networks in Hong Kong and in India was one of the reasons why Muslims culturally integrated more closely with the Chinese population in Hong Kong, that is, through marriage.

Starting in the early twentieth century, the economic activities of Parsees, Indian Muslims and Sephardim became less linked to trade with India, which had created a niche for them in Hong Kong's economy. These traders continued to use their links with co-religionists in China and the Far East, but they began also to invest in Hong Kong-based ventures for which diasporic networks became less important. Concomitantly, the ways in which these merchants ran their businesses became more independent from their ethnic characteristics. They increasingly hired employees from outside their own group. In the case of Parsees, links with the subcontinent in the twentieth century remained crucial to assure their historical continuity, providing networks through which to recruit spouses, so that the children of younger generations in Hong Kong would retain their parents' group membership. The number of Sephardim in Hong Kong declined sharply in the early twentieth century, and many Sephardim who resided in India migrated to other places (such as to the West) from which they did not wish to depart. Sephardim in Hong Kong found it increasingly difficult to maintain community cohesion through marrying spouses through their transregional networks. They integrated more with Western residents. An interesting case of how assimilation to the characteristics of the Chinese majority in Hong Kong was combined with maintaining primordial ethnic identities rooted in India is the case of 'local boys'. Despite adopting many elements from Chinese culture, and frequently intermarrying with Chinese residents, the memory of their forefathers' residence in India remained a strong element in their ethnicity, accounting for the exclusion of Chinese Muslims from their communal associations.

Conclusion

For diaspora merchants and entrepreneurs, being members of a diaspora and being engaged in transregional commercial exchange supported the construction of multiple identifications. Diaspora merchants integrated elements from different cultures into their identities and developed globalized ethnicities that were rooted in several geographical regions. Diaspora entrepreneurs were minorities in their places of abode, and therefore, at least to some extent, they were excluded from access to resources controlled by the majorities in their host societies. In order to have better prospects, some of them wanted to enter into networks with the majority, or to improve their positions in such networks. To support these processes, they adopted elements from the majority's culture. However, they also maintained elements from their own diasporic cultures. This, at times, also supported their economic and social aspirations, because maintaining common characteristics with co-ethnics helped them to draw on the skills and resources available within their networks. The willingness of diaspora traders to maintain the cohesion of their own ethnic group (often through asserting a number of exclusive identifiers) provided them with some assets to negotiate their positions in networks with the majority. Diasporic links provided traders with attributes that the majority did not necessarily share, and in a number of cases, the majority recognized that these characteristics had the potential to make contributions to their economic and political pursuits. Hence they included some diaspora traders more closely into their midst, and this changed also the characteristics of the majority, making them more cosmopolitan. This research does not yield a single pattern according to which identifications of diaspora traders changed over time. Rather it points toward a multiplicity of processes that differed from one another according to the relations these merchants could, and wished to, maintain with co-ethnics, and the networks they hoped to enter with other groups of people. Changes in diasporic identities were motivated not only by economic aspirations alone but also by the degree to which the members of a diaspora wished to maintain their social cohesion in order to assure historical continuity. Oftentimes, the consciousness of being a member of a diaspora remained important in terms of differentiating oneself culturally from outsiders by drawing boundaries around everyday social conduct. This applied also to cases in which commercial links with a homeland and with co-ethnics in the diaspora became less relevant to the pursuit of economic activities, and in which diaspora members relatively freely interacted with other ethnic communities, taking up economic pursuits that no longer distinguished them from other members in a society of residence. Nevertheless, most members of a diaspora still wished to maintain their distinct traditions by linking their cultural identifications to their places of ethnic origin.

Notes

1. Thanks to Raj Brown for her comments on an earlier version of the material for this chapter. The grants from the following bodies have contributed to the research on which this chapter is based: The Committee for Research and Conference Grants of The University of Hong Kong, The Freemasons Fund for East Asian Studies, The Hang Seng Bank Golden Jubilee Education Fund, the Incorporated Trustees of the Jewish Community of Hong Kong and The Lord Wilson Heritage Trust. The content is solely the author's responsibility.
2. For a discussion of deterritorialization and cosmopolitanism see for example Cohen (1997: 155–76) and Papastergiadis (2000: 100–21). For a classic discussion of the multiple loyalties of members of diasporas and their perceptions by host societies see Bonacich (1973: 583–94).
3. And personal communication from a descendant of this family residing in Hong Kong.
4. And personal communication from a Hong Kong Parsee.

5. These characteristics of middlemen are loosely adopted from Bonacich 1973: 583.
6. Personal communication from a Hong Kong Parsee who was born in India.
7. Nevertheless, through the centuries of their history in India, Indians appear to have been included in Parsee communities. An interviewee explains that this is visible in the racial features of Parsees.
8. Personal communication from a Hong Kong Parsee.
9. This designation remains in use today.
10. Personal communication from a Hong Kong Parsee.
11. Personal communication from an Indian resident in Hong Kong who worked previously for the British administration in India.
12. There appear to have been no intermarriages between Parsees and British, or Europeans, in Hong Kong until the second half of the twentieth century.
13. Personal communication from a member of his family.
14. The number of Parsees in Bombay (now Mumbai) is drastically falling, given the prohibition on converting outsiders and Parsees' migration to other countries.
15. Personal communication from a member of the Ebrahim family.
16. Personal communication from a member of the Ebrahim family.
17. In the year 2000, there were around 170–180 Bohras in Hong Kong. Personal communication from a member of the Ebrahim family.
18. Although Borah Muslims never prayed in the Sunni mosque, given ritualistic differences and diverging interpretations of Islam, they wished to join the Trustees. Borah Muslims were buried in the Muslim cemetery, albeit in a separate part. They desired to join this organization to participate in the cemetery's administration.
19. On the functions of diasporic networks of Pakistani Muslim in Hong Kong, see Weiss's discussion of their *deras* (1991: 432–40).
20. This point has been developed in Plüss 2000: 22.
21. Jackson (1968: 22) claims the company was founded in Bombay in 1832.
22. Personal communication from a member of the Jewish community.
23. For a brief history of the different synagogues in Hong Kong see Plüss (2003: 61).
24. Nevertheless, Benjamin Disraeli had converted to Catholicism, which Belilios was not inclined to do.
25. Benjamin Disraeli became Lord Beaconsfield.

References

Anonymous (n.d.), 'Late Mr. J.H. Ruttonjee', unidentified newspaper clipping, no page number.

Anonymous, 'Spreading Risks', in M. Keswick (ed.) (1982), *The Thistle and the Jade: A Celebration of 150 Years of Jardine, Matheson & Co.*, Hong Kong: Mandarin Publishers: 181–95.

Bard, S. (1993), *Traders of Hong Kong: Some Foreign Merchant Houses, 1841–1899*, Hong Kong: Urban Council.

Bonacich, E. (1973), 'A Theory of Middleman Minorities', *American Sociological Review*, 38(5): 583–94.

Bourdieu, P. (1977), *Outline of a Theory of Practice*, London: Cambridge University Press.

The China Mail (1897), 'Supreme Court: In Original Jurisdiction', 2 December, no page number.

Cohen, R. (1997), 'Diasporas in the Age of Globalisation', in *Global Diasporas: An Introduction*, Seattle: University of Washington Press.

Criswell, C.N. (1991), *The Taipans: Hong Kong's Merchant Princes*, Hong Kong: Oxford University Press.

Dobbin, C. (1996), 'Bombay: The Parsee-British Affinity', *Asian Entrepreneurial Minorities: Conjoint Communities in the Making of the World-Economy 1570–1940*, Richmond: Curzon.

Eitel, E.J. (1983), *Europe in China*, Hong Kong: Oxford University Press.

Endacott, G.B. (1964), *Government and People in Hong Kong, 1841–1962: A Constitutional History*, Hong Kong: Hong Kong University Press.

England, V. (1998), *The Quest of Noel Croucher: Hong Kong's Quiet Philanthropist*, Hong Kong: Hong Kong University Press.

Gans, H.J. (1996), 'Symbolic Ethnicity', in J. Hutchinson and A.D. Smith (eds), *Ethnicity*, Oxford: Oxford University Press.

Hall, P. (1992), *In the Web*, Wirral (UK): Peter Hall.

Hall, S. (1991), 'The Local and the Global: Globalization and Ethnicity', in A.D. King (ed.), *Culture, Globalization and the World-System*, London: Macmillan.

Incorporated Trustees of the Islamic Community Fund of Hong Kong, *ITICFHK* (1985), Hong Kong: Incorporated Trustees of the Islamic Community Fund of Hong Kong.

Incorporated Trustees of the Zoroastrian Charity Funds of Hongkong, Canton and Macao (2002), *Directory of Hong Kong Zoroastrians, 2001–2002*, Incorporated Trustees of the Zoroastrian Charity Funds of Hongkong, Canton and Macao.

Ingrame, H. (1952), *Hong Kong*, Her Majesty's Stationery Office: (presumably) London.

Jackson, S. (1968), *The Sassoons*, London: Heineman.

The Jewish Chronicle (1879), 'Hong Kong: From an Occasional Correspondent', 29 August, p. 13.

Kadoorie, L. (1985), 'The Kadoorie Memoir', in D.A. Leventhal (ed.), *Sino-Judaic Studies: Whence and Whither*, Sino-Judaic Monograph Series, Hong Kong: Jewish Historical Society of Hong Kong, Vol. 1.

Keswick, M. (1982), *The Thistle and the Jade: A Celebration of 150 Years of Jardine, Matheson & Co.*, Hong Kong: Mandarin.

Kotkin, J. (1993), *Tribes: How Race, Religion, and Identity Determine the Success in the New Global Economy*, New York: Random House.

Papastergiadis, N. (2000), 'The Deterritorialization of Culture', in *The Turbulence of Migration: Globalization, Deterritorialization and Hybridity*, Cambridge: Polity Press.

Pavri, J.K. (n.d.), *Honourable Dr. Dhunjishah J.H. Ruttonjee O.B.E., C.B.E., J.P. of Hong Kong*, unpublished typescript: 1–3.

Plüss, C. (2000), 'Hong Kong Muslim Organisations: Creating and Expressing Collective Identities', *China Perspectives*, 29, May/June: 19–23.

—— (2003), 'Sephardic Jews in Hong Kong: Constructing Communal Identities', *Sino-Judaica*, Vol. 4, Palo Alto: The Sino-Judaic Institute.

Reid, A. (1982a), 'The Steel Frame', in M. Keswick (ed.), *The Thistle and the Jade: A Celebration of 150 Years of Jardine, Matheson & Co.*, Hong Kong: Mandarin.

—— (1982b), 'Sealskins and Singsongs', in M. Keswick (ed.), *The Thistle and the Jade: A Celebration of 150 Years of Jardine, Matheson & Co.*, Hong Kong: Mandarin.

—— (1982c), 'Merchant Consuls', in M. Keswick (ed.), *The Thistle and the Jade: A Celebration of 150 Years of Jardine, Matheson & Co.*, Hong Kong: Mandarin.

—— (1982d), 'East Point', in M. Keswick (ed.), *The Thistle and the Jade: A Celebration of 150 Years of Jardine, Matheson & Co.*, Hong Kong: Mandarin.

Reid, M. (1982), 'Jamsetjee Jejeebhoy', in M. Keswick (ed.), *The Thistle and the Jade: A Celebration of 150 Years of Jardine, Matheson & Co.*, Hong Kong: Mandarin.

Roth, C. (1941), *The Sassoon Dynasty*, London: Robert Hale Limited.

Silliman, J. (1998), 'Crossing Borders, Maintaining Boundaries: The Life and Times of Farah, a Woman of the Baghdadi Jewish Diaspora (1870–1958)', *The Journal of Indo-Judaic Studies*, 1(1): 57–79.

Smith, C. (1995), 'The Establishment of the Parsee Community in Hong Kong', in C. Smith, *A Sense of History: Studies in the Social and Urban History of Hong Kong*, Hong Kong: Hong Kong Education Publishing.

—— (n.d. a), *The Shelley Street Mosque and Muslims in Hong Kong in the Nineteenth Century*, Hong Kong: unpublished manuscript.

—— (n.d. b), *Genealogies of Hong Kong Muslims Families*, Hong Kong: unpublished typescript.

Tang, K. and Y. Tian (1995), 'Xiang Gang yi si lan jiao de qi yuan yu fa zhan' (The Development of Hong Kong's Islam'), *Dong nan zu yan jiu lun cong (Southeast Asian Studies)*, 6: 48–51.

Taraporevata, S. (2000), *The Zoroastrians of India: Parsis*, Mumbai: Good Books.

Thompson, P. (1994), 'Between Identities: Homi Bhabha Interviewed by Paul Thompson', in R. Benmayor and A. Skotnes (eds), *Migration and Identity: International Yearbook of Oral History and Life Stories*, vol. 3, Oxford: Oxford University Press.

Toraval, J. (1991), 'Zhang li yu qi dao an pai: Xiang gang mu si lin ji jin zong hui li shi gai mao' ('Managing Death and Prayer: A Historical Sketch of the Board of Trustees of the Hong Kong Muslim Community (1850–1885)'), *Guangdong min zu yan jiu lun cong (The Collection of Studies of Ethnic Groups of Canton)*, no. 5: 221–48.

Vaid, K.N. (1972), *The Overseas Indian Community in Hong Kong*, Hong Kong: Centre of Asian Studies, University of Hong Kong.

Welsh, F. (1977), *A History of Hong Kong*, London: HarperCollins.

Weiss, A. (1991), 'South Asian Muslims in Hong Kong: Creation of a "Local Boy" Identity', *Modern Asian Studies*, 25(3): 417–53.

White, B.S. (1994), *Turbans and Traders: Hong Kong's Indian Communities*, Hong Kong: Oxford University Press.

–12–

The Trade Diaspora of Baghdadi Jews: From India to China's Treaty Ports, 1842–1937
Chiara Betta

The treaty of Nanking signed by Great Britain and Qing China at the end of the Opium War (1839–42) brought the demise of the Canton trade system, a monopolistic commercial regime that had tightly regulated and closely monitored maritime cross-cultural trade between the Middle Kingdom and the rest of the world for about a century. Restrictions on international trade were consequently eased with the cession of Hong Kong to the British and the opening of the first five treaty ports: Canton (Guangzhou), already a thriving international emporium, Shanghai, Amoy (Xiamen), Ningbo and Fuzhou. Half a century later, at the turn of the twentieth century, more than thirty treaty ports had been forcefully created in Chinese territory by unequal treaties, ratified by an increasingly weak Qing government, with the result that an integrated and aggressive system of foreign trade had taken shape in Chinese territory. At the centre of this system were foreign concessions and settlements, self-governing enclaves, whose status was fraught with legal complexities. The ambiguities of these 'grey zones' are exemplified by the fragmentation of the foreign area of Tianjin into nine concessions under nine foreign flags and by the equivocal status of the Shanghai International Settlement which was controlled by a bellicose British oligarchy rather than by the local British Consular authorities.

Treaty ports attracted enterprising traders and unscrupulous adventurers from the four corners of the globe eager to exploit the many commercial interstices and legal loopholes available to foreigners who could claim extraterritoriality rights. As a result of their strategic alliance with British private capitalism, Baghdadi Jews from British India (mainly Bombay) became deeply entrenched in the treaty-port system and founded one of the main centres of their trade diaspora in Shanghai, China's main commercial and manufacturing hub the in first decades of the twentieth century.[1] They also established peripheral bases in the smaller treaty ports where their presence was confined to a handful of bachelors and a few individuals with their families. My narrative will concentrate on Shanghai but will nevertheless make numerous references to the Baghdadis' commercial networks in the smaller treaty ports and will also mention the Baghdadi Jewish community of Hong Kong, another important outpost of the Baghdadi diaspora. The aim of this chapter is threefold. First, it will delineate Baghdadi Jewish spatial networks in the treaty ports through a detailed examination of the Sassoon firms, secondly it will use opium commerce as an analytical tool to compare the Baghdadi and Parsi diasporas in China; and finally it will briefly dissect the commercial strategies of Baghdadi firms in Shanghai.

The Nineteenth-Century Spice Route: the Sassoon Firms in the Chinese Treaty Ports

In the second half of the nineteenth century, Jews from Baghdad and its adjacent areas in the Ottoman Empire formed a trade diaspora that stretched from Bombay to China, with London as the main base in the metropole. The spatial structure of Baghdadi Jewish commercial networks replicated the eastward expansion of the formal and informal British Empire and, accordingly, the vital nodes of Baghdadis' enterprises were located in Bombay, Calcutta, Rangoon, Singapore and Hong Kong, and in the Shanghai foreign settlements (Ristaino 2003: 105–24). Within a broader historical framework, nineteenth-century Baghdadi Jewish networks in South, Southeast and East Asia might also be seen as an offshoot of ancient Jewish commercial patterns rather than entrepreneurial endeavours which simply reflect the framework of the British Empire. We could therefore consider Baghdadi Jewish presence in China within a *longue durée* framework of cross-cultural commercial contacts conducted through the overland Silk Road(s) and the maritime Spice Road(s) between China, India, Central and West Asia (Curtin 1984).

Such a perspective leads us to draw intriguing comparisons between ancient and modern Jewish settlements in India, as well as in China, and highlights the continuity of Jewish trade in the Indian Ocean and its adjacent regions. As early as 1905 the German sinologist Berthold Laufer pointed out that the Jewish community of Kaifeng, formed during the Northern Song dynasty (960–1127) and Baghdadi Jewish settlements established in China at the twilight of the Qing (1644–1911) shared common historical patterns. Laufer took for granted that Jews in the Song as well as in the late Qing travelled to China using the maritime Spice Road, an assumption which cannot, however, be validated since Jews might have reached the Song capital Kaifeng using the overland Silk Road. Nevertheless, Laufer's (1905: 31) stimulating insight retains its validity on the grounds that Jews with roots in West Asia travelled to China in the eleventh century as well as in the nineteenth century for the same reason: long-distance trade.

New commercial opportunities did indeed draw the Baghdadi trader Elias David Sassoon to sail (steamers were not used until 1845) from Bombay to Canton in the immediate aftermath of the Opium War. Elias David was the first Baghdadi Jew to set foot in the Middle Kingdom, though his father's company had already started to ship Indian opium to Canton in 1834, a first attempt to become involved in the contraband trade of the drug which was then monopolized by British and Parsi traders (*North China Herald*, 11 May 1880: 416; Trocki 1999: 112). The Sassoons, Baghdad's most eminent Jewish family, had migrated to Bombay as late as 1832 to escape persecution by the local Ottoman governor and, within a short period, they established a commercial empire which stretched over vast areas of Asia. As the Shanghai publication *North China Herald* summarized in 1881 (8 February), 'The name of Sassoon is less known in Europe than that of Rothschild, but among Arab or Banyan traders, even with Chinese and Japanese merchants, in the Straits as well as on both sides of the Ganges, it is a name to conjure with.'

Most importantly, the patriarch of the family, David, with the help of his eight sons and the family firm D. Sassoon, Sons & Co., performed a crucial role in the expansion of Baghdadi Jewish networks in Southeast and East Asia (Roland 1999: 141–53). In China the Sassoons' commercial interests took the shape of a spatial grid, characterized by overlapping trading networks after the foundation of a second Sassoon firm, E.D. Sassoon & Co., by Elias David shortly after the death of his father in 1867. By the early 1870s the core commercial bases of the Sassoons in China were situated in the treaty port of Shanghai and in the British colony of Hong Kong; secondary offices functioned in the smaller treaty ports of Hankou, Jinjiang, Zhifu, Ningbo, Tianjin and Niuzhuang (*The Chronicle & Directory for China, Japan, & the Philippines for the Year 1868*: 155, 201, 223, 234, 236, 238; *The China Directory for 1874*, 1971: 28–9[J], 1[K], 4[M], 3[N], 3[P], 2[Q]). As for Canton, it had swiftly lost its commercial clout, and the southern Chinese business of the Sassoons was entirely taken over by their Hong Kong offices. We should then not overlook the fact that the Japanese cities of Nagasaki, Yokohama and Kobe could be viewed as the eastern extension of the Sassoons' spatial networks in China (Earns 1999: 159–60).

In the early days the Sassoons recruited the staff for their Chinese offices directly in Bombay, often among young Jews who attended the local Sassoon school where they received a basic education and probably also learnt the rudiments of trade. Employees were usually circulated between Bombay, the smaller treaty ports, Shanghai and Hong Kong and, finally, Bombay again. In the second half of the nineteenth century both Sassoon firms routinely employed brothers in their Chinese offices: the Shanghai tycoon Silas Aaron Hardoon moved to China with his elder sibling Elias Aaron; Sir Ellie Kadoorie (Eleazar Silas), the founder of the Kadoorie family fortunes, arrived in Hong Kong in 1880, in the footsteps of his elder brother Moshi and three years before his younger brother Sir Ellis. The Sassoon firms provided secure work to entire families yet obedience was expected and an autocratic style of management was readily applied especially with the lower ranks of employees. When Sir Ellie used, without permission from his superiors, a barrel of disinfectant during a plague epidemic in Ningbo he was 'severely reprimanded' and, after lodging a protest in Shanghai, 'he was told not to argue but to obey' and was eventually dismissed. This unfortunate episode marked the beginning of Sir Ellie's commercial success – after being fired he set up a successful brokerage firm and became one of China's wealthiest Baghdadi Jews. His Hong Kong-based grandson, Lord Michael Kadoorie, still presides over a vast economic empire and ranks among Asia's billionaires (Leventhal 1995: 83–4).

The Sassoon firms and their *modus operandi* in China in the second half of the nineteenth century epitomized the transition of Baghdadi Jews in British India, Singapore and China from a traditional trade diaspora deeply rooted in West Asia into a trade diaspora integrated within the European-dominated world economy. My own understanding of trade diasporas in the course of the nineteenth century, which is shaped by the study of Baghdadi Jews, is slightly different from that expounded by Philip Curtin in his classic *Cross-cultural Trade in World History* (1984: 198). In this respect I have been strongly influenced by Claude Markovits's recent work on Sindhi's commercial networks and I therefore suggest that the trade diaspora of Baghdadi Jews flourished rather than disappeared under the increased Westernization of international commerce in South, Southeast and East Asia. My analysis does not take into account the fact that trade diasporas lost their function as cross-cultural brokers in the late nineteenth century, but rather stresses the vitality and resilience of West Asian commercial networks that had left the tutelage of the declining Ottoman empire to find fresh opportunities under the aegis of the British Empire (Marcovits 2000: 20–4).

In order to survive under the new circumstances Baghdadi Jewish merchants were compelled to re-assess their trading strategies and partially re-invent their commercial practices. By the 1880s the Sassoons had already given up traditional accounting techniques, used double-entry in their business files, recorded their commercial transactions in English rather than Judaeo-Arabic and had adopted a business organization modelled after European trading firms.[2] Nevertheless, the Sassoon firms continued to function on the grounds of shared kinship ties and personal trust with Baghdadi co-religionists. They hired, in fact, almost exclusively Jews of 'Baghdadi' extraction, a term that in India as well as in China comprised Jews from many areas of the Ottoman empire as well as Persia and even Afghanistan. That said, the core of the Sassoons' employees traced their roots to Mesopotamia and only a minority originated from other regions, an apt example being the Egyptian Jew Simon A. Levy who spent most of his life working for E.D. Sassoon & Co. (London PRO, 1 May 1907: FO 372/47/21695). As a rule the Sassoons' offices in China did not employ Russian Jews, who in Shanghai formed the great majority of the Ashkenazi community prior to the arrival of Central European refugees in the 1930s. Relations between Baghdadi and Russian Jews were, in effect, marked by diffidence on the grounds of their different cultural background and economic conditions, and the two communities led largely separate lives. Occasionally, the East Asian branches of the Sassoon companies employed British gentiles and, in one case, the Englishman Arthur Barnard was entrusted with the management of the Yokohama branch of D. Sassoon, Sons & Co. In the 1860s Yokohama was clearly a peripheral office of the Sassoon empire, which could be easily supervised by non-Jews, something that was, however, out of question in China. In the nineteenth century the main branches of the Sassoons' operations in the Middle Kingdom were usually headed by members of the Sassoon clan who therefore maintained direct control over the family's commercial affairs in the country. One exception was represented by S.A. Hardoon, the managing partner of E.D. Sassoon & Co. between the 1890s and 1911, who was, however, initially regarded with a degree of suspicion by some members of the Sassoons' entourage.[3]

During their stay in China Baghdadi Jews were, most likely, not fully proficient in local business practices and almost certainly could not communicate fluently in the many dialects that are spoken in the country. In the second half of the nineteenth century the Sassoons firms, like other foreign merchant houses, heavily relied on the services of *compradors*, Chinese merchants who acted as the prime collaborators of Western business enterprise in China and strongly profited from their association with foreign firms (Curtin 1984: 250–1). *Compradors* working for the Sassoons acquired notable independent wealth, especially by trading commodities, such as Indian opium, independently. Carl Trocki (1999: 120) has suggested that the *comprador* of one of the Sassoon firms in the smaller treaty port of Jinjiang sold one and a half million *taels* of opium in only one year (probably in the 1880s), thus making a considerable profit within a short period of time. Most significantly, the Sassoons' *compradors* shrewdly exploited kinship relations and common place-of-origin ties in the business dealings they conducted on behalf of their foreign employers and, in some cases, passed on their job to their descendants, therefore building a long-term system of reciprocal trust which benefited both sides. However, by the beginning of the twentieth century the golden age of *compradors* in China was over and their services became increasingly superfluous for the Sassoon firms as well as for other foreign concerns in China (Zhang and Chen 1985: 127–44).

The legal position of *compradors* vis-à-vis foreign firms was highly ambiguous; in some circumstances they were considered employees while in others they were regarded as independent brokers. Therefore, serious conflicts arose when *compradors* incurred heavy financial losses since it was not immediately clear who was liable to pay their creditors. This pivotal question was debated in two court proceedings that involved D. Sassoon, Sons & Co., their Tianjin *comprador* Hou Meiping, and two of the latter's Chinese creditors (Motono 1992: 44–70). Besides working for the Sassoons and for other foreign firms, Hou was an independent entrepreneur who traded Mongolian furs, owned confectionery and opium shops in Beijing and Tianjin, ran a gold pawnshop in Shanghai and managed the Tianyuan *qianzhuang* (native bank) (Zhang and Chen 1985: 127–8). Notwithstanding his wide-ranging business connections Hou did not survive a severe financial crisis which unfolded in 1883 and, subsequently, his Chinese creditors requested the Sassoons to honour the payment for his purchase of gold bullion. Their request was based on the fact that Hou had issued receipts in the name of his foreign employers even when he conducted private business (Motono 1992: 48–53). The final judgments on the Hou cases and an additional third lawsuit brought against D. Sassoon, Sons & Co. were, however, of contradictory nature in regard to the legal position of *compradors* and had 'the effect of undermining the credibility of the *comprador* system among the Chinese and Western mercantile people in China' (Motono 1992: 69). From the point of view of Baghdadi Jewish business, the Hou cases illuminate how D. Sassoon, Sons & Co. operated in conjunction with *compradors* in the treaty ports and demonstrates that the import to China of Indian opium and the export to India of gold bullion were part of an integrated and parallel trade which still needs to be fully researched.

Baghdadi Jews, Parsis and Opium

These [Jews and Parsis] came almost entirely from India, or parts adjacent, and they were all British subjects. There were two large Jewish houses, the two Sassoons, and the remainder of the Jews, and all the Parsees, were either brokers or merchants in a very small way [*sic*]. They were quite inoffensive, and their raison d'être was chiefly the opium trade. (Dyce 1906: 50)

Baghdadi Jews' economic achievements in the Chinese treaty ports were, on a local level, favoured by the intimate relationship they enjoyed with British communities in China and, from a more global perspective, were fostered by the close cooperation that Baghdadi Jews forged with the British Empire in India (Betta 2003a: 999–1024). Since this question has been dissected extensively elsewhere and does not necessitate any further treatment, I merely specify that Chinese did not easily differentiate between Baghdadi Jews and European traders and that they usually considered the Sassoon firms and their employees as 'British'. Such a perception is illustrated by Hou Meiping's arbitrary and unauthorized translation of 'D. Sassoon, Sons & Co.' into Chinese as *Yingshang jiu Shaxun*, literally the 'British firm "Old" Sassoon' (Motono 1992: 50). Hou's addition of 'British' was unquestionably dictated by his eagerness to reassure Chinese clients about the status of the firm he was acting for; being 'British' in the Chinese treaty ports signified commercial strength and political and military might.

It would be incorrect to argue that the Baghdadi Jewish trade diaspora was the only trade diaspora in China associated with the British Empire. Parsis, Gujarati Muslims, Hindu Sindhis and even Peshawari Muslims occupied functional niches in India-China trade under the aegis of the British Empire at different times in the nineteenth and early twentieth centuries. Baghdadi Jews, Parsis and Gujarati Muslims imported cotton yarn and opium from Bombay and Calcutta to China, Sindhis from Hyderabad were engaged in the commerce of cheap varieties of silk, while Peshawari Muslims traded tea, silk and furs.[4] More specifically, between the mid-nineteenth and mid-twentieth centuries 'Britain in China' comprised at its periphery concentric circles of merchants based in British India, which were formed by the commercial elite of Baghdadi Jews, Parsis and Guajarati Muslims. As for Hindu Sindhis and Peshawari Muslims, they constituted the outer circle of British commercial interests in the Chinese treaty ports and held rather tenuous links with 'Britain in China'.[5]

To understand the development of Baghdadi Jewish trading networks in the treaty ports, especially in Shanghai, it is essential to compare the mercantile endeavours of Baghdadi Jews and Parsis. At the outset of the treaty port system in the 1840s Parsis enjoyed a substantial commercial superiority over Baghdadi Jews in the India-China trade. Numbers clearly illustrate the Parsis' predominance: in 1846 more than 60 Parsi merchants were sojourning in Canton, Hong Kong and Macao whereas Baghdadi presence in China was restricted to Elias David Sassoon and Moses Dahood (*The Hongkong Almanac and Directory for 1846*). The Parsis' extensive commercial networks in China had taken shape at the time of the Canton trade system, as early as the middle of the eighteenth century, when they acted as guarantee brokers for British private traders. At the same time, as leading ship-owners in India, the Parsis had brought cotton and smuggled opium into Canton, thus accumulating enormous riches which contributed to their overall economic achievements in Bombay. Yet, despite their initial advantage over Baghdadi Jews, the Parsis failed to capitalize on their mercantile expertise in the India-China trade and, especially after the 1870s, adopted a defensive rather than an aggressive commercial strategy in the Chinese treaty ports (Kamerkhar 1999: 134–40; Marcovits 2000: 56–8). Conversely, Baghdadi Jews, under the enlightened guidance of the Sassoons' firms, sought fresh lines of trade, shrewdly invested in real estate and did not eschew financial activities, with the result that the Parsis were gradually sidelined in the treaty ports by the more enterprising Baghdadi Jews.

The Parsis' commercial history in China is epitomized by Cowasjee Pallanjee & Co., a firm with headquarters in Bombay. Founded in Canton in 1832, fourteen years later the office was staffed by three people: Cooverjee Bomanjee, Cawasjee Framjee, and Sapoorjee Bomanjee. In 1849 it opened a branch in Shanghai, at a time when the Parsis were forcefully expanding their commercial enterprises toward northern China. At the turn of the twentieth century the Hong Kong and

Shanghai branches were still leading dealers of opium, yarn and silks but the firm had already lost its original entrepreneurial zeal and, by the 1920s, it was in the process of scaling down its operations in China. Apparently Cawasjee Pallanjee & Co. gave its employees the option to return to Bombay after a three- or four-years' stint in their Chinese offices, probably a routine practice among the Parsis who, as a rule were not accompanied by their families (*The Hongkong Almanac for 1846*; Smith 1995: 393–4; Wright 1908: 228). The Parsi community in China was, in effect, formed by sojourning men, a condition that, in some cases, encouraged sexual entanglement with prostitutes and attracted vehement condemnation from co-religionists in Bombay (*North China Herald* 6 July 1906: 36; Smith 1995: 397). Baghdadi Jews took the opposite path from that of their Parsi competitors: they brought their families to China and settled in Shanghai and Hong Kong, thus establishing communities formed by a few hundred families which constituted the crucial nodes of the Baghdadi trade diaspora.

Baghdadi Jews, Parsis, Gujarati Muslims and Persians based in British India shared common interests in the India-China trade and competed over the import of cotton, cotton yarn and especially opium to China. Before the opium trade was legalized in 1858 by the treaty of Tianjin, opium contraband in the newly opened treaty port of Shanghai was dominated by Britons, Americans, Parsis and Baghdadi Jews. Fast clippers, heavily armed to defend their valuable cargoes from the threat of pirates who infested the China coast, smuggled opium consignments to Wusong, in the vicinity of Shanghai. According to F.L. Hawks Potts (1928: 46), until 1854 ten receiving ships would wait in Wusong: 'four for opium consigned to British firms, four to Jewish or Parsee firms and two to American firms. In 1854 the two American ships were withdrawn from service.' The legalization of opium commerce in 1858 prompted an increasing 'Asianization' of the trade which, in the Chinese treaty ports, became increasingly controlled by Baghdadi Jews. From as early as the 1870s the bulk of the opium trade between India and China was handled by the Sassoon firms which, according to some estimations, might have controlled as much as 70 per cent of the opium in India as well as in China (Trocki 1999: 112–15). The Sassoons, who had been latecomers to the Indian opium markets in the 1830s, turned into principal players when they started to act as bankers 'to finance the Malwa opium crop, making advances to an already established group of dealers and, in effect, purchasing the crop before it was even planted' (Trocki 1999: 113). As a result, the Sassoons became directly involved in the cultivation of opium, a gamble that other traders were not willing to take, and that gave the family direct control over opium production. We need also to highlight the fact that in Calcutta and Bombay the Sassoons maintained a tight grip on local opium auctions with the assistance of other Baghdadi Jews since, as a traditional diaspora, Baghdadi Jews tended to trust only co-religionists and whenever possible operated in association with each other.

Despite the control which Baghdadi Jews, especially the Sassoon firms, extended over the opium trade in the late nineteenth century, the Parsis were never entirely displaced from this lucrative business and firms such as Cawasjee Pallanjee & Co., Tata & Co., R.S.N. Talati & Co., Talati & Co., P.B. Petit & Co. continued to import large quantities of Indian opium to China. In this respect, in 1894 the Shanghai branch of Tata & Co. employed four steamers to import opium, cotton yarn and other merchandise from Bombay to Shanghai and then exported coal and other commodities to India (*North China Herald*, 19 January 1894). Gujarati Muslims based in Bombay, who had already been active in Canton before the Opium War, maintained a considerable stake in the opium trade through E. Pabaney & Co. and Abdoolally Ebrahim & Co., concerns with branch offices in Shanghai and Hong Kong. The first, E. Pabaney & Co. had been founded by Sir Currimbhoy Ebrahim, a leading Khoja Ismaili whose shipowning family had held trading interests as far as the Arabian peninsula and the African coast. The second, Abdoolally Ebrahim & Co., had been set up by Ebrahim Noordin, a Bohra Ismaili, in Canton shortly after the end of the Opium War. Scholars have often overlooked the fact that two Persian firms, M.M.B. Afshar & Co. and Nemazee & Co., were also active in the opium trade in China. Nemazee & Co. was a Shiraz concern that held extensive businesses in India as well as in Hong Kong and Shanghai where branches were opened respectively in 1857 and 1895. The headquarters of M.M.B. Afshar & Co. were located in Bombay. In 1897 the firm opened in Shanghai a branch which was engaged in import–export trade between China, Persia and India and also acted as commission agents and held a number of agencies (Wright 1908: 225–8, 638, 652, 654). In a few words, by the late nineteenth century the opium trade between India, Persia and China was almost totally dominated by non-Europeans – Baghdadi Jews, Parsis, Gujarati Muslims, Persians – who had filled the vacuum left by the British and Americans' hasty retreat from the business. Baghdadi Jews were the principal actors in the opium traffic but it would be highly incorrect to downplay the commercial weight of the other groups who remained credible competitors until the trade became illegal at the end of 1917.

Whenever the opium trade came under scrutiny, Baghdadi Jews and Parsis strenuously defended the commerce. Not surprisingly, they forcefully minimized the effects of the drug on Chinese users in the interviews they granted to the Royal Opium Commission which had been set up in India between 1893 and 1894 (Blue 2000: 39). They stressed that opium, if used in moderation, was a safe form of entertainment rather than a dangerous drug with deleterious effects. The Baghdadis consciously exploited the various strands of the leisure discourse on opium constructed by the Chinese, and maintained that the use of opium as a recreational activity for the upper classes usually brought no visible harm to the Chinese (Des Forges 2000: 167–85). Accordingly, M.S. Howard of David Sassoon, Sons & Co. maintained that 'opium had debilitating effects on those who could not afford it whilst it was a mere entertainment activity for the upper classes' (*North China Herald*, 19 January 1894). S.A. Nathan, an employee of E.D. Sassoon & Co., added that 'if taken moderately opium was very beneficial' (*North China Herald*, 30 March 1894). Baghdadi traders also skilfully employed the commonly used Western stereotype that while Europeans naturally indulged in drinking alcohol, the Chinese were instinctively drawn to opium. E.S. Gubbay, who had spent many years in the treaty ports of Ningbo and Shanghai, contended that 'the Chinese who smoked or imbibed opium were better behaved, more quiet, and far more sensible than those addicted to alcoholic drinks' (*North China Herald*, 30 March 1894). The high status of opium traders among the Chinese was further upheld by the Parsi Hormasji Kuvarji who stressed that opium merchants 'enjoyed as much respect and credit as tea and silk merchants' (*North China Herald*, 30 March 1894).

By the turn of the twentieth century the opium trade was no longer justifiable in Great Britain, and a policy of gradual reduction of opium imports from India to China was introduced in 1907 with the aim of terminating the trade a decade later. In reality, the import of Indian opium virtually stopped already in 1913 not on moral or diplomatic considerations but to suit the pressing needs of opium merchants in the treaty ports who had accumulated enormous supplies of the drug after a series of commercial miscalculations. Amid these uncertain circumstances, Baghdadi Jewish and Parsi traders formed a cartel, the Shanghai Opium Merchants' Combine, which aimed to monopolize the distribution of Indian and Persian opium and bring huge profits to its members before the final dismissal of the trade (Blue 2000: 40–3; Trocki 1999: 128–30). However, not every Baghdadi Jewish trader involved in the opium trade joined this organization; Silas Aaron Hardoon most probably dealt in the drug on an individual basis and, according to a Chinese source, made huge profits by selling as much as 5 tons of opium (Yu 1990: 4). In the middle of 1918 a Shanghai merchant was still attempting to acquire 1,600 pounds of opium from the Hardoon Company and specified that 'the goods were for Japanese buyers' (London PRO, 12 July 1918: FO 671/452/212–3). Eventually Hardoon, like the great majority of Baghdadi Jews, complied with the ban on the opium trade, though some individuals were reluctant to give up what had been a profitable and legal business.

This was the case with the Ezra family whose misfortunes started after the premature death in 1921 of the patriarch of the family, Edward, the main promoter of the Opium Combine. In the aftermath of a financial crisis Edward's younger siblings, Judah and Isaac, moved to San Francisco where they became entangled in a smuggling ring of opium and narcotics from China to California. In May 1933 both brothers were charged with illegal importation and sale of narcotics in the United States, thus bringing their family's fortunes to an abrupt and dramatic conclusion (*North China Herald*, 24 May 1933; 14 June 1933; 4 October 1933).

The Ezras, who had been respected merchants in Shanghai's foreign settlements in the 1910s, had turned into dangerous narcotics-traffickers in San Francisco in the 1930s. In reality their line of trade – drugs – was always the same; only circumstances, times and attitudes had changed. With the Ezra case in San Francisco, the Baghdadi Jews' connection to drugs, which had initiated to compete with the Parsis in the India-China trade, had come full circle. By then opium profits made legally in Shanghai by Baghdadis, as well as by other foreign merchants and Chinese, had already been reinvested in other lines of trade in industrial and financial endeavours and in real estate.

Business Strategies in the Treaty Port of Shanghai

Altogether we can distinguish between three generations of Baghdadi Jewish firms in the treaty port of Shanghai in the period taken into consideration in this chapter. The first generation was formed by the Sassoon firms, which in the decades between 1845 and the early 1880s set the foundations for a permanent Baghdadi community in Shanghai. The second generation of Baghdadi firms was founded by ex-Sassoon employees who broke away from the shackles of the Sassoons and started to operate as individual brokers and general merchants from the middle of the 1870s onward. These entrepreneurs were still firmly anchored in Baghdadi Jewish culture and did not always utilize Western accounting practices since their business records and correspondence were often kept in Judaeo-Arabic. The third generation of Baghdadi firms was founded in the course of the early twentieth century by Baghdadis who were often born in Shanghai and whose world-view was largely shaped by the close commercial and social ties they maintained with the local British community (Betta 2000: 41–2; Betta 2003a: 90–3). Despite the Anglicization of Baghdadi Jewish traders of the third generation, their businesses did not differ substantially from those of the previous generation. In fact, with the exception of the Sassoon firms and David & Co., Baghdadi firms in Shanghai were usually small family affairs, engaged in various forms of brokerage, general commerce and real estate, that employed relatives or Baghdadi Jewish acquaintances and did not develop into sophisticated international business operations. On the whole, business partnerships between Baghdadis and non-Jewish businessmen were extremely rare, two exceptions being the firms Benjamin & Potts and Toeg & Read, formed by Baghdadi Jewish and British brokers. Of the two, only Benjamin & Potts became a unique example of long-term commercial co-operation involving Baghdadi Jewish and British businessmen in Shanghai.[6] Obviously, not all Baghdadi Jews owned or worked for companies: some ran shops that catered for co-religionists, others serviced the Sephardic community, and many of those who resided in Shanghai for shorter periods were indigent.

What is interesting to remark is that jobs, including those for the least well-off, were created within the Baghdadi community, and only a minority worked outside the confines of Shanghai's Baghdadi Jewish world.

Besides opium, Baghdadi Jews traded in a large number of commodities such as cotton, cotton yarn, silk, porcelain, bullion and metals, and acted as general, stock, and bullion brokers. Baghdadi Jews also counted among Shanghai's main real-estate owners as they took full advantage of the rise of a modern real-estate market in the city's foreign settlements. Real estate was regarded as a safe investment in the early twentieth century as properties continuously rose in value, especially in the Central District of the International Settlement where prices increased tenfold between 1900 and 1930. Land values depreciated only once, in 1910, at the height of the rubber boom. The reasons behind the constant re-evaluation of real estate can be ascribed to a number of factors such as the complex system of land tenure envisaged in the foreign settlements, which guaranteed foreign protection not only to foreign landowners but also to Chinese landowners who employed foreign trustees (Feetham 1931: 328–9, 338, 342–3). Among Baghdadi Jews, Silas Aaron Hardoon, who was a British subject by act of 'grace', most likely registered under his own name the properties of some of his powerful Chinese acquaintances so that they could rely on British protection to guarantee the safety of their possessions.[7]

It is well known that opium profits in Shanghai were often re-invested in real estate in the foreign settlements, though the link between the two still needs to be researched. Among Baghdadi opium dealers, E.D. Sassoon & Co. and Silas Aaron Hardoon invested heavily in real estate. E.D. Sassoon & Co. acquired its first property in 1877 and by 1921 owned 29 properties in the foreign settlements, comprising a total area of almost 300 *mu* and a value of over 13 million *taels* (Zhang and Chen 1985: 33–62). At the very end of the 1920s Sir Victor Sassoon, the grandson of the founder of the firm, embarked on a series of ambitious real-estate developments and erected architectural landmarks such as the Cathay mansions and the Cathay Hotel, the latter being heralded as 'the most modern hotel of the Far East' (*North China Herald*, 23 December 1930). The least famous, Silas Aaron Hardoon, enjoyed a brilliant career at E.D. Sassoon & Co., for whom he acted as managing partner until his retirement in 1911 when he concentrated only on the management of his real-estate portfolio through his own company. Starting with the ownership of a shack in the 1870s, Hardoon gradually built a real-estate empire by mortgaging his properties to raise cash to finance further real-estate purchases. At the turn of the century Hardoon already had a clear insight of the commercial potential of properties situated along Nanking Road, a thoroughfare which gradually blossomed into the commercial heart of Shanghai, and he pursued a strategy of purchasing all the available properties along the road. Whenever possible he leased, for enormous amounts of money, his Nanking Road properties to commercial ventures such as the Wingon and Sincere companies, department stores that introduced to Shanghai new and revolutionary concepts of shopping. When he died in 1931 he was the main landowner in Nanking Road and was one of the wealthiest foreigners in East Asia, if not the wealthiest (Betta 1997: ch. 3). Hardoon was undoubtedly the most successful Baghdadi real-estate owner, but we should also note that other co-religionists played a prominent role in Shanghai's real-estate market as well. Toward the end of the 1920s Baghdadi families such as the Somekhs and Toegs erected expensive and fashionable residential housing which boasted the most up-to-date appliances and the latest architectural styles and therefore contributed to the evolution of a Western shape to Shanghai's skies (*Israel's Messenger*, 4 January 1929: 4; 7 February 1930; 4 July 1930: 12; 2 January 1931: 4).

To conclude, dealings in opium and land typify the entrepreneurial and pragmatic spirit of the Baghdadi trade diaspora, which in the course of the nineteenth century and early twentieth century was willing to take remarkable risks in order to expand its commercial networks in China. Opium speculations represented the main incentive that prompted 'Asian' traders like Baghdadi Jews, Parsis, Gujarati Muslims and Persians to become enmeshed in the India-China trade (in the case of the Parsis already at the end of the eighteenth century). Real estate was a longer-term investment, attractive for those Baghdadi Jews who settled in the treaty port of Shanghai and in the colony of Hong Kong and for whom China had become a permanent home. In a few words, we could posit that opium attracted Baghdadi Jews to China and real estate kept them there.

From London to Shanghai, Baghdadi Jews acted as a cultural and economic unit welded together by common heritage; geographical distance did not weaken their strongly shared sense of identity. In this respect, Baghdadi Jews in the treaty ports – whether independent opium merchants, real-estate developers, brokers, managers, salaried clerks or shopkeepers – formed intertwining and layered commercial networks that constituted an integral segment of the wider trade diaspora of Baghdadi Jews. Most importantly, Baghdadi traders that operated in China perpetuated traditional Baghdadi networks by creating close-knit commercial ties – impenetrable even to Ashkenazi Jews – that functioned largely on the basis of personal relations, kinship ties and a shared Judaeo-Arabic heritage. Quite clearly, at least in my opinion, the Baghdadi trade diaspora did not evaporate as a result of the Westernization of commerce and the consequent creation of large ecumenical trade zones in the course of the nineteenth century (Curtin 1984: 230). Under the pressures of nineteenth-century formal and informal colonialism, Baghdadi Jews envisaged skilful solutions for energizing their traditional trading networks in an environment which, undoubtedly, required a degree of Anglicization but did not demand thorough homogenization of business practices or the overall repudiation of a commercial identity and memory that had taken shape on the caravan routes of West Asia and in the maritime lanes of the Asian seas. In the treaty ports Baghdadi

Jews relied on the commercial wisdom which their ancestors had acquired over the centuries, and were therefore not operating merely in the guise of British merchants. In short, they were placed at the crossroads of many worlds – the disintegrating Ottoman empire, British India, the British Empire, China, the treaty ports – and were able to juggle between them by operating as a trade diaspora as late as the first decades of the twentieth century.

Notes

1. On Baghdadi Jews in Shanghai see Betta 2000: 38–54; 2003a: 999–1024; 2003b: 81–104), and Meyer 2003.
2. My observation are based on the viewing of some commercial files of the Shanghai branch of E.D. Sassoon, Sons & Co. which are kept in the Shanghai House Property Administration Bureau Archives; I have formulated the observation on double-entry after reading Goody 1996: 49–81.
3. My conclusions are based on the readings of commercial directories of China between 1868 and 1928; interesting insights can be found in Jackson 1968: esp. 24, 64. However, this source needs to be used with great discretion since it contains many factual mistakes.
4. For an insight on the commercial activities of these groups in Shanghai see the *Comacrib Directory* 1928, esp. 1–162 [D1].
5. I have here re-interpreted the concept of 'Britain in China' formulated in Bickers 1999.
6. My comments are based on the analysis of the Shanghai sections of *The Directory & Chronicle for China... & C.*, 1906, 1910, 1919; and of the Shanghai section of the *Comacrib Directory* 1928.
7. Hardoon managed the properties of a number of Chinese warlords such as Lu Yongxiang. See Shanghai House Property Administration Bureau Archives. Archives of the Hardoon Company, Jia 267, S0069.

References

Primary Sources

I. Archival Material

London. Public Record Office (PRO). FO 372. Foreign Office General Correspondence, Treaty.

London. Public Record Office. FO 671. Shanghai Correspondence, 1845–1948.

Shanghai. Shanghai House Property Administration Bureau Archives. Archives of the Hardoon Company.

II. Newspapers, Magazines

Israel's Messenger, 1929-1931.

North China Herald, weekly edition of the *North China Daily News*, 1880–1, 1894, 1906, 1930, 1933.

III. Contemporary Directories, Memoirs, Reportage

The China Directory for 1874 (1874). Reprint. Taipai: C'heng Wen Publishing, 1971.

The Chronicle & Directory for China, Japan, & the Philippines for the Year 1868 (1868) Hong Kong: Daily Press Office.

The Comacrib Directory of China, 1928 (1928), Shanghai: Commercial and Credit Information Bureau.

The Directory & Chronicle for China, Japan, Corea, Indo-China, Straits Settlements, Malay States, Siam, Netherlands's India, Borneo, the Philippines & C (1906, 1910, 1919), Hong Kong: Hong Kong Daily Press Office.

Dyce, C.M. (1906), *Personal Reminiscences of Thirty Years' Residence in the Model Settlement Shanghai*, 1870–1900, London: Chapman & Hall.

The Hongkong Almanac and Directory for 1846, with an Appendix (1846), Hong Kong: China Mail.

Wright, A. (ed.) (1908), *Twentieth Century Impressions of Hong Kong, Shanghai and Other Treaty Ports in China: Their History, People, Commerce, Industries, and Resources*, London: Lloyd's Greater Britain Publishing Company.

IV. Official Papers, Published

Feetham, R. (1931), *Report of the Hon. Justice Feetham, C.M.G., to the Shanghai Municipal Council*, Vol. 1, Shanghai: North China Daily News and Herald.

Secondary Sources

Betta, C. (1997), 'Silas Aaron Hardoon (1851?–1931): Marginality and Adaptation in Shanghai', PhD diss., University of London, School of Oriental and African Studies.

—— (2000), 'Marginal Westerners in Shanghai: The Baghdadi Jewish Community, 1845–1931', in R. Bickers and C. Henriot (eds), *New Frontiers: Imperialism's New Communities in East Asia, 1842–1952,* Manchester: Manchester University Press.

—— (2003a), 'The Baghdadi Jewish Diaspora in Shanghai: Community, Commerce and Identities', in *Sino-Judaica* 4: 81–104.

—— (2003b), 'From Orientals to Imagined Britons: Baghdadi Jews in Shanghai', *Modern Asian Studies*, forthcoming.

Bickers, R. (1999), *Britain in China: Community, Culture and Colonialism, 1900–1949*. Manchester: Manchester University Press.

Blue, G. (2000), 'Opium for China: The British Connection', in T. Brook and B. Tadashi Wakabayashi (eds), *Opium Regimes: China, Britain and Japan, 1839–1952*, Berkeley: University of California Press.

Curtin, P. (1984), *Cross-cultural Trade in World History*, Cambridge: Cambridge University Press.

Des Forges, A. (2000), 'Opium/Leisure/Shanghai: Urban Economies of Consumption', in T. Brook and B. Tadashi Wakabayashi (eds), *Opium Regimes: China, Britain and Japan, 1839–1952*, Berkeley: University of California Press.

Earns, L. (1999), 'The Shanghai-Nagasaki Judaic Connection, 1859–1924', in Jonathan Goldstein (ed.), *The Jews of China: Historical and Comparative Perspectives*, Vol. 1, Armonk, NY: M.E. Sharpe.

Goody, J. (1996), 'Rationality and *Ragioneria*: the Keeping of Books and the Economic Miracle', in J. Goody, *The East in the West*, Cambridge: Cambridge University Press.

Hawks Potts, F.L. (1928), *A Short History of Shanghai: Being an Account of the Growth and Development of the International Settlement*, Shanghai: Kelly & Walsh.

Kamerkhar, M.P. (1999), 'Parsis in Maritime Trade on the Western Coast of India from the Seventeenth to the Nineteenth Century', in N.B. Mody (ed.), *The Parsis in Western India, 1818 to 1920*, Bombay: Allied Publishers.

Jackson, S. (1968), *The Sassoons*, New York, E.P. Dutton.

Laufer, B. (1905), 'Zur Geschichte der chinesischen Juden', *Globus* 87(14), April.

Leventhal, D.A. (1995), 'The Kadoorie Memoir', in D.A. Leventhal, *Sino-Judaic Studies: Whence and Whither, An Essay and Bibliography*, Hong Kong: Jewish Historical Society of Hong Kong.

Marcovits, C. (2000a), *The Global World of Indian Merchants, 1750–1947: Traders of Sind from Bukhara to Panama*, Cambridge: Cambridge University Press.

—— (2000b), 'Indian Communities in China, *c*.1842–1949', in R. Bickers and C. Henriot (eds) *New Frontiers: Imperialism's New Communities in East Asia, 1842–1953*, Manchester: Manchester University Press.

Meyer, M.J. (2003), *From the Rivers of Babylon to the Whampoo: A Century of Sephardi Life in Shanghai*, Lanham MD: University Press of America

Motono, E. (1992), 'A Study of the Legal Status of the Compradores during the 1880s with Special reference to the three Civil Cases between David Sassoon

Sons Co. and Their Compradores, 1884–7', *Acta Asiatica*, no. 62 (February): 44–70.

Ristaino, M. (2003), 'Reflections on the Sephardi Trade Diaspora in South, Southeast and East Asia', *Sino-Judaica* 4: 105–24.

Roland, J.G. (1999), 'Baghdadi Jews in India and China in the Nineteenth Century: A Comparison of Economic Roles', in Jonathan Goldstein (ed.), *The Jews of China: Historical and Comparative Perspectives*, Vol. 1, Armonk, NY: M.E. Sharpe.

Smith, C.T. (1995), 'The Establishment of the Parsee Community', in C.T. Smith, *A Sense of History: Studies in the Social and Urban History of Hong Kong*, Hong Kong: Hong Kong Educational Publishing.

Trocki, C.A. (1999), *Opium Empire and the Global Political Economy: A Study of the Asian Opium Trade,* London: Routledge.

Yu Bohai (1990), 'Hatong' (Hardoon), Unpublished paper.

Zhang Zhongli and Chen Zengnian (1985). *Shaxun jituan zai jiu Zhongguo* [The Sassoon firms in Old China], Beijing: Renmin chubanshe.

–13–

Western Corporate Forms and the Social Origins of Chinese Diaspora Entrepreneurial Networks
Wai-keung Chung

Introduction

It is undebatable that the economic growth of the last few decades in Southeast Asia can largely be attributed to the business activities of the Chinese diaspora.[1] The ethnic Chinese, who constitute fewer than 10 per cent of the population in Southeast Asia, hold a significant proportion of its wealth. While different perspectives are available to explain this economic miracle created by the Chinese, one major argument is that the success of the Chinese can be attributed to their unique pattern of business organization. This pattern of organization has created what some scholars would call a 'network-based economy', as opposed to a 'firm-based economy' that is commonly found in many Western economies.[2]

A network-based economy is an economy based on relational networks – economic actors connect to each other through various personal networks. Because of the functionalities of the networks, it is the networks, rather than the individual firms, that are the key contributors to the economy. Firms, in this case, are therefore embedded in networks. Conversely, in a firm-based economy, there are individual firms in the market that are competing with each other to maximize their profits. Firms are the key contributors of the economy, and networks, if they ever exist, are secondary. Through legal individuation of economic actors, networking becomes a functional strategy between individual firms. Networks, in a firm-based economy, are therefore embedded in firms.

A typical Western economy develops an institutional foundation that facilitates autonomous individual economic actors, therefore facilitating a firm-based economy; Asian economies, notably Chinese, Japanese and Korean economies, are rooted in social and economic institutions that encourage personal ties and network formation.[3] With different institutional settings in the societies, the organizational logics of the economies will be different.

This chapter provides a socio-historical analysis of the emergence of the network-based economy among the Chinese business communities in Southeast

Asia. I argue that fundamental characteristics of post-Second World War Chinese diaspora economic activities can be traced back to both the long history of Chinese business practices and to the institutional transformation of the Chinese economy since the turn of the last century. Modern organizational logics of the economy developed in Mainland China beginning in the early twentieth century, and spread overseas along with the development of overseas Chinese communities.[4] While local factors were also crucial in shaping particular business strategies of overseas Chinese in different Southeast Asia countries, their general practices were influenced by Mainland China (Limlingan 1986). After all, we can see a general pattern of business practices among the Chinese entrepreneurs in Southeast Asia that are consistent with practices in other Chinese communities, including Hong Kong and Taiwan.

I will first discuss the basic features of the Chinese diaspora entrepreneurial networks in Southeast Asia and the social mechanism behind their business practices. Personal trust based on social norms, rather than contracts backed by a legal system, is the key component of these very adaptive entrepreneurial networks, working both within and among Chinese communities in Southeast Asia. I will then illustrate the socio-historical origin of the network-based capitalism created in China. The origin of this network economy can be traced back to the late Qing economy in the nineteenth century. The institutional transformations initiated by the introduction of Western corporate forms during that time eventually changed the economy – they transformed traditional business networks by preparing the business community for a fundamental structural change, and through the process created a new setting for the rise of Chinese entrepreneurship. Rather than being replaced by the economic mechanism of Western capitalism during the transition, the use of personal networks survived by reinventing itself, and has since remained a vital element of the overseas Chinese economy.

Chinese Diaspora Business Networks in Southeast Asia

Ethnic-specific networking as a business strategy can be found in many societies where overseas Chinese are conducting economic activities. Research indicates that ethnic ties among overseas Chinese are particularly crucial in capital formation and information flow (Weidenbaum and Hughes 1996). While the impact of this ethnic-based networking among Chinese can be found in many places around the world,[5] the role of Chinese capital and its contribution to local economies in Southeast Asia has attracted particular attention since the 1980s (Lim and Peter 1983).[6]

Being referred to as the 'Lords of the Rim' (Seagrave 1995), 'Merchant Princes' (Hodder 1996) and 'Essential Outsiders' (Chirot and Reid 1997) of Southeast Asia, it is undeniable that overseas Chinese have made their mark in this part of the world. The Chinese played a leading role in the economic life of different parts of Southeast Asia as early as the seventeenth and eighteenth centuries (Trocki 1997; Yoshihara 1988). Economic activities in Southeast Asia have since then proliferated largely because of Chinese settlement in the region. In recent years, elite Chinese entrepreneurs in East and Southeast Asia have increasingly engaged in multi-million-dollar joint ventures (Redding 1995). Liem Sioe Liong of the Salim Group in Indonesia, Robert Kuok of the Kuok group in Malaysia, Chin Sophonpanich of the Bangkok Bank Group in Thailand, to name a few, have all contributed to the economies of the countries where they reside, and at the same time have formed joint ventures among each other that have contributed to regional prosperity. Informal linkages between regions and countries through the ethnic ties of the Chinese have facilitated an integration of the economies in the Southeast Asia region (Peng 2002).[7]

This kind of inter-country economic activities would happen much less frequently without the informal personal ethnic-specific ties, especially since the legal framework for international business transactions within Southeast Asia is weak (Rauch and Trindade 2002).[8] The creation of these ethnic-specific networks is based on a social mechanism existent in all Chinese communities, to different extents, that guarantees the relative advantage of using personal connections as social capital in business transactions.[9]

The Social Foundation of the Network Economy

A network economy is an economy that is based on personal connections backed by social trust. When trust is being confident that your trustee is not going to engage in opportunistic behaviour even though it is in his or her own best interest. A social trust is one that is regulated by social norms, rather than by an authoritarian third party, typically the government. Chinese business transactions have long been depended on a trust-based, self-regulated mechanism. For centuries, Chinese society had developed without government intervention sets of norms and rules that could guarantee an acceptable degree of certainty in economic transactions and which had never been replaced with any institutional alternative.[10]

Business transactions among overseas Chinese, including Southeast Asian Chinese, depend on the same social foundation that has evolved in China after centuries of commercialization. It is a practice that is based on personal trust which allows non-contractual business exchange. Personal trust among Chinese is built on the assumption that there is a shared moral culture of honesty that is expected to be the ethical code of anyone doing business. To be a Chinese, or even better, to be someone from the same native place, is advantageous in that it assumes a mutual expectation of honesty between each other and therefore a good partnership.

The reasons why Chinese businessmen prefer non-contractual rather than contractual relationships are not simply based on a lack of contract tradition in China, or the fact that there is no institutional support for the contract.[11] More importantly, it is the availability of a social-trust mechanism that can guarantee the reliability of a non-contractual relationship, which in turn allows the kind of flexibility that the Chinese businessmen may actually prefer to have as a strategy to tackle the ever-changing market situation. Accordingly, trust is not just for risk and uncertainty reduction, it is also essential for the transaction to be more predictable, efficient and flexible.

Organizational studies on inter-firm relationships suggest that the availability of trust can be a positive source of competitive advantage if it can be maintained (Barney and Hansen 1994). A trust-based transaction is supposed to be more flexible and efficient (Nooteboom et al. 1997; Uzzi 1996, 1997). In a transaction that is based on pre-existing *guanxi* – personal relationships – between two business parties, business decisions can be made more quickly than transactions that are based on contracts since an informal phone call may be all that is required to solve a business problem (Chen 1994; Yao 1987).[12] A 'loose' contractual form – or even a verbal promise – can often be more cost-effective than a written legal form, provided there is a personal trust to guarantee it (Charny 1990). If the exchange is based on a contract rather than mutual trust, it will be less flexible to change, and will be slower and more costly to alter the terms to respond to external fluctuations of conditions.

This kind of flexibility is significant especially for the small- to medium-sized manufacturing enterprises that are commonly found in East and Southeast Asia. Smaller manufacturers have to respond to the changing market in a quicker and more flexible way. In order to survive, they have to be flexible enough to capture different kinds of business opportunities. What they may prefer are business partners who can be flexible and willing to cooperate when specific needs of production or services arise. The economic opportunities that are created through these flexible and cooperative relationships are difficult to replicate via markets, contracts or vertical integration (Uzzi 1997). The choice of flexibility might be a rational one, but to fulfil this choice one has to depend on the embedded norms that govern the social relationships of Chinese society. Seeking flexibility in a business transaction therefore may be less feasible in a Western context, or at least it requires a totally different social mechanism to achieve it.[13]

Particularly in overseas Chinese communities, people from the same native place are expected to be closer to each other than Chinese from other communities, as native fellows have a higher density of social connections back home. Groups with a high density of overlapping relationships can establish an internal mechanism through invisible codes of ethics to maintain a higher level of trust among the group members (Landa 1994). Also, the relative interconnectedness of every individual with other group members will facilitate positive personal traits such as greater sense to exhibit reliability and sincerity among the group members, since if these traits are not kept, most people within the group will know it. The existence of groups with overlapping relationships traditionally provided some guarantee for those doing business within the network.[14] *Tongxiang,* or the native fellows, among Chinese who share a common dialect and collective memory of their hometown, find it easier to create social ties with each other.[15] While their decisions were based on business, the fact that both Robert Kuok of Malaysia and Liem Sioe Liong of Indonesia are Hokkien and speak the same dialect certainly helped to establish the cross-border joint ventures between them.

The use of *guanxi* in Chinese business practices therefore facilitates inter-firm transactions in the Chinese business community. Rather than making transactions of various kinds through arm-length relationships, Chinese entrepreneurs tend to seek business partners whom they can trust. Networks of firms are created among Chinese entrepreneurs through the *guanxi* social logic. In the Chinese business context, a network is the resulting configuration of a set of *guanxi*. It represents the structure of how a person relates him/herself to a group of people through personal connections. Chinese networks in general can be used to avoid opportunistic behaviour by mutual trust without using costly monitoring apparatus. For Chinese firms, trust-building seems to be less of an issue, although it is certainly cannot be said that there are no problems establishing trust among Chinese firms, as dishonesty happens everywhere. Trust in Chinese societies, however, as different from that of the West, is supported by a moral community which sees the practice of *guanxi* logic and trust as a 'normal' and 'expected' social practice among those who are related. Daily-life experience, which emphasizes sincerity and honesty, has given every individual a shared understanding of what is trust, how to be trustworthy and how to interpret another's actions in terms of trustworthiness, even if one does not intend to practice these social conventions. This common cultural awareness and practice of trust has facilitated the establishment of trust among business partners.

The interconnectedness of Chinese firms in Southeast Asia, as in other Chinese communities, also becomes an essential tactic for the growth of their firms. In typical Chinese family firms, top management positions are always filled by family members, and sometimes close relatives or employees who have been working for the family for decades. One of the common critiques of Chinese business practices is the closed system of its decision-making process, which in turn can limit the growth of the firm. In the past, most Chinese firms were small- to medium-sized, and indeed were limited by their own management style. However, the Chinese family firms typically found in Southeast Asia have overcome their scale limitations by networking with other Chinese family firms, not just within their place of residence, but also beyond to other parts of the region (Hamilton 1996a; 2000; Redding 1995).

A well-established trust-based business *guanxi* can, therefore, serve as a preset channel of business transaction where both sides are willing to do business on a personal basis. Here we see a 'moral' contract in contrast to a legal one, between the two parties, one which represents a tacit agreement on any transaction. In this sense, business networks represent an extension of social networks. This socially-based business network then can provide access to credit, market information, services and trading opportunities, etc., which makes Chinese firms more competitive. The connections of firms turn them into much bigger business entities with a combination of the resources from this collection of firms. Family business, as the most typical organizational form of Chinese business, can therefore benefit from this networking strategy to increase its competitiveness by increasing its opportunities and flexibility. Personal relationships can turn into a direct joint-investment relationship, e.g. joint-family business, or if not, at least can be a supportive network for one's business.

Chinese business networks are therefore an extension of social networks. This social nature of Chinese networks is supported by the *guanxi* logic that every Chinese, including those overseas, practices on a daily base (Chung and Hamilton 2001). Social logic is used to maintain and strengthen business networks.[16] Even though some may do better than others, every Chinese has the shared understanding of the logic on how to relate to others. On the contrary, in the American business community, for example, networking basically represents a learned behaviour with little social basis. Western business networks may also be an outgrowth of one's social network, since a firm's prior social ties can help to identify alliance partners and opportunities (Gulati 1998), but the social dimension ends there, the remainder typically being replaced by business logic.[17] Personal trust, if it ever exists in a typical Western context, will remain at the personal level between the involved parties and will not be monitored by any social mechanism.

Traditional Chinese Business Networks

These business practices and their related social dimensions can be identified in almost every Chinese community. The practice of network economy has a long history in China and can especially relate to the 'traveller economy' in the traditional Chinese economy. Merchants from all parts of the country travelled to different locations and did business in that location much like a diaspora community. They had to face a high level of uncertainty in places that were 'foreign' to them. Networks in the traditional Chinese business community were used to extend business opportunities, and more importantly, to stabilize the transactions. Merchants from the same native place who settled in the same location were connected together through native-place associations and professional guilds where regulations would be set and reinforced to regulate the business. Traditional networks, while helping individuals to maximize the utilization of one's business opportunities, were at the same time promoting cooperation among those who were linked.

Chinese Native Banks as an Example

The organization of native banks (*qian zhuang*) in modern China provides a good example of how traditional networks worked in late nineteenth- and early twentieth-century Chinese economy. Serving as the principal financial institution in China's advanced commercial economy during late imperial times, Chinese native banks were among the most traditional forms of Chinese business. Through an ownership analysis of all native banks in Shanghai during 1927, we can see how these native banks stand out as vibrant examples of how interpersonal networks function in a traditional Chinese business setting.[18]

Native banks normally provided services to a known group of merchants and tradesmen.[19] Wealthy merchants who had some capital to invest and many good connections in the commercial community usually started the banks.[20] Although a few were single proprietorships, most native banks were organized through partnerships of four to six people.[21] In most cases partners would have no kinship ties among them and instead would be predominantly friends and business colleagues of the same native place. Reputable individuals from outside the native regions who possessed good business contacts, possibly linked to foreign and Western-style modern banks, were also involved. In Shanghai, the guild of native banks linked all the banks together to form an overarching financial network that guaranteed and ensured the continuity of commercial transactions in the City.

A key characteristic of native-bank investment was cross-investment patterns. Rather than investing one's capital in only one place, as a sole proprietor for instance, native banks' investors would rather diversify their investments in different banks than place all their money in one bank. Partnerships created from such cross-investments neither created nor reflected a core business elite in each location. Rather, these partnerships represented interpersonal networks allowing investors to bridge multiple and distinct groups within the commercial community.[22] Native-bank organizers would also solicit partners who could bridge some of the regional cleavages that existed in most immigrant urban settings.

The operating capital of the native banks was usually quite small.[23] Different from modern Western banks which required very large pools of capital to support and guarantee business operations, Chinese native banks depended more on reputation as an asset and on personal ties as a guarantee. Partnerships in the Chinese native banks thus represented not only a pooling of capital, but also sets of relations that could potentially be tapped by each partner.

The membership list for the Shanghai native-bank guild provides information on partnerships for seventy-eight native banks operated in Shanghai during 1927. Only five of the seventy-eight native banks were sole proprietorships. The rest were formed by partnerships. Because of cross-ownership, most of the banks were directly or indirectly linked up with each other. Representing by a line between two banks when there is at least one interlocking ownership, Figure 13.1 shows that fifty of the seventy-eight native banks were linked through cross-ownership. This web of relations represents the personal linkages of individuals in Shanghai's

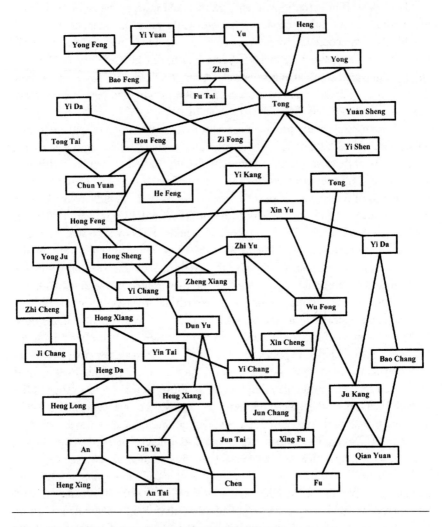

Source: Shanghai Native Banks Guild membership list 1927

Figure 13.1 Shanghai Native Banks Partnership Networks in 1927

native-bank community. The linkages facilitated a very efficient flow of market information which was essential for this banking institution.

This pattern of interlocking demonstrates a collection of 'weak ties' to create an extensive interpersonal network across Shanghai's native banks. Most of the interlocks are singular, i.e. no more than one partner has cross-investment in the same two banks and there appear to be no family groups represented among the interlocks. Rather than forming into one closed group, native-bank investors extended their connections by linking themselves directly and indirectly to multiple groups of people which in turn provided the foundation for native banks to operate as a financial system.

The system, which functioned without the intervention of state officials or the state's legal framework, worked quite well until after the Second World War.[24] Partnerships were made on the basis of unlimited liability, and bank loans were unsecured. The entire system operated on the basis of reputation: the banks' reputations, the partners' reputations, and the borrowers' reputations or that of their guarantors.[25] The system worked because the entire commercial community acted as third-party monitors backing every transaction. Information about misdeeds on the part of merchants or banks would circulate throughout the community, making it impossible to do business again in the community.

Since trust among banks was so important for the maintenance of the efficiency and stability of this traditional financial institution, native banks relied on a collective mechanism to guarantee the trustworthiness of the system: the local association of native bankers. Associational membership was monitored closely. To be a member of the guild, a bank needed to invite a person of high prestige within the community to serve as its guarantor. One's native-place origin was also very important. While there was never a rule restricting anyone from entering the business, the majority of the native banks' owners were from Ningpo and the surrounding areas. Ties based on native-place origin were certainly used as a tool to monitor and control this high-risk business.

Personal ties served at least one more function for native banks. When a bank began to run out of cash, for example when it issued more bank notes than it could afford to clear, the bank would have to ask for help from other banks with which they maintained connections. Personal ties helped to establish these 'strategic alliances' so that the amount of operating capital could be minimized and the chance of long-term survival maximized.

The nature of the traditional economy as illustrated here is that networks represent a web of mutual trust across a group of interrelated people. This web serves as a web of capital and information flow on the one hand, but also as a vehicle to exercise control and regulation from which the larger group can benefit. There was no centre within this kind of network. While there were merchants who were doing better than others, they were still supposed to be subordinate to the broader networks that encompassed people from the same native place, or people doing the same business. The operation of the native bank illustrates that personal ties were necessary for a merchant to get into the bank business, but the same ties also acted as a constraint on one's business conduct. So long as one was a member of the guild, one was supposed to conform to the rules and regulations set by the group. The networks in a traditional business community therefore performed the function of guaranteeing the stability and functioning of the business through which conformity to the group norms could be reinforced.

What we find among contemporary overseas Chinese communities, however, is a rather different kind of network. Originating from the traditional mode, the 'modern' network has become more 'personal'. Individual entrepreneurs, while attached to the networks, now can have more personal influence on how these networks will be created. These are not networks above individuals; rather, these are networks over which individuals have more control. I argue that this personalization of Chinese business networks was largely a result of the adoption of Western corporate forms, which eventually became an institutional device for individual entrepreneurs to consolidate their social capital into one legally independent entity.

The Transformation of the Traditional Chinese Economy

One could argue that the reason why contemporary Chinese are still using personal networks in economic transactions is that the Chinese economy has never been 'modernized'. Economic and legal institutions which are comparable to those in the West have never developed well. The continuous use of personal networks results from the fact that better alternatives do not exist. While this has some truth, the Chinese economy did transform itself by following a Western model with the development of Western-style institutions. The traditional business networks described above began to change gradually in the early twentieth century when Western ideas of business organization were more widely adopted.

Since the mid-1800s, foreign economic invasion had been progressively destroying the traditional economic system in China (Richardson 1999). Foreign goods were replacing traditionally domestic-made goods in many major sectors (e.g. textile). Foreign companies, involved at the beginning mostly in trading and finance but later on also in manufacturing, increased in number over time and put tremendous pressure on China's economy. This extreme competition had stimulated enormous discussion among the government, intellectuals and the business community in China, and had fostered tremendous institutional changes (most of which can be described as Westernization) in the economy which had never occurred before in Chinese history.

In the late nineteenth century, there was a shared belief in China that in order to increase national strength, commerce had to be developed and modernized, and in order to develop commerce, the economy should be organized under Western-style corporate forms (Guo 1995; Zhu 1996). In order to compete with their foreign counterparts, Chinese merchants mobilized to join together and establish *gongsi* (company). The introduction of corporate forms into China, especially the corporate form with limited liability, constituted a key landmark on the capitalistic transformation of the country's economy. The early stages of Chinese capitalism can therefore be characterized partly by the ways Chinese merchants reorganized themselves into companies in order to capture capital and to regain control of the national market. New business and organizational concepts such as the board of directors, shareholders, the general meeting, and limited liability, etc. were introduced into China and gradually changed the contours of commercial life in China.

China Incorporated

The result of this institutional transformation in the economic sector, however, was not as progressive as expected, and one could argue that the introduction of corporate forms and the related institutional transformation (e.g. legal reform) were not very successful. In terms of the number of firms registered as companies under the company law, the transformation was not significant. Between 1904, the first year of the promulgation of the first Chinese company law in China, and 1912 (end of the Qing Dynasty), the total number of registered companies was less than 200. There were only 1,185 more companies registered as limited companies between 1912 and 1927 (Shanghai Municipal Archives 1996). Compared with what happened in Britain, for example, where thousands of companies registered in the first few years after the liberalization of the limited-liability company and have increased rapidly in number since then, China did not experience such rapid growth in company establishment after the introduction of company law and there was no immediate effect on the organization of the Chinese economy.

However, when we look at the history of the emergence of corporate forms in the West, it appears that it actually took a few centuries for the company form to mature and become accepted by the public. It took about two hundred years for the joint-stock company to develop before it finally acquired its legal status in the 1800s and further developed into its mature form (Scott 1910). Without a long tradition of joint-stock business operation in China, it is only reasonable to expect that the Chinese would take some time to accommodate to, and to understand, this new institution before they would be more willing to adopt it.

Based on the statistics that are available, however, it is clear that a transformation of how business was organized did indeed happen in China, and that the sort of

Wai-keung Chung

capital accumulation which characterized a modern economy did occur over time. Table 13.1 shows that there was an increase in the size of corporations' capital size from 1915 to 1920. Companies with a capital size of more than 1 million yuan (the Chinese currency at that time) composed only 2.3 per cent of all registered companies in 1915, but had jumped up to 8.6 per cent in five years.

Table 13.1 Percentage Distribution of Investment Capital Size in Corporations (in yuan)

	10,000–50,000	50,000–200,000	200,000–500,000	500,000–1,000,000	1,000,000 and above	Total
1915	31.9%	57.8%	6.0%	2%	2.3%	100%
1920	24.4%	49.6%	12.4%	5%	8.6%	100%

Source: Chen (1989: 261) (modified)

The global economic conditions during the First World War were very favourable to China. Institutional reform had benefited from this and had created a 'golden age' for Chinese capitalists (Bergère 1989). Accumulation and investment in the 'new economy' – the industrial production – had increased a few fold in less than a decade (especially between 1914 and 1921; see Table 13.2).

Table 13.2 Rate of Increase in Private Industrial Investment (in 10,000 yuan)

Industry	1913	1921	Growth Rate (%)	Average Annual Growth Rate (%)
Cotton Spinning	1,423	9,842	691.6	27.35
Flour	885	3257	368.0	17.69
Silk Reeling	1,603	2253	140.6	4.00
Tobacco	138	1,680	403.2	15.13
Cement	294	746	308.8	12.34
Matches	294	746	308.8	12.34
Total	4,628	18,658	403.2	19.04

Source: Huang and Yu (1995: 114) (modified)

While the statistics indicate that the total number of companies established per year was not impressive, they do suggest that the limited liability company was the most preferable organizational form. More than 70 per cent of those who registered between 1929 and 1935 were in this form. Even more significant is that the capital size of the limited-liability company was always much larger than that of other corporate forms. We can therefore argue that even though most economic activities were still conducted through traditional partnership or sole proprietorship, a significant percentage of national capital was incorporated.

The Emergence of Chinese Entrepreneurs

The way that the Chinese business community was organized started to experience changes at about the same time as the 1904 Company Law was officially introduced to the public. While traditional merchant organizations continued to exist for a longer time, new forms of business associations began to emerge at the turn of the century. The major change was the transformation of traditional business associations into modern, Western business associations like the chambers of commerce.[26] One of the later developments of the chambers of commerce in China was the further relaxation of membership criteria. This change signalled the emergence of relatively independent economic actors in the Chinese economy.

The Shanghai General Chamber of Commerce, as the most influential chamber of commerce in early twentieth-century China, gives us a representative example of this change. Its membership at the beginning was composed mostly of traditional merchants with gentry-status from different places of origin and different businesses. With representatives from only a few key Chinese modern enterprises, most of the members were representatives from guilds and trade associations (Xu and Qian 1991). In 1912, the association was reorganized into a more mature form – the Shanghai Chamber of Commerce. One of the major changes in this association was that the regulations on membership had been largely revised. The annual membership fee was significantly lowered from 300 *taels* of silver to 100 *taels* which eventually led to a broadening of membership to include individual members outside the traditional guilds and associations. More and more enterprises formed as companies became members of the Chamber. Younger elites from the new entrepreneur class also finally took more control in this modern Western business association.[27]

The impact of the emergence of this modern form of business association was the breakdown of traditional organizational patterns of the economy. The traditional structure of the business community was organized into sectors from different native places and different businesses. Since most traditional businesses were dominated by people from a particular native place, cross-sector investment was not common unless it was a business that one's fellow-regionals were also conducting.[28] Ties between each business (and each native place) were relatively tight. The changing composition of the Shanghai Chamber of Commerce reflected the changing structure of the economy with more and more business activities being conducted by individual firms, and cross-investment becoming less restricted as a practice. At the same time, the proliferation of the chambers of commerce in China at the same time at least partly led to a structural change in the business community. It was a transformation that signified the emergence of modern firms in the Chinese economy.

As discussed previously, traditional merchants were supposed to be embedded in business networks rather than existing as individuals. Individual merchants were always recognized as part of a larger group – a *bang* or trade coalition. The social recognition of merchants in the past was based on where they were from or what business they were in and very little on who they were as individuals. Merchants from the *Jin* region – the Shanxi province – of China would be *Jin* merchants and were embedded in the *Jin* merchants' networks. Merchants who traded tea would be tea merchants and were embedded in the tea traders' networks. As part of a larger group, merchants were expected to be cooperative and not compete with each other. Rules and regulations were set by associations of their professions and high conformity was expected as a way to guarantee the stability of trade. No matter how successful the merchant was, he was expected to be subordinate and conform to the networks to which he belonged. Since business opportunities were highly constrained and regulated by guilds or trade associations,[29] opportunities for the emergence of business elites and expanding businesses were rare.[30]

Because of the changing institutional settings in the late nineteenth and early twentieth centuries, merchants were allowed to free themselves from traditional constraints and to engage in competition rather than cooperation. In contrast to the traditional merchants who were confined to those traditional businesses, 'new-style' merchants during the turn of the last century were referred to as merchants who invested in 'new-style' enterprises – manufacturing, banking and finance, public utilities, etc. The social consequences, however, were more than just alternative patterns of investment. Those who invested in these modern businesses were at the same time more likely to use Western corporate forms to organize their businesses and therefore much less likely to be confined by the traditional guild-related economy. Chu Baosan, for example, was one of those who had successfully transformed themselves into modern entrepreneurs by engaging in a diversity of modern businesses organized in Western corporate forms. He had been involved in forty-nine different companies, mostly as founder or co-founder, ranging from public utilities, mining, shipping, manufacturing and insurance to banking over the course of twenty-five years (Tao 2000). Liu Hongshen's business conglomerate, as another example, was organized as a group of related limited-liability companies that had diverged investments into a wide range of modern businesses – harbour, matches, cement, wool spinning, coal mining, enamel, banking and insurance (Shanghai Shehuikexueyuan Jingji Yanjiusuo 1981). Modern corporate forms that assume regulation from the government rather than from the guilds had helped Chinese merchants to break the traditional ties which promoted more cooperation than competition.

Firms as Carriers of Personal Resources

The adoption of corporate forms to establish one's business typically occurs because the design allows easier capital consolidation and at the same time offers relevant legal protection according to company law. In China, however, the introduction of this Western institutional design served more than that purpose and had turned out to be a *carrier* of personal resources – a device that made personal resources much more effective. To a large extent, the availability of this institutional device facilitated the emergence of business elites in China.

It is certainly true that it was the engagement in modern businesses in China that allowed the creation of much greater wealth for modern businessmen in China in comparison to that of those who engaged in traditional businesses. And corporate forms, especially the form of the limited-liability company, became the most obvious choice for the organization of those modern businesses, as a larger amount of capital was usually needed. This institutional transformation of business organizations, however, should be understood as a path-dependent process that was influenced by traditional business practices. The introduction of corporate forms in China had established new rules of the game in organizing business, but at the same time these corporate forms provided a device that allowed some of the traditional business practices in China to be revitalized and sustained. Corporate forms provided an institutional device to consolidate capital in modern China, but it was the direct and indirect personal connections that helped to make it possible (Chung 2004).

Through subscriptions of shares from the public, the limited-liability company allows entrepreneurs to create a much bigger enterprise than those based on sole proprietorship or a partnership. At the same time, by using the governance structure of the modern corporate form, entrepreneurs can distance themselves from the shareholders – the real owner – and can gain more control of the decision-making process. Also, limited liability allows investors and, at the same time, the entrepreneurs to be able to spread out of their investments to more companies and create a much larger network.

Rather than depending solely on personal capital, a corporation with the ownership divided into shares of equal value can help the entrepreneurs to create a firm that incorporates outsiders' resources. In the context of China, individual entrepreneurs can use this 'Western' institutional design to consolidate resources that are directly or indirectly connected to oneself, with the hope that a considerable amount of total strangers will also be interested in investing in the corporation. Compared with traditional partnerships that would permit the pooling of resources only among a small group of people, corporate forms provide the institutional construct that allows more people to participate with basically any amount they are willing to invest.

Because of the particular route of economic transformation in China, entrepreneurs using Western corporate forms to organize their businesses were able to exercise a degree of control that would not be found in a Western context. Individual merchants were able to consolidate a much larger quantity of resources then before without the typical constraints from the guilds. Old practices governing interpersonal business transaction continued to function, but at the same time allowed individual entrepreneurs to coordinate social capital in a more flexible way, and to increase one's competitiveness in the marketplace. By relaxation of membership in modern business and trade associations, the transformation of the traditional business networks represented a broadening of the scope of possible connections (Rowe 1984). Geographical and professional dividing lines that used to exist in Chinese business communities were finally disappearing.

Since the 1920s, large business conglomerates have been formed by individual entrepreneurs in China through the creation of multiple personal networks by connecting oneself to both the traditional networks (e.g. native-bank networks) and a contemporary one (e.g. the industrialists' networks) (Li 2000). The construction of multiple layers of networks, which would transgress native places and business sectors, and now companies as well, become possible in the new institutional setting.

The Emergence of Chinese Diaspora Entrepreneurial Networks

The changes described above shed light on the changes in the institutional framework in which business was being conducted in China. The emergence of corporations signified the emergence of new economic actors and a change in the business logic of the past. At the same time, capitalism developed in China, but with a logic different from that of the West.[31] Rather than replacing traditional business practices in China, the Western model of business organization – the corporate form – was modified by being incorporated with traditional Chinese networking practices. The new networking practices maintained the same social-trust mechanism of the traditional model, but allowed for individuals to take personal advantage of the network resources in a more flexible way.

While the Western model of business organization was being adopted almost everywhere around the world after the Second World War, the innovative use of it by the Chinese can simultaneously be found in all Chinese business communities. Companies were set up by the Chinese according to the local company law, but they were at the same time connected together, in one way or another, through personal networks. Chinese entrepreneurs who were competent further expanded their businesses by using various levels of networks.

Robert Kuok of Malaysia, for example, diversified his 'silent empire' through cross-investment in many companies that were based on his personal connections.

As described by Cottrell (1986), his empire was composed of a group of core family businesses linked to an extended network well beyond the family firms and to a wide variety of businesses. This level of networks indicates a highly diversified investment strategy, representing the kinds of personal connections that Kuok has accumulated all these years. Cottrell (1986) has documented a very complex web of companies with a wide range of businesses and with all levels of cross-investment. While the holdings in Kuok's core business were always high, with some as high as 100 per cent, the holdings of Kuok family cross-investment varied a great deal: many of them were less than 10 per cent, with some of them as low as 1 per cent.[32] These networks of investment were very likely the results of broad kinship and friendship ties, representing a way to retain all the potential business opportunities for further use.[33]

The networks continued to expand on yet another level. Chinese diaspora entrepreneurs, each with their own business conglomerates, teamed up to 'cooperate' and to explore even more business opportunities. Redding (1995) identified the fact that intensive cross-border entrepreneurial networks existed among major ethnic Chinese diaspora entrepreneurs. Based on the companies' official announcements, the business deals that were generated between 1990 and 1994 by these Chinese diaspora entrepreneurial networks in Asia amounted to tens of millions of US dollars. The network-based economy originated from the commercialization of late Imperial China. It had then been transformed because of the introduction of the Western corporate forms. The same transformation has now further developed into an even more vibrant system among the overseas Chinese diaspora societies.

Notes

1. There is much literature describing the Chinese Diaspora economy; see for example Brown 1995; Hamilton 1996a; Kao 1993; Lever-Tracy et al. 1996; Omohundro 1983; Redding 1995; Weidenbaum and Hughes 1996; Yeung and Olds 2001.
2. For a discussion of firm-based economy, see Biggart and Hamilton 1992. For a discussion of the nature of a network-based economy, see Hamilton 1996b.
3. The network-based economy, however, is not restricted to Asia. Both general networking and ethnic-specific networking as a business strategy are also not unique to the Chinese. Italian, Jews and Greeks, for example, are commonly identified as using personal networks for business.
4. An interesting twist that is happening now is the reverse influence of the overseas Chinese capitalism on the Mainland. See, for example, Lever-Tracy et al. 1996.

5. The networks of the Chinese-owned computer firms in California, United States, for example, is a widely mentioned example of how this ethnic-based business networking can create competitive advantages (Zhou 1996).

6. While there is evidence on its significance in the region, we should, however, be careful not to exaggerate the overall role of Chinese capital within each Southeast Asia country and for the interconnectedness of these economies. A more country-specific historical sociology of ethnic Chinese enterprises should replace the notion of a pan-Southeast Asian universalism (Gomez and Hsiao 2001).

7. The smallest estimated average increase in bilateral trade in recent years in Southeast Asia in differentiated products attributable to ethnic Chinese networks is about 60 per cent (Rauch and Trindade 2002). Studies also indicate that Chinese ethnic business networks did not just extend regionally but also internationally in recent years (Yeung 1999).

8. In Southeast Asia, however, connections with the government are just as important as the ethnic ties. Social capital has to be incorporated with political capital.

9. Whether the use of *guanxi* – or personal connections – is becoming significant in the growing post-socialist economy of Mainland China is still controversial. See Guthrie 1999 and Yang 2002.

10. This mechanism of course will never be perfect. Merchant manuals during the Ming-Qing period, for example, the *Jianghu Bidu* (Essential Reading for Travellers), constantly warned merchants about all kinds of possible dishonesties that they might come across. How to determine who is and who is not honest by their appearance, by the way they talk, etc. is a common theme of these manuals (Chen 1987; Lufrano 1997).

11. As a matter of fact, China has a very long history of using contracts in business transactions and other matters (Hansen 1995; Faure and Pang 1997). More research has to be done before reaching any conclusions, but it may possibly be true that the Chinese use contracts in situations where things can be specified, and depends less on contracts when flexibility is preferred. So it may be wrong to say that China lacks the culture of contracts, even though the base of it may still be different from that in the West.

12. If a part is needed to assemble a product, one can simply call up the business partner with a good *guanxi*. No time is needed to spend to go through all the details, e.g. price, delivery time, specification, etc., because one can assume that the best possible offer will be given (Uzzi 1997).

13. Arrighetti et al. (1997) shows how in Western business practice, flexibility beyond contract can actually be achieved, under some conditions, on a foundation of formalized contractual understandings.

14. Traditional organizations such as lineage or native-place association in Chinese societies carry the same group dynamics described, and therefore

can provide pressure on ethical conformity within the organization. In a contemporary context, however, it is certain that the in-group control of these kinds of organizations has lost most of its energy because of the weakening of group involvement and interpersonal bonds.

15. It is not because they are necessarily more trustworthy, but because the personal connection or trust is more easily established between *tongxiang* since they have either known each other for years (all coming from the same village or town), or they know people who have known the other side for years.

16. There is, however, a debate on whether Chinese social logic in business practices will eventually be replaced by Western business logic. Some suggest that *guanxi* practice will change when a more mature legal framework is developed (Landa 1994); others, however, maintain that Chinese business practices will resist change since its persistence goes beyond functional necessity (Tong and Yong 1998).

17. Studies suggest that Western firms depend on network relationships only when they are small or weaker, or those who need the benefit of networking more, but once their corporate power increase to a certain level, they will shift back to market governance (Baker 1990; Podolny and Page 1998). Also, once the firm is bigger, it has the capacity to internalize the transaction rather than depending on inter-firm exchanges which are considered to be risky. Chinese business, on the other hand, still depends on personal relationships even after they are big (e.g. Weidenbaum and Hughes 1996; Yeung 1997).

18. The analysis is based on a 1927 ownership list published by the native-bank guild included in People's Bank of China 1960: 264–8.

19. Native banks provided services similar to those of a modern bank, including services such as short-term loans, issuing guaranteed promissory notes and currency exchange.

20. In the guild membership list it appears that many investors used to be opium traders or dyestuff merchants.

21. In a few cases, the number of partners involved was as few as two and as many as seven or eight.

22. Even if one family owned a bank, the family would expand its business by opening multiple native banks with different names and with different managers. For example, the Cheng family of Suzhou invested in twelve different banks between 1876 and 1953 through different combinations of family members (People's Bank of China 1960: 738–41).

23. The average is 100,000 *taels* in 1927. It used to be even less in previous decades.

24. Traditionally, the Chinese government always welcomed a 'self-regulated' economy so long as sufficient revenue could be generated. With limited administrative power, the Chinese government in the past simply granted

exclusive rights to guilds, brokers (*yiahang*) or small groups of merchants to either control and regulate the market or to monopolize certain businesses (e.g. salt trade). Taxes and fees were collected from owners with exclusive rights rather than directly from every individual economic actor.

25. Chinese merchants consider it a disgrace if the bank requires a mortgage for loan. Reputation, and not property, is traditionally used as a mortgage.

26. For an excellent treatment on the transformation of business and trade associations in modern China, see Yu 1993. For an overview description of the same process in Shanghai, see Zhang 1990. For discussion on exemplars of other modern business organizations which were established during that time, see for example Bergère (1992). By 1908, there were 39 general chambers of commerce and 223 branch chambers established in China. By 1912, the total number rose to 794, and in 1915, to 1,262 (Chan 1977: 226).

27. The average age for the thirty-five directors before the reorganization in 1920 was 57.2; the average age after the reorganization dropped to 44 (Xu and Qian 1991).

28. Depending on how much capital they had, *Hui* merchants for example would usually be involved only in a few kinds of trade such as salt trading, tea trading, pawnshops, lumber, food and textiles (Wang 1997).

29. In some manufacturing sectors, for example, the number of apprentices the shop owner could have was set by the guild. In this case, the shop could rarely expand and produce more, even if more buyers could have been found.

30. The time at which business elites could emerge was usually when either a particular merchant or a particular *bang* had secured exclusive resources from the Imperial state. Hu Xiuyang, a prominent native-bank merchant in the Late Qing, became extremely rich and high-status not because of his success in his native-bank business which could be very profitable, but largely because he had extensive personal connections with high-level state officials. A lot of *Jin* merchants from the Shanxi province became very wealthy mainly because they were engaged in the salt trade in the earlier stage – a business that needed licences that were exclusively franchised by the government, and *Piaohao* at the later stage – a financial business that involved huge amounts of government remittances and deposits (Zhang 1989).

31. More and more of the literature suggests that there is more than one kind of capitalism, each coming from a different institutional tradition. See for example Whitley 1999 and Guillén 2001.

32. Another 'model' of control adopted by the Chinese family business is to establish an unlimited company as a holding company and use this company to 'invest' and to 'own' other limited companies – many of them being public companies. With the holding company as an unlimited company, the family does not have to disclose the family asset to the government and the public, while at the same time, they can use the institution of modern business

organizations – limited-liability companies – to expand and coordinate the family's business empire.

33. To invest a minimal amount of capital, in Kuok's case some as low as 1 per cent, in a friend's company is a way to maintain the *guanxi* between them that might become worthy in the future. This is also a way to expand one's business by extending the web of potential opportunities with an unlimited boundary.

References

Arrighetti, A., Bachmann, R. and Deakin, S. (1997), 'Contract law, social norms and inter-firm cooperation', *Cambridge Journal of Economics* 21(2): 171–95.

Baker, W.E. (1990), 'Market Networks and Corporate Behavior', *American Journal of Sociology*, 96: 589–625.

Barney, J.B. and Hansen, M.H. (1994), 'Trustworthiness as a Source of Competitive Advantage', *Strategic Management Journal*, 15: 175–90.

Bergère, M. (1989), *The Golden Age of the Chinese Bourgeoisie, 1911–1937*, Cambridge MA: Harvard University Press.

—— (1992), 'The Shanghai Bankers' Association, 1915–1927: Modernization and the Institutionalization of Local Solidarities', in F. Wakeman, Jr., and W. Yeh (eds), *Shanghai Sojourners,* Berkeley: Institute of East Asian Studies, University of California.

Biggart, N.W. and Hamilton, G.G. (1992), 'On the Limits of a Firm-Based Theory to Explain Business Networks: The Western Bias of Neoclassical Economics', in N. Nohria and R.G. Eccles (eds), *Networks and Organizations: Structure, Form, and Action*, Boston: Harvard Business School Press.

Brown, R.A. (1995), *Chinese Business Enterprise in Asia*, London: Routledge.

Chan, W.K.K. (1977), *Merchants, Mandarins and Modern Enterprises in Late Ch'ing China,* Cambridge MA: Council on East Asian Studies, Harvard University Press.

Charny, D. (1990), 'Nonlegal Sanctions in Commercial Relationships', *Harvard Law Review*, 104: 373–467.

Chen, C.H. (1994), *Xieli Wangluo yu Shenhuo Jiegou. Taiwan Zhongxiao Qiye de Shehui Jinji Fenxi* (Cooperative Network and the Structure of Daily Life), Taipei: Lianjin Publishing Company.

Chen, X. (1987), *Mingqing Shiqi Shangyeshu ji Shangrenshu zhi Yanjiu* (A Study of the Ming Qing Commerce Manual and Merchant Manual), Taipei: Hungye Wenhua.

Chirot, D. and Reid, A. (eds) (1997), *Essential Outsiders: Chinese and Jews in the Modern Transformation of Southeast Asia and Central Europe*, Seattle: University of Washington Press.

Chung, W.K. (2004), 'The Emergence of Corporate Forms in China 1872–1949: An Analysis on Institutional Transformation', Dissertation Manuscript, Department of Sociology, University of Washington.

—— and Hamilton, G.G. (2001), 'Social Logic as Business Logic: *Guanxi*, Trustworthiness, and the Embeddedness of Chinese Business Practices', in R.P. Appelbaum, W.L.F. Felstiner and V. Gessuer (eds), *Rules and Networks: The Legal Culture of Global Business Transactions*, Oxford: Hart Publishing.

Cottrell, R. (1986), 'The Silent Empire of the Kuok Family', *Far Eastern Economic Review*, 30 October: 59–65.

Faure, D. and Pang, A. (1997), 'The Power and Limit of the Private Contract in Ming-Qing China and Today', in L. Douw and P. Post (eds), *South China: State, Culture and Social Change During the 20th Century*, Amsterdam: Koninklijke Nederlandse Akademie van Wetenschappen.

Gomez, E.T. and Hsiao, M.H. (eds) (2001), *Chinese Business Networks in South-East Asia: Contesting Cultural Explanations, Researching Entrepreneurship*, Richmond, Surrey: Curzon.

Guillén, M.F. (2001), *The Limits of Convergence. Globalization and Organizational Change in Argentina, South Korea, and Spain*, Princeton: Princeton University Press.

Gulati, R. (1998), 'Alliances and Networks', *Strategic Management Journal*, 19: 293–317.

Guo, X. (1995), *Zhongguo Jindai Zhenxing Jingji zhi Dao de Bijiao* (A Comparison on the Ideas of Promoting Economy in Modern China), Shanghai: Shanghai Caijing Daxue Chubanshe.

Guthrie, D. (1999), *Dragon in a Three-piece Suit. The Emergence of Capitalism in China*, Princeton: Princeton University Press.

Hamilton, G.G. (1996a), 'Overseas Chinese Capitalism', in W.M. Tu (ed.), *Confucian Traditions in East Asian Modernity: Moral Education and Economic Culture in Japan and the Four Mini-dragons*, Cambridge, MA: Harvard University Press.

—— (1996b), 'The Theoretical Significance of Asian Business Networks', in G.G. Hamilton (ed.), *Asian Business* Networks, Berlin: Walter de Gruyter.

—— (2000), 'Reciprocity and Control: The Organization of Chinese Family-Owned Conglomerates', in H.W.C. Yeung and K. Olds (eds), *Globalization of Chinese Business Firms*, NY: St Martin's Press.

Hansen, V. (1995), *Negotiating Daily Life in Traditional China. How Ordinary People Used Contracts 600–1400*, New Haven: Yale University Press.

Hodder, R. (1996), *Merchant Princes of the East: Cultural Delusions, Economic Success and the Overseas Chinese in Southeast Asia*, Chichester: John Wiley.

Kao, J. (1993), 'The Worldwide Web of Chinese Business', *Harvard Business Review*, March/April: 24–35.

Landa, J.T. (1994), *Trust, Ethnicity, and Identity: Beyond the New Institutional Economic of Ethnic Trading Networks, Contract Law, and Gift-Exchange*, Ann Arbor: The University of Michigan Press.

Lever-Tracy, C., Ip, D. and Tracy. N. (1996), *The Chinese Diaspora and Mainland China. An Emerging Economic Synergy*, London: Macmillan.

Li, J. (2000), *Shanghai de Ningpo Ren* (Ningpo People in Shanghai), Shanghai: Shanghai Renmin Chubanshe.

Lim, L. and Peter, L.A. (1983), *The Chinese in Southeast Asia.* 2 vols, Singapore: Maruzen Asia.

Limlingan, V.S. (1986), *The Overseas Chinese in ASEAN: Business Strategies and Management Practices*, Manila: Vita Development Corporation.

Lufrano, R.J. (1997), *Honorable Merchants: Commerce and Self-cultivation in Late Imperial China*, Honolulu: University of Hawaii Press.

Nooteboom, B., Berger, H. and Noorderhaven, N.G. (1997), 'Effects of Trust and Governance on Relational Risk', *Academy of Management Journal*, 40(2): 308–38.

Omohundro, J.T. (1983), 'Social Networks and Business Success for the Philippine Chinese', in L. Lim and P. Gosling (eds), *The Chinese in Southeast* Asia, Singapore: Maruzen Asia.

Peng, D. (2002), 'Invisible Linkages: A Regional Perspective of East Asian Political Economy', *International Studies Quarterly*, 46: 423–47.

People's Bank of China (1960), *Shanghai Qianchuan Shiliao* (Historical Materials on Shanghai Native Bank), Shanghai: Shanghai Renmin Chubanshe.

Podolny, J.M. and Page, K.L. (1998), 'Network Forms of Organization', *Annual Review in Sociology*, 24: 57–76.

Rauch, J.E. and Trindade, V. (2002), 'Ethnic Chinese Networks in International Trade', *Review of Economics and Statistics*, 84: 116–30.

Redding, S.G. (1990), *The Spirit of Chinese Capitalism*, Berlin: Walter de Gruyter.

—— (1995), 'Overseas Chinese Networks: Understanding the Enigma', *Long Range Planning*, 28: 61–9.

Richardson, P. (1999), *Economic Change in China, c.1800–1950*, Cambridge: Cambridge University Press.

Rowe, W.T. (1984), *Hankow: Commerce and Society in a Chinese City, 1796–1889*, Stanford: Stanford University Press.

Scott, W.R. (1910), *The Constitution and Finance of English, Scottish and Irish Joint-Stock Companies to 1720*, Cambridge: Cambridge University Press.

Seagrave, S. (1995), *Lords of the Rim: the Invisible Empire of the Overseas Chinese*, New York: Putnam's Sons.

Shanghai Municipal Archives (1996), *Jiu Zhongguo Gufenzhi* (The Joint-Stock System in Old China), Beijing: Dangan Chubanshe.

Shanghai Shehuikexueyuan Jingji Yanjiusuo (1981), *Liu Hongshan Qiye Shiliao* (Historical Materials on Liu Hongshan's Enterprises), Shanghai: Shanghai People's Publisher.

Tao, S. (2000), *Zhejiang Shangbang yu Shanghai Jingji Jindaihua Yanjiu* (A Study on Zhejiang Business Clique and the Shanghai Economic Modernization), Shanghai: Shanghai Joint Publisher.

Tong, C.K. and Yong, P.K. (1998), '*Guanxi* Bases, *Xinyong* and Chinese Business Networks', *British Journal of Sociology*, 49(1): 75–96.

Trocki, C.A. (1997), 'Boundaries and Transgressions: Chinese Enterprise in Eighteenth- and Nineteenth-Century Southeast Asia', in A. Ong and D. Nonini (eds) *Ungrounded Empires: The Cultural Politics of Modern Chinese Transnationalism*, London: Routledge.

Uzzi, B. (1996), 'The Sources and Consequences of Embeddedness for the Economic Performance of Organizations: The Network Effect,' *American Sociological Review*, 61: 674–98.

—— (1997), 'Social Structure and Competition in Interfirm Networks: The Paradox of Embeddedness', *Administrative Science Quarterly*, 42: 35–67.

Wang, S. (1997), *Fujiayifang de Hui Shang* (One of the Richest Hui Merchants), Hangzhou: Zhejiang People's Publisher.

Weidenbaum, M. and Hughes, S. (1996), *The Bamboo Network: How Expatriate Chinese Entrepreneurs are Creating a New Economic Superpower*, NY: Martin Kessler.

Whitley, R. (1999), *Divergent Capitalisms. The Social Structuring and Change of Business Systems*, Oxford: Oxford University Press.

Xu, D. and Qian, X. (1991), *Shanghai Zongshanghui Shi* (History of the Shanghai General Chamber of Commerce), Shanghai: Shanghai Shehui Kexueyuan Chubanshe.

Xue, Z. (1985), *Mingdai Huishan ji qi Shangye Jingyin* (Ming Hui Merchants and their Commercial Operation), in Jianghuai Luntan (ed.) *Huishan Yanjiu Lunwenji* (A Collection of Papers on the Study of Huishan), Hefei: Anhui People's Publisher.

Yang, M.M.H. (2002), 'The Resilience of *Guanxi* and its New Deployments: A Critique of Some New *Guanxi* Scholarship', *China Quarterly*, 170: 459–76.

Yao, S. (1987), 'The Fetish of Relationships: Chinese Business Transactions in Singapore,' *Sojourn*, 2: 89–111.

Yeung, H.W.C. (1997), Business Networks and Transnational Corporations: A Study of Hong Kong Firms in the ASEAN Region', *Economic Geography*, 73(1): 1–25.

—— (1999), 'The Internationalization of Ethnic Chinese Business Firms from Southeast Asia: Strategies, Processes and Competitive Advantage', *International Journal of Urban and Regional Research*, 23: 103–27.

—— and Olds, K. (eds) (2001), *Globalization of Chinese Business Firms*, NY: St Martin's Press.

Yoshihara, K. (1988), *The Rise of Capitalism in South-East Asia,* Singapore: Oxford University Press.

Yu, H. (1993), *Shanghui yu zhongguo zaoqi xiandaihua* (Chambers of Commerce and the Early Modernization of China), Shanghai: Shanghai Renmin Chubanshe.

Zhang, G. (1989), *Wanqing Qianzhuang he Piaohao Yanqiu* (A Study of Late Qing Native Bank and Piaohao), Beijing: Zhonghua Shuju.

Zhou, Y. (1996), 'Inter-firm Linkages, Ethnic Networks, and Territorial Agglomeration: Chinese Computer Firms in Los Angeles', *Papers in Regional Science: The Journal of the RSAI*, 75: 265–91.

Zhu, Y. (1996), *Wanqing Jingji Zhengce yu Gaige Cuoshi* (The Late Qing Economic Policies and Reform Measure), Wuchang: Huazhong Shifan Daxue Chubanshe.

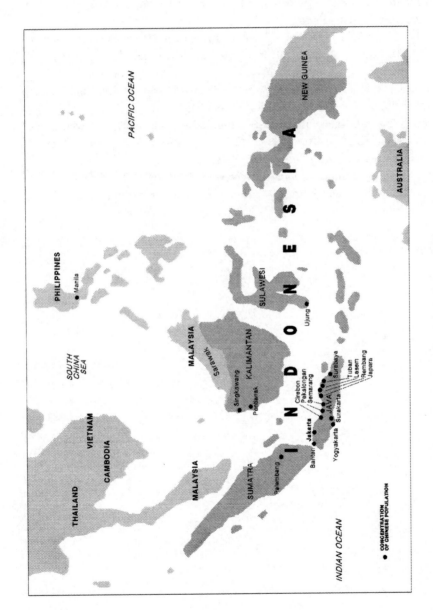

Map 5 Overseas Chinese in Indonesia, 20th century

–14–

Irrational Exuberance: The Fatal Conceit of Chinese Financial Capitalism in Contemporary Indonesia

Rajeswary Ampalavanar Brown

This chapter examines an important phenomenon – that of volatile growth within Chinese financial institutions in Indonesia since the early 1980s. This volatile growth is scrutinized through a detailed study of four Chinese financial-industrial conglomerates: the family business of Salim and Bank Central Asia; Mochtar Riady and the Lippo Bank; Bob Hasan and Bank Umum Nasional and Bank Duta; and Eka Tjipta Widjaja and Bank International Indonesia. An additional one *pribumi* (indigenous) bank – Bank Niaga – is included as a comparison of a non-Chinese private bank.

A critical part of this analysis is focused on financial instability resulting from the patterns of growth and alliances forged by these Chinese bankers, their attitudes to risk, the very processes of risk assessment and capital accumulation as important precipitating factors in the 1997 financial crisis. The literature on the Asian Financial Crisis, while admitting the part played by defects in the corporate economy, provided no detailed empirical evidence or analysis (Agénor et al. 1999; De Brouwer and Pupphavesa 1999; Edwards 2000; Jones et al. 2001; Jomo 1998; Radelet and Sachs 1998; Sharma 1998; Masayoshi Tsurumi 2001; Warr 1999).[1] Stijn Claessens (Claessens, Djankov and Lang 2000a; Claessens, Djankov and Xu 2000b; Bongini et al. 2001) admits to difficulties in securing such data. The primary aim of this chapter therefore is to fill this gap, through an examination of Chinese financial groups and their role in the creation of a volatile capitalism. Crucial here was an 'irrational exuberance' in Indonesian economic growth driven by highly optimistic domestic and foreign investors and swayed by the 'fatal conceit' prevailing among Indonesian financial groups as they embraced a prodigious growth fuelled by risky capital accumulation. Such positions provided an 'amplification mechanism' to the commodity-price falls, trade deficits, declining asset prices, and volatile short-term capital flows (Shiller 2000). These problems were further exacerbated by the 'psychological anchors' provided by the state and Chinese capitalist networks at home and abroad. The crisis and the distorted recovery could have provided 'learning and unlearning' in methods of capital accumulation and risk and volatility inherent in such capitalist growth, but it is not apparent that this has occurred, not even after 1997.

In order to extract the patterns of growth and volatility from these four case studies, we need detailed analysis of performance over the crucial two decades – the 1980s and 1990s. These banks were chosen on the criteria of size, importance of state connections and ethnic networks, diverse experience during the crisis and subsequent restructuring following the brutal shake-out that occurred in 1997. This sample also includes a cross-section of *pribumi* banks, valuable in identifying ethnic influences in the growth of the Indonesian financial system. Although this variation in ethnic role and performance may be difficult to quantify, individual or collective strengths and weaknesses of ethnic groups can be crudely evaluated. The most simple and direct observations of the differences in performance between Chinese and *pribumi* banks are sought as part of the broad institutional non-economic factors shaping performance and volatility in finance. This too requires verification through the use of detailed empirical data.

Structural Factors: Corporate Organization and Concentration

Chinese banks in Indonesia were family-controlled, with ownership concentrated in the hands of one large shareholder – the family.[2] This concentration was intensified through cross-holding and pyramid structures, with links to other Chinese corporations and to government and other capitalist networks. Separation of ownership from management rarely existed because family members dominated the Board of Directors, the Executive Committees and the Audit Committees. This concentration by the family was further strengthened by the fact that sixteen large family-owned conglomerates with several banks within them owned 70 per cent of the total equity on the Jakarta Stock Exchange in the period 1989–97.

Privatization had intensified the concentration within Chinese and *pribumi* entrepreneurs. The mergers and acquisitions during the rapid growth in the 1980s and 1990s further encouraged concentration. Patron-client clusters centred around Suharto and his cronies. Lucrative projects went to those with political and military connections, all sustained by 'soft loans' from the state and through state and foreign capital investments. Concentration within Indonesian corporate and financial institutions is thus extremely pervasive. In 1995, 17 per cent of the total value of listed corporate assets could be traced to a single family, the Salim group (Indonesian Securities, Clearing and Depository Institution, *Periodic Reports* [hereafter *Periodic Reports*] 1993–1995; BAPEPAM 1993–95: *Annual Reports*; *ICMD* 1993–2002; Claessens et al. 2000a: 103).

Corporate empires were often built around a family bank, as in the Salim Group where Bank Central Asia was the core family bank in Indonesia with First Pacific

Holdings dominating its expansion overseas. Having established themselves in government-assisted industries, such as cement and food, with generous credit from state banks, these groups participated in the privatization of commercial banking in the 1980s. The private commercial-banking sector was a major recipient of oil revenues, foreign aid, foreign direct and portfolio investments. These private banks, as part of large conglomerates, also had access to offshore banks as well as to more diverse and innovative sources of finance. Competition from foreign banks was negligible; they had been nationalized under Sukarno while their growth under Suharto was constrained. State banking dominated throughout and was an important source of funds for private Chinese banks. Until 1983, government controlled 75 per cent of all bank assets, attracted 75 per cent of all funds and was responsible for 77 per cent of total credit (McKendrick 1989: 192). This dominance of state banking continued into the 1990s. However, it is the proliferation of private commercial banking that is impressive, rising from 70 in 1982 to 162 in 1994, (see Table 14.1).

Table 14.1 Number of banks by ownership category

Type of Banks	1969	1982	1988	1991	1994	1998
State Banks	5	5	5	5	5	7
Regional and Development Banks	25	29	29	29	29	27
Private Domestic Foreign Exchange Banks	7	10	12	28	51	–
Private Domestic Non-foreign Exchange Banks	123	60	51	101	111	130
Foreign and Joint-Venture Banks	11	11	11	29	40	58
Others	12	3	3	3	3	0
Total	183	118	111	195	239	222

Source: Bank Indonesia, Financial Statistics 2000.

The state banks channelled cheap credit to a select group of Chinese and *pribumi* financial elites, guaranteeing an uncompetitive banking sector. The consequence of this was that Chinese banking emerged as 'network banking', sustained by state, foreign multinationals and Chinese conglomerates. The majority of deposits were with state banks while Chinese banks and their clients had access to these deposits through patronage.

Chinese capitalists were also linked to state finance through the interbank money market established by the Suharto government in 1974 to help banks with liquidity. This was boosted by the establishment of a foreign-exchange swap facility in 1979 to help banks attract overseas funds and avoid foreign-exchange risks. Bank Indonesia would buy currencies and sell to domestic entrepreneurs at no risk. Foreign-exchange earnings derived from oil exports were channelled to private Chinese banks. The subsidizing of funding and preferential credit was highest in the period 1974–90, facilitated by the surge in oil reserves. Chinese and a few *pribumi* financial institutions were the major recipients.

Even with financial liberalization from 1988, state patronage was crucial in determining who had access to large foreign direct and portfolio capital. Thus state funds and subsidized credit were critical for the growth of Chinese banks in the 1980s and 1990s. Large syndicated loans arranged by foreign banks meant that external debt owed to foreign banks more than doubled between 1990 and 1997 while short-term liabilities to foreign banks rose to 181 per cent of foreign reserves in 1996 (Moody 1997: teleconference proceedings). Foreign currency borrowings were high and a large proportion was short-term and nominated in dollars. The result was unstable gearing ratios for Chinese banks. When the rupiah fell in August 1997, the foreign-currency debt of Chinese banks reached unprecedented levels. Corporate borrowing alone amounted to $38 billion (US) – a large proportion of this was from Chinese banks (*Asia Development Outlook* 1999: 26; *Panji Masyarakat*, 24 June 1998: 69; *Jakarta Post*, 9 October 1999; Claessens et al. 1999: 5–6). The ability of Chinese banks to lend while maintaining a sufficient loan-deposit ratio was possible because of generous support from state funds. This practice of excessive lending and yet preserving smaller reserve ratios accelerated in the 1990s with financial liberalization. Forsaking prudent banking, Chinese banks were less restricted because of increased inflows of foreign capital, in particular short-term portfolio capital.

A further practice was the concentration of loans to individuals or to select groups of conglomerates, the majority of them Chinese. There was also distribution of loans to related firms. When Bank Summa failed in 1992, 55 per cent of its loans were to its subsidiaries in the PT Astra Group.[3] In June 1995, there were 6 banks which had made loans to related firms that constituted more than 200 per cent of the bank's own capital, and 23 banks for whom the ratio was over 100 per cent; 42 banks had loans to linked companies, exceeding 50 per cent (Sharma 1998: 29; ING Barings 2000). Hence almost half of the total of private banks' debt in 1995 was comprised of loans to their own firms (*Tempo*, 20 February 2000: 31). Here the capital-loans ratio exceeded the legal lending limit, particularly on loans to individual clients. In April 1996, 15 banks failed to meet the 8 per cent capital-asset ratio, while 41 banks did not comply with the legal lending limit on individual clients (Claessens et al. 2000a: 11; Bongini et al. 2001: 5–25). Many banks also exceeded the limits on foreign-exchange exposures.

Another source of capital concentration among Chinese banks came about through the assistance of foreign partners. Financial liberalization from 1988 eased the restrictions on foreign participation in Indonesian banking and they found willing partners in Chinese and *pribumi* bankers who tapped into foreign equity to finance new shares issues and grow. Thus in 1996, there were 11 listed Chinese banks which raised Rp 1.6 billion through new share issues. In 1997 they raised 3 trillion rupiahs (*ICMD* 2002: 469–559; BKPM *Annual Report* 1999). Bank Dagang Nasional Indonesia (BDNI – Gajah Tunggal Group) secured expansion through a joint venture with a Japanese bank. The state directed funds borrowed from Japanese banks to BDNI as well.

Capital concentration also occurred through the diversification of financial subsidiaries within a single bank; the creation of finance houses, leasing and factoring subsidiaries and insurance companies within single banking groups continued to accelerate in the 1990s.

Chinese corporations were able to retain their core family ownership through the use of the holding company and interlocking shareholding; the only outsiders were government and loyal institutional shareholders facilitating easy access to outside capital and colluding in each others' interests. This concentrated family ownership in listed banks, with no separation between ownership and control and management, remained even after the crisis. In addition, different Chinese families held stock in each other's corporations. Moreover, high-profile politicians and their families held not only shares but also managerial positions in the Chinese corporate groups. There was a core controlling group comprised of powerful Chinese capitalists, Indonesian bureaucrats and politicians. This concentration persisted throughout the life-cycle of the conglomerate. The evolution of such a concentration can be traced to privileges from government: export-import licences, monopolies in marketing and distribution of essential commodities including rice, cooking oil and clove cigarettes, and privileged access in the procurement of large government contracts. This method of collusive growth, aided by preferential cheap credit from government and foreign sources, with direct participation of government officials, bureaucrats and army in banking, distorted the already weak legal, institutional framework and inadequate corporate governance.

Finally, this capital and ownership concentration was further induced by the growth of the Jakarta Stock Market. The ability to raise capital on the Jakarta Stock Exchange from state, domestic and foreign sources was exploited without diluting family ownership. The Jakarta Stock Exchange witnessed a dramatic expansion in market capitalization from $8 billion (US) in 1990 to $91 billion (US) in 1996 before shrinking to $29 billion (US) in 1997. A state/IMF-assisted rescue in 1999 bolstered the Exchange with $64 billion (US) but declined to $25 billion (US) in 2001.[4] The increase in foreign investors on the Jakarta Stock Exchange from 10 per cent of total value in 1989 to 30 per cent in 1993 doubled the value of foreign investors to that of local private investors (Jakarta Stock Exchange 1989–95: *Factbook*). For Chinese banks, this raising of equity was critical because they could not attract sufficient retail or wholesale deposits to maintain their lending levels.

Another critical source for Chinese financial growth was through country and mutual funds. By 1990 there were sixteen country-funds available for Indonesia

(BAPEPAM 1990: *Factbook of the Indonesian Capital Market*; BAPEPAM 1992, 1993: *Annual Report*). These were frequently directed by the state to its preferred private Chinese capitalists and *pribumi* elite. This increased participation in the capital-market sector led to risky diversification in the portfolio of Chinese financial firms. They now undertook securities business, and also participated in bond markets. Such highly diverse forms of corporate finance, and the accompanying growth of plural financial institutions, increased the potential for volatility after 1989. However, bank loans rather than equity finance continued to be more important for corporate finance. Banks were central to the growth and concentration of financial capital. Of the total assets of financial institutions, 84 per cent was vested in the commercial banking sector (Lindgren et al. 1999: 13) (see Table 14.1). Each Chinese banking group had a dense pattern of interlocks with state institutions, networks and also overseas and domestic investors, which intensified their financial power and influence. Mergers and acquisitions rampant after 1988 added to this cohesion and concentration with less competition. Chinese capitalists euphoric over prophecies of accelerated economic growth in Indonesia circulated by World Bank economists now sought to purchase banks in the US, Australia, Hong Kong and China (*ICMD* 2002: 490–1).

Foreign Capital Inflows and Financial Volatility

As noted earlier, a critical element in the expansion of Chinese financial capitalism was the large foreign-capital surges, sustaining a boom in the diversification of financial institutions. This also provided the Chinese with the resources for global financial moves, by creating banks, finance houses and insurance companies in Hong Kong, Southeast Asia, China and the US in the 1990s.

Indonesian Chinese capitalists mimicked each other in investment behaviour and strategies. Capital became highly sensitive to perceived market potential and the magnitude of these shifts, into both new industries and new regions, resulted in a phenomenal expansion in finance, ultimately creating great potential volatility. Capital was responding to rumours and perceptions as well as to the inordinate global ambitions of a few Indonesian Chinese entrepreneurs. This herd mentality – induced and sustained by both rapid economic growth in contemporary Asia and the highly concentrated oligopolies, with increased availability of capital and opportunities – propelled these groups into sophisticated financial ventures beyond their traditional strongholds in commodity production and trade. Chinese nonchalant attitudes to risk and risk management had been nurtured by years of state patronage while capital inflows fuelled exuberance – an 'irrational exuberance'.

Foreign direct investment into Indonesia rose in the 1990s. In particular, an impressive acceleration occurred between 1993 and 1996 (see Tables 14.2a and

Table 14.2(a) Indonesian capital inflows as a percentage of gross domestic product (GDP)

Year		Percentage (%)
1990	FDI	1.03
	Portfolio	0.09
	Others	3.29
1991	FDI	1.27
	Portfolio	−0.01
	Others	3.62
1993	FDI	1.27
	Portfolio	1.14
	Others	1.38
1994	FDI	1.19
	Portfolio	2.19
	Others [Bank Loans]	−0.87
1995	FDI	2.16
	Portfolio	2.04
	Others	1.20
1996	FDI	2.72
	Portfolio	2.20
	Others	0.11
1997	FDI	2.18
	Portfolio	−1.23
	Others	−0.21

Source: IMF, International Financial Statistics 1998 (cited in Takatoshi Ito 2000).

Table 14.2(b) Indonesia: FDI as a percentage of gross domestic capital formation

Year(s)	Percentage
1980–1984	0.9
1985–1989	1.8
1990–1994	3.8
1995	7.6
1996	9.2
1997	7.7
1998	−1.4
1999	−9.0
2000	−12.2

Source: UNCTAD, World Investment Report, various years.

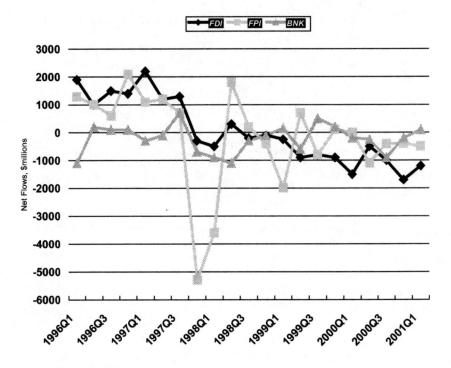

Source: Athukorala 2002

Figure 14.1 Net Capital Flows to Indonesia 1996Q1–2001Q1

14.2b). A major segment of this increase was private portfolio capital attracted by higher interest rates in Asia compared to those in Europe and the US. The relationship between this portfolio capital and the unstable, almost precarious, nature of Chinese financial growth lies at the heart of this chapter: the volatility of both and the magnitude of the impact need to be understood if Chinese attitudes to risk, to financial capital accumulation and their contribution to the financial crisis are to be more accurately grasped. FDI inflows into Indonesia rose from $8,751 million (US) in 1990 to $23,724 million (US) in 1994, then doubled in 1995 and even in 1997 approximated $33,833 million (US) (Takatoshi Ito 2000: 264; IMF 1998, September. Portfolio capital rose in 1993 and continued to rise again in 1995/96 before collapsing in 1997 (see Table 14.2a).

Lending by foreign banks experienced a major rise during 1990/91 with a slight contraction in 1992 and followed by an accentuated fall in 1993 before rising in 1994/95 and 1996 (Takatoshi Ito 2000: 258) (see Table 14.3). Volatile inflows were in short-term bank lending. In June 1997, Indonesia held $58,726 million (US) in cross-border bank lending of which half were short-term (up to a year).

Table 14.3 The level and variability of capital inflows 1996–2000 in Indonesia (in millions of US dollars)

Year	4th Quarter					Coefficient of Variation	
	1996	*1997*	*1998*	*1999*	*2000*	*1994–2001 1st Quarter*	*1994–1997 2nd Quarter*
FDI Inflow	6194	2702	–356	–2745	–4550	1281.4	102.5
FDI Net	5594	2551	–400	–2817	–4700	2680.9	109.5
Portfolio Flows Net	5005	–3558	–1878	–1792	–1909	–1008.0	152.1
Bank Credit	–758	–117	–2270	126	–1420	–229.3	–934.3
Total	9841	–1123	–4548	–4483	–8092	–754.6	90.3

Source: Athukorala 2002: 23–4; IMF International Financial Statistics.

The majority of the loans in June 1997 were from the Japanese approximating 39 per cent, European 38 per cent and the US only 8 per cent (cited in Takatoshi Ito 2000: 277).

This level of bank lending, together with increases in portfolio and foreign direct investment, led to unstable increases in corporate debt nominated in US dollars. There was a serious mismatch between short-term liabilities of Indonesian banks' and their liquid assets (see Tables 14.4a and 14.4b). Thus the boom in bank lending in the mid-1990s resulted in serious distortions. The distortions were made worse by the fact that during this period asset prices on the stock market and in real estate were falling.[5]

Equity participation by foreigners on the Jakarta Stock Exchange had been slow. In the 1990s, joint ventures were sought in the new industries – telecommunications, electronics. The involvement of foreigners was high in 1993 – 57 per cent – but dropped to 36 per cent in 1999 and 25 per cent in 2000.[6] This mirrored the decline in foreign capital investment. Despite the lifting of restrictions on foreign

Table 14.4(a) Corporate debt composition: Indonesia 1996

Foreign Debt (in %)		Domestic Debt (in %)	
Short-term	*Long-term*	*Short-term*	*Long-term*
20.5	19.6	31.4	28.5

Table 14.4(b) Short-term external debt and international reserves 2nd quarter, 1997

Short-term Debt (Billion US Dollars)	*International Reserves (Billion US Dollars)*	*Debt-Reserve Ratio*
34.66	20.34	1.70%

Source: Asian Development Bank, Asia Development Outlook 1999: 26.

participation on the Jakarta Stock Exchange in 1999, local investors constituted 65 per cent of trading volume, in contrast to figures in 1995 when foreign investors contributed to a higher value of investment than local investors (BKPM 1999: *Annual Report*). Mergers and acquisitions, encouraged by the state after 1997, saw an increase in value from $36 million (US) in 1998 to $1,441 million (US) in 2000.[7] The majority of these mergers with foreign capitalists failed because of the persistent suspicion that Indonesian entrepreneurs were not disclosing the true level of financial distress, despite the guarantees offered by BKPM and BPPN.[8]

The impact of foreign-capital inflows, in particular short-term portfolio capital, was crucial in sustaining the casino capitalism of financial growth, speculation on the Jakarta Stock Exchange and the real-estate sector. Indonesian banks did not register a decline in net profits from 1995 as Claessens claims. To the contrary, they were recording net profits until after July 1997. Earlier declines in 1996 were only in their earnings per share (see Tables on banks). My explanation for this continuous growth is that Indonesian banks were exploiting money borrowed from abroad and only the financial crisis of 1997 forced any disclosure of weakness in real earnings. The actual gravity of financial distress was concealed through increased borrowing, most of it from abroad.

The Asian Financial Crisis thus was preceded by a good number of profit rises and asset expansion within the corporate sector. Only stock-price decreases were discernable, and that too only from December 1996. Investors then reacted to the bad news and asset prices and financial reserves were wiped out in the frenzy. Thus the crisis was not foreseen.

Besides the volatility created by the short-term, unhedged private external debt of banks, the lending between banks added to instability.[9] Loans were often concentrated because banks of one conglomerate lent to those of another: this interrelated lending was through political and ethnic loyalties rather than from purely financial motives. Poor risk assessments and further concentration of loans to a tiny elite added to this hazard.

Finally, foreign-capital inflows introduced volatility to financial institutions through added volume, mobility and increased risk sensitivity through perhaps poorer information or just 'irrational exuberance', a euphoria induced by the high expectations which fuelled Asian economic growth in the 1980s and 1990s.

Banks and Volatility

Having established some of the causes of macro-economic vulnerability in Indonesia, this study now focuses on the volatility and inefficiency of six banking groups. This is an attempt to identify and locate volatility, the timing, the areas and the long-run causes of disequilibrium. Internal corporate data on earnings, share-price performance, dividend payments, liability structure, in particular net income after tax, total assets, return on assets, and capital increases over the 1990s will provide valuable insights on the critical turning points in volatile growth. The banks investigated here are Bank Central Asia, Bank International Indonesia, Bank Duta, Bank Lippo, Bank Niaga and Bank Bali.

First I will appraise how financial and stock-market volatility was reflected in the organizational development of Chinese banks. This includes several political variables including business links with political leaders, the privatization of state-owned enterprises since the 1980s and the accelerated influx of foreign capital. Second, I need to identify the precise mechanism by which each factor affected financial stability. Third, I will evaluate the alternative plausible explanations for the phenomena including that of global influence. Fourth, the impact of these factors has to be assessed for the *pribumi* banks too, in order to determine whether Chinese financial groups had greater instability than other ethnic groups or whether the volatility was endemic in Indonesia. Such a comparative approach demands further scrutiny into Chinese strategies of growth and diversification, their predatory instincts and the impact on corporate governance: are these strategies ethnically cast or are they fostered by other market and non-market forces? Fifth, do large block holdings of shares by single owners introduce volatility? Do intimate interlocking relationships between banks and their investment and securities subsidiaries contribute to mercurial growth in a liberated but poorly regulated financial system? The increasing concentrations and polarization of powerful capitalist groups in the Indonesian financial infrastructure need to be explored to understand the lurch to financial collapse in 1997. Finally, there is a need to examine whether the pace and nature of the privatization of banks that took place in the late 1980s gave rise to weak structures in corporate governance, including a weakening bureaucracy and enhanced private-sector power in finance, without enhanced public access to information.

The growth and financing strategies of Indonesian Chinese banks are therefore central to this study on the institutional volatility of the Indonesian financial system. A crucial segment of this analysis will therefore focus on the Asian financial crisis of 1997. An appraisal of the ownership structure, the performance and the political and ethnic networks permeating these financial groups between 1983 and 2000 will assist in identifying the origins of the crisis in banking and the difficulties for a successful resolution there.

Salim, Bank Central Asia and First Pacific Holdings

The Salim conglomerate has been the largest trading group in Indonesia since 1950. Its bank, the Bank Central Asia (BCA) was established in Indonesia in

1957. First Pacific Holdings was purchased in 1982 and listed in Hong Kong in 1988. The acquisitions of Hibernia Bank in 1983 and United Savings Bank of California in 1986, Wells Fargo Bank and Crocker National Bank in 1985, and Hong Nin Bank (Hong Kong) in 1987 were critical to the group's global and product transformation. From the import–export trade, the Salim group moved into manufacturing, with the establishment of international manufacturing, first in import-substitution industries and later in export-led manufacturing, with the establishment of international manufacturing and financial concerns in Hong Kong, China, the Netherlands and the US. These financial transplants corresponded to the influx of oil revenues, foreign capital inflows (Arab, Japanese and American) from the early 1970s, and the rise of the Suharto-family business empire. Privileged access to finance both from domestic and external sources prepared the way for the emergence of concentrated, oligopolistic business groups in strategic industries in Indonesia. The Liem Group carved out powerful shares in flour-milling, cloves, cement, steel and telecommunications, all predicated on access to government contracts, state credit and foreign capital. This reinforced the explosion in the banking and financial interests of the group.

From 1957 to 1978, BCA emerged as the largest private commercial bank in Indonesia. The initial period of impressive growth was between 1974 and 1978. In 1973, BCA had no foreign-exchange facilities, possessed one branch, and was ranked twenty-third among fifty-eight private commercial banks in terms of total assets. The Indonesian oil boom catapulted the bank into a dominant position. The assets of BCA rose from 211 million rupiah in 1970 to 16,903 million rupiah in 1975, to 1,542,116 million rupiah in 1987, and to 7,439,999 million in 1990 (see Table 14.5; Bank Central Asia 1970–91: balance sheets and *Annual Reports*).

Close liaisons with the state introduced Suharto's family as share-holders. Sigit Harjojudanto (the eldest son) and Siti Hardijanti (the eldest daughter) held 6 per cent and 14 per cent respectively. Liem himself held only 8 per cent. The remaining 42 per cent was held by 18 shareholders, mainly foreigners. Indifference to minority shareholders was fostered by the dominance of the Liem family, the Suharto family and their allies.[10] Mochtar Riady owned 18.7 per cent shareholding in BCA in 1987 but soon left to form his own banking empire – the Lippo Bank.

Liem's links to Suharto date from the 1940s. In the 1950s Liem was involved in the export of primary products. From 1968, Liem held exclusive rights to import cloves for the tobacco industry. In the 1980s, with export-led industrialization, he moved into the manufacture of cement, textiles, steel, aluminium and timber, and mineral extraction. Three-quarters of the group's expansion in the 1970s and 1980s was in manufacturing. The aggressive expansion in manufacturing stimulated a parallel growth in banking.

Table 14.5 Bank central Asia 1973–1990 in million rupiah

Year	Total Assets	Total Deposits	Loans Outstanding	Paid up Capital	Net Profit	Number of Branches	Number of Employees
1973	NA	NA	NA	2.5	NA	1	NA
1974	998	24	426	500	39	4	112
1975	12,800	10,766	5,800	1,800	39	4	298
1976	17,523	12,401	8,961	2,500	203	12	620
1977	24,843	19,100	12,607	2,500	203	13	828
1978	37,274	29,045	21,729	2,500	323	15	975
1979	64,628	51,845	27,496	NA	NA	NA	NA
1980	107,462	88,178	44,239	6,000	1,104	22	1,527
1981	174,462	143,388	68,933	6,000	1,479	24	1,871
1982	240,580	202,121	95,248	15,860	2,050	26	2,207
1983	386,681	290,835	133,649	22,000	5,053	27	2,084
1984	464,798	345,462	287,254	22,000	7,647	29	2,741
1985	707,909	534,047	425,824	22,000	NA	NA	NA
1986	1,045,290	792,088	626,245	32,000	8,276	34	3,474
1987	1,526,283	1,128,929	928,517	32,000	11,023	40	3,904
1988	2,311,055	1,736,229	1,254,755	32,000	16,234	50	4,641
1989	4,172,054	3,409,471	2,327,099	42,678	21,794	173	8,119
1990	7,439,999	5,890,264	4,972,200	42,678	36,714	321	12,883

Source: Yuri Sato 1993: 417

Multinational banking and investment services were essential to maintain growth. The main argument here is that the expansion and performance of financial interests within the Salim Group were sustained by the group's pre-eminence in critical non-financial industries. The Salim Corporation diversified not from its core specialization in commodities but rather through acquisitions, absorbing a whole range of industrial projects through government contracts and procurement policies in regard to strategic goods such as flour, textiles, clove cigarettes, cement, steel, tyres and cords. This pattern of state-led growth created appropriate financial structures. There was horizontal and vertical integration of production and manufacturing, and integration with state-owned enterprise to maintain this oligopolistic grip. Thus financial institutions were created to tap into state-capital and foreign-capital sources. The varying combinations of banking and finance with the non-financial sectors of the Salim Corporation are captured in these figures. Banking contributed 27.2 per cent of net profits in 1989, rising from 10 per cent in 1975. The share declined to 13.5 per cent in 1991, rising slightly to 15.6 per cent in 1993. The relative decline of banking was due to the increased importance of new capital-intensive industries attracting foreign capital. Telecommunications, which accounted for 1.8 per cent of total profits in 1989, was responsible for 26.3 per cent of company profits in 1992. The property sector also grew, with a contribution of 11.2 per cent of net profits in 1989, rising to 19.6 per cent in 1993. Production and marketing and distribution, which accounted for 59.8 per cent in 1989, fell to 48.5 per cent in 1993.[11] Therefore, the growth stages and critical turning points for BCA were contingent on the fortunes of the non-financial segments within the Salim Group.

Multinational banking was also essential for Indonesian private banks, because state banks dominated the domestic financial system. To tap into foreign capital as well as channelling lucrative earnings available from rising military expenditure in Indonesia in the 1980s, Liem acquired suitable financial institutions in Hong Kong, the Virgin Islands and the US to mobilize and hoard these funds. First Pacific Holdings was typical of this capital movement in the 1980s.

The international ambitions of Liem are covered in some detail in the account of First Pacific Holdings (FPH) to illustrate how international expansion increased risk for Chinese capitalists. Under-capitalized Indonesian banks and finance companies borrowed heavily and invested both at home and abroad, confident that the government would bail them out. The hazards behind that guarantee and the privileged access to funds had the most serious consequences in the 1997 crisis. Non-performing loans were the result of poor investment decisions, the collapse of the property market, the decline in exports and the current-account deficit and falling reserves. Foreign capital began to flow out, creating a further squeeze on liquidity, which bankrupted financial institutions and the corporate sector.

FPH is principally an investment holding company with four divisions: banking, property (FP Davis), telecommunications (Pacific Link, Smart Communications and Indo Link), and marketing (Hagemeyer, Berli Jucker and Metro Pacific). FPH was acquired in May 1982. Originally called Shanghai Land Investment Company, FPH was incorporated in 1888 by British expatriate merchants in Shanghai investing in land and real estate in China and Hong Kong. Chinese investors bought FPH in 1949. Liem bought and listed FPH on the Hong Kong stock exchange in 1983 for $1.25 billion (HK), fourteen times its original equity. FPH underwent radical restructuring in 1988 with separate listings in Hong Kong and Bermuda, and became an investment company trading in land, mortgages, equity, currency, bonds and securities, as well as developing banking. The directors of FPH were family members, Chinese and *pribumi*, as well as business associates and Filipino, American and British bankers and managers.

FPH's largest interest was in banking, with Hibernia Bank and United Savings Bank (USB) in California, and First Pacific Bank (Hong Nin Bank) in Hong Kong. USB was acquired in March 1986, having been established in 1974 in San Francisco as a bank catering for the large Asian population. USB had moved into property development and mortgage lending, but this was risky, and the bank failed in 1986 just prior to its takeover. USB expanded rapidly in its first year after takeover, with a 24 per cent increase in total assets, from $641 million (US) to $792 million (US) in 1987. With increased capital in 1988, USB expanded into southern California. FPH had already acquired another bank in San Francisco in 1983 – the Hibernia Bank. After acquiring Wells Fargo Bank and Crocker National Bank in 1986, Salim was involved in corporate finance as well as trade finance in the United States. The Hibernia Bank expanded into Hong Kong in 1987, where FPH had acquired Hong Nin Bank, and renamed it First Pacific Bank. This was to mobilize capital in East Asia, and to specialize in mortgage lending as well as trade financing.

The growth of FPH was impressive. Net profits rose from $33.4 million (US) in 1989 to $135.3 million (US) in 1994. Turnover rose from $1,622.9 million (US) to $3,681.9 million (US) in the same period; total shareholder funds increased from $261.3 million (US) in 1989 to $439.8 million (US) in 1994. By 1993 it had also undergone another important restructuring, transferring Hibernia Bank to a unit within FPH. The reason for this restructuring – transferring firms, swapping equities and assets between separate units within the group – is clouded in mystery. In the same year (1993), family members, including Antony Salim, and other Indonesian partners left the FPH Board. Manuel Panglinan, a Filipino executive, rose to the top and FPH strengthened through product diversification rather than focusing on its major core financial interests. The more flexible joint-ownership and joint-management, with Liem in overall control, had survived until the mid-1980s. Then the directors' own interests conflicted with those of the board, leading to important restructuring. In contrast, the core Salim family group in Indonesia tightened control and ownership – with Liem, his second and third sons, together with professional managers, the board of directors and eleven divisions, each with a committee, deciding on strategy, and sub-division committees deciding on day-to-day operations. This pyramid controlled 400 companies. In short there was a centralized ownership – management, with delegation of operations and policy to divisional managers. Domestic and overseas operations could be managed through this system. The ownership and family management of the core financial interests within FPH was more diffused and less dominated by the Liem family. Manuel Panglinan ushered in radical change in growth and diversification in the early 1990s. This change corresponded with increased activity in the Philippines, both in finance and property.

There were dramatic changes in the Salim group as a result of the currency crisis of 1997. Bank Central Asia, the largest private bank in 1998, possessing 12 per cent of total liabilities of the Indonesian banks, faced a series of runs in November 1997 and on 16 May 1998, triggered by rumours of capital flight by Chinese bankers (Sharma 1998: 26–7). Twenty trillion rupiahs were withdrawn on a single day, 6 May 1998. The state provided thirty trillion rupiahs to rescue the bank after Liem promised to repatriate some of his capital from abroad (*Forum Keadilan*, 15 December 1997; *Suara Pembaruan*, 12 January 1998; Van Dijk 2000: 90).

Salim, who had been a close friend of Suharto, now faced the latter's wrath. Salim already facing a debt of $3.2 billion (US) to overseas banks, now had to hand over BCA and sell his stake in firms in Hong Kong before the Bank could be restructured and returned to the family.

In May 2000, BCA was relisted subsequent to BPPN's recapitalization and restructuring. Foreign investment and state involvement reduced the Salim-family holdings to 2.8 per cent (held by Antony Salim) and 2.1 per cent (held by Soedano Salim). Farindo Investment Mauritius possessed 52.6 per cent, the Indonesian government held 6.5 per cent and the remaining 33 per cent was held by the public (*ICMD* 2002: 476–7).

FPH faced a $3 billion (US) debt. To reschedule this, it had to sell its most lucrative asset – Hagemeyer, the Dutch trading company – in January 1998 for $1.7 billion (US). FPH also divested itself of its telecommunications units for $2 billion (US) and sold USB in California and First Pacific Bank in Hong Kong. These difficulties were closely linked to the crisis in the Salim Corporation in Indonesia, where government subsidies and finance were withdrawn in 1998. Indofood Sukses Makmur – the largest noodle manufacturer in the world- alone had debts in foreign currencies of $1 billion (US). FPH's turnover fell from $3,774 million (US) in January-June 1997 to $2,285 million (US) in January-June 1998. Operating profits fell from $300 million (US) to $190 million (US) between January and June (*International Herald Tribune*, 17 May 1999). Initially, Salim lost control of BCA to the government and sold his flour mills, cement factories, oil-palm plantations and property. He had debts of $5 billion (US). The fall of Suharto, the riots in Jakarta, and the massive debts of the corporation precipitated the sale of its lucrative food interests to an Australian firm. The decline of Liem Sioe Leong and sons had already been anticipated by the rise of Manual Panglinan and the shift to the Philippines and a new patron in Estrada.

Changes in performance were reflected in changes in management. For example, in the early phase, family control was maintained while partial management was delegated to executive non-family members such as Sudwikatmono (Suharto's cousin) and Risjad, and to professional managers – Filipinos, American, British, and Japanese. The Board of Directors remained with family and friends. With the rise of Manuel Panglinan there was a return to increased investment in the Philippines in property (Fort Bonifacio City), banking, telecommunications, and marketing (*Far Eastern Economic Review*, 12 March 1998). In 1998, FPH made $1.7 billion (US) in investment in the Philippines.

The developments in the financial system outlined above contained the ingredients for a crisis. The dominance of state-owned banks and their relations with powerful capitalists – often guaranteeing credit as well as absorbing losses – made it inevitable that during the crisis non-performing loans were concentrated in the state-owned banks. The lack of effective state regulation of domestic and offshore banking led to the quadrupling of external debt owed to foreign banks between 1990 and 1997. Short-term liabilities to foreign banks rose by 181 per cent in the same period (*Indonesian Financial Statistics*, 1990–8). The pegging of the rupiah to the US dollar, with only limited movement of 5 per cent, encouraged over-borrowing. Between 1990 and 1997, the real exchange rate appreciated by 8 per cent in Indonesia (*Key Indicators of Developing Asian and Pacific Countries*, 1997: 136–7). The private corporate sector had absorbed much of the domestic credit, which rose by 160 per cent. The domestic corporate sector was therefore over-leveraged, creating a volatile situation. A large proportion of this credit leaked into the real-estate sector, as well as into stock-market speculation and investment in new industries such as telecommunications throughout Asia. By June 1997, bank lending to the property sector had grown by 40 per cent from 1995.

The deregulation of domestic financial markets, the liberalization of international capital flows, the rapid innovation in financial instruments and the diffusion of information technology encouraged speculators in both currency and equity markets. The inflow of short-term portfolio capital created bubbles in asset markets which, when combined with the dramatic expansion in domestic credit and weakness in accountancy mechanisms, fostered a volatile situation. This volatility was also exhibited by Lippo Bank.

The Lippo Group

The Lippo Bank was founded in 1948 as Bank Perniagan Indonesia but the Riady family was associated with it only from 1989. In 1987 it merged with Central Commercial Bank and in 1989 with Bank Umum Asia. The purchase of Lippo Bank in 1989 coincided with their expansion in global finance. Lippo acquired financial interests in Hong Kong and China. It purchased a bank in Hong Kong to finance and manage infrastructural projects in mainland China. It held 40 per cent equity in China Mercantile Bank, and its branch in Shenzhen coordinated power projects and financed export trade. The Lippo Group used Lippo Bank to finance their joint-venture initiatives in Singapore, Shanghai and Hong Kong. It raised Rp142.8 billion ($98.5 million [Australian]) in 1993 through a rights issue, to fund projects in China (*ICMD* 2002: 490–1). The Group was active in Sydney, Australia, concentrating principally in property, finance and export–import trade. Its fame, however, was in the purchase of Arkansas Bank, and in 1994 Bill Clinton appointed John Huang, who was the Vice-Chairman of Lippo USA, as the Principal Deputy Secretary of the US Department of Commerce (*South China Morning Post*, 8 October 1994). A major criticism of the Lippo Group in Indonesia was that it was stealthily moving capital away from Indonesia into Australia, Hong Kong and China since 1990 and into the US since 1994.

The growth of Lippo Bank between its listing in November 1989 and collapse in November 1997 was spectacular. Its highly impressive expansion occurred in November 1994 and December 1996, but collapsed in July 1997 (see Table 14.6). It was taken over by BPPN for recapitalization in December 1998, succumbing to devastating losses in December 1999 before a strong revival in December 2000 and a gradual recovery into June 2001 (*ICMD* 2002: 490–1). Throughout the crisis the family retained some equity and Mochtar Riady remained President of the Bank during the course of reconstruction.

Bank Duta

The following account of Bank Duta again identifies the three major factors that contributed to the financial crisis of 1997. The first factor was that links with the state and the Suharto family complicated the regulation and supervision of financial institutions. The relationship compromised government regulations on capital adequacy rates for banks, tighter rules for loan provisions and in particular loans to the real-estate sector. The second factor was the cross-ownership between the bank and industrial firms which produced further confusion in the monitoring of debt. Large loans and excessive borrowing dominated the Hasan group. The continuous creation of financial institutions, whereby Hasan had five banks, underestimated risk. The third factor was Hasan's speculation on offshore capital markets, borrowing in US dollars (most of it short-term and unhedged).

Bob Hasan (head of Nusamba Group) controlled a number of banks largely through acquisitions: Bank Umum Nasional, Bank Umum Tugu, Bank Duta which he rescued in 1995 and Bank Bukopin, acquired in 1989. He was also a major shareholder of Bank Muamalat, an Islamic bank formed in the mid-1990s. These numerous banks and their close association to Hasan's corporate interests in timber and newsprint introduced volatility in the financial sector. His monopolies in timber and paper and in the marketing and distribution of these products were financed by state banks, foreign banks and his personal banks. He secured a giant share of the state's development funds for his regional interests in Kalimantan through his corporation Kiani Kertas (*Merdeka*, Minggu ke, July 1998). His banks and the credit they secured from the state and foreign interests also helped finance his joint ventures in shipping, oil exploration and refining, and sustained his contracts with Pertamina, the state oil company. In 1995, of the loans from Bank Umum Nasional 80 per cent had been distributed to Kiani Kertas (Bank Umum Nasional, 1996: *Annual Report*, December; *Merdeka*, July 1998). In addition, as a Suharto crony, he had substantial loans from the state, enjoyed tax holidays and had privileged access to government contracts (*Jakarta Post*, 15 June 1999; *Kompas*, 30 September 1999; *Panji Masyarakat*, 24 June 1998: 69).

Table 14.6 Lippo Bank

Key Ratios	1993	1994	1995	1996	1997	1998	1999	2000	2001
Profitability									
ROE (After Tax)	11.80%	15.01%	16.55%	12.85%	12.85%	11.78%	146.81%	-70.90%	9.73%
Net Profit/Total Assets	0.92%	0.95%	1.10%	1.14%	1.14%	0.91%	-57.87%	-6.90%	1.09%
Net Interest Margin*	6.10%	6.28%	5.45%	5.12%	4.48%	4.85%	-9.08%	-5.73%	2.84%
(Net Interest Income/Average Total Assets)									
Net Interest Margin*	17.46%	8.52%	7.06%	6.73%	5.99%	6.22%	-12.51%	-16.17%	16.65%
(Net Interest Income/Average Total Advances)									
*1993 Ratio not calculated on Average Assets but on Closing Assets									
Capital Adequacy									
Total Liability/Equity	11.79	14.82	14.07	10.23	10.23	11.92	-3.54	9.28	7.93
Total Equity/Deposits+Borrowings	8.97%	7.19%	7.60%	10.70%	10.70%	9.63%	-32.76%	13.95%	15.28%
Total Equity/Total Advances	11.19%	8.26%	8.53%	11.92%	11.92%	9.61%	-60.24%	56.61%	66.26%
Liquidity									
Total Advances/Deposits+Borrowings	80.17%	87.00%	89.11%	89.76%	89.76%	100.15%	54.39%	24.65%	23.06%
Liquid Asset Ratio (liquid assets/Total Assets)	2.49%	2.78%	3.13%	5.44%	5.44%	9.10%	13.76%	8.90%	10.58%
Liquid Assets/Deposits+Borrowings	2.85%	3.16%	3.59%	6.53%	6.53%	11.32%	11.44%	12.76%	14.44%
Net Loans/Deposits	83.58%	88.91%	98.74%	85.54%	85.54%	90.94%	24.35%	16.71%	18.26%
Free Capital/Total Capital	-38.33%	-54.46%	-7.57%	6.69%	6.69%	68.44%	159.71%	-22.09%	-65.14%
Share Related									
Share Price RI	8,180.36	5,834.94	6,049.46	9,391.26	2,449.89	3,372.68	2,500.00	550.00	450.00
No. of Shares ''000s	1,997,000	1,997,000	1,997,000	2,519,000	2,519,000	2,519,000	1,103,000	856,980	856,980
EPS RI	274.22	229.72	293.20	163.14	163.14	137.82	-9,749.00	-80.40	6.29
PER	29.83	25.40	20.63	57.57	15.02	24.47	-0.26	-6.84	71.54
PER (Pres. Price)	1.6410	0.0000	0.0000	0.0000	0.0000	0.0000	0.0000	0.0000	0.0000
BV/Share RI	191.90	218.88	253.41	360.09	360.09	398.25	-5,158.00	2,700.00	2,956.00
P/B Ratio	42.63	26.66	23.87	26.08	6.80	8.47	-0.48	0.20	0.15
Dividend/Share RI	4.77	8.58	7.15	20.42	20.42	11.23	0.00	0.00	0.00
Dividend Yield	0.06%	0.15%	0.12%	0.22%	0.83%	0.33%	0.00%	0.00%	0.00%

Source: Datastream

As a result of these privileges and uncontrolled borrowing, Bank Duta alone had a bad debt of $704 million (US) and all of Hasan's banks were closed in June 1998. To settle these debts he had to sell his companies (thirty-three of them). Bank Duta's failure in 1998 was surprising. Though it had a history of failure – having failed in 1990 and been rescued by Salim and Pangetsu, then failed in 1995 with debts of $419 million (US) and taken over by Hasan and collapsed in April 1998, and taken over by BPPN (*Forum Keadilan*, 14–12, 1998: 83; *Panji Masyarakat*, 26 June 1998: 69) – between 1995 and 1997, Bank Duta had revealed a spectacular rise in revenues and an increase in net profits before experiencing clear financial distress in 1998 (see Table 14.7 for returns on assets, net income, turnover, capital adequacy ratio and dividend yields).

Bank Duta had been suspected of fraud throughout the 1990s, linked to three major charitable foundations of Suharto and to his prestigious projects (Van Dijk 2000: 276, 408). In 1995 it had been listed, just three months before its failure, revealing an absence of rigorous supervision by Bank Indonesia and BAPEPAM (Capital Market Supervisory Agency). Even after the 1997 collapse, Hasan was accused of using the Central Bank's liquidity funds for property speculation and capital transfers abroad between September 1997 and September 1999. Indonesian capitalists had allegedly transferred around $80 billion (US) to foreign banks in these two years (*Kompas*, 30 September 1999).

Bank International Indonesia

Bank International Indonesia, belonging to the Sinar Mas Group, failed in April 1998 with a debt of $4.6 billion (US) and was recapitalized through nationalization in April 1999. This was the largest foreign debt owed by an Indonesian corporation in 1997 (*Panji Masyarakat*, 24 June 1998: 69).

The Bank, established in 1959, was only acquired by Eka Tjipta Widjaja in 1982 and was listed on the Jakarta Stock Exchange in 1989. The rise in capitalization occurred between July 1990 and October 1996. Total assets grew from Rp 99 million in 1970 to Rp 803 million in 1975, to Rp 12,249 million in 1980, to Rp 102,314 million in 1987, and to Rp 388,808 million in 1989. By 1993, this had risen to Rp 7,139 billion and by 1996 expanded to Rp 17,707 billion (see Table 14.8).

After July 1997, asset growth was through an injection of capital from government and foreign sources. It also undertook recapitalization through a new share issue for Rp 967.1 billion in July 1997 to raise the capital adequacy ratio of the bank. This share issue introduced a foreign equity of 47.4 per cent, though the family still retained 51 per cent (Bank Indonesia and Bank International Indonesia 1993–98: balance sheets).

Table 14.7 Bank Duta

Key ratios	1993	1994	1995	1996	1997
Profitability					
ROE (After Tax)	12.34%	7.42%	9.60%	10.62%	10.65%
Net Interest Margin	3.10%	3.47%	4.18%	3.51%	2.75%
(Net Interest Income/Average Total Assets)					
Net Interest Margin	5.91%	5.94%	6.45%	5.84%	4.34%
(Net Interest Income/Average Total Loans and Advances)					
*Ratios for 1993 calculated on Closing Assets and not Average Assets					
Asset Quality					
Loan Loss Prov/Loans & Advances	0.50%	0.44%	2.60%	0.41%	1.64%
Capital Adequacy					
Total Liability/Equity	9.93	2.83	6.36	10.22	12.55
Total Equity/Deposits+Borrowings	10.07%	35.29%	15.73%	9.78%	7.97%
Total Equity/Total Loans & Advances	16.45%	24.86%	19.22%	14.43%	10.12%
Liquidity					
Total Loans & Advances/Deposits+ Borrowings	61.20%	141.94%	81.82%	67.79%	78.70%
Liquid Asset Ratio (liquid assets/Total Assets)	1.93%	2.28%	2.02%	3.07%	3.97%
Liquid Assets/Deposits+Borrowings	2.25%	5.00%	2.54%	3.64%	4.58%
Net Loans/Deposits	72.87%	164.52%	106.36%	97.79%	111.43%
Free Capital/Equity Capital	−88.84%	81.70%	88.10%	24.32%	36.10%
Share Related					
Share Price (RI)	1,053.96	458.24	297.86	366.59	274.95
EPS (RI)	43.63	38.72	48.22	56.47	61.70
PER	24.16	11.83	6.18	6.49	4.46
BV/Share (RI)	353.52	477.94	502.51	531.51	579.14
P/B Ratio	2.98	0.96	0.59	0.69	0.47
Dividend/Share (RI)	45.82	22.91	22.91	28.64	59.57
Dividend Yield	4.35%	5.00%	7.69%	7.81%	21.67%

Source: Datastream

Return on assets grew from 2.02 per cent in 1970 to 3.59 per cent in 1980 but fell to 1.97 per cent in 1983 though rising to 2.84 per cent in 1986. In the same period net income as a ratio of assets too rose from 9.02 per cent in 1980 to 13.5 per cent in 1982, falling to 5.9 per cent in 1987. Net income as a percentage of total operating income was 27.53 per cent in 1980, fell to 7.48 per cent in 1984 but rose to 11.82 per cent in 1987. The economic depression of the mid-1980s was responsible for the slight decline in ROA and net income as ratio of assets (Bank Indonesia *Annual Reports*) (for statistics on growth between 1993 to 2001, see Table 14.8).

Table 14.8 Bank International Indonesia

Key Ratios	1993	1994	1995	1996	1997	1998	1999	2000	2001
Profitability									
ROE (After Tax)	21.72%	16.86%	19.07%	20.78%	9.56%	129.97%	–108.11%	11.44%	187.86%
Net Interest Margin*	4.06%	4.34%	4.44%	4.14%	4.80%	–5.00%	–3.08%	1.98%	0.12%
(Net Interest Income/Average Total Assets)									
Net Interest Margin*	6.22%	6.24%	6.52%	6.23%	7.14%	–8.51%	–7.62%	4.98%	0.29%
(Net Interest Income/Average Total Advances)									
*Ratios for 1993 calculated on Closing Assets and not Average Assets									
Asset Quality									
Loan Loss Prov/Advances	0.74%	0.46%	1.50%	0.73%	3.15%	56.22%	4.62%	0.14%	33.90%
Capital Adequacy									
Total Liability/Equity	12.79	10.08	11.80	13.13	8.66	–4.84	19.76	14.91	–14.99
Total Equity/Deposits+Borrowings	10.93%	11.77%	9.93%	10.18%	19.31%	–30.34%	7.26%	8.00%	–8.14%
Total Equity/Total Advances (Gross)	11.10%	12.41%	12.06%	10.44%	15.51%	–48.97%	16.40%	12.31%	–24.66%
Liquidity									
Total Advances/Deposits+Borrowings	98.51%	94.87%	82.29%	97.57%	124.50%	61.95%	44.30%	64.96%	33.01%
Liquid Asset Ratio (liquid assets / Total Assets)	2.23%	1.65%	3.07%	4.21%	4.79%	8.59%	11.82%	10.05%	6.79%
Liquid Assets/Deposits+Borrowings	3.37%	2.15%	3.90%	6.07%	8.93%	10.01%	17.82%	12.79%	7.73%
Net Loans/Deposits	104.04%	108.71%	96.39%	91.32%	117.41%	40.79%	38.49%	57.89%	18.66%
Free Capital/EquityCapital	–254.42%	–141.47%	–138.13%	–223.62%	–59.55%	222.05%	–815.50%	–110.39%	163.80%
Share Related									
Share Price RI	5,339.38	3,781.54	5,508.68	10,339.39	1,980.04	1,370.80	1,500.00	400.00	200.00
EPS	427.00	468.00	608.00	135.00	118.00	–3,038.00	–39.00	3.00	–45.00
PER	12.50	8.08	9.06	76.59	16.78	–0.45	–38.46	133.33	–4.44
BV/Share	1,287.00	1,936.00	2,316.00	2,880.00	4,814.00	–17,088.00	4,988.00	6,025.00	–5,666.00
P/B Ratio	4.15	1.95	2.38	3.59	0.41	–0.08	0.30	0.07	–0.04
Dividend/Share RI	65.51	72.72	72.72	266.82	140.13	0.00	0.00	0.00	0.00
Dividend Yield	1.23%	1.92%	1.32%	2.58%	7.08%	0.00%	0.00%	0.00%	0.00%

Source: Bank International Indonesia, Annual Reports, Balance Sheets, 1993–2002

What is clear from the data above is that between 1970 and 1990, the growth was gradual and sustainable, based on domestic expansion. After 1990, the growth was global as well and fuelled by access to foreign capital. This dual growth had serious repercussions for the Bank's survival in Indonesia. This globalization of Chinese capitalists was at the heart of the volatility in Chinese capitalism in Indonesia in the 1990s. Ironically, this vulnerability at the close of the twentieth century repeated the demise of Chinese-revenue farming syndicates in Southeast Asia and Southern China at the close of the nineteenth century (Brown 1994: 142–50). Lucrative global fortunes built on revenue farming by Chinese capitalists in Indonesia and the rest of Southeast Asia disintegrated with rapid economic diversification and globalization between 1870 and 1914. This cyclical growth in Chinese entrepreneurship is a response to changing political patrons and changing responses to the global economy.

There are three critical factors in Bank International's growth. The first is that the bank had a diverse financial portfolio in insurance, leasing and corporate banking. More than 70 per cent of its business was with its own firms or with large corporate customers. The second factor was its joint-venture relations; since 1989 with Bank Fuji and from 1993 with Korean Daehan Investment Trust Company. This ability to impress foreign investors added to their hubris – being awarded in 1996 'The Emerging Markets Chief Executive Officer of the Year' by the New York International Media Partners and ING Bank. The same year, *Asia Money* ranked it as the best commercial bank in Indonesia and the fifteenth in Asia.

The third factor triggering growth and ultimate decline was rapid globalization. In Singapore the bank acquired a partnership in United Industrial Corporation, whose Chairman Lee Kim Yew was Lee Kuan Yew's brother. This global explosion led to a series of offshore companies in pulp and paper, food industry and financial services. In China, the bank's China Strategic Holdings had equity in thirty state-owned firms involved in beer production and tyre manufacture. In early 1995 the Sinar Mas Group acquired Ming Pao Daily News. In the same year they moved into property management and financial services in Australia through the firm Lend Lease. In late 1996 the group moved into the Indian pulp industry with an investment of $100 million (US). Many of these ventures abroad were regarded as essential lifeboats in a racially volatile and politically insecure Indonesia. Ironically it was this packaging abroad that undid their fate at home.

Despite the increase in bank revenues from Rp 853,558 million in 1993 to Rp 2,332,750 million in 1996 and rise in net profits from Rp 112,434 million in 1993 to Rp 260,410 million in 1996, the bank collapsed in 1997. The bank's reserves and provision for bad debts rising from Rp 125,631 million in 1995 to Rp 518,449 million in 1997, could not cover their high exposures to foreign exchange contracts both in Indonesia and abroad (see Table 14.8).

It was only their stock-market performance that hinted at the gathering storm clouds. Bank International Indonesia saw share prices rising since 1990, with dramatic increases in 1994 and further spectacular rises from 1996 continuous to July 1997 before collapsing. A precipitous decline continued from 1998 to 2000 with brief recoveries.

The family lost its stake in the Bank. The restructuring completed in 2001 resulted in the Indonesian government owning 93.69 per cent of the Bank. Unfettered ambition abroad had cost the family the ownership of one of Indonesia's largest banks.

Bank Niaga

Bank Niaga, a *pribumi* bank, mimicked the same pattern of growth and collapse as the Chinese banks outlined above. The bank was founded in 1955 but only recorded impressive growth after 1974 when it secured a licence to operate in foreign-exchange transactions. The Bank belonged to the Tirtamas group (formed by Hashim S. Djojohadikusumo, the brother of Probowo, Suharto's son-in-law and a relative of the Governor of Bank Indonesia, Soedradjad Djiwandono) expanded into Hong Kong, Cayman Islands and California. This group had four other banks including Bank Arya Panduarta and Bank Papan Sejahtera. This powerful presence in finance attracted investors like Rashid Hussein from Malaysia, who in January 1997 purchased a 20 per cent controlling stake in Bank Niaga. This was relinquished in May 1999 when the Indonesian government through BPPN, acquired 97 per cent equity – in effect nationalizing the bank. All the other banks owned by Djojohadikusumo were closed. Bank Papan Sejatera held massive bad debts on loans to Semen Cibinong, a firm in the Tirtamas group (*Ummat*, 8 March 1999: 31–2; *Media Indonesia*, 30 and 31 March 1999). Bank Niaga continued to make serious losses. In 2001, it recorded losses of Rp 9,069 trillion and the state issued new share issue in April 2001 to cover these loans (*ICMD* 2002: 498–9; Bank Niaga 2001: financial accounts). However, a glance at Table 14.9 again shows no indication of impending distress. Positive growth is recorded until 1998.

The descriptions and analyses of the five banks clearly reveal the disastrous misjudgment not only by the state and foreign capital but also by international financial-rating agencies such as Moodys and Standard and Poor. Bank Danamon, which had been ailing for a long time, received a BB rating from both Moodys and Standard and Poor in 1996. Its vulnerable position on long-term and short-term debt, incredible volatilities in net profits and share prices were evident in 1990, 1992 and 1994. It was taken over in April 1998 by BPPN and merged with eight other private banks in June 2000, with BPPN absorbing a 99 per cent equity

Table 14.9 Bank Niaga

Key Ratios	1993	1994	1995	1996	1997	1998	1999	2000	2001
Profitability									
ROE (After Tax)	16.39%	16.58%	21.71%	16.31%	5.06%	127.67%	66.56%	6.09%	16.58%
Net Profit/Total Assets	0.87%	0.85%	1.00%	1.27%	0.33%	-32.60%	-84.26%	0.36%	0.88%
Net Interest Margin*	4.02%	4.30%	4.15%	4.44%	4.77%	-10.87%	-16.87%	-1.03%	0.89%
(Net Interest Income/Average Total Assets)									
Net Interest Margin*	5.41%	5.62%	5.48%	5.98%	5.90%	-11.07%	-14.53%	-1.66%	2.43%
(Net Interest Income/Average Total Advances)									
*1993 Ratios are not calculated on Average Assets but closing Assets									
Asset Quality									
Loan Loss Prov/Advances	0.98%	1.27%	0.86%	1.10%	2.22%	18.87%	46.74%	-8.96%	0.00%
Capital Adequacy									
Total Liability/Equity	17.84	18.49	20.79	11.79	14.40	-4.92	-1.79	16.07	17.88
Total Equity/Deposits+Borrowings	5.99%	5.65%	4.99%	9.06%	7.51%	-22.77%	-61.19%	7.00%	6.35%
Total Equity/Total Advances	7.16%	6.55%	6.22%	10.43%	7.64%	-23.22%	-99.33%	15.00%	15.32%
Liquidity									
Total Advances/Deposits+Borrowings	83.69%	86.27%	80.29%	86.89%	98.33%	98.05%	61.61%	46.70%	41.44%
Liquid Asset Ratio (liquid assets / Total Assets)	2.62%	2.77%	2.45%	3.16%	3.92%	8.67%	14.68%	8.09%	6.30%
Liquid Assets/Deposits+Borrowings	2.96%	3.05%	2.67%	3.67%	4.54%	7.73%	7.10%	9.67%	7.55%
Net Loans/Deposits	95.92%	103.00%	95.21%	102.03%	123.73%	110.98%	48.67%	43.66%	40.03%
Free Capital/Total Capital	-113.49%	-67.85%	-76.54%	-44.58%	15.71%	109.01%	105.53%	39.66%	-8.95%
Share Related									
Share Price RI	1,223.55	903.70	924.01	1,231.64	396.98	208.94	175.00	70.00	55.00
No. of Shares ''000s	569	569	569	860	860	860	719	719	719
EPS RI	600.00	721.00	553.00	613.00	62.00	-5,552.00	-7,800.00	1.00	2.60
PER	2.04	1.25	1.67	2.01	6.40	-0.04	-0.02	70.00	21.15
BV/Share	371.81	441.68	530.80	714.31	827.58	-3,653.00	-11,719.00	13.72	1,693.00
P/B Ratio	3.29	2.05	1.74	1.72	0.48	-0.06	-0.01	5.10	0.03
Dividend/Share RI	20.31	11.17	47.72	31.23	129.54	0.00	0.00	0.00	0.00
Dividend Yield	1.66%	1.24%	5.16%	2.54%	32.63%	0.00%	0.00%	0.00%	0.00%

Source: Datastream

holding. Return on assets for Bank Danamon fell from 5.93 per cent in 1994 to 2.94 per cent in 1995; its return on equity fell from 15.74 per cent to –22.60 per cent in the same years. Net income fell from 61.85 per cent in 1995 to 45.39 per cent in 1996, to –93.46 per cent in 1997, to –151754.15 per cent in 1998, to –81.31 per cent in 1999, to –105.88 per cent in 2000 but rose to 146.33 per cent in 2001 because of recapitalization. Asset quality too fell from 0.94 per cent in 1994 to 0.61 per cent in 1995. World Bank economists and international rating agencies were providing the 'anchors' for this continued irrational exuberance and 'fatal conceit'.

The 1997 Financial Crisis

The following discussion on the crisis again highlights the three major characteristics of the Indonesian financial system: flawed corporate structure, strong political and ethnic networks traversing these organizations, and an almost recessive, corrupt economic behaviour by capitalists distorting any attempts by the bureaucracy to achieve reform and recovery. These three characteristics form part of the common explanations for Indonesian financial turbulence. The diasporic element of Chinese capitalism merely enhances this endemic volatility, but is not a cause nor an emphatic factor in determining the nature and course of this turbulence. Indonesian Chinese bankers were part of this internal endemic volatility, and their external diasporic alliances can be said to have only partially influenced this deep-rooted economic instability. My hypothesis is that diasporas become indigenized, almost vernacularized, creating and responding directly to their environment rather than to an ethnic trademark or to diasporic loyalties. This is clear when one compares the upheavals surrounding Indonesian Chinese financial growth with Chinese banks in Singapore and Malaysia. Hong Leong Bank, Southern Bank, Tat Lee Bank and OCBC were all prudently sculptured models of their immediate environment and not simply products of ethnic entrepreneurial evolution. The phases of financial instability in Malaysia and Singapore when Chinese banks were trapped, either in the quagmire of the 1930s depression or in the financial crisis of 1997, revealed critical problems of transitional growth in finance only in the 1930s or the agonies of a global emergency as in the late 1990s. They were not strictly peculiarities of diasporic Chinese financial behaviour. The severity and length of the crisis reflected the environment, not the ethnic background of the financiers.

The 1997 financial crisis in Indonesia was not precluded by any powerful indication of weak corporate performance or seriously volatile macro-economic factors on the ascendant. The stock market which peaked in 1995 and 1996 declined only after December 1996. Yet on 8 July 1997, the crisis thrashed Indonesia with more devastating consequences than in the rest of Southeast Asia, including Thailand. The rupiah was attacked by speculators and continued its downward spiral despite the dedication of Bank Indonesia to support it with foreign reserves. Finally the IMF had to intervene in 1998 with a package of $43 billion (US), dependent on trade reform and the dismantling of cartels in essential commodities – rice, flour and tobacco. The IMF also sought the closure of some banks and the restructuring of others.

The causes and outcomes have received the attention of numerous scholars. What this chapter has consistently argued is that the serious structural defects in the Indonesian financial system, its macro- and micro-inefficiencies provided the environment for a contagion effect to take hold after Thailand had come under attack in May 1997. The highly positive indicators of economic growth peeled away to reveal nepotistic and fraudulent financial institutions. Iriana and Sjoholm (2002: 149–50) argue that the Indonesian crisis was partly a product of contagion where 'relatively small macro-economic imbalances can generate large economic difficulties if they are combined with regional turbulence … economic crises typically spread across borders through changing international investor sentiment'. The account so far has demonstrated the reverse: the major defects in the financial system required only a tiny external pressure for the edifice to crumble.

Hal Hill (2000) in his article 'Indonesia: The Strange and Sudden Death of a Tiger Economy' does admit that weak corporate structures, inadequate regulation and cronyistic conspiracies and influences created serious moral hazards. However, he emphasizes and concentrates on the critical role of weakening external trade, unstable capital flows and declining manufacturing as critical causes for the crisis. He identifies the role of capital mobility in creating volatility but concedes that Indonesian external debt 'never reached [the] high levels of most of its neighbours' (Hill 2000: 124). Banks accounted for only 8 per cent of Indonesia's total external debt in 1997 (ibid.: 91–2).

What should be stressed here first is the concentrated nature of debt-holding in the hands of a tiny Chinese and *pribumi* elite. High levels of this corporate debt were short-term and nominated in US dollars. The rise in domestic credit by 5 per cent per annum by 1996 was less than that of Thailand, but the density of such holdings in the hands of a preferred few created the turbulence (*Panji Masyarakat*, 24 June 1998: 69; *Far Eastern Economic Review*, 17 December 1998: 51–2). This rise in private corporate debt coincided with a phase of decline in the autonomy and rigour of financial bureaucrats in Jakarta. This weakness contributed decisively to and lengthened the Indonesian crisis.

Second, although the stock market did not experience so dramatic an increase in size and value as in Malaysia and Singapore, many of the listed companies in Indonesia belonged to this small group; hence the transfer of risk was further intensified. Public enthusiasm for the Jakarta Stock Exchange was restrained by this dominance and the clear evidence of insider trading. The market index was only 50 per cent higher in 1996 than in its 1990 figures (Hill 2000: 94).

The volatility here was located in the magnified inflows of foreign portfolio capital in the 1990s and its major recipients, the Chinese and *pribumi* capitalists. Of the top-listed corporations, 61 per cent were in the hands of these fifteen families. Their extensive cross-ownership produced further confusion in the monitoring of debt. The links between political, economic elites in Indonesia and foreign capitalists meant that Chinese capitalists could avoid important rules on listing and the protection of the minority shareholder. Risk too was underestimated in this vast avenue of capital creation. Bank Duta, which failed in August 1990, had been listed in June 1990. Such cases raise the suspicion that listing was sought to avert immediate default.

Restructuring

The first phase of Indonesia's financial restructuring involved the closure of some banks: 64 out of 237 were closed. BPPN took over some while injecting public funds into other failing banks. Bad debt was removed from these banks and taken over by BPPN. There was pressure to create large banks through mergers, and foreign investors were encouraged to buy into these banks. Such proposals had two serious implications for Indonesian Chinese banks with close links to industrial and commercial conglomerates. These banks were not in a position to cover interest expenses from operational cash flows. This proposition of distressed corporations thus rose from 12.6 per cent in 1995 to 40 per cent in 1997, to 58 per cent in 1998, to 63.8 per cent in 1999 and fell back to 57.4 per cent in the period 2000–2002. In contrast, 26 per cent and 28 per cent of corporations in Malaysia and Thailand were unable to meet interest payments in 1998 respectively (Claessens 2000b: 2, 19). The high leverage of Indonesian bank-corporate groups meant that even a slight contraction in credit aggravated their difficulties in maintaining interest payments.

The bank bailout that accompanied the crisis pumped in liquidity with no safeguards. The major Chinese capitalists and the Suharto family benefited initially from this. The total cost of this recapitalization was 660 trillion rupiah in 1999. In addition, the state acquired overvalued assets from these banks and faced difficulties in selling these assets. They only succeeded in increasing state ownership of the banking structure – 70 per cent, reversing the privatization programme of the early 1990s. At the end of January 1999, Bank Central Asia had interest repayments of 18.3 trillion rupiah before recapitalization measures by the state reduced it to 8.3 trillion in 2000. Bank International Indonesia recorded interest repayments of 3.2 trillion rupiah in 2000, half that of its 6.2 trillion rupiah repayment in 1999 (*ICMD* 2002: 476, 480, 488, 490).

A second difficulty was in the restructuring of these financial institutions. In April 1998, BPPN took over management of seven private banks including BUN (Hasan), BDNI (Nursalim of Gajah Tunggal), BCA (Salim), and Danamon (Admadjaja). In return, the banks handed over assets as guarantees. These included land, property, factories and cash. The value of much of these was exaggerated and government reassessment proved this serious shortfall in value (Van Dijk 2000: 401).

The banks that were closed were largely those belonging to Suharto and the *pribumi* elite who had acquired many of them in the euphoric boom of the late 1980s and early 1990s. The restructured banks were largely Chinese banks with a few exceptions such as Bank Niaga (*Tempo*, 20 February 2000: 31). All this resulted in a reduction in the number of private banks from 212 to 28 by January 1998 (Bank Indonesia 2000: *Indonesia Financial Statistics*).

As part of this restructuring of Chinese banks, they were persuaded to repatriate some of their capital from Hong Kong, Singapore and the USA through the purchasing of equity by their multinationals. Thus, in June 1999, Salim's Hong Kong subsidiary First Pacific purchased 52 per cent equity in Indofood in Indonesia. Salim also streamlined his interests in Indonesia by disposing of equity in Astra, Indocement, Indofood, Indomobil and QAF (Quality Asian Food). This was part of the strategy to reduce the level of bad debt in BCA.

Difficulties in the restructuring of debt arose from the inadequate method of loan classification and government guarantees on bank liabilities and payments by BPPN. The close links of individual banks to non-financial firms confused these liquidity payments and hampered bank restructuring.

In 1995 the volume of non-performing loans amounted to 9 per cent of total bank credit; it rose to 10 per cent in 1996, with dramatic increases in 1997 and 1998 to 55 per cent and 65 per cent respectively (Bank Indonesia 2000: *Indonesia Financial Statistics*; Bank Indonesia 1995–9: *Annual Reports*).[12] State banks held 68 per cent of such bad debt. A major segment of these loans had been distributed through 'memo-lending' by the government to selected Chinese and *pribumi* capitalists (Sharma 1998: 29). By August 1999, only 13 per cent of non-performing loans had been restructured. This injection of public funds in the recapitalization of these banks – Rp 132 trillion ($21.7 billion [US]) by June 1998 rising to Rp 164.5 trillion by January 1999 and to Rp 200 trillion by April 1999 – only increased volatility and did not achieve any stability in the banking system (Van Dijk 2000: 401). These figures may not be accurate but are useful estimates in appraising the crude level of liquidity support provided by Bank Indonesia.

Another strategy was the issuing of medium- and long-term government bonds at high interests rates of 14 per cent. These bonds were directly exchanged for the worst of non-performing loans. The state was simply taking over useless assets of these banks and corporations. The Indonesians should have emulated Thailand's aggressive strategy of closing failing banks or providing incentives and guarantees for their safe takeover by foreign multinationals. In addition, the Thai government provided state funds only after restructuring. In contrast, BPPN absorbed the non-performing loans without securing prior guarantees. Hence, Indonesian debt restructuring was lowest, at 13 per cent of rescheduled debt as a percentage of total bad debt, when compared to that in Malaysia of 32 per cent of restructured debt out of the total non-performing loans and that in Thailand where the Thais succeeded in restructuring 20 per cent of total bad debt (Bongini et al. 2001: 5–25; Claessens et al. 2000a: 81–112; Lindgren et al. 1999: 65).

The third plank in the restructuring platform was mergers and joint-venture alliances. Bank Danamon merged with Bank Tiara and PDFIC in December 1999 and eight other banks before recapitalization. Bank Buana Indonesia, which already held foreign partners (Tat Lee Bank and Development Bank of Singapore), had increased this foreign shareholding with Keppel and Tat Lee Bank in 1999. However, by early 2000 the Singapore partners had withdrawn because of inadequate guarantees and suspicions of unauthorized capital transfers. The Indonesian government then assisted with recapitalization through the Jakarta Stock Exchange in May 2000. This again implied increased state ownership. In 1996, 40 per cent of bank liabilities rested with the state, by December 1999 this ratio rose to 70 per cent (Bank Indonesia 2000: *Financial Statistics*; Sharma 1998: 29).

Attracting foreign capital and partnership in bank restructuring was fraught with difficulties. This was constantly marked by prevarication because of the unstable nature of the financial sector and continuing political unrest. Bank International Indonesia, which previously held joint-venture ties with the Commonwealth Bank of Australia and Inter Pacific Bank, which had ties with French and Japanese banks before 1997, now failed to attract foreign partners. The first was taken over by the state, while Inter Pacific Bank was forced to shed its capital-market subsidiaries and concentrate on commercial banking (*ICMD* 2002: 514).

However, it was in the debacle over Bank Bali and its foreign suitor, Standard Chartered, that the reluctance of prospective foreign buyers highlighted the three major inhibiting factors in Indonesian bank reform: political corruption, lack of strict corporate governance and pervasive and confusing inter-bank, inter-corporate linkages.

Bank Bali had been established by Djaja Ramli. It was in serious difficulty in the 1997 crisis. Standard Chartered was persuaded to acquire a 20 per cent stake in the bank for $56 million (US) in April 1999. This was withdrawn in July 1999 when it was apparent that because of serious corruption, a higher capital-asset ratio was necessary and recapitalization costs were rising. The level of inter-bank loans too was high. The majority of these loans were with banks that had been frozen by BPPN (*Jakarta Post*, 16 August 1999, 21 September 1999). Bank Dagang Nasional Indonesia alone owed Bank Bali Rp 904 billion. Bank Bali had been lending to Golkar and Cabinet Ministers (including Habibie) Rp 550 billion for election expenses. There were illegal transfers by BPPN to Bank Bali to cover these inter-bank losses. This was concealed and only an audit by Pricewaterhouse Coopers revealed this. In September 1999, IMF suspended its loans to Indonesia, further intensifying the crisis. Rudy Ramli and three directors of the Bank were arrested the same month and Standard Chartered withdrew (*Jakarta Post*, 17 December 1999).

This scandal now increased the pressure for checks on how far bankers were using state credit for unauthorized lending – lending to politicians or friends, or speculating on the capital market. Bank Bali's net losses of Rp 132.2 billion and interest expense of Rp 1.2 trillion in 2000 were difficult to reconcile with its positive performance indicators before 1997 (*ICMD* 2002: 472) (see Table 14.10). The Bank was finally taken over by BPPN after selling its operations in Hong Kong.

This case study again supports my conclusion that endogenous structural factors rather than ethnic groups and their ethnically determined modes of operation, determined the success or failure of financial institutions. Success in restructuring and reform of banks also rested on similar endogenous factors in Indonesia. The dramatic but unstable growth in the banking sector and the inadequate regulatory structure in finance were further exacerbated when, in the mid-1980s, the Governor of Bank Indonesia lost some of his supervisory powers to the Ministries of Planning and Finance. This meant intensification of corruption, collusion and nepotism. Uncertainty and vulnerability inbred in the dependence on large foreign-capital inflows and borrowing from abroad provided only a mere trigger to the eroding edifice. Historically determined and flawed institutions – political, social and economic – were the culprits.

Pribumi banks such as Bank Niaga were just as exposed to volatility as Chinese banks such as BCA, BUN and Danamon. This emphasis on endogenous patterns of growth is sustainable when we compare Indonesian Chinese banks with Chinese banks in Malaysia (Hong Leong) and Singapore (Tat Lee, OCBC and UOB) which were successful in restructuring after the crisis (Brown 2000). Financial volatility is not a disease of the Chinese diaspora, it was the environment, the institutional framework and the levels of regulatory supervision which determined volatility. The financial crisis in Indonesia provided further evidence of this endemic volatility, institutional flaws and bank vulnerability. In 1967, thirty private banks failed (McKendrick 1989: 174). Failures were more frequent following the financial deregulation in 1988. Bank failures grew with the boom in commercial banking,

Table 14.10 Bank Bali

Key Ratios	1993	1994	1995	1996	1997	1998	1999	2000	2001
Profitability									
ROE (After Tax)	28.52%	28.44%	24.34%	29.13%	12.65%	149.92%	55.44%	-235.46%	44.99%
Net Profit/Tot. Assets	2.24%	2.06%	2.05%	2.24%	0.85%	-26.69%	-32.04%	-9.33%	1.78%
Net Interest Margin* (Net Int Inc/Avg Tot Assets)	3.97%	4.59%	4.60%	4.64%	4.59%	1.97%	-5.49%	-2.80%	0.62%
Net Interest Margin* (Net Int Inc/Avg Tot Advances)	5.67%	6.42%	6.31%	6.57%	7.44%	3.24%	-9.59%	-11.75%	4.21%
*Ratios for 1993 calculated on Closing Assets and not on Average Assets									
Asset Quality									
Loan Loss Provision/Advances	0.46%	0.51%	0.90%	0.59%	2.69%	39.68%	15.70%	41.14%	5.56%
Capital Adequacy									
Total Liability/Equity	11.66	12.73	10.82	11.96	13.90	-6.61	-2.72	24.18	24.23
Total Equity/Total Advances	7.86%	7.25%	8.44%	7.70%	6.70%	-17.80%	-57.79%	3.96%	3.95%
Liquidity									
Total Advances/Deposits+Borrowings	81.98%	85.56%	85.90%	84.51%	69.13%	63.36%	34.69%	15.93%	21.03%
Liquid Asset Ratio (Liquid assets / Total Assets)	2.24%	2.70%	2.52%	3.40%	4.19%	7.15%	13.01%	8.46%	6.07%
Liquid Assets/Deposits+Borrowings	2.62%	3.17%	2.98%	4.19%	5.06%	6.94%	10.11%	10.69%	7.56%
Net Loans/Deposits	107.65%	107.88%	105.39%	109.62%	89.12%	40.89%	18.48%	11.15%	19.34%
Free Capital/Total Capital	-12.29%	-1.03%	-5.67%	-50.66%	-85.62%	190.64%	110.11%	-64.35%	-1302.73%
Share Related									
Share Price SLRs	1,016.45	954.84	638.56	611.58	242.83	179.43	215.31	75.00	40.00
No. of Shares ''000s	1,208	1,208	1,397	1,404	1,404	1,404	1,404	672	669
EPS	30.80	30.80	40.47	35.97	61.16	0.00	0.00	0.00	0.00
PER	33.00	31.00	15.78	17.00	3.97	N/a	N/a	N/a	
BV/Share	269.26	298.94	382.70	438.51	600.58	-1,269.00	-2,644.00	704.04	768.63
P/B Ratio	3.77	3.19	1.67	1.39	0.40	-0.14	-0.08	0.11	0.05
Dividend/Share	30.81	30.81	34.63	35.96	38.68	0.00	0.00	0.00	0.00
Dividend Yield		3.23%	5.42%	5.88%	15.93%	0.00%	0.00%	0.00%	0.00%
CFPS									
P/CF									

Source: Bank Bali, *Annual Reports and Balance Sheets*

from 112 banks in 1988 to 239 in 1996. Bank Summa collapsed in 1992 with bad debts totaling $700 million (US). Bank Duta failed in 1990 owing to foreign exchange speculation. The collapse of Bapindo (Bank Pembangun Indonesia) in 1994, a state-owned bank, was due to the loan of $430 million (US), 5 per cent of the total loans of the bank, to Edy Tansil for a leisure project (Cole and Slade 1996: 85, 137, 182, 277, 340). This form of memo-lending by banks to Chinese capitalists, senior military and political personnel (including Finance Minister Johannes Sumarlin and the Soeharto family) persisted. All this compromised the achievement of an effective reconstruction of banks and financial organizations in contemporary Indonesia.

Notes

1. Nasution's chapter 'Capital Inflows and Policy Responses: the case of Indonesia in the 1990s' (Jones et al. 1998: 117–43) covers only the period 1990–94, neglecting the period 1994–96 which is the most critical phase in determining how portfolio inflows distorted the financial system. The neglect of this crucial period affects the entire analysis. Sharma's paper (1998) contains good information on the banks and their difficulties.
2. For an excellent study on the Indonesian financial system see Cole and Slade 1996. See also McKendrick 1989: ch. 10.
3. Bank Summa had losses of Rp 591 billion (Barings Securities, *Report on PT Astra International*). Its non-performing loans were valued at 1.5 billion rupiah ($720million [US]). See Brown 2000: 64.
4. The composite index of the Jakarta Stock Exchange rose from 66.35 to 305.12 per cent in 1988, to 588.765 in 1993 and 637.43 in 1996 before collapsing to 401.71 in 1997, to 398.038 in 1998 and to an artificially supported rise to 679.919 in 1999 (Bank Indonesia 2002: *Indonesia Financial Statistics*; Jakarta Stock Exchange 2000 and 2002: *Factbook*; Siregar 2000).
5. Bank lending to property and real estate sectors increased by 40 per cent in the period 1995–96, again rising in 1996–97, a 21 per cent increase from 1996 (Sharma 1998: 9–13).
6. After 1997, foreign investors were allowed to form holding companies, could absorb equity in pioneer industries outside Java and were given fiscal incentives to encourage investments (BKPM 1999–2000: *Annual Reports*).
7. As cited in Athukorala 2002: 27. These figures are only announced values. The Coordinating Body for Investment (BKPM) noted an increase of 37 per cent of

FDI approvals for 2000. Yet Japanese inward investment for 2001 dropped to 1 per cent from 5 per cent for 2000.

8. BKPM is Badan Koordinasi Penaman Modal (Investment Coordination Board) while BPPN is Badan Penyehatan Perbankan Nasional (Indonesian Bank Restructuring Agency).

9. Short-term debt owed to foreign commercial banks was $33 billion (US), which was 1.75 times that of Indonesian foreign-exchange reserves in 1998 (Radelet 1999: 3–4). Japan provided more than 40 per cent of total foreign credit and their reduction increased distress for Indonesian banks.

10. See First Pacific Holdings (1995: *Annual Report*) for Salim Group's consolidated group accounts. See also Yuri Sato 1993.

11. First Pacific Holdings (1995: *Annual Report*).

12. Non-performing loans were calculated to account for 60–85 per cent of all loans; bank recapitalization would cost Rp 643 trillion ($89 billion [US]). By November 1998 it was clear that private corporations held $118 billion (US) debt, 60 per cent of this owed to foreign creditors; 40 per cent of debt was in foreign currency. See Sharma 1998: 29–30 and Lindgren et al. 1999: 13.

References

1 Primary Sources

1.1 Official Publications
Asian Development Bank. *Asia Development Outlook.* Various years.
Bank Bali, *Annual Reports.* Various years.
Bank Central Asia (B CA), *Annual Reports.* Various years.
Bank Duta, *Annual Reports.* Various years.
Bank Indonesia, *Annual Report.* Various years.
——, *Indonesia Financial Statistics.* Various years.
Bank International Indonesia, *Annual Reports.* Various years.
Bank Lippo, *Annual Reports.* Various Years.
Bank Niaga, *Annual Reports.* Various years.
Bank Umum Nasional (BUN), *Annual Reports.* Various years.
BAPEPAM (Badan Pelaksana Pasar Modal, Capital Market Supervisory Agency), *Annual Reports*, Various years.
BKPM (Badam Koordinasi Penanman Modal, Capital Investment Coordinating Board), *Annual Report.* Various years.
——, *Factbook of the Indonesian Capital Market.* Various years.
First Pacific Holdings (FPH), *Annual Report.* Various years.
Indonesian Securities, Clearing and Depository Institution (Kiliring, Deposit Efek Indonesia), *Periodic Reports.* Various years.

Institute for Economic and Financial Research, Jakarta, *Indonesian Capital Market Directory [ICMD)*,Various years.

International Monetary Fund (IMF), *International Capital Markets.* Various issues.

Jakarta Stock Exchange, *Factbook.* Various years.

Key Indicators of Developing Asian and Pacific Countries. Various issues.

1.2 Journals and Periodicals

Far Eastern Economic Review. Various issues.

Forum Keadilan. Various issues.

Global Credit Research, Moody Investors Service. Various years.

International Herald Tribune. Various issues.

Jakarta Post. Various issues.

Kompas. Various issues.

Media Indonesia. Various issues.

Merdeka. Various issues.

Panji Masyarakat. Various issues.

South China Morning Post. International Weekly. Various issues.

Suara Pembaruan. Various issues.

Tempo. Various issues.

Ummat. Various issues.

2 Secondary Sources

Agénor, P.R., Miller, M., Vines, D. and Weber, A. (eds) (1999), *The Asian Financial Crisis: Causes, Contagion and Consequences*, Cambridge: Cambridge University Press.

Athukorala, P.C. (2002), 'Foreign Direct Investment in Crisis and Recovery: Lessons from the Asian Economic Crisis'. Paper presented at XIII International Economic History Congress, Buenos Aires.

Barings Securities (1994), *Report on PT Astra International.*

Bongini, P., Claessens, S. and Ferri, G. (2001), 'The Political Economy of Distress in East Asian Financial Institutions'. *Journal of Financial Services*, 19(1): 5–25.

Brown, Rajeswary Ampalavanar (1994), *Capital and Entrepreneurship in South East Asia*, Basingstoke: Macmillan.

—— (2000), *Chinese Big Business and the Wealth of Asian Nations*, Basingstoke: Palgrave.

—— (2002), 'An Inefficient Stock Market and the Performance of Chinese Banks in Malaysia and Singapore', Unpublished paper. May 2002.

Claessens, S., D. Simeon and Klingebiel, D. (1999), 'Financial Restructuring in East Asia: Halfway there?', Financial Sector Discussion Paper No. 3, World Bank, September.

——, Djankov, S. and Lang, L.H.P. (2000a), 'Separation of Ownership and Control in East Asian Corporations'. *Journal of Financial Economics*, 58: 81–112.

——, Djankov, S. and Lixin Colin Xu (2000b), 'Corporate Performance in the East Asian Financial Crisis', *World Bank Research Observer*, 15(1), February: 23–46.

Cole, D.C. and Slade, B.F. (1996), *Building a Modern Financial System*, Cambridge: Cambridge University Press.

De Brouwer, G. and Pupphavesa, W. (eds) (1999), *Asia Pacific Financial Deregulation*, London: Routledge.

Edwards, S. (ed) (2000), *Capital Flows and the Emerging Economies: Theory, Evidence and Controversies*, Chicago: University of Chicago Press.

Hill, H. (2000), 'Indonesia: The Strange and Sudden Death of a Tiger Economy', *Oxford Development Studies*. 28(2) June: 117–39.

ING Barings Indonesia Research (2000), Stock Market Review. Slow Road to Recovery. Company Review. May.

Iriana, R. and Sjoholm, F. (2002), 'Indonesia's Economic Crisis: Contagion and Fundamentals', *Developing Economies*, 2 June: 135–51.

Jomo, K.S (ed.) (1998), *Tigers in Trouble: Financial Governance, Liberalization and Crises in East Asia*, London: Zed.

Jones, S.G., Montes, M.F. and Nasution, A. (eds) (2001), *Short-term Capital Flows and Economic Crises*, Oxford: Oxford University Press.

Lindgren, C.J., Balino, T., Enoch, C., Gulde, A.M., Quintyn, M. and Teo, L. (1999), 'Financial Sector Crisis and Restructuring: Lessons from Asia', *IMF Occasional Paper 188*, Washington DC.

Masayoshi Tsurumi (2001), *Financial Big Bang in Asia*, Aldershot: Ashgate.

McKendrick, D.G. (1989), 'Acquiring Technological Capabilities: Aircraft and Commercial Banking in Indonesia', Unpublished PhD dissertation, University of California at Berkeley.

Moodys Investor Service (1997), Global Credit Research, Teleconference Proceedings, 'The Impact of Market Turmoil in South East Asia and Korea on Japanese Banks and other Financial Institutions', 24 October.

Nasution, A. (2001), 'Capital Inflows and Policy Responses: the case of Indonesia in the 1990s', in S.G. Jones, M.F. Montes and A. Nasution (eds), *Short-term Capital Flows and Economic Crises*, Oxford: Oxford University Press.

Radelet, S. (1999), 'Indonesia: Long Road to Recovery', Unpublished paper, Harvard Institute for International Development, March.

—— and Sachs, J.D. (1998), 'The East Asian Financial Crisis: Diagnosis, Remedies, Prospects', *Brookings Papers on Economic Activity*, I: 1–74, 88–90.

Sato, Yuri (1993), 'The Salim Group in Indonesia: The Development and Behaviour of the Largest Conglomerate in South East Asia', *Developing Economies*, 21(4), December: 408–41.

Sharma, S.D. (1998), 'The Indonesian Financial Crisis: From Banking Crisis to Financial Sector Reforms 1997–2000', in World Bank, *Indonesia in Crisis: A Macroeconomic Update*, Washington: World Bank.

Shiller, R.J. (2000), *Irrational Exuberance*, Princeton: Princeton University Press.

Siregar, A. (2000), 'Demokratisasi dan Ekonomi Pasar' (Democratization and Market Economy), in *Warta Ekonomi*.

Takatoshi Ito (2000), 'Capital Flows in Asia', in S. Edwards (ed.), *Capital Flows and the Emerging Economies: Theory, Evidence and Controversies*, Chicago: University of Chicago Press.

Van Dijk, K. (2000), *A Country in Despair: Indonesia between 1997 and 2000*, Leiden: KITLV Press.

Warr, P.G. (1999), 'What Happened to Thailand', *World Economy*, 22(5), July: 631–50.

Appendix

Rupiah Exchange Rate to US Dollar

1985	1,125 rupiah
1990	1,901 rupiah
1992	2,062 rupiah
1997	2,392 rupiah
1998	10,175 rupiah
1999	7,455 rupiah
2000	8,945 rupiah
2001	10,455 rupiah

Source: Bank Indonesia Financial Statement, 2001.

Part III
Perspectives on Diaspora

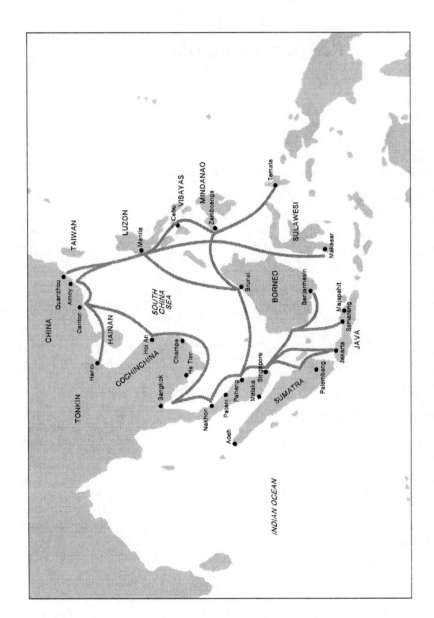

Map 6 Chinese trade routes in southeast Asia, 16th–18th centuries

–15–

Diaspora Networks in the Asian Maritime Context

Anthony Reid

'Asia' was invented, first by Phoenicians, then Greeks, as an antithesis to Europe. Its subsequent place in the historiography of the West has often been as a corrective or counter-factual to Europe, demonstrating the irreducible presence of some dynamic element in Europe by its absence in Asia. Marx began a huge industry of pondering why capitalism was born in Europe and not in Asia. John Hicks was convinced he had found 'the principal key to the divergence between the history of Europe and the history of Asia' in the prominence of the city-state phase in the former (Hicks 1969: 68). Jacob van Leur (1955: 63–79), despite an anti-colonialism iconoclastic for his day, could not break out of a Weberian dichotomy between European capitalist trade and an unchanging 'Oriental trade' in which urban patriciates were divided by a huge gap from the mass of travelling pedlars.

Fortunately, the work of the past three decades has gradually abandoned the notion that either Europe or Asia can be essentialized in these ways. Japanese economic history is as different from India's as either is from that of France. My own view was that the fine balance between the market and the palace was tilted differently in different times and places, giving merchants better protection for property in some European cities than in many Asian ones (Reid 1993: 267–70). Others have gone further. Victor Lieberman (1999, 2003) suggests that the eastern and western margins of Eurasia show more parallels than those within, say, Southeast Asia. Some recent contributors to the debate have reacted so far against any kind of European uniqueness that they have needed to find late and almost accidental reasons for European power in the nineteenth century (Frank 1998; Blaut 2000).

Among the more striking divergences in the economic history of different parts of Asia is the role of entrepreneurial diasporic networks. Northeast Asia, and particularly Japan and Korea, represent one extreme of the global experience, where entrepreneurial networks of foreign or ethnic minority origins were unusually marginal. On the other hand South and Southeast Asia appear at the other extreme, a marvellous laboratory for the study of entrepreneurial networks of all sorts. As is apparent even from the sample of studies in this book, the rich variety of diaspora networks in early modern Southeast Asia gradually gave way in the twentieth century to a perceived dichotomy between 'indigenous' and 'Chinese' economies. In South Asia, on the other hand, diversity has remained, partly because twentieth-century nationalism was able to perceive the networks of Parsees, Jains, Chettiars, Sikhs, Baniars and so forth as part of the inherently diverse Indian nation.

Most of the chapters in this section are concerned with the late nineteenth and twentieth centuries, while the seventeenth-century Japanese diaspora described by William Wray is atypical in its tendency to disappear through intermarriage and assimilation within a couple of generations. Some further information on the pre-colonial situation will therefore be helpful to make clear the subsequent transitions.

In the sixteenth century, the richest diasporic networks in Southeast Asia appear to have been the Hindu commercial castes, notably Gujarati sharafs and South Indian chettiars. The Portuguese report the richest merchants, bankers and money changers in Melaka, Pasai and Pegu to have been of these castes at their arrival on the scene. Castanheda (1552: 458) described the chettiars of Melaka as the richest merchants in the world, financing voyages from that city to various ports in Southeast Asia and China. Malay sources of the same period confirm their great commercial prowess, and explain it with reference to the temple fund from which the chettiar community could borrow. This was an effective proto-bank, taking one-twentieth of the sum borrowed as a donation to the fund, and providing a supernatural sanction against defaulting. 'If the merchant wanted to default on the gold of the idol, wherever he went he would be destroyed' (*Hikayat Hang Tuah*, cited Reid 1993: 111–12).

This is one type of commercial diaspora, a tiny minority of financiers held together by a religious system which reinforced their financial activities. Usually strongly endogamous, they have some resemblance to the Jewish and Parsee diasporas discussed in preceding chapters. We will call this type A – religiously-bounded, endogamous, financiers.

To conduct their shipping activities, such financiers had, however, to rely on the much more numerous commercial diasporas of type B – porous, hybrid-ized, traders. In Melaka those who took ships to China were typically labelled Javanese, Malay or Luzon, though I have argued that each of these at this time was a commercial and hybrid or bicultural group with much Chinese (Fujianese) admixture (Reid 1996). Those who sailed to Burma were labeled Pegu (Mon of coastal Burma), Javanese or Malay, and those travelling to India usually Gujarati, Kling (South Indian Muslim) or Malay (Pires 1515). Type B were much looser identities associated with language rather than descent, and all in the process of profound change through intermarriage in the trading ports. What each group had in common was an orientation to commerce, a foothold in more than one port and culture, and a mobility which helped protect them from any one ruler's greed. All except the Mon were Muslim and almost all Sunni, so the boundaries between them were also porous.

Chinese per se (as opposed to the Sino-Southeast Asians carrying some of the above labels) played a relatively small part in this commercial world of the early sixteenth century. The Ming regime maintained a strict ban on private trade, and had long lost interest in the tribute relations of the early 1400s. Chinese were more prominent around 1600 when we have copious Dutch reportage, since in 1567 the Middle Kingdom had begun licensing junks to sail to southern ports. Fifty junks each year were initially licensed, but by 1597 the figure was 117 and it appears to have grown subsequently. The period between 1567 and the 1630s represented the exceptional period referred to by Wray in Chapter 4 of this volume, when Chinese and Japanese both visited Southeast Asian ports such as Manila, Hoi An, Cambodia, Ayutthaya and Banten to exchange Chinese silk and porcelain for Japanese silver. While Wray's Japanese diaspora fits my type B quite well, Chinese commercial diasporas could also be of a third type.

China has had at least the demographic and economic weight of Europe for most of the last thousand years, and we should not expect a single type of diasporic interaction. On the other hand China did not, like India, generate specific money-handling castes or religious minorities of type A. Those who travelled overseas on a large scale were members of a relatively small number of speech-groups scattered along the south China coast, but their religious practices and social mores were part of the Chinese mainstream and they had no necessary concern for endogamy. Indeed because women seldom evaded the bans on leaving the Middle Kingdom, while Southeast Asian women were indispensable partners in the market as well as the bedroom, Chinese migrants had every reason to marry locally. Hybridized or bicultural communities were thereby often formed, filling particular niches in the trade by dint of accessing more than one culture.

In the seventeenth century, however, a situation arose in the most active ports for the China trade (Ayutthaya, Hoi An, Cambodia, Manila, Banten and Batavia) where a constant flow of Chinese migrants provided a labour force that was relatively skilled without being yet hybridized. The diaspora in these cases, led by bicultural traders able to mobilize capital, grew by the mobilization and gradual absorption of a labour force active in production as well as exchange. In the seventeenth century this production was largely in urban trades such as carpentry, metalwork, and the production of food and drink. A beginning was made also with sugar-milling in Java and the Vietnamese hinterland of Hoi An. In the eighteenth century new migrants moved into the mining of gold, silver and tin, and cash-cropping in pepper, gambier and cloves. Thus Chinese diasporas spanned both type B and another type-C diaspora – mobilizing migrant labour for production.

Each of these diasporas tended to occupy different niches in the economy, and these certainly changed over time. The first Dutch expedition to the east described with some wonder (and probable inaccuracies) the diverse pattern they found at the great Javanese pepper market of Banten in 1597:

> The Persians, who are called Khorasans in Java, are those who usually earn their living in [precious] stones and medicines... The Arabs and Pegus [Mons, of southern Burma] are the ones who mostly conduct their trade by seas, carrying and bringing merchandise from one city to another, and buying up much Chinese merchandise, which they exchange against other wares from the surrounding islands, and also pepper, against the time when the Chinese return to buy. The Malays and Klings [south Indian Muslims] are merchants who invest money at interest and in voyages and bottomry. The Gujaratis, since they are poor, are usually used as sailors, and are those who take money in bottomry, on which they often make one, two, and three times profit...
>
> The Chinese live at Banten in their own quarter, which is surrounded with a strong palisade... When they first come from China, like other merchants they buy a wife, who serves them until they again return to China, when they again sell her, taking the children with them that they have produced. Those who live here are the ones who buy up pepper from the farmers, going through the countryside with their scales in hand ... gathering the pepper against the return of the Chinese ships... They are so clever in their handiwork and trade, that they exceed all other nations. (Lodewycksz 1598: 120–2, 124).

If we follow these three types of diaspora through time, we might expect type B to be the least stable, unless it absorbs elements of type A, to preserve the boundaries of the group, or of type C, to absorb a flow of new recruits. Most chapters in this volume, concerned with the colonial and post-colonial periods, do in fact suggest something of this pattern.

Clarence-Smith and Plüss are nicely matching chapters primarily concerned with type-A diasporas. They raise fascinating questions about why such diasporas should derive so frequently from the Middle East – the geographic label Clarence-Smith uses to group his seemingly very disparate Jews, Armenians, Maronites, Druze, Syrian Orthodox, Gulf Shi'ites and Hadhrami Arabs. Plüss adds the Parsees of India to the list, as well as her own take on Baghdadi Jews in the Hong Kong context. With the exception of the Hadhramis, these are all clear examples of type-A diaspora, very small in numbers, tight-knit through endogamous bonds primarily religious in motivation, and active in finance.

Is there a common secret to their success in these niches? Clearly the tightness of the communal bonds is one factor, establishing trust within the tiny group and minimizing claims on its wealth from those outside the circle. But there must also be some factor linked to colonialism itself, since it is especially in the high-colonial era of the nineteenth and twentieth centuries that these small type-A communities flourish. In most of the cases in question, it does appear that type-A characteristics, and especially the vulnerability of the tiny group to popular pressures against them, made them seek a role of broker to the colonial power itself. In British and Dutch colonies these groups became disproportionately strong in urban landholding, understanding better than most the colonial legal system that gave security of property to the otherwise powerless, and often using foreclosure to claim the landed assets of their debtors. The ability of Armenians and Jews to dominate the hotel sector is another example of the advantage of understanding the ruling authority and its social habits.

If we may readily understand why the majority communities did not readily grasp these opportunities, why did not Europeans themselves take advantage of their knowledge of the colonial system to exploit them? The answer seems to be in motivation. If commercial and especially money-lending occupations long had somewhat disreputable associations among European landed elites, the colonial situation increased the importance of status considerations for Europeans. The system discouraged them, in other words, from 'getting their hands dirty' in commerce.

The Hadhramis discussed by Clarence-Smith, and the Indian Muslims in Hong Kong by Plüss, are in some respects also type-A diasporas, usually small in numbers and active in financing and urban real estate. The Indian Muslims were also close to the colonial government in Hong Kong, and useful to it in brokering roles. But as mainstream Muslims the boundaries of these communities need not have been so clear. Hadhramis did widely intermarry with host Muslim societies, and only the Sayyids among them needed to stress the purity of their descent from the Prophet as a status marker. They therefore had aspects of type-B behaviour. Indian Muslims in Hong Kong, however, seemed to be protected by the diasporic status from extensive intermarriage. The gap to the majority Chinese community was simply too great to bridge.

The chapters by Chung and Brown bring us to contemporary times, in which Chinese have become very dominant among the commercial diasporas of Southeast Asia, and are widely credited for the recent economic growth of that region. Both are concerned with the techniques employed by Chinese businesses, and how far these may diverge from orthodox entrepreneurial theory. Both reveal a mature form of diaspora with very strong roots in the communities where they live. They are no longer limited to the niche areas of financing or trade typical of types A or B, but nor are they refreshed by a constant inflow of new migrants as the older type C was. Networks and entrepreneurship are here the more relevant terms than diasporas.

Chung demonstrates the adaptability of Chinese business over the past century. Although he portrays a dichotomy between the firm-based economy of Europe and its offshoots, and the network-based economies of eastern Asia, he cautions against seeing these as unchanging stereotypes. In fact he sees contemporary entrepreneurship in China as essentially a modern creation out of competition with Western firms. Raj Brown is more inclined to stress continuities in the habits of Chinese business networks despite their very different modus operandi in adapting to the new Asian stock markets.

In short, diaspora networks are very different over time and place, and only by categorizing them more finely can we begin to see the utilities of concepts such as diaspora and network.

References

Blaut, J.M. (2000), *Eight Eurocentric Historians*, New York: Guilford Press.

Castanheda, F. Lopez de (1924 [1552]), *Historia do Descobrimento y Conquista da India pelos Portugeses*, Vol. II, Reprint Coimbra: Imprensa da Universidade.

Frank, A.G. (1998), *ReOrient: Global Economy in the Asian Age*, Berkeley: University of California Press.

Hicks, J. (1969), *A Theory of Economic History*, Oxford: Oxford University Press.

Leur, J.C. van (1955), *Asian Trade and Society: Essays in Asian Social and Economic History*, The Hague: van Hoeve.

Lieberman, V. (1999), 'Transcending East-West Dichotomies: State and Culture Formation in Six Ostensibly Disparate Areas', in V. Lieberman (ed.), *Beyond Binary Histories: Re-imagining Eurasia to c.1830*, Ann Arbor: University of Michigan Press.

—— (2003), *Strange Parallels*, Vol. I: *Integration on the Mainland: Southeast Asia in Global Context, c.800–1830*, Ann Arbor: University of Michigan Press.

Lodewycksz, W. (1915 [1598]), 'D'eerste Boeck: Historie van Indien vaer inne verhaelt is de avontueren die de Hollandtsche schepen bejeghent zijn', in G.P. Rouffaer and J.W. Ijzerman (ed.), *De eerste schipvaart der Nederlanders naar Oost-Indië onder Cornelis de Houtman 1595–1597*, Vol. I, The Hague, Nijhoff for Linschoten-Vereniging.

Pires, T. (1944 [1515]), *The Suma Oriental of Tomé Pires*, ed. Armando Cortesão, London: Hakluyt Society.

Reid, A. (1993), *Southeast Asia in the Age of Commerce, c.1450–1680*, vol. II: *Expansion and Crisis*, New Haven: Yale University Press.

—— (1996) 'Flows and Seepages in the Long-term Chinese Interaction with Southeast Asia', in A. Reid (ed.), *Sojourners and Settlers: Histories of Southeast Asia and the Chinese*, Sydney: Allen & Unwin.

–16–

A Profile of Ethno-national Diasporas
Gabriel Sheffer

The Need for a Comprehensive Profile of Ethno-National Diasporas

The purpose of this chapter is to provide a comprehensive, yet focused and updated, portrayal of historical and new ethno-national diasporas (that is, diasporas which are parts of ethnic nations).[1] The emphasis is on the essential internal and external political dimension of the existence and behaviour of these groups. Short and focused definitions of social and political phenomena may be elegant, easy to digest and remember. Occasionally, therefore, such sharply crafted definitions may have an enduring impact on the development of entire academic disciplines in both the natural and social sciences. However, when a field of study is relatively recent and the available definitions of the subject matter are still inadequate and insufficient for developing useful theoretical and analytical perspectives, and when the subject is intricate, the need is not for such short, elegant, generalized definitions but for more elaborate charcterizations. This is particularly true in the study of ethno-national diasporas. In this field of study, such a characterization or profile, with a strong emphasis on politics, is necessary for four main reasons.

First, like other aspects of current ethnicity and nationalism, since the mid-nineteenth century the ethno-national diasporic phenomenon has undergone some transformations. Nevertheless, those diasporas have not lost their essential (not essentialist) perennial characteristics. Differently put, it is true that because of the changes in domestic, regional and global environments, older (such as the Jewish, Armenian Greek[2] and Chinese) and newer (such as the Irish, Croatian and Korean) diasporas have acquired some novel features, yet these new features only complement the characteristics of such entities that had been established in antiquity or the middle ages. It means that veteran diasporas have not lost their older characteristics and newer ones resemble them.

Second, the term 'diaspora' has been applied to other types of groupings: various kinds of tourists, refugees, legal and illegal guest workers and, especially, religious dispersals. All these groups are lumped together with ethno-national diasporas that exhibit different characteristics. The third reason for the need to present a profile emphasizing the political angle is that when the current multifaceted features of these groups are discussed, frequently this aspect is neglected, and other features are more extensively emphasized. Fourth, the realities of diasporic existence have been more multifaceted than those depicted and analysed in the available theoretical and analytical discussions, especially those based on examination of the roles of historical diasporas in various multi-ethnic empires (see for example Armstrong 1976; Chaliand and Rageau 1995; Clifford 1994). This also applies to previous attempts to delineate the 'common features of a diaspora' that focus on the social attributes and goals of such entities (Cohen 1997: 26).

The Various Types of Ethno-National Diasporas

Basically there are two overarching types of ethno-national diasporas. First, the dispersed segments of ethnic nations or groups which, due to historical circum-stances, have been unable to establish their own independent states are 'stateless diasporas'. The second type of dispersed groups is that connected to societies that constitute a majority or a dominant group in established states – and these are the 'state-linked diasporas'. Of the two, stateless diasporas form the smaller category, including such ethnic groups, or 'trans-state nations', as the Palestinians, Kurds, Gypsies, Tibetans and Sikhs. The larger state-linked category includes all other ethno-national diasporas, regardless of their age, organization, or nature of relations with homeland and host country.

Both stateless and state-linked ethno-national diasporas can be arranged on one spectrum. At one pole of the spectrum are individuals, families and extended families of guest workers, refugees and other sojourners who stay in host countries for very long periods and, despite explicit agreements or solemn vows to the contrary, never return to their homelands. Members of these groups are either 'proletarian' – namely, from poorer segments of their homeland societies such as Pakistanis and Indians in the UK, Moroccans in France, and many Palestinians in the US and Kuwait – or 'capitalists' – that is, middle-class and richer migrants such as the recent emigrants from Hong Kong to Canada and the US and white South Africans who migrated to other Anglo-Saxon countries such as Australia. Some of these groups are unorganized (as is the case with the white South Africans), some are loosely organized (such as the Palestinians in the US and Canada), and some are highly organized (such as the Jewish and Armenian diasporas).

The main interest of this chapter, however, is in two types in tandem: the 'historical state-linked diasporas' (such as the Chinese, Jews and Armenians) and the fully fledged 'modern state-linked diasporas' established from the nineteenth to the mid-twentieth centuries (such as the Greeks in the US, South Africa and Australia, and the Indians in Africa and Europe). The profile of those two types is the same.

Because of the immense diversity and complexity of ethno-national diaspora communities they should be characterized accordingly and in a manner that defies normative disparaging definitions or characterizations influenced by the traditional Marxist, Liberal and Assimilationist approaches to ethnicity in general, and to ethno-national diasporas in particular. The following portrayal also jettisons the assumptions that these groups constitute merely a temporary phenomenon, that their members are bound to assimilate and shed their unique identity, that they are in exile, and that these are artificial or purely 'imagined' social and political entities. What follows is in fact an elaboration and refinement of the 'operational definition of ethnic diasporas' that I proposed in the mid-1980s (Sheffer 1986: 8–11) and then elaborated in further publications (see especially Sheffer 2003).

The Profile of Ethno-National Diasporas

As noted, the profile elaborated below comprises the main features fitting most, if not all, existing ethno-national diasporas. It is based on the common attributes and organizational and behavioural patterns of historical, modern and incipient diasporas. As noted, this profile takes into account the perennial elements of diasporism as well as elements pertaining to contemporary diasporas which have emerged in conjunction with globalization and liberalization. It also indicates the political ramifications of some of the features.

Ethno-national diasporas are created as a consequence of both voluntary and imposed migration to one or various host countries. However, contrary to the view widely held by laymen, politicians and scholars, identifying the reasons for migration from homelands is not crucial to understanding diasporic organization and behaviour in host countries. This is true regardless of the cultural, social, political and economic background of such migrants: that is, whether at the time of migration from their homeland they are rich or poor, whether they have a-priori intentions of returning to their homeland or intend to settle permanently in the new host country, and whether they are well versed in the homeland's traditions and politics or only superficially acquainted with them. As global political conditions change it is more difficult to stop persons from both leaving their homelands and entering desired hostlands.

Most migrants make the critical decisions about whether to settle permanently in a host country and join an existing diaspora, or help establish one, only after arriving in the host country. Recent surveys have confirmed the fact that upon their arrival in a host country only very few migrants are emotionally or cognitively in a position to decide whether they intend to live permanently outside their homeland or whether they wish to maintain connections with it. Thus, for example, upon arrival in new host countries, only a small number of Palestinians who for political reasons fled from the Israeli-occupied territories were ready to affirm that they had left for ever, that they intended to assimilate into the new society, or become fully integrated (Burghuti 1988: 8; Van Hear 1998: 200). Various studies have shown that, similarly, few Israeli Jews, Filipinos and Koreans who voluntarily migrated to the US are unequivocal about their intention to permanently settle there (Gold and Philips 1996; Gold 1997; Magnifico 1988; Sheffer 1998). On the other hand, voluntary migrants and refugees who decide to leave their homelands for ideological reasons, such as the Germans who left their fatherland for the US after the failure of the 1848 revolutions, or the Chinese scientists who left mainland China because they were seeking freedom to conduct their research, may be driven by an a priori intention to organize or join diasporic entities, on the one hand, or to integrate and assimilate into the new homeland, on the other. Thus it is clear that during this phase of the emergence of diasporas political factors play a major role and influence the migrants' decisions.

Occasionally migrants leave their homeland, head to a certain host country but stay there only temporarily, moving on to another host country because of local political-legal restrictions on their permanent settlement, or because of other economic, political and social difficulties. In extreme cases they may move to a third or fourth host country. Namely these are secondary or tertiary migrations of the same individuals, families, small groups or their descendants. This was the case recently with some Russian Jews who, in the last days of the Soviet Union, were permitted to emigrate only to Israel. Some regarded Israel only as an interim refuge while, in fact, their final intended destinations were the US, Canada and Australia (Sicron and Leshem 1998). Other East European migrants, such as Poles and Ukrainians, are another case in point. When they realized that local social and economic conditions in Germany, France or Britain were difficult, they too continued their sorrowful journey to the US, Canada, Latin America, Australia and South Africa (Rex 2000).

Generally, only when they reach a host country that out of political and economic reasons permits longer stay, or where they intend to reside permanently, do migrants begin to ponder integration and assimilation. The alternative is to join or establish diasporic entities and thus avoid full integration and assimilation. This juncture in the personal and collective history of migrants is important not only for an accurate understanding of the development of particular diasporas, it is also a most significant element for distinguishing various groups of transient migrants from diasporas. The difference is that those who either a priori do not intend to settle in a certain host country, or consider it too unfriendly, are not interested in organizing or joining diaspora communities, and therefore do not face the dilemma concerning assimilation or full integration vs creating new or joining existing diasporic communities. Such patterns occurred during the large waves of migration at the end of the nineteenth century and into the twentieth, which resulted in the establishment of some of the largest ethnic diasporas that now exist.

Large groups of migrants that established new societies in host countries, that eventually gained independence and that either became a majority or acquired the status of a predominant group (such as the British who settled in America, Canada and Australia) are not considered here to be ethno-national diasporas. This notwithstanding, the fact is that members of such groups may feel sympathy toward the old homeland and maintain cultural affinity and political and economic ties with it. The reasons for excluding these groups from this category are that they either forged or adopted a new identity, and consequently their loyalty lies with the new state and society that they had formed or joined. In fact, they regard these countries as their exclusive homeland. Thus, although contacts have been maintained between Anglo-Saxon Americans and England and between French Canadians and France, from every perspective it is extremely difficult to regard these Americans as a British diaspora or these French Canadians as a diaspora of France.

Hence, ethno-national diasporas are those groups that remain a minority in their host countries, and thus are potentially faced with the dangers of expulsion, social, political and economic hardships, or alienation. There are, however, some borderline cases, such as the Chinese in Taiwan. Though the Taiwanese Chinese form a majority on that island, they are embroiled in questions concerning their identity, the centrality of Mainland China and consequently their relations with that homeland. As the arguments that have been made and the political and diplomatic clashes that have occurred in the late 1990s between Mainland China and Taiwan show, these questions are of a political nature and therefore the answers have not only interesting theoretical but also significant political ramifications.

The readiness and capability of migrants to maintain their ethnic identity in the host country and to publicly identify with their community and homeland are two other crucial features of the present profile. While most observers stress the structural, social and political environmental impacts on migrants' movement and capability to maintain their identity in a new host country (Gold 1992: 4–14), here the emphasis is on migrants' capability – and readiness – to take tough emotional and cognitive decisions with political implications that greatly influence their behaviour in the new host country. Hence, the critical formative stage in the creation of a diaspora occurs only after migrants overcome the initial shock involved in leaving their homeland. Only afterward do they cope with the overwhelming problems involved in reaching a new host country: encountering the new culture, confronting the daunting task of finding permanent jobs, renting or buying suitable housing, establishing social relations, and finding political support systems.

After migrants make initial adjustments and solve immediate problems involved in settling down in a host country, their main dilemma is whether to opt for eventual assimilation or maintain their ethno-national identity and contacts with the 'old homeland'. In addition to the solution of those strategic dilemmas, this phase also requires tactical decisions, especially in view of the migrants' expectations about better political and economic opportunities that may facilitate their assimilation or full integration. These dilemmas and questions are aggravated when migrants become involved in mixed marriages or when the receiving society offers visible incentives and rewards if the migrants are ready to give up their identity and undertake the problematic process of full integration that eventually may lead to assimilation. At that stage another issue may arise: how will the host country react to the migrants' inclination to integrate and eventually assimilate?

In some host countries, these issues and dilemmas are not relevant for migrants, especially if these are non-democratic states that restrict the arrival and the prolonged sojourn of migrants and guest workers. For example, the Korean, Filipino and especially Palestinian guest workers in Kuwait were not permitted to integrate and certainly not to assimilate into the host society or to establish a permanent organized diaspora there. In fact, they were kept at bay as second-class citizens (Brand 1988: 107–48; Lesch 1994). This, however, was not the end of their tribulations – out of security and political considerations and, like the Yemenites in Saudi Arabia and the Egyptians in Iraq, the Palestinians were expelled from Kuwait during the Gulf War (Van Hear 1993 and 1998: 199–202). In other host countries, the social and political environment may be so hostile that even when there are no formal constraints, migrants find it extremely difficult to entertain the idea of assimilation and integration into the host society or of establishing an organized diaspora. In any event, the decisions the migrants make at this stage of their residence in the host country are of crucial consequence for them, for their kin in the homeland and for the homeland's government.

Migrants base their decisions regarding the future in their host country on a complex mix of emotional and rational considerations. This is connected to the basic observation that both their primordial and psychological/symbolic identity and instrumental considerations influence these decisions.

Individual and collective decisions to maintain ethnic identity are not sufficient for the establishment, revival or maintenance of diasporas. These must be followed by equally critical decisions concerning membership in communal organizations or, when these do not exist, by decisions to assist in establishing and operating them. An intensive effort on this score is essential since without such organizations diasporas can neither exist nor thrive in what basically are socially and politically hostile environments for these groups.

Hence, the existence of communal organizations, which has far-reaching political implications, is an essential feature of diasporas. This is probably the most vital aspect distinguishing the various types of transient migrants that stay for longer periods in host countries and incipient and established diasporas. Yet, usually, only certain segments of each of the ethno-national migrant groups actually become seriously involved in the operation of such bodies. Because of relative tolerance shown toward migrants, mainly in Western host countries, in certain cases assimilation and integration may cause severe demographic losses to an incipient as well as to an established diaspora.

During the initial period after arriving in the host country, most decisions concerning the migrants' future behaviour are taken by individuals or small groups: nuclear families, extended families, fraternities and social circles. As soon as larger diasporic communal organizations are formed, or as soon as migrants join existing diasporic organizations, they face the need to make additional strategic and tactical collective choices.

Then they decide especially about the main strategy organized diasporas pursue vis-à-vis their host societies and governments, homelands and other dispersed segments of the same nation. The political angle in this phase is pretty clear.

The menu of available strategies is large, ranging from assimilation through various modes of accommodation to separation and, in the case of stateless communities, to secession. More specifically, this spectrum includes the following: full assimilation, integration, acculturation, communalism, corporatism, isolation, autonomism, secession, separation and irredentism (Iwanska 1981; Sheffer 1994; Smith 1981 and 1986; Weiner 1991).

Memories about their forced or voluntary uprooting from the homeland, initial hardships in the new host country, the need to make critical decisions about settling there, the compelling necessity to decide whether to refrain from total assimilation, and the efforts migrants invest in establishing and running communal organizations, all result in the rise of solidarity among members of these groups. In other words, diaspora solidarity is not based solely on ties to the homeland; rather, it fully emerges in the host country and in view of the political and economic conditions there.

Based on such solidarity, there emerges a degree of coherence within such groups. Sentiments of solidarity and group coherence can be traced back to the primordial and cultural elements in their collective identity. But by no means are these highly homogenous entities in all aspects. To ensure the survival, continuity and prosperity of a diaspora these sentiments must overcome generational, class, educational, social and political ideological differences within the group. Otherwise such diasporas disintegrate and ultimately dissipate. Similarly, without a degree of solidarity and coherence, their social, political and economic domestic and trans-state activities are almost impossible. Furthermore, identity and solidarity serve as the twin bases for maintaining and promoting constant contacts among the diasporas' elites and grass-roots activists. These relations are of great social, political, economic and cultural significance for ethno-national diasporas, their host countries, homelands and other interested actors.

The traits mentioned in the previous paragraph constitute also the bases for the organized activities of the diasporas. One of the purposes of these activities is to create and promote the readiness and ability of diaspora members to preserve a

Gabriel Sheffer

continuous interest in the homeland and cultural, economic and political exchanges with it.

Organized diasporas take care of their cultural, social, political and economic needs in a way that complements the services provided by host governments. Yet, the establishment of diaspora organizations and membership in these organizations create the potential for dual or divided authority and, consequently, of loyalty vis-à-vis the host country. Such a development may result in conflicts between a diaspora and its host society and government.

To avoid undesirable conflicts between diaspora norms and the norms and laws set by the host government or dominant group, most state-linked diasporas accept the basic rules of the game that exist in each host country. At certain periods in diasporas' development, however, real or alleged dual or divided loyalty that is generated by dual and divided authority patterns may create tension between social and political groups in both the host country and the diaspora. Sometimes this leads to the intervention of homelands in host countries on behalf of their diasporas, or to homelands' direct intervention in the affairs of the diasporas.

Communal cohesion and solidarity, recurrent social, political and economic problems facing the diasporic entity in the host country, diaspora members' wish to support the homeland as well as pressure from homeland to provide such support, and the sheer bureaucratic logic of diaspora organizations lead diasporas to become engaged in a range of diaspora cultural, social, political and economic activities. These activities are intended to meet certain basic needs of the diaspora that no other social or political organization in the host country can, or wish to, furnish.

Diasporic organizations function on a number of levels: the local diaspora community, the host-country society and government and the trans-state level. In this context of particular importance – and, therefore, of particular theoretical and analytical interest – are diasporas' exchanges with their homelands. In addition to the activities aimed at sustaining the diaspora communities themselves, exchanges with the homeland and the help that diasporas extend to it constitute an essential element in the *raison d'être* of these communities and the networks that they create.

The conduct of such exchanges becomes difficult without the existence of elaborate, sometimes even labyrinthine, trans-state networks. These allow the transfer of various significant resources to the homeland, to other segments of the same diaspora and to other interested states and organizations outside the host countries. The creation and regular operation of such networks are critical elements in the life cycles of all diasporas.

Because of their range of functions, these networks may also be a source of trouble for diasporas. They may cause clashes with various segments in host societies, including other diasporas, and they may deeply disturb host governments because they are regarded as the most blatant expressions of a diaspora's dual or divided loyalties. In extreme cases, their existence may be regarded as a clear indication that these ethnic communities constitute a fifth column in the host country. This was the case, for example, with members of the German diaspora in the Middle East and America, who, on the eve of the Second World War, joined the Nazi Party and provided the Nazi regime with intelligence and other services.

Some, but not all, of these trans-state networks are linked to other networks that serve legitimate and peaceful interests of their diasporas and homelands. It is therefore understandable why host governments become suspicious of these networks as they may function as conduits for activities such as international terrorism, supply of weapons and illegitimate money transfers. The existence of these networks may also provoke clashes with international organizations such as the UN or Interpol.

As a result of a combination of the above characteristics, diasporas are pre-disposed to become locked in conflicts with their homelands, host countries and other international actors. The likelihood of such conflicts is closely related not only to economic competition with other groups in the host countries or to absolute and relative deprivation (Gurr 1993) but, primarily, are caused by 'soft' factors related to diaspora members' identity and social and political needs. They are also related to the complex patterns of ambiguous, divided and dual authority and loyalty that emerge as a consequence of their existence in host countries, on the one hand, and concern about their homelands on the other. In turn, these factors affect diasporas' strategies and behaviour.

Although clashes between diasporas and other domestic or international actors win attention in the media and in political circles, and they may cause damage and grief to all sides, basically state-linked ethno-national diasporas are interested in cooperation with host societies and governments.

In this vein, diasporas are capable of significant contributions to host societies' well-being. They can serve as bridges between friendly segments in the host society, on the one side, and their homelands and the international arena, on the other. These contacts may spur significant economic, scientific and political benefits to all parties involved. This was certainly the case with the Lebanese diaspora in the US, South America (especially Brazil and Argentina), West Africa, Australia, Canada, and elsewhere (Chaliand and Rageau 1995; Hourani and Shehadi 1992).

The Applicability of the Profile

As noted, some features of contemporary ethno-national diasporism that have been elaborated in the previous section are not unlike those found in earlier periods. The most significant common aspects are that all diasporas have been created as a result of voluntary or imposed migration; that after settling in host countries and wherever political conditions permitted they faced the dilemma of whether to assimilate and fully integrate or to maintain their ethno-national identity; that core members were capable of maintaining their ethnic identity, which is the basis for continued solidarity; that based on that solidarity and the wish to maintain their links to their brethren, they establish intricate organizations in their host countries as well as international networks; and that they maintain continuous contacts with their homelands and other dispersed segments of the same nation. However, because of the changed conditions that prevailed in almost all corners of the globe in the late twentieth century, perforce, modern and incipient diasporas have acquired some new features that complement the traditional characteristics of diasporas and add to the complexity of the diasporic phenomenon.

This greater complexity is reflected in behaviour patterns in the triangular relationship – diaspora, homeland and host country – as well as with international organizations and groupings. These include, for example, diversified migration patterns that constitute the backdrop factors for the establishment of new diasporas and for the growth and sometimes the revival of older ones. The ways through which homelands become involved in migrants' exit also fall into this framework. These extend to the agency roles of homeland governments, the timing of departure from the homeland, the arrangements involved in their arrival in the host countries, the forms of migrants' settlement in host countries, the formation of diaspora organizations, diasporas' multiple connections with their homelands through the trans-state networks, the multiplicity of exchanges they conduct with other diaspora communities, the distribution of power between diasporas and homelands, and contradictory patterns of authority and loyalty.

I do believe that all the considerations about the profile as well as about the exclusion and inclusion of groups in the category of ethno-national diasporas can serve as a more fruitful conceptual basis for discussion about these diasporas around the world.

Notes

1. This is a much abridged and updated version of Gabriel Sheffer, 'Defining Ethno-National Diasporas', *Migration, Special Issue: Globalization and Diasporas*, 2002.
2. The controversy about the Greeks being a classical diaspora is addressed in this book by Gelina Harlaftis. See Chapter 7 for details.

References

Armstrong, J.A. (1976), 'Mobilized and Proletarian Diasporas', *American Political Science Review*, 70(2), June: 393–408.

Brand, L. (1988), *Palestinians in the Arab World: Institutions Building and the Search for State,* New York: Columbia University Press.

Burghuti, I. (1988), *Palestinian Americans: Socio-Political Attitudes of Palestinian Americans Towards The Arab Israeli Conflict,* Occasional Papers Series no. 38, Centre for Middle Eastern and Islamic Studies, University of Durham (UK): 4–35.

Chaliand, G. and Rageau, J.-P. (1995), *The Penguin Atlas of Diasporas,* New York: Viking.

Clifford, J. (1994), 'Diasporas', *Current Anthropology,* 9(9): 302–38.

Cohen, R. (1997), *Global Diasporas,* London: UCL Press.

Gold, S. (1992), *Refugee Communities: A Comparative Field Study*, Newbury Park, CA: Sage.

—— (1997), 'Transnationalism and Vocabularies of Motive in International Migration: The Case of Israelis in the US', *Sociological Perspectives,* 40(3): 409–27.

—— and Philips, B.A. (1996), 'Israelis in the US', *The Jewish Yearbook 1996,* New York: American Jewish Committee: 51–101.

Gurr, T.R. (1993), *Minorities at Risk,* Washington, DC: United States Institute of Peace California Press.

Hourani, A. and Shehadi, N. (eds) (1992), *The Lebanese in the World: A Century of Emigration,* London: Tauris.

Iwanska, A. (1981), *Exiled Governments: Spanish and Polish,* Cambridge MA: Schenkman.

Lesch, A. (1994), 'Palestinians in Kuwait', *Journal of Palestine Studies,* 20(4).

Magnifico, L. (1988), *Contemporary American Immigrants: Patterns of Filipino, Korean and Chinese Settlement in the US,* New York: Praeger.

Rex, J. (2000), 'Communities, Diasporas and Multiculturalism', a Paper presented in the EUROFOR conference no. 31 on Immigrant Communities, Diasporas and Politics, Athens, 25–28 May 2000.

Sheffer, G. (1986), 'A New Field of Study: Modern Diapsoras in International Politics', in G. Sheffer (ed.), *Modern Diasporas in International Politics,* London: Croom Helm.

—— (1993), 'Ethnic Diasporas: A Threat to their Hosts?' in M. Weiner (ed.), *International Migration and Security,* Boulder CO: Westview.

—— (1994), 'Ethno-national Diasporas and Security', *Survival,* 36(1), Spring: 60–79.

—— (1998), 'The Israeli Diaspora', *The Jewish Yearbook,* London: Vallentine Mitchell.

—— (2003), *Diaspora Politics: At Home Abroad*, Cambridge: Cambridge University Press.

Sicron, M. and Leshem, E. (eds) (1998), *A Profile of an Immigration Wave,* Jerusalem: Mganes Press.

Smith, A.D. (1981), *The Ethnic Revival in the Modern World*, Cambridge: Cambridge University Press.

—— (1986), *The Ethnic Origins of Nations*, New York: Blackwell.

—— (1992), 'Chosen Peoples: Why Ethnic Groups Survived', *Ethnic and Racial Studies,* 15(3): 436–56.

Van Hear, N. (1993), 'Mass Flight in the Middle East: Involuntary Migration and the Gulf Conflict, 1990–91', in R. Black and V. Robinson (eds), *Geography and Refugees: Patterns and Processes of Change*, London: Belhaven.

—— (1998), *New Diasporas,* London: UCL Press.

Weiner, M. (1991), *The Impact of Nationalism, Ethnicity and Religion on International Conflict*, Boston: MIT Center for International Studies.

Greek Merchant Networks in the Age of Empires (1770–1870)

Maria Christina Chatziioannou

The formation and evolution of Greek merchant capitalism within the Ottoman Empire, particularly since the last quarter of the eighteenth century, is a subject that has attracted the research of many Greek historians. From very early on, transport and trade activities within the Ottoman economy attracted groups from different ethnic origins and religions. The Greek population in the Ottoman lands was characterized by great mobility until the first decades of the nineteenth century, and commercial emigration was influenced by both non-economic and economic factors.[1]

The non-economic factors that determined commercial emigration during the early industrial period were place of origin and family and local ethic-value systems (including religion, language, customs, knowledge/technical know-how). The economic factors behind this mobility are mainly equated with commercial activities and the specialization of certain groups of particular areas in certain crafts: stone building from the regions of Epirus and the Peloponnese; painting from the regions of Epirus and western Macedonia; sponge fishing from the Dodecanese islands.

The commercial emigration of Greeks spread throughout the unified territory of the Ottoman Empire from the seventeenth century onward and was subordinate to local and central Ottoman authorities. The vast area of the Ottoman Empire that extended from the Balkans to Asia Minor, the Middle East and North Africa included the geographical area which later became the modern Greek state in the southeast tip of the Balkan peninsula. Trade in agricultural products, raw materials and manufactured goods (mainly cloth) developed in the ports and inland markets of the Ottoman Empire, which were in close contact with corresponding ports from the Black Sea to the Italian peninsula, France, Holland and Great Britain. The activities of the Greek traders were not usually connected to local production, but were the link in the chain of the movement of trade from the East to the West. As Ina McCabe indicates for the Armenians, organized groups of Greek trading families were formed in the Ottoman Empire and eventually expanded in the East and West and formed the extended networks of Greek diaspora entrepreneurship (see also Harlaftis, Chapter 7 in this volume).

Thus sea trade became the axis of the economic development of the eastern Mediterranean, and the port cities of Smyrna, Constantinople, Thessaloniki, Alexandria, Taganrog and Odessa provided the mechanism for linking the agricultural production of the hinterland of the Ottoman and Russian Empires with western Europe. Nevertheless, an extended network of inland routes, despite its inferior infrastructure, developed and spread from the southern Balkan peninsula of the Ottoman Empire to central Europe and thus to the adjacent Hapsburg and Russian Empires.

An interesting and under-researched subject is the coexistence of various ethnic groups within the borders of the great empires, ethnic groups that could offer competitive, similar or complementary services to an economic centre. For example, historical research might be able to confirm the withdrawal of Jewish merchants from certain Mediterranean markets in the seventeenth century and their replacement in these economic gaps by Greeks, or the coexistence of Greeks and Armenians in other cases. The establishment of these mobile, organized ethnic groups of trading families in the main economic centres of the great empires offered them access to a vast area for the expansion of their networks, and the ability to manage their business from a centre that provided commercial intelligence. Great empires, like the Hapsburg, the Russian and the British, attracted these organized ethnic groups of trading families and provided them an ideological framework, a sense of economic belonging, often with conciliatory advantages.

Different ethnic minorities mobilized by the same economic motives migrated toward the economic centres of these Empires offering a unique experience for migration and for gaining knowledge of new countries, new ideas and new practices of trading. The experience of ethnic coexistence may be the subject of social anthropology, but it is certainly an important issue in regard to the economic and social behaviour of migrant entrepreneurs. For example, we come across Greeks living, operating and competing as merchants along with Slavs in Pest, Trieste and Vienna, with Jews in Odessa, and with Germans and Italians in London and Manchester. The 'homogeneous' social and economic environment offered entrepreneurial opportunities. The host countries, as new social and economic environments, offered new entrepreneurial opportunities along with new cultural and entrepreneurial models.

It is to be expected that all trade diasporas were not identical, although we can draw interesting comparative characteristics, whether we are referring to the Armenians of the seventeenth century in New Julfa, or to the Greeks in eighteenth-century Smyrna. As Jonathan Israel clearly indicates in Chapter 1 of this volume, the diasporas are not homogeneous even in regard to their own internal organization. Recent studies of merchant communities, diasporas and trade networks provide new dimensions and perspectives through a comparative approach. Finally, we may have to completely reconsider this major issue that is generally known as

Greek Diaspora, a concept that has frequently been promoted in a rhetorical way for political reasons by Greek national historiography (Tomadakis 1953; Psiroukis 1975).

In the discussion about ethnicity,[2] various approaches have been undertaken, tackling the concepts of 'ethnic group' and 'ethnic community'; the underlying question, however, is always the issue of national identity. From these various analytical approaches to the issue of ethnicity, we will choose that of the ethnic network. Thus an ethnic network based on group solidarity, kinship and common culture provides to its members economic advantages plus economic resources.

The close relationship between the ethnic group and entrepreneurship has taken the forefront recently in the relevant literature. Particularly, when entrepreneurial groups with common historical background and cultural values – the Jews, for example – found themselves in different host countries under different circumstances, they followed different entrepreneurial models (for example see Godley 2001). The entrepreneurial activity was often based on family and national bonds that provided financial, social and psychological security along with specialized knowledge. The concept of entrepreneurship has various definitions in economic theory. The importance of entrepreneurship in trade is brought to the fore by the Austrian school of Hayek and Kirzner, who focus their attention on the way private information is used in competitive markets in order to counterbalance continuous fluctuations. According to this theory, the entrepreneur acts as the agent whose aim is profit earned particularly under the irregular circumstances of the market (Casson 1990: 46, 73).

The analysis of the ethnic group and entrepreneurship brings out the cultural features of this relationship. Studying entrepreneurial groups such as the Jews with their common historical background and common cultural values, scholars come across different entrepreneurial paths and models that developed in their different places of settlement. This interesting point has been raised in recent research and has been further enriched by sociological and social anthropological approaches. Why should we study the relation between ethnic group and entrepreneurship? It is well known that ethnic groups adjust themselves to the conditions and circumstances found in their place of establishment. It is indispensable to focus on the collateral relation between ethnicity and entrepreneurship and to analyse a system of relations and values shared between people with common ethnic background and migrant experience.

In order to understand the relationship of the ethnic group and entrepreneurship we shall examine three interrelated factors: first, the structure of the conditions of the market; second, the special features of the group (selective migration, culture, creation of social networks); and third, the strategy of the group (the relation between opportunities and ethnic characteristics) (Aldrich and Waldinger 1990: 115–35). These factors developed in different periods of time and geographical areas, and can be traced in the merchant networks that were formed by diaspora trading groups. The cohesion of the period from 1780s to 1870s enables us to study common characteristics and entrepreneurial practices in the Greek merchant networks.

The Chiots and the Vlachs formed networks that expanded from their place of origin to their place of settlement. The two networks shared three well-known common characteristics: religion, language and place of origin.[3] However, they present a distinct difference: the Vlachs are considered to be an ethnic group distinguished by specific cultural features, while the Chiots are characterized by their place of origin.

It is of particular interest that the Chiots were conscious of being a distinct entrepreneurial group (and their contemporaries regarded them as such), whereas the Vlachs, who were an entrepreneurial group with special cultural characteristics (language), did not regard themselves as an entrepreneurial group, nor were they regarded as such by the others.[4] Nevertheless the importance of both groups was pivotal for the social and economic formation of Greek-diaspora merchant communities.

The economic emigration during the Ottoman Empire leads us to the history of the trade diaspora. The theoretical discussion of the 'trade diaspora' was initiated by Abner Cohen. This concept refers to an ethnic group socially interdependent but dispersed in various communities. The field of research initially focused on entrepreneurial groups in Western Africa and Southeast Asia (Cohen 1971; Dobbin 1996).[5] A central issue was whether the emergence of these entrepreneurial minorities should be attributed to the sorts of economic factors that exist in every society of capitalist development or whether it is just a vague response to economic and political circumstances. Commercial transactions provided new sources of income to the powerful states that were formed in Europe during the seventeenth and eighteenth centuries and in southeast Asia during the nineteenth century. Within this framework, and under these circumstances, certain groups of minorities – such as the Jews and the Chinese – were activated with an immediate response to the needs of the commercialization of goods. The reasons for this response do not lie only in economic or cultural interpretations (Reid 1997: 36–7).

My purpose here is to examine closely the case of the different sub-groups that made up part of the central core of the Greek diaspora from the last quarter of the eighteenth century until mid-nineteenth century. We will focus on three types of network, the first and the second belonging to a lesser-known part of the Greek diaspora, the inland trade routes. The first is the network of the Vlachs from Epirus and western Macedonia, particularly from the mountain region of Pindos (northwest of modern Greece), which concentrated on inland transport trade toward the Ottoman and the Hapsburg Empires (Pest, Vienna). The second network is one that was composed of organized commercial groups from Epirus which directed their entrepreneurial activities toward the Adriatic port-cities of Venice and Trieste, as well as to the inland routes that led to the Russian Empire (Nizna, Moscow). The third network is the most famous one, the islanders of the Chiot maritime transport trade who conducted their activities from the Ottoman to the British Empire (London, Manchester) and covered almost every corner of the Greek entrepreneurial diaspora (Chatziioannou, forthcoming).

One of our main questions here is whether we can identify sub-groups in the Greek diaspora with special internal features and external motives.[6] We know that Greek, Serb, Vlach and Albanian merchants, inhabitants of regions of the Ottoman Empire, had been trying in the eighteenth century to acquire economic access mainly to Hungary and Transylvania, but to Russia as well (Cicanci 1981, Bur 1986: 17–85; Papastathi-Tsourka 1994). What is mainly missing is to confront sub-groups of the same ethnic group, or different ethnic groups in the same territorial domain: on one hand inland migrations and entrepreneurial ventures in the Ottoman, Hapsburg and Russian Empires and on the other sea-route migrations and business activities in the British Empire.

Greek merchants who traversed the overland routes in the Ottoman period departed mainly from towns in Thessaly, Epirus, Albania and Macedonia, heading for transit stations in the Balkans, Central Europe and Russia. Overland trade routes started from Yannina and Metsovo in Epirus, or Siatista, Kozani and Serres in Macedonia, frequently using old Roman routes such as the *Via Egnatia*, passing through such cities in the Balkans and Central Europe as Sibiu, Brasov, Kecskemét, Miskolc, Zemun, and in many cases terminating in Pest and Vienna, capital of the Hapsburg monarchy, or accordingly in Nizna and Moscow in the heart of the feudal economy of imperial Russia.

Traian Stoianovich, in his classic study 'The Conquering Balkan Orthodox Merchant', describes the gradual evolution of Balkan merchants since the seventeenth century, from land carriers, thieves and pirates, to agents accepting orders and dabbling in money-lending, then to independent merchants and bankers aiming to political activities, and finally to politicians with parallel business activities (1992: 63–4). The above hierarchy of the Balkan merchant, predicated on a linear evolution, corresponds to a more complex historical reality. It is difficult to identify the activities, in the case of Balkan and Ottoman merchants at least, before the middle of the nineteenth century. To complicate matters further, the Austrian authorities, in the framework of a bureaucratic evaluation and registration of the population, imposed a categorization of 'classes' on all Balkan merchants which could not possibly include the variety and complexity of their business activities. The most appropriate approach, that of Stoianovich, evaluates business activities in the main city-centres of the Balkan overland trade, where the geographical place of origin provides a first criterion for the classification of merchants on land routes.

A region/cradle of commercial tradition and business culture can be located along the overland trade routes: the settlements in the Pindos mountains in both Epirus and western Macedonia (Siatista, Kastoria, Kozani, Vlasti, Moschopolis), the homeland of Greeks, Vlachs and Albanians, all Ottoman subjects who can be categorized as 'minorities' within the Ottoman state, and who competed with Serbs and local merchants in the main economic centres where they emigrated. Moschopolis has been described as the place of origin of a large percentage of merchants of Vlach origin: in the registration of merchants in 1766 (1767) in Vienna, 12 out of 82 Greek merchants were from Moschopolis[7] and in the overall table for the same period (1770), compiled by Stoianovich, Moschopolis is listed as the place of origin of 98 merchants out of 362–70 in Croatia, Srem, Semlino, Vienna and Tokai (Stoianovich 1992: 17)[8].

Thus, these small mountain towns with domestic wool industry, commercial connections, and experience in organizing land transport produced an organized group of Vlach merchants with expanded networks, among which are included many distinguished entrepreneurs, the most illustrious of whom are the three generations of the Sinas family in Budapest and Vienna (Laios 1972). The Moschopolis merchants' business methods in Pest and Vienna remain to be identified and will probably prove to be similar to those of the Chiots in many respects.

The degree of success of entrepreneurial ventures depends on various factors, both external and internal, and comparison of the economic emigration of sea and land routes can fill out the picture of the Greek merchant-entrepreneur. I submit the following hypothesis: sea trade opened up business horizons for most of the members of the Greek economic diaspora and created a commercial tradition contrary to what happened to the corresponding overland trade. It is known that sea trade created surplus commercial capital through the captain-merchant who offered both services in sea transport and the means of transport, the ship. The carriers on land routes (*kiratzidhes*) do not seem to have played the same role in Greek commercial transactions. Particularly important for land trade are non-economic factors, such as Ottoman assaults as well as local national uprisings, which threatened economic practice and upset commercial transactions in most of the small Balkan markets, the cradles of Greek merchants, such as Moschopolis, Philippoupolis, Meleniko, etc. The importance of the quest for national identity, a quest that impregnated the multi-ethnic communities of the diaspora, combined with the political absolutism and economic feudalism of the places of settlement, should be stressed in connection with the early commercial diaspora of overland emigration to the Balkans, Central Europe and Russia. We can trace two common features in the formation of Greek merchant networks inside great empires. The first is that Greek merchant communities (*paroikies*) embraced all sub-groups of the same ethnic group. The comparison between the Greek communities in Austro-Hungarian and Russian economic centres (Pest, Vienna, Trieste, Nizna, Moscow, Odessa) during 1780–1830 and those in Britain (London, Manchester) during 1830–1870 share many similarities, namely the creation of a community, at the heart of which lay the Church, religion being central to the cohesion of the group as it offered social philanthropy to the weaker members of the community, thus providing a common and stable background for economic survival and differentiation. The second feature is that maritime transport and inland transport of foodstuffs, furs, leathers and cloth were organized on the same model – that is, social networks. The sub-groups present the same characteristics of an introvert social group that is reproduced through endogamy and reproduction of common cultural patterns, offering certain similarities with guilds. The transformation of social networks to trade networks was easily achieved through chain emigration, based on close relations with persons living in the place of origin.

Until the mid-nineteenth century, Greeks in the commercial enclaves of the Italian peninsula were engaged in a general import-export trade with the centres of the Ottoman Empire. Trade was based on tightly controlled merchant-commercial information and markets. One of the main functions of Greek merchants in the Italian peninsula, and particularly in the large Austrian port of Trieste (as is revealed by the relevant sources, see Katsiardi-Hering 1986), was commissioning merchandise from Ottoman lands and Greece, alongside personal business affairs. The client in the eastern port commissioned the buying and selling of merchandise or currency of interest to him, and the merchant in the western port executed these orders in the most profitable way, charging credit and issuing bills of exchange in his client's name, and keeping the agreed commission. Thus the expatriate-merchant provided his fellow merchant in Ottoman territory and Greece with knowledge of the western market through his active participation in commercial negotiations (Chatziioannou 2003). The same trade practices would follow similar patterns in other Greek merchant communities as well.

Knowledge of trade and transport of the same commodities, ways of penetrating the local market and a common language or dialect are some of the basic reasons for cooperation between the first immigrants. The transition from simple middle-man trade to complex multi-national entrepreneurial activity indicates the formation of primary capital accumulation, the consequent successful management of a limited capital through social connections which led to access to abundant financial sources. The Mediterranean ports of the Italian peninsula had open, extra-dependent economies and did not belong to a unified state until 1862. The diaspora entrepreneurial group that stood out during the late eighteenth century in the Italian peninsula is that of the emigrants from the region of Epirus in northwest

Greece. Emigrants from this region were found in all Greek settlements in the Italian peninsula in the eighteenth century.[9]

The Epirotes, the Vlachs and the Chiots constituted distinct groups within the Greek merchant communities. They formed different merchant networks sustained by maritime and inland transportation that traded agricultural, pastoral and manufactured goods within and outside the borders of the Ottoman Empire. The strengthening of the Chiot network in comparison to that of the Epirotes and that of the Vlachs may be attributed to the comparative advantages of maritime trade over land trade. Epirotes and Vlachs never managed to constitute a homogeneous force in the diaspora trade centres in which they settled, namely Moscow, Venice and Vienna, whereas Chiots formed 'cartels', wherever they established immigrant communities, particularly in London, maintaining strong ties with their native island (Chatziioannou and Harlaftis forthcoming). The Chiot success can equally be attributed to the more mature capitalist conditions that sustained it. The structure, the patterns and the evolution itself of the entrepreneur in the Habsburg Empire were strongly influenced by the court as well as by the imperial bureaucracy.

In contrast, in the British Empire the development of the liberal businessman provided different social patterns for the newcomers, the Chiot merchants. Establishment in Britain offered the Greek-diaspora merchants of the nineteenth century the unique experience of a competitive entrepreneurial environment, in addition to living within a society with a rigid class system which provided a variety of social and cultural patterns. Every diaspora Greek was aware of the social and economic rules of Victorian England. The archetype of the British entrepreneur, his business culture and practices, gave the prototype to Chiot entrepreneurship. England became the most important junction for the path and development of Greek trade networks. The liberal British political and economic framework provided all the right conditions for entrepreneurial competition: Greeks were brought face to face with the Germans, the Jews, the Scottish, the Irish – all ethnic groups that developed due to the family formation of their companies. That the Greeks competed with these ethnic groups is evident, and the ones that were able to withstand and were more resilient during the nineteenth century were able to assimilate socially and culturally into British bourgeois life, with the prime examples being Eustratius Ralli and Michael Rodocanachi.

The presence of the Vlachs in the Austro-Hungarian Empire can be detected from early on. The central administration in Vienna, in order to defend the southern borders of the Empire against the Ottomans, had formed, according to one historiographic interpretation, an informal defensive system that used the Vlachs as a 'zone-fence' which expanded from Belgrade along the river Sava to Vidin and Bucharest. The organization of this defensive system was facilitated by the particular social organization (*zantruga*) that was common in the southern

Balkans (Wace and Thomson 1914; Nouzille 1991: 255–6). The concentration of the population of Vlachs along the boundaries brought the Vlach groups in contact with the roads of communication from the southern Balkans to central Europe. It is obvious that during a time and place when the differences between transporter and merchant were rather blurred, land transport could be made easy by the chain establishment of various groups of Vlachs in the main trading urban centres of the Balkans and central Europe. A known land route that led from Moschopoli to Salonica, then to Zemun and finally to Budapest, made the Vlachs, if not the only at least one of the few closely knit groups of merchants which carried on commerce between the Ottoman and Hapsburg Empires (Kasaba 1988: 20–1).

In short, we would characterize land economic emigration more limited than maritime economic emigration. Sea trade gave more opportunities for capital formation since the merchant captain not only owned the ship but also participated in the ownership of the cargo and in any profit. The equivalent *kiratzides* (land transporters) did not play the same role in the commercial transactions. In this way, land transport did not lead to the formation of an entrepreneur of the type which sea transport produced and which consequently led the Chiots to ship ownership (Harlaftis 1996). And in this case the place of establishment of the diaspora merchants proved the most important factor in the transformation of their business.

The period between 1875 and 1914 has been described by E. Hobsbawm under the old-fashioned title *The Age of Empires*. His study emphasizes the beginning of a new era for the international economy, focusing on the colonial features of the new imperialistic economy, affecting mostly the distribution of international trade (Hobsbawm 2000 [1987]: 61). The diaspora merchants, closely connected with the evolution of international transport and trade, would confront a critical turning point by the last quarter of the nineteenth century.

Looking back to the Ottoman-based Greek commercial migration that had been moving for over a century and had expanded through sea and land routes to Amsterdam, Calcutta, Beirut, Alexandria, Tunis, Minorca, etc., we may observe that by the last third of the nineteenth century such commercial migration was almost over. A major factor here was the slow disintegration of the Ottoman Empire and the formation of the Greek national state. The formation of the Greek state (1828) and the associated return and settlement of expatriates marks the first watershed in the history of Greek emigration. This was a crucial historical moment for the whole of the Greek merchant diaspora[10], offering a strategic turning point for declining merchant communities or a reorganization of business firms. Some of the old merchant networks of the Vlach and Epirote groups vanished, whereas others like the Chiot networks modified their organization and strategy following the paths of imperialistic expansion.

Maria Christina Chatziioannou

Notes

1. For a bibliography on the Greek diaspora, as well as evaluation of the meaning of terms such as 'diaspora', 'enclave', 'community', see Hassiotis 1993. For a brief note on Greek commercial migration, see Chatzioannou 1999: 22–38.
2. On the meaning of ethnicity, see Hutchinson and Smith 1996.
3. For the dynamics of these characteristics in Greek diaspora communities, see Kitromilides 1999: 131–45.
4. The matter here is not Vlach identity but the economic activities of a population group of Vlach-speakers from the southern Balkans, known mainly from place of origin and surname. The learned class of Vlachs had Greek education. On the topic of education, see Konstantakopoulou 1988 and Katsiardi-Hering 1995: 153–77.
5. For common culture as evidence of solidarity in mercantile diaspora groups, see Curtin 1984: 1–3.
6. These sub-groups have been described by Scott (2000: 20) as '… an informal association of people among whom there is a degree of group feeling and intimacy and in which certain group norms of behaviour have been established'.
7. Registrations of the population in Austria and Hungary started during the reign of Maria-Theresia. See for example Gurther 1909 and Enepekides 1959. The registration mentioned here is reproduced in Stoianovich 1992: 17.
8. A bibliography for Moschopolis is gathered in Peyfouss 1989.
9. Emigrants from Epirus constituted 13 per cent of the Greek community of Venice from the late sixteenth century until 1866 (Kyriakopoulou-Kyriakou 1978: 263–6. The history of the Durutti family, migrants from a small village of Epirus in the port of Ancona in the early nineteenth century, is a typical example (Chatziioannou 1997: 17–41.
10. For a political view of the term 'diaspora' see Constas and Platias 1993: 3–28.

References

Aldrich, H. and Waldinger, R. (1990), 'Ethnicity and Entrepreneurship', *Annual Review of Sociology*, 16: 111–35.
Bur, M. (1986), 'Das raumergreifen Balkanischer Kaufleute im Wirtschaftsleben der Ostmitteleuropäischen länder im 17. und 18. Jahrhundert', in V. Bàcskai (ed.), *Bürgertum und Bürgerische Entwicklung in Mittel und Osteuropa*, Studia Historiae Europae Medio-Orientalis 1, Budapest.
Casson, M. (1990), *Enterprise and Competitiveness: A System View of International Business*, Oxford: Clarendon.

Chatziioannou, M.C. (1997), 'The Development of a Traditional Firm during the First Half of the Nineteenth Century', in C. Agriantoni and M.C. Chatzioannou, *Metaxourgeion: The Athens Silkmill*, Athens: Institute of Neohellenic Research, no. 61.

—— (1999), 'L'emigrazione commerciale greca dei secoli XVIII–XIX: una sfida imprenditoriale', *Proposte e ricerche*, 42(1): 22–38.

—— (2003), *Family strategy and Commercial competition: The Geroussi Merchant House in the Nineteenth Century*, Athens (in Greek).

—— (forthcoming), 'New Approaches in Diaspora Ethnic Merchant Networks: The Greek Community in Manchester', *Tetradia Ergasias*, I.N.R./N.H.R.F.

—— and Harlaftis, G. (forthcoming), 'From the Levant to the City of London: Mercantile Credit in the Greek International Commercial Networks of the 18th and 19th centuries', paper at the Conference of the European Association for Banking History, 'Centres and Peripheries in Banking', Stockholm, 30 May–1 June 2002.

Cicanci, O. (1981), *Companiile Grecesti din Transilvania si comertul european in anii 1636– 1746*, Bucarest.

Cohen, A. (1971), 'Cultural Strategies in the Organization of Trading Diasporas', in C. Meillassoux (ed.), *The Development of Indigenous Trade and Markets in West Africa*, London: Oxford University Press.

Constas, D. and Platias, A.G. (eds) (1993), *Diasporas in World Perspective*, London: Macmillan.

Curtin, P. (1984), *Cross-cultural Trade in World History*, Cambridge: Cambridge University Press.

Dobbin, C. (1996), *Asian Entrepreneurial Minorities. Conjoint Communities in the Making of the World-Economy*, London: Curzon.

Enepekides, P.K. (1959), *Griechische Handelsgesellschaften und Kaufleute in Wien aus dem Jahre 1766 (ein Konskriptionbuch)*, Thessalonike: Institute for Balkan Studies, no. 27.

Godley, A. (2001), *Jewish Immigrant Entrepreneurship in New York and London 1880–1914: Enterprise and Culture*, Basingstoke: Palgrave.

Gurther, A. (1909), *Die Volkszahlungen Maria Theresias und Josef II, 1753–1790*, Innsbruck.

Harlaftis, G. (1996), *A History of Greek-owned Shipping, from 1830 to the Present Day*, London: Routledge.

Hassiotis, I.K. (1993), *A Survey of the History of Modern Greek Diaspora*, Thessaloniki: Vanias.

Hobsbawm, E. (2000 [1987]), *The Age of Empires 1875–1914*, Athens (Greek translation).

Hutchinson, J. and Smith, A. (1996), *Ethnicity*, Oxford: Oxford University Press.

Kasaba, R. (1988), *The Ottoman Empire and the World Economy: The Nineteenth Century*, Albany NY: State University of New York Press.

Katsiardi-Hering, O. (1986), *The Greek Community in Trieste, 1751–1830*, 2 vols, Athens: University of Athens, Department of Philosophy (in Greek).

—— (1995), 'Education in Diaspora: Toward a Greek Education or Toward a "therapy" of multilingualism', in *Neohellenic Education and Society*. Proceedings of an International Congress dedicated to the memory of K.Th. Dimaras, Athens: OMED (in Greek).

Kitromilides, P. (1999), 'Orthodox Culture and Collective Identity in the Ottoman Balkans during the Eighteenth Century', *Oriente Moderno*, 18(1): 131–45.

Konstantakopoulou, A. (1988), *Greek Language in the Balkans (1750–1850): The Quadrilingual Dictionary of Daniel Moshopolites*, Ioannina.

Kyriakopoulou-Kyriakou, A. (1978), *The Greek Community of Venice (1797–1866)*, Thessaloniki: Aristoteleio Panepistimio.

Laios, G. (1972), *Simon Sinas*, Athens: Academy of Athens (in Greek).

Nouzille, J. (1991), *Histoire de frontières: L'Autriche et l'Empire Ottoman*, Oxford and New York: Berg.

Papastathi-Tsourka, D. (1994), *The Greek Trade Company in Sibiou of Transylvania 1636–1848: Organization and Law*, Thessaloniki: Institute for Balkan Studies, no. 246.

Peyfouss, M.D. (1989), *Die Druckerei von Moschopolis 1731–1769: Buchdruck und Heiligenverehrung im Erzbistum Achrida, Wiener Archiv für Geschichte des Slawentums und Ostereuropas*, Vol. 13, Böhlau Verlag.

Psiroukis, N. (1975), *The Phenomenon of Neohellenic Diaspora*, Athens (in Greek).

Reid, A. (1997), 'Entrepreneurial Minorities, Nationalism and the State', in D. Chirot and A. Reid (eds), *Essential Outsiders: Chinese and Jews in the Modern Transformation of Southeast Asia and Central Europe*, Seattle: University of Washington Press.

Scott, J. (2000), *Social Network Analysis*, 2nd edn, London: Sage.

Stoianovich, T. (1992), 'The conquering Balkan Orthodox Merchant', in *Between East and West*, Vol. 2, *Economies and Societies: Traders, Towns and Households*, New Rochelle NY: A.D. Caratzas.

Tomadakis, N. (1953), *The Contribution of Greek Communities Abroad to the War of Independence*, (in Greek).

Wace A.J.B. and Thomson, M.S. (1914), *The Nomads of the Balkans*, London.

–18–

The Concept of 'Diaspora' in the Contemporary World
Stathis Gourgouris

The shortcomings of this chapter, particularly in this disciplinary context and in the company of such experts in the social sciences, should be rather obvious. Although I will speak wearing my hat of historian of national (and nationalist) culture, I acknowledge nonetheless that my general framework of understanding and addressing these issues will be drawn inevitably from the epistemological inventory of literary studies and my own disciplinary boundaries. On the other hand, it may perhaps be reassuring that the impetus and indeed departure point for the brief meditations that follow is the problematic usage of 'diaspora' precisely in, and by, the domain of literary studies. Thus, whatever may be said to condition this shortcoming will be subjected to critique.

To get on with the matter at hand: I find the contemporary proliferation of uses of the notion of diaspora exceedingly curious. In the last two decades, particularly in the broader terrain of the humanities in American universities, diaspora has attained the full-fledged status of a concept with a multiplicity of philosophical, psychological, linguistic and literary references. In literary studies especially, it has become by now entirely conventional (one might say, it has assumed the order of self-evidence) to speak in terms of 'diasporic language' – of the 'diaspora of meanings' over a supposedly unchartable textual terrain. Jacques Derrida's legendary treatise *La dissémination* (1968) is now over thirty years old and so deeply inscribed – one is tempted, in like spirit, to say diffused, disseminated – within the institutional language of literary studies that it has been laid aside, nearly forgotten, as faint tradition. Yet, this literal translation from the Greek – the transposition from diaspora to dissemination – is emblematic of a whole set of terms that seem intertwined with the meaning of diaspora and are themselves implicated in a general process of 'autonomous conceptualization': cosmopolitanism, migration, exile, displacement, homelessness, border identity, crossover culture, transnationalism, long-distance nationalism, nomadism, hybridity, and so on.

What do I mean by saying that diaspora has achieved an 'autonomous conceptualization'? In a most basic sense, I am referring to an act of disjoining the notion of diaspora from its various historical manifestations – from the *evidence* of diaspora (political, economic, sociological, psychological, cultural) in specific communities under specific historical conditions. Even though such historical instances may yield very productive results under comparison (which is precisely the work that concerns us here), so much that we may even begin to theorize certain elemental figures pertaining to diaspora communities as such, we would all agree, I believe, that the historical particularity can never be placed under erasure, as one would say in philosophy. And yet, this is precisely what happens when 'diaspora' becomes the key word to describe a conceptual pattern, a semantic condition.[1]

We have thus reached – in American universities at least – the phenomenon of an emerging (but nonetheless wholly underwritten institutionally) discipline of Diaspora Studies. This seems to me the most puzzling of all. How does one 'do' Diaspora Studies? What does it mean to do Diaspora Studies? Though often the personnel sought for such positions targets scholars of actual diasporic communities, fully versed in the social-historical details needed in order to pursue this object of study, the rubric enabling this whole edifice to stand institutionally is the autonomization of diaspora as a concept of general utility. At the limit, this seems to delineate and qualify a field of study (which entails no less than the assumption of an autonomous epistemological terrain), or an area of study (and here, the geographical basis of so-called 'area studies' has surely served as a model, even if inadvertently). It is, of course, absurd to pose the question: 'what is the area of diaspora studies?' The multiple but precise geographies of diasporic communities render such a quest inoperative.

I find it difficult to provide a concise explanation for this phenomenon. If one is to take seriously the residual power of cultural tendencies and trends, it is possible to attribute the newfangled fashion of alleged diasporic phenomena to an increasing preference for structures of decentring and dispersal, as the positivist hold of grand narratives, linear progression, binary logic or causal stability on the methodology of social and historical sciences has significantly weakened in the last two or three decades. Admittedly, we cannot ignore the significant shift in social-historical reality throughout the globe during this same period: the magnitude of mass migrations due to the rapid deterioration of safe political and economic conditions in many places in the world; the questioning and redrafting of national boundaries, often with acts of remarkable violence that tear the social fabric and create conditions of mass refugee populations; and the enormous changes in communication and transportation technologies that facilitate mobility and speed on an unprecedented scale, so that the *topos* of inhabitance itself comes to bear the mark of uncertainty. In other words, today's assessment of diasporic communities cannot be easily disentangled from the examination of globalized transnational social-political structures or the resurgence of fierce micronationalisms often within previously uncontested national boundaries. As a result, a basic conflation (indeed confusion) between migration and diaspora emerges, not merely within the scholarly ranks but also at the level of societal self-representation. Migrant communities seem to turn themselves into diasporic communities, perhaps in an attempt to invent for themselves a frame of reference different from the standard one that hearkens back to nineteenth-century immigration.

For instance – and I use an example that does not pertain to the specific focus of our work on this occasion but nonetheless illustrates the conceptual abuse I am describing – the Greek-American community has shifted its own self-identification from that of an immigrant culture that aspired toward national conformity in accord with the assimilationist (melting-pot) ideology of Americanism to that of a self-styled diaspora community whose distinct voice jostles for position in the newfangled multicultural marketplace. The consequence of this shift is greater attunement to both the symbolic existence and the real politics of motherland Greece, with actual links being forged so that the American-born community might act occasionally as foreign-policy lobby power for the ancestral country. Schematically perhaps, but not inaccurately, this particular characteristic may be considered as the forging of diasporic culture out of immigrant culture, whereby the national ancestral centre presides not as the departure point of dispersal across other national boundaries but as the retroactive symbolic centre whose claim can be cashed in for an improvement of social and cultural status within the land of immigration. This is a peculiar phenomenon, wholly commensurate to the times we live in, whereby the so-called 'post-modern' and 'post-colonial' reality has spawned a resurgence (albeit in mutated form) of nationalist passion.

In contrast to this forging of diaspora out of immigration, proper diasporic communities – at least in ethno-social terms – can only be those communities existing within specific national boundaries not as immigrant but as indigenous populations that do not possess national sovereignty of their own: the Kurdish and Palestinian cases are currently the most significant, given the profoundly complex geopolitics involved. On the other hand, one can hardly say that the cultural issue of the Armenian diaspora, for example, is resolved by the sheer inauguration of an Armenian nation after the break-up of the Soviet republics. Nor is the issue of Jewish diaspora resolved by virtue of the existence of the state of Israel, though here – both because of the enormous historical and geographical scale of the Jewish diaspora and the internal and highly problematic complexities of the various Jewish populations returning to claim a national position, often in order to buttress the nationalist claims of State power – the matter is singular and indeed pushes the categorization to the limit.

Ironically – and this is what really concerns us here – the real social and economic history of diaspora in the nineteenth century (and before) is rendered absent from this (re)invention of diaspora in the late twentieth going on to the twenty-first. This goes hand in hand with how the 'elevation' of diaspora into a methodological-epistemological concept worthy of institutional recognition seems to coincide either with the retreat of diasporic culture in the real world (its absorption by either transnational or micronationalist determinations) or with its diffusion into phenomena of mass migration. Any explanations here eschew the realm of self-evidence. One is tempted perhaps to speak of the shift in the 'nature' of capitalism – by all accounts, more of a shift in means than in nature – which is conceived, in the prevalent idiom of the day, as the shift from industrial capital and its reliance on labour to so-called finance capital and its reliance on information technology. You hear often these days from the gurus of financial markets the term 'techonomy' as a way of denoting the extreme dependence of today's economy on technology. (It's doubtful that the more accurate etymological dimension of this awkward 'Greekism' registers at all; 'techonomy' might mean literally the condition in which technology has become the law.) Yet, whatever this shift may signify, or however it may be determined, the foundational ways of capitalist relations have hardly been changed or overcome. And since, according to the premises of this conference, the very conditions of diaspora are implicated in the history of capitalism (including its long prehistory in mercantile relations, strictly speaking), to discover that 'diaspora' has become an autonomous concept devoid of its social-historical content at the very point when capitalism's entrepreneurial networks are operating with a breadth and speed of unequal scale is at the very least puzzling.

Perhaps I may be revealing a certain prejudice, but the incapacity of newly constituted 'Diaspora Studies' to take into account the long-term historical coincidence between diaspora communities and capitalism is due to the profoundly narrow understanding of 'societies of the East' (for lack of a more precise term) that characterizes the Anglo-American academic institution of our time. One of the first things inscribed in my memory as a young student of contemporary Greek history was that the benefactors of this tiny emergent nation in the mid-nineteenth century were all 'Greeks from abroad' – *heterochthonous* Greeks, as the term of the day had it – that is, people whose capital (not merely financial but also cultural) was always external to the national boundaries. That my earliest reading of Marx a few years later revealed to me that capital was constitutively external to national boundaries drew strength not just from the theory's powerful rhetoric but also from coming to confirm an already understood historical condition.

Yet, ironically, this sort of national-historical knowledge does not seem to have achieved an institutional existence in this odd new 'discipline'. The vast history of the 'societies of the East' – diasporic in an essential way, both socially and economically – does not seem to have found paradigmatic status in the context of a 'discipline' that would have had no meaning (indeed, no name) without this history. Likewise, I might add, the obsession with the notion of 'multiculturalism' that I encountered in American campuses in the 1980s – which, incidentally, fed even further the empty autonomization of the concept of diaspora – was utterly mystifying in its ignorance of the inimitable historical conditions of actual multi-culturalism in the southeastern Mediterranean that had gone on for millennia.

Such historical slippages become abundant, it seems, the more the terminology of social-historical conditions stretches out into greater and greater generalization and permeable all-inclusiveness. The current academic obsession in certain circles with globalization emulates the ahistorical conceptual abuse of the old arguments on multiculturalism. What does it mean to say that we live in the era of globalization? The globality of capitalism is at the very least basic to its constitution, though here too those who argue that globalization was in existence in the mercantile economy of the Italian Renaissance or the earliest instances of European colonial exploration (following, wittingly or not, the pattern of Immanuel Wallerstein's world-system theory) labour under the same degree of conceptual abuse, even if in the opposite direction. In both cases, historical differences are outmanoeuvred on the basis of economic formalism of one sort or another. The point is surely not whether capitalism is now, or has always been, global – because no doubt the very logic of capitalist markets is to seek to exceed boundaries – but whether the globality of capitalism achieves meaning according to its specific historical content, which is to say, according to the political dimensions that characterize it. The 'exploration' of the African continent and the slave trade from Africa to the Americas for the financial profit of European national states were surely instances of a 'global' economy. Yet, their political dimensions are hardly similar to those of American technological patents currently being manufactured by cheap Asian labour for the benefit of multinational corporations, which market products worldwide and are accountable for the validity or legality of their profit margins not to some national State tax structure but to the ruthless logic of the global stock exchange. It is the *political* economy of today's globalization that matters, not globalization itself as some sort of chimeric condition of capitalism.

Both the diasporic phenomenon as such and the history of the concept of diaspora cannot be evaluated outside an assessment of the historical particularities of capitalism as *political* economy. For example, the fact that the large diasporic populations in the fringes of Europe (Jews, Greeks, Armenians) distinguished themselves as entrepreneurial networks of the first order is entirely commensurate with the imperial framework within which (and because of which) they flourished socially and culturally, as well as economically. Their mobile 'family-centred' mode of mercantile enterprise was particularly successful against the grain of the colonialist economies of the industrial-capitalist powers, where private enterprise benefited consistently from its alliance with the administrative apparatus of the colonialist State. Diasporic entrepreneurial networks took advantage of the more open-ended administrative structure of their host State (the multi-ethnic and multicultural *laissez-faire* of, say, the Ottomans or the Hapsburgs), as well as the more than less politically-centralized apparatus of colonialist power with which they did business abroad. Broadly speaking, it is just this *co-incidence* between the residual 'feudal'-imperial framework of 'societies of the East' and the advancing colonialist framework of rapidly expanding industrial capitalism of 'societies of the West' that enables diasporic capitalism to flourish in eighteenth- and nineteenth-century Europe and its periphery.

Likewise, the shift in the significance of diaspora from a designation of a social phenomenon that had distinct economic parameters to a rather historically disembodied concept whose parameters are at most strictly cultural is due to the shift in political economy that characterizes capitalism in the latter half of the twentieth century, namely the conditions whereby both age-old imperial administrations and colonialist structures collapse dramatically in favour of the political triumph of the nation-form and the ensuing transnational ('globalized') labour, technology and commodity markets. One can see how, according to the political-economic terms of this shift, the prominence of diaspora as a designation of an entrepreneurial network gives way to a designation of mass migrant labour. Similarly, the social-cultural significance of diaspora, which once underlay the economic force of such communities beyond their state borders, now fades and is replaced by the discursive formation of so-called 'minority culture' and more recently 'identity politics'. It is a matter of elementary historical thinking that the very notion of minority culture is inconceivable in an imperial or even colonialist framework. Communities that identify themselves as minorities (social, ethnic, linguistic, religious or broadly cultural – it makes no difference) can only arise – that is, can only give themselves meaning – within a national, if not indeed nationalist, configuration. The concept of minority meant nothing to the Ottomans and to the communities subjected to their political and economic control. But it begins to take shape, even if not yet identified as such, precisely during the time of the general nationalization of society that takes place in the Empire's Balkan provinces during the mid- to late nineteenth century.[2] Only if the Bulgarians can be conceptualized as an ethnic minority population within the boundaries of the Ottoman Empire can they then graduate to full-fledged national status. On the other hand, precisely because the historically multi-ethnic and multicultural infrastructure in this region cannot be so easily eradicated, the Bulgarians – I am only taking this case as an example – must deal with the Turkish, Romanian or Gypsy minorities within their assumed national boundaries even a century past their national institution. In other words, both minority discourse and identity politics, as they are fashionably designated nowadays, emerge out of and obey the tenets of nationalist logic, oftentimes against the social-historical terms of the communities they represent.

But next to this extensive nationalization of society during the latter half of the twentieth century, which goes hand in hand with the transnationalization of capital, the significance of diaspora as a socio-economic category is rapidly eroded. On the socio-economic front, diaspora is replaced by discourses of migration and eventually by the more abstract and rather lazy designation of 'post-coloniality'. On the strictly semantic or more conceptual front (but what could this mean?), diaspora remains viable, even though its content becomes now more elusive than ever. Of course, one can understand how and why the concept of diaspora in the contemporary world comes to be occupied by references to communities of migrant labour, as this is after all the chief social and cultural element of transnational capitalism following the era of decolonization and Third World national independence movements. What is striking, however, is how often this designation slips into explicit articulations of the nationalist logic that generates it: diasporic communities now come to embody the symbolic cohesion of ancestral nationality, often even voluntarily assuming the agency of the nation abroad, in a bizarre (ultimately paradoxical) simultaneity of both confirming and exceeding national boundaries. This seems to be followed in scholarly considerations as well; diasporic communities have become nations themselves, even if of a different sort. Anthony Reid, for example, explicitly adopts as stalwartly common and modern Abner Cohen's definition of diaspora as 'a nation of socially interdependent, but spatially dispersed communities'[3] – showing directly that the spatial fluidity or social heterogeneity of the diasporic community does not seem able to stand on its own signification but needs the reliability of the nation-form.

The option to identify diasporas under the logical rubric of national communities ultimately compromises their idiomatic historical character: the fact that diasporic networks are not only comprehensible within the particularity of their social-historical conditions but that, even more, they are exemplary in harnessing the forces of their social-historical particularity to the utmost advantage of their reproductive capacities – which is to say, in effect, their actual survival. More than the allegedly nostalgic anchor to the presumed national home that might provide the security of self-reference, diasporas are fuelled by an idiomatic ethos, built into the very terms of their historical resilience.[4] The remarkably successful economic capacity of diasporic entrepreneurial networks during the height of industrial-colonialist capitalism, without necessarily subscribing or submitting to its institutional apparatus, might be explained according to such an ethos. From this standpoint, it is precisely the fact of this success, based largely on the evasion of a centralized or state-propelled relation to historical contingency, that gives diasporic communities both their extraordinary mobility and the articulate image of social-ethnic cohesion, not the other way around. To consider diasporic communities as traces of a national community, or even at best as non-ideological extensions of the nation-form, is to read this historical equation backwards. It is also, by extension, to misread the problematic conceptual significance of diaspora in the contemporary world, thus risking the possibility that the profoundly rich history of diasporic communities until the recent past is either fetishized as a once-upon-a-time glorious achievement or, conversely, occluded by a formalist or ahistorical conceptualization believed to encapsulate some sort of epistemological essence. In either case, diaspora falls right off history's field of vision.

Notes

1. Even the best intentions to take on this conflation of terms by resisting its tendency to efface historical particularity do not evade, in the last instance, the trap of autonomous conceptualization. See indicatively the important but maculate (because it supposes itself as all-inclusive) issue on *Diaspora and Immigration* (Mudimbe and Engel 1999).
2. The concept of 'nationalization of society' belongs to Etienne Balibar (1990: 329–61). I elaborate on this concept in my *Dream Nation: Enlightenment, Colonization, and the Institution of Modern Greece* (1996: 10–46).
3. Quoted in Anthony Reid (1997: 33–71). The same national designation of diaspora communities, even when acknowledging their problematic relation to the ancestral centre, characterizes Gabriel Sheffer's introductory essay to his *Modern Diasporas in International Politics* (1986: 1–15).
4. In a very intelligent article, Vassilis Lambropoulos (1997: 19–26) has argued in favour of this point as diaspora's 'ethos of dwelling'.

References

Balibar, E. (1990), 'The Nation Form: History and Ideology', *Fernand Braudel Center Review*, 12(3), Summer: 329–61.

Derrida, J. (1986), *La dissémination*, Paris: Seuil.

Gourgouris, S. (1996), *Dream Nation: Enlightenment, Colonization, and the Institution of Modern Greece*, Stanford: Stanford University Press.

Lambropoulos, V. (1997), 'Building Diasporas', *Crossings*, 1(2), Fall: 19–26.

Mudimbe, V.Y. and Engel, S. (eds) (1999), *Diaspora and Immigration*, special issue, *South Atlantic Quarterly*, 98(1–2), Winter/Spring.

Reid, A. (1997), 'Entrepreneurial Minorities, Nationalism, and the State', in D. Chirot and A. Reid (eds), Seattle: University of Washington Press.

Sheffer, G. (1986), 'Introduction', in *Modern Diasporas in International Politics*, New York: St Martin's.

Epilogue
In Memoriam

A Scottish Merchant in Batavia (1820–1840): Gillean Maclaine and Dutch Connections*[1]

Frank Broeze

'…if she were only Scottish I am convinced she is everything they could desire…'

(*AP* 3/5: Maclaine to his brother Angus Maclaine, Batavia, 16 June 1832)

Introduction

As Jaap Bruijn's oeuvre demonstrates in eloquent abundance, the real stuff of life is people. Maritime history – as all other types of history – is sterile without its human dimensions. Navies and East India Companies need to be commanded, crewed and administered. Overseas trade and merchant shipping requires entrepreneurs as well as clerks, captains and sailors. Each of the individuals involved in any of these and other pursuits had a public, professional, as well as a domestic, private identity. The motives for and objectives of public actions and ambitions can often be found in the latter realm, locked away in the personality, ideology, loyalty and family environment of the individual. Only rarely, however, does the surviving documentation allow for an understanding of private dimensions, drives and dynamics. This applies, in particular, to the thousands of European and American businessmen who after the opening of the British, Spanish, Dutch and other colonial systems and, for Asia more specifically, the abolition of the trading monopolies of East India Companies, helped forge the single world economic system. During the first half of the nineteenth century they swarmed out in an unprecedented entrepreneurial diaspora over all the inhabited continents, creating dynamic networks of trade, transport and investment.

The subject of this chapter is one of these businessmen, the Scot Gillean Maclaine.[2] As the historian of one of the most prominent Scottish companies operating in the Asian seas wrote (Blake 1956: 15): '…the release of India from John Company's long monopoly was a wonderful opportunity for precisely such people as the Scots, who, in their own opinion, were "uniquely industrious, shrewd and correct in all their financial dealings".'[3] Maclaine made his career as a merchant in Batavia, spanning the two decades from 1820 to 1840, during which time the Dutch metropolitan and colonial governments implemented a host of policies and measures designed to recapture the full economic advantages of colonial possession. The purpose of this brief sketch of Maclaine's career is to enable us to experience and understand the life of a merchant in Batavia from his particular vantage point and as a particular example of the dialectic coexistence of an ambitious Scottish businessman in diaspora and the rapidly changing Dutch colonial system.[4] As

will be seen, the interests of both were not necessarily mutually exclusive or contradictory. The second theme running through Maclaine's business life is the relationship with his Scottish principals in the City of London who sent him out to the East as one of their employees. But his aim was not to remain an agent, acting for and on account of others. He craved both independence and what he termed 'independency', the accumulation of wealth sufficient to be able to retire from business into a comfortable and respectable lifestyle. And here his Scottish identity was of crucial importance. He imagined retirement always in terms of returning home to Scotland and, more specifically, to the western parts of Argyll from which he hailed, Ardtornish, Ardnamurchan, and the islands of Mull, Iona and Staffa. Maclaine's Scottish networks had as much to do with his relatives and the places of his birth and youth as with his business interests. From the very moment he left Britain, Maclaine lived and worked for his successful repatriation. A second imagined aspect of retirement was the conclusion of marriage with a suitable Scotswoman. And here is the final and most intriguing dialectic of Maclaine's life, in which dream and reality were sweetly juxtaposed, as he fell in love with a Dutch girl and, while committed to marrying her, begged for the approval of his fiercely Scottish relatives.

The following story will, therefore, be one in which the Scottish and the Dutch will be entwined on three levels. First, there is the conjunction of the public history of British trade and Dutch reaction on Java. Second, there is Maclaine's private objective, to make his fortune with the Dutch in order to retire to Scotland. And, third, there is his most private of dreams, which could not be bought with money, to make his bride love Scotland and his family as much as he did himself. Only when he retired under those circumstances, could he call his life fulfilled. Thus, Maclaine's career on Java would be like a double helix, business and private ambition interlocked in a never-ending embrace.[5]

I

Gillean Maclaine was born in 1798 as the eldest son of Allan Maclaine, of Ardtornish (county Argyll in Scotland) and his wife Marjorie, née Gregorson. His father died when he was still young and his uncle, the wealthy John Gregorson, who soon afterward bought Ardtornish Castle, became guardian of Gillean and his younger brother, Angus (born 1800). Gillean benefited from the excellent Scottish education system and, as so many of his countrymen, after graduation from college struck out to make his fortune in commerce.[6] Through the mediation of his uncle, in late 1816 he got a job in the counting house of Messrs MacLachlan & Co. of London, which was rapidly assuming primacy of the recently-opened private trade east of the Cape of Good Hope with India, Southeast Asia and Australia. MacLachlan's were among the first Scottish firms drawn to the great metropolis, a phenomenon that increased in intensity as the nineteenth century wore on. They ran an agency house, as were so many at the time, involving the financing and shipment of orders overseas, arranging freight and insurance, and performing all the ancillary tasks that were necessary to keep the wheels of imperial trade and shipping turning. Maclaine applied himself with great vigour to his new position, 'the more actively I am employed, the greater pleasure it yields me' (*AP* 1/2: Maclaine to Angus, London, 12 March 1817). He kept cash books, copied correspondence, checked the accounts, and at night studied 'my favourite science, arithmetics [*sic*]' (*AP* 2/3: Maclaine to Angus, London, 28 July 1917). He quickly mastered the routine business of the counting house and learned to write business letters in French (*AP* 1/1: Maclaine to Angus, London, 21 November 1817).

Maclaine was a trusted force at MacLachlan's in 1819 when the firm was embarrassed by the failure of its Indian connections to make timely shipments of produce, the proceeds of which were to supply the firm with the necessary funds to meet its commitments. The episode would teach Maclaine a lesson for life. 'Not a ship has yet come in', he lamented as the financial crisis deepened and many firms waited in vain for remittances and were forced to close their doors (*AP* 4/4: Maclaine to Gregorson, London, 24 April 1819). As it happened, MacLachlan's had sufficient funds to weather the crisis, but for the time being they reduced their exports to India. And, in a strategic shift of interest that was to determine the further course of Maclaine's life, they decided to enter the trade with the Dutch East Indies. In late 1819 they began preparing an expedition to Batavia to which, in recognition of his accomplishments, they appointed Maclaine as supercargo to accompany and dispose of the cargo. At the same time they made arrangements for the expansion of their entrepreneurial network in the East by asking their Calcutta relations to establish an agency in Batavia. Should that house be established when Maclaine arrived, his task was to deliver the cargo and proceed to Calcutta. Although no firm promises were made, Maclaine could expect to become a partner in the firm after his return from India; in the meantime he would draw a handsome salary (*AP* 4/4: Maclaine to Gregorson, London, 5 January 1820). If, however, no agency was in place, Maclaine was to stay in Batavia. He would make arrangements with a local agency house to represent MacLachlan's business and then return directly to London, again with the prospects of joining the firm in due course as a partner.

Maclaine seems to have had some reservations about leaving Britain, but, as he wrote his brother, if he did not take this opportunity, 'I fear my chance of securing an independency would not be so good' (*AP* 2/3: Maclaine to Angus, London, 28 January 1820). This desire to accumulate enough wealth to become financially independent was indubitably the strongest motive driving Maclaine to go into business. That it was not mere wealth he craved can be understood from his response to his brother Angus when the latter chose a career in the Church. 'As a clergyman you could make sure of an independence in this world, have abundance of leisure for literary pursuits, and certainly run a fairer chance of living an easy life than if engaged in any other profession' (*AP* 2/3: Maclaine to Angus, London, 8 January 1819).[7]

Maclaine sailed on 17 April 1820 from London on the ship *Mary Ann*, chartered by MacLachlan & Co. and largely loaded with goods on their account. A fortunate passage brought him in around one hundred days to Batavia (*Bataviasche Courant*, 5 August 1820). On landing, he found no agency to handle the firm's business. Maclaine was now in charge of disposing of the cargo and arranging for remittances to be made. Although there is no specific documentation that can inform us about his operations, it is evident that he arrived at a crucial time in the development of free trade in Batavia and, more generally, in the Dutch East Indies. Since the conquest of Java by Raffles in 1810, a number of British merchants and firms had established themselves there and its foreign commerce had very much fallen into their hands and those of American traders. In 1819, of all 171 European and American ships calling at Java, no fewer than 62 were British, 50 American and only 43 Dutch, with many of the latter hailing from Belgian ports (Mansvelt 1924, I:41). Only a handful of Dutch agency houses existed against a fast growing number of English, Scottish and German firms. By 1823, fifteen out of the twenty-three firms in Batavia were British (*Regeeringsalmanak voor Nederlandsch-Indië* 1823). Several of these dated from the British occupation, such as Miln Haswell & Co., R. Thornton and Macquoid Davidson & Co., and others had joined the rush after 1815. Among these was Maclaine, who in 1822 with his close friend Edward Watson established his own firm, Maclaine & Co, which five years later was restyled as Maclaine Watson & Co. (Campbell 1915, 1: 648).

Evidently, by staying in Batavia, Maclaine had grasped a golden opportunity to share in what was a rapidly growing market – or, rather, two markets. On the one hand, there were the imports of British manufactured goods, above all cheap textiles, that rapidly captured British India and the East Indies (*Regeeringsalmanak* 1828; Nusteling 1992: 19). In this manner the British were able to compete profitably with Americans who mainly travelled to Asia with silver dollars bought at home or in South America and with the struggling Dutch merchants. The latter could match neither the products of Britain's Industrial Revolution nor the bullion amassed by the Yankees through Atlantic networks or trans-pacific expeditions. Their imports were of far lesser value than their purchases of colonial produce, and for finance they often had to resort to the expensive practice of drawing bills of exchange.[8] The prices for Javanese exports, and in particular coffee, were driven up to such levels that severe losses were suffered and many merchant-shipowners reduced or stopped their operations. By 1823 only nine ships left Amsterdam for the East Indies, against twenty in 1820 and seventeen in 1816.[9] It is, of course, one of the best-known stories of Dutch economic history that the losses suffered by these merchants and the prospect of the total collapse of Dutch trade with the East Indies were the immediate cause of the foundation, in 1824, of the *Nederlandsche Handel-Maatschappij* which for many decades was to remain the dominant force in the trade between the East Indies and the Netherlands.[10]

Dutch merchants suffered their losses, above all, in the second market they were facing – the export of colonial produce, mainly coffee, to Europe. As they were unable to generate the profits of their foreign competitors in the East Indies, they found that coffee prices at auction or private sale in Java were much higher than they could afford. Millions were lost in the coffee trade and the foreign share of colonial imports in Dutch ports rose to 40 per cent. The British were capturing the Dutch coffee market as Americans had taken over the tea trade (Broeze 1979a: 103–11). In addition, they had begun to make inroads into the inter-insular trade from Singapore. This is not the place to provide an outline of all the measures taken in The Hague and Batavia to recapture the East Indies trade and boost the declining economies of the major port cities in the Netherlands. What must be emphasized here is that what were severe problems for the Dutch were brilliant chances for ambitious young Scotsmen like Maclaine.

Instead of returning to London, Maclaine stayed in Batavia, but rather than engaging in commercial pursuits, he first went into the plantation business. Most probably he could do so with money advanced by his London principals, MacLachlan's. The exact nature of their financial relationship cannot be fully understood because of the lack of documentation, but considerable sums must have been put at his disposal. As Maclaine was able to move quickly, it is likely that he could use at least part of the proceeds of the *Mary Ann*'s cargo. In 1820 Maclaine, in partnership with two other British merchants, leased an estate in the *Vorstenlanden*; soon afterward he became part-owner of an estate in Buitenzorg and leased a much bigger one at Malambong, upland from Samarang (Campbell 1915, 1: 654–6). Although he found country society not much to his liking, as his Dutch neighbours were either dissipate or ignorant, he was thoroughly satisfied with his new career, even if a position in Bengal might have been more lucrative (*AP* 1/2: Maclaine to Gregorson, Malambong near Samarang, 19 September 1821). In 1822 Maclaine left Malambong, leaving its management to one of his partners, and with Edward Watson established his own firm, Maclaine & Co., in Batavia. He took up the import-export business, in financial association with his principals, MacLachlan's of London. These commercial activities soon took him to Singapore where J.A. Maxwell was established as his regular agent (Campbell 1915, 1: 622). While the British and Dutch governments had delineated their territories and spheres of influence in the 1824 *Sumatra tractaat*, merchants bothered little about political boundaries. Maclaine also began acting as an agent for other coffee planters, including the prominent Dézentjé family (Campbell 1915, 1: 622). He prospered and through his many and diverse business connections established his standing in the British merchant community in Batavia and with Dutch businessmen and authorities.[11] He was 'merchant and planter, householder and landed proprietor', and applied for and gained local citizenship (*NA*: Koloniën 827, Exh. 11 February 1832, N32, La. 32 Spoed). Thus, he perfectly fitted the image of the 'Gentleman Capitalist' recently depicted by Anthony Webster (1998). He probably was already beginning to think of returning home to Argyll in early 1826 when he wrote letters of introduction for Thomas Miln, 'the senior partner of one of our most respected houses here', who after a career of almost fifteen years in Batavia repatriated with 'a very independent fortune' (*AP* 2/3: Maclaine to Gregorson, Batavia, 5 February 1826; *AP* 1/2: Maclaine to Angus, Batavia, 6 February 1826).

Unfortunately, larger events intervened which left Maclaine for several years in extremely uncomfortable circumstances. First, the Sultan of Jogyakarta, Dipanegara, rose in rebellion against the Dutch regime on Java, and later in 1825 the great financial crisis, which started with the collapse of a number of South American government loans, hit the East Indies trade.[12] The Java War, mainly caused by the rapid expansion of coffee and sugar cultivation in the *Vorstenlanden* and the resulting social and cultural dislocations to indigenous society (Carey 1976: 52–78; Lubis 1987: 138–40), led to the destruction of many estates and heavy physical losses to Maclaine's own plantations – some half a million coffee shrubs were ravaged at Malambong alone. At the same time, MacLachlan's insisted on the restructuring of Maclaine's affairs and the remittance of considerable sums to London. Two of MacLachlan's partners became part-owners in the plantations as the Batavia government decided that Maclaine and others, instead of compensation in cash, would receive leases under a new system (Campbell 1915 I. 654–6; *NA*: Collectie Schneiter, report 20 May 1825, bijlagen D and L; *NA*: Koloniën 3098, land leases 1826–9). Maclaine, according to his own calculation, now had some ƒ240,000 sunk in his two plantations (the third had earlier been taken over by Dézentjé), and needed all his resources to keep his commercial operations going (*NA*: Collectie Van Hogendorp, Aanwinsten 1913 no. 190, Maclaine to Hogendorp, Batavia, 12 January 1828). He was faced with 'extremely severe' losses which, at least for the time being, had 'annihilate[d]' his prospects of joining his relatives in Scotland (*AP* 1/2: Maclaine to Angus, Batavia, 25 October 1827).

Already in 1826, before the financial crisis struck, he had bitterly complained about his treatment at the hands of MacLachlan & Co. and he now vowed to establish himself in complete entrepreneurial independence from London. But, while he did not succeed in that objective until 1832, the reputation he had built up helped him to lay the foundations of his future fortune. In early 1827 Maclaine was approached by John Palmer, one of the most prominent businessmen in British India, to become his Batavia agent. Head of the largest agency house in Calcutta and known as the 'prince of merchants', Palmer had many interests between India and Sydney, including shares in a large estate in western Java (*Palmer Papers*: English Letters, Palmer to Prinsep, 21 January 1827).[13] With Palmer's introduction came also the highly profitable agency of the Calcutta Insurance Company that for some years, with another British Indian company, dominated the Batavia market (Mansvelt 1924: I. 193). Palmer's support gave Maclaine the leverage to wind up his old firm and, again with Edward Watson, to establish Maclaine Watson & Co. (*Bataviasche Courant*, 21 April 1827). This reorganization enabled the partners to strike out independently, while Maclaine resolved his differences with MacLachlan's and their partners. He again visited Malambong and also travelled to Singapore, returning via Riau and Muntok (*Palmer Papers*: English Letters, c. 109, p. 188, Palmer to Watson, 13 December 1828; *Bataviasche Courant* 6 November and 11 December 1827). He observed the failure of Riau as a free port and the 'very substantial increase in the trade of Singapore' (*NA*: Collectie Van Hogendorp, Maclaine to Hogendorp, Batavia, 10 November 1827; Campbell 1915: I.622). In due course, the growing traffic between Batavia and Singapore was to induce Maclaine to invest in a small fleet of fast sailing ships. But, before he reached that point, he first made a return trip to Europe to sever his links with MacLachlan's and to place his connection with Britain on a new basis.

II

In February 1830 Maclaine departed from Batavia on the *North Briton*, bound for the Netherlands (*Javasche Courant*, 23 February 1830).[14] From there he travelled first to London and then to Scotland to visit his relatives. In England, his experiences had, at first, been less than fortunate.

MacLachlan's and, in particular, their partner, D. MacIntyre, 'fleeced' Maclaine of an unsubstantiated but 'enormous' sum. But that price, though high, he felt had been worth paying: 'As a house of business, we are ... now perfectly independent of support in a pecuniary way either from London or Bengal. Our own capital will I trust now carry us on.' (*AP* 3/5: Maclaine to Angus, Batavia, 16 June 1832) Equally importantly, while in London Maclaine had made new business connections (*AP* 1/2: Maclaine to his mother, London, 6 January 1832). One of these concerned

Finlay Hodgson & Co., the London branch of the great Glasgow house of James Finlay & Co. With Finlay's and a number of smaller firms Maclaine re-established his connection between Britain and Batavia. He was to act as commission agent for the exports of the London firms and, in return, to consign to them both the produce bought as his remittances and his own consignments. The Finlay connection extended to Calcutta and Canton, where they also possessed branch firms, both styled Gladstone Finlay & Co. Maclaine's other major new connection was John Deans, the senior partner of the long-standing Batavia agency house of Deans Scott & Co. (*AP* 3/5: Maclaine to his mother, Glasgow, 21 November 1831). To Maclaine's happy surprise, Deans put £15,000 at the disposal of Maclaine Watson & Co., to be used entirely at Maclaine's discretion. As can be imagined, Maclaine was elated with these signs of confidence. For a brief moment he regretted having made a commitment to the assignees of MacLachlan's to return to Batavia. In his view, there were so many business opportunities in London that he might do better to stay there and leave Watson in charge at Batavia.

Maclaine's trip turned out to be successful in other respects as well. In March 1831 he was summoned to appear as a witness before a Select Committee of the House of Lords which investigated the affairs of the East India Company to provide evidence of the land-lease system in the Dutch East Indies (Great Britain *Parliamentary Papers* 1831: 320, vol 221, qq. 1566–1840). Afterward he set out on a trip to Holland and Germany, during which he visited several of his Dutch colonial friends, including Louis d'Anethan and G.K. van Hogendorp, and was received by the British Ambassador, Sir Charles Bagot. Evidently, his financial troubles had not harmed his social standing; Maclaine had well and truly arrived in high society. His experiences in Holland confirmed the close relationship between political authorities and businessmen which he had already observed at Batavia.

Maclaine had always enjoyed the cityscape and ambience of Batavia and he now took great pleasure in travelling as a tourist through the country from which its inspiration originated. Although he did not waver in his loyalty to Scotland as his future home, he was very much taken with Holland.

Rotterdam '…is really an exceedingly pretty town and its convenience for commerce remarkable. The ships unload in front of the merchants' houses so close that the yards almost touch the windows. The canals running (by the bye, they don't run very fast) in the middle of the streets and long avenues of trees, style of architecture &c put me quite in mind of Batavia which is in every respect a complete imitation of a Dutch town.' (*AP* 4/6: Maclaine to Gregorson, Frankfurt am Main, 9 May 1831)

Haarlem was 'really worth going to', and then came Amsterdam. Maclaine saw Rembrandt's *Nachtwacht* and some other of the 'most famous paintings of Europe' (*AP* 4/6: Maclaine to Gregorson, Frankfurt am Main, 9 May 1831). The city itself was '... most curious and has a much more foreign look than Rotterdam. The streets are magnificent, and the buildings along the quays superior to anything I have seen in a seaport town. The very Wapping of Amsterdam is equal to the first rate streets in the City of London in point of appearance and cleanliness' (*AP* 4/6: Maclaine to Gregorson, Frankfurt am Main, 9 May 1831).

In early 1832 Maclaine could finally depart for Batavia. He travelled via Rotterdam where he had booked passage on the *Anthony*, 'an uncommonly fine ship' belonging to the local merchant prince Van Hoboken (*AP* 1/2: Maclaine to his mother, Rotterdam, 9 and 14 February 1832).[15] Captain Bruhn seemed 'good natured and I understand is a very experienced sailor having made nine voyages in the Java trade'. Maclaine spent a last few pleasant days with friends in Rotterdam and The Hague. The *Anthony* sailed on 20 February and made an excellent passage of ninety-eight days from Hellevoetsluis. Maclaine was much impressed by Captain Bruhn, his officers and crew who worked together in perfect harmony and without swearing.[16] He also thought 'the Rotterdam Eastindiamen far superior to the general run of our Free Traders' (*AP* 1/2: Maclaine to Angus, off Cape St Nicholas near Batavia, 30 May 1832).[17] The social life on board was pleasant, with a total of ten passengers, including Maclaine and the twenty-year-old Arthur Fraser who was to join Maclaine Watson & Co. in Batavia. Fraser and a young navy Lieutenant earned themselves sneering comments from Maclaine for falling in love with the two young ladies on board. They had only just recovered from their infatuation when Maclaine, somewhat to his own surprise, himself fell prey to the same emotion. The subject of his feelings was the eighteen-year-old Katherine van Beusechem who was travelling with her parents and a younger brother. Her father, Nicolaas Philippus van Beusechem, was returning to the Indies to take up the position of acting member of the Batavia Orphan Chamber (*NA*: Koloniën, stamboeken O.I. ambtenaren, deel E, f.25). More important than this relatively modest position was the fact that his brother, Jan Michiel van Beusechem, was a wealthy and successful Batavia bureaucrat whose career culminated in 1832 when he was appointed President of the Court of Justice (Christiaans 1992: vol. 5). He moved in the circles of the Governor-General, thus conveying on all his relatives the stamp of social respectability.

Maclaine's fuse may have burned slowly, but the result was all the more spectacular as it was to cause another sea change in his life. For some time he tried to control his feelings, believing that it was 'right, before getting dangerously wounded, ... to write down coolly all the *Pros* and *Cons* for & against my encouraging this growing attachment'. Maclaine drew up the balance sheet of his emotional future in a remarkable memorandum, dated 'Ship *Anthony*, off the Cape of Good Hope, 30 April 1832'. He listed no fewer than six '*Cons*' and eight '*Pros*' (*AP* 2/2; for the full text of this memorandum see Appendix). The latter list sang the praises of 'Miss V. Beusechem' in all possible variations on her looks and accomplishments. It culminated in the highest praise imaginable from a born and bred Scotsman: 'I esteem the Dutch more than any other people after my own countrymen [and] I consider a Dutch girl less a foreigner than an English girl.' Despite the probable objections of his mother and uncle, which 'weigh more than all others at present', Maclaine acknowledged the '*Pros*' had clearly won the day.

Two weeks after his return to Batavia Maclaine wrote a long letter to his brother Angus. Talking business first, he rejoiced in the prosperous state in which he had found his firm, thanks to the hard work of Watson (*AP* 3/5: Maclaine to Angus, Batavia, 16 June 1832). Having put Angus in a good mood, he then warned him to prepare himself for 'a piece of intelligence which I am sure will surprise you: I am to be married in August to one of my fellow passengers in the *Anthony*!' Followed another paean on Katherine's sweetness and her many other qualities. Anxious about the impression this news would make on his mother and guardian and hoping to reconcile them to his choice, Maclaine stressed, 'none of my relatives need be ashamed of her, for if she were only Scottish I am convinced she is everything they could desire'. Maclaine was also at pains to demonstrate the high social status of Katherine's family and especially her uncle, 'a man of the highest character here and the bosom friend of our Governor'. And, though Katherine's father had only modest means, the uncle, a man of 'considerable property', had no children and might, Maclaine hoped, make his relatives his heirs. His appeal to Angus for his approval and that of his mother and uncle did not stop here. In an extraordinary display of filial loyalty, Maclaine enclosed the memorandum he had written at sea to sort out his own feelings. A month later he wrote directly to his mother, and a week before the wedding followed the first letter from Katherine, in French (*AP* 3/5: Maclaine to his mother, Batavia, 12 July 1832; *AP* 3/5: van Beusechem to her mother-in-law, Batavia, 15 August 1832).[18]

As it turned out, Maclaine was more than comforted by the reactions from home. All fully approved of his choice and a regular correspondence developed between his mother and Katherine, who was quick to learn English. Maclaine, who had never liked the wild bachelor's parties that characterized much of mercantile and colonial society, took very much to his new circumstances. All signs point to a married life filled with love and happiness. Although explicitly materialistic, Maclaine and Katherine had not lost 'God and Church ... at sea',[19] alternatively attending Scottish and Dutch Reformed religious services. Both he and Katherine enjoyed good health and the only sadness in their life was the early death of their first-born child, Margery. A second daughter, Sarah, and a son, Gillean, survived infancy. Over the years Katherine's affection for Gillean's family and Scotland grew, and Maclaine could confidently look forward to being able to realize his dream of a happy retirement with his family near his relatives in Scotland (*AP* 3/5: Maclaine to his mother, Batavia, 24 August 1835).

The financial foundation for that retirement had to be created first, but Maclaine viewed his business prospects with optimism. Watson had restructured the firm's affairs and Maclaine found them in 'a prosperous state' (*Palmer Papers*: English Letters, c.122, p.9, Palmer to Maclaine, 2 August 1832). Most importantly, felt Maclaine, they were now 'perfectly independent of support in a pecuniary way either from London or Bengal... Our own capital will I trust now carry us on' (*AP* 3/5: Maclaine to Angus, Batavia, 16 June 1832). He also discovered he possessed a vigorous new attitude to his work: 'I take now a pleasure in business that I never before experienced when fettered by associates at home, and have a confidence, I hope a humble confidence, in my own exertions...' (*AP* 2/3: Maclaine to Angus, Batavia, 25 December 1832). With business rolling along nicely, in early 1833 Watson could travel to Europe and visit Maclaine's relatives in Argyll. He returned in August 1835 with a 'nice, blooming wife' – 'lucky fellow', he could expect her to inherit some £12,000 to 15,000 (*AP* 3/5: Maclaine to his mother, Batavia, 24 August 1835). Now it had been Maclaine's turn to work very hard during Watson's two years absence. But the firm had progressed so well that Watson claimed that, had he been aware of its financial state, he would not have sailed again.

Maclaine had indeed been highly successful but not, as he had expected on his return in 1832, in the agency business with Britain. Instead, he had been forced to radically shift the firm into new fields. The main reason for his strategic reorientation was the sudden and almost total loss of consignments from Finlay & Co., who 'now receive precious more than they give', and other 'manufacturing friends' in Britain (*AP* 3/5: Maclaine to his mother, Batavia, 28 December 1833). In consequence, Maclaine had been forced 'to make business for ourselves', which caused him both more anxiety and more hard work than ever before. No evidence is available to document the reasons for Finlay's decision, but they probably lay primarily in Bengal and the Calcutta trade, which during the early 1830s were hit by a severe crisis (Tripathi 1979: ch. 5).[20] They may also have been influenced by the severe short-term disruption of the trade caused by the political crisis in the relationship between Britain and the Netherlands over the Belgian question and/or he may have doubted the prospects for British exports to the Dutch East Indies. The Hague and Batavia worked hard to recapture the trade in coffee and other colonial produce and to conquer the markets of the East Indies for Dutch nationals. Great changes did occur in the Java trade during these years, resulting from the rapid expansion of the *Nederlandsche Handel-Maatschappij*, the introduction of the *cultuurstelsel*, discriminatory import duties on Java, the prohibition of foreigners becoming citizens or permanent residents on Java, and the secret contracts with Dutch manufacturers. But, although the Dutch cotton industry gained a powerful boost, British merchants were not entirely eliminated. They retained a sizeable, though relatively declining, share in the importation of textiles from Europe. While the value of Dutch textile imports rose from f1.3 million in 1831 to 3.2 million in

1836 and 8.8 million in 1840, the comparable figures for Britain were ƒ1.2 million, 2.6 million and 2.8 million, respectively (Mansvelt 1924: I.333).

Whatever the reasons for the sharp decline in his consignments from Finlay's, Maclaine moved quickly to shift his resources into the 'country trade', a field that stretched from India through Southeast Asia and the East Indies to the China coast.[21] The firm's business rapidly increased in volume and complexity. In a few years it developed into a classic multi-functional firm conducting merchant-banking operations, general commission and shipping-agency work, and representing banking and insurance interests. In addition to acting for planters such as Dézentjé, Maclaine rapidly built up a network of new connections, especially on the Javanese coast and with Singapore. (There is no evidence that he used Singapore to try to establish contact with Belgian industrialists in order to benefit from their exclusion from the Dutch East Indies.)[22] Batavia benefited from the opening of the trade between China and Britain to private traders, for example by providing rice and other cargoes from Java to Canton for British ships arriving from Australian ports. Already in 1834 Maclaine bought several cargoes for such China-bound vessels and he was the agent for the famous *Earl of Balcarres*, the largest Eastindiaman of the time (*AP* 1/2: Maclaine to his mother, 29 April–1 May 1834 and 24 August 1835). Indicative of his own high standing and the close social nexus between government and business in Batavia, he introduced the latter's Captain Hine to the Governor-General. Besides his earlier partnership, with James McNeill at Samarang (styled McNeill & Co.), he established a second subsidiary at Surabaya, where the young Arthur Fraser became the founder of Fraser, Eaton & Co. (*AP* 3/5: Maclaine to his mother, Batavia, 24 August 1835). It is a moot question whether Maclaine might have been selected to be the first British Consular Agent in the Dutch East Indies. When the British government sounded out The Hague, the Dutch government in 1836 confirmed its earlier position to exclude foreign agents from its colonial possessions (*ARA*: Staatssecretarie 5799, 8 December 1836, La. C43 Geheim).

An important new field for the firm became shipowning. As the intra-colonial trade was reserved for vessels registered in the Dutch East Indies an extensive and high-quality shipbuilding industry had developed on Java (Earl 1837: 24; Phipps 1840: 184–7; Raffles 1817, 1: 183–5). Between November 1833 and January 1834 Maclaine Watson & Co., in partnership with their Singapore firm, bought two newly built schooners, 'very beautiful vessels', especially for the trade between Batavia and Singapore (*AP* 1/2: Maclaine to his mother, Batavia, 2 November 1833 and Pondok Pinang, 28 December 1833–14 January 1834; Maclaine to Gregorson, Batavia, 6 April 1835). The *Catharina Cornelia* (the baptismal names of his wife) and *Amelia* measured 60 and 82 lasts, about 140 and 190 tons English measurement, and were perfectly suited for the trade. They were armed with eight guns and carried an indigenous crew of twenty. During the next few years

Maclaine expanded his shipping interests further, occasionally also buying and selling a vessel on speculation.[23] Much of the profits of the 'very fortunate' year 1835 (*AP* 3/5: Maclaine to his mother, Batavia, 12 February 1836) were ploughed back into shipping and by 1836 his fleet totalled 389 last. It counted one brig of 130 last and four schooners, ranging between 50 and 82 lasts. Maclaine Watson & Co.'s shipping interests were not as large as those built up by other British firms such as Miln Haswell & Co. (four vessels, 459 last) and Douglas, Mackenzie & Co. (six vessels, 535 last), or the NHM's connection Tissot, Lagnier & Co. (eight vessels, 760 last), but they reflected the boom in Java-based shipping of the mid-1830s.[24]

In late 1836 Maclaine branched out into the Australian trade which, from its very beginning in the late 1780s had been closely linked to China, Batavia and India (Broeze 1998: 26–36, 79–85; Tweedie 1994: chs 1 and 3). As the Australian colonies entered a sharp boom period under the combined effects of ample supplies of cheap land (from which the Aborigines were dispossessed without any compensation), heavy investment and renewed migration, he saw good chances for Javanese exports. He sent his brig *Courier*, under the command of one of his 'most experienced country captains', Captain J.C. Ross,[25] to Sydney and accepted the Batavia agency of the Bank of Australasia (Nicholson 1977: 168; *AP* 2/3 Maclaine to Angus, Pondok Pinang, 29 December 1837). After the successful return of the first expedition, with Ross as part-owner, he bought a larger vessel for the trade (*AP* 1/2: Maclaine to Angus, Batavia, 18 August 1838). The Java-built fully rigged three-master *Justina*, was a 'superior' ship, 'built upon the improved principle laid down by Sir William Symonds, of no hollow lines' (*Sydney Herald*, 17 May 1838). In February 1838 Ross made his second voyage to Sydney, this time via Adelaide (Nicholson 1977: 189). A third expedition to Sydney departed in July 1838. One of Maclaine's friends, Loudon, travelled on the ship with liberty to call at any of the new settlements in South Australia to investigate their conditions and invest up to £2,000 each in land, should prospects appear to be favourable. Although Ross this time bypassed Adelaide (Nicholson 1977: 197), he and Loudon returned full of enthusiasm about the prospects of the new colony and Maclaine was determined to share in the boom. This time, moreover, he had an even greater incentive to deepen his interest in Australia: his brother Angus had decided to leave the Church and seek his future as a sheep farmer in Australia. There was deep irony as well as potential tragedy in Angus' disenchantment with home: just as Gillean was finalizing his plans to retire to Scotland, he would leave the Old World! It was uncertain whether they would ever meet again, either away from home or in Scotland, although Gillean hoped Angus would follow him after a few years, 'for dear old Scotland after all must be our home' (*AP* 1/2: Maclaine to Angus, Schoonered near Batavia, 17 May 1839). Once Maclaine knew of Angus' intentions, he did not lose time. In December 1838 the *Justina* was sent out on its third Australian voyage, to Adelaide.[26] Ross arranged the purchase of a block measuring 800 acres (ca 112 ha), some 30 km distant from Adelaide, and leased another 12,000 acres for pasturage. Maclaine also made £5,000 available to his brother for use on joint account and moved to appoint an agent in Adelaide. Angus arrived at his destination in June 1840, his first impression was that he liked the colony's prospects and found the climate 'delightful' (*AP* 1/1: Angus Maclaine to Gregorson, Adelaide, 17 June 1840).

While Gillean thus prepared the way for his brother, he was also making the arrangements for his repatriation with Katherine and the children. Already in early 1835 he had contemplated retiring with 'a moderate fortune' (*AP* 1/2: Maclaine to Angus, Batavia, 15 February 1835), but business had been so good that he had aimed at a higher sum for his 'independency'. In addition, Watson was to return permanently to Scotland and Maclaine needed more time in order to arrange his firm's succession (*AP* 1/2: Maclaine to his mother, Batavia, 1 December 1836). By late 1837 he decided on the arrangements, the timing of which then also helped determine when he himself could repatriate. On the return from Scotland of his trusted partner and 'worthy friend' at Samarang (*AP* 3/5: Katherine Maclaine to her mother-in-law, Batavia, 2 February 1837), James MacNeill, Maclaine intended to hand over the firm to his 'hard working and faithful assistant' in Batavia, J.L. Bonhote, as 'chief' and MacNeill as junior partner (*AP* 3/5: Maclaine to his mother, 12 February 1836). These two were ideally suited together, Maclaine felt, as Bonhote was 'perhaps the most thoroughbred man of business in the colony' and MacNeill possessed the '*suaviter in modo*' (*AP* 2/3: Maclaine to Angus, Pondok Pinang, 29 December 1837). Maclaine anticipated being able to leave by late 1838 or early 1839.

Unfortunately, Maclaine was delayed by more than a year as MacNeill spent much longer in Europe for the restoration of his health than anticipated, leaving Holland only in July 1839. By then Maclaine had continued to prosper, achieving more than just his 'independency': '... in a pecuniary point of view my ambition has been more than gratified' (*AP* 1/2: Maclaine to Gregorson, Schoonoord, 26 December 1839). He had accumulated a larger capital than necessary for an estate in the Highlands. In a fateful decision, he bought, with Captain Ross, 'a splendid new ship ... fitted up with every convenience for our accommodation and comfort' (*AP* 1/2: Maclaine to Angus, Batavia, 8 October 1839, p. 74). Maclaine had had excellent experiences with the products of the Java shipbuilding industry, and he intended the 196-last (ca 550 tons burthen) *Regina* (named to celebrate the young queen Victoria) to become a regular trader between Britain and the East Indies. Registered in Batavia in the name of Maclaine Watson & Co., and flying the red-white-and-blue flag of the Dutch East Indies (*Regeeringsalmanak* 1840), the *Regina*'s first employment was to carry Maclaine and his family home. Home to his mother at Ardnamuchan Manse and his guardian uncle and aunt John and Mary

Gregorson at Ardtornish Castle, and home also to his beloved Morvern and the islands of Mull, Iona, and Staffa with its famous Fingal's Cave which he always asked his relatives to show to his business friends.[27]

In a bitter blow, however, not long before his intended departure in February 1840, Maclaine learned of the death of his mother (*AP* 1/2: Maclaine to Gregorson, Schoonoord, 26 December 1839). With Angus bound to leave soon for Adelaide, he vowed he would do all to take the place of his brother in the lives of those left behind. Reminding them of his 'Iona lucky pebble', he looked forward to entering the Channel by late May. Tragically, such was not to be. On 31 August Maclaine's London connections, Finlay, Hodgson & Co., had not received any reports about the ship since its departure on 17 March (*AP* 1/2: Finlay, Hodgson & Co. to Gregorson, London, 31 August 1840). A small ray of hope resided in the thought that Captain Ross might have found refuge with his brother at Cocos Island but by late October the insurers were prepared to regard the vessel as lost ((*AP* 1/2: Watson to Angus Maclaine, London, 21 October 1840). A devastated John Gregorson acknowledged in November that the *Regina* must have foundered at sea and that all aboard, including Gillean and his young family, had perished. Sadly, he recorded, 'they were I believe a happy family' (*AP* 1/2: Gregorson to Angus Maclaine, Ardtornish, 16 November 1840). More practically, he reminded Angus that it was his duty to come home immediately. In doing so, he speculated about the possible cause for the loss of the *Regina*: 'I trust you will only come in a well tried ship commanded by a man of experience and having a good crew. I always dread a new ship, they generally carry away spars from the rigging shortening ... I fear the *Regina* must have been dismasted from her being a new ship...'

III

No trace was ever found of the *Regina* or its crew and passengers; it was presumed the ship had foundered in one of the frequent heavy gales near Mauritius. There was some thought of Angus travelling to Batavia to help arrange Maclaine Watson & Co.'s affairs but it was rightly assumed that Gillean would have taken care of all eventualities. Inevitably, there were complications, and Gillean's estate was not settled until 1846. But the firms he had founded continued to thrive under the partners he had appointed and those who followed them. Their high standing in Batavia's business world was confirmed when Maclaine Watson & Co. assisted the NHM in the re-privatization of the so-called *Kendalsche fabrieken* (Mansvelt 1924: II.366). By the late 1870s the Batavia firm, and its affiliates McNeill & Co. (Samarang) and Fraser Eaton & Co. (Surabaya), were the largest East Indian connections of the leading Amsterdam merchant banking house, Van Eeghen & Co. (Rogge 1949: 353). Maclaine Fraser & Co. looked after the network's interests in Singapore. In January 1880 the sheer volume of its operations in northern Europe necessitated the creation of a subsidiary, Maclaine Watson & Co., in London (Rogge 1949: 329). The culmination of the corporate expansion of the firm completed the entrepreneurial circle with the City, from which Maclaine had set sail for Batavia in April 1820. When the Dutch flag was finally lowered over Batavia in 1949, the Scottish house Maclaine Watson & Co. was still one of the major commercial business houses of the Indonesian capital.

Appendix: Gillean Maclaine's Memorandum

[front page]
Being [or fancying myself] in love with Miss Katherine Van Beusechem, I think it right before getting 'dangerously wounded' which may probably be the case, ere we reach Java, to write down coolly all the *Pros* and *Cons* for & against my encouraging this growing attachment.

To begin with the *Cons* –
1. Being a Foreigner & not acquainted as yet with the English language –
2. Manners somewhat different from those of my Countrywomen –
   – Sometimes awkward from timidity & want of mixing in society
   – This awkwardness I however admire – so it goes for nothing
3. Miss K. Beusechem has no Fortune –
4. Marrying a Dutchwoman, may estrange me from my Native Country –
5. Probable objections from my Relatives
   weigh more than all others at present
   I think I hear my Mother & Uncle say
'We thought Gillean had HOME more deeply engraved on his heart than to think of a Foreign connexion – & and more firmness of mind & purpose, than to get married before settling in his native country & arranging his affairs – Poor fellow! He has been captivated by the personal attractions of that cunning Dutch girl – merely from being cooped up in the same ship with her – on shore he would never have thought of her.'
6. Difference of age too great
she being only 18 and I alas! nearly 34 – nearly double hers –
[back page]
Pros –
1. Miss V. Beusechem has a sweet expression of countenance, indicating much modesty and good sense, her face when animated strikingly beautiful –
her figure tall & handsome, perhaps a little too slender –

2. She possesses a mild, retiring feminine disposition, & manners which exactly suit my taste –

3. Her temper without exception is the most amiable I ever met with –

4. Her abilities are above the common – her mind well cultivated – I am at this moment more attracted by her mind than by her personal appearance – she understands French perfectly – also a little German – draws a little – & has made wonderful progress in English since she came on board –

5. She sings very sweetly – & plays the piano tolerably well –

6. She appears of a serious turn of mind – her Religion is the same as mine.

7. Her relations are respectable – her mother a delightful ladylike woman.

8. I have been advised by Deans & other friends to get married were it merely for prudential reasons – Being a married man will keep me out of the noisy roaring Bachelors parties at Batavia, which I always detested – and save me expences [*sic*] even in my housekeeping – I hope it will make me a steadier & fitter man – as a man of business it will rather increase than diminish my credit.

It is true I formed plans of marrying on my return to my native country & thought of forming connexions, it is unnecessary to mention, but how few long projected matches are realized – or if they take place, are they happy ones? No person of feeling likes to be controlled in the selection of a wife – Taking the most favourable view of things, I have not a chance of settling myself in Scotland before my 40th year – a period of life I consider too far advanced for marrying, although there are many instances to the contrary – my uncles for instance – I esteem the Dutch more than any other people after my own countrymen – I consider a Dutch girl less a foreigner than an English girl –

Ship *Anthony* – off the Cape of Good Hope – 30 April, 1832 –

Notes

*This chapter has also been published in Leo Akveld et al. (eds) (2003), *Maritime-historische studies aangeboden aan Jaap R. Bruijn bij vertrek also hoogleraar zeegeschiedenis*, Universiteit Leiden, Amsterdam: De Bataafsche Leeuw, 2003.

1. The main source for this essay is a collection of letters, which were contained in the Ardtornish Papers, temporarily housed in the Argyll & Bute Regional Council Archives, Lochgilphead, Scotland. I gratefully acknowledge permission from the Greenfield family, Old Rectory, Kinnersley, Hertfordshire, England, to peruse this collection. The letters are kept in a number of boxes,

each containing several files. The exact location of each document is indicated as follows: *Ardtornish Papers*, Box 1, File 1; abbreviated as *AP* 1/1.

2. On the concept of diaspora see Chaudhuri 1985: 224–6.

3. British India Steam Navigation Company was founded by the Calcutta firm Mackinnon Mackenzie & Co. who built up a network of connections stretching from East Africa and the Persian Gulf via India to Australia and China. See also Jones 1986: ch.1; Gibb (1937) regrettably only discussed the Scottish diaspora within the British Empire.

4. For a highly interesting sketch of the Dutch mercantile community one generation after Maclaine see Nieuwenhuys 1963: 69–93. A general social history of Batavia in the nineteenth century can be found in Abeyasekere 1989: ch. 2.

5. A very short and unreliable account of Maclaine's career on Java, containing many factual errors, can be found in the history of the Amsterdam firm who, in due course, became Maclaine's firm's closest business connections (Rogge 1949: 248).

6. In April 1819 Maclaine met no fewer than four old school mates who also worked in London offices (*AP* 2/3: Maclaine to Angus, London, 14 April 1819).

7. On Angus' career see *Fasti Ecclesiae Scoticanae*, vol. 4 (Edinburgh 1915) 107–8. I owe this reference to my colleague, Iain Brash.

8. See, for many examples, *Nationaal Archief*, The Hague [*NA*], Collectie Bezemer, 15 and 18, documenting the practice of N. J. de Cock & Frère of Antwerp and Ghent; and A. Hoynck van Papendrecht, *A. van Hoboken & Co, 1774–1824* Amsterdam 1924: chs 10–11 and 18–19.

9. Calculated from the ship's muster rolls in the Gemeentearchief Amsterdam, Particulier Archief 38, Waterschout, 113–21.

10. See, e.g., Mansvelt 1924, 1: 49–64; de Vries 1931; Furnivall 1939: 80–147; Wright 1955, esp. 186–206; Brugmans 1960; Broeze 1978; LittD thesis, Rijksuniversiteit Leiden, 1–9; Oosterwijk 1983: chs 8 and 10. Of some use are also H. W. Tijdeman's anti-protectionist thesis (1967) and the contemporary prize-winning essay written by an Amsterdam insider, J. van Ouwerkerk de Vries (1827).

11. A good description of the structure of the manifold operations of British merchants at Batavia was given by John Deans (of Deans Scott & Co., resident at Batavia from 1813 to 1828), in his testimony to the Select Committee on the Affairs of the East India Committee (18 March 1830; Great Britain, *Parliamentary Papers*, 1830, vol. 644, qq. 3470–3659). Maclaine's Singapore connection J.A. Maxwell appeared before the same committee (16 March 1830, qq. 3660–3826), but, apart from one reference to the abundance of British ships from New South Wales calling at Batavia, his evidence was entirely focused on the China trade.

12. On the 1825 crisis see Dawson (1990).
13. On Palmer see, e.g., Tripathi (1979): *passim*.
14. The ship had arrived on 7 January from Sydney, New South Wales.
15. The *Anthony* had been built in 1827. A watercolour of the vessel, by the famous ship's portrayist Jacob Spin, of 1838, is in the collection of the Rotterdam Maritiem Museum, Rotterdam.
16. Maclaine described his passage in a long letter to Angus, in diary style and completed on 17 May 1832 (*AP* 1/2).
17. Maclaine's positive view of the Dutch Eastindiamen of the time was fully shared by George Windsor Earl (1837: 13) who called them 'the finest class of merchant vessels in the world'.
18. The marriage took place on 22 August 1832.
19. As most Dutch merchants by the early 1860s had done (Nieuwenhuys 1963: 89).
20. A partner of Finlay testified to the 1833 Select Committee on Manufactures (Tripathi 1979: 168).
21. It should be noted that Maclaine did not sever his links with Finlay Hodgson Co. Their relationship remained warm and the London firm, for example, handled the annual payments Maclaine made to his mother and brother (see, e.g., *AP* 2/3, Maclaine to Angus, Batavia, 25 December 1832, and Maclaine to Angus, 8 September 1835).
22. On the possibility of such trade see *Algemeen Handelsblad*, 17 December 1834.
23. The development of his fleet can be followed in the shipping lists of the annual *Regeeringsalmanak*.
24. For a more general overview of the merchant fleet registered on Java see Broeze (1979: 251–69).
25. Captain Ross was a brother of J. Clunies Ross, the proprietor-colonizer of Cocos Island.
26. This was also the last Australian voyage made by a Dutch East Indies vessel. The British Navigation Acts in principle prohibited such contacts, but Maclaine had benefited from an oversight by Australian customs officials. This was rectified in 1839 as a result of the intervention of planters from Mauritius who thus were able to exclude Javanese sugar from the lucrative Australian market. See Broeze (1994: 125); and *AP* 1/2, Maclaine to Angus, Batavia, 8 October 1839.
27. I have not been able to find out whether Maclaine knew of Felix Mendelssohn's visit to Argyll in 1829 or of the young composer's *Hebrides* (or *Fingal's Cave*) overture which was only completed in 1832 after Maclaine had returned to Batavia.

References

Abeyasekere, Susan (1989), *Jakarta: A History*, Oxford: Oxford University Press

Algemeen Handelsblad.

AP = Ardtornish Papers (see note 1 above)

ARA, Staatssecretarie

Bataviasche Courant.

Blake, George (1956), *B.I. Centenary 1856-1956*, London.

Broeze, Frank (1978), *De Stad Schiedam: De Schiedamsche Scheepsreederij en de nederlandse vaart op Oost-Indië omstreeks 1840*, The Hague: LittD thesis, Rijksuniversiteit Leiden.

—— (1979a), 'Atlantic Rivalry: The Struggle for the Dutch Tea Market 1813-1850', *Low Countries History Yearbook*, vol. 11 (1978), The Hague: 103-11.

—— (1979b), 'The Merchant Fleet of Java 1820-1850', *Archipel*, 18: 251-69.

—— (1994), 'The transfer of Technology and Science to Asia 1780–1880: Shipping and Shipbuilding', in Yamada Keiji (ed.), *The Transfer of Science and Technology between Europe and Asia, 1780–1880*, Kyoto.

—— (1998), *Island Nation: A History of Australians and the Sea*, Sydney: Allen & Unwin.

Brugmans, I.J. (1960), *Paardenkracht en Mensenmacht: Sociaal-Economische Geschiedenis van Nederland 1795-1940*, The Hague.

Campbell, Donald Maclaine (1915), *Java, Past and Present*, London.

Carey, Peter (1976), 'The Origins of the Java War (1825-30)', *English Historical Review*, 91: 52-78.

Chaudhuri, K.N. (1985), *Trade and Civilisation in the Indian Ocean: An Economic History from the Rise of Islam to 1750*, Cambridge.

Christiaans, P.A. (1992), 'De belagnrijke Indische ambtenaren van 1834', *De Indische Navorscher*, 5.

Dawson, F.B. (1990), *The First Latin American Debt Crisis*, New Haven.

de Vries, A. (1931), *Geschiedenis van de handelsbetrekkingen tusschen Nederland en Engeland in de negentiende eeuw (1814-1872)*, The Hague.

Earl, G.W. (1837), *The Eastern Seas, or Voyages and Adventures in the Indian Archipelago in 1832-33-34*, London.

Fasti Ecclesiae Scoticanae (1915), Edinburgh.

Furnivall, J.S. (1939), *Netherlands Indies*, Cambridge.

Gemeentearchief, Amsterdam.

Gibb, A.D. (1937) *Scottish Empire*, London.

Hoynck van Papendrecht, A. (1924), *A. van Hoboken & Co. 1774-1924*, Rotterdam.

Javasche Courant.

Jones, Stephanie (1986), *Two Centuries of Overseas Trading: The Origins and Growth of the Inchcape Group*, London.

Keiji, Yamada (ed.) (1994), *The Transfer of Science and Technology between Europe and Asia, 1780-1880*, Kyoto.

Lubis, Mochtar (1987), *Indonesia: Land under the Rainbow*, Manila.

Mansvelt, W.M.F. (1924), *De Nederlandsche Handel-Maatschappij 1824-1924*, Haarlem, vol. I.

Nationaal Archief, The Hague.

Nicholson, I.H. (1977), *Shipping Arrivals and Departures Sydney, 1826-1840*, Canberra.

Nieuwenhuys, Rob (1963), 'The young merchant in the Indies of 1863', in H. Baudet (ed.), *Trade World and World Trade: One Hundred Years of Internatio*, Rotterdam.

Nusteling, Hubert P.H. (1992), 'Strijd om de commerciële suprematie in de zeventiende en achttiende eeuw', *NEHA-Bulletin*, 6(1): 19.

Oosterwijk, Bram (1983), *Koning van de koopvaart: Anthony van Hoboken (1756-1850)*, Rotterdam.

Parliamentary Papers, Great Britain

Palmer Papers, English Letters.

Phipps, John (1840), *A Collection of Papers Relative to Shipbuilding in India &c. &c.*, Calcutta.

Raffles, T.S. (1817), *The History of Java*, London, vol. 1.

Regeeringsalmanak voor Nederlandsch-Indië (1823).

Rogge, J. (1949), *Het Handelshuis Van Eeghen: Proeve eener Geschiedenis van een Amsterdamsch Handelshuis*, Amsterdam.

Sydney Herald.

Tijdeman, H.W. (1967), *De Nederlandsche Handel-Maatschappij*, Leiden.

Tripathi, Amales (1979), *Trade and Finance in the Bengal Presidency 1793-1833*, Calcutta.

Tweedie, Sandra (1994), *Trading Partners: Australia & Asia 1790-1993*, Sydney.

van Ouwerkerk de Vries, J. (1827), *Verhandeling over de oorzaken van het verval des Nederlandschen handels en de middelen tot herstel van denzelven*, Haarlem.

Webster, Anthony (1998), *Gentlemen Capitalists: British Imperialism in South East Asia, 1770-1890*, London.

Wright, H.R.C. (1955), *Free Trade and Protection in the Netherlands, 1816-1830*, Cambridge.

Index

Index

Index

Index

Mendelssohn family 192, 201, 204, 208
Mennonites 198, 203, 207
merchant networks 44–5, 161, 165, 166, 245–7, 374
   Armenian 39–40, 51, 54, 64, 66
   Baghdadi Jews 281–2
   Chinese diasporas in Southeast Asia 287–303, 338, 357–8
   Greek maritime diaspora 97, 147, 151–2, 155, 176, 182, 378, 379
   Indian Muslim traders 261–2, 262
   Jewish trade diaspora 196, 261–2, 270, 271
   Maltese 137–9
   Parsees 261–2, 262–3
merchant princes, Bengal 54, 55, 59
Messina 157
Messina, Calogero 131
Metaxá family 108–9
Meulen, D. van der 227
Mexico, Iberian conquest of 12
Meyer, Manasseh 225–6
Michel, B. 207
Middelburg 20
Middle Ages
   Armenian trade diaspora 5–6
   Christian-Islamic divide 10, 11
   Julfa's prosperity 27
Middle East 4, 18, 356
   Jews 5, 258, 259, 261
Middle Eastern entrepreneurs, in Southeast Asia 217–19
middlemen minority
   Jews 195
   Parsees 252, 261
migration 30, 204–5
   Chinese diasporas in Southeast Asia 355–6
   and contemporary concept of diaspora 385, 386
   and economic accomplishment 134
   ethno-national diasporas 361–5, 368
   of Iranians to India 32
   Jewish bankers 205–6, 209–10
   magnitude of in recent decades 384
   Maltese diaspora 135–7
   of Middle Eastern entrepreneurs to West 238
   opportunities afforded by empires 372
   and rise of City of London 201
   Sephardic Jews 195–6
   see also emigration

Miln, Thomas 398
Miln Haswell & Co. 396, 405
Ming Pao Daily News 335
mining, Chinese labour in Southeast Asia 355
Minorca 127, 152–3
minority culture 388
Minorsky 32
Mintoff, Dom 139–40
Mir Jafar Khan, Nawab 56, 63
Mirès, Jules Isaac 208
mixed marriages
   ethno-national diaspora 355, 364
   Japanese diaspora 76, 88–9
M.M. Warburg & Co. 192, 198
M.M.B. Afshar & Co 277
Mocha 58, 64
Modone 98
mohair trade 8, 14
Mohamat Aldjuffrie & Co. 225
Moluccas 218, 224, 231
Mon (of coastal Burma) 354, 355, 356
Monemvasia 98
moneylenders
   Hadhramis in Southeast Asia 225, 227–8
   Parsees 251–2
Mongolia 5
Moniteur Officiel du Commerce 219
Moors, expulsion from Spain 75–6
Morawitz, Karl 193
Morea/Morean Greeks 98, 109
Moresini, Taddeo 106
Moroccans 360
Morocco 20, 191
Morowska, Eva 134
Moschopolis 376, 379
Moscow 6, 164, 375, 377
Mosdeen, Shaik 255
Moses Ezechiëls & Zoonen 192
mosques, Hong Kong 255, 257
Mosse, W.E. 194
Mountbatten, Louis, 1st Earl Mountbatten of Burma 249
Mughal Empire 36, 52, 53, 67
Muhammad bin Talib, Salim bin 233
Multan 64
multiculturalism, and concept of diaspora 385, 386–7, 388

–430–

Index

Index